Young Children with Special Needs

Fifth Edition

Stephen R. Hooper
University of North Carolina School of Medicine
Chapel Hill, North Carolina

Warren Umansky
Children's Clinic
Augusta, Georgia

Merrill
is an imprint of

Upper Saddle River, New Jersey
Columbus, Ohio

Library of Congress Cataloging-in-Publication Data

Hooper, Stephen R.
  Young children with special needs / Stephen R. Hooper, Warren Umansky.—5th ed.
      p. cm.
  Includes bibliographical references and index.
  ISBN-13: 978-0-13-159014-4 (alk. paper)
  ISBN-10: 0-13-159014-6 (alk. paper)
  1. Children with disabilities—Education—United States. 2. Perceptual-motor learning. 3. Child development—United States. I. Umansky, Warren. II. Title.
  LC4031.U425 2008
  371.9'0472—dc22

                                                                                    2008002495

Vice President and Executive Publisher: Jeffery W. Johnston
Executive Editor: Ann Castel Davis
Senior Managing Editor: Pamela D. Bennett
Editorial Assistant: Penny Burleson
Production Editor: Sheryl Glicker Langner
Production Coordination: Mary Tindle, S4Carlisle Publishing Services
Design Coordinator: Diane C. Lorenzo

Cover Designer: Ali Mohrman
Cover Art: Corbis
Production Manager: Laura Messerly
Director of Marketing: Quinn Perkson
Marketing Manager: Erica DeLuca
Marketing Coordinator: Brian Mounts

This book was set in 10/12 Berkeley Book by S4Carlisle Publishing Services. It was printed and bound by R. R. Donnelley & Sons Company. The cover was printed by R. R. Donnelley & Sons Company.

Chapter Opening Photo Credits: p. 2, Todd Yarrington/Merrill; pp. 42, 344, Courtesy of Lisa Harris; p. 114, Courtesy of Carole Dennis; p. 168, Courtesy of Jean Patz; p. 236, Scott Cunningham/Merrill; pp. 308, 418, 462, Anne Vega/Merrill; p. 382, Courtesy of Stephen Hooper

Pearson® is a registered trademark of Pearson plc
Merrill® is a registered trademark of Pearson Education, Inc.

Pearson Education Ltd., London
Pearson Education Singapore, Pte. Ltd.
Pearson Education Canada, Inc.
Pearson Education—Japan

Pearson Education Australia PTY, Limited
Pearson Education North Asia, Ltd., Hong Kong
Pearson Educación de Mexico, S.A. de C.V.
Pearson Education Malaysia, Pte. Ltd.
Pearson Education Upper Saddle River, New Jersey

Merrill
is an imprint of

10 9 8 7 6 5 4 3 2 1
ISBN 13: 978-0-13-159014-4
ISBN 10:   0-13-159014-6

Dedication

To my children, Lindsay Rae and Madeline Grace, who are my lifelong teachers of child development. Thank you for your guidance and youthful wisdom as each of you has moved through your own unique developmental processes. I know I will continue to learn from you. I am extremely proud of both of you. To my wife, Mary Anne, whose support has been essential to the completion of this project. You have kept me grounded (and sane), and I could not have done it without you and your constant encouragement.

Stephen R. Hooper,
Chapel Hill, NC

I dedicate this book to the memory of my parents, Dorothy and George, whose vision and efforts in getting my brothers and me to where we are provide a model of parenting to be emulated. My wife, Jean, and I have tried to remain loyal to their model in raising our three children, Derrick, Aaron, and Neely. To all of them, who make us so proud, this book also is dedicated.

Warren Umansky,
Augusta, GA

As we prepare to offer the fifth edition of our text, we are saddened to know that the field of early childhood special education lost one of its strongest advocates, Dr. Pascal Louis "Pat" Trohanis, who passed away on June 23, 2007. Pat Trohanis was Director of the National Early Childhood Technical Assistance Center and truly served in one of the major leadership roles in the field. During his tenure of over 30 years with NECTAC, Pat was a guiding force in bringing information to the field and in making services more available and user/family-friendly. He was also a good friend to those fortunate enough to know him. The field will miss his presence, his wisdom, and his optimism.

Stephen R. Hooper and Warren Umansky

Foreword

All children with special needs deserve the best in terms of supports and services. But young children differ from older children in at least three ways. First, although some will have obvious delays or disabilities, many have genetic conditions or other risk factors (e.g., prematurity) that could lead to a delay or disability but are not currently obvious. As a result, early intervention has to take a prevention perspective, keeping close watch on children's development and implementing programs that minimize the likelihood of delay or disability.

Second, teaching young children is not the same as teaching older children. Young children learn primarily through play and social experiences, not by sitting in a desk with formal lessons. As a result, parents of young children with disabilities and the professionals who work with them must be creative in the ways they systematically embed teaching in the context of ongoing activities and routines. Finally, young children and their families are inextricably connected, and any attempt to teach children without working with families is likely to have limited results.

These and other factors mean that professionals who work with young children with special needs need specialized knowledge, training, and experience. This book, now entering its 5th Edition, provides an excellent overview for the beginning professional. The editors and the chapter authors provide a solid introduction to the field, keeping the best of previous editions and adding new information so that the book is current, informative, and evidence-based. The ongoing focus of this text on developmental processes remains a critical cornerstone of the field.

As we look toward the future of early intervention and early childhood special education, the core values and approaches that have long been advocated by early childhood specialists and developmental psychologists will continue to guide the development and evaluation of effective practices in working with both children and families. But in an era of accountability, programs for young children with special needs will increasingly be asked to demonstrate that the services provided result in improved outcomes for children and families. This text provides a great beginning for students who are willing to accept this challenge and this responsibility.

Don Bailey, Ph.D.,
Distinguished Fellow
RTI International
January, 2008

Contributors

Carole White Dennis, Sc.D., OTR/L
Assistant Professor and Chair
Occupational Therapy Department
Ithaca College
Ithaca, New York

Tashawna Duncan, Ph.D.
Pediatric Neuropsychologist
Bradenton, Florida

Susan R. Easterbrooks, Ed.D.
Professor
Department of Educational Psychology
    and Special Education
College of Education
    Georgia State University
Atlanta, Georgia

Katy Gregg
Graduate Associate
Institute on Human Development and Disability/UCEDD
The University of Georgia
Athens, Georgia

Jennifer L. Harman
School Psychology Program
Department of Educational Psychology
University of Florida
Gainesville, Florida

Jennifer Hiemenz, Ph.D.
Assistant Professor
Department of Psychiatry
Clinical Center for the Study of Development and Learning
The University of North Carolina School of Medicine
Chapel Hill, North Carolina

Stephen R. Hooper, Ph.D.
Professor
Departments of Psychiatry, Psychology, and Education
Associate Director
The Clinical Center for the Study of Development
    and Learning
The University of North Carolina School of Medicine
Chapel Hill, North Carolina

Rita Kahng, Ph.D.
Postdoctoral Fellow in Psychology
The Clinical Center for the Study of Development
    and Learning
University of North Carolina School of Medicine
Chapel Hill, North Carolina

Joan Lieber, Ph.D.
Professor
Department of Special Education
University of Maryland—College Park
College Park, Maryland

Rose M. Messina, M.S., OTR
Madison Metropolitan School District
Madison, Wisconsin

Tanya L. Parker, M.Ed.
Deaf Education Instructor
Special Student Services
Cobb County School District
Marietta, Georgia

Jean Ann Patz, M.S., OTR/L
Instructional Specialist
Department of Kinesiology, Occupational
    Therapy Program
Medical Sciences Center and
Assistant Researcher
Epidemiology of Developmental Disabilities Unit
Waisman Center
University of Wisconsin–Madison
Madison, Wisconsin

Rebecca Edmondson Pretzel, Ph.D.
Assistant Professor
Department of Psychiatry
Psychology Section Head
The Clinical Center for the Study of Development
    and Learning
The University of North Carolina School
    of Medicine
Chapel Hill, North Carolina

Mary E. Rugg, M.Ed.
Early Intervention Coordinator
Institute on Human Development and Disability/UCEDD
University of Georgia
Athens, Georgia

Kathleen A. Schlough, P.T., D.Sc., PCS
Pediatric Physical Therapy Services
Ithaca, New York

Tina M. Smith–Bonahue, Ph.D.
Associate Professor
Department of Educational Psychology
College of Education
University of Florida
Gainesville, Florida

Zolinda Stoneman, Ph.D.
Director
Institute on Human Development and Disability/UCEDD
Professor
College of Family & Consumer Sciences

The University of Georgia
Athens, Georgia

Warren Umansky, Ph.D.
Director
Children's Clinic
Augusta, Georgia

Crista E. Wetherington, Ph.D.
Assistant Professor
Department of Psychiatry
University of Texas–Southwest
Center for Pediatric Psychiatry
Children's Medical Center Dallas
Dallas, Texas

Jaclyn M. Wetherington, M.S.
School Psychology Program
Department of Educational Psychology and Instructional
    Technology
The University of Georgia
Athens, Georgia

Preface

When the first edition of *Young Children with Special Needs* was published, Nancy Fallen, its editor, had a vision for a nascent field that was laid out in the text. However, there was little history to present about the field at that time. In the three decades since, early childhood special education has grown in ways few others would have imagined. From the first few experimental personnel preparation programs, there have grown dozens, many aligned closely with regular early education and child development training programs. From a few model demonstration early intervention programs for preschoolers in each state, there have grown thousands of programs, and early intervention is mandatory in every state for eligible children beginning at birth. From a few experimental curricula and homemade materials, there has grown an industry geared to serving the needs of young children with special needs and their families. The introductory chapter in this fifth edition traces the unprecedented evolution of early childhood special education from the seedling stage that characterized the field when this book was first published to the current stage of emerging maturity with an appetite for evidence-based best practices.

Growth of the field is likely to continue—even in the face of competing political and economic priorities. There has been a true commitment to early childhood special education on the part of state and federal governments, university training programs, and local communities. This commitment likely will be rewarded with better services and evidence-based interventions for young children with special needs, better-trained personnel, more informed and more involved families and communities, and increasingly child-friendly public policies. In turn, we already have gained increased respect for young children with special needs and their families and appreciate the valuable contributions to our society this population makes.

The modifications in this edition either reflect what early interventionists have said about the importance of a specific issue and their need for more comprehensive knowledge or they reflect our own impressions of what early interventionists need to know. In either case, while the material often can be complex and technical, mastery of this information will lead to mastery on the job. Any redundancy in information among chapters is intentional because it reflects the natural overlap in material from one developmental area to another and because repetition facilitates learning.

The key to successful early intervention has not changed over the years. Therefore, this edition continues to be driven by a developmental theoretical perspective. We place great emphasis on the reader gaining a deep and broad perspective of how and why children develop as they do and what can go wrong. We know that successful early intervention revolves around competent professionals who are knowledgeable about children, families, and the tools of intervention, and who apply that knowledge in a sensitive and skillful way. The early interventionist who knows child development can feel confident and be supportive of children's and parents' needs.

We have made a great effort to present the very latest information and to challenge the reader to think beyond the facts. We believe this formula will yield the greatest benefits to the reader.

For this revision, we also listened to our consumers. As a result of peer reviewer comments, and of remarks of users of the fourth edition, we have subdivided the chapters a bit differently from the previous edition into three separate sections. This is consistent with the knowledge-content-application approach that guides the structure of this text as well as the curricula and associated courses for many early childhood training programs. We lay the foundation for this perspective in chapter 2, and the contributors have done an exceptional job of integrating this developmental theme into the chapters in Part II. We also have continued to emphasize some key content areas in early childhood special education such as historical foundations, basic growth and development, families, assessment and intervention, technology, and cultural competency, with many of these topics being woven into the fabric of each chapter. The knowledge-content-application approach guided us in rearranging the book's structure and content in other ways as well. For example, we moved the family, assessment, and intervention chapters to form a Part III of the book. The emphasis of the assessment chapter is on the array of assessment approaches and the process of assessment rather than on specific instruments. This gives the student much more flexibility to apply knowledge in a multitude of settings. The family and intervention chapters bring the reader the most current knowledge in areas that are so dynamic in their theories and models. Some of the chapters, such as those on motor development, are expansive, as they incorporate diverse human functions. We have deleted the separate chapter on technology, but have integrated its most important elements into the content chapters. This in no way implies a disregard for the importance of technology; rather, it should be viewed as an attempt to address the extraordinary impact that technology has on all aspects of child development and how it should be viewed as a key candidate for inclusion in any assessment and/or intervention process.

All of the chapters in the current edition have been aligned to emphasize the information that is most important for early interventionists and to provide as broad a perspective as possible to the reader. Philosophically, we see development as the basis of assessment and diagnosis; it is the foundation upon which interventions are built. To this end, the central chapters of this text in Part II provide the information necessary to make the reader comfortable and confident in his or her knowledge of how children develop.

The fifth edition of *Young Children with Special Needs* also maintains the changes that were made in the fourth edition and that were well-received. The text has a user-friendly appearance with a number of helpful instructional aids. Specifically, each chapter begins with an outline of the chapter-specific topic and ends with questions and discussion points. In addition, each chapter provides a number of recommended resources for additional reading, research, and projects. All chapters have additional instructional technologies, including introductory case vignettes, key points listed in a sidebar format, text boxes highlighting a topic directly or indirectly related to the chapter, and boldfaced key terms. It is hoped that these instructional features will facilitate the teaching and learning of this material.

Finally, for the sake of clarity and consistency we have standardized terminology. For example, we use the term *early interventionist* to refer to the many different professionals, including and most specifically the early childhood special educator, who provide early intervention services. We provide these professionals and professionals-in-training with a clear philosophy and knowledge base from which to work. We believe this approach is more logical and more conducive to incremental learning by the student.

We are indebted to our contributors whose hard work, expertise, and judgment have resulted in a comprehensive, contemporary, and clinically useful text. We also would like to express appreciation to the professionals who reviewed our manuscript: Karen Applequist, Northern Arizona University; Robin Hasslen, Bethel University; Marjorie Schiller, Central Arizona College; and Victoria Wilcox, Marywood University. Special thanks to Ann Davis, Executive Editor, and Penny Burleson, Editorial Assistant, at Pearson/Merrill for their constant guidance in completing this revision. We are confident you will find this book both intellectually stimulating and practical. Your comments and anecdotes are welcome.

Stephen R. Hooper, Ph.D.

Warren Umansky, Ph.D.

Brief Contents

Contents

CHAPTER 7 SOCIAL AND EMOTIONAL DEVELOPMENT   344

Joan Lieber

Note: Every effort has been made to provide accurate and current Internet information in this book. However, the Internet and information posted on it are constantly changing, so it is inevitable that some of the Internet addresses listed in this textbook will change.

Foundations

Introduction to Young Children with Special Needs

Warren Umansky

Chapter Outline

- A Rationale for Early Childhood Special Education
- The Early Interventionist
- Young Children with Special Needs and Their Families
- The Family and the Community

Alex and Margie

*A*lex and Margie got married in their mid-30s. Soon afterward, they tried to satisfy one of their mutual goals in life—that of having a child. After several years of marriage, Margie finally became pregnant. Joy was mixed with apprehension. Had they waited too long? They had heard that the chances of problems occurring increased with the age of the parents. Did their family history doom their chances of having a typical child? After all, Margie's older brother had Down syndrome, two of her nephews were being treated for attention deficit hyperactivity disorder, and an elderly uncle had what probably was a mild case of cerebral palsy. Alex's family also had its share of problems, from autism in his sister's youngest son to his father's congenital deafness in one ear. Maybe they shouldn't have tried to have kids after all, Margie and Alex thought to themselves.

Margie was in good health and she was committed to taking excellent care of herself during pregnancy. The couple also planned to have prenatal testing done that would alert them to any suspected problems. Although Margie and Alex wanted desperately to envision a healthy and perfect baby, they knew there were no guarantees. They looked forward to the first sonogram that would allow them to see the fetus in the uterus. They also eagerly anticipated the quickening, when Margie would begin to feel their baby moving. They would be more comfortable when they saw a healthy-looking image on the sonogram and felt the baby's movements. They tried hard to concentrate on positive thoughts of a wonderful baby and happy family experiences, but they were aware that resources in their community provided early intervention services to their nephew with autism and would be available to them if the need arose. They hoped this would not be the case.

There is mounting evidence that early intervention can have a markedly positive effect on the development of infants and preschoolers with some types of disabilities. Partly because of the influence of professional and advocacy organizations, such as the Council for Exceptional Children, Children and Adults with Attention Deficit Disorders (CHADD), United Cerebral Palsy, the Autism Society of America, and the Epilepsy Foundation of America, decision makers have become more responsive to the needs of children with disabilities and children who are at risk for disabilities. In addition, the experiences of agencies that offer early intervention programs, such as the community resources referred to in the vignette, have contributed to an atmosphere of urgency. These experiences have revealed such benefits of early intervention as long-term savings in program costs as children's needs for complex and expensive services decrease with time.

Not everyone is convinced that early education is successful or necessary, however. Certainly the goal of early childhood special education is an ambitious

The goal of early intervention is to prevent or reduce negative environmental and biological influences on the child.

one: to intervene during the early years to prevent or lessen the effects of harmful biological or environmental influences and to maximize a child's development and learning. It is the broad scope of early education efforts that has provided fuel for the fires of both proponents and skeptics.

The idea of early education did not develop overnight; rather, it evolved slowly and on many fronts simultaneously. For example, classic animal research conducted by Harlow (1974) with monkeys and by Denenberg and his colleagues (Denenberg, 1981; Denenberg et al., 1981) with rats and rabbits related characteristics of early experience to the animals' subsequent behavior and development. For example, rats that are raised in a complex environment have brains that are different from those of rats raised in a nonstimulating environment (Card, Levitt, Gluhovsky, & Rinaman, 2005). The preponderance of evidence from psychological research supports the significant impact of early experience on development (Cashmore, 2001; Shonkoff & Phillips, 2000). Enriched experiences can maintain or accelerate development, and deprivation and abusive experiences can contribute to retarded or deviant development.

Medical and sociological research has contributed further evidence of the effects of early experiences on development. The generalized influence of poverty on development is profound, but can be mitigated by early intervention (Chung, Hawkins, Gilchrist, Hill, & Nagin, 2002; Gottlieb & Blair, 2004). The specific effects of nutrition on brain growth and mental development have been found to be significant (Guesry, 1998; Lucas, Morley, Isaacs, & Youdim, 2001; Liu, Raine, Venables, & Mednick, 2004) as well. Malnourished children tend to develop at a retarded rate and exhibit learning and behavioral deficits as they get older (Galler, Waber, Harrison, & Ramsey, 2005). Prenatal malnutrition may have a particularly negative impact on the later development of children (Lecours, Mandujano, Romero, Arroyo, & Sanchez-Perez, 2001); however, many of the adverse effects of malnutrition may be overcome by sensory stimulation. Benefits of early intervention also were reported for young children prenatally exposed to cocaine (Bono et al., 2005; Claussen, Scott, Mundy, & Katz, 2005).

In theory, as in practice, attention has focused on early experiences. The works of Freud (1965), Erikson (1963), and Piaget and Inhelder (1969) portray a building-block concept in which development is viewed as a structure made up of different levels. The strength and integrity of the lower levels of the structure—the early years—are necessary for stability as more levels are added. Similarly, this chapter lays the foundation for a logical and supportable approach to the education of young children with special needs. Subsequent chapters focus on characteristics of these children and the process of providing high-quality services to them and their families to maximize their development and independence.

:: A RATIONALE FOR EARLY CHILDHOOD SPECIAL EDUCATION

Particularly during times of economic hardship and competition for limited resources, programs that remain and grow are often those with advocates who present the most logical and compelling arguments. Many arguments can be made for

---

One basis for early childhood special education is found in animal research.

Children who are malnourished may achieve typical ranges of development with comprehensive early intervention.

committing resources to the education of young children with special needs. Programs throughout the country that have served these children provide firsthand evidence of the benefits of doing so.

Legislation

Until the last half of the 20th century, education for children with disabilities was primarily a local and state concern. The federal government made few specific commitments to children with special needs. Its first commitment to special education was the establishment in 1864 of Gallaudet College for the Deaf in Washington, DC. It was not until 1930, however, that the federal government directly addressed the issue of special education and established a Section on Exceptional Children and Youth in the Office of Education of the Department of Health, Education, and Welfare. The needs of young children were also addressed through the Children's Bureau of the same department.

The federal government's role in special education remained limited, however, until the 1960s. It did support programs for children with special needs by (1) supplying matching funds to state and local agencies, (2) granting funds for research in all areas of exceptionality, (3) disseminating information, (4) providing consultative services to state and local groups, and (5) distributing fellowships for the training of professionals in all areas related to special education. A major turning point for federal support of education came in 1965, when Congress passed the Elementary and Secondary Education Act (ESEA). This act and its subsequent amendments made available to schools large amounts of money with which to serve children from 3 to 21 years of age who were educationally disadvantaged and who were disabled, it created the Bureau of Education for the Handicapped, and it provided funds for research and demonstration projects to improve special education services. In the 2001–2002 school year, more than 300,000 disadvantaged preschool children were served under Title I of ESEA (U.S. Department of Education, 2004).

The Handicapped Children's Early Education Assistance Act of 1968 represented the first major federal recognition of the specific importance of early education. The purpose of this legislation was to support model programs throughout the nation that would demonstrate exemplary practices and share their information with others. The act established the Handicapped Children's Early Education Program (HCEEP) to administer and provide technical support for 3-year demonstration programs, called *First Chance* projects. Over the years, the act also funded outreach programs and a Technical Assistance and Development System (TADS) to assist these projects. Called *NECTAS* for many years, the name was changed in 2002 when it was refunded as the **National Early Childhood Technical Assistance Center (NECTAC).** The center still is engaged in technical assistance, publication, and other support activities and continues to be located at the University of North Carolina at Chapel Hill. HCEEP was renamed the Early Education Program for Children with Disabilities (EEPCD) in 1990, but the program was significantly changed by the Amendments to IDEA in 1997, and EEPCD is no longer a separate program. Rather, early childhood initiatives are now included in many parts of IDEA.

Garnering support for early childhood special education programs requires that the professional can make clear and compelling arguments that justify their benefits.

The federal government has played a growing role in supporting and encouraging the growth of early intervention programs.

The National Early Childhood Technical Assistance Center provides a wealth of resources for the early childhood special education community.

Several hundred demonstration programs have been funded since 1968. Many former demonstration programs continued to receive funds after the initial funding cycle to help other agencies adopt their documented models for delivering services to young children with special needs in other geographical areas. Outreach programs now are encouraged to work closely with state agencies rather than with individual programs and agencies to replicate their exemplary service models with young children and their families.

During the early years of demonstration projects, two large studies were funded by the federal government to evaluate the projects' efforts in meeting their goals. A Battelle Institute report (1976), although criticized for lack of stringent research procedures, cited developmental gains in children beyond those that would have been expected had intervention not been provided. Subsequent to that study, Littlejohn & Associates (1982) followed up on programs and children who once had been part of the First Chance network and found that 84% of the programs continued to serve children when eligibility for federal funding expired. The outcomes for the children who had been served in the programs also appeared to be favorable. The legislative incentive offered in 1968, then, recognized the importance of the early years; it appears that mandate has been exercised prudently and effectively.

Yet, early intervention programs have evolved dramatically in the decades since the Littlejohn report. While research on individual early intervention programs has been substantial during this period and will be discussed later in this chapter, the 1997 Amendments to IDEA authorized funding for two national early intervention studies. The National Early Intervention Longitudinal Study (NEILS) was a descriptive study that examined a nationally representative sample of more than 3300 infants and toddlers with disabilities or who were at risk for disabilities and their families. The study period lasted from 1997 to 2001. The study was not intended to assess the effectiveness of early intervention and did not utilize a control or comparison group. Five questions were examined: (1) Who are the children and families receiving EI services? (2) What EI services do participating children and families receive? (3) What are the costs of EI services? (4) What outcomes do participating children and families experience? (5) How do outcomes relate to variations in children's and families' characteristics and services received? (Hebbeler et al., 2007). The results provided some illuminating and some intuitive results, such as that children with the greatest disabilities face the greatest challenges and are likely to show the least developmental progress. In addition, these children require the highest program expenses (Levin, Perez, Lam, Chambers, & Hebbeler, 2004). Nevertheless, parents who were most involved in their children's program learned valuable advocacy and improved parenting skills regarding their own children. See Recommended Resources at the end of this chapter for access to additional information regarding NEILS.

The second early intervention study authorized by the 1997 Amendments to IDEA was the six-year Pre-Elementary Education Longitudinal Study (PEELS). This descriptive study followed a nationally representative sample of more than 3000 children aged 3 to 5 who received special education services through the year 2009. The questions that were posed for examination were: (1) What are the characteristics of children receiving preschool special education? (2) What preschool program and services do they receive? (3) What are their transitions like—between early intervention and preschool and between preschool and elementary school? (4) How do these children function and perform in preschool, kindergarten, and early elementary school? (5) Which child, service, and program characteristics are associated with children's performance over time on assessments of academic and adaptive skills? (Markowitz et al., 2006). See Recommended Resources at the end of this chapter for access to additional information regarding PEELS.

Both NEILS and PEELS had substantial limitations in that they were descriptive and did not reflect the great variations in characteristics or quality of services at the local level. It is likely that the results of these studies, however, will provide a model for state and local programs to evaluate the effectiveness of their early intervention efforts.

Other federal legislation also has played an important role in supporting early intervention programs. **The Economic Opportunity and Community Partnership Act of 1974** and subsequent amendments to the law required Head Start programs in each state to serve a minimum of 10% children with disabilities. In addition, 14 Resource Access Projects were funded to provide training and technical assistance for improved services to children with disabilities in Head Start programs. During the 2004–2005 school year, approximately 907,000 children and their families were served in Head Start programs; more than 12½% were disabled. The Early Head Start Program has provided services to 61,500 children under 3 years of age and their families during the same period in 708 community-based programs. One of the challenges of the program was to identify and serve children with disabilities (Peterson et al., 2004). This program also has generated an interesting body of research relative to factors in a home visitation service delivery model that contribute to program outcome (Brookes, Ispa, Summers, Thornburg, & Lane, 2006; Love, Kisker, Raikes, Constantine, & Boller, 2005; Raikes et al., 2006).

In addition to these programs, the **Even Start Family Literacy Program,** a part of Title I of the Elementary and Secondary Education Act discussed earlier, offers services to low-income families with children birth through age 7 by integrating early childhood education, adult education, parenting education, and interactive literacy activities. Even Start serves about 27,000 children younger than 5 years of age.

In 1974, amendments to the Education of the Handicapped Act required states without conflicting laws to establish a plan to identify and serve all children with disabilities from birth to 21 years of age. The same philosophy and a similar age range were included in Public Law (P.L.) 94–142, the Education for All Handicapped Children Act of 1975. (Unfortunately, few states fell within this act's mandate because of state laws that defined an older mandatory school age.) In addition, priorities for serving children were established such that states first had to serve school-aged children who were receiving no education, then children with severe disabilities who were in inappropriate placement, and, finally, preschool children. Nevertheless, several states passed local legislation to serve young children with special needs. Texas, for example, made programs available from birth to children who needed special services. California offered state funds to any school system that served preschool-aged children with disabilities. Virginia maintained a statewide technical assistance system for preschool teachers of children with disabilities and reimbursed the school system for a large portion of the teachers' salaries. P.L. 94–142

Head Start programs have served an increasing number of young children with special needs and their families.

is viewed by some as one of the major pieces of legislation ever passed that has motivated states to provide high-quality education to children with special needs. Amendments to the original law have further expanded and refined services.

P.L. 94–142 contains numerous provisions that apply to children with disabilities of all ages and some that apply to preschool-aged children specifically. Some of the requirements of the original law follow (Kirk, Gallagher, Anastasiow, & Coleman, 2005):

1. Public education agencies must ensure that all children who need special education and related services are identified and evaluated.
2. Parents have numerous procedural safeguards that protect the rights of each child with a disability to receive a free and appropriate education. These safeguards include the rights of parents to do the following:
   a. Review the child's educational records.
   b. Obtain an independent evaluation of the child.
   c. Receive written notice before the school begins the special education placement process.
   d. Request a hearing before an impartial hearing officer to challenge placement or program decisions.
3. The child must receive a comprehensive multidisciplinary educational assessment. Various types of intellectual, social, and cultural information must be considered in the assessment. The process must be repeated at least every 3 years.
4. An individualized education plan (IEP) must be written for every child in special education. Development of the document is a joint effort of school personnel and the parent. The IEP must be reviewed at least annually.
5. To the maximum extent possible, children with disabilities must be educated with their nondisabled peers. Special classes and separate schools can be used only when the nature or severity of the child's disability prohibits education in a more typical setting.

P.L. 94–142 also provided Preschool Incentive Grants to states that identified preschool children in need of special education services. The act allowed states to receive up to $300 for each 3- to 5-year-old child in addition to the funds the act already made available to all children with disabilities. In actuality, considerably less than that amount was available for each child with disabilities when the law was first implemented; initially, only about an additional $100 was provided by the federal government to states for each identified 3- to 5-year-old in need of special education services.

P.L. 99–457 was a major turning point for services to infants, toddlers, and preschoolers with disabilities.

Legislative action during the past 30 years has left little doubt about the federal commitment to young children with special needs. Congress took a major step in 1986 with the passage of **P.L. 99–457.** In addition to continuing authorization for services to preschool children with disabilities from age 3 under Section 619 of Title B of the law (the Preschool Grants Program), Title H of the law provided incentives to states to serve children from birth who had special needs or were at risk for later problems. The law specified an increased role for families in services to children from birth through 2 years of age and introduced the individualized family service plan (IFSP), which is the equivalent of the IEP but must consider the needs of the whole family relative to the child. States had 5 years to implement a comprehensive, coordinated interagency system of services and resources, including an emphasis on serving infants and toddlers. States that adopted this initiative were required to have 14 components in place based on a timeline specified by the law wherein states had to be prepared to provide full services to infants and toddlers by the fifth year of funding. By the 1993–1994 school year, all states were required to ensure full implementation. There are now 16 components required by P.L. 99–457 as a consequence of subsequent amendments to the law (P.L. 105–17). These components are presented in Box 1.1.

In 1991, Congress reauthorized funds for special education programs as the Individuals with Disabilities Education Act (IDEA). This revision of the original law made services for the 3- to 5-year-old population mandatory for states rather than optional. A subsequent authorization changed the funding formula to increase the amount of money that states received for each identified child. The **1997 Amendments to IDEA (P.L. 105–17)** and **IDEA 2004 (P.L. 108–446)** further solidified the funding of services. Figure 1.1 presents funding levels and the number of children served under Part B of IDEA for the period from 1977 to 2006. The amendments of 1997 also moved provisions for services to infants and toddlers from Part H to Part C.

The specific wording of the law formalized a philosophy of **inclusiveness** promoted by early intervention professionals for many years. According to Odom et al. (2000), "*inclusion* is the active participation of young children with disabilities and typically developing children in the same classroom . . . and community settings" (p. 1). The purpose of inclusion is to expose children with disabilities to typical settings, activities, and peers, allowing typically developing children to interact with their peers with disabilities. IDEA also promoted the principle of **natural environments,** which means that the child should receive early intervention services where the child naturally would be—in the home or at a child care center, for example. With increasing numbers of children receiving early intervention, programs are being challenged to develop new service delivery models. A significant change in procedures for reassessment of children was made in the reauthorized IDEA of 2004. P.L. 94–142, as noted earlier, required that a comprehensive multidisciplinary educational assessment be performed at least every three years. This was changed such that assessments can be performed no more frequently than annually if the needs of the child warrant and at least every three years unless the parent and local education agency agree that reassessment is not necessary.

The number of children served by early intervention programs and the amount of money spent for services are significant. About 702,000 children with disabilities aged 3 through 5 were served by preschool programs supported by IDEA (Part B, Section 619) during the 2004–2005 school year. More than one-third of them were served exclusively in regular early childhood settings, while about a third were served exclusively in early childhood special education settings. The remainder of the children were served in home, clinical, or a combination of early childhood settings. Table 1.1 shows the number of infants and toddlers through age 2 served from 1987 to 2007 under Part C of IDEA and the amount of money appropriated. During the 2005–2006 school year, almost 298,000 infants and toddlers and their families received early intervention services. This represents an increase of more

Inclusiveness is the participation of children with disabilities in settings with typically developing children.

Natural environments enable delivery of services to young children with special needs in settings that are typical for other children of that age.

BOX 1.1   MINIMUM COMPONENTS UNDER IDEA FOR A STATEWIDE, COMPREHENSIVE SYSTEM OF EARLY INTERVENTION SERVICES TO INFANTS AND TODDLERS WITH SPECIAL NEEDS (INCLUDING AMERICAN INDIAN AND HOMELESS INFANTS AND TODDLERS)

1. A rigorous definition of the term 'developmental delay'
2. Appropriate early intervention services based on scientifically based research, to the extent practicable, are available to all infants and toddlers with disabilities and their families, including Indian and homeless infants and toddlers
3. Timely and comprehensive multidisciplinary evaluation of needs of children and family-directed identification of the needs of each family
4. Individualized family service plan and service coordination
5. Comprehensive child find and referral system
6. Public awareness program including the preparation and dissemination of information to be given to parents, and disseminating such information to parents
7. Central directory of services, resources, and research and demonstration projects
8. Comprehensive system of personnel development, including the training of paraprofessionals and the training of primary referral sources
9. Policies and procedures to ensure that personnel are appropriately and adequately prepared and trained

10. Single line of authority in a lead agency designated or established by the governor for carrying out:
    a. General administration and supervision
    b. Identification and coordination of all available resources
    c. Assignment of financial responsibility to the appropriate agencies
    d. Development of procedures to ensure that services are provided in a timely manner pending resolution of any disputes
    e. Resolution of intra- and interagency disputes
    f. Development of formal interagency agreements
11. Policy pertaining to contracting or otherwise arranging for services
12. Procedure for securing timely reimbursement of funds
13. Procedural safeguards
14. System for compiling data on the early intervention system
15. State interagency coordinating council
16. Policies and procedures to ensure that to the maximum extent appropriate, early intervention services are provided in natural environments except when early intervention cannot be achieved satisfactorily in a natural environment

Note: Adapted from 20 U.S.C. §1435(a).

than 30,000 children served since the last edition of this book was published. These children are served in many different settings. The trend over the years has been for more infants and toddlers to receive services in the home rather than in other settings (see Table 1.2) and is consistent with the principle of natural environments.

IDEA provides other programs that indirectly benefit young children with special needs and their families. For example, the law provides continued funding for

FIGURE 1.1

Number of children served, total appropriations, and allocation per child from 1977 to 2006 under Part B, Section 619 (Preschool Programs) of the Individuals with Disabilities Education Act.

Key:

Dollars (Millions) appropriated for distribution to states

Children (Thousands) receiving FAPE in the Fall of each federal fiscal year, U.S. & Outlying Areas.

Dollars Per Child allocation of Section 619 dollars

FFY (**Federal Fiscal Year**): For example, in FFY 1986, 261,000 children were reported to be receiving services as of December 1, 1985.

FFY	'77	'86	'87	'88	'89	'90	'91	'92	'93	'94	'95	'96	'97	'98	'99	'00	'01	'02	'03	'04	'05	'06
Dollars (Millions)	12	28	180	201	247	251	292	320	326	339	360	360	360	374	374	390	390	390	387	387	385	381
Children (Thousands)	197	261	265	288	323	352	369	398	430	479	528	549	562	572	573	587	599	647	647	680	702	704
Dollar Per Child	63	110	679	697	769	713	797	803	750	707	683	656	641	654	653	664	650	630	599	570	548	541

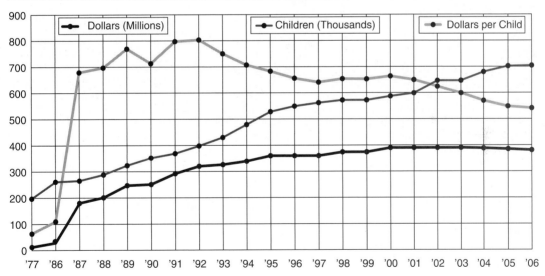

Sources: www.ideadata.org (Fall 2005 child count data updated *July 17, 2006*, and downloaded March 8, 2007) and http://www.ed.gov/about/overview/budget/budget07/07action.pdf. Reproduced with permission of the National Early Childhood Technical Assistance Center from Lazara, A., Danaher, J., & Kraus, R. (Eds.) (2007). Section 619 profile (15th edition). Chapel Hill: The University of North Carolina, FPG Child Development Institute, National Early Childhood Technical Assistance Center.

Note: The number represents US and outlying areas.

			TABLE **1.1**	Summary of the Infant and Toddler Program (Part C) of the Individuals with Disabilities Education Act. Annual appropriations and number of children served under Part C of IDEA Federal Fiscal Years 1987–2007.

FFY	Appropriations (Millions $)	Children Number	Percentage
1987	50		
1988	67		
1989	69		
1990	79		
1991	117	194,363	1.77
1992	175	166,634	1.41
1993	213	143,392	1.18
1994	253	154,065	1.30
1995	316	165,253	1.41
1996	316	177,734	1.54
1997	316	187,348	1.65
1998	350	197,376	1.70
1999	370	188,926	1.63
2000	375	205,769	1.78
2001	383.6	230,853	1.99
2002	417	247,433	2.14
2003	434	268,331	2.24
2004	444	272,454	2.24
2005	440.8	282.733	2.30
2006	436.4	298,150	2.40
2007	436.4	n/a	n/a

Source: Reproduced with permission of the National Early Childhood Technical Assistance Center from Danaher, J., Good, S., & Lazara, A. (Eds.) (2007). Part C updates (9th edition). Chapel Hill: The University of North Carolina, FPG Child Development Institute, National Early Childhood Technical Assistance Center.

		TABLE **1.2**	Number of infants and toddlers in different settings receiving services under part of the Individuals with Disabilities Education Act as of July 17, 2006.

Setting	Number of Children
Developmental delay programs	12, 415
Home	231,529
Hospital (inpatient)	280
Service provider location	15,826
Typically developing programs	12,339
Residential facility	153
Other setting	7,587

Source: U.S. Department of Education, Office of Special Education Programs, Data Analysis System (DANS), OMB #1820-0557.

demonstration service projects (formerly First Chance projects), for replication of successful demonstration projects (called *outreach*), for research projects and demonstration personnel training projects, for research institutes and other research activities, and for technical assistance. During the 2004–2005 school year, the following activities were funded through IDEA: 10 model demonstration projects; 6 outreach projects; 22 research projects; 38 research institutes, centers, and studies; 3 Institute of Education science projects; 21 general supervision grants; 16 technology and media projects; 10 congressionally mandated activities; 52 deaf-blind state projects; and 1 national technical assistance center.

Finally, IDEA provides funds to states for personnel training programs and specifies that each state must have a Comprehensive System of Personnel Development (CSPD) plan to prepare its personnel. There were 104 personnel preparation projects and 49 state improvement/personnel development grants funded for 2004–2005. Recipients of demonstration and outreach grants are encouraged to coordinate activities with the state agency responsible for administering early intervention programs. The law gave the governor of each state authority to appoint the state agency to oversee the infant and toddler (Part C) program in the state. The responsible agencies in each state are listed in Table 1.3. The successful application of other federal laws to young children with special needs offers further support for the rights of these children to early education opportunities.

The reauthorization of IDEA in 2004 called for states to establish goals for students with disabilities that were aligned with the **No Child Left Behind (NCLB) Act of 2001**. NCLB had as its primary goal that every child would be reading at grade level by third grade. The law also focused on the application of evidence-based strategies (i.e., using approaches that have research support). The movement toward using documented approaches has been at the foundation of early childhood programs and has been addressed with respect to special needs populations (Odom et al., 2005; Schweinhart, 2002). While IDEA emphasizes individual student progress and NCLB emphasizes school accountability through measurement of a school's Adequate Yearly Progress (AYP), both laws focus on improving academic achievement through high quality programs and high expectations. In order for young children to meet the goals of NCLB, especially those with special needs, it was understood that high quality programs must begin before kindergarten. Consequently, the *Good Start, Grow Start* initiative was enacted in 2002 as an offshoot of NCLB. This program had three components: strengthening Head Start, promoting a federal-state partnership to improve early childhood programs, and improving dissemination of information on current practices and research to early childhood personnel.

Section 504 of the Rehabilitation Act of 1973 prohibits discrimination on the basis of disability in any state or local government program or activity that receives federal funds. A regulation added in 1977 specifies the applicability of Section 504 to public school districts and other recipients of federal funds in education, health, and social services. These agencies, including schools, must ensure that children with disabilities are not excluded from services or denied benefits. However, whereas the law ensures the participation of children with disabilities in school programs, it does not require that the school provide expensive or extensive services. Rather, the law refers to "reasonable accommodations." These may include a special aide providing assistance, modifications to the class program, monitoring of medications,

Section 504 of the Rehabilitation Act of 1973 requires that "reasonable accommodations" be made in school for children with disabilities.

TABLE 1.3	List of Part C lead agencies.
State/Jurisdiction [1,2]	**Lead Agency**
Alabama	Rehabilitation Services
Alaska	Health and Social Services
American Samoa	Health
Arizona	Economic Security
Arkansas	Human Services/Developmental Disabilities
California	Developmental Services
Colorado	Human Services/Developmental Disabilities
Commonwealth of Northern Mariana Islands	Education
Connecticut	Mental Retardation
Delaware	Health and Social Services
District of Columbia	Human Services
Florida	Health (Children's Medical Services)
Georgia	Human Resources/Division of Public Health
Guam	Education
Hawaii	Health
Idaho	Health & Welfare/Developmental Disabilities
Illinois	Human Services
Indiana	Family and Social Services
Iowa	Education
Kansas	Health and Environment
Kentucky	Health Services
Louisiana	Health & Hospitals
Maine	Education
Maryland	Education
Massachusetts	Public Health
Michigan	Education
Minnesota	Education
Mississippi	Health
Missouri	Education
Montana	Public Health and Human Services
Nebraska	Education and Health and Human Services (Co-Lead)
Nevada	Human Resources/Health
New Hampshire	Health and Human Services
New Jersey	Health and Senior Services
New Mexico	Health
New York	Health
North Carolina	Health and Human Services
North Dakota	Human Services
Ohio	Health
Oklahoma	Education
Oregon	Education
Pennsylvania	Public Welfare
Puerto Rico	Health
Rhode Island	Human Services
South Carolina	Health and Environmental Control
South Dakota	Education
Tennessee	Education
Texas	Assistive and Rehabilitative Services
Utah	Health
Vermont	Education and Human Services (Co-Lead)
Virgin Islands	Health
Virginia	Mental Health, Mental Retardation & Substance Abuse Services
Washington	Social and Health Services
West Virginia	Health and Human Resources
Wisconsin	Health and Family Services
Wyoming	Health

[1] Federated States of Micronesia, Republic of Marshall Islands and Republic of Palau are not currently eligible for this federal program.

[2] The Department of the Interior (DOI) receives allocation from the U.S.Department of Education, which then is distributed by DOI to tribes.

Source: National Early Childhood Technical Assistance Center (NECTAC). Chapel Hill: The University of North Carolina, FPG Child Development Institute. Retrieved from http://www.nectac.org/partc/ptclead.asp

counseling, using assistive technology, or application of a behavior management plan. Under Section 504, children may receive related services, such as speech therapy, occupational therapy, or physical therapy, even if the child does not receive services through IDEA. However, no funds are provided to schools for these services.

The **Americans with Disabilities Act of 1990 (ADA)**, like Section 504, is an antidiscrimination law. Whereas mostly aimed at employment settings, two provisions affect students. The first applies protections in nonsectarian private schools, including preschools. Furthermore, ADA requires that public schools make accommodations for students with disabilities. These may include accessibility to facilities, program modifications, and use of assistive technology. The law provides no funds to fulfill these requirements.

Through legislative authority, the U.S. Department of Health and Human Services's Administration for Children and Families and the Administration on Developmental Disabilities also provide specialized funds for some early intervention activities. Funds are allotted through state developmental disabilities councils which may support a variety of child development activities, such as training programs and workshops. University Centers for Excellence in Developmental Disabilities Education, Research, and Service (UCEDDs), of which there are 61 in the United States, provide interdisciplinary training, exemplary services, technical assistance, and information and dissemination activities for a population beginning at birth. Finally, Projects of National Significance (PNS) are funded annually to address critical needs in the area of developmental disabilities. Among these are projects that develop training and ongoing programs for inclusion of children with developmental disabilities in child care settings.

Clearly, there is now tangible evidence to support the prudence of government involvement in early childhood intervention. Although government action initially was a response to pressure from advocacy groups and legislators with family members or friends with disabilities, federal and state legislative and regulatory activities currently reflect growing acceptance of early education.

The Americans with Disabilities Act of 1990 states that public schools must provide accessible accommodations for students with disabilities, including modified programs and adaptive technology.

Review the legislative actions that had a significant impact on early intervention. What would be the status of early childhood special education without legislation?

Empirical Evidence

Factors that cause impairment in a child are present even before birth. The gene pool of the mother and father, as well as the level and extent of prenatal care, contribute to the outcome of pregnancy. These are among the many concerns that weigh heavily on the minds of prospective parents like Alex and Margie. As will be seen in chapter 2, research literature continues to identify specific factors that have an impact during pregnancy and influence the subsequent health and well-being of the child. Intervention in the areas of maternal nutrition and child-rearing attitudes have yielded optimistic results (Dombrowski, Timmer, Blacker, & Urquiza, 2005). Further, revelations from the Human Genome Project offer hope of prenatal identification and even prenatal treatment for many genetically based disorders. The Human Genome Project initially was planned as a 15-year, federally-funded program whose goal was to identify the functions of each of the human genes. After just a few years of the program, several private companies and laboratories began to do the same work. Progress was rapid and the structure of the human genome, and those of many other organisms, was revealed ahead of schedule. The findings from the program already have provided revolutionary changes in the search for prevention and treatment of broad-based diseases and disorders.

Once a child is born with a disabling condition, of course, a different set of factors must be addressed. The accumulating evidence indicates that results of efforts to remediate or attenuate children's deficits also can be successful.

Investigations of early intervention have focused on two major groups of children: those who exhibit developmental deficits as a result of environmental factors and those who are disabled as a result of biological factors. These two groups of children comprise the majority of the special education population in public school programs. A question that must be asked is: If these children had been identified and served earlier, could something have been done to make special education placement less likely or, at least, to reduce the severity of the children's problems? Although more evidence exists to support the benefits of early intervention for children at environmental risk (Anderson et al., 2003; Nelson, Westhues, & McLeod, 2003; Vandell, 2004), research that supports services for young children with biological impairments also is growing. For example, Black, Dubowitz, Krishnakumar, & Starr (2007) examined the influence of home visiting on infants with failure to thrive syndrome. In particular, the home intervention curriculum concentrated on maternal sensitivity, parent-infant relationships, and child development. This group was compared with a group of typical infants and with a group of other infants with failure to thrive who did not receive home intervention, but were seen in a medical clinic for routine care. At 8-year follow-up, children in the typical growth group were taller, heavier, and had better arithmetic scores than the clinic-only group. The home intervention group had intermediate results. There were no group differences in IQ, reading, or mother-reported behavior problems. However, children in the home intervention group had fewer teacher-reported problems and better work habits than the clinic-only group. Whereas failure to thrive makes a child vulnerable to poor outcomes, including short stature, poor arithmetic achievement, and poor work habits, home intervention attenuates some of these negative effects.

> Even with procedural problems with the research, the evidence tends to support the benefits of early intervention with a variety of young children with special needs.

In general, the body of research on biological risk is riddled with procedural problems, such as small sample size, lack of comparison groups, a short period of intervention, and poorly defined intervention procedures. It is no surprise, therefore, that outcome research in early intervention with children with biological impairments has yielded equivocal results (Baker & Feinfield, 2003; Johnson, Ring, Anderson, & Marlow, 2005).

Some components of early intervention may have greater impact than others (Shonkoff, Hauser, Krauss, & Upshur, 1992). For example, the impact of child–family interaction (Keogh, Garnier, Bernheimer, & Gallimore, 2000) and biological traits (Hauser-Cram, Warfield, Shonkoff, & Kraus, 2001) was examined in various groups of infants, toddlers, and preschoolers with developmental disabilities in early intervention programs. In general, biological characteristics of the child with disabilities are the best predictors of development during the infant and toddler years. Family factors, which may be influenced by focused early intervention programs, manifest changes in development into the middle preschool years and beyond (Sameroff, 1998).

The earliest study of contemporary importance concerning children at environ-mental risk was the classic work of Skeels (1966). A group of children in an institu-tional facility were moved to an orphanage where they received individualized attention from older residents, in contrast to the considerable deprivation experi-enced by the children who remained in the institution. As time passed, children who remained in the original setting showed an average decrease in measured intel-ligence, whereas children in the new setting showed significant increases in mea-sured intelligence, apparently as a result of the greater attention they received.

Research on the influence of early education received great impetus when prominent scholars such as Benjamin Bloom (1964) and J. McVicker Hunt (1961) emphasized the sensitive nature of children's earliest years. Federal funding of pro-grams to serve preschool children from low-income families provided researchers with an opportunity to explore the application of their theories through various ap-proaches to early intervention. In the mid-1970s, a group of individuals who had directed these model programs gathered to review the progress of the children they had served. The Consortium for Longitudinal Studies (1983) issued several reports based on its review. Longitudinal results continued to be reported for the Perry Preschool Project over the years (Schweinhart, 2004). The Consortium for Longitu-dinal Studies and Perry Preschool reports described the following outcomes for children who had received early intervention compared to children who had not:

1. The number of special education placements and children who were retained in grade was significantly smaller for the early intervention groups when they entered school.
2. These children attained higher achievement test scores and were more commit-ted to school.
3. Members of this group were less likely to show delinquent behavior outside of school or to get into legal trouble.

These are the more conservative outcomes of early intervention, representing the human aspect of the benefits. That is, children are more productive and per-form better within and outside of school when they receive early intervention. Another aspect of the benefits is equally meaningful: Significant financial gains are realized as a result of serving preschoolers with disabilities from the youngest age possible (Burr & Grunewald, 2006; Federal Reserve Bank of Minneapolis, 2003; Reynolds, Temple, Robertson, & Mann, 2002). Studies on the cost-effectiveness of early intervention generally have examined disadvantaged children and fami-lies and are in agreement that schools quickly recover the costs of early interven-tion through savings in the lesser amount of special services required and in less retention in grade. The cumulative cost of serving a child through age 18 de-creases in proportion to how early intervention begins. Savings to society con-tinue outside of school and even after the child leaves school altogether. Children who need services and who receive early intervention are less likely than those who do not to use public funds for maintenance in prison, for welfare payments, or for unemployment compensation. They are more likely to obtain gainful em-ployment after leaving school and to pay taxes and are more likely to complete high school and avoid trouble with the law (Campbell, Ramey, Pungello, Sparling,

The benefits of early inter-vention can be measured in many dimensions.

& Miller-Johnson, 2002; Karoly, Kilburn, Bigelow, Caulkins, & Cannon, 2001; Lynch, 2004; Schweinhart, 2004).

Palmer (1983), one of the Consortium for Longitudinal Studies members, urged caution in interpreting and generalizing the results. Gray (1983), another member, responding to comments that the outcome of her own project did not match the enthusiastic results of some other projects, placed intervention into perspective by noting that the families with whom her project worked had multiple and severe problems, including extreme poverty. She also noted that, compared with the amount of time a project child spent in impoverished surroundings, "the total input from our program occupied about two-thirds of one percent of the waking hours of the participants from birth to 18 years" (p. 128). Cole, Mills, Jenkins, & Dale (2005) also have questioned the results of differential social benefits reported for two preschool models of the Perry Preschool Project, finding no differences in their follow-up study of 174 15-year-olds.

Several longitudinal studies provide additional insight into the influences of early intervention. For example, in a review of results of three long-term studies of children from low-income and undereducated families, Ramey and Ramey (1994) concluded the following:

> Maternal intelligence is a key factor in children's intellectual development, especially when these children are not provided with intensive early intervention. Fortunately, children whose mothers have low IQs respond positively to intensive, high-quality early intervention, which leads to a dramatic reduction in their rates of mental retardation during the intervention program. (p. 1066)

Another study followed a large cohort of infants living in poverty (Bradley, Whiteside, Mundfrom, & Casey, 1994). The Infant Health and Development Program found that, at 3 years of age, certain home factors and participation in the early intervention program differentiated those children who showed early signs of coping with environmental demands ("resiliency") from those who did not. The latter group was identified as having a poorer developmental prognosis. A study of specific types of early intervention, including home visits and enriched day care, with a low-birth-weight subgroup of this cohort found that, at an 18-year follow-up of 636 of the original 984 baby cohort, the heavier low birth weight treatment group had significantly higher IQ and math scores than the children who did not receive early intervention services. The lighter low birth weight group did not do as well in a reading achievement test as the group that received no early intervention. This might indicate that different types of early intervention are needed for children who experience severe biological risk compared with those who experience environmental or milder biological risk (McCormick et al., 2006).

More recently, Barlow et al. (2007) reported on a British study of home visitation with infants of families at risk for abuse and neglect. Home visitors provided intervention following the Home Partnership Model involving weekly visits from six months prenatally to 12 months postnatally. Outcome measures included mother-child interaction, maternal psychological health attitudes and behavior, infant functioning and development, and risk of neglect or abuse. At 12 months, the intervention group versus a comparison group showed significant positive differences in maternal sensitivity and infant cooperativeness. While these results would be promising were the changes sustained beyond the intervention period, an earlier study of adolescent mothers by this author and colleagues (Baskin, Umansky, & Sanders, 1987) sheds concerns on longer-term benefits. Indeed, adolescents who received the home intervention were significantly more responsive to their infants than mothers in the comparison group, but these changes were not sustained at six months following the end of intervention. The authors identify numerous factors that must be addressed to maximize the long-term outcome of children from high-risk families. These include family encouragement to continue one's own education, financial help, availability of day care, transportation, and the maturity level and motivation of the mother.

Finally, an excellent and comprehensive presentation of the long-term outcomes of early childhood programs in the United States and elsewhere was published about a decade ago (Behrman, 1995) and is worthwhile reading.

A summary review of the evidence supports the benefits of early intervention on both personal and financial levels with most young children with special needs. More systematic research on children with biological impairments is needed, but the available evidence suggests a justification for early intervention.

> Take a moment to review the empirical evidence supporting early intervention. What additional research is needed for you to be forceful in your justification for early childhood special education programs?

Ethical Considerations

Individuals with special needs are likely to be dependent on others throughout their lives. Their dependence can be extremely burdensome financially and in terms of the quantity of resources. The cost of maintaining one person who is disabled in a state institution, for example, can exceed $60,000 per year. Within the community, adults with disabilities often require special housing, transportation, health services, sheltered employment or work training, food and clothing subsidies, and other support. The constant dependence of the individual on others and the inability to break away from the dependency promotes "learned incompetence." Continued dependence also contributes to negative attitudes on the part of the public toward people with disabilities. When so much public money is spent on expensive services for a small percentage of the population, a society under economic stress often looks for a scapegoat. The problem is compounded when resources are channeled to individuals with disabilities when it is too late to do more than support a subsistence level of living. Certainly, the evidence shows only limited success for intervention with older school-aged children and adults with disabilities.

> Ethics is a system of moral principles that govern conduct.

The ethical arguments for early intervention, then, encompass three issues: (1) preventing the child from learning incompetence by promoting greater independence, (2) removing the continued burden to society by reducing the child's long-term needs for intensive and expensive resources, and (3) changing the public's attitudes toward individuals who are disabled by demonstrating the success of early intervention programs in decreasing their dependence on public support.

Ethical considerations in support of early childhood special education should be as important as empirical evidence. The forces that motivated passage of the Americans with Disabilities Act and those that refocused the attention of Americans on the future of our youth appear to be maintaining momentum to support

> Congress reauthorizes special education laws every few years. Advocates must be knowledgeable and current to offer a rationale for supporting early childhood special education.

educational opportunities for young children with special needs. But this trend could change quickly because Congress and the states reconsider funding and priorities on a regular basis. Early interventionists play a critical and challenging role in this advocacy process as well as provide competent delivery of high-quality services. They are in a position that demands both the persuasive discourse and oratory of a journalist and the controlled militarism of one who has seen battles on the front lines. The challenge is keen, but the outcomes are tangible and offer a significant contribution to individuals and to society.

:: THE EARLY INTERVENTIONIST

Teacher Roles

The professional who works with young children with special needs and their families is called by many titles and wears many hats: those of teacher, social worker, psychologist, counselor, and public relations person. This is not always by design, but often out of necessity. The early interventionist may, after all, work in a public school classroom, in a center-based program operated by a nonschool agency, in a clinical setting, in a consulting capacity, or in the home, and he or she works with a population with which few people have much experience. Consequently, this professional becomes the resource for the parent, for education colleagues, and for community agency personnel.

> The early interventionist as teacher should be able to verbalize the basis for the early intervention strategies being used.

The teacher has several primary tasks. Ultimate responsibility for program planning and implementation belongs to the teacher, who may base the intervention approach on a central theoretical scheme or on a more generalized eclectic scheme. (See chapter 9 for a discussion of program models.) In either case, the teacher should be able to justify the particular program used with any child.

Program implementation for a young child often demands identification of the many factors that influence development and learning. Recognition of the importance of the home environment and family members in this process frequently draws early intervention programs toward a homebound model, but, as we shall see, there are many ways to make an impact on a young child.

The role of early interventionist encompasses great diversity and requires certain personal qualities: quick thinking, flexibility, diplomacy, scholarship, and an inner drive for accomplishment. The daily schedule of a professional in a school system reflects the uniqueness of the job, as described in the following vignette.

VIGNETTE 1.1

AN EARLY INTERVENTIONIST'S DAILY SCHEDULE

The first thing I do when I arrive in the morning is go over the daily schedule with my "parapro" (paraprofessional), Ken. He's the best; I couldn't do without him! We have two groups of six parents and their children who come into school three times each week. One group comes Monday, Wednesday, and Friday; the other group Tuesday, Thursday, and Friday. Fridays get a little hairy, but it does the parents and kids so much good to get together with each other.

So my "parapro" and I start the day reviewing what we will do with the morning group. They are here from 9 until 11:30 and get our total attention during that time. From 11:30 to 12, we talk over what occurred, jot down notes, and transfer any data we collected to the kids' folders. It helps for us to keep an ongoing record of the kids' progress just so we can feel we're making a difference. And the parents appreciate it, too.

We usually brown-bag lunch at one of the local agencies in the area or go out for lunch with a few of the welfare caseworkers, public health nurses, school psychologists, or whoever is available. It helps us to know what's going on in other agencies and it sure helps for them to know us. A lot of our kids use other community resources, and it's nice to be able to pick up the phone and say, "Hi, Nick. Enjoyed lunch yesterday. By the way, I think Ms. Jones is having some problems again with Toni's braces. I'd appreciate it if you'd give her a call today." It works! And our colleagues around town do the same with us. Martha called me yesterday because she knew Ken had a visit scheduled with one of our mutual families. Martha wanted Ken to remind the family about their appointment at the orthopedic clinic next week. Happy to do it! It's also a lot more efficient than professionals tripping over each other trying to get to the family. Some of our families are followed by five or more agencies. Can you imagine all those visitors coming and going in your home!

Well, Ken and I each have two home visits scheduled for the afternoon. One of my visits today is to screen a new child for the program. The others are to continue working through our curriculum with the children and families.

I head back to school today after the visits for a staffing on another new child. Sometimes the special education director runs the staffing, but I'll be running this one. I was a little scared the first few times I ran staffings. I've settled in now and just try to get the parent and the other people there to share their thoughts on what the child needs. Everyone's concern for the child and desire to do the best thing usually come through loud and clear. And I think that some of my colleagues who hadn't thought much about serving preschoolers with disabilities are becoming strong advocates for the program!

Today's a little longer day than usual. I speak to a church group this evening. They have several kids in their neighborhood who have dropped out of school or have graduated but don't have jobs. I think I'd like to use some of them on a volunteer basis in our class. Maybe after they're trained, they'll be able to get a good job at a local child care center. The programs need good people, and we could sure use a few extra sets of trained hands around our kids.

No question about it, it's a challenging job. But we love it. Ken and I enjoy working with the children, of course, but the opportunities to work with parents and other community people make us feel that we're doing the most efficient job of addressing the total needs of the kids and helping to change community attitudes, too.

The early interventionist who works with the infant and toddler program of the community public health agency also brings personal perspectives, as described in the following vignette.

VIGNETTE 1.2

PERSPECTIVE ON THE INFANT AND TODDLER PROGRAM

Sometimes my first visit with the child and parent is in the hospital right after the child is born. When an obvious disability is identified, the physician or hospital social worker calls us to begin the process of parent education and preparation for what is likely to be ahead. Having a young child of my own has made me a lot more sensitive to how I approach the parents. I recognize their many months of building happy expectations for a healthy baby, their desire but sometimes reluctance to accept and love the child, and the complications resulting from the impact that early medical interventions (neonatal intensive care units, technological devices, and limited physical contact, for example) may have on the parent–child relationship. And we talk about these issues. We talk about how I can help the family when the baby gets home and start talking about other family and community support resources that are available.

Teacher Competencies

It is relatively easy to see that an untrained person will not do well in the tasks just described. The complex roles that early interventionists take on require careful training and ongoing clarification of professional responsibilities. Certain minimum entry-level skills and knowledge are necessary to do an adequate job. Experience as well as further knowledge and skill allows the teacher to meet the challenges of the position with confidence and competence.

The complexity of the teacher's role may be thought of as a matrix with at least four dimensions:

1. The age of the child may range from newborn to 5 years or older.
2. The setting may be a hospital, the home, a clinic, a special preschool classroom, a parent–child group, or an inclusive setting with children with and without disabilities together.
3. The individuals involved in the intervention may be the child, the parents and other family members, community agency personnel, health professionals, and others representing a variety of cultures and backgrounds.
4. The task may be assessment, intervention, counseling and education, evaluation, report writing, case management, or coordination of staffing.

Even without complete agreement among professionals about the order of importance of skills and knowledge, several competencies stand out logically for the early interventionist, as one teacher tells us in the following vignette.

VIGNETTE 1.3

COMPETENCIES NEEDED BY THE EARLY INTERVENTIONIST

I couldn't believe all I was called upon to do and all I felt that I needed to do. It helps to enjoy the work and to be really committed to it. I believe it was Weikart (1981) who found that one's commitment to whatever approach is used is more closely related to the child's outcome than any one particular approach over another. Of course, the interventionist should know child development backward and forward and be ready to be amazed when a child does something unexpected!

I think I know what I'm doing. Each time I interact professionally with a child or parent or colleague I know what I want to accomplish and I have a plan to accomplish it. I also keep some alternate plans in my "back pocket." Flexibility helps!

I find it important to speak several languages, also. A language for parents and volunteers that is free of the professional jargon. Jargon can lose them really quickly. And there are the languages of the other professionals. I've learned a lot about occupational therapy, speech therapy, physical therapy, medications, and all types of physical and health problems that my kids have. I've had to if I am to keep my credibility with my colleagues. They've learned my language, too. I like the continuous learning aspect of the job anyway. It does a lot to prevent burnout.

Screening and assessing kids came pretty easy to me because I had done a lot in my university training program. I learned about a few more testing instruments pretty quickly, which let me concentrate on the child and parent instead of the test manual during a testing session. The school psychologist hasn't had much experience testing really young kids, so we work together most of the time. Testing young kids is tough even when you know what you're doing. I want to be sure we do everything possible to get an accurate assessment, so it's good that we work together.

What blew me away the most in my job was a late-night call I got from one of my parents. We had become close—it happens when you go into people's homes regularly and share their emotional highs and lows. Her child had been in the hospital with respiratory complications. The child had just died and I was the first person that the mom had thought to call. I wasn't prepared for that moment and was pretty disappointed that I couldn't do more. But maybe the fact that I was there to listen was enough for the parent at the time. I at least know now how, ideally, to deal with a situation like that—what to say, what to do. I've done some reading and talking to people about it.

It's a difficult balance to maintain when you work with parents of kids with disabilities. You want to remain objective but you need to give them support and get them actively involved in supporting their kids. I've got lots more learning to do but I'm sure working on it.

I get a lot of satisfaction out of seeing how far the classroom part of the program has progressed. It's taken a bunch of work to make the parents feel comfortable with me and with each other, and I think they could run the program themselves now (with a little guidance every once in a while). The routine we established for the sessions has helped. We try hard to model for the parents and to give them good feedback when they interact with their kids. Our parents also are becoming better able to identify the resources that they and their children need in the community. They seem more confident calling the health department or physician or counseling center, for example. I hope that we've helped to build their skills to mobilize community resources. Just as we're trying to teach the children to be more independent in making choices and decisions, we're trying to make parents less dependent upon us. That's not easy and sometimes I feel so tempted to make the call for the parent or handle a child's temper tantrum or bring toys into the home or do for the parents what they are ready to do for themselves. It's taken some time for me to know how fast to move with different families, and I still make mistakes. But I feel pretty comfortable now discussing my fallibility with the parents and they understand!

The early interventionist must have a broad knowledge base and diverse skills. For a good foundation, teachers must know where to seek needed information and skill-building experiences. Above all, they must recognize their own limitations. Teachers should use, to the maximum extent possible, public and university libraries, teacher centers, community resource people, and the Internet.

Over the course of the past several years, communities have made efforts to offer programs to young children with disabilities in the same settings as their peers without disabilities. This movement toward capitalizing on inclusive settings has demanded an examination of the practices used by programs that serve young children.

The National Association for the Education of Young Children (NAEYC) published a position paper in 1991 that was revised in 1997 titled *Developmentally Appropriate Practice in Early Childhood Programs Serving Children from Birth to Age 8* (Bredekamp & Copple, 1997). This document of general philosophy and program guidelines for early childhood educators led to the publication of a similar document for early interventionists by the **Division for Early Childhood (DEC)** of the Council for Exceptional Children. *DEC-Recommended Practices in Early Childhood/Special Education* (Sandall, McLean, Hemmeter, & Smith, 2004) provides the early interventionist with excellent guidelines against which to evaluate her or his philosophy, knowledge, and skills. A workbook also has been published to accompany these guidelines (Hemmeter, Smith, Sandall, & Askew, 2005). There are many similarities between the developmentally appropriate practices (DAPs) presented by NAEYC and DEC. The philosophical differences, characterized by a developmental approach in early childhood education (ECE) versus a remedial–prescriptive approach in early childhood special education (ECSE), spurred considerable debate in the literature at the time the NAEYC document was published (Fox, Hanline, Vail, & Galant, 1994; Odom & McEvoy,

> The Division for Early Childhood of the Council for Exceptional Children is one of the major professional organizations for early interventionists.

1990), but less discussion across disciplines since then. The differences do not appear to be an impediment for either discipline to work together for the good of each child and family. Furthermore, the changing faces of both ECE and ECSE within the community setting encourage a drawing together of the content of both documents:

> Analyses of the components of DAP reveal that practices valued by ECSE are not incompatible with what has been stated as important in educating typically developing children. In the areas of curriculum, adult-child interaction, and developmental evaluation, the practices that are important to ECSE fit within the breadth of what is considered developmentally appropriate. Furthermore, there appears to be a trend in ECSE, with a growing empirical base, to move towards interventions that reflect the practices articulated by NAEYC and away from a narrow, remedial approach to early intervention. (Fox et al., 1994, p. 253)

The unity of ECE and ECSE is reflected in the collaborative position paper by DEC, the Association of Teacher Educators, and NAEYC (1994) titled *Personnel Standards for Early Education and Early Intervention: Guidelines for Licensure in Early Childhood Special Education* (reaffirmed in 2000). This document offers a framework for the preparation of professionals to serve a unique population and a standardization of minimum competencies. The competent early interventionist is one who

- is knowledgeable about child development and disabilities
- follows a theoretical intervention model and can justify the approach
- supports and responds to children and parents but promotes their independence
- adapts quickly to new and demanding situations
- administers and interprets preschool test instruments
- interacts productively with colleagues, children, and parents
- evaluates program success routinely and systematically
- uses available resources to better understand and meet the needs of children and their families
- functions well in a variety of settings
- adapts to the cultural differences of families
- encourages and accepts input related to development and modification from families and other sources.

A comprehensive guide to these recommended practices in personnel preparation is available from DEC (Sandall, McLean, & Smith, 2002).

:: YOUNG CHILDREN WITH SPECIAL NEEDS AND THEIR FAMILIES

Who Are Young Children with Special Needs?

IDEA defines children with disabilities as those children with mental retardation, hearing impairments including deafness, speech or language impairments, visual impairments including blindness, serious emotional disturbance, orthopedic impairments, autism, traumatic brain injury, other health impairments, specific learning disabilities, deaf-blindness, or multiple disabilities, and who because of those impairments need special education and related services (34 C.F.R. Ch. 111, Section 300.7 (a) (1), p. 13). Any child from birth through 21 years of age who meets the specific criteria for any of these categories may be eligible for services. Infant and toddler services (for children under 3 years of age) are described in Part C of IDEA. States may choose to serve, under Part C of IDEA, children who are at biological or environmental risk for one of the specified disabilities. The 2004 Amendments to IDEA also provide parents with the option of having their young child continue to be served under Part C. Heretofore, services for all children from 3 years of age were described in Part B of IDEA. However, concerns have been expressed about having to identify young children categorically by the type of disability. Changes in the law over the years acknowledged these concerns (Danaher, Armijo, & Lazara, 2006). In 1991, IDEA permitted states to serve children who are experiencing "developmental delays" as defined by the state using objective measures of physical, cognitive, social-emotional, and adaptive development. The 1997 Amendments to IDEA extended the use of the "developmental delay" category to age 9 and also reinstated the requirement that states report the number of children served by category, but with the addition of "developmental delay." The Improvement Act of 2004 maintained the 3 through 9 age range for developmental delay.

> The use of the "developmental delay" category allows services to be provided to children who do not yet meet the criteria for traditional categories. Services to these children might lessen or eliminate the need for services later in childhood.

Barbara Schwartz/Merrill

For children with disabilities, legislation and research have provided support for early intervention services.

There is a sound rationale for serving young children in at-risk and developmentally delayed categories. The range of variations in development is considerable, even in a group of children of the same chronological age, gender, and ethnic group. In some children, the variation is so extreme that identification of a problem is relatively easy. In such cases, a child may clearly fit into a category described by IDEA. In most situations, however, the child's pattern of development may appear atypical without clearly falling into one of the disability categories. For these children, the developmental delay category is most beneficial, providing less of a stigma and more opportunity to move forward without the categorical burden.

The more flexible definition for young children with special needs, in particular, acknowledges that serving a child early often can prevent serious impairments. Children from poor environments are overrepresented in special education classes in the public schools relative to their number in the general population. Successful efforts have been reported with many different high-risk populations to prevent minor developmental delays from becoming serious impairments (Campbell et al., 2002; McCormick et al., 2006; Peterson et al., 2004). By supporting programs to serve young children prior to the appearance of a clearly identifiable disability, the government may provide a vehicle for preventing more serious impairments as children grow up and reducing the costs of care for these individuals far into the future.

In our discussions in this text, we approach children's needs from a developmental perspective. A framework of typical development underlies descriptions of how children vary from the typical pattern and what programmatic modifications are helpful to support learning. We also have included information on how specific types of disabilities influence development in each skill area. Table 1.4 presents the number of young children by disability area who are receiving special education under IDEA. A brief description of these disability areas follows.

TABLE 1.4	Number of 3- to 5-year-old children served under IDEA, Part B by disability during the 2004–2005 school year.
Disability Category	**Number of Children**
Autism	30,305
Deafness/blindness	236
Traumatic brain injury	1,077
Developmental delay	260,692
Specific learning disability	12,065
Speech/language impairment	330,043
Multiple disability	8,515
Hearing impairment	7,846
Orthopedic impairment	8,201
Other health impairment	13,135
Mental retardation	22,759
Emotional disturbance	5,789
Visual impairment	3,424

Source: From the U.S. Department of Education, Office of Special Education Programs, Data Analysis System (DANS).

Speech and Language Disorders   Because of differences in the rates of development of young children, it is difficult to clearly define what is and what is not a disorder. Certainly, some structural and functional aspects stand out as being atypical. For example, a child with a cleft palate who uses no words at 4 years of age or a child whose language is limited to repetition of what others say clearly can be categorized as having disordered speech and language. But the absence of certain speech sounds at times may reflect a disorder and at other times may reflect normal variations in development. Great care must be taken in identifying a child as fitting this category, particularly when cultural diversity and environment play such critical roles in forming children's speech and language patterns.

Impairments of speech and language frequently accompany other disabilities and, in fact, may be the first suggestion of problems. Children with hearing impairments, cerebral palsy, emotional disturbances, or mental retardation all may exhibit atypical speech and language.

The ability of a child to communicate functionally is a requirement for independent living. A child who is unable to express needs and wants or to interact verbally and appropriately with other children and adults is at a serious disadvantage. Consequently, speech and language disorders must receive careful attention as soon as problems are identified.

Language must be viewed in the context of the child's environment and culture.

Developmental Delay   Other than speech and language impairment, more preschool children are served under this category than any other. IDEA permits this label to be used with children from birth through 9 years of age. The Division for Early Childhood (2000) issued a position paper supporting the use of this category and defined developmental delay as

> a condition which represents a significant delay in the process of development. It does not refer to a condition in which a child is slightly or momentarily lagging in development. The presence of developmental delay is an indication that the process of development is significantly affected and that without special intervention, it is likely that educational performance at school age will be affected. (p. 1)

Supporters of this category believe that the early childhood years are too early to use traditional labels due to the plasticity of development. That is, there is a greater chance of making errors in diagnosis because children's development is molded by changes in the environment and by maturity, and guided by genetic factors, as well. Furthermore, some children show global problems during their early years, although they might not meet the criteria for traditional disability categories. These children would go unserved without a mechanism to make them eligible for appropriate services at a young age. The potential exists for those problems to become more serious and complex as time goes on without appropriate services.

During the 2003–2004 school year, more than 258,000 3- to 5-year-old children were served under the developmental delay category. IDEA mandates that states develop guidelines to determine eligibility of children. Children may be eligible for services under the developmental delay category if they satisfy two conditions: if they currently have a disabling or established risk condition or if they are considered to have a condition that, through informed clinical opinion, is deemed to place them at risk for a disabling condition in the future. States must develop a list of established risk conditions (e.g., Down syndrome and blindness) and set up a process to make children with other problems eligible using **informed clinical opinion.** Through this process, experts use all available information (intake reports, progress notes, test results, medical discharge summaries, etc.) to determine if a child's condition is likely to result in a disability at school entrance were the child not to receive early intervention services. The child's status is reviewed on a regular basis and a determination is made as to whether the child is eligible for services under one of the traditional categories and whether it is in the child's best interests to be served in that category.

Intellectual Disability (Mental Retardation)   While the term *mental retardation* continues to be used in federal law, the preferred term in common use is *intellectual disability*. Nevertheless, these terms are equivalent. The definition of **mental retardation** used most often was developed by the American Association on Mental Retardation (AAMR): Mental retardation refers to "significant limitations both in intellectual functioning and in adaptive behavior as expressed in conceptual, social, and practical adaptive skills. This disability originates before age 18" (American Association on Mental Retardation, 2002).

Intellectual functioning has traditionally been assessed by performance on intelligence tests. Figure 1.2 shows the theoretical distribution of scores on a standardized intelligence test. Although not part of the current definition, it has become commonplace to provide labels for different levels of retardation. A score between 1 and 2 standard deviations below the mean (70–85) characterizes a child with borderline intellectual functioning. Children who score greater than 2 standard deviations below the mean of 100, an intelligence quotient of less than approximately 70, would fall in the category typically classified as intellectually disabled. The levels of disability, as defined by IQ, are as follows:

Mild intellectual disability	55–69
Moderate intellectual disability	40–54
Severe intellectual disability	25–39
Profound intellectual disability	Below 25

The AAMR modified the definition of *mental retardation* to abolish levels based on cognitive dysfunction, as described previously, to differentiate cases of mental retardation based on "needed levels of support" (Bellini, 2003).

The term *adaptive behavior* refers to a child's ability to deal with worldly demands. This may encompass components of communication skills, self-help skills, social skills, and psychomotor skills. Demands vary from setting to setting. A child, therefore, may show deficits in adaptive behavior and be considered mentally retarded in some settings but not in others. What constitutes intellectual disability, however, is both subaverage intellectual functioning *and* deficits in adaptive behavior.

An individual must show deficits in both intellectual functioning and adaptive behavior to be considered mentally retarded or intellectually disabled.

FIGURE 1.2   The theoretical distribution of IQ scores.

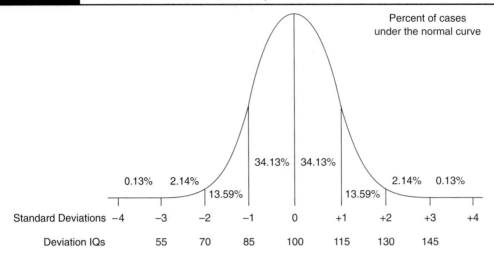

The characteristics of a child who has an intellectual disability depend predominantly on the child's mental age, which is derived from an intelligence test. The more severely disabled a child is, the greater the disparity between mental age and chronological age. Children of the same chronological age, then, may display very different characteristics. Mental age, more than chronological age, reflects a child's current level of ability and determines educational needs. It should be noted that few standardized intelligence tests are available and statistically sound for preschool children, particularly for infants and toddlers. Consequently, other strategies and instrumentation may be employed to measure the intellectual capabilities of these children.

Hearing Impairments   Hearing losses are characterized by degree and type. Hearing is measured in units of intensity (i.e., loudness) and frequency (i.e., pitch). A child with normal hearing can hear sounds as soft as 0 to 25 decibels (dB) within a frequency range of approximately 40 to 4,000 hertz (Hz). Most conversational speech has an intensity of about 55 dB and a frequency range of 500 to 2,000 Hz. A child with a hearing loss of greater than 40 dB will probably miss a considerable amount of spoken information; a profound loss of greater than 90 dB will severely disable a child.

A hearing loss may be conductive or sensorineural. Conductive losses are caused by interference with the sequence of sound vibrations reaching the auditory nerve. Sensorineural losses are caused by defects in the inner ear or in the auditory nerve, which transmit electrical impulses to the brain for interpretation.

Hearing impairments may result from infection during the prenatal or postnatal period, from an accident, or from exposure to certain prescription drugs. The severity of the impairment depends on the degree of loss and the age of onset. A mild loss may allow a child to benefit completely from an auditory environment. A more severe loss may require alternative communication systems and modifications to the environment. In addition, a hearing loss that occurs prior to a child's learning language requires greater environmental modifications than a loss that occurs after mastery of language. *Deafness* is defined in IDEA as a hearing impairment that is so severe that a child is impaired in processing linguistic information through hearing, with or without amplification, and that the child's educational performance is thus adversely affected. Further discussion of hearing impairments is provided in chapter 6.

Infection, accidents, and drugs may contribute to hearing loss.

Visual Impairments   A child is considered to be blind if visual acuity is poorer than 20/200 in the better eye after correction or if the field of vision is limited to an angle of less than 20 degrees. A child with partial sight has an acuity of less than 20/70 but greater than 20/200. An acuity of 20/200 indicates that a child can see at 20 feet what a person with normal vision can see at 200 feet.

In education, children often are categorized in terms of their potential as either print or braille readers. Preschool children with visual impairments whose vision is too poor for them to benefit from even large-print materials should begin a program that sensitizes them to tactile learning materials. This provides an introduction to subsequent learning of pre-braille and braille reading skills.

Most vision problems in young children are attributable to prenatal factors. Infections, such as rubella, and certain hereditary factors may manifest themselves in blindness at birth or create a likelihood that a child will require special education services.

Serious Emotional Disturbance   The causes of severe emotional disturbance in young children are not well understood. Some experts attribute such problems to environmental factors and others to structural or neurochemical abnormalities in the brain. Strategies used to remediate emotional disturbance usually reflect the theoretical orientation of the program staff. Some programs may adjust the child's diet, others may restructure the child's physical environment, and still others may plan the child's interactions with other objects and people. It is most likely, however, that emotional disturbance encompasses many different types of problems, some biologically based and others environmentally based. Certainly, the variety of behaviors that characterize a child with emotional disturbance may be quite diverse: anxiety, withdrawal, aggression, impulsiveness, extreme fear, and so on. Diagnosis is based on the frequency, duration, and intensity of these behaviors. However, the conceptualization of diagnosing such a young child with a psychiatric disorder is not universally accepted. Many of these children will be on one or more medications. It is beneficial for the early intervention professional to be familiar with characteristics of the medications, including their purpose and potential side-effects.

Emotional disturbance probably encompasses many types of problems that are defined by their frequency, intensity, and duration.

Serious emotional disturbance is defined in IDEA as a condition exhibiting one or more of the following characteristics over a long period and to a degree that adversely affects a child's educational performance:

- An inability to learn that cannot be explained by intellectual, sensory, or health factors
- An inability to build or maintain satisfactory interpersonal relationships with peers and teachers
- Inappropriate types of behavior or feelings under normal circumstances
- A general pervasive mood of unhappiness or depression
- A tendency to develop physical symptoms or a physical focus associated with personal or school problems.

Orthopedic Impairments   The category of orthopedic impairments is so broad that it is difficult to identify many general characteristics. Any condition that interferes with the health or normal functioning of bones, joints, or muscles qualifies as an orthopedic impairment. Defects such as spina bifida, club feet, or cerebral palsy may be present at birth; other problems, such as amputations, may occur later in childhood.

Causes of orthopedic impairments are as diverse as the problems themselves. Some are a result of hereditary factors and some are a result of the influence of infection or toxic substances on the mother, particularly during the first trimester of pregnancy. Other impairments may be traced to birth injuries or to diseases or accidents after birth.

Many children with orthopedic impairments require no special education services. Adaptive equipment for some children may help them function independently in a typical setting. Special education staff may help children adjust to their impairment and adapt to the demands of their environment.

Some children with orthopedic impairments require only adaptive equipment and training to adjust to environmental demands.

Other Health Impairments (OHI)   Based on the definition in IDEA, children in this category have limited strength, vitality, or alertness as a result of chronic or acute health problems related to a heart condition, tuberculosis, rheumatic fever, nephritis, asthma, sickle cell anemia, hemophilia, epilepsy, lead poisoning, leukemia, diabetes, or other conditions that adversely affect a child's educational performance. A significant subgroup in this category are children diagnosed with attention deficit-hyperactivity disorder (ADHD). Between 3 and 7% of the school-age population is estimated to have ADHD. In 1991, the Office of Special Education and Rehabilitative Services of the U.S. Department of Education (OSERS, 1991) issued a Joint Policy Memorandum which clarified the circumstances under which children diagnosed with ADHD are eligible for special education services under the OHI category. The memorandum encouraged general and special education personnel to coordinate their efforts to best meet the needs of these children. In addition, the role of Section 504 was discussed for children with ADHD who do not meet the criteria to be served under IDEA.

Autistic Spectrum Disorder (ASD)   As defined by the law, **autism** is a developmental disability that significantly affects verbal and nonverbal communication and social interaction, is generally evident before age 3, and adversely affects a child's educational performance. Other characteristics often associated with autism are engagement in repetitive activities and stereotyped movements, resistance to environmental change or change in daily routines, and unusual responses to sensory experiences. The ASD category also includes Asperger syndrome, Rett syndrome, and pervasive developmental disorder, all of which are characterized by apparent normal early infancy and, during the late stage of infancy and early toddlerhood, development of different *degrees* of atypical performance in the social, communication, and cognitive domains as described for children with autism.

Traumatic Brain Injury (TBI)   TBI is an acquired injury to the brain caused by an external physical force, resulting in total or partial functioning disability or psychosocial impairment, or both, that adversely affects a child's educational performance. Although this definition appears to be fairly simple in its presentation, a plethora of issues surround this disability category (e.g., type of brain injury, severity of brain injury, and age at time of injury). In fact, this special education classification may be especially challenging for the early interventionist, particularly in regard to understanding the nature of recovery from a traumatic brain injury as well as specialized rehabilitation and intervention techniques. It is especially important to coordinate services with medical personnel who can provide guidance relative to safety issues and supportive therapies.

:: THE FAMILY AND THE COMMUNITY

It is difficult for even the experienced professional to have an accurate understanding of the dynamics of families with young children who are disabled. Prospective parents who have waited so many months for the birth of a baby may suddenly find that the child does not even approximate their idealized expectations. The amount of stress imposed on the family may depend on how radically parental expectations are violated (Raina et al., 2005; Ray, 2003; Waisbren, Rones, Read, Marsden, & Levy, 2004). The degree of family stress is related to the specifics of the child's disability, with the greatest stress occurring in families with children who are most severely disabled or in families with limited access to resources (Duarte, Bordin, Yazigi, & Mooney, 2005; Eisenhower, Baker, & Blacher, 2005; Farmer, Marien, Clark, Sherman, & Selva, 2004; Hastings et al., 2005; Johnson, Ring, Anderson, & Marlow, 2003). On the other hand, parenting style and parenting competence can have a significant impact on the quality of life of the child. In a study of children with cerebral palsy, for example, Aran, Shalev, Biran, & Gross-Tsur (2007) reported that parenting style was the only significant factor to have an impact on the child's psychosocial development, exceeding the influence of disease severity. In other developmental domains, the effect of parenting style was greater than the influence of IQ, anxiety, and socioeconomic status. So, while the degree of stress that the disabled child brings to the family is imposing, the influence of parenting style on the child can enhance the child's outcome. Nevertheless, an outgrowth of dealing with the multiple needs of children with disabilities is isolation from normal community activities and interactions (Ehrmann, Aeschleman, & Svanum, 1995).

Consider for a moment the parents for whom every feeding session is a struggle because the child thrusts the food out with the tongue as soon as the parent spoons it in, or the parents who must still change diapers on their 4½-year-old child, or the parents who must keep constant vigilance over their 3-year-old, who sleeps only 2 hours per night and is on the move the remainder of the time! One teacher's experiences with families coping with children with disabilities are described in the following vignette.

VIGNETTE 1.4

COPING WITH DISABILITIES

I don't ever spend time anymore feeling sorry for myself. One of the first families I worked with cured me of that, and it's been reinforced by family after family. Myrna had twin boys. Both were deaf and had cleft palates and hip problems. John also had a cleft lip and a congenital cataract. Myrna was in an auto accident recently and has had medical problems of her own. She's spent most of her time since I've known her running from doctor to doctor and clinic to clinic for John and James. I bet she's had more experience with community agency people than anyone in the state. And she's shared with me a lot of her frustrations about the "hurry up and wait" games and not getting understandable answers from professionals. Yep, she's been through a lot, and I hope her struggles will make things easier for those who follow.

Myrna's husband left soon after the kids were born so she has been pretty much on her own. The kids are 5 years old now, and she's still shuttling them to the speech and hearing clinic regularly for hearing aid checks and to the medical center for monitoring of their cleft palate surgery, making sure they get to school, and trying to keep the house in order. I've never seen happier kids or a mom who could cope the way Myrna has. Sometimes when I'm driving in my car, I just think about her and wonder how she's handled it. I go crazy if my checkbook doesn't balance! Myrna's really given me an education. I hope I've helped her.

Another family that sticks out in my mind has taught me a lot, also. Vicky and Larry's daughter is 2 years old now and has Down syndrome. Her pediatrician recommended immediately after birth that Annie be institutionalized "for her own good and the good of the other children." Imagine that! It's been a tough few years for the family but somehow they manage to come through crisis after crisis a bit stronger and more reflective. Annie has had heart and respiratory problems, and Vicky spends most of her nights keeping watch while Larry gets some rest. He works the first shift at a local plant and rushes home after work to help feed Annie and the other kids, run errands, and handle chores. I don't think Vicky and Larry have been out alone together since Annie was born. They're still scared to leave her with a babysitter, and they have no relatives in the area. I've watched her for a few hours on a couple of nights so that the rest of the family could go out and eat casually at a restaurant. But those moments have been few for them. Mostly, it's feed, change diapers, run to doctors, come to school, and start the cycle again. Vicky and Larry have recently relaxed enough to talk with some of the other parents. I believe it's helped. Hopefully, they'll begin swapping childsitting chores and give each other support.

Sometimes I feel very limited. At other times I know I'm very limited. It's clear to me that I don't know about a child until I know about the child's family. And often the only way to help the child is to help the family. This takes getting to know and understand, as much as possible, the family and home environment. Fortunately, there have been some good folks working in the community who have been more than willing to get me through some rough moments and to help me get families through even more trying times. I remember people telling me about how I should stay away from Cathy Sue at the health department or Jimmy at the welfare office because they're so tough to work with. But these very colleagues—and I choose the word carefully—are my best friends now and some of the strongest advocates for my kids and families.

It's taken me a long time to be comfortable visiting homes routinely, but there's no other way to do my job well. At first, I also thought I was wasting my time stopping by different community agencies to say hello. But it's all helped; it really has. Parents need to know that I'm not interested in their child just as a clinical entity—because it's my job—but that I care about them, the whole family and the child together. Agency people also need to know that I take my job seriously. It makes them feel that their jobs are as important as they really are! I think I've made a difference.

IDEA mandates parent-related activities. Parents must approve individualized testing of their child, must be invited to and may attend the program staffing, must approve the child's special education program and placement, and must have the right to question and challenge decisions that are made for the child. In addition, the needs of the family are a central point of the IFSP. This principle has not changed in the years since P.L. 94–142 was passed.

> The evidence indicates that the family is the most effective and economical system for fostering and sustaining the development of the child. . . . Without family involvement any effects of intervention, at least in the cognitive sphere, appear to erode rapidly once the program ends. In contrast, the involvement of the parents as partners in the enterprise provides an on-going system which reinforces the effects of the program while it is in operation, and helps to sustain them. (Bronfenbrenner, 1974, p. 55)

SUMMARY

The proliferation of early childhood special education programs represents a significant sociological and educational event. The long-term impact of early intervention has been demonstrated in terms of human and financial resources. Furthermore, early intervention offers opportunities to prevent or reduce deficits in children and stress in their families. However, the effectiveness of early intervention efforts depends to a great extent on the competence of the early interventionist. The diversity of children, families, and communities poses both problems and challenges. The ability of the teacher to apply a broad base of knowledge, to communicate well with families and other professionals, to use available resources effectively, and to monitor progress maximizes the ultimate benefits of programs for children.

The first years of children's lives are the most important for establishing a foundation for later learning. Young children with special needs require careful attention by trained individuals to ensure a path of development that, as closely as possible, parallels that of children without disabilities. This is achieved by providing for the child's physical and biological needs and by providing an environment rich in opportunities to learn. Although legal and ethical precedents have spawned an increase in the number of programs available, only the commitment of knowledgeable and skilled professionals can ensure that a high level of quality accompanies the increase in services.

REVIEW QUESTIONS AND DISCUSSION POINTS

1. Describe the historic and current involvement of government in the education of young children with special needs.
2. You are asked to make a presentation to a legislative committee that is considering funding for early childhood special education programs. Make a case for funding based on empirical research in the area.
3. What qualities and characteristics contribute to being a successful early interventionist?
4. Discuss the similarities and differences between an IEP and an IFSP.
5. What are the differences between mandates for services to infants and toddlers and those for preschoolers with special needs?
6. How has the use of the "developmental delay" category affected the eligibility process?
7. Describe at least five changes from the passage of P.L. 94–142 to passage of the most recent reauthorization of IDEA regarding young children with special needs.
8. What influence does the No Child Left Behind Act have on early intervention services?

RECOMMENDED RESOURCES

Websites

American Speech-Hearing-Language Association (ASHA)
http://www.asha.org

Autism Society of America
http://autism-society.org

Children and Adults with Attention Deficit Disorders (CHADD)
http://www.chadd.org

Council for Exceptional Children
http://www.cec.sped.org

Division for Early Childhood (DEC)
http://www.dec-sped.org

Epilepsy Foundation of America
http://www.epilepsyfoundation.org

National Dissemination Center for Children with Disabilities
http://research.nichcy.org

National Early Childhood Technical Assistance Center (NECTAC, formerly NECTAS)
http://www.nectac.org

National Early Intervention Longitudinal Study (NEILS)
http://www.sri.com/neils

Pre-Elementary Education Longitudinal Study (PEELS)
http://www.peels.org

United Cerebral Palsy
http://www.ucp.org

U.S. Department of Education, Office of Special Education Programs
http://www.ed.gov/about/offices/list/osers/osep/index.html

Publications and Other Media

DEC Recommended Practices Collection—available at www.dec-sped.org
Journal of Early Intervention—subscribe at http://www.dec-sped.org
Young Exceptional Children—subscribe at http://www.dec-sped.org
The Young Exceptional Children Monograph Series—available at http://www.dec-sped.org
ZERO TO THREE—subscribe at http://www.zerotothree.org

REFERENCES

American Association on Mental Retardation. (2002). *Mental retardation: Definition, classification, and systems of supports* (10th ed.). Washington, DC: Author.

Anderson, L. M., Shinn, C., Fullilove, M. T., Scrimshaw, S. C., Fielding, J. F., Normand, J., & Carande-Kulis, V. G. (2003). The effectiveness of early childhood development programs: A systematic review. *American Journal of Preventive Medicine, 24*(3S), 32–46.

Aran, A., Shalev, R. S., Biran, G., & Gross-Tsur, V. (2007). Parenting style impacts on quality of life in children with cerebral palsy. *The Journal of Pediatrics, 151*(1), 56–60.

Baker, B. L., & Feinfield, K. A. (2003). Early intervention. *Current Opinions in Psychiatry, 16*(5), 503–505.

Barlow, J., Davis, H., McIntosh, E., Jarrett, P., Mockford, C., & Stewart-Brown, S. (2007). Role of home visiting in improving parenting and health in families at risk of abuse and neglect: Results of a multicentre randomized controlled trial and economic evaluation. *Archives of Disease in Childhood, 92*, 229–233.

Baskin, C., Umansky, W., & Sanders, W. (1987). Influencing the responsiveness of adolescent mothers to their infants. *Zero to Three, 3*(2), 7–11.

Battelle Institute of Columbus, Ohio. (1976). *A summary of the evaluation of the Disabled Children's Early Education Program.* Columbus: Author.

Behrman, R. E. (Ed.). (1995). Long-term outcomes of early childhood programs. *The Future of Children 5*(3). Washington, DC: Woodrow Wilson School of Public and International Affairs and the Brookings Institute.

Bellini, J. (2003). Mental retardation: Definition, classification, and systems of supports. *Mental Retardation, 41*(2), 135–140.

Black, M. M., Dubowitz, H., Krishnakumar, A., & Starr, R. H. (2007). Early intervention and recovery among children with failure to thrive: Follow-up at age 8. *Pediatrics, 120*(1), 59–69.

Bloom, B. (1964). *Stability and change in human characteristics.* New York: Wiley.

Bono, K. E., Bolzani-Dinehart, L. H., Claussen, A. H., Scott, K. G., Mundy, P. C., & Katz, L. F. (2005). Early intervention with children prenatally exposed to cocaine: Expansion with multiple cohorts. *Journal of Early Intervention, 27*(4), 268–284.

Bradley, R. H., Whiteside, L., Mundfrom, D. J., Casey, P. H., Kelleher, K. J., & Pope, S.K. (1994). The contribution of early intervention and early caregiving experiences to resilience in low birth weight premature children living in poverty. *Journal of Clinical Child Psychology, 23,* 425–434.

Bredekamp, S., & Copple, C. (1997). *Developmentally appropriate practice in early childhood programs serving children from birth to age 8.* Washington, DC: National Association for the Education of Young Children.

Bronfenbrenner, U. (1974). *A report on longitudinal evaluations of preschool programs.* Vol. 2: *Is early intervention effective?* DHEW Publication No. (OHD) 76-30025. Washington, DC: U.S. Department of Health, Education, and Welfare.

Brookes, S., Ispa, J. M., Summers, J. A., Thornburg, K., & Lane, V. (2006). Building successful home visitor-mother relationships and reaching program goals: A qualitative look at contributing factors. *Early Childhood Research Quarterly, 21,* 25–45.

Burr, J., & Grunewald, R. (2006). *Lessons learned: A review of early childhood development studies.* Draft. Minneapolis, MN: Federal Reserve Bank of Minneapolis.

Campbell, F. A., Ramey, C. T., Pungello, E. P., Sparling, J., & Miller-Johnson, S. (2002). Early childhood education: Young adult outcome from the Abecedarian Project. *Applied Developmental Science, 6,* 42–57.

Card, J. P., Levitt, P., Gluhovsky, M., & Rinaman, L. (2005). Early experience modifies the postnatal assembly of autonomic emotional motor circuits in rats. *Journal of Neuroscience, 25*(40), 9102–9111.

Cashmore, J. (2001). Early experience and brain development. *Journal of the HEIA, 8*(3), 1–4.

Chung, I-J, Hawkins, J. D., Gilchrist, L. D., Hill, K. G., & Nagin, D. S. (2002). Identifying and predicting offending trajectories among poor children. *Social Science Review, 76,* 663–685.

Claussen, A. H., Scott, K. G., Mundy, P. C., & Katz, L. F. (2005). Effects of three levels of early intervention services on children prenatally exposed to cocaine. *Journal of Early Intervention, 26*(3), 204–220.

Cole, K. C., Mills, P. E., Jenkins, J. R., & Dale, P. S. (2005). Early intervention curricula and subsequent adolescent social development: A longitudinal examination. *Journal of Early Intervention, 27*(2), 71–82.

Consortium for Longitudinal Studies. (1983). *As the twig is bent . . . Lasting effects of preschool programs.* Hillsdale, N.J.: Lawrence Erlbaum Associates.

Danaher, J. (2005). *Eligibility policies and practices for young children under Part B of IDEA.* (NECTAC Notes No. 15). Chapel Hill, NC: The University of North Carolina, FPG Child Development Institute, National Early Childhood Technical Assistance Center.

Danaher, J., Armijo, C., & Lazara, A. (Eds.). (2006). *Part C updates: Eighth in a series of updates on selected aspects of the Early Intervention Program for Infants and Toddlers with Disabilities, (Part C), of IDEA.* Chapel Hill, NC: The University of North Carolina, FPG Child Development Institute, National Early Childhood Technical Assistance Center.

Denenberg, V. H. (1981). Hemispheric laterality in animals and the effects of early experience. *Behavioral and Brain Sciences, 4,* 1–49.

Denenberg, V. H., Zeidner, L., Rosen, G. D., Hofman, M., Garbanati, J. A., Sherman, G. F., & Yutzey, D. A. (1981). Stimulation in infancy facilitates interhemispheric communication in the rabbit. *Brain Research, 227,* 165–169.

Division for Early Childhood. (2000). *DEC position statement on developmental delay as an eligibility category.* Retrieved from http://www.dec-sped.org

Dombrowski, S. C., Timmer, S. G., Blacker, D. M., & Urquiza, A. J. (2005). A positive behavioral intervention for toddlers: Parent-child attunement therapy. *Child Abuse Review, 14*(2), 132–151.

Duarte, C. S., Bordin, I. A., Yazigi, L., & Mooney, J. (2005). Factors associated with stress in mothers of children with autism. *Autism, 9*(4), 416–427.

Ehrmann, L. C., Aeschleman, S. R., & Svanum, S. (1995). Parental reports of community activity patterns: A comparison between young children with disabilities and their nondisabled peers. *Research in Developmental Disabilities, 16,* 331–343.

Eisenhower, A. S., Baker, B. L., & Blacher, J. (2005). Preschool children with intellectual disability: Syndrome specificity, behaviour problems, and maternal well-being. *Journal of Intellectual Disabilities Research, 49*(9), 657–671.

Erikson, E. H. (1963). *Childhood and society.* New York: Norton.

Farmer, J. E., Marien, W. F., Clark, M. J., Sherman, M. A., & Selva, T. J. (2004). Primary care supports for children with chronic health conditions: Identifying and predicting unmet family needs. *Journal of Pediatric Psychology, 29*(5), 355–367.

Federal Reserve Bank of Minneapolis. (2003). *The economics of early childhood development: Lessons for economic policy. Conference proceedings.* Minneapolis: Author.

Fox, L., Hanline, M. F., Vail, C. O., & Galant, K. R. (1994). Developmentally appropriate practice: Applications for young children with disabilities. *Journal of Early Intervention, 18,* 243–254.

Freud, A. (1965). *Normality and pathology in childhood: Assessments of development.* New York: International Universities Press.

Galler, J. R., Waber, D., Harrison, R., & Ramsey, F. (2005). Behavioral effects of childhood malnutrition. *American Journal of Psychiatry, 162*(9), 1760–1761.

Gottlieb, G., & Blair, C. (2004). How early experience matters in intellectual development in the case of poverty. *Prevention Science, 5*(4), 245–252.

Gray, S. W. (1983). Controversies or concurrences: A reply to Palmer. *Developmental Review, 3*, 125–129.

Guesry, P. (1998). The role of nutrition in brain development. *Prevention Medicine, 27*(2), 189–194.

Harlow, H. F. (1974). Syndromes resulting from maternal deprivation: Maternal and peer affectional deprivation in primates. In J. H. Cullen (Ed.), *Experimental behavior: A basis for the study of mental disturbance.* New York: Wiley.

Hastings, R. P., Kovshoff, H., Brown, T., Ward, N. J., Espinosa, F. D., & Remington, B. (2005). Coping strategies in mothers and fathers of preschool and school-age children with autism. *Autism, 9*(4), 377–391.

Hauser-Cram, P., Warfield, M. E., Shonkoff, J. P., & Kraus, M. W. (2001). Children with disabilities: A longitudinal study of child development and parent well-being. *Society for Research in Child Development Monographs, 66*, 1–131.

Hebbeler, K., Spiker, D., Bailey, D., Scarborough, A., Mallik, S., Simeonsson, R., Singer, M., & Nelson, L. (2007). *Early intervention for infants and toddlers with disabilities and their families: Participants, services, and outcomes: Final report of the National Early Intervention Longitudinal Study (NEILS).* Menlo Park, CA: SRI International.

Hemmeter, M. L., Smith, B., Sandall, S. R., & Askew, L. (2005). *DEC recommended practices workbook.* Missoula, MT: Division for Early Childhood.

Hunt, J. McV. (1961). *Intelligence and experience.* New York: Ronald Press.

Johnson, S., Ring, W., Anderson, P., & Marlow, N. (2005). Randomised trial of parental support for families with preterm children: Outcome at 5 years. *Archives of Disease in Children, 90*, 909–915.

Karoly, L. A., Kilburn, M. R., Bigelow, J. H., Caulkins, J. P., & Cannon, J. S. (2001). Benefit-cost findings for early childhood intervention programs. In L.A. Karoly et al. (Eds.). *Assessing costs and benefits of early childhood intervention programs: Overview and application to the Starting Early, Starting Smart Program.* (pp. 49–71) Santa Monica, CA: Rand.

Keogh, B., Garnier, H. E., Bernheimer, L. P., & Gallimore, R. (2000). Models of child-family interactions for children with developmental delays: Child-driven or transactional. *American Journal on Mental Retardation, 105*, 32–46.

Kirk, S. A., Gallagher, J. J., Anastasiow, N. J., & Coleman, M. R. (2005). *Educating exceptional children* (11th ed.). Boston, MA: Houghton Mifflin.

Lecours, A. R., Mandujano, M., Romero, G., Arroyo, P., & Sanchez-Perez, C. (2001). Ontogeny of brain and cognition: Relevance to nutrition. *Nutrition Reviews, 59*, 57–511.

Levin, J., Perez, M., Lam, I., Chambers, J. G., & Hebbeler, K. M. (2004). *National Early Intervention Longitudinal Study: Expenditure Study. NEILS Data Report No 4.* Menlo Park, CA: SRI International.

Littlejohn & Associates, Inc. (1982). *An analysis of the impact of the Disabled Children's Early Education Program.* Washington, DC: Author.

Liu, J., Raine, A., Venables, P. H., & Mednick, S. A. (2004). Malnutrition at age 3 and externalizing behavior problems at ages 8, 11, and 17 years. *American Journal of Psychiatry, 161*, 2005–2013.

Love, J., Kisker, E. E., Raikes, H., Constantine, J., & Boller, K. (2005). The effectiveness of Early Head Start for 3-year-old children and their parents. *Developmental Psychology, 41*(6), 885–901.

Lucas, A., Morley, R., Isaacs, E., & Youdim, M. B. (2001). Nutrition and mental development. *Nutrition Reviews, 59*, 524–533.

Lynch, R. G. (2004). *Exceptional returns: Economic, fiscal, and social benefits of investment in early childhood development.* Washington, DC: Economic Policy Institute.

Markowitz, J., Carlson, E., Frey, W., Riley, J., Shimshak, A., Heinzen, H., et al. (2006). *Preschoolers with disabilities: Characteristics, services, and results. Wave 1 overview report from the Pre-Elementary Education Longitudinal Study (PEELS).* Washington, D.C.: National Center for Special Education Research, Institute of Education Sciences, U.S. Department of Education.

McCormick, M. C., Brooks-Gunn, J., Buka, S. L., Goldman, J., Yu, J., Salganik, M., Scott, D. T., Bennett, F. C., Kay, L. L., Bernbaum, J. C., Bauer, C. R., Martin, C., Woods, E. R., Martin, A., & Casey, P. H. (2006). Early intervention in low birth weight premature infants: Results at 18 years of age for the Infant Health and Development Program. *Pediatrics, 117*(3), 771–780.

NAEYC. (1994). Personnel standard for early education and early intervention: Guidelines for licensure in early childhood special education. Washington, DC: Author.

Nelson, G., Westhues, A., & McLeod, J. (2003). A meta-analysis of longitudinal research on preschool prevention programs for children. *Prevention and Treatment,* 1–67.

Odom, S. L., Brantlinger, E., Gersten, R., Horner, R. H., Thompson, B., & Harris, K. R. (2005). Research on special education: Scientific methods and evidence-based practices. *Exceptional Children, 71*(2), 137–148.

Odom, S. L., & McEvoy, M. A. (1990). Mainstreaming at the preschool level: Potential barriers and tasks for the field. *Topics in Early Childhood Special Education, 10,* 48–61.

Odom, S. L., Peck, C. A., Hanson, M., Beckman, P. J., Kaiser, A. P., Lieber, J., et al. (2000). *Inclusion at the preschool level: An ecological systems analysis.* Olympia, WA: Office of State Superintendent of Public Instruction (Special Education, P.O. Box 47200, Olympia, WA 98504).

Palmer, F. (1983). The continuing controversy over the effects of early childhood intervention: A perspective and review of Gray, Ramsey, and Klaus's *From 3 to 20: The Early Training Project. Developmental Review, 3,* 115–124.

Piaget, J., & Inhelder, B. (1969). *The psychology of the child.* New York: Basic Books.

Peterson, C. A., Wall, S., Raikes, H. A., Kisker, E. E., Swanson, M. E., Jerald, J., Atwater, J. B., & Qiao, W. (2004). Early Head Start: Identifying and serving children with disabilities. *Journal of Early Childhood Special Education, 24*(2), 76–88.

Raikes, H., Green, B. L., Atwater, J., Kisker, E., Constantine, J., & Chazan-Cohen, R. (2006). Involvement in Early Head Start home visiting services: Demographic predictors and relations to child and family outcomes. *Early Childhood Research Quarterly, 21*(1), 2–24.

Raina, P., O'Donnell, M., Rosenbaum, P., Brehaut, J., Walther, S. D., Russell, D., Swinton, M., Zhu, B., & Wood, E. (2005). The health and well-being of caregivers of children with cerebral palsy. *Pediatrics, 115*(6), 626–636.

Ramey, C. T., & Ramey, L. R. (1994). Which children benefit the most from early intervention? *Pediatrics, 94*(2), 1064–1066.

Ray, L. D. (2003). The social and political conditions that shape special-needs parenting. *Journal of Family Nursing, 9*(3), 281–304.

Reynolds, A. J., Temple, J. A., Robertson, D. L., & Mann, E. A. (2002). Age 21 cost-benefit analysis of the Title I Chicago Child-Parent Centers. *Education Evaluation and Policy Analysis, 24*(4), 267–303.

Sameroff, A. J. (1998). Management of clinical problems and emotional care: Environmental risk factors in infancy. *Pediatrics, 102*(5). Supplement. 1287–1292.

Sandall, S., McLean, M., Hemmeter, M. L., & Smith, B. (2004). *DEC Recommended Practices in early childhood/special education.* Missoula, MT: Division for Early Childhood.

Sandall, S., McLean, M., & Smith, B. (2002). *Personnel preparation in early childhood special education: Implementing the DEC Recommended Practices.* Missoula, MT: Division for Early Childhood.

Schweinhart, L. J. (2002). *Making validated educational models central in preschool standards.* Ypsilanti, MI: High/Scope Educational Research Foundation.

Schweinhart, L. J. (2004). *The High/Scope Perry Preschool Study through age 40: Summary, conclusions, and frequently asked questions.* Ypsilanti, MI: High/Scope Press.

Shonkoff, J. P., & Phillips, D. (Eds.). (2000). *From neurons to neighborhoods: The science of early childhood development.* Washington, DC: National Academies Press.

Shonkoff, J. P., Hauser, C. P., Krauss, M. W., & Upshur, C. C. (1992). Development of infants with disabilities and their families: Implications for theory and service delivery. *Monographs of the Society for Research in Child Development* (Serial No. 230).

Skeels, H. M. (1966). Adult status of children with contrasting early life experiences. *Monographs of the Society for Research in Child Development* (Serial No. 105).

United States Department of Education. (2004). *Serving preschool children under Title I: Non-regulatory guidance.* Washington, DC: Author.

Vandell, D. L. (2004). Early child care: The known and the unknown. *Merrill-Palmer Quarterly, 50*(3), 387–414.

Waisbren, S. E., Rones, M., Read, C. Y., Marsden, D., & Levy, H. L. (2004). Brief report: Predictors of parenting stress among parents of children with biochemical genetic disorders. *Journal of Pediatric Psychology, 29*(7), 565–570.

Weikart, D. P. (1981). Effects of different curricula in early childhood intervention. *Educational Evaluation and Policy Analysis, 3,* 25–35.

Typical Development and Factors Affecting Development

Stephen R. Hooper, Crista E. Wetherington, and Jaclyn M. Wetherington

Chapter Outline

- Definitional Issues and Developmental Processes
- Typical Development
- Factors Affecting Development

Denise and Nathaniel

Nathaniel is Denise's third child. Denise is 21 years old and has struggled with a cocaine addiction for the past 4 years. She has been drug-free for the past year, although she was using a variety of substances during her pregnancy with Nathaniel. As a single parent, she works hard to keep her part-time job and care for her three children. Although she receives some financial support from the WIC program, she does not receive any child support. Her family is considered to be of low socioeconomic status and can afford only a one-bedroom apartment in an extremely old and poorly maintained building. Her first two children demonstrated some delays in their early development and are currently exhibiting some challenging behavioral difficulties in the classroom. Denise did not seek medical services during her pregnancy with Nathaniel, in large part because of her struggles with cocaine, but she is now becoming increasingly concerned about his lack of developmental progress—even when compared to her other two children. At 23 months of age he is not able to stand without assistance, or walk, and is just beginning to use one-word utterances. Apprehensive about his slow progress, she made an appointment at the local child development clinic. Denise is frustrated with her lack of resources, feels alone in the process, and is overwhelmed by thoughts of what lies ahead for her and her family.

A sound knowledge of typical growth and development is essential for anyone interested in children, particularly for those who work with children in educational and developmental settings. For the student aspiring to work with young children with special needs, as well as for professionals already engaged in clinical practice serving such children, an understanding of typical growth and development provides a foundation from which many of the needs of children can be met. Not only does such knowledge contribute to an understanding of how children typically develop, but it also provides a basic yardstick for recognizing children with all kinds of exceptionalities and differences, and appropriately addressing their needs. Further, this knowledge base facilitates an understanding of the plethora of factors that can impinge on a child's developmental progress, some of which are illustrated in the vignette at the beginning of the chapter. An understanding of typical child development, including deviations and differences, along with an awareness of factors that affect development will guide the efforts of early interventionists in addressing the needs of young children with special needs.

This chapter provides an overview of the basic processes and principles of development. In addition to discussing definitional issues and specific stages of child development through the preschool years, selected risk factors that can impede development are highlighted.

:: DEFINITIONAL ISSUES AND DEVELOPMENTAL PROCESSES

Several questions arise in any attempt to define *development:* "Is there a time frame for the development of a specific behavior or repertoire of behaviors?" "How much change is needed in a behavior before it is recognized as development?" "Are there componential aspects to development?" How one conceptualizes human behavior and its development is a determining factor in how *development* is defined.

Definition

Development fundamentally involves systematic, cumulative change.

At its most fundamental level, development involves change. This change must be cumulative and systematic; random change is not considered to be developmental in nature. Whereas the concept of *growth* refers to the addition of new components or skills through the appearance of new cells, **development** refers to the refinement, improvement, and expansion of existing skills through the refinement of cells already present (Schuster, 1992). More specifically, three basic criteria must be met before change can be considered to be development:

Unlike growth, through which new skills are acquired, development involves refining, improving, and expanding existing skills.

1. The change must be orderly—not random fluctuations of behavior.
2. The change must result in a consistent modification in behavior.
3. The change must contribute to a higher level of functioning in the individual.

When a specific change in behavior satisfies these three criteria, development has occurred.

Development may be either qualitative or quantitative. For example, increases in height, weight, creativity, activity level, and vocabulary are quantitative changes; that is, they are directly measurable. Progression toward maturity and the integration of complex physiological and psychological processes are qualitative changes; in other words, it is more difficult to gain an exact measure of these changes, but the changes are still noticeable. We see both types of change when children's shoes no longer fit, when they run faster and jump higher, when their increased proficiency in language helps them control their surroundings and their behaviors in a more accomplished manner, and when old toys and games lose their fascination in favor of new friendships and increased social contacts.

Through the processes of growth and development, an individual's characteristics and behavior unfold or mature.

With these definitional components in mind, it also becomes important to distinguish between development and maturation. The concept of maturation is similar to that of development in that skills and functions are refined and improve over time. The concepts differ, however, in that **maturation** refers to the unfolding of personal characteristics and behavioral phenomena through the processes of growth and development. The concept of maturation reflects the final stages of differentiation of cells, tissues, and organs in accordance with a genetic blueprint wherein full or optimal development of a specific skill can be achieved (Schuster, 1992).

Individual Differences

Another factor to consider in relation to development is the concept of individual differences. Children develop at different rates. This, in turn, creates variations among individuals (i.e., individual differences). Again, these differences can be either qualitative or quantitative. For children in any preschool classroom setting, the differences in temperament, personality, intelligence, achievement, and physical factors such as height and weight, are noteworthy and reflect a wide range of normal variation. Some children grow rapidly and others grow more slowly. There also are racial and gender developmental variations. During the fetal stage, for example, females mature faster than males do. Further, at birth, the skeletal development of females is about 4 weeks ahead of that of males, and African American children show more rapid skeletal maturation than white children do (Puckett & Black, 2004; Russell et al., 2001; Tanner, 1990).

It is important to understand that the concept of individual differences is the basis upon which one child is compared to another. Also, the existence of these differences constitutes the fundamental premise underlying the development of standardized educational and psychological tests. An understanding of individual differences provides the foundation for recognizing normal variations as well as extreme differences among children and, thus, for identifying those who may have special needs. In general, understanding of the various developmental levels is enhanced by familiarity with the concept of individual differences. As illustrated in the case vignette, Denise has observed some distinct developmental differences between Nathaniel and her other two children. She is worried that these differences could represent developmental delays or deficits.

> Recognizing individual differences among children is the basis for determining special needs and for many testing procedures.

Principles of Development

Although children develop at different rates and, therefore, the notion of *interindividual* differences exists, a single child can show more rapid change in some developmental areas than in others; thus, *intraindividual* differences also exist. Regardless of the perspective, there are certain principles of development that apply to all children. These include the following:

> Most principles of development apply to all children.

> Children develop at varying rates, just as an individual child develops at varying rates in different areas.

- Development progresses in a step-by-step fashion. It is orderly, sequential, and proceeds from the simple to the complex. Each achieved behavior forms the foundation for more advanced behaviors.
- Rates of development vary among children as well as among developmental areas in a single child.
- Development is characterized by increasing specificity of function (differentiation) as well as integration of these specific functions into a larger response pattern. A good example of this principle is the infant startle reflex. When an infant is startled, his entire body tenses and his arms move out to the side. With age, this reflex becomes integrated into more specific behavioral patterns such that a startled preschooler will tense only the shoulder and neck muscles.

- Neurological development contributes significantly to the acquisition of physical skills in young children. Physical development proceeds in cephalocaudal and proximodistal directions. **Cephalocaudal development** describes the progression of body control from the head to the lower parts of the body. For example, an infant will achieve head, upper trunk, and arm control before lower trunk and leg control. **Proximodistal development** describes progress from the central portions of the body (i.e., the spinal cord) to the distal or peripheral parts. In this developmental progression, gross motor skills and competencies precede fine motor skills. This developmental progression continues throughout early childhood, with upper trunk control being achieved first, then arm control, and finally finger control. According to this principle, each change in the child's development should result in an increasingly refined level of skill development.

- Development of any structure follows a sequential pattern; however, there appear to be specific times during development in which a developing structure is most sensitive to external conditions. These **sensitive periods,** or **critical periods,** are the times during which a specific condition or stimulus is necessary for the normal development of a specific structure. Conversely, these periods also represent times when a structure may be most vulnerable to disruption (Rice & Barone, 2000). The concept of critical periods has created much debate in theoretical circles, particularly with respect to parent–infant bonding (Anisfeld et al., 1983) and language development (Lenneberg, 1967).

- All development is interrelated. Although it is convenient for the student or early interventionist to discuss development in terms of discrete developmental areas, such as motor skills, development in other areas such as social-emotional or communication functions does not cease, nor is it necessarily separate from other areas. The student or child practitioner must recognize how different areas of development are interrelated to understand how a particular child develops.

- Development is influenced by heredity and environment. Although there has been much discussion by experts in the field about which is more important, there is no doubt that they both play a role in a child's development. A child's genetic inheritance (i.e., heredity) provides the basic foundation for many physical and personality attributes, but the influences of social, cultural, and familial variables (i.e., environment) also contribute to development.

During sensitive, or critical, periods, a child must receive specific stimuli in specific conditions to develop normally.

Processes of Development

An understanding of development requires resolution of a fundamental question: Do we develop primarily because we learn from our surroundings (environment) or because we are predisposed to grow in certain ways (heredity)? An explanation of each position provides an interesting framework for examining contemporary theories of child development.

The term heredity *refers to the inborn attributes of an organism.*

Heredity   **Heredity** is the totality of characteristics transmitted from the parents to the offspring. The view that behavior and development are primarily directed by heredity, or nature, was initially set forth by **Jean Jacques Rousseau** in the eighteenth century. Rousseau was a French philosopher who believed that a child's growth and

Normal variation is the rule in the development of a young child.

development were ultimately determined by nature, and that the child's surroundings had little influence on development. According to this viewpoint, nature provides the primary guidance for healthy growth and development. This philosophy has been advocated by Gesell (Gesell & Ilg, 1943), Jensen (1980), and others.

Rousseau believed that a child's growth and development were determined by nature.

Environment   The position that environment is primarily responsible for how a child develops can be traced to the work of seventeenth-century British philosopher **John Locke.** Locke resurrected many of the teachings of Aristotle in describing the mind of an infant as a **tabula rasa,** or "blank slate." Locke believed that all of an individual's experiences contribute to filling the blank slate. The child was perceived as a passive receiver of information and thus easily shaped by environmental influences.

John Locke believed that the environment was primarily responsible for growth and development.

Watson (1924) and many other theorists (e.g., Skinner, 1961) have been strong advocates for the environmentalist position. Watson was a prominent force in American psychology and adhered almost exclusively to the nurture philosophy of the nature–nurture controversy. The basic tenets of his thinking are revealed in one of his earlier works (Watson, 1924):

> Give me a dozen healthy infants, well-formed, and my own specified world to bring them up in, and I'll guarantee to take any one at random and train him to become any type of specialist I might select—doctor, lawyer, merchant, chief, and yes, even beggar man and thief, regardless of his talents, penchants, tendencies, abilities, vocations, race of his ancestors. (p. 104)

Watson represented an extreme environmentalist position that downplayed biological influences on development and truly emphasized Locke's *tabula rasa* philosophy.

Interaction of Heredity and Environment   As a resolution to these seemingly opposing positions, common sense dictates that neither heredity nor environment alone explains a child's typical growth and development. Heredity does not dominate development, nor are environmental influences solely responsible for one's personality, talents, or physical abilities. It seems that an interaction between these two positions most likely accounts for the multiple facets or elements of development. Although the interaction between heredity and environment is well accepted from a contemporary viewpoint, the exact degree of interaction remains a mystery; however, current scientific discoveries in the area of *genomics* (the study of genes and their expression) should provide clearer guidance with respect to the degree or magnitude of this interaction in the next several decades. The task for observers of child behavior and development should be to focus on describing the specific aspects of each philosophical position that may be affecting the development of any particular child. For Nathaniel, the interaction of heredity and environment clearly is present; but, how this interaction will manifest over time remains to be seen.

> Both heredity and environment influence a child's development.

:: TYPICAL DEVELOPMENT

This section explores the development of a child from conception through the early childhood years, and includes a brief discussion of the prenatal period, the neonatal period, infancy, toddlerhood, and the preschool period. To complement the other chapters in this text, the emphasis here is placed on the prenatal and neonatal periods, although later developmental periods also will be described briefly.

Prenatal Development

> Growth and development begin at the time of conception.

Prenatal refers to the time from conception to birth. The prenatal period may be divided into three stages. The first stage is called the **germinal stage** and lasts for about 2 weeks. The **embryonic stage** is next and lasts from about 2 to 8 weeks. The third stage, the **fetal stage**, follows and continues until birth. Although the variation of ovulation among women, as well as within the same woman, creates minor difficulties in accurately dating the pregnancy, this sequence of prenatal development holds true for all children. According to Deiner (1997), a general guideline to estimate the due date is to count back 3 months from the first day of the last menstrual cycle and then add 7 days, resulting in approximately 266 days postconception.

> To estimate a baby's due date, count back 3 months from the first day of the last menstrual cycle and then add 7 days.

Germinal Stage   The cell created by the union of the sperm and the egg is the zygote. Within 36 hours of fertilization, mitosis begins; this single cell rapidly divides. During the beginnings of mitosis, the zygote slowly moves down the fallopian tube toward the uterus. This process takes about 3 to 4 days. Once its destination is reached, the zygote has transformed into a liquid-filled structure called a **blastocyst,** which floats in the uterus for about 24 to 48 hours. Mitosis continues and some of the cells of the blastocyst begin to clump on one side of the uterus to form the **embryonic disk.** This is the group of cells from which the baby will develop.

As the embryonic disk thickens, it begins to divide into three layers: the ectoderm, the endoderm, and the mesoderm. The **ectoderm** is the upper layer of cells in the embryonic disk and ultimately will become the epidermis, nails, hair, teeth, sensory organs, and central nervous system. The lower layer of cells, the **endoderm,** will eventually become the child's digestive system, respiratory system, and various other internal organs. The **mesoderm** is the last of the three layers to develop. It will evolve into the dermis, muscles and connective tissue, the skull, and parts of the circulatory and reproductive systems. The remaining parts of the blastocyst will create the prenatal structures required for intrauterine life. These include the **placenta,** which will nourish and protect the developing infant; the **umbilical cord,** which will connect the placenta to the developing child; and the **amniotic sac,** which will house the baby for the entire prenatal period. The outer layer of the blastocyst, called the **trophoblast,** eventually will produce microscopic, hair-like structures called **villi.** These villi adhere to the uterine lining until the blastocyst is totally implanted. Once uterine implantation is complete, the germinal stage is over, and the embryonic period begins.

Embryonic Stage   This stage of development has been divided into 23 separate stages termed **Carnegie Stages.** It is beyond the scope of this chapter to review each of these stages in detail (for a review, see O'Rahilly & Muller, 1996); the main point to note is that during the embryonic stage, the embryo, as it is now called, experiences rapid growth. The amniotic sac, placenta, and umbilical cord are fully developed, and mitosis has progressed to the point that the **embryo** resembles a miniature human being. During this period, the developing embryo is extremely sensitive to toxic and infectious agents. Nearly all major birth defects, such as malformed limbs, cleft palate, blindness, and deafness, occur during this period or slightly after, but typically within the first 3 months of pregnancy (O'Rahilly & Muller, 1996). In fact, as noted earlier, many embryos spontaneously abort when their defects are markedly severe. Prenatal surgery is now possible to correct certain abnormalities (see Box 2.1).

Many major birth defects occur during the embryonic stage of development.

By the end of this period, at about 8 weeks, the embryo has a beating heart, the beginnings of a skeleton, and a rapidly growing brain. This tiny developing human is now only about 2.5 to 3.8 cm (1–$1^{1}/_{2}$ in) long and weighs about 0.9 gm ($^{1}/_{30}$ oz), but it clearly has begun to show distinct human characteristics (Moore, Persaud, & Torchia, 2007). For example, the head and brain are now visible, with the head accounting for approximately one half the length of the fetus, and a thin pink skin covers the body.

By about 8 weeks of prenatal age, the embryo is about 2.5 to 3.8 cm (1 to $1^{1}/_{2}$ in) long and about 0.9 gm ($^{1}/_{30}$ oz) in weight.

Fetal Stage   The fetal stage begins with the development of the first bone cell, which is produced from the cartilage of the developing skeleton at about 8 to 9 weeks. The embryo now becomes a **fetus.** This final stage of the prenatal period lasts until birth. It is during this time that the organism experiences the most extensive rate of growth in its lifetime. The length of the fetus increases until normal body proportions

---

BOX 2.1   PRENATAL SURGERIES

Typical prenatal care activities may include obtaining a family and medical history, screening for hereditary conditions, conducting a variety of medical procedures such as blood work and urinalysis, discussing nutritional and physical needs, and perhaps performing genetic counseling. In addition to these important prenatal care activities, pioneering work in the field of fetal surgery is now being conducted. These delicate surgeries may involve inserting a shunt into the brain of the fetus to allow excess fluid to escape (thus minimizing brain damage), correction of urinary tract abnormalities, placement of the bowels back into the body, and fixing of abdominal hernias. Many of these procedures are still in their experimental stages and surrounded by many ethical concerns; however, the possibilities for contributing to positive growth and development are quite promising. See DeCherney, A. H., Nathan, L., & Goodwin, T. M. (2006). *Current obstetric and gynecologic diagnoses and treatment* (10th ed.). New York: McGraw-Hill for additional information about these procedures.

During the last 7 months of pregnancy, called the *fetal stage*, the baby experiences the most extensive rate of growth.

After 3 months, the baby measures 8 cm (3 in) in length and is humanlike.

Life outside of the uterus is possible beginning around the fifth month of prenatal life.

are achieved, and all internal systems and organs continue to increase their efficiency. At the end of the third month, the fetus is approximately 8 cm (3 in) long and begins to show human characteristics. Its musculature is developing, and some spontaneous movements may be noted by the mother. Eyelids, teeth, fingernails, toenails, and external genitalia begin to form, and the gender is easily distinguished. During the fourth month the fetus grows another 2.5 to 5 cm (1 to 2 in) in length and begins to develop hair, called **lanugo**, on its body. The eyelids begin to blink, the mouth begins to open, and the hands are capable of grasping. The fifth month is characterized by the mother typically feeling the fetus move for the first time. Eyebrows and hair appear, and the skin begins to take on the human shape. The length of the fetus is now roughly 25 cm (10 in). At the end of the second trimester, the fetus has eyes that can open, taste buds on the tongue, and a functional respiratory system; it also is capable of making crying sounds. The fetus now weighs approximately 680 gm (1 lb 8 oz), and life outside of the uterus is possible.

The final trimester is a period of further growth and development of the fetus. This is manifested in greater structural differentiation and definition. At this point the fetus is viable; that is, its respiratory system and central nervous system are developed to a point at which it could survive independently outside of the uterine environment without undue difficulty. This growth continues until the point of delivery, or birth, typically somewhere between weeks 37 to 41 of the pregnancy. Table 2.1 presents a month-by-month summary of the growth and development during the prenatal period.

The Birth Process

As delivery time nears, the mother's calcium level drops. This decrease is particularly marked in the pelvic area so that the mother's pelvis can be extended as widely as possible to accommodate the fetus. Simultaneously, muscles around the uterus and cervix also become larger and more flexible to accommodate the fetus during

| TABLE 2.1 | A month-by-month summary of development in the prenatal period. |

First Month *(1 to 4 weeks after conception)*

Conception, rapid growth
Fertilized egg embeds in uterine wall
Differentiation of individual from accessory structures
Three germ layers differentiated
Rudimentary body parts formed
Cardiovascular system functioning
Yolk sac begins to diminish

Second Month *(5 to 8 weeks)*

Formation of head and facial features
Very rapid cell differentiation and growth
Beginning of all major external and internal structures
External genitalia present, but gender not discernible
Heart functionally complete
Some movement by limbs
Yolk sac incorporated into the embryo
Weight: 1 gm

Third Month *(9 to 12 weeks)*

Eyelids fused, nail beds formed
Teeth and bones begin to appear
Kidneys begin to function
Some respiratory-like movements exhibited
Begins to swallow amniotic fluid
Grasp, sucking, and withdrawal reflexes present
Moves easily (not felt by mother)
Gender distinguishable
Weight: 30 gm (1 oz)

Fourth Month *(13 to 16 weeks)*

Much spontaneous movement
Moro reflex present
Rapid skeletal development
Meconium present
Uterine development in female infant
Downy hair (lanugo) appears on body
Weight: 120 gm (4 oz)

Fifth Month *(17 to 20 weeks)*

Begins to exchange new cells for old, especially in skin
"Quickening"—fetal movement felt by mother
Vernix caseosa appears
Eyebrows and head hair appear
Skeleton begins to harden
Strong grasp reflex present
Permanent teeth buds appear
Heart sounds can be heard with a stethoscope
Weight: 360 gm (12 oz)

Six Month *(21 to 24 weeks)*

"Miniature baby"
Extrauterine life first possible (but very unlikely)
Mother may note jarring but rhythmic movements
    of infant indicative of hiccups
Body becomes straight
Fingernails appear
Skin has a red, wrinkled appearance
Alternates periods of sleep and activity
May respond to external sounds
May try to find comfortable position
Weight: 720 gm (1½ lb)

Seventh Month *(25 to 28 weeks)*

Respiratory system and central nervous system
    sufficiently developed that many babies may
    survive with excellent and intensive care
Eyelids reopen
Assumes head-down position in uterus
Respiratory-like movement
Weight: 1,200 gm (2½ lb)

Eighth Month *(29 to 32 weeks)*

Begins to store fat and minerals
Testes descend into scrotal sac in male
Mother may note irregular, jerky, cryinglike movements
Lanugo begins to disappear from face
Skin begins to lose reddish color
Can be conditioned to environmental sounds
Exhibits good reflex development
Good chance of survival if born
Weight: 2,000 gm (4 lb)

Ninth Month *(33 to 36 weeks)*

Continues fat deposits
Body begins to round out
Increased iron storage by liver
Increased development of lungs
May become more or less active because of space
    tightness
Excellent chance of survival if born
Lanugo begins to disappear from body
Head hair lengthens
Weight: 2,000 gm (6 lb)

Tenth Month *(37 to 40 weeks)*

Lanugo and vernix caseosa both begin to disappear
High absorption of maternal hormones
Skin becomes smooth, plump
Firming of skull and bones
Continued storage of fat and minerals
Ready for birth
Weight: 3,400 to 3,400 gm (7 to 7½ lb)

Source: Adapted from Schuster, C. S. (1992). In C. S. Schuster & S. S. Ashburn (Eds.), *The Process of Human Development: A Holistic Life-Span Approach* (3rd ed., pp. 68, 70). Philadelphia: J. B. Lippencott Company. Adapted by permission.

birth. In preparation for birth, the fetus rotates in the womb so that it will be born head first. This rotation is triggered by hormonal action in the mother and is the first indication of the onset of labor. If fetal rotation does not occur, the baby will be born feet first. This awkward type of delivery is called a **breech delivery** and occurs in about 3 to 4% of births, with increased frequency noted in preterm deliveries (i.e., 25% prior to 28 weeks gestation, 14% at 29 to 32 weeks gestation, 7% at 32 weeks gestation) (Lee et al., 1998). A breech delivery can cause anoxia (lack of oxygen), intracranial hemorrhage (bleeding), and transient lowering of the fetal heart rate, particularly in the premature infant (DeCherney, Nathan, & Goodwin, 2006). Although a breech delivery typically is not of major consequence to outcome, some association has been made to abnormalities in the child, with central nervous system anomalies being noted most frequently (Mazor, Hagay, Leiberman, Biale, & Insler, 1985). In addition, nearly half of all cases of hydrocephalus, myelomeningocele, Prader-Willi syndrome, and trisomy are associated with breech presentation (Krebs & Langhoff-Roos, 2006).

> The fetus rotates in the uterus so that it will be born head first; if this rotation does not occur, a breech delivery will result.

Other factors that can affect the baby include pressure in the birth canal, the use of forceps during delivery, and the sedation of the mother. This latter factor can be critical because the baby's immature liver and excretory systems experience difficulties eliminating maternal medications and anesthesia from the body. This may contribute to sedation and, consequently, to a baby who initially may be less responsive to environmental stimulation—including its parents (Murray, Dolby, Nation, & Thomas, 1981).

When there is a possibility of an abnormal vaginal delivery, a **cesarean section** (c-section) can be performed. In this procedure, the mother's abdomen and uterus are surgically opened, and the baby and placenta are removed. This procedure eliminates many of the risks associated with an abnormal delivery for the mother as well as for the child. One factor that can indicate the need for a c-section is **postmaturity**. Postmaturity refers to a baby being post-term, or after the 41st week. About 10% of babies are born after the 41st week of gestation (Coustan, 1995). Although most babies show no permanent signs of being post-mature, largely because of routine and careful prenatal monitoring, some post-mature babies do not obtain sufficient nutrients and oxygen from the placenta to meet the demands of labor (White, 2004), and thus brain injury or death can occur.

> A C-section can eliminate many of the risks of an abnormal delivery for the mother and baby.

Despite reports of significant morbidity of later occurring disorders following perinatal complications (Dean & Davis, 2007), from this point forward, the baby grows and develops in a remarkable fashion. One area that the early interventionist should be well versed in is developmental milestones. In addition to the discussion below, Table 2.2 provides an overview of many of the major developmental milestones from infancy through the preschool years. These milestones should be "hard wired" into the knowledge base of the early interventionist.

Neonatal Period

The **neonatal period** is the transitional time from intrauterine to independent existence. Defined as approximately the first 4 weeks after delivery, the neonatal period is possibly the most tenuous in a human's lifetime. Of the nearly 4 million babies

TABLE 2.2 Major developmental milestones from infancy through preschool (obtained by > 90% of children within 2 to 3 months).

Developmental Domain	Age In Months											
	1–2	3–5	6–8	9–11	12	18	24	30	36	42	48	60
Gross Motor	Lifts head in prone; balances head in supine.	Bears weight on forearms (elbows ahead of shoulders); brings hand to midline in supine.	Rolls from prone to supine without rotation; rolls from supine to prone with rotation; sits alone steadily.	Creeps on hands and knees reciprocally; cruises around furniture without rotation.	Maintains squatting position.	Creeps up steps; creeps down steps backwards.	Jumps off floor using both feet.	Climbs and descends stairs with both feet on each step.	Climbs stairs alternating feet.	Descends stairs alternating feet.	Hops on one foot; may gallop.	Skips.
Fine Motor	Grasp reflex, but no voluntary release; arms activate upon sight of object.	Hands mostly open, but loosely closed in prone; involuntary release after sustained grasp; swipes at object; raking grasp; emergent grasp; emergent transfer of object from hand-to-hand.	Over-reaches for object; circular reach in sitting with 1 arm; reaches in prone on extended arms; direct reach in sitting with 1 arm; direct transfer from hand-to-mouth-to-hand; clumsy release into large container.	Emergent pincer to precise pincer grasp; controlled release into large container; drops object from high chair; chewing skills develop.	Forearm supination with reach; precise release with cube; begins to stack blocks.		Emergent smooth, graded release of objects; can drink from a straw.	Digital pronate on crayon.	Emergent adult grasp of spoon.		Emergent static tripod grasp on pencil.	Dynamic tripod grasp on pencil.

(Continued)

TABLE 2.2 (Continued)

Developmental Domain	Age In Months											
	1–2	3–5	6–8	9–11	12	18	24	30	36	42	48	60
Expressive Language	Makes sucking sounds.	Vocalizes pleasure and displeasure sounds.	Babbles; tries to communicate with gestures; repeats sounds; vocalizes with intonation.	Points to objects, pictures, and family members.	Uttering recognizable words; says 2–3 words to label a person or object.	Vocalizes 8–10 words and makes animal sounds; expressed worded are typically nouns; begins to combine words; begins to use pronouns; correctly pronounces most vowels and n, m, p, and h.	Rapid topic change; Emergent use of auxiliary system; uses at least 40–50 words; speech is more accurate, but may leave off some endings.	Asks simple questions; uses 2–3 word phrases; begins to use plurals.	Emergent code switching; begins to assume the perspective of another person; begins to identify colors; has most speech sounds with some distortions; repeats sentences; emergent rhyming; expresses feelings and ideas.	Begins to establish verbal control over behavior; increased self-regulation.	Says 200–300 words; describes how to do things; defines words.	Engages in conversation; describes objects with increased details; speech is generally grammatically correct.
Receptive Language	Reacts to sounds.	Turns head to sound source; watches faces of speaker, particularly familiar faces.	Understands "no"; responds to friendly and angry tones.		Begins to follow simple directions with accompanying gestures.	At least 50 words in vocabulary; points to body parts; follows simple commands.	Begins to understand some spatial concepts (e.g., on, up, down); 150–300 words in vocabulary.		Understands functional uses for objects; begins to understand simple humor; 900–1000 words in vocabulary.		Understands complex questions; answers "shy" questions.	Carries out 2- and 3-step directions; understands time sequences; has over 2000 words in vocabulary.

TABLE 2.2 (Continued)

Cognitive	Does not actively search for objects that have moved out of sight; discrimination of novel and familiar stimuli.	Begins to search for partially concealed objects; anticipates destination of a moving object that is lost from sight.	Begins to search for objects seen being hidden.	Begins to search for objects hidden in visible changes in location.	Begins to search for objects in hidden displacements by recreating the sequence; begins to formulate plans, remembers them, and shows persistence in trying to achieve a goal.	Full object permanence achieved.	Generalization of information and "chunking" information into categories continues to increase.		Cause-and-effect relationships begins to emerge; use of fantasy to solve problems and dilemmas.
Social-Emotional	Smiles when caregiver/parent appears.	Recognizes familiar and unfamiliar faces; stranger anxiety may surface; initiates interactions; emergent interest in relationships.		Egocentric view of the world and own immediate needs.	Begins to engage in play with peers (solitary, parallel); "terrible twos" emerge as child experiences discrepancy between own needs and the caregiver's.	Awareness of gender identity.	Imitation of caregiver behaviors; emergent negotiation and conflict resolution skills; begins to engage in rule-governed behaviors.	Emergent inhibition of emotional expression, arousal, and general self-monitoring.	Use of words to mediate social interactions and conflicts; emergence of guilt; increasing interest in peer relationships and friendships. Increased coping skills contribute to growing self-esteem; racial identity begins to emerge.

Sources: Piper, M. C., & Darrah, D. (1995). *Motor assessment of the developing infant.* Philadelphia: W. B Saunders; Erhardt, R. (1994). *Developmental hand dysfunction* (2nd ed.). San Antonio, TX: Therapy Skill Builders; Hulit, L. M., & Howard, M. R. (2001). *Born to talk* (3rd ed.). Upper Saddle River, NJ: Merrill/Pearson Education; Puckett, M. B., & Black, J. K. (2004). *The young child: Development from prebirth through age eight* (4th ed.). Upper Saddle River, NJ: Prentice Hall.

The neonatal period—the first 4 weeks after birth—is considered a high-risk stage in human life.

who are born alive annually in the United States, approximately 1% die within the first 24 hours, 1% die within the first week, and 1% die within the first year. Behrman and Kliegman (1983) note that an infant experiences a greater risk of death during the first 7 days of life than at any other time during the next 65 years. The largest number of deaths occurring during the first year of life is attributed to sudden infant death syndrome (SIDS). See Box 2.2 for further discussion.

The average newborn enters the world weighing between 2,500 and 4,300 gm (5 lb 8 oz) and (9 lb 8 oz), with the overall average being about 3,200 to 3,400 gm (7 lb to 7 lb 8 oz). About 90% of newborns are approximately 46 to 56 cm (18 to 22 in) in length, with the average being about 51 cm (20 in) (O'Rahilly & Muller, 1996). The baby's size is associated with a variety of factors including parental size, race, gender, maternal nutrition, and overall maternal health. Male newborns tend to be slightly longer and heavier than their female counterparts, and the first child in the birth order generally weighs less than any of the siblings who follow (Puckett & Black, 2004). The skin of newborns is often pale and thin. The skin also may be covered with lanugo—a light, fuzzy body hair—or **vernix caseosa,** an oily fluid that protects the baby from infection. Both of these substances disappear shortly after birth.

The average full-term baby weighs about 3,400 gm (7 lb 8 oz) and is about 51 cm (20 in) long.

The skeletal system of the neonate is not totally developed, and consequently many of the bones are soft and pliable. For example, the **fontanelles** are the gaps between the bones in the skull that permit the skull bones to overlap during the birth process and allow for additional brain growth. The posterior fontanelle gradually

BOX 2.2   SUDDEN INFANT DEATH SYNDROME (SIDS)

Each year approximately 2,100 deaths of infants under 12 months of age are attributed to "crib death"—a problem best known as sudden infant death syndrome (SIDS). This accounts for the largest number of deaths occurring during the first year of life in developed countries with a rate of about 1–2.5 deaths per 1,000 live births, or about 7.7% of infant fatalities, according to the National Center for Health Statistics (Kung, Hoyert, Xu, & Murphy, 2005). Researchers and medical professionals are still in the process of trying to understand the causes of this condition, particularly given that the majority of cases occur in apparently healthy infants. Although there are some indications that this condition is related to delayed development of physiological arousal and cardiorespiratory control, the actual mechanisms behind this problem remain unknown. Recent research findings suggest that there may be an ab-

normality in the lower part of the brain stem that controls breathing, blood pressure, body heat, and neurotransmission of serotonin, a chemical messenger in the brain. What we do know is that premature infants have a five times greater risk for SIDS than full-term infants, that SIDS is seen more frequently in boys than girls, and that there also is higher risk for infants born to mothers who smoke, are not married, and/or come from impoverished backgrounds. In addition, many of the parents of babies succumbing to SIDS reported mild cold symptoms prior to the event. As might be expected, parents are devastated at the unexpected loss of their infant, and often experience intense guilt and grief. Prevention measures, such as keeping infants on their back as much as possible, avoiding overheating, and avoiding soft, loose bedding, all have contributed to reducing the occurrence of SIDS (American Academy of Pediatrics, 2000).

closes up through the third month of life, whereas the anterior fontanelle is closed by 18 months of age.

The respiratory system of the newborn must adapt to a gaseous environment. Although the newborn consumes about twice the amount of oxygen as an adult does (Klaus & Fanaroff, 2001), respiration tends to be rapid, shallow, irregular, and unsynchronized, with the abdomen doing more work than the chest. The neonate may make peculiar wheezing and coughing sounds because the entire respiratory system is underdeveloped and inexperienced with the demands of the extrauterine environment. The digestive and circulatory systems also must make the transition to independent functioning. The visual system is incomplete because of underdevelopment of the retina and optic nerve; however, the newborn's eyes can follow a moving light as well as a moving target. In general, neonates can see best at a distance of about 19 cm (7$^1/_2$ in). There also seems to be a preference for visually following human faces more than any other type of object (Johnson, Dziurawiee, Ellis, & Morton, 1991) and they seem to prefer faces judged by adults to be more attractive, regardless of age, gender, or race (Slater et al., 1998). Interestingly, these features may not be as true for newborns with emergent neurodevelopmental disorders (e.g., autism).

The neonate also maintains physiological reactivity to sound intensity, as indicated by increased heart rate and motor activity, as well as an orienting reflex in which the baby turns in the direction of the sound stimulus. The other senses of olfaction, taste, and tactile sensitivity also are intact (Puckett & Black, 2004). For example, the neonate is capable of distinguishing among sweet, sour, and bitter tastes, as well as distinguishing the odor of its mother's breast milk (Winberg & Porter, 1998). Motor skills of the neonate are mainly characterized by primitive reflexes and random gross motor activity. Reflexes are automatic inborn behaviors of which the newborn has many. Further discussion of reflexes and motor development is provided in chapters 3 and 4. Many neonates who experience medical difficulties are served in neonatal intensive care units. Box 2.3 discusses neonatal intensive care facilities for infants with special developmental needs.

Infant Period

Infancy describes the growth and development of the child from about the fourth week through the second year of life. The infant experiences rapid physical growth during this time. The birth weight doubles by the fifth month and triples by the end of the first year, and the infant gains about 2,300 to 2,700 gm (5 to 6 lb) per year for the next several years (Puckett & Black, 2004). The infant grows approximately 25 cm (10 in) by the end of the first year, an average of 13 cm (5 in) by the end of the second year, and 7 cm (3 in) the following year (Deiner, 1997). In addition to weight and length, **head circumference** is an important physical feature to measure at regular intervals. Changes in head circumference are important because they denote brain growth. During the first year of life, head circumference increases from 33 or 36 cm (13 or 14 in) at birth to about 43 or 46 cm (17 or 18 in), with most of this growth occurring during the early months of development. The circumferences of the chest and abdomen are about the same in the neonate, but during infancy the

Newborns can see best at a distance of about 19 cm (7$^1/_2$ in), and they seem to prefer attractive human faces.

The infancy period—from 4 weeks of age to 2 years—is a time of rapid physical growth.

Changes in head circumference indicate brain growth.

BOX 2.3   THE NEONATAL INTENSIVE CARE UNIT (NICU)

Premature, low-birth-weight, and medically involved infants may need to spend time in a closely monitored environment where they can receive complex medical care and attention. The newborn or neonatal intensive care unit (NICU) is a specialized facility that can meet the needs of medically fragile infants and their parents. Length of stay in the NICU is determined by a number of factors including severity of the illness or condition and the rate of progress during care. Although the infant mortality rate has decreased 90% from 1915 to 1997 to about 7.2 per 1,000 live births (Centers for Disease Control and Prevention [CDC], 1999), the United States continues to have one of the highest rates of infant mortality among industrialized nations. Whereas the mortality rates have decreased with advances in medical technology, reducing the morbidity rates

(i.e., negative outcomes) increasingly has become the focus of caregivers in the NICU environment.

A strong movement in NICUs within the United States and abroad is to integrate developmental care into the NICU environment. A training model and protocol developed by Heidelise Als around 1986, titled the Neonatal Intervention and Developmental Care Assessment Program, is a forerunner to the family-centered developmental care movement. This model suggests that the environment should be modified to simulate the in utero setting, yet stimulate and encourage development of the newborn on its schedule. Modifications in lighting, handling of the infant, and feeding practices are examples of variables that may need to be changed to suit the infant's specific developmental needs (Als, 1997, Als & Lawhon, 2004; Als et al., 2003).

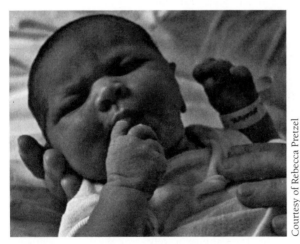

Courtesy of Rebecca Pretzel

Infants begin learning about themselves and their environments as early as the first day of life.

African American and female children typically grow faster than do white children and males.

chest circumference becomes larger than that of the abdomen. Deciduous, or primary, teeth appear at about 6 to 8 months and continue to erupt until all 20 are in place by toddlerhood. The skeletal structure of the infant hardens, and the musculature increases in weight and density. Typically, African American children show more rapid skeletal growth than white children do, and the bones of females generally grow faster than those of males (Puckett & Black, 2004; Tanner, 1990).

Another manifestation of infancy is the apparent disappearance or, more accurately, the integration of many of the primitive reflexes into the baby's developing nervous system. This occurs as the cerebral cortex matures and begins to exert control over the lower central nervous system. This control is accomplished, in part, by a process called **myelinization.** Myelin is a soft, white, fatty substance that coats and protects many nerve cells. It allows for rapid transmission of neural messages from the brain to other parts of the body. Myelinization begins in utero at about the fourth gestational month, with some neural pathways (e.g., the brain stem) being fully myelinated by the 30th gestational week (Amand, Phil, & Hickey, 1987); however, myelinization is not complete at birth (Biese & Wang, 1994). Although it will not be complete until adulthood, by 6 months many of the cortical fibers have been sheathed with myelin, thus facilitating greater cortical control and enabling the infant to achieve various developmental milestones such as sitting up, grasping, and walking, and various cognitive and adaptive skills necessary for maturation (Tanner, 1990).

> Myelinization is the process by which myelin, a soft, white, fatty substance, coats and protects nerve cells.

Toddler Period

The **toddler period** generally encompasses development during the second and third years of life. Strang (1969) has labeled this period "the first adolescence." It is a transitional time between infancy and early childhood, just as adolescence links childhood to adulthood. The toddler period is characterized by a slowing of physical development, although the toddler maintains a growth rate faster than any subsequent period except adolescence. At age 2 the average toddler is 81 to 89 cm (32 to 35 in) tall and weighs approximately 11 to 14 kg (25 to 30 lb). The child now is capable of maintaining an upright physical posture, and development in all areas becomes more refined. Bones continue to calcify and harden, with the composition of wrists and ankles changing from cartilage to bone. Nonetheless, the toddler still has a larger proportion of cartilage than hard bone, making possible skeletal damage resulting from disease or poor diet. A toddler normally has a full set of baby teeth by age 2. Muscle and fat tissues develop slowly during this period, with fatty tissue growth actually decreasing up to about age 30 months when it again begins to increase. Motor development improves, and well-balanced walking, jumping, and climbing without adult assistance are common. In the case of Nathaniel, he is unable to walk at 23 months of age and may be as much as one year behind in his gross motor development. Fine muscle control is evident in the child's finger coordination in learning to handle pencils, crayons, and paintbrushes.

> Toddlerhood—the second and third years of life—is a transitional period of continued growth and development.

Memory and language skills also show significant gains during this period. The child learns the names of people, objects, and places and can recall them for later use. In the language domain, the child moves from word combinations at age 2 to sentences at age 3. With only one-word utterances, Nathaniel is showing very few of these language related behaviors at 23 months of age. Words and actions become more coordinated near the end of the toddler period. Social-emotional development moves from adult-assisted activities to more independent social-emotional activities, with play being exploratory and egocentric in nature. Self-help and adaptive behaviors also emerge during toddlerhood, with the major one being toilet training. In general, the toddler begins to use thought, language, movement, and emotions in a coordinated fashion and is learning to gain verbal control over actions (Tinsley & Waters, 1982).

> The toddler begins to coordinate thinking and language skills, as well as motor and emotional skills.

Preschool Period

As will be seen from the chapters in Part II of this text, the **preschooler** continues to experience refinement in growth patterns, particularly in physical structures and motor skills. Self-help skills, such as dressing, toileting, and language usage, become

Courtesy of Stephen Hooper

Play during the toddler period is increasingly exploratory and self-directed.

The preschooler integrates self-help skills, such as dressing, toileting, and language usage, into daily behavior.

Nearly all of the preschooler's developmental activity forms the foundation for future learning and social challenges.

a regular part of day-to-day behaviors. Gender differences are minimal, although boys usually are heavier and have more muscle tissue than girls do.

The preschool child is willing to try new games, tricks, and stunts, and self-confidence in this realm is growing. Preschoolers are excited about their surroundings and are curious enough to ask "Why?" questions. Speech and language skills have become more grammatically correct in their manifestations, and the child uses language in a functional manner. Social-emotional development is characterized by increased child-to-child and child-to-adult interactions as fears, fantasies, and a sense of self-respect emerge. Much of the preschooler's developmental activity forms the foundation for the social and learning challenges to be encountered when formal schooling begins around age 6 (Puckett & Black, 2004).

Neurodevelopment

Concurrently with the developmental changes observed across the motor, language, cognitive, and social domains, underlying neurodevelopmental changes are occurring. In fact, one of the primary reasons for the observed developmental changes seen from birth through the preschool years is associated brain development. Needless to say, it is rapidly developing during this time period and fuels many of the wonderful changes that can be seen in children as they move through the infant,

Courtesy of Stephen Hooper

Even typically developing preschoolers will demonstrate a wide range of physical, cognitive, communication, and social-emotional skills.

toddler, and preschool years. It is important for the early interventionist to have a working understanding of how the brain contributes to the various behaviors exhibited by a child. Box 2.4 illustrates how age and neurodevelopment interact to influence what you can and cannot recall about your infancy.

While a review of the neurological development of various brain structures and their associated functions is beyond the scope of this book (see Swaiman, Ashwal, & Ferrier, 2006, for a comprehensive examination of this topic), it is important to note that brain development begins in the womb with an overproduction of neurons. During that time period it is extremely susceptible to negative factors (e.g., maternal illness) but as well as to positive factors (good maternal health and nutrition). At birth, the brain has the neurons in the correct places, in general, and it weighs approximately 25% of its final adult weight. In healthy children, brain volume increases steadily until about age 10 to 12 years, with about 75% of the adult brain weight occurring by 24 months; by age 3 it is closer to its mature size than any other body part (Puckett & Black, 2004); and by age five years it has attained approximately 96% of its adult size and weight (Carmichael, 1990; Pfefferbaum et al., 1994). This brain growth is largely fueled by the rapid branching and increased connections among neurons as well as the increased myelination that occurs on the axons. The myelination process is critical not only to increasing the capacity of brain structures, but also to increasing the rate of speed with which information is communicated along the axons. Conversely, while the brain is growing and maturing, and concomitant behaviors are changing, the brain also

By the end of the preschool years, the head grows to 90% of its adult size and the brain to 75% of its adult weight.

BOX 2.4   CAN YOU REMEMBER EVENTS FROM WHEN YOU WERE A YOUNG INFANT?

Unfortunately (or fortunately!), you probably can't. If you do, the memories more than likely are ones that have been shared about you by your parents and caregivers. In fact, you were probably pretty forgetful as a young infant—typically remembering information for only about 24 hours at 6 months of age and up to a month at about 9 months of age. So, although your memory clearly began to develop as you approached the second year of life, it probably contributes to why you don't recall much of being a young infant. One of the reasons for this relates to the neurological development of specific areas of the brain that deal with memory and retrieval,

specifically the hippocampus and the frontal lobes. Interestingly, it has been speculated that these brain regions undergo increased development during that time period between 9 and 17 months of age. Additionally, language abilities are increasing rapidly during this time period, and these skills also could have contributed to better recall during the second year of life. So, while you may have a well developed memory today, such as for remembering facts and information for your classes, when you were a young infant, you probably didn't remember too much, and you more than likely don't remember your first birthday!

Pruning refers to the elimination of ineffective or inefficient neurons.

is striving to be more efficient. In this regard, the brain also engages in a process called **pruning,** wherein ineffective and/or inefficient neuronal connections are eliminated. This process begins around age 4 years, but will continue throughout much of childhood and young adulthood (Whitaker, Bub, & Leventer, 1981). Epstein (2001) has noted that many of these changes in neurodevelopment actually seem to coincide with Piaget's stages of cognitive development.

Suffice it to say that certain aspects of the overall anatomy of very young children make them more vulnerable to the negative effects of neurological insult and injury. For example, with respect to traumatic brain injury (TBI), infants and toddlers have proportionally larger heads than older children and adults. The disproportional distributions of the head, neck, and trunk result in TBI impacting the bodies and brains of very young children differently than older children or adults (Ewings-Cobb et al., 1995; Keenan, Hooper, Wetherington, Nocera, & Runyan, 2007). Neck muscles may not yet be strong enough to protect the head and brain stem from injury as well as they would in older individuals. The developing skulls of infants have soft membranes (i.e., sutures and fontanelles) that differ significantly from the rigid skulls of adults, contributing to the differential impact of a trauma to the brain (Goldsmith & Plunkett, 2004). Other characteristics of the skull and brain that make infants especially susceptible to injury are the skull's thinness and pliability, the brain's softness, a lack of a myelin sheath for many axons, a flatter base of the skull, and immature neck muscles (Case, Graham, Corey-Handy, Jentzen, & Monteleone, 2001). These characteristics, in tandem with a subsequent insult or injury, can disrupt the developmental trajectories of a variety of skills and abilities which, in turn, may negatively affect the development of motor, language, cognitive, social-emotional, and adaptive behaviors and learning.

In addition to trauma-induced neurological differences, sometimes neurodevelopment is simply different, but different enough to create problems with attention and behavior (e.g., attention deficit-hyperactivity disorder), language (e.g., specific language disorder), and related learning (e.g., learning disabilities, intellectual disabilities, autism). As we move into the next section, Factors Affecting Development, think about how brain development and function may be a major part of the behaviors that are described in young children. As an exercise, you may want to do some research to see what brain functions might be affected by the various factors that will be discussed. Indeed, there is a rapidly growing body of literature in that regard, one that should be of interest to the early interventionist in increasing understanding of overall child development.

:: FACTORS AFFECTING DEVELOPMENT

Although the unfolding of the developmental process is a fairly remarkable set of events, there are many factors that can influence the viability of the developing embryo and the subsequent condition of the young child. Some of these factors, such as maternal age and parity, exist prior to conception; some, such as maternal nutrition, substance use during pregnancy, and maternal illness, exist at or following conception, but prior to birth; some, such as prematurity and low birth weight, appear at the time of birth; and others, such as child abuse or neglect, occur after birth. Many of these factors are interrelated, such as when poor maternal nutrition during the prenatal period contributes to low birth weight; however, these factors will be considered separately for the purposes of discussion. Further, it is important to note that this section is not meant to be an exhaustive listing of factors that can disrupt development; it is intended merely to illustrate the many possible factors that can disrupt the developmental process.

Maternal Age and Parity

Maternal age and parity (i.e., number of previous pregnancies) provide clues relating to the course of development of the fetus. Women between the ages of 20 and 30 are in the prime of their childbearing years. Although today more women are waiting until their mid-30s or early 40s to have children (Martin et al., 2002), emergent research suggests that female fertility begins to decline in the early to mid-30s (Auyeuna, Klein, Ratts, Odem, & Williams, 2001). While rates have fluctuated over the last 75 years, about 14% of births in the United States in 2002 were to women of advanced maternal age (i.e., 35 years or older at delivery; Resta, 2005). Further, although the risks during pregnancy at a later age are still relatively small, they do increase with advancing age (Dildy et al., 1996).

Risks to the unborn child increase with advancing maternal age.

The effects of delayed childbearing has demonstrated effects on gestational age and birth weight across multiple studies, but some variability exists in the way that maternal age was classified and its effects measured (Newburn-Cook & Onyskiw, 2005). Advanced maternal age has been associated with a host of negative outcomes ranging from greater incidence of preterm delivery (Delbaere et al., 2006; Machado, 2006; Seoud et al., 2002); cesarean delivery (Delbaere et al., 2006; Seoud et al., 2002); low birth weight (Machado, 2006); very low birth weight and intensive neonatal care (Delbaere et al., 2006) to antepartum complications (Seoud et al.,

2002); stillbirth (Reddy, Ko, & Williger, 2006); and perinatal death (Delbaere et al., 2006). Additionally, factors such as ethnicity may mediate the effects of maternal age on outcomes. For example, advanced maternal age was more likely to be associated with low birth weight for African American and Puerto Rican mothers, and somewhat more likely with Mexican American women relative to non-Hispanic whites (Khoshnood, Wall, & Lee, 2005).

In addition, mothers over 25 years of age are at increased risk of having babies with congenital malformations, such as clubfoot, not associated with chromosomal abnormalities (Hollier, Leveno, Kelly, McIntire, & Cunningham, 2000). Maternal age greater than 35 years, however, has been identified as a risk factor for cerebral palsy (Wu, Croen, Shah, Newman, & Najjar, 2006) and other abnormalities in newborns, as well as for difficult pregnancies characterized by high blood pressure, diabetes, cardiovascular disease, preterm labor, and postpartum hemorrhage. In some older mothers, a decrease in muscle tone and joint flexibility also may contribute to more difficult labor, but this may not be a problem for women who have maintained good physical condition prior to and during pregnancy.

The risk of Down syndrome also increases with age, with rates being approximately 1 in 10,000 for 20-year-old mothers, about 3 in 1,000 for 35-year-old mothers, and 1 in 100 for 40-year-old mothers (Murkoff, Eisenberg, & Hathaway, 2002), with some variability noted in this pattern as a result of ethnicity (Forrester & Merz, 2003). Demographic shifts are evident in maternal age and Down syndrome, with 25% of Down syndrome pregnancies in 1980 and 50% in 2002 related to advanced maternal age. Fetal loss rates in these pregnancies are thought to be higher as maternal age increases (Savva, Morris, Mutton, & Alberman, 2006). In contrast, older maternal age (>35 years) is related to greater rates of survival of quadruplets and quintuplets (Salihu, Aliyu, Kirby, & Alexander, 2004).

In general, women over the age of 35 and teenagers are more likely to have high-risk pregnancies. For example, Machado (2006) found more positive outcomes with regard to prematurity and low birth weight in Brazilian women between the ages of 20 and 30 than in women younger and older than this age range. Reasons for the increased risk associated with teenage pregnancy may include limited prenatal care and poor nutrition, as well as a number of negative social and emotional consequences. Denise, our young mother in the chapter vignette, clearly would be at-risk here. For teenagers specifically, evidence points to lower IQ as a key contributor to early childbearing (Shearer et al., 2002) and has identified increased levels of postnatal depression relative to older mothers (Shaw, Lawlor, & Najman, 2006). This combination of factors may increase the teenage mother's chances of premature labor, delivery of a low-birth-weight child, and efficacy as a parent. Both teenage and older mothers have a greater likelihood of developing toxemia (Batshaw, Pellegrino, & Roizen, 2007). Children of adolescent mothers also are at greater risk for a number of social-behavioral, academic, and cognitive problems (Byrne, Agerbo, Ewald, Eaton, & Mortensen, 2003; Shaw et al., 2006), although it is important to note that the rate of births to teenagers has been steadily dropping over the past decade (Martin et al., 2002).

Parity, or the number of times a woman has previously given birth, has been correlated with outcomes of other pregnancies. Regardless of the mother's age, the

Teenagers and women over age 35 are more likely to face risks during pregnancy.

first birth carries an added risk because all of the maternal systems involved in pregnancy and delivery have yet to be tested. Subsequent births less than 2 years apart and after the third child also carry additional risks (Apgar & Beck, 1972; Holley, Rosenbaum, & Churchill, 1969), although many of these risks have been linked to poor prenatal care (Blondel, Kaminsky, & Breart, 1980).

Extremely high parity (e.g., 15 or more prior live births), for example, has been linked with a greater risk of stillbirth (Aliyu et al., 2005a). Findings regarding the relationship between Down syndrome and parity have been equivocal. Increasing parity may be related to increased risk of Down syndrome for both younger (age < 35 years) and older (age ≥35 years) mothers (Doria-Rose, Kim, Augustine, & Edwards, 2003). The magnitude of this trend weakened, however, when excluding mothers who had had amniocentesis and may have been more likely to terminate the pregnancy due to a prenatal diagnosis of Down's syndrome. Other research suggests that higher parity is associated with greater risk for Down syndrome only in mothers who are 35 years or older (Clementi, Bianca, Benedicenti, & Tenconi, 1999). Maternal age also appears to be related to the differential impact of parity on very preterm births of twins (Branum & Schoendorf, 2005). Differences in parity also have been demonstrated in cortisol levels (a naturally occurring steroid hormone secreted by the adrenal cortex as part of the body's response to stress), with second-time bottle feeding mothers demonstrating higher cortisol levels than breastfeeding mothers; however, such an effect was not found for first-time mothers (Tu, Lupien, & Walker, 2006).

> The first birth carries added risks to the child and mother.

Paternal Factors

Until recently, it was believed that a father's sole responsibility in the reproductive process consisted of egg fertilization; however, this may not be an accurate reflection of the paternal role. While scientists have long decided that the sperm decides the gender of the baby, more recently researchers have debated the influence of an older father's sperm on the prevalence of (1) birth defects (Yang et al., 2007); (2) miscarriage (Maconochie, Doyle, Prior, & Simmons, 2007) and spontaneous abortions (Kleinhaus et al., 2006); (3) autism (Reichenberg et al., 2006); (4) neural tube defects (Fear, Hey, Vincent, & Murphy, 2007); (5) schizophrenia (Byrne, Agerbo, Ewald, Eaton, & Mortensen, 2003; Dalman & Allebeck, 2002; Malaspina et al., 2005; Malaspina et al., 2002; Malaspina et al., 2001); (6) breast cancer (Choi et al., 2005); and (7) Down syndrome (Abroms & Bennett, 1981). Some researchers have challenged these findings (Luetjens, Rolf, Gassner, Werny, & Nieschlag, 2002) and ongoing research is needed to provide greater clarification, particularly as it may apply to *genetic counseling* (Hook, 1987).

Scientists have speculated that, just as in the case of the eggs of the older mother, the undeveloped sperm of the older father have had longer exposure to environmental hazards or teratogens and, consequently, might contain altered or damaged genes or chromosomes (Eisenberg, Murkoff, & Hathaway, 1991). Others have postulated that a father's sperm may be a vehicle for transporting drugs, such as cocaine, to the egg during fertilization (Yazigi, Odem, & Polakoski, 1991). Wyrobek et al. (2006) suggested that paternal age may have some effect on the genomic integrity of sperm and the risk of Apert syndrome, but not Down, Klinefelter, Turner, triple X, and XYY syndromes. Furthermore, damage to sperm chromatin has also been associated with male infertility (Wyrobek et al., 2006). Therefore, many obstetricians now consider paternal age and related factors (e.g., substance abuse) as risk factors to development in addition to the age of the mother.

Maternal Nutrition

Approximately 40 years ago, the Food and Nutrition Board published a landmark report titled *Maternal Nutrition During the Course of Pregnancy* (National Research Council, Committee on Maternal Nutrition/Food and Nutrition Board, 1970), which examined the relationship between nutrition and the course and outcome of pregnancy. This report made recommendations for weight gain and nutritional intake during pregnancy. It also suggested that women should be concerned about their nutritional habits from puberty through the childbearing years because these habits can help prepare them for childbirth. Adequate maternal nutrition is important to the health of the expectant mother as well as to that of her unborn child. Poor maternal nutrition will affect the child by not sufficiently meeting the nutritional requirements of the developing fetus and by weakening the mother and, consequently, the intrauterine environment (Herbert, Dodds, & Cefalo, 1993). Mahajan et al. (2006) suggest that inadequate maternal nutrition requires the fetus to adapt to a restricted environment, which alters the growth of the fetus.

Good nutritional health is important for both the expectant mother and the unborn child.

During pregnancy, many substances are exchanged between mother and baby as their blood passes through the placenta. Thus, dietary intake by the mother influences the developing fetus. Both quality and quantity of nutrient intake required by a woman increase during pregnancy. Qualitative deficiencies relate to the imbalance of proteins, vitamins, and minerals in the mother's diet. Quantitative deficiencies are simply those in which the mother lacks sufficient caloric intake. A review of data on nutrient intakes during pregnancy indicates that, on average, women probably meet their recommended daily allowance (RDA) for protein, thiamin, riboflavin, niacin, and vitamins A, B_{12}, and C. Expectant mothers are less likely to meet requirements for folic acid, iron, calcium, zinc, magnesium, and vitamins B_6, D, and E. This does not necessarily mean that a woman's diet is deficient, however, as many of the RDA requirements are somewhat generous. Although a sensible, balanced diet, consisting of approximately 2,700 calories, is considered the optimal way for an expectant mother to pass nutrients to her baby, vitamin and mineral supplementation is common.

Iron and folate are primary nutrients that typically require supplementation during pregnancy.

For example, for women who are on restricted diets, are carrying more than one fetus, are very young, use drugs, or have poor pre-pregnancy nutritional or physical status, selective supplementation may be warranted. For women who regularly follow suggested dietary guidelines, iron and folic acid appear to be the primary nutrients for which requirements cannot be met reasonably by diet alone. The RDA for iron during pregnancy is more than twice as high as the average daily intake for a nonpregnant female. Further, a deficiency in folic acid in the expectant mother's diet has been associated with **neural tube defects** (i.e., problems with the closing of the primary tubular structure that develops into the brain and spinal cord; Smithells et al., 1983), orofacial clefts (Shaw, Lammer, Wasserman, & O'Malley, 1995), and low birth weight (Scholl, Hediger, Schall, Khoo, & Fischer, 1996). While folic acid continues to be considered important in preventing neural tube defects, more recent research has not supported the protective factors of folic acid on other birth defects (Bower, Miller, Payne, & Serna, 2006). In a study of Australian women, for example, folic acid intake during pregnancy was not associated with a reduction in orofacial clefts, congenital heart defects, urinary tract defects, limb reduction defects, or other birth defects (Bower et al., 2006).

The Centers for Disease Control and the U.S. Public Health Service encourage all women who could become pregnant to consume 400 micrograms (400 mcg) of synthetic folic acid daily (CDC, 2007). In addition, the Department of Health and Human Services and the Food and Drug Administration (FDA) announced that many foods in the United States would be fortified with folic acid to prevent birth defects (U.S. Food and Drug Administration, 1996).

Despite the evidence that folic acid is key for preventing neural tube defects, the use of folic acid supplements continues to lag. Indeed, Denise did not take folic acid and her diet likely was compromised by her generally low socioeconomic status and polysubstance abuse. While the rate of folic acid supplement consumption appeared to increase from prepregnancy to the first trimester, rates decreased by the eighth month of pregnancy in a large sample of Norwegian women (Nilsen et al., 2006). Factors that corresponded to taking supplements prior to pregnancy and during the first trimester included higher education levels, plannned pregnancies, infertilitiy treatments, and chronic dieases. These women were also more likely to be older, married, of higher income, of lower parity, and nonsmokers. In a study examining the timing of initiation of iron and folic acid supplements, Korean women seemed to benefit from such supplementation earlier in their pregnancy (Lee, Lee, & Lim, 2005). In addition to its benefits in preventing neural tube defects, studies of rat embryos suggest that folic acid may prevent malformations when the embryos are exposed to diabetes (Wentzel, Gäreskog, & Eriksson, 2005). Despite some research suggesting that folate consumption might protect against depression, Miyake and colleagues (2006) did not find a relationship between intake of folate and postpartum depression, but found some support that riboflavin might protect against postpartum depression.

Several other dietary components, such as choline, iodine, calcium, and antioxidants, are essential in the diet of a pregnant woman and may have an impact on brain growth and subsequent cognitive development. For example, recent work has targeted choline as a key nutrient in this regard (see Box 2.5). Choline is one of the building blocks of cell membranes that aids functions such as the neurotransmissions that control memory. Following a dose of choline to a pregnant rat during the third trimester, her pups could negotiate a maze nearly 40% better than pups of mothers who were not given choline (Zeisel, 2000, 2006). Other findings have shown choline to increase the size and activity of neurons in rat pups post-birth following prenatal ingestion of choline, and improved their memory as adults (Glenn et al., 2007). Although the generalization of these findings to humans awaits confirmation, these findings generally suggest that the dietary needs of women of

Deficient folate during pregnancy has been associated with a variety of developmental problems including neural tube defects such as spina bifida.

BOX 2.5   CAN PRENATAL INGESTION OF CHOLINE MAKE BRAINS LARGER AND FASTER?

Scientists at Duke University, Boston University, and the University of North Carolina think so. These research groups have shown that choline, a nutrient typically found in egg yolks, milk, nuts, soy products, liver and other meat, fish, and chocolate, can increase the size of brain cells and increased the efficiency of the cells in the rat's brain when ingested by the expectant mother during a narrow window of prenatal development. Choline is a fundamental component for a key brain chemical, or neurotransmitter, acetylcholine, that is involved in memory functions. Once born, rat pups showed more dendritic surface than rat pups whose mothers did not ingest choline, and the neurons fired more rapidly. Further, rat pups whose mothers ingested choline prenatally actually negotiated a maze about 40% faster than rat pups whose mothers did not ingest choline. Indeed, they appeared to be smarter and have improved learning capabilities. These findings stress the importance of maternal prenatal nutrition, but also offer hope for lessening the effects of neurodevelopmental abnormalities via careful prenatal nutrition. It will be exciting to see how these findings may generalize to humans. See Glenn et al., 2007, and Zeisel, 2006 for additional reading on the importance of choline to brain development.

childbearing age should be monitored because preconception nutrition deficits may affect the developing fetus in positive as well as negative ways (House, 2000; King, 2000).

Research has also examined the impact of iodine supplements during pregnancy, with a review of the research suggesting that most European women demonstrate iodine deficiency during pregnancy, with only about half of them receiving iodine supplements (Zimmermann & Delange, 2004). Iodine deficiency has the potential to affect thyroid functioning of the mother and both thyroid functioning and mental development of the child. In a community sample in India, consumption of calcium-rich foods was measured at 18 and 28 weeks gestation in an observational study. In addition to child and parent characteristics such as socioeconomic status and parent height, calcium intake was associated with higher bone density (Ganpule et al., 2006). Higher antioxidant intake during pregnancy, especially vitamin E and zinc, appears to have a beneficial impact on wheezing in children at 2 years (Litonjua et al., 2006). Effects were found when the antioxidants were consumed through foods alone as well as through supplements alone. Glycemic index may also impact pregnancy outcomes, with a low glycemic index associated with more positive outcomes (Moses et al., 2006).

Poor prenatal care and insufficient food intake both are associated with poor pregnancy outcomes. Between the 1960s and 1980s it became common for doctors to recommend a **gestational weight gain** averaging 11 kg (24 lb) or more rather than the 9 kg (20 lb) or less recommended prior to the 1960s. Contemporary best practices suggest a range of weight gain for pregnant women based on prepregnancy weight-for-height. This change in recommended weight gain for expectant mothers has been accompanied by an increase in mean birth weight of their infants and a reduction in low birth weight (Institute of Medicine, National Academy of Sciences, 1990a; Susser, 1991). A large body of evidence indicates that gestational weight gain during pregnancy, particularly during the second and third trimesters, is an important determinant of fetal growth. For example, inadequate nutritional intake during the last trimester can permanently reduce the number of brain cells by as much as 40%, and improved nutritional intake after such a period of malnourishment ultimately will not increase the number of brain cells (Winick, 1971). Poor fetal nutrition also has previously been associated with increased risk for problems in adulthood, such as coronary heart disease (CHD), stroke, and diabetes (Barker & Clark, 1997; Godfrey & Barker, 2000; Petry & Hales, 2000). More recent research has not, however, supported the finding that maternal nutrition affects risk factors for coronary heart disease in adulthood (Huxley & Neil, 2004). A longitudinal study that tracked the impact of dietary rations during World War II did not support a relationship between birth weight and maternal nutrition in pregnancy with CHD risk factors later in life in the offspring.

In general, low weight gain during pregnancy is associated with intrauterine growth retardation (IUGR), which in turn can have adverse consequences for subsequent growth and possible neurobehavioral problems. It also increases the risk of infant mortality. IUGR results from a combination of genetic and environmental influences and is thought to occur in approximately 5% of U.S.-born infants (Wu, Bazer, Cudd, Meininger, & Spencer, 2004). It tends to be more common in mothers whose diets are not adequately rich in certain nutrients, young mothers who themselves are continuing to grow and need the nutrients, and pregnancies with multiple fetuses as the fetuses compete for nutrients. IUGR places fetuses at greater risk for both mortality (e.g., stillbirth) and morbidity (e.g., neurological, respiratory, intestinal, and circulatory problems; Wu et al., 2004). Women with total individual weight gains of less than 10 kg (22 lb) were two to three times more likely to have growth-retarded full-term babies (Luke, Dickinson, & Petrie, 1981).

While undernutrition has long been a focus of research on fetal development, a review of recent research on maternal nutrition of humans and animals suggests that both maternal undernutrition and overnutrition can negatively impact fetal development, affecting the intrauterine environment and contributing to intrauterine growth retardation (Wu et al., 2004). Overweight and obesity in pregnant women is often related to excessive amounts of energy and protein consumption, which can also slow fetal and placental growth. Excessive weight gain in pregnancy can be associated with high birth weight and, secondarily, prolonged labor, shoulder dystocia (i.e., a disconnecting of the upper arm from the shoulder during the birth process in which muscles and nerve fibers can be damaged or destroyed), cesarean delivery, birth trauma, and asphyxia (Institute of Medicine, 1990a).

Breastfeeding is thought to have beneficial effects on development after birth. A combination of breastfeeding, parental education, and family income predicted intellectual functioning at 5 and 14 years of age in a study of women and their offspring in Australia (Lawlor et al., 2006). Breast milk appears to have a dose-response effect on very low birth weight infants as well, with scores on the Bayley Scales of Infant

Weight gain during gestation is important in determining fetal growth.

Poor fetal nutrition has been associated with problems at developmental stages across the life span.

Developmental Mental Development Index, Psychomotor Development Index, and Behavior Rating Scales increasing with breast milk consumption. Risk for rehospitalization decreased in the breastfed group. The ingredients in breast milk, particularly the fatty acids, appear to facilitate brain development in this population of infants. Interestingly, although approximately 75% of new mothers in the United States breastfeed their babies, only about 30% continue to feed their babies breast milk three months after birth, and only 11% are breastfeeding exclusively at six months past birth. While there are many reasons for this (e.g., mothers need to go back to work), it does appear that new mothers are not breastfeeding their infants long enough (i.e., about six months) to capitalize fully on the benefits of breast milk (Center for Disease Control and Prevention, 2007).

The **Special Supplemental Food Program for Women, Infants and Children (WIC),** which is administered by the U.S. Department of Agriculture, has had an increasing impact on the provision of food to low-income pregnant women since 1974. In addition to food or food vouchers, WIC provides education, counseling, and referrals for women who meet state criteria for nutritional risk during pregnancy and the early childhood years of their babies. This program has had a positive impact on the health of pregnant mothers from lower socioeconomic strata and their babies, with increasingly more mothers participating in the program early in their pregnancies (U.S. General Accounting Office, 2006). Despite some concerns with the WIC program, research suggests that it is effective in improving birth outcomes (Bitler & Currie, 2005) and positive health and weight gain outcomes in infants (Black et al., 2004).

> The WIC program has had a positive impact on the health of pregnant mothers from lower socioeconomic strata and their babies.

Exposure to Toxins During Pregnancy

Exposure to various toxins during child development has the potential for significant deleterious effects. A conceptual framework to organize neurotoxins, or teratogens, and their developmental consequences has been presented by Trask and Kosofsky (2000). A **teratogen** is anything external to the fetus that causes later structural or functional disabilities. Teratogens typically fall under two main categories: exposure to environmental toxins, such as lead and mercury (see Stein, Schettler, Wallinga, & Valenti, 2002, for review), and exposure to drugs, such as alcohol and tobacco. Research indicates that the earlier the exposure, particularly during the prenatal period, the greater the potential for negative developmental outcomes as a result of the exposure. In addition to the direct effects of teratogens on the child, indirect effects of the teratogens may compromise other maternal systems (Williams & Carta, 1997). For instance, smoking or alcohol consumption may inhibit the availability of critical nutrients in the bloodstream, and further hinder the development of the fetus. Research that attempts to quantify the impact of teratogens on children, both short-term and long-term effects, are often hindered by the frequency with which potential negative influences, such as poverty and poor nutrition, tend to co-occur (Abel & Hannigan, 1995).

> As a general rule, the earlier the exposure to a substance, the greater the potential for negative developmental sequelae.

Substance Use During Pregnancy

Substance use during pregnancy is an area of serious concern, with contemporary estimates suggesting a prevalence of about 11% (Chasnoff, 1991). Given her polysubstance use, our young single mother, Denise, would certainly fall into that group. Annually, the number of women who use tobacco, alcohol, or illicit drugs during pregnancy in the United States is approximately 1.2 million, 800,000, and 200,000, respectively (Chasnoff, 2003). This figure could be even higher given that many expectant mothers do not report their use of illegal substances. This issue was brought to the fore during the early 1960s, when a number of babies were born with no limbs and with other malformations because their mothers had taken thalidomide, a German-made tranquilizer, to control vomiting during pregnancy. About 20% of the pregnant women who took thalidomide gave birth to babies with birth defects. This incident dramatically underscored the risks involved in taking any drug during pregnancy. Although detrimental effects have been suggested for a variety of drugs, such as heroin, marijuana, and lysergic acid diethylamide (LSD), it is difficult to document the individual impact of these specific substances because many users of illegal drugs experiment with a variety of substances, not to mention variants of the same drug. In addition to the negative effects of direct exposure to substances prenatally, infants and children are also affected by the parental illnesses related to substance use and are at risk for future substance abuse themselves (Richter & Richter, 2001). Many women who use illicit drugs often place their babies at additional risk resulting from poor nutrition and lack of adequate prenatal care.

> The use of thalidomide by expectant mothers about 50 years ago dramatically highlighted the risks involved in taking any drug during pregnancy.

In general, the specific effects of a drug on a developing fetus are determined by at least two key factors: the dosage level and the stage of pregnancy during which the drug is taken. In fact, drugs with addictive properties, such as heroin, can cross the placenta barrier and cause the baby to be born addicted to that particular substance. Unfortunately, the infant then must go through withdrawal symptoms similar to those of adult addicts to get the drug out of its system. It is not clear how Nathaniel's mother's polysubstance abuse has affected his development, but it likely has contributed, in part, to his apparent developmental delays.

> The use of addictive drugs can cause the baby to be born addicted to that substance.

In a recent examination of over 100 research papers and reviews, Williams and Ross (2007) analyzed various trends related to prenatal toxin exposure. While prenatal exposure to multiple drugs negatively affects child development, relationships between specific drugs and outcomes are less clear, as they are often confounded by the presence of multiple drugs. Of the trends Williams and Ross studied, PCBs and lead appear to affect brain development, marijuana and alcohol seem linked to attentional deficits, the relationship between smoking and later delinquency appear influenced by genetic variables, and cocaine effects tend to decrease with age and seemed influenced by other psychological factors.

For the sake of the unborn child, the use of any drug for recreational purposes during the prenatal period should be avoided. This precaution should be extended to include both over-the-counter and prescription drugs, and all medications should be used only when they are recommended *and* monitored by the expectant mother's physician (see Shehata & Nelson-Piercy, 2001).

Alcohol   Alcohol is the drug most frequently used by women in the United States, with approximately 10% of pregnant women, aged 15 to 44, reporting alcohol consumption in the past month, 4% reporting binge drinking, and less than 1% engaging in heavy drinking (Wright, Sathe, & Spagnola, 2007; Wright & Walker, 2001). Approximately 40,000 infants born each year are affected by prenatal alcohol exposure (National Organization on Fetal Alcohol Syndrome, 2007). Alcohol use during pregnancy is cited as one of the leading causes of preventable birth defects and developmental disabilities in the United States (Weber, Floyd, Riley, & Snider, 2002), and, unfortunately, appears to have the most direct long-term effects relative to other drugs (Chiriboga, 2003). Some of the most consistent manifestations of significant alcohol exposure are intrauterine growth deficiency, low birth weight, cardiac defects, microcephaly (i.e., small head and brain) (Chiriboga, 2003), shortened fetal length, and subsequent cognitive delays (Abel, 1998; Sowell et al., 2001). Cognitive delays have been documented across nearly every area of functioning including motor, sensory, attention, language, visual-spatial abilities, learning and memory, problem solving, and overall intelligence (Rasmussen, 2005; Streissguth & Kanter, 1997). Burden, Jacobson, Sokol, and Jacobson (2005) reported specific working memory weaknesses in $7\frac{1}{2}$-year-old children who were exposed to alcohol during gestation, with heightened effects seen for children whose mothers aged 30 or older when pregnant. Further, abnormalities in specific brain structures (e.g., corpus callosum, basal ganglia, cerebellum) also have begun to be documented (Mattson & Riley, 1998; Sowell et al., 2001). Researchers have begun to explore the use of technology, such as electroencephalography (EEG), to assess brain functioning and to identify neurological markers associated with prenatal exposure to alcohol (D'Angiulli, Grunau, Maggi, & Herdman, 2006).

A distinct cluster of characteristics, which have been linked to comprise a disorder termed **fetal alcohol syndrome** (FAS), has been identified in children of alcoholic mothers. These characteristics include (a) pre- and postnatal growth retardation; (b) abnormalities of major organ systems such as the heart and liver; (c) central nervous system abnormalities including microcephaly, mental retardation, or specific neurodevelopmental delays; (d) gray matter density in the brain, and (e) distinctive facial characteristics (e.g., short palpebral fissures, a thin upper lip, a flattened and elongated philtrum, minor ear anomalies, and micrognathia) (National Organization on Fetal Alcohol Syndrome, 2007; Riley, McGee, & Sowell, 2004; Stoler & Holmes, 2004). These latter features are illustrated in Figure 2.1. It should be noted that many of the facial features may not be present if the mother did not consume alcohol during the time that these facial characteristics were forming (i.e., about the 20th day of pregnancy) and, when present, they may be seen most clearly between the ages of 2 and 10 (Stoler & Holmes, 2004).

The estimated prevalence of FAS in the United States is approximately 0.5 to 2 cases per 1,000 births (May & Gossage, 2001). The incidence of FAS is approximately 1 to 3 per 1,000 live births (Gardner, 1997), and it is estimated that thousands more children may exhibit **fetal alcohol effects** (FAE); that is, they have some, but not the full range of FAS characteristics. The Institute of Medicine (1990b) termed brain dysfunction in the presence of significant prenatal exposure to alcohol but no physical deformities **alcohol-related neurodevelopmental disorder**; this may

FIGURE 2.1   Distinctive facial characteristics of FAS.

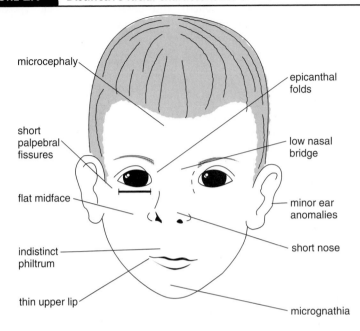

occur with at least 10 times the prevalence of FAS. Mattson, Schoenfeld, and Riley (2001) and others noted that children with FAE may show a variety of maladaptive behaviors, learning disabilities, speech and language problems, hyperactivity, and attention deficit-hyperactivity disorder.

Along with fragile X syndrome in males, FAS is one of the leading known causes of mental retardation in the United States (Deiner, 1997; National Organization on Fetal Alcohol Syndrome, 2007). Current research also indicates that there may be a dose-response relationship to development; in other words, detrimental effects on development seem to increase with the amount and frequency of alcohol consumption (Day et al., 2002; Day & Richardson, 1991; Sood et al., 2001). Binge drinking appears to be more harmful than more continuous drinking patterns even if less alcohol is consumed during the period of binge drinking (Maier & West, 2001). However, recent data suggest that environmental, behavioral, and genetic variables may also influence the risk of developing FAS following prenatal alcohol exposure (May et al., 2004). In general, there may be no safe level of alcohol consumption during pregnancy (National Organization on Fetal Alcohol Syndrome, 2007; National Clearinghouse for Alcohol and Drug Information, 1995), although it appears that moderate-to-high levels of alcohol consumption early in pregnancy cause the most severe problems. A woman is thought to be at increased risk of delivering a baby with FAS when her daily alcohol intake exceeds 80 gm ($2\frac{1}{2}$ oz) of alcohol per day (10 gm = one glass of wine or half a pint of beer). In fact, fetal growth may be compromised by as little as 40 gm ($1\frac{1}{2}$ oz) of alcohol per day (Shubert & Savage, 1994). It is thought that one of the primary mechanisms of damage occurs when high

One of the leading known causes of mental retardation in the United States is fetal alcohol syndrome.

There are no safe levels of alcohol consumption during pregnancy.

blood concentrations of alcohol hinder the transfer of amino acids and other necessary nutrients from the mother to the fetus, thus contributing to fetal hypoxia, subsequent decreased brain weight, and perhaps brain abnormalities. The rate at which alcohol is metabolized also may contribute to these anomalies (Autti-Ramo & Granstrom, 1991). Recent evidence indicates that exposure to alcohol in utero may even contribute to a preference for alcohol later in life (Molina, Chotro, & Dominguez, 1995).

Given the range of negative effects of prenatal alcohol exposure, some scientists have recommended the use of a continuum, appropriately coined, **fetal alcohol spectrum disorders** (FASD). This spectrum of disorders includes fetal alcohol syndrome, partial fetal alcohol syndrome, alcohol-related birth defects, and alcohol-related neurodevelopmental disorder (Autti-Ramo et al., 2006). Approximately 1 in 100 babies are born with some form of FASD, a disorder that is not outgrown and is associated with tremendous neurodevelopmental, physical, and financial costs (Elliott, Payne, Morris, Haan, & Bower, 2007; Lupton, Burd, & Harwood, 2004; National Organization on Fetal Alcohol Syndrome, 2007).

Tobacco   While the percentage of women who smoke during pregnancy has decreased over the past decade, almost half a million American women continued to smoke while pregnant in 1999. Nearly 11% of low birth weight cases involved mothers who smoked when pregnant (CDC, 2007). Unfortunately, the prevalence of women who smoke while pregnant in the United States is estimated to be between 13 and 30% and is often obscured by unreliable self-report data (Cnattingius, 2004; Hoyert, Freedman, Strobino, & Guyer, 2001; Slotkin, 1998). In one study, pregnant women between the ages of 15 and 25 were twice as likely to have smoked in the last month as were expectant mothers aged 26 to 44 (Wright et al., 2007). The potential impact of this problem has led to the identification of **fetal tobacco syndrome** (FTS) (Nieburg, Marks, McLaren, & Remington, 1985). This syndrome is characterized by mothers who (1) smoke five or more cigarettes per day, (2) have no maternal history of hypertension in pregnancy, (3) have babies with fetal growth retardation at term, and (4) manifest no other causes for their baby's intrauterine growth retardation. A likely mechanism for FTS involves the vasoconstrictive properties of nicotine. Nicotine actually binds to fetal hemoglobin and, consequently, reduces oxygen availability to the fetus (Longo, 1976). This effect has also been found in cases where the mother is exposed to passive or secondhand smoke (Dollberg et al., 2000).

There have been additional risks associated with smoking during pregnancy including spontaneous abortion, premature delivery, and stillbirth later in pregnancy (Cnattingius, 2004; Kleinman & Madans, 1985), with the overall mortality rate being twice as high for women who smoke during pregnancy versus those who do not smoke. Prenatal exposure to nicotine is associated with general physiological dysregulation and higher risk for psychiatric problems (Ernst, Moolchan, & Robinson, 2001; Wakschlag, Leventhal, Pine, Pickett, & Carter, 2006) including early onset conduct disorder and adolescent-onset drug dependence (Weissman, Warner, Wickramarante, & Kandel, 1999), an increased risk of cleft lip and cleft palates (Kallen, 1997), and a significant negative impact on the behavior of toddlers

---

Smoking accounts for about 11% of all low-birth-weight babies.

Passive or secondhand smoke may have a negative impact on the developing fetus.

(Wakschlag et al., 2006) and preschoolers (Day, Richardson, Goldschmidt, & Cornelius, 2000). More recent concerns also have focused on the effects of passive exposure to smoking, and correlations have been made to delays in intellectual, academic, and social-emotional development (Cnattingius, 2004; Rush & Callahan, 1989). Infants whose mothers were exposed to passive smoking also have been found to be at increased risk for illnesses such as pneumonia, bronchitis, laryngitis, otitis media (i.e., chronic ear infections; Floyd, Zahniser, Gunter, & Kendrick, 1991), and lung-related problems at birth (Milner, Marsh, Ingraham, Fox, & Susiva, 1999).

As is suspected with alcohol, a strong dose-response relationship seems to exist for smoking; that is, the more a woman smokes during pregnancy, the greater the likelihood that her baby will have low birth weight (Cnattingius, 2004). In fact, Cnattingius reported that the incidence of low birth weight is significantly higher for infants born to women who smoke than for those born to women who do not. More specifically, the rate of having infants with low birth weight is high for women who smoke less than 10 cigarettes per day versus those who don't smoke, but it is even higher for women who smoke more than 10 cigarettes per day. Further, Cnattingius reported that age is a significant mediating factor affecting these rates. For example, the risk of a baby being small for gestational age is about twofold for teenage mothers who smoke compared to teenage mothers who do not smoke, but the rate more than doubles to about 4.5 times for women over 40 years of age who smoke during pregnancy. In addition, women who stopped smoking within the first trimester reduced the risk for stillbirth and infant mortality to levels comparable to the rates for children of nonsmoking mothers, suggesting that whether or not a mother stops smoking by the 16th week of gestation may be critical (Wisborg, Kesmodel, Henriksen, Olsen, & Secher, 2001). Despite these findings, only about 25% of women who smoke stop smoking during pregnancy, and it may be more difficult to encourage older smokers to quit than younger ones. Nonetheless, smoking remains one of the most preventable risk factors and quitting smoking, even as late as the seventh or eighth month of gestation, may have a positive influence on an infant's birth weight (Frank, McNamee, Hannaford, & Kay, 1994; Vogler & Kozlowski, 2002).

> A strong dose-response relationship seems to exist for smoking.

Other Substances　Since the mid-1980s, a number of studies have examined the impact of prenatal cocaine exposure on infant development. Early reports suggested that cocaine use during pregnancy was associated with a host of adverse effects spanning a continuum of severity from significant physical and neurological impairments to very subtle neurobehavioral differences. More recent studies, however, have been less conclusive, in part because of complex methodological issues (Zuckerman & Frank, 1994). The direct impact of cocaine is difficult to document because of its many variants, the concern that women using cocaine are likely to be using other drugs concomitantly (including tobacco), and the problem that there often are coexisting environmental factors of poverty and malnutrition, which can lead to less than optimal pregnancy outcomes. It is likely that these are all conditions that have affected both Denise and Nathaniel. Children exposed to high-frequency cocaine use prenatally had poorer neurobehavioral outcomes (Schuler & Nair, 1999), significant cognitive deficits, were twice as likely to have a developmental delay

(Singer et al., 2002), and were at increased risk for motor dysfunction (Swanson, Streissguth, Sampson, & Olsen, 1999). In contrast, other investigators have suggested that the effects of prenatal cocaine exposure are similar to the effects of other teratogens (Frank, Augustyn, Knight, Pell, & Zuckerman, 2001). In fact, one study did not reveal significantly lower IQ scores in a sample of prenatally exposed preschoolers tested at age 4 (Hurt et al., 1997). Nonetheless, studies have linked cocaine exposure to smaller babies, either as a result of early delivery or intrauterine growth retardation, or both (Datta-Bhutada, Johnson, & Rosen, 1998; Frank, Bresnahan, & Zuckerman, 1993; Richardson, Hamel, Goldschmidt, & Day, 1999; Robins & Mills, 1993).

Findings from neuroimaging studies of the brain have even revealed structural differences in the white matter pathways in the frontal lobes of children exposed prenatally to cocaine compared to controls. Additionally, controls outperformed cocaine-exposed children on executive functioning tasks (Warner et al., 2006). Cone-Wesson's (2005) review of fetal alcohol- and cocaine-related research provided support for the relationship between FAS and deleterious effects on cognitive impairment, learning, behavior, and the acquisition, expression, and receipt of language. However, the association between prenatal cocaine exposure and postnatal functioning was less evident (Cone-Wesson, 2005). In another study, Morrow et al. (2006) assessed intellectual functioning, learning impairments, and academic achievement of approximately 400 children with and without prenatal cocaine exposure. While there were no significant differences on measures of intellectual functioning between groups, children who were exposed to cocaine in utero had almost triple the risk of a learning disability diagnosis by age 7.

In an evaluation of preschool-aged children on multiple measures of attention, cocaine and cigarette use during pregnancy were related to selective attention difficulties. Difficulties on sustained attention tasks were positively associated with prenatal marijuana exposure (Noland et al., 2005). A four-year longitudinal study published in the *Journal of the American Medical Association* (*JAMA*) found no significant differences between children with and without prenatal cocaine exposure on measures of IQ and performance at age four. On visual-spatial, general knowledge, and arithmetic skills subscales, however, nonexposed children significantly outperformed exposed children. Interestingly, the strongest independent predictor of outcome was the quality of the home environment (Singer et al., 2004). Expressive language difficulties and increased frustration reactivity have also been reported for preschoolers whose mothers used cocaine during pregnancy (Dennis, Bendersky, Ramsay, & Lewis, 2006; Morrow et al., 2004); however, such findings have been documented up through age six, but become negligible by nine years of age (Beeghly et al., 2006). Despite these findings, the 23-month-old in our case vignette would be at-risk for negative developmental outcomes.

Heroin use by expectant mothers also has received recent attention. The use of heroin during pregnancy is associated with decreased birth weight and length (Little et al., 1990; Wright & Walker, 2001), along with other perinatal and postnatal complications. Heroin quickly crosses the placenta, so if the mother is addicted, the infant is, too. This addiction results in neonatal withdrawal symptoms affecting both the central and autonomic nervous systems (Strauss & Reynolds, 1983). Symptoms frequently include tremulousness and hyperirritability, a high-pitched cry, and possible neurologic regulation difficulties manifested by sleeping and eating disturbances. Methadone maintenance often is recommended for heroin-addicted women in conjunction with adequate prenatal care. This treatment has been shown to reduce the incidence of medical complications resulting from prematurity (Kaltenbach & Finnegan, 1987; Kandall, Doberczak, Jantunen, & Stein, 1999). Although the use of methadone during pregnancy also may have some early effects on the baby, long-term developmental problems are not suspected or, at least, have not been documented.

Although minimal research has been conducted on the effects of prenatal exposure to marijuana, recent cross-sectional and longitudinal studies have reported deficits in specific areas of cognitive function, such as attention (Fried & Smith, 2001). Likewise, the effect of inhalant abuse during pregnancy is limited, yet appears to indicate several negative fetal outcomes (Jones & Balster, 1998).

> Because heroin quickly passes through the placenta, the infant becomes addicted, too.

Maternal Illness

Some diseases minimally affect the expectant mother but can devastate her unborn child. Diseases and infections have the greatest influence during the first trimester, when the major body systems are being formed. The effects of rubella on the mother, for example, may be mild or even go unnoticed; however, the unborn child may experience heart malformation or disease, microcephaly, retardation, vision and hearing deficits, or death. There is now a vaccine for rubella that can be administered to prepubescent females to prevent this from becoming a factor during pregnancy. Other maternal illnesses and conditions that develop during the prenatal period, such as venereal diseases, toxoplasmosis, toxemia, pica, chicken pox, mumps, measles, scarlet fever, tuberculosis, and urinary tract infections, also may cause children to have various intellectual, motor, physical, and/or sensory differences or deficits.

> Some diseases that severely affect a fetus have minimal impact on the mother-to-be.

Diabetes   With incidence rates between 1.5 to 11.3%, diabetes in expectant mothers can have negative effects on their infants (Magee, Walden, Benedetti, & Knopp, 1993). In pregnancy, there are two main forms of diabetes: **gestational diabetes mellitus (GDM)** and **pregestational diabetes mellitus (PGDM)**. GDM generally is limited to pregnancy and is not considered to be a maternal disease; it usually is resolved about 6 weeks after the birth of the baby (Blackburn, 2007). GDM occurs in about 2 to 6% of pregnancies (Sullivan, Henderson, & Davis, 1998). In contrast, PGDM is a maternal disease that can begin to exert an impact on the pregnancy at the point of conception, particularly if the mother-to-be has not achieved adequate control of blood sugar levels (Kitzmiller et al., 1991). This impact may be seen in the form of major and minor abnormalities in the fetus, with the incidence of major abnormalities between 5 and 13% (Gotto & Goldman, 1994; Omori et al., 1994). Although these abnormalities can involve nearly all of the body systems (Cousins, 1983), in particular there is a 2- to 19-times higher risk of central nervous system disruption (McLeod & Ray, 2002) and a 4- to 7-times higher risk of cardiac anomalies (Ferencz, Rubin, Mc-Carter, & Clark, 1990). The most frequent central nervous system malformation is anencephaly (no brain development), followed by spina bifida (McLeod & Ray, 2002).

More generally, infants born to diabetic mothers tend to be larger, heavier, and born somewhat earlier than infants of nondiabetic mothers; they also tend to be more prone to critical levels of hypoglycemia (low blood sugar) after birth (Blackburn, 2007). Women with poorly controlled PGDM also experience a higher rate of spontaneous abortion (Katz & Kuller, 1994), intrauterine growth retardation (Van Assche, Holemans, & Aerts, 2001), and complications during delivery (Scholl, Sowers, Chen, & Lenders, 2001).

The offspring of diabetic mothers, whether diabetes is preexisting or limited to the gestational period, are at increased risk for a number of undesirable developmental outcomes, such as difficulties with attention span and motor function (Ornoy, Ratzon, Greenbaum, Wolf, & Dulitzky, 2001), obesity (Silverman, Rizzo, Cho, & Metzger, 1998), and a greater number of hospitalizations (Aberg & Westbom, 2001). One of the most significant fetal complications of GDM or PGDM is **macrosomia** (i.e., "large body," or an absolute birth weight greater than 4,000–4,500 gm [9–10 lb]), which occurs 10 times more frequently in infants with diabetic mothers than in infants with nondiabetic mothers. Macrosomia can lead to birth trauma, such as brachial plexus palsy, and asphyxia in labor secondary to difficulties in extracting the baby from the mother. Approximately 25 to 30% of fetuses born to diabetic mothers have macrosomia (Carrapato & Marcelino, 2001). Macrosomia, low birth weight, and preterm birth are more common for mothers with insulin-dependent diabetes (dos Santos Silva et al., 2005). Longer duration of diabetes also was related to decreased incidence of macrosomia.

A number of etiological factors have been described as contributing to the formation of congenital abnormalities in babies of women with diabetes. These include metabolic abnormalities, such as hyperglycemia (high blood sugar levels), hypoglycemia (low blood sugar levels), hyperinsulinemia (high insulin levels), hyperketonaemia (high ketone [a sugar-based metabolic agent typically found in the blood and urine] concentrations), and general genetic susceptibility. Although a description of these etiological factors is beyond the scope of this chapter, the main point to note is that one of the key factors necessary for fetal development is glucose. For the fetus, glucose is completely derived from the blood circulation of the mother via diffusion through the placenta. Therefore, the condition of the mother's metabolic system is a critical determinant in fetal growth. Circulating glucose levels that are too high or too low force the fetus to adjust to these conditions because it is completely dependent upon these circulating levels, and this condition sets the stage for the potential of the abnormalities just described (Aerts, Pijnenborg, Verhaeghe, Holemans, & Van Assche, 1996).

Research has also begun to suggest that gestational diabetes, as well as higher birth weight, might be predictive of being overweight in adolescence (Gillman, Rifas-Shiman, Berkey, Field, & Colditz, 2003).

> Babies of diabetic mothers typically are larger, heavier, and born earlier than babies of nondiabetic mothers.

Maternal Infections

Maternal infections can have significant deleterious effects on the developing fetus. An acronym to delineate various maternal infections that can cause similar malformations is **STORCH**. This acronym stands for syphilis, toxoplasmosis, other infections, rubella, cytomegalovirus, and herpes simplex virus. In addition, there are other maternal infections that can disrupt the developing fetus.

Acquired Immunodeficiency Syndrome   One of the most serious conditions that infants can acquire from their mothers is acquired immunodeficiency syndrome (AIDS). AIDS in young children primarily is the result of congenital or perinatal maternal transmission of the human immunodeficiency virus (HIV) to the fetus or newborn infant. This transmission also can occur across the placenta or in utero, during delivery, or via breast milk (Deiner, 1997; Miotti et al., 1999). Transmission of the AIDS-causing virus ranges from 20 to 30% of infants born to HIV-infected mothers (UNICEF, 2006), to 65% (Deiner, 1997), with recent advances in treatment of pregnant women who are infected with HIV having decreased these estimates substantially. The Centers for Disease Control and Prevention (CDC, 2006a) report that the implementation of HIV screening, antiretroviral drug use, avoidance of breastfeeding, and cesarean delivery have been instrumental in reducing rates of prenatal and perinatal HIV transmission from 25–30% to just 2%. Perinatal HIV infections in the United States reached a high of 1,650 in 1991, with more recent estimates suggesting approximately 142 in 2005 (Center for Disease Control, 2006a). Emergent research suggests, however, that some of the antiretroviral therapies (e.g., AZT), when combined with maternal undernutrition, also affect weight at birth, onset of diabetes in rats (Morten et al., 2005), and anemia in humans (Myers, Torrente, Hinthorn, & Clark, 2005), but are not necessarily detrimental to weight, height, and head circumference in newborns (Hankin, Thorne, & Newell, 2005).

> Infants affected with HIV can experience slowed, arrested, or even reversed development in cognitive, physical, and social domains.

In addition, the mortality rate for prenatally and perinatally infected infants is high, with a median survival rate of approximately 38 months once the child exhibits symptoms of the virus. Although most infected infants may appear to be healthy at birth, symptoms reportedly can occur as early as 8 months of age (Scott et al., 1989) with early motor and cognitive development being affected (Chase et al., 2000). Initially, the incubation period in young children appeared to be much shorter than in adults, estimating that approximately one-third of the infected children die during infancy, another third before kindergarten, and another third before 20 years of age (Grubman, Gross, Lerner-Weiss, & Hernandez, 1995). More recent reports (Lindegren, Steinberg, & Byers, 2000) suggest that about 15 to 20% of children with HIV rapidly deteriorate and die within the first 4 years after infection, whereas the majority show disease progression at a rate similar to adults. Survival rates have improved over time with the use of antiretroviral drugs for extended periods (McConnell et al., 2005).

HIV affects the body's immune system, leaving the individual vulnerable to various illnesses. The leading cause of death in HIV-positive children is opportunistic infections secondary to this compromised immune system (Gilbert, 2006). Even those children who are fortunate enough to remain uninfected by the virus face a life

> HIV affects the body's immune system, leaving the individual vulnerable to various illnesses.

filled with uncertainty because of their mother's infection and higher rates of anxious and depressive symptoms (Esposito et al., 1999). A serious problem discovered in Africa, where AIDS-infected women were discouraged from breastfeeding their infants, was that the infants died at higher rates from other diseases. The infants did not benefit from the natural immunity conferred by the breastmilk and they died from other opportunistic infections. Other infections such as the flu may also impact the developing fetus. For example, mothers who reported having experienced a flu-like illness and/or an episodic illness during the first trimester of their pregnancy were more likely to have babies with renal anomalies, as were mothers who reported both having a fever and using medication (Abe, Honein, & Moore, 2003). The transmission of various infections between mother and fetus is not always clear. In one study, researchers studied the maternal and fetal tissue of women who terminated their pregnancies after contracting West Nile Virus in their second trimester (Skupski, Eglinton, Fine, Hayes, & O'Leary, 2006). They did not find evidence of transmission of West Nile Virus from the mother to the fetus. Other infections, such as bacterial vaginosis, have been associated with preterm delivery and spontaneous abortion (Leitich et al., 2003). Work with rat models suggests that impacts of maternal influenza on the developing fetus likely follows an indirect rather than direct path, as the infection was not found in the fetus or placenta (Shi, Tu, & Patterson, 2005), with infections affecting the fetus differently at different times during development (Meyer et al., 2006).

Maternal Emotional State

It is clear that children of mothers with depression are at greater risk for developing depression or other forms of psychopathology than children of nondepressed mothers (Chronis et al., 2007). Other differences noted in children of depressed mothers include sleep problems in infancy (Diego, Field, & Hernandez-Rief, 2005), lowered neurobehavioral assessment scores (Hernandez-Reif, Field, Diego, & Ruddock, 2006), and poorer growth in infancy (Rahman, Iqbal, Bunn, Lovel, & Harrington, 2004). Prenatal and postpartum depressive symptoms predicted behavior problems in toddler boys, while it was the quality of early interactions that predicted problem behaviors in girls (Carter, Garrity-Rokous, Chazan-Cohen, Little, & Briggs-Gowan, 2001). Parent vulnerability to depression may also be an important determinant of child outcome, specifically negative affectivity and effortful control (Pesonen, Räikkönen, Heinonen, Järvenpää, & Strandberg, 2006) and the presence of internalizing problems in first grade (Anhalt, Telzrow, & Brown, 2007). Additionally, complications during pregnancy were found to predict anxiety disorders in children, with effects above and beyond what would be expected based on parent mental health status (Hirshfeld-Becker et al., 2004).

Despite considerable research on maternal depression, the pathways that influence the child's developmental trajectory and increase the likelihood of transmission from parent to child is not well elucidated (Cummings, Davies, & Campbell, 2000; Moehler, Brunner, Wiebel, Reck, & Resch, 2006). A combination of genetic and environmental factors, particularly interactions between the parent and child, may contribute to depressive disorders in children. Preliminary findings suggest that adverse prenatal conditions, such as the exposure of the fetus to abnormal neuroendocrine functions, increased cortisol levels, or constricted blood flow to the fetus, may increase a child's vulnerability to future psychopathology (Goodman & Gotlib, 1999). Therefore, although the emotional state of the mother may not directly affect her developing child, the hormonal releases that accompany her emotions, particularly those associated with stress and anxiety, affect the baby both before and after birth (Glover, 1999). These hormonal releases have been associated with the neuroanatomical and biochemical organization of the brain of the fetus as early as 8 weeks following conception. Exposure of the mother to life stress appears to result in physiological changes, which in turn affects the future behavior and stress reactivity of her offspring (Fifer, Monk, & Grose-Fifer, 2001). In fact, even the physical health of the infant has been suggested as being compromised by maternal stress. For example, peptic ulcers related to maternal stress have been found in newborns (Herrenkohl, 1988).

Stress creates changes in the nervous system that contribute to reduced blood flow to the uterus and, consequently, reduced flow of nutrients and oxygen to the fetus. One of the hormones triggered by increased stress is cortisol. Cortisol is a recognized teratogen to body organs, especially the organs of the reproductive system (Schuster, 1992). Herrenkohl (1988) has noted that the "prenatal stress syndrome" may contribute to the feminization and demasculinization of male offspring, and it may contribute to reproduction dysfunction in females. More generally, women who are highly anxious or who experience prolonged stress have complicated deliveries, spend about 5 more hours in labor, and have more spontaneous abortions and premature births than their less-stressed counterparts. The presence of malformations in babies of mothers with critical stress during the first trimester is higher than in babies of mothers with lower levels of stress (Gilbert, 2006). Anxiety in the prenatal period predicted cortisol levels of 10-year-olds, suggesting that the effects of maternal emotional state may have impacts into early adolescence (O'Connor et al., 2005).

Both prepartum and postpartum levels of maternal depression were found to be related to high levels of cortisol and norepinephrine in newborns (Diego et al., 2004). DaCosta, Dritsa, Larouche, and Brender (2000) found that mothers reporting less satisfaction with their social supports experienced greater stress during pregnancy, had more difficult deliveries, and delivered children of lower birth weight. For low-income women, the relationship between social support and positive pregnancy outcomes is particularly strong (Hoffman & Hatch, 1996). Examination of other maternal lifestyle variables has the potential to provide new insights about the effects of maternal emotional states on the fetus (Nathanielsz, 1995). In fact, Van den Bergh and Marcoen (2004) found associations between prenatal maternal anxiety and symptoms of attention deficit-hyperactivity disorder, anxiety, and other types of psychiatric difficulties when the children were 8 and 9 years of age. These findings were present even after controlling for a variety of variables, such as gender, parent socioeconomic status, smoking, or birth weight. Further, in a group of women between 16 and 29 weeks' gestation, researchers have reported levels of stress to correspond to cortisol and norepinephrine levels (Diego et al., 2006).

Taken together, these findings support the idea that stress during pregnancy (e.g., maternal sociodemographic characteristics, daily hassles) was related to levels of cortisol and norepinephrine. When controlling for other factors, cortisol also related to fetal weight. Diego et al. (2006) suggested the impact of the cortisol was likely related to its crossing directly through the placenta to the fetus. In addition, dopamine levels were found to be lower than those of a comparison group and EEGs reflected asymmetry in the right frontal lobe.

Evidence also suggests that maternal depression compromises a mother's ability to bond effectively with her child. Some researchers have found that maternal depressive symptoms, even those subthreshold or mild in nature, may hinder bonding between the mother and her infant at 2 weeks, 6 weeks, and 4 months postnatally, but not at 14 months (Moehler et al., 2006). Such findings support the idea of a sensitive period of bonding between a mother and her infant, with these researchers suggesting that this sensitive period peaks at 6 weeks and decreases after 4 months. Their study should be generalized with caution, however, as the mothers who participated were not very diverse and did not have a high incidence of clinically significant depression. One wonders how Denise bonded with Nathaniel during his early infancy, particularly given the possible stressors in her life.

Focused, well-carried-out interventions have the potential to significantly improve the quality of attachments between toddlers and mothers who had experienced an episode of major depression since their child's birth (Toth, Rogosch, & Manly, 2006). Therapy sessions focused on both mother and infant as well as the interaction between the two. The distribution of different types of attachment of the intervention group was similar to a nonintervention comparison group at baseline; both these groups differed from a nondepressed control group. After treatment, the group receiving the intervention had significantly more dyads with secure attachments relative to both the comparison and control groups. The results of this study should be generalized with caution, however, as the sample was comprised of well-educated families who were not of low SES in order to study effects of treatment without the complex factors of intensive psychosocial needs.

While maternal depression has been identified as a risk factor for negative child outcomes, little research has examined the effect of taking antidepressants while pregnant on the infant. Oberlander, Warburton, Misri, Aghajanian, and Hertzman (2006) found that neonates whose mothers had taken selective serotonin reuptake inhibitors (SSRIs) during pregnancy to treat depression had significantly lower birth weight, younger gestational age, increased respiratory distress, jaundice, and feeding problems. A similar issue could be raised for many of the medicaitons used to treat psychiatric disorders. More generally, it is important to note that most inserts for psychotropic medications advise against using the medication during pregnancy, or indicate that there is too little information to state level of risk.

Blood Incompatibility

Early in pregnancy all women are tested to determine blood type (A, B, AB, or O) and Rh factor (positive or negative). If a woman's blood type is Rh positive (which is true of approximately 85% of women), or if both she and the baby's father are Rh negative, there is no cause for concern. If the mother is Rh negative and the father is Rh positive, however, the baby could inherit the father's positive blood type, which could cause a problem during pregnancy or at the time of delivery if the condition is not treated. When the baby's blood enters the Rh-negative mother's circulatory system during pregnancy, the mother's body produces antibodies to destroy the "foreign substance" in a natural protective immune response. The antibodies are intended to attack the baby's blood cells in the mother's circulatory system, but they can cross the placenta and destroy the fetus's Rh-positive blood cells. These antibodies may not be a problem during a first pregnancy, but they can lead to serious hemolytic or Rh disease in subsequent newborns. When there is a high level of antibodies produced by the mother, many of the fetus's red blood cells are destroyed, eventually leading to severe anemia or possible fetal death. If this condition is left untreated, live births can be complicated by severe jaundice, which can lead to mental retardation, hearing loss, or cerebral palsy.

Fortunately, hemolytic disease of the newborn can be prevented most of the time by injections of gamma globulin, or **RhoGam**. RhoGam acts to prevent the mother's immune system from reacting to the fetus's red blood cells and producing antibodies. At 28 weeks, an expectant Rh-negative mother who shows no antibodies in her blood receives an injection of RhoGam, and another dose is administered within 72 hours following delivery, miscarriage, abortion, amniocentesis, or bleeding during pregnancy if the baby is Rh positive. If it is determined that the Rh-negative mother has begun producing antibodies during pregnancy and that her blood is incompatible with the fetus's blood, maternal antibody levels are carefully monitored. When the incompatibility is severe, which is rare, a fetal transfusion of Rh-negative blood may be necessary. In most cases, however, a transfusion is not necessary or can be done at the time of delivery.

Genetic Abnormalities

Although most babies are born healthy and develop normally, approximately 3 to 4% have defects that are detected prenatally, at birth, or within the first few years of life (Batshaw et al., 2007). Some birth defects are inherited, others are a result of environmental influences, and still others are attributable to the interaction of heredity and environment. Families with a history of genetic abnormalities may wish to consider genetic counseling, testing, or both as part of their family-planning process. It may be important for an expectant couple to be aware of any increased genetic risk so they can consider the possibility of prenatal screening. Parents of a child with developmental difficulties may decide, along with their pediatrician, to have a **karyotype** (i.e., chromosomal analysis) performed or to have other, more sophisticated genetic testing conducted to diagnose abnormal chromosome patterns.

Abnormalities caused by hereditary factors are of three types: autosomal inheritance, X-linked inheritance, and defective chromosomes. Table 2.3 shows examples of problems resulting from the three types of genetic abnormalities, their causes, their characteristics, and what is known about the developmental course of individuals with the abnormality.

In nearly 3 to 4% of newborns, defects are detected prenatally, at birth, or within the first few years of life.

TABLE **2.3** Examples of genetic abnormalities.

Abnormality	Cause/Early Detection	Characteristics	Developmental Course
Autosomal Inheritance Cystic fibrosis	Recessive gene/prenatal testing	Glands controlling production of mucus, sweat, tears, and saliva function incorrectly and make breathing difficult. Coughing, recurring pneumonia, large appetite, small size, and enlarged fingertips are symptoms.	Increased risk of severe respiratory infection; possible future candidate for gene therapy.
Phenylketonuria (PKU)	Recessive gene located on chromosome #12/ possible prenatal DNA analysis and routine newborn screening	Inborn error of metabolism; newborn lacks ability to process phenylalanine found in products like milk. If left untreated, can cause mental retardation.	Dietary restriction of phenylalanine beginning in infancy minimizes any effects.
Sickle-cell anemia	Recessive gene/prenatal screening and blood test after birth	Shortage of red blood cells causes pain, damage to vital organs, possible death in childhood or early adulthood.	Chronic illness; often treated medically but there is no cure.
Tay-Sachs disease	Recessive gene/prenatal screening	Progressive nervous system disease that allows a toxic product to accumulate in the brain as a result of enzyme deficiency. Leads to brain damage and death.	Normal development until 6 months of age. Neurological deterioration includes seizures, blindness, mental retardation, and death by age 5.
Achondroplasia	Dominant gene/prenatal testing	Disproportionately short stature, relatively large head, short limbs, trident hand, normal intelligence.	Possible delay in developmental milestone attainment; occasional deafness.
Marfan's syndrome	Dominant gene/no prenatal testing at this time; usually diagnosed by physical exam	Tall, thin with hypermobile joints; long, thin spiderlike fingers; spinal curvature, dislocated eye lens.	Prone to lung collapse with high incidence of heart and blood vessel defects; associated with ADHD and learning disabilities.
Neurofibromatosis	Dominant gene; linked to chromosome #17/no prenatal tests; diagnosis based on physical exam	Multiple "cafe-au-lait" spots on body; small nerve tumors on body and skin; some affected persons may have large heads, scoliosis, or variety of bone defects.	No known treatment. Wide variability in expression; may be associated with mild mental retardation or learning disabilities.
X-Linked Inheritance Color blindness	X-linked recessive gene	Red-green color blindness.	No known cure.

(Continued)

Abnormality	Cause/Early Detection	Characteristics	Developmental Course
Hemophilia	X-linked recessive gene	Blood lacks important clotting factor.	Blood-clotting factor is needed to stop bleeding. Frequent hospitalizations and chronic problems. No known cure.
Duchenne muscular dystrophy	X-linked recessive gene/prenatal testing	Normal development until 6 to 9 years of age; then muscular weakness appears and progresses.	Progressive disease affecting all muscles including heart and diaphragm; usually results in death during young adulthood.
Fragile X syndrome	X-linked fragile site/ chromosomal testing available pre- and postnatally	The most common hereditary form of mental retardation in males, with associated physical features of prominent jaw, large ears and testes.	Children may have associated behavioral problems, hyperactivity, and some autisticlike features.
Defective Chromosomes Cri du chat syndrome	Deletion on top portion of #5 chromosome	Microcephaly, widely spaced eyes, small chins, and high-pitched cry ("cat cry"); severe retardation.	No known cure.
Down syndrome	Extra chromosome of 21st pair/ prenatal testing	Cognitive deficits, hypotonia, facial characteristics, short stature, congenital heart disease.	Developmental progress appears to slow.
Klinefelter's syndrome	Extra X chromosome (45XXY)/prenatal testing	Male child with inadequate testosterone production resulting in abnormal sexual development. Usually tall, slender, with breast development and small genitalia. Close to normal intelligence.	Psychological and psychiatric abnormalities; small percentage has mental retardation, language delays. Medical treatment involves administration of male hormones.
Turner's syndrome	Missing X chromosome (XO or 45X)/prenatal testing	Only disorder associated with survival despite loss of chromosome. All are female, very short, and have webbed necks, widely spaced nipples, and nonfunctional ovaries. Usually of normal intelligence, with visual perceptual difficulties.	Majority of girls have learning disabilities; medical treatment with hormones.
XYY syndrome	Extra Y chromosome/ prenatal testing	Usually tall with normal sexual development but low intelligence. Aggressive behavior; severe acne.	Associated with behavioral problems and learning disabilities. No known cure.

Autosomal inheritance is a natural process by which traits are transmitted from parents to their children. Two autosomal patterns of inheritance are the autosomal recessive pattern and the autosomal dominant pattern, of which the chances of inheritance are equal for males and females. For an **autosomal recessive disorder** to occur, both parents must be carriers of a defective recessive gene and transmit this gene to their child; the risk of occurrence is 25% for each conception, as shown in Figure 2.2. Carriers are not usually clinically symptomatic.

One example of the autosomal type of inheritance pattern is the disorder phenylketonuria (PKU). PKU is an inherited inborn error of metabolism for which infants are routinely screened at birth. It is a condition whereby the body is unable to process adequately the food it consumes, particularly with respect to a component of protein called phenylalanine. This incomplete metabolic process creates a toxin that can be damaging to neurological development. The fetus is unaffected by this metabolic defect prior to birth because excess materials pass freely from child to mother via the placenta (White, 2004). Following birth, however, and without treatment, the body accumulates excess phenylalanine within tissues, which causes central nervous system damage including mental retardation by 1 year of age. Various white matter abnormalities have also been associated with phenylalanine hydroxylase deficiency (Leuzzi et al., 2007; Sirrs et al., 2007). Early identification of PKU can lead to restriction of the intake of phenylalanine (i.e., to reduce the amount of toxin in the body) in the diet within the first few weeks of life. Although this special diet may need to continue indefinitely, it has been proven to be effective in preventing adverse outcomes (Poustie & Rutherford, 2000).

FIGURE 2.2   **Pattern of an autosomal recessive disorder.**

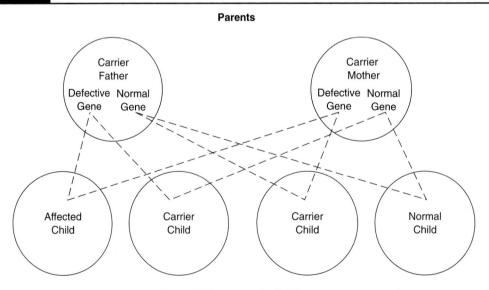

Autosomal dominant disorders are different from autosomal recessive disorders in that the individual has the disease when he or she has a single abnormal gene; thus the risk of transmission is increased to 50%. Autosomal dominant disorders usually involve structural abnormalities (Batshaw et al., 2007). This type of inheritance pattern can be seen in Figure 2.3. An example of the autosomal dominant pattern is neurofibromatosis. Neurofibromatosis is one of the most common genetic disorders, with an incidence rate of approximately 1 per 3,000 births. One of the common signs of this disorder is the presence of large tan spots, or "cafe-au-lait" spots, on the skin. These spots often are present at birth, and they may increase in size, number, and pigmentation with age. Small, benign tumors under the skin may appear at any age, and other tumors may be present in and damage major neurological systems. Tumors in the auditory nerve, for example, result in hearing impairment or deafness. The degree of involvement in any single case can vary widely, ranging from relatively few problems to significant learning and developmental problems (Perek-Polnik et al., 2006). Recent neuroimaging research indicates that the *brain location* (e.g., thalamus) that displays discrete, high signal intensity during a brain scan (i.e., **Magnetic Resonance Imaging**) may be linked to cognitive impairment (Hyman, Gill, Shores, Steinberg, & North, 2007). Currently, there is no prenatal test that can detect neurofibromatosis; the diagnosis is made by physical exam.

The second form of genetic inheritance of abnormalities is referred to as sex-linked, or **X-linked**, because it involves genes located on the X, or female, chromosome. With this type of disorder, females typically are carriers and males are affected—largely because males have only one X chromosome. One variant of an

---

FIGURE 2.3   **Pattern of an autosomal dominant disorder.**

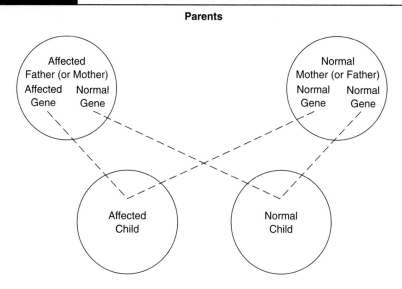

Parents

Affected Father (or Mother)
Affected Gene   Normal Gene

Normal Mother (or Father)
Normal Gene   Normal Gene

Affected Child

Normal Child

Potential Outcomes in Children

X-linked inheritance pattern can be seen in Figure 2.4. An example of an X-linked inheritance pattern is fragile X syndrome.

As noted in Table 2.3, fragile X syndrome is the leading cause of inherited developmental delay in males (Alanay et al., 2007; Hagerman & Cronister, 1996). The prevalence of fragile X syndrome in males is about 1 per 4,000 compared to about 1 per 8,000 for females. As its name implies, this abnormality relates to a mutation at the bottom of the X chromosome. This mutation can result in a variety of physical (e.g., elongated face, large ears, increased head circumference), behavioral (e.g., attention deficits, self-injury), emotional (e.g., social anxiety) (Hall, DeBernardis, & Reiss, 2006), and learning problems ranging from subtle deficits in mildly affected children to severe levels of mental retardation (Bailey et al., 2004; Cohen, 1995; Hagerman & Cronister, 1996). Disproportionate deficits also have been noted in attention and general regulatory functions (Hooper et al., 2008). Both males and females are affected by this disorder, although females tend to have less impairment (Hagerman & Cronister, 1996). In one study comparing girls with either fragile X or Turner syndrome to controls on a series of visuospatial tasks, girls with fragile X performed worse on the visuospatial location task, which was correlated with math performance (Mazzocco, Singh Bhatia, & Lesniak-Karpiak, 2006). Social anxiety behaviors (e.g., abnormal gaze) have been linked to cortisol reactivity in children with fragile X syndrome (Hessl, Glaser, Dyer-Friedman, & Reiss, 2006).

The third type of genetically inherited abnormalities are caused by **chromosomal malformations** in which chromosomes are added to or deleted from the normal 23 pairs or they are damaged. Any of these disruptions can result in birth defects or death.

FIGURE 2.4   **Example of an X-linked disorder inheritance pattern.**

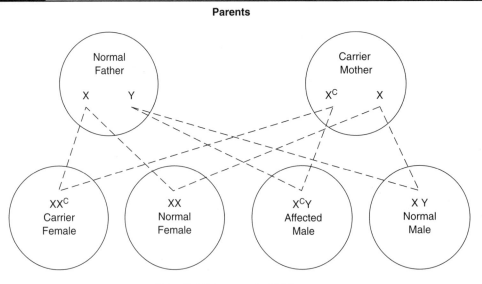

Parents

Potential Outcomes in Children

Courtesy of Lisa Harris

Children with Down syndrome and other genetic disorders can show positive development and growth when provided with a nurturing environment and early intervention.

The incidence of chromosomal aberrations is about 0.4%. Autosomal chromosomal abnormalities usually lead to mental retardation and are characterized by distinct physical characteristics (Batshaw, Pellegrino, & Roizen, 2007).

Down syndrome is an example of this type of genetic abnormality, with an incidence rate of about 1 in 700 to 800 live births. As noted earlier, this rate tends to increase for expectant mothers over the age of 35 (Chan, McCaul, Keane, & Haan, 1998). The diagnosis of Down syndrome is typically suggested by clinical observations of physical characteristics and then confirmed by obtaining a karyotype (Cohen, 1999); however, prenatal testing also can determine its presence. Selected physical features include a variety of minor anomalies (e.g., flat nasal bridge and flat profile), although most individuals manifest only some of these features (Cohen, 1999). More severe involvement of musculoskeletal, hematological, neurological, endocrine, and cardiac systems also is common (McBrien, Mattheis, & Van Dyke, 1996). Although children diagnosed with Down syndrome tend to show pervasive developmental delays, they also manifest steady rates of positive development with appropriate educational and family interventions.

Prematurity and Low Birth Weight

Historically, the risk factors of prematurity and low birth weight have been used interchangeably. Certainly, these factors are intimately related in that prematurity tends to be a cause of low birth weight; however, it is important to note that infants born prematurely do not always have low birth weight and, conversely, infants with low birth weight are not always born prematurely. In fact, about 33% of babies with a birth weight of less than 2,500 gm (5 lb 8 oz) are actually small for their gestational age, perhaps secondary to **placental insufficiency**. Placental insufficiency reduces the flow of oxygen and nourishment to the fetus (Kliegman et al., 2007).

A baby is defined as **premature** if the period of gestation is less than 37 full weeks (March of Dimes, 2007). In the United States in 2004, about 12.5% of newborns were classified as premature; this rate reflected an 18% increase since 1990 (Hamilton, Martin, Ventura, Sutton, & Menacker, 2005). It is important to note, however, that the births of twins, triplets, and babies with diabetic mothers inflate this figure somewhat because prematurity is an expected outcome in these cases (Lin, Verp, & Sabbagha, 1993), with prematurity 6 times more likely in multiple births than in singleton births (March of Dimes, 2007). Rates of premature singleton births also continue to rise (Hamilton et al., 2005), however, with recent data noting that preterm birth rates differ by ethnicity. They are highest for blacks (17.7%) and Native Americans (13.2%), decreasing somewhat for Hispanics (11.6%), whites (11.0%), and Asians (10.4%) (March of Dimes, 2007).

Although most babies born after 37 weeks usually experience few problems and have good survival rates, babies born before this time can experience a myriad of problems and risks, including heightened mortality. Of the 636 infants born at 22–27 weeks in Norway in 1999 and 2000, 41% died in the delivery room or NICU (Markestad et al., 2005). In the United States, rates of premature births continue to rise and now represent the leading cause of infant deaths, accounting for approximately 34% of all infant deaths (Callaghan, MacDorman, Rasmussen, Qin, & Lackritz, 2006). The survival rates tended to increase with gestational age but with some variability (i.e., 0% at <23 weeks, 16% at 23 weeks, 44% at 24 weeks, 66% at 25 weeks, 72% at 26 weeks, 82% at 27 weeks, and 69% for >27 weeks). Factors related to premature delivery include inadequate prenatal care (Krueger & Scholl, 2000), multifetal pregnancy, uterine and cervical abnormalities, infection, diabetes, hypertension, smoking, alcohol, and illicit drug use (March of Dimes, 2007). Increased risk of premature or low birth weight has also been associated with being first born, being born to a young mother, having a single, separated, or divorced mother, maternal smoking during pregnancy, or being Aboriginal (Moshin, Wong, Bauman, & Bai, 2003). According to March of Dimes (2007) estimates, approximately $26.2 billion was spent in medical, educational, and lost productivity costs to prematurity in 2005.

Many preterm infants manifest spasmodic and weak reflex movements and crying, show periods of apnea (i.e., not breathing), have problems maintaining body temperature, and may require respiratory assistance until the lungs mature. Lanugo and vernix may still cover the body of the preterm infant. Cerebral hemorrhaging, or bleeding in the brain, also is common in these infants. Improved medical technology

A premature baby is one that is born before 37 weeks of gestation.

has increased the survival rate of premature babies; however, as we shall see with the low-birth-weight babies, this higher survival rate has increased the vulnerability of surviving premature infants to a host of developmental abnormalities.

Relative to infants born at term, a cohort of infants born in France between 22 and 32 weeks gestation in 1997 were more likely to have behavioral problems (e.g., overall behavioral problems, hyperactivity, conduct problems, emotional symptoms, peer problems, and other behavior problems) when they were 3 years old than a group of term children, based on parent report (Delobel-Ayoub et al., 2006). Length of NICU stay (i.e., greater than 13 weeks), duration of time intubated (i.e., greater than 10 days), and presence of cerebral lesions, as well as psychosocial characteristics (e.g., young maternal age, low education) were related to these behavioral difficulties. Effects of prematurity may follow children into the teenage years, with 15- and 16-year-olds who were born at less than 29 weeks' gestation showing a higher incidence of hyperactivity, peer relationship problems, and emotional problems relative to term-born peers (Gardner et al., 2004). The preterm group did not, however, demonstrate more conduct problems; in fact, they reported less delinquency, alcohol, and drug use. In a review of literature from 1980–2001 examining impact of prematurity on outcomes after the age of 5 years, Bhutta, Cleves, Casey, Cradock, and Anand (2002) found evidence that cognitive scores, internalizing problems, and externalizing problems were all negatively affected by prematurity and that prematurity increases risk of later diagnosis of ADHD.

Many professionals consider fetal birth weight to be one of the most important indices in the prediction of fetal outcome (Figueras et al., 2007). In general, a baby is deemed to be small at birth because it was born too soon (i.e., it is premature), because it grew too slowly in utero (i.e., it is small for its gestational age), or because of a combination of these two factors. More specifically, an infant is viewed as having low birth weight with weight less than 2,500 gm (5 lb 8 oz). It has been estimated that, at present, about 8% of all infants are born with low birth weight (Hamilton et al., 2005), with about 62% of these births culminating in neonatal deaths (Hoyert et al., 2001). In 2004, 1.47% of infants born in the United States were of very low birth weight, weighing less than 1,500 gm (3 lb 5 oz; Hamilton et al., 2005).

Survival rates for infants born with low birth weight have improved dramatically over the past decade, with infants weighing over 1,000 gm (2 lb 3 oz) having a survival rate of over 90%, and infants weighing 751 to 1,000 gm (about 1 lb 10 oz to 2 lb 3 oz) having a survival rate approaching 86% (Lemons et al., 2001). Infants with birth weights of 501 to 750 gm (1 lb 2 oz to 1 lb 10 oz) are thought to have about a 59% chance of survival (Finer, Horbar, & Carpenter, 1999). Infants weighing less than 500 gm (1 lb 2 oz) at birth rarely survive; however, rates of approximately 11 to 15% have been reported (Gould, Benitz, & Liu, 2000), and this likely will continue to increase with ongoing improvements in neonatal technology and prenatal care (e.g., prenatal surgery). Recent research suggests that the survival rates of extremely low birth weight infants (500–999 grams) has increased over the past several years, from 49% in a cohort of infants born between 1982–1989 to 68% for those born between 1990 and 1999 to 71% in 2000–2002 (Wilson-Costello et al., 2007). To date, the smallest baby on record to survive was born at

Fetal birth weight may be one of the most important predictors of fetal outcome.

The farther a newborn is from the 2,500 gm birth weight, the greater are the chances for problems to arise.

Nearly 50% of school-aged children receiving some form of special education had birth weights less than 2,500 gm.

approximately 22 weeks post conception and was about 9.5 inches long and about 283 gm (<10 ounces)—a remarkable feat, but highly unusual.

As a general rule of thumb, the farther the infant is from the 2,500-gm criterion, the greater the problems it experiences. The closer the infant is to the 2,500-gm birth-weight criterion, the better the prognosis. Although most low-birth-weight children function within the normal range across a variety of domains when compared to normal-birth-weight children, these children tend to show higher rates of mental retardation, cerebral palsy, blindness and deafness, psychomotor problems, school failure, subnormal growth, and related health problems (Hack, Klein, & Taylor, 1995). In addition, children with very low birth weight demonstrated significantly lower intellectual abilities, academic achievement skills, and adaptive behavior (Peterson, Taylor, Minich, Klein, & Hack, 2006) as well as greater impairments in visual-motor skills, spatial memory, and executive function (Taylor, Minich, Bangert, Filipek, & Hack, 2004). In fact, cognitive factors, such as intelligence level (IQ), show a direct relationship to birth weight; that is, as birth weight declines, so does IQ (Bhutta et al., 2002). Further, school-aged children with birth weights of less than 2,500 gm are nearly 50% more likely than their normal-birth-weight counterparts to be receiving some form of special education (Lewit, Baker, Corman, & Shiono, 1995) and three times more likely than normal-birth-weight peers to receive special education if they did not receive early intervention services (Hollomon & Scott, 1998). A group of very-low-birth-weight (<1,000 g) or preterm (<28 weeks) infants in Australia were assessed at 8 years of age and found to demonstrate significant differences in overall intellectual functioning, verbal comprehension, perceptual organization, freedom from distractibility, processing speed, reading, spelling, arithmetic, attention difficulties, internalizing problems, and adaptive skills, relative to a normal-birth-weight comparison group (Anderson & Doyle, 2003). In one of the few studies that has tracked premature very-low-birth-weight infants into adulthood, Hack et al. (2002) found that, despite the presence of learning disabilities and physical problems, many of these individuals were likely to complete high school and to engage in less risky behaviors (i.e., they were not prone to use alcohol and drugs, experience problems with the law, or become teenage parents). Some effects of low birth weight may still be evident in adulthood, however. Pregnant women who themselves were of low birth weight are more likely to develop impaired glucose tolerance and diabetes than women with higher birth weight (Bo, Marchisio, Volpiano, Menato, & Pagano, 2003).

Recent research has offered some conflicting evidence about change over time in outcomes of their populations of extremely low-birth-weight infants. Tommiska et al. (2007) found no differences in mortality rates or incidence of many medical complications in their samples of infants in Finland in 1996–1997 and 1999–2000. When comparing outcomes of infants in two cohorts born before 2000 and another born between 2000 and 2002, Wilson-Costello et al. (2007) found significant and encouraging changes in survival rates as well as morbidity. For example, fewer infants born after 2000 had sepsis or severe intraventricular hemorrhage as neonates and fewer developed cerebral palsy and neurodevelopmental impairments.

Other complications of prematurity and low birth weight also have been shown to have an impact on later development. For example, children born prematurely, with very low birth weight (less than 1,500 gm [3 lb 5 oz]), or both, are at risk for chronic lung disease because of their lack of lung maturity. In fact, chronic lung disease, specifically bronchopulmonary dysplasia, is the most common chronic illness among very-low-birth-weight infants who survive the neonatal period, and occurs with an estimated prevalence of 17 to 54% (Marshall et al., 1999). Outcome studies of infants born with chronic lung disease indicate that this condition is associated with an increased risk for developmental abnormalities over and above the problems attributed to very low birth weight (Farel, Hooper, Teplin, Henry, & Kraybill, 1998; O'Shea et al., 1996; Taylor et al., 2004). In fact, the longer infants require mechanical oxygenation, the greater the likelihood of cognitive delay (Stephens, Richardson, & Lewin, 1997) with learning difficulties being documented into late childhood and early adolescence (Vohr et al., 1991).

The use of artificial surfactant, a medication designed to facilitate the transfer of gases in the lungs until natural surfactant can form, has become part of the routine treatment for infants with immature lungs, and its use has increased the survival rate of infants with **respiratory distress syndrome** (RDS) (Fujiwara, 1996); however, available research suggests that it has not lowered the risk for chronic lung disease nor its associated morbidity (Ferrara et al., 1994; Schwartz, Luby, Scanlon, & Kellogg, 1994). Medical advances have introduced new techniques to address the needs of these fragile infants, with mixed findings. Antenatal steroids have also been found to be effective in reducing the incidence and severity of RDS and related disorders (Crowther, Haslan, Hiller, Doyle, & Robinson, 2006; Hagedorn, Gardner, & Abman, 2002). Prenatal corticosteroid use to prevent chronic lung disease has not been supported, however (Halliday, 2004; Halliday, Ehrenkranz, & Doyle, 2003). Other changes in treatment protocol, such as high frequency oscillatory ventilation, do not appear to be any more effective than conventional methods (Marlow et al., 2006).

Another problem resulting from prematurity and low birth weight involves the flow of oxygen to the fetus. **Anoxia** results from a lack of oxygen during the birth process, whereas **hypoxia** results from a reduced flow of oxygen. These conditions can occur during prolonged labor, when excessive pressure can rupture a blood vessel in the brain (intraventricular hemorrhage), or during the birth process when the umbilical cord can become tangled or restricted. In each case, oxygen flow to the baby is disrupted and brain damage can result. In fact, chronic hypoxia has been found to be the cause of at least 60% of postnatal fetal deaths (Manning, Morrison, Lange, & Harman, 1982). In many instances, hypoxia and anoxia cause damage in the motor areas of the brain, and a variety of motor disorders can occur. These disorders, as a group, are called *cerebral palsy*, and the astute reader will note the various descriptions of children with these problems scattered through the development section of this text. Although most babies who experience anoxia or hypoxia do not suffer mental retardation or central nervous system involvement, the risk is higher for these babies than for their problem-free counterparts (Mecham, 1996; White, 2004). Rates of cerebral palsy among infants weighing less than 1,500 gm appear to have declined over the last two decades (Platt et al., 2007). Other research, however, has resulted in conflicting findings, suggesting that decreases in infant mortality may be related to increased incidence of cerebral palsy (Vincer et al., 2006) and that rates continue to be high in infants born very preterm (Ancel et al., 2006).

At least 60% of all postnatal fetal deaths are the result of chronic hypoxia.

Failure to Thrive

Failure to thrive (FTT) is a chronic, potentially life-threatening disorder of infancy and early childhood. It strikes as many as 3 to 5% of all infants under 1 year of age (Kessler & Dawson, 1999), and up to 27% of infants were found to meet at least one of the seven criteria used in a Danish birth cohort (Olsen et al., 2007). Failure to thrive accounts for 3% of all pediatric hospitalizations (Dacey & Travers, 2002). The criteria used to diagnose FTT historically have varied (Drotar, 1990), but generally the term refers to infants and young children whose weight is persistently below the third percentile for age on appropriate standardized growth charts (Dacey & Travers, 2002). The use of **anthropometric** criteria (i.e., comparative measurements of the human body such as height, weight, and head circumference) has also been employed (Olsen et al., 2007). Psychosocial interventions targeting the needs of children who failed to thrive had mixed results, but one consistent finding emerged: abused children who experienced a "positive and sustained change in their lives" (e.g., adoption, mothers remarried) had good outcomes (Iwaniec, Sneddon, & Allen, 2003). For the entire group, the relationship between parent and child as well as the etiology of failure to thrive were related to outcomes 20 years later. Similar effects on their own parenting experiences were evident in this group (Iwaniec & Sneddon, 2002). For example, those who had experienced positive gains from psychosocial interventions and life changes tended to report lower stress and greater enjoyment from parenting.

> Three percent of all pediatric hospitalizations are due to FTT.

In the past, some researchers (e.g., Homer & Ludwig, 1981) suggested three etiological categories for FTT: organic, nonorganic, and a combination of these. Most cases are of the combined type, however, and the organic-versus-nonorganic distinction is not used by most pediatricians practicing today (White, 2004). Regardless of etiology, the common trait for all infants with FTT is the inadequate intake, retention, or use of calories. In addition to medical malnutrition, many of these children show poor physical growth; delayed motor, language, and cognitive skills; and emotional listlessness (Homer & Ludwig, 1981). Significant evidence exists to suggest that failure to thrive is associated with impaired intellectual outcomes (Corbett & Drewett, 2004), but some specific studies have not found significant differences in cognition and emotion between children with FTT as infants and those without (Drewett, Corbett, & Wright, 1999; Drewett, Corbett, & Wright, 2006).

Although adequately controlled studies in FTT are rare, it appears that the prognosis is more favorable for the child's physical growth than for cognitive growth (Berwick, 1980). Sturm and Drotar (1989) noted in their longitudinal study of 59 infants with FTT that about 67% of their group achieved normal growth parameters at age 3; however, intellectual functioning for the group tended to fall within the borderline range. With respect to treatment, the earlier and more vigorous the intervention is, particularly when the parents are involved and multiple etiological factors are considered, the better the chances of recovery from FTT (Spinner & Siegel, 1987).

A constellation of factors related to failure to thrive has emerged. For example, failure to thrive is more commonly found in preterm infants, with mothers of these infants more likely to be depressed than mothers of infants born at term (Drewett, Blair, Emmett, & Emond, 2004). In addition, maternal attachment seems to be related to failure to thrive (Ward, Lee, & Lipper, 2000). Specifically, children with failure to thrive are less likely than typical peers to have secure attachments and more likely to show disorganized and anxious attachments. Cognitive and academic outcomes for children with failure to thrive appear to be exacerbated by a history of maltreatment (Kerr, Black, & Krishnakumar, 2000), with findings supporting a cumulative risk model. Mothers of infants with failure to thrive also appear to be more limited in their problem-solving strategies than mothers with healthy children (Robinson, Drotar, & Boutry, 2001).

Child Abuse and Neglect

In addition to the medically based factors that can influence development, child abuse and neglect can exert a significant influence on the developing child. In 2004, approximately 3.5 million suspected child abuse and neglect cases were reported in the United States, at a rate of 47.8 per 1,000 children (Children's Bureau, 2006; U.S. Department of Health and Human Services, 2006). About 872,000 of these cases were confirmed (i.e., a victim rate of 11.9 per 1,000 children). Approximately 48% of the victims were boys and 52% were girls. The rate of victimization tended to be inversely related to age, with young children being disproportionately represented (e.g., 10.3% of victims were under the age of 1 year). Neglect was more likely to be the cause of a report in the younger children (73% for birth to 3 years) than older children (52% for 12–15 years). Rates of victimization were lower for Asian (2.9 per 1,000), white (10.7 per 1,000), and Hispanic (10.4 per 1,000) children than for African-American (19.9 per 1,000), Pacific Islander (17.6 per 1,000), and Alaska Native (15.5 per 1,000) children. Of the victims, 53.8% were white, 25.2% were African-American, and 17% were Hispanic.

Abuse can come in several forms: physical, sexual, and psychological/emotional. All represent a significant and profound assault on a developing child. Child abuse occurs across racial, ethnic, and socioeconomic groups, and it may be difficult to recognize. Researchers have identified a variety of factors that may increase the risk of child maltreatment. These include parent, child, and family characteristics as well as features of the community or culture (Belsky, 1993; Cicchetti & Toth, 1998). In addition to the risk of abuse, the actual occurrence of abuse or neglect in the child may be a function of a combination of these characteristics, such as abuse of the parent as a child (Yehuda, Halligan, & Grossman, 2001). Factors such as poor social networks, young parental age, low educational levels, parental psychiatric history, and parental childhood abuse have been implicated in increased risk of suspected maltreatment.

Physical abuse and neglect may be the easiest forms to detect; other forms may be manifested by a child's internalizing behaviors (e.g., withdrawal, depression, anxiety) or by inappropriate externalizing behaviors (e.g., conduct problems, sexual acting out). Neglect refers to the failure of the caregivers to meet the child's emotional, physical, or medical needs, and can be difficult to substantiate.

Child abuse and neglect have been associated with many negative short-term and long-term effects, including abnormal brain development.

Because the circumstances under which abuse occurs vary dramatically from case to case, and because data are often based on retrospective, or speculative, information from hesitant reporters (e.g., a single parent who could be in and out of jail), it is difficult to determine a direct causal relationship between detrimental developmental outcomes and various forms of abuse. Nonetheless, child abuse and neglect have been associated with negative short-term and long-term effects on children's physical development and mental health. Emergent data have begun to document structural abnormalities in the brains of these children with associated cognitive dysfunction (Beers & De Bellis, 2002; De Bellis, 2001).

For example, physical abuse in infancy can result in scarring or other deformities, as well as in problems such as mental retardation, seizures, cerebral palsy, or blindness following head trauma (e.g., shaken baby syndrome). Neglect of young children puts them at increased risk for poisoning, burns, cuts, and similar types of injuries (Rosenberg & Krugman, 1991). Abuse and neglect during infancy also have been associated with difficulties in the regulation of emotions, poor attachment, language delays, and problems with peers (Cicchetti & Rogosch, 1994). Early stress can influence neurotransmitter systems and brain structures, thereby altering the development of the child. More research on the interaction of genes, the environment, and the development of future mental disorders is necessary (Heim & Nemeroff, 2001; Kaufman, Plotsky, Nemeroff, & Charney, 2000).

Maltreatment in childhood may lead to behavioral or psychiatric problems that manifest themselves in childhood or adulthood. Conditions such as posttraumatic stress disorder, depression, anxiety, personality disorders, self-injurious behaviors, substance abuse, eating disorders, interpersonal difficulties, and other forms of psychopathology also have been linked to child abuse (Briere & Elliot, 1994; Rosenberg & Krugman, 1991). Even physical punishment that may not be classified as abuse has been associated with increased odds of developing adult psychopathology relative to a group who did not sustain physical punishment or abuse. In addition, abused children often demonstrate lower cognitive and academic performance (Crozier & Barth, 2005). Indeed, young children with special needs may be at increased risk for abuse and neglect because of the very nature of their needs and disabilities (Alexander & Sherbondy, 1996; Ammerman, Hersen, Van Hasselt, Lubetsky, & Sieck, 1994). Maltreatment during early and middle childhood appears to have an impact on behavior in the adolescent years, with findings supporting a cumulative risk model (Appleyard, Egeland, van Dulmen, & Sroufe, 2005). Problems may persist into adulthood, with history of abuse during childhood related to poorer self-reported health and more frequent visits to the emergency room in adulthood (Chartier, Walker, & Nainmark, 2007).

Increased social support in families has been tied to reduced risk of neglect as well as "psychologically harsh parenting, and domestic violence" (Zolotor & Runyan, 2006). Maternal employment has also been identified as a protective factor against maltreatment (Sidebotham & Heron, 2006).

SUMMARY

The development of an individual from conception through childhood is a complex unfolding that is influenced by the processes of heredity and environment. Numerous theories have been proposed to explain how these processes interact; however, no single theory appears to provide a satisfactory explanation for all the intricate events that comprise development—typical or atypical. Certainly, children inherit many characteristics from their parents, and neurodevelopmental processes unfold in an orderly fashion. The environment also shapes the way children behave, how and what they learn, and their rate of development, and selected aspects of the environment may interact with neurological growth and development, as well.

Typical development is characterized by major milestones, but even these milestones can vary widely within the broad range of "normal." From the point of conception, the developmental process begins, with major organ systems being refined so that the fetus is prepared for entry into the world. During the gestational period, the developing mother's experiences also are key contributors to this process. For example, food and beverage intake, exposure to toxic substances and disease, and other activities of the mother (e.g., smoking) have an impact on intrauterine life—some positive and some negative. Once born, the child's interactions with the environment and the quality of parental care appear to be critical influences on the child's development. Furthermore, observations of developing children over time reinforce the concept that areas of development are interrelated. For example, as you will see in the following chapters of this text, language development and cognitive skills parallel each other in many ways, and in turn both of these are further influenced by a child's physical health, social-emotional development, family dynamics, school, and cultural expectations. No single theory integrates all of the factors of child development. Consequently, a holistic perspective of the child more readily lends itself to understanding the multitude of factors that are involved in development.

In reading the following chapters, it is important to consider how each area of development affects the others. With an understanding of the complexity of these phenomena, the early interventionist will be prepared to identify and address the many needs that young children with disabling conditions, such as Nathaniel, can manifest.

REVIEW QUESTIONS AND DISCUSSION POINTS

1. Describe the differences among growth, development, and maturation. What three basic criteria must be met before change can be considered to be development?
2. Describe major developmental milestones from each of the developmental domains, and find a heuristic that will enable you to keep this knowledge at your fingertips.
3. Discuss potential factors that could affect typical development. Be sure to note which factors are positive and which ones are negative.
4. How does nutrition influence a developing fetus? With respect to having a baby, why is it worthwhile for a woman to think about such things as nutrition and physical health prior to pregnancy?
5. Discuss the linkage of neurodevelopment to subsequent behavior in young children.
6. What information would be important to gather from a woman who is planning to become pregnant? What information would be important to know about a man who is planning to be a father?

RECOMMENDED RESOURCES

Websites

America's Children—Key National Indicators of Children's Well-Being: 2002
http://www.childstats.gov/americaschildren/

March of Dimes Birth Defects Foundation
http://www.modimes.org

National Clearinghouse on Child Abuse and Neglect Information
http://www.calib.com/nccanch/stats/index.cfm

Parenting Resources for the 21st Century
http://www.parentingresources.ncjrs.org

Women, Infants, and Children Program, U.S. Department of Agriculture
http://www.fns.usda.gov/wic/

Books

Fogel, A. (2001). *Infancy: Infant, family, and society* (4th ed.). Australia: Wadsworth Group.

Shonkoff, J. P., & Phillips, D. (2000). *From neurons to neighborhoods: The science of early childhood development.* Washington, DC: National Academy Press.

Swaiman, K., Ashwal, S., & Ferriero, D. (2006). *Pediatric neurology: Principles and practice* (4th ed.). New York: Elsevier Mosby.

REFERENCES

Abe, K., Honein, M. A., & Moore, C. A. (2003). Maternal febrile illnesses, medication use, and the risk of congenital renal anomalies. *Birth Defects Research (Part A): Clinical and Molecular Teratology, 67,* 911–918.

Abel, E. L. (1998). *Fetal alcohol abuse syndrome.* New York: Springer-Verlag.

Abel, E. L., & Hannigan, J. H. (1995). Maternal risk factors in fetal alcohol syndrome: Provocative and permissive influences. *Neurotoxicology and Teratology, 17,* 445–462.

Aberg, A., & Westbom, L. (2001). Association between maternal pre-existing or gestational diabetes and health problems in children. *Acta Paediatrica, 90,* 746–750.

Abroms, K. I., & Bennett, J. W. (1981). Age dispersion of parents of Down and non-Down syndrome children. *American Journal of Mental Deficiency, 86,* 204–207.

Aerts, L., Pijnenborg, R., Verhaeghe, J., Holemans, K., & Van Assche, F. A. (1996). Fetal growth and development. In A. Dornhorst & D. R. Hadden (Eds.), *Diabetes and pregnancy: An international approach to diagnosis and management* (pp. 77–97). New York: Wiley.

Alanay Y., Unal, F., Turanli, G., Alikasifoglu, M., Alehan, D., Akyol, U., et al. (2007). A multidisciplinary approach to the management of individuals with fragile X syndrome. *Journal of Intellectual Disabilities Research, 51,* 151–161.

Alexander, R. C., & Sherbondy, A. L. (1996). Child abuse and developmental disabilities. In M. L. Wolraich (Ed.), *Disorders of development and learning: A practical guide to assessment and management* (2nd ed., pp. 164–184). Boston: Mosby.

Aliyu, M. H., Salihu, H. M., Keith, L. G., Ehiri, J. E., Islan, M. A., & Jolly, P. E. (2005). Extreme parity and the risk of stillbirth. *Obstetrics & Gynecology, 106,* 446–453.

Als, H. (1997). Earliest interventions for preterm infants in the Newborn Intensive Care Unit. In M. J. Guralnick (Ed.), *The effectiveness of early intervention* (pp. 47–76). Baltimore: Brookes.

Amand, K. J. S., Phil, D., & Hickey, P. R. (1987). Pain and its effects in the human neonate and fetus. *New England Journal of Medicine, 317,* 1321–1329.

Ammerman, R. T., Hersen, M., Van Hasselt, V. B., Lubetsky, M. J., & Sieck, W. (1994). Maltreatment in psychiatrically hospitalized children and adolescents with developmental disabilities: Prevalence and correlates. *Journal of the American Academy of Child and Adolescent Psychiatry, 33,* 567–576.

Ancel, P. Y., Livinec, F., Larroque, B., Marret, S., Arnaud, C., & Peirrat, V. (2006). Cerebral palsy among very preterm children in relation to gestational age and neonatal ultrasound abnormalities: The EPIPAGE cohort study. *Pediatrics, 117,* 828–835.

Anderson, P., & Doyle, L. W. (2003). Neurobehavioral outcomes of school-age children born extremely low birth weight or very preterm in the 1990s. *Journal of the American Medical Association, 289,* 3264–3272.

Anhalt, K., Telzrow, C. G., & Brown, C. L. (2007). Maternal stress and emotional status during the perinatal period and childhood adjustment. *School Psychology Quarterly, 22,* 74–90.

Anisfeld, E., Curry, M. A., Hales, D. J., Kennell, J. H., Klaus, M. H., Lipper, E., et al. (1983). Maternal-infant bonding: A joint rebuttal. *Pediatrics, 72,* 569–572.

Apgar, V., & Beck, J. (1972). *Is my baby all right? A guide to birth defects.* New York: Trident Press.

Appleyard, K., Egeland, B., van Dulmen, M. H. M., & Sroufe, L. A. (2005). When more is not better: The role of cumulative risk in child behavior outcomes. *Journal of Child Psychology and Psychiatry, 46,* 235–245.

Autti-Ramo, I., Fagerlund, A., Ervalahti, N., Loimu, L., Korkman, M., & Hoyme, H. E. (2006). Fetal alcohol spectrum disorders in Finland: Clinical delineation of 77 older children and adolescents. *American Journal of Medical Genetics A, 140,* 137–143.

Autti-Ramo, I., & Granstrom, M. (1991). The psychomotor development during the first year of life of infants exposed to intrauterine alcohol of various duration: Fetal alcohol exposure and development. *Neuropediatrics, 22,* 59–64.

Auyeuna, A., Klein, M. E., Ratts, V. S., Odem, R. R., & Williams, D. B. (2001). Fertility treatment in the forty and older woman. *Journal of Assisted Reproduction and Genetics, 18,* 638–643.

Bailey, D. B., Roberts, J., Hooper, S. R., Hatton, D., Mirrett, P., Roberts, J. E., et al. (2004). Research on fragile X syndrome and autism: Implications for the study of genes, environments, and developmental language disorders. In M. L. Rice & S. F. Warren (Eds.), *Developmental language disorders: From phenotypes to etiologies.* Mahwah, NJ: Lawrence Erlbaum Publishing.

Barker, D. J., & Clark, P. M. (1997). Fetal undernutrition and disease in later life. *Review of Reproduction, 2,* 105–112.

Batshaw, M. L., Pellegrino, L., & Roizen, N. J. (2007). *Children with disabilities.* Baltimore: Brookes.

Beeghly, M., Martin, B., Rose-Jacobs, R., Cabral, H., Heeren, T., Augustyn, M., et al. (2006). Prenatal cocaine exposure and children's language functioning at 6 and 9.5 years: Moderating effects of child age, birthweight, and gender. *Journal of Pediatric Psychology, 31,* 98–115.

Beers, S. R., & De Bellis, M. D. (2002). Neuropsychological function in children with maltreatment-related posttraumatic stress disorder. *American Journal of Psychiatry, 159,* 483–486.

Behrman, R. E., & Kliegman, J. M. (1983). Jaundice and hyperbilirubinemia in the newborn. In R. E. Behrman, V. C. Vaughan, & W. E. Nelson (Eds.), *Neslon textbook of pediatrics* (12th ed., pp. 378–381). Philadelphia: W. B. Saunders.

Belsky, J. (1993). Etiology of child maltreatment: A developmental-ecological analysis. *Psychological Bulletin, 114,* 413–434.

Berwick, D. (1980). Nonorganic failure to thrive. *Pediatric Review, 1,* 265.

Bhutta, A. T., Cleves, M. A., Casey, P. H., Cradock, M. M., Anand, K. J. S. (2002). Cognitive and behavioral outcomes of school-aged children who were born preterm: A meta-analysis. *Journal of the American Medical Association, 288,* 728–737.

Bitler, M. P., & Currie, J. (2005). Does WIC work? The effects of WIC on pregnancy and birth outcomes. *Journal of Policy Analysis and Management, 24,* 73–91.

Black, M. M., Cutts, D. B., Frank, D. A., Geppert, J., Skalicky, A., Levenson, S., et al. (2004). Special Supplemental Nutrition Program for Women, Infants, and Children participation and infants' growth and health: A multisite surveillance study. *Pediatrics, 114,* 169–176.

Blackburn, S.T. (2007). *Maternal, fetal, and neonatal physiology: A clinical perspective* (3rd ed.). New York: Elsevier Health Sciences.

Blondel, B., Kaminsky, M., & Breart, G. (1980). Antenatal care and maternal demographic and social characteristics: Evolution in France between 1972 and 1976. *Journal of Epidemiology and Community Health, 34,* 157–163.

Bo, S., Marchisio, B., Volpiano, G., Menato, G., & Pagano, G. (2003). Maternal low birth weight and gestational hyperglycemia. *Gynecological Endocrinology, 17,* 133–136.

Bower, C., Miller, M., Payne, J., & Serna, P. (2006). Folate intake and the primary prevention of non-neural birth defects. *Australian and New Zealand Journal of Public Health, 30,* 258–261.

Branum, A. M., & Schoendorf, K. C. (2005). The influence of maternal age on very preterm birth of twins: Differential effects by parity. *Paediatric and Perinatal Epidemiology, 19,* 399–404.

Briere, J. N., & Elliott, D. M. (1994). Immediate and long-term impacts of child sexual abuse. *The Future of Children: Sexual Abuse of Children, 4,* 54–69.

Burden, M. J., Jacobson, S. W., Sokol, R. J., & Jacobson, J. L. (2005). Effects of prenatal alcohol exposure on attention and working memory at 7.5 years of age. *Alcohol Clinical and Experimental Research, 29,* 443–452.

Byrne, M., Agerbo, E., Ewald, H., Eaton, W. W., & Mortensen, P. B. (2003). Parental age and risk of schizophrenia: A case-control study. *Archives of General Psychiatry, 60,* 673–678.

Callaghan, W. M., MacDorman, M. F., Rasmussen, S. A., Qin, C., & Lackritz, E. M. (2006). The contribution of preterm birth to infant mortality rates in the United States. *Pediatrics, 118,* 1566–1573.

Carmichael, A. (1990). Physical development and biological influences. In B. J. Tonge, G. D. Burrows, & J. S. Werry (Eds.), *Handbook of studies on child psychiatry.* New York: Elsevier Science Publishing Company.

Carrapato, M. R., & Marcelino, F. (2001). The infant of the diabetic mother: The critical developmental windows. *Early Pregnancy, 5,* 57–58.

Carter, A. S., Garrity-Rokous, F. E., Chazan-Cohen, R., Little, C., & Briggs-Gowan, M. J. (2001). Maternal depression and co-morbidity: Predicting early parenting, attachment security, and toddler social-emotional problems and competencies. *Journal of the American Academy of Child and Adolescent Psychiatry, 40,* 15–26.

Case, M. E., Graham, M. A., Corey-Handy, T., Jentzen, J. M., & Monteleone, J. A. (2001). The National Association of Medical Examiners ad hoc Committee on shaken baby syndrome position paper on fatal abusive head injuries in infants and young children. *American Journal of Forensic Medicine and Pathology, 22,* 112–122.

Centers for Disease Control. (2006a). Achievements in public health. Reduction in perinatal transmission of HIV infection—United States, 1985–2005. *Morbidity and Mortality Weekly Report, 55,* 592–597.

Centers for Disease Control and Prevention. (2006b). Revised recommendations for HIV testing of adults, adolescents, and pregnant women in health-care settings. *Morbidity and Mortality Weekly Report, 55,* 1–17.

Center for Disease Control and Prevention. (2007). Breast-feeding practices: Results from the National Immunization Survey. Atlanta, GA: Author.

Chan, A., McCaul, K. A., Keane, R. J., & Haan, E. A. A. (1998). Effect of parity, gravidity, previous miscarriage, and age on risk of Down's syndrome: Population based study. *British Medical Journal, 317,* 923–924.

Chartier, M., Walker, J., & Nainmark, B. (2007). Child abuse, adult health, and health care utilization: Results from a representative community sample. *American Journal of Epidemiology, 10,* 1093.

Chase, C., Ware, J., Hittelman, J., Blasini, I., Smith, R., Llorente, A., et al. (2000). Early cognitive and motor development of infants born to women infected with human immunodeficiency virus. Women and Infants Transmission Study Group. *Pediatrics, 106,* E25.

Chasnoff, I. J. (2003). Prenatal substance exposure: Maternal screening and neonatal identification and management. *NeoReviews, 4,* 228–235.

Children's Bureau, Administration on Children, Youth, and Families. (2006). *Child maltreatment 2004.* Retrieved February 26, 2007, from http://www.acf.dhhs.gov/programs/cb/pubs/cm04/chapterthree.htm#first

Chiriboga, C. A. (2003). Fetal alcohol and drug effects. *Neurologist, 9,* 267–279.

Chronis, A. M., Lahey, B. B., Pelham, W. E., Jr., Williams, S. H., Baumann, B. L., Kipp, H., et al. (2007). Maternal depression and early positive parenting predict future conduct problems in young children with attention-deficit/hyperactivity disorder. *Developmental Psychology, 43,* 70–82.

Cicchetti, D., & Rogosch, F. A. (1994). The toll of child maltreatment on the developing child. *Child and Adolescent Psychiatric Clinics of North America, 3,* 759–772.

Cicchetti, D., & Toth, S. L. (1998). Perspectives on research and practice in developmental psychology. In I. E. Sigel & K. A. Renninger (Eds.), *Handbook of child psychology* (Vol. 4). (5th ed., pp. 479–582). New York: Wiley.

Clementi, M., Bianca, S., Benedicenti, F., & Tenconi, R. (1999). Down syndrome and pairty. *Community Genetics, 2,* 18–22.

Cnattingius, S. (2004). The epidemiology of smoking during pregnancy: Smoking prevalence, maternal characteristics, and pregnancy outcomes. *Nicotine & Tobacco Research, 6,* S125–S140.

Cohen, I. L. (1995). A theoretical analysis of the role of hyperarousal in the learning and behavior of fragile-X males. *Mental Retardation and Developmental Disabilities Research Reviews, 1,* 286–291.

Cohen, W. I. (1999). Down syndrome: Care of the child and family. In M. D. Levine, W. B. Carey, & A. C. Crocker (Eds.), *Developmental-behavioral pediatrics* (3rd ed., pp. 240–248). Philadelphia: W. B. Saunders.

Cone-Wesson, B. (2005). Prenatal alcohol and cocaine exposure: Influences on cognition, speech, language, and hearing. *Journal of Communicative Disorders, 38,* 279–302.

Corbett, S. S., & Drewett, R. F. (2004). To what extent is failure to thrive in infancy associated with poorer cognitive development? A review and meta-analysis. *Journal of Child Psychology and Psychiatry, 45,* 641–654.

Cousins, L. (1983). Congenital anomalies among infants of diabetic mothers: Etiology, prevention, prenatal diagnosis. *American Journal of Obstetrics and Gynecology, 147,* 333.

Coustan, D. R. (1995). Obstetric complications. In D. R. Coustan (Ed.), *Human reproduction: Growth and development* (pp. 431–455). Boston: Little Brown.

Crowther, C. A., Haslan, R. R., Hiller, J. E., Doyle, L. W., & Robinson, J. S. (2006). Neonatal respiratory distress syndrome after repeat exposure to antenatal corticosteroids: A randomised control trial. *Lancet, 367,* 1913–1919.

Crozier, J. C., & Barth, R. P. (2005). Cognitive and academic functioning in maltreated children. *Children & Schools, 27,* 197–206.

Cummings, E. M., Davies, P. T., & Campbell, S. B. (2000). *Developmental psychopathology and family process: Theory, research and clinical implications.* New York: Guilford Press.

DaCosta, D., Dritsa, M., Larouche, L., & Brender, W. (2000). Psychosocial predictors of labor/delivery complications and infant birth weight: A prospective study. *Journal of Psychosomatic Obstetrics and Gynaecology, 21,* 137–148.

Dacey, J. S., & Travers, J. F. (2002). *Human development across the lifespan* (5th ed.). Boston: McGraw-Hill.

Dalman, C., & Allebeck, P. (2002). Paternal age and schizophrenia: Further support for an association. *American Journal of Psychiatry, 159,* 1591–1592.

D'Angiulli, A., Grunau, P., Maggi, S., & Herdman, A. (2006). Electroencephalographic correlates of prenatal exposure to alcohol in infants and children: A review of findings and implications for neurocognitive development. *Alcohol, 40,* 127–133.

Datta-Bhutada, S., Johnson, H. L., & Rosen, T. S. (1998). Intrauterine cocaine and crack exposure: Neonatal outcome. *Journal of Perinatology, 18,* 183–188.

Day, N. L., Leech, S. L., Richardson, G. A., Cornelius, M. D., Robles, N., & Larkby, C. (2002). Prenatal alcohol exposure predicts continued deficits in offspring size at 14 years of age. *Alcoholism: Clinical and Experimental Research, 26,* 1584–1591.

Day, N. L., Richardson, G. A., Goldschmidt, L., & Cornelius, M. D. (2000). Effects of prenatal tobacco exposure on preschoolers' behavior. *Journal of Developmental and Behavioral Pediatrics, 21,* 180–188.

Dean, R. S., & Davis, A. S. (2007). Relative risk of perinatal complications in common childhood disorders. *School Psychology Quarterly, 22,* 74–90.

De Bellis, M. D. (2001). Developmental traumatology: The psychobiological development of maltreated children and its implications for research, treatment, and policy. *Developmental Psychopathology, 13,* 539–564.

DeCherney, A. H., Nathan, L., & Goodwin, T. M. (2006). *Current obstetric and gynecologic diagnoses and treatment* (10th ed.). New York: McGraw-Hill.

Deiner, P. L. (1997). *Infants and toddlers: Development and program planning.* Fort Worth, TX: Harcourt Brace.

Delbaere, I., Verstraelen, H., Goetgeluk, S., Martens, G., De Backer, E., & Temmerman, M. (2006). Pregnancy outcome in primiparae of advanced maternal age. *European Journal of Obstetrics and Gynecology, 10,* 1016.

Delobel-Ayoub, M., Kaminski, M., Marret, S., Burguet, A., Marchand, L., N'Guyen, S., et al. (2006). Behavioral outcomes at 3 years of age in very preterm infants: The EPI-PAGE study. *Pediatrics, 117,* 1196–2005.

Dennis, T., Bendersky, M., Ramsay, D., & Lewis, M. (2006). Reactivity and regulation in children prenatally exposed to cocaine. *Developmental Psychology, 42,* 688–697.

Diego, M. A., Jones, N. A., Field, T., Hernandex-Reif, M., Schanberg, S., Kuhn, C., et al. (2006). Maternal psychological distress, prenatal cortisol, and fetal weight. *Psychosomatic Medicine, 68,* 747–753.

Diego, M. A., Field, T., & Hernandez-Reif, M. (2005). Prepartum, postpartum, and chronic depression effects on neonatal behavior. *Infant Behavior & Development, 28,* 155–164.

Dildy, G. A., Jackson, G. M., Fowers, G. K., Oshiro, B. T., Varner, M. W., & Clark, S. L. (1996). Very advanced maternal age: Pregnancy after age 45. *American Journal of Obstetrics and Gynecology, 173,* 668–674.

Doria-Rose, V. P., Kim, H. S., Augustine, E. T. J., & Edwards, K. L. (2003). Parity and the risk of Down's syndrome. *American Journal of Epidemiology, 158,* 503–508.

dos Santos Silva, I., Higgins, C., Swerdlow, A. J., Laing, S. P., Slater, D. K., Pearson, D. W. M., et al. (2005). Birthweight and other pregnancy outcomes in a cohort of women with pre-gestational insulin-treated diabetes mellitus, Scotland, 1979–1995. *Diabetic Medicine, 22,* 440–447.

Drewett, R. F., Corbett, S. S., & Wright, C. M. (1999). Cognitive and educational attainments at school age of children who failed to thrive in infancy: A population-based study. *Journal of Child Psychology and Psychiatry, 40,* 551–561.

Drewett, R. F., Corbett, S. S., & Wright, C. M. (2006). Physical and emotional development, appetite and body image in adolescents who failed to thrive as infants. *Journal of Child Psychology and Psychiatry, 47,* 524–531.

Drewett, R., Blair, P., Emmett, P., & Emond, A. (2004). Failure to thrive in the term and preterm infants of mothers depressed in the postnatal period: A population-based birth cohort study. *Journal of Child Psychology and Psychiatry, 45,* 359–366.

Drotar, D. (1990). Sampling issues in research with nonorganic failure-to-thrive children. *Journal of Pediatric Psychology, 15,* 255–272.

Eisenberg, A., Murkoff, H. E., & Hathaway, S. E. (1991). *What to expect when you're expecting.* New York: Workman.

Elliott, E. J., Payne, J. M., Morris, A., Haan, E., & Bower, C. A. (2007). Fetal alcohol syndrome: A prospective national surveillance study. *Archives of the Diseases of Childhood, 1136,* 120–220.

Epstein, H. T. (2001). An outline of the role of brain in human cognitive development. *Brain and Cognition, 45,* 44–51.

Ernst, M., Moolchan, E. T., & Robinson, M. L. (2001). Behavioral and neural consequences of prenatal exposure to nicotine. *Journal of the American Academy of Child & Adolescent Psychiatry, 40,* 630–641.

Esposito, S., Musetti, L., Musetti, M. C., Tornaghi, R., Corbella, S., Massironi, E., et al. (1999). Behavioral and psychological disorders in uninfected children aged 6 to 11 years born to human immunodeficiency virus-seropositive mothers. *Journal of Developmental and Behavioral Pediatrics, 20,* 411–417.

Ewings-Cobb, L., et al. (1995). American Academy of Pediatrics: Shaken baby syndrome: Rotational cranial injuries—Technical report. *Pediatrics, 108,* 206–210.

Farel, A., Hooper, S. R., Teplin, S., Henry, M., & Kraybill, E. (1998). Very low birth weight infants at 7 years: An assessment of the health and neurodevelopmental risk conveyed by chronic lung disease. *Journal of Learning Disabilities, 31,* 118–126.

Fear, N. T., Hey, K., Vincent, T., & Murphy, M. (2007). Paternal occupation and neural tube defects: A case-control study based on the Oxford Record Linkage Study register. *Paediatric Perinatal Epidemiology, 21,* 163–168.

Ferencz, C., Rubin, J. S., McCarter, R. J., & Clark, E. B. (1990). Maternal diabetes and cardiovascular malformations: Predominance of double outlet right ventricle and truncus arteriosus. *Teratology, 41,* 319.

Ferrara, T. B., Hoekstra, R. E., Couser, R. J., Gaziano, E. P., Calvin, S. E., Payne, N. R., et al. (1994). Survival and follow-up of infants born at 23 to 26 weeks of gestational age: Effects of surfactant therapy. *Journal of Pediatrics, 124,* 119.

Fifer, W. P., Monk, C. E., & Grose-Fifer, J. (2001). Prenatal development and risk. In G. Bremner & A. Fogel (Eds.), *Blackwell handbook of infant development* (pp. 503–542). Oxford, England: Blackwell.

Figueras, F., Figueras, J., Meler, E., Eixarch, E., Coll, O., Gratacos, E., et al. (2007). Customized birthweight standards accurately predict perinatal morbidity. *Archives of Disease in Childhood: Fetal and Neonatal Edition, 92,* F277–F280.

Finer, N. N., Horbar, J. D., & Carpenter, J. H. (1999). Cardiopulmonary resuscitation in the very-low-birth-weight infant: The Vermont Oxford Network experience. *Pediatrics, 104,* 428–434.

Floyd, R. L., Zahniser, C., Gunter, E. P., & Kendrick, J. S. (1991). Smoking during pregnancy: Prevalence, effects, and intervention strategies. *Birth, 18,* 48–53.

Forrester, M. B., & Merz, R. D. (2003). Maternal age-specific Down syndrome rates by maternal race/ethnicity, Hawaii, 1986–2000. *Birth Defects Research Part A: Clinical and Molecular Teratology, 67,* 625–629.

Frank, D. A., Augustyn, M., Knight, W. G., Pell, T., & Zuckerman, B. (2001). Growth, development, and behavior in early childhood following prenatal cocaine exposure: A systematic review. *Journal of the American Medical Association, 285*(1), 1613–1625.

Frank, D. A., Bresnahan, K., & Zuckerman, B. (1993). Maternal cocaine use: Impact on child health and development. *Advances in Pediatrics, 40,* 65–99.

Frank, P., McNamee, R., Hannaford, P. C., & Kay, C. R. (1994). Effect of changes in maternal smoking habits in early pregnancy on infant birthweight. *British Journal of General Practice, 44,* 57–59.

Frank, D. A., Augustyn, M., Knight, W. G., Pell, T., & Zuckerman, B. (2001). Growth, development, and behavior in early childhood following prenatal cocaine exposure: A systematic review. *Journal of the American Medical Association, 285*(12), 1613–1625.

Fried, P. A., & Smith, A. M. (2001). A literature review of the consequences of prenatal marijuana exposure: An emerging theme of a deficiency in aspects of executive function. *Neurotoxicology and Teratology, 23,* 1–11.

Fujiwara, T. (1996). Surfactant therapy for neonatal respiratory distress syndrome. In F. A. Chervenak & A. Kurjak (Eds.), *The fetus as a patient* (pp. 603–616). New York: Parthenon.

Ganpule, A., Yajnik, C. S., Fall, C. H., Rao, S., Fisher, D. J., Kanade, A., et al. (2006). Bone mass in Indian children—relationships to maternal nutritional status and diet during pregnancy: The Pune Maternal Nutrition Study. *Journal of Clinical Endocrinology & Metabolism, 91,* 2294–3001.

Gardner, F., Johnson, A., Yudkin, P., Bowler, U., Hockley, C., Mutch, L., et al. (2004). Behavioral and emotional adjustment of teenagers in mainstream school who were born before 29 weeks' gestation. *Pediatrics, 114,* 676–682.

Gardner, J. (1997). Fetal alcohol syndrome—Recognition and intervention. *American Journal of Maternal and Child Nursing, 22,* 318–322.

Gesell, A., & Ilg, S. (1943). *The infant and child: The culture of today.* New York: Harper Brothers.

Gilbert, E. S. (2006). *Manual of high-risk pregnancy and delivery*. New York: Elsevier Health Sciences.

Gillman, M. W., Rifas-Shiman, S., Berkey, C. S., Field, A. E., & Colditz. G. A. (2003). Maternal gestational diabetes, birth weight, and adolescent obesity. *Pediatrics, 111*, e221–e226.

Glenn, M. J., Gibson, E. M., Kirby, E. D., Mellott, T. J., Blusztajn, J. K., & Williams, C. L. (2007). Prenatal choline availability modulates hippocampal neurogenesis and neurogenic responses to enriching experiences in adult female rats. *European Journal of Neuroscience, 25*, 2473–2482.

Glover, V. (1999). Maternal stress or anxiety during pregnancy and the development of the baby. *Practicing Midwife, 2*, 20–22.

Godfrey, K. M., & Barker, D. J. (2000). Fetal nutrition and adult disease. *American Journal of Clinical Nutrition, 71* (Supplement 5), 1344S–1345S.

Goldsmith, W., & Plunkett, J. (2004). A biochemical analysis of the causes of traumatic brain injury in infants and children. *The American Journal of Forensic Medicine and Pathology, 25*, 89–100.

Goodman, S. H., & Gotlib, I. H. (1999). Risk for psychopathology in the children of depressed mothers: A developmental model for understanding mechanisms of transmission. *Psychological Review, 106*, 458–490.

Gotto, M. P., & Goldman, A. S. (1994). Diabetic embryopathy. *Current Opinions in Pediatrics, 6*, 486.

Gould, J. B., Benitz, W. E., & Liu, H. (2000). Mortality and time to death in very-low-birth-weight infants: California, 1987 and 1993. *Pediatrics, 105*, E37.

Grubman, S., Gross, E., Lerner-Weiss, N., & Hernandez, M. (1995). Older children and adolescents living with perinatally acquired human immuno-deficiency virus infection. *Pediatrics, 95*, 657–663.

Hack, M., Flannery, D. J., Schluchter, M., Cartar, L., Borawski, E., & Klein, N. (2002). Outcomes in young adulthood for very-low-birth-weight infants. *New England Journal of Medicine, 346*, 149–157.

Hack, M., Klein, N. K., & Taylor, H. G. (1995). Long-term developmental outcomes of low-birth-weight infants. *The Future of Children, 5*, 176–196.

Hagedorn, M. E., Gardner, S. L., & Abman, S. H. (2002). Respiratory diseases. In G. B. Merenstein & S. L. Gardner (Eds.), *Handbook of neonatal intensive care* (5th ed., pp. 485–575). St. Louis, MO: Mosby.

Hagerman, R. J., & Cronister, A. (Eds.). (1996). *Fragile X Syndrome: Diagnosis, treatment, and research* (2nd ed.). Baltimore: Johns Hopkins University Press.

Hall S., DeBernardis, M., & Reiss, A. (2006). Social escape behaviors in children with fragile X syndrome. *Journal of Autism and Developmental Disorders, 36*, 935–947.

Halliday, H. L. (2004). Use of steroids in the perinatal periods. *Paediatric Respiratory Review, 5*, Supplement A, S321–327.

Halliday, H. L., Ehrenkranz, R. A., Doyle, L. W. (2003). Early postnatal (<96 hours) corticosteroids for preventing chronic lung disease in preterm infants. *Cochrane Database System Review, 1*, 1146.

Hamilton, B. E., Martin, J. A., Ventura, S. J., Sutton, P. D., & Menacker, F. (2005). Births: Preliminary data for 2004. *National Vital Statistics Report, 54*, 1–18.

Hankin, C., Thorne, C., & Newell, M. L. (2005). Does exposure to antiretroviral therapy affect growth in the first 18 months of life in uninfected children born to HIV-infected women? *Journal of Acquired Immune Deficiency Syndrome, 40*, 364–370.

Heim, C., & Nemeroff, C. B. (2001). The role of childhood trauma in the neurobiology of mood and anxiety disorders: Preclinical and clinical studies. *Biological Psychiatry, 49*, 1023–1039.

Herbert, W. N. P., Dodds, J. M., & Cefalo, R. C. (1993). Nutrition in pregnancy. In R. A. Knuppel & J. E. Drukker (Eds.), *High-risk pregnancy: A team approach* (2nd ed.). Philadelphia: W. B. Saunders.

Hernandez-Reif, M., Field, T., Diego, M., & Ruddock, M. (2006). Greater arousal and less attentiveness to face/voice stimuli by neonates of depressed mothers on the Brazelton Neonatal Behavioral Assessment Scale. *Infant Behavior and Development, 29*, 594–598.

Herrenkohl, L. R. (1988). The impact of prenatal stress on the developing fetus and child. In R. L. Cohen (Ed.), *Psychiatric consultation in childbirth settings: Parent- and child-oriented approaches*. New York: Plenum Medical Books.

Hessl, D., Glaser, B., Dyer-Friedman, J., & Reiss, A. L. (2006). Social behavior and cortisol reactivity in children with fragile X syndrome. *Journal of Child Psychology and Psychiatry, 47*, 602–610.

Hirshfeld-Becker, D. R., Biederman, J., Faraone, S. V., Robin, J. A., Friedman, D., Rosenthal, J. M., et al. (2004). Pregnancy complications associated with childhood anxiety disorders. *Depression and Anxiety, 19*, 152–162.

Hoffman, S., & Hatch, M. C. (1996). Stress, social support, and pregnancy outcome: A reassessment based on research. *Paediatric and Perinatal Epidemiology, 10*, 380–405.

Holley, W. L., Rosenbaum, A. L., & Churchill, J. A. (1969). Effects of rapid succession of pregnancy. In *Perinatal factors affecting human development*. Pan-American Health

Organization, Pan-American Sanitary Bureau, Regional Office of World Health Organization.

Hollier, L. M., Leveno, K. J., Kelly, M. A., McIntire, D. D., & Cunningham, F. G. (2000). Maternal age and malformations in singleton births. *Obstetrics and Gynecology, 96,* 701–706.

Hollomon, H. A., & Scott, K. G. (1998). Influence of birth weight on educational outcomes at age 9: The Miami site of the Infant Health and Development Program. *Journal of Developmental & Behavioral Pediatrics, 9,* 404–410.

Homer, C., & Ludwig, S. (1981). Categorization of etiology of failure to thrive. *American Journal of the Disabled Child, 735,* 848.

Hook, E. B. (1987). Issues in analysis of data on paternal age and 47, + 21: Implications for genetic counseling for Down syndrome. *Human Genetics, 77,* 303–306.

Hooper, S. R., Hatton, D., Sideris, J., Sullivan, K., Hammer, J., Schaaf, J., et al. (2008). *Neuropsychology,*

House, S. (2000). Stages in reproduction particularly vulnerable to xenobiotic hazards and nutritional deficits. *Nutrition and Health, 14,* 147–193.

Hoyert, D. L., Freedman, M. A., Strobino, D. M., & Guyer, B. (2001). Annual summary of vital statistics: 2000. *Pediatrics, 108,* 1241–1255.

Hurt, H., Malmud, E., Betancourt, L., Braitman, L. E., Brodsky, N. L., & Giannetta, J. (1997). Children with in utero cocaine exposure do not differ from control subjects on intelligence testing. *Archives of Pediatric and Adolescent Medicine, 151,* 1237–1241.

Huxley, R. R., & Neil, A. W. (2004). Does maternal nutrition in pregnancy and birth weight influence levels of CHD risk factors in adult life? *British Journal of Nutrition, 91,* 459–468.

Hyman, S. L., Gill, D. S., Shores, E. A., Steinberg, A., & North, K. N. (2007). T2 hyperintensities in children with neurofibromatosis type 1 and their relationship to cognitive functioning. *Journal of Neurology, Neurosurgery, and Psychiatry, 78,* 1088–1091.

Institute of Medicine, National Academy of Sciences. (1990a). *Nutrition during pregnancy.* Washington, DC: National Academy Press.

Institute of Medicine, National Academy of Sciences. (1990b). *Broadening the base of treatment of alcohol problems.* Washington, D.C.: National Academy Press.

Iwaniec, D., & Sneddon, H. (2002). The quality of parenting of individuals who had failed to thrive as children. *British Journal of Social Work, 32,* 283–298.

Iwaniec, D., Sneddon, H., & Allen, A. (2003). The outcomes of a longitudinal study of non-organic failure-to-thrive. *Child Abuse Review, 12,* 216–226.

Jensen, A. R. (1980). *Bias in mental testing.* New York: Free Press.

Johnson, M. H., Dziurawiee, S., Ellis, H., & Morton, J. (1991). Newborns' preferential tracking of the face-like stimuli and its subsequent decline. *Cognition, 40,* 1–19.

Jones, H. E., & Balster, R. J. (1998). Inhalant abuse in pregnancy. *Obstetrical and Gynecological Clinics in North America, 25,* 153–167.

Kallen, K. (1997). Maternal smoking and orofacial clefts. *Cleft Palate and Craniofacial Journal, 34,* 11–16.

Kaltenbach, K., & Finnegan, L. P. (1987). Perinatal and developmental outcome of infants exposed to methadone in utero. *Neurotoxicology and Teratology, 9,* 311–313.

Kandall, S. R., Doberczak, T. M., Jantunen, M., & Stein, J. (1999). The methadone-maintained pregnancy. *Clinical Perinatology, 26,* 173–183.

Katz, V. L., & Kuller, J. A. (1994). Recurrent miscarriage. *American Journal of Perinatology, 11,* 386.

Kaufman, J., Plotsky, P. M., Nemeroff, C. B., & Charney, D. S. (2000). Effects of early adverse experiences on brain structure and function: Clinical implications. *Biological Psychiatry, 48,* 778–790.

Keenan, H. T., Hooper, S. R., Wetherington, C. E., Nocera, M., & Runyan, D. K. (2007). Neurodevelopmental consequences of early traumatic brain injury in 3-year-old children. *Pediatrics, 119,* e616–e623.

Kerr, M. A., Black, M. M., & Krishnakumar, A. (2000). Failure-to-thrive, maltreatment and the behavior and development of 6-year-old children from low-income, urban families: A cumulative risk model. *Child Abuse and Neglect, 24,* 587–598.

Kessler, D. B., & Dawson, P. (1999). *Failure to thrive and pediatric undernutrition. A transdisciplinary approach.* Baltimore: Paul H. Brookes Publishing Company.

Khoshnood, B., Wall, S., & Lee, K. (2005). Risk of low birth weight associated with advanced maternal age among four ethnic groups in the United States. *Maternal and Child Health Journal, 9,* 3–9.

King, J. C. (2000). Physiology of pregnancy and nutrient metabolism. *American Journal of Clinical Nutrition, 71* (Supplement 5), 1218S–1225S.

Kitzmiller, J. L., Gavin, L. A., Gin, G. D., Jovanovic-Peterson, L., Main, E. K., & Zigrang, W. D. (1991). Preconception care of diabetes: Glycemic control prevents congenital anomalies. *Journal of the American Medical Association, 265,* 731.

Klaus, M. H., & Fanaroff, A. A. (2001). *Care of the high-risk neonate.* New York: Elsevier Health Sciences.

Kleinhaus, K., Perrin, M., Friedlander, Y., Paltiel, O., Malaspina, D., & Harlap, S. (2006). Paternal age and spontaneous abortion. *Obstetrics and Gynecology, 10,* 369–377.

Kleinman, J., & Madans, J. H. (1985). The effects of maternal smoking, physical stature, and educational attainment on the incidence of low birth weight. *American Journal of Epidemiology, 121,* 832–855.

Kliegman, R. M., Behrman, R. E., Jenson, H. B., Stanton, B. F., Zitelli, B. J., & Davis, H. W. (Eds.). (2007). *Nelson textbook of pediatrics e-edition* (18th ed.). New York: Elsevier Health Sciences.

Krebs, L., & Langhoff-Roos, J. (2006). Elective cesarean delivery for term breech. *European Journal of Obstetrics & Gynecology and Reproductive Biology, 127,* 26–28.

Krueger, P. M., & Scholl, T. O. (2000). Adequacy of prenatal care and pregnancy outcome. *Journal of American Osteopathy Association, 100*(8), 485–492.

Kung, H-C, Hoyert, D., Xu, J., & Murphy, S. L. (2005). Deaths: Preliminary data for 2005. Hyattsville, MD: National Center for Health Statistics.

Lawlor, D. A., Najman, J. M., Batty, G. D., O'Callaghan, M. J., Williams, G. M., & Bor, W. (2006). Early life predictors of childhood intelligence: Findings from the Mater-University study of pregnancy and its outcomes. *Paediatric and Perinatal Epidemiology, 20,* 148–162.

Lee, J. I., Lee, J. A., & Lim, H. S. (2005). Effect of time of initiation and dose of prenatal iron and folic acid supplementation on iron and folate nutrition of Korean women during pregnancy. *American Journal of Clinical Nutrition, 82,* 843–849.

Lee, K. S., Khoshnood, B., Sriram, S., Hsieh, H. L., Singh, J., & Mittendorf, R. (1998). Relationship of cesarean delivery to lower birth weight-specific neonatal mortality in singleton breech infants in the United States. *Obstetrics & Gynecology, 92,* 769–774.

Leitich, H., Bodner-Adler, B., Brunbauer, M., Kaider, A., Egarter, C., & Husslein, P. (2003). Bacterial vaginosis as a risk factor for preterm delivery: A meta-analysis. *Amercian Journal of Obstetrics and Gynecology, 189,* 139–147.

Lemons, J. A., Bauer, C. R., Oh, W., Korones, S. B., Papik, L., Stoll, B. J., et al. (2001). Very-low-birth-weight outcomes of the National Institute of Child Health and Human Development neonatal research network, January 1995 through December 1996. NICHD Neonatal Research Network. *Pediatrics, 107,* E1.

Lenneberg, E. H. (1967). *Biological foundations of language.* New York: Wiley.

Leuzzi, V., Tosetti, M., Montanaro, D., Carducci, C., Artiola, C., et al. (2007). The pathogenesis of the white matter abnormalities in phenylketonuria. A multimodal 3.0 tesla MRI and magnetic resonance spectroscopy (^{1}H MRS) study. *Journal of Inherited Metabolic Disease, 30,* e209–e216.

Lewit, E. M., Baker, L. S., Corman, H., & Shiono, P. H. (1995). The direct cost of low birth weight. *The Future of Children, 5,* 35–56.

Lin, C. L., Verp, M. S., & Sabbagha, R. E. (1993). *The high-risk fetus: Pathophysiology, diagnosis, and management.* New York: Springer-Verlag.

Lindegren, M. L., Steinberg, S., & Byers, R. H. (2000). HIV/AIDS in infants, children, and adolescents: Epidemiology of HIV/AIDS in children. *Pediatric Clinics of North America, 47,* 1–19.

Litonjua, A. A., Rifas-Siman, S. L., Ly, N. P., Tantisira, K. G., Rich-Edwards, J. W., Camargo Jr., C. A., et al. (2006). Maternal antioxidant intake in pregnancy and wheezing illnesses in children at 2 years of age. *American Journal of Clinical Nutrition, 84,* 903–911.

Little, B. B., Snell, L. M., Klein, B. R., Gilstrap, L. C., Knoll, K. A., & Breckenridge, J. D. (1990). Maternal and fetal effects of heroin addiction during pregnancy. *Journal of Reproductive Medicine, 35,* 159–162.

Longo, L. D. (1976). Carbon monoxide: Effects on oxygenation of the fetus in utero. *Science, 194,* 523–525.

Luetjens, C. M., Rolf, C., Gassner, P., Werny, J. E., & Nieschlag, E. (2002). Sperm aneuploidy rates in younger and older men. *Human Reproduction, 17,* 1826–1832.

Luke, B., Dickinson, C., & Petrie, R. H. (1981). Intrauterine growth: Correlation of maternal nutritional status and rate of gestational weight gain. *European Journal of Obstetrics, Gynecology, and Reproductive Biology, 12,* 113–121.

Lupton, C., Burd, L., & Harwood, R. (2004). Cost of fetal alcohol spectrum disorders. *American Journal of Medical Genetics, 127C,* 42–50.

Machado, C. J. (2006). Impact of maternal age on birth outcomes: A population-based study of primiparous Brazilian women in the city of Sao Paulo. *Journal of Biosocial Science, 38,* 523–535.

Maconochie, N., Doyle, P., Prior, S., & Simmons, R. (2007). Risk factors for first trimester miscarriage—results from a UK-population-based case-control study. *British Journal of Obstetrics and Gynaecology, 114,* 170–186.

Magee, M. S., Walden, C. E., Benedetti, T. J., & Knopp, R. H. (1993). Influence of diagnostic criteria on the incidence of gestational diabetes and perinatal morbidity. *Journal of the American Medical Association, 269,* 609.

Mahajan, S. D., Aalinkeel, R., Singh, S., Shah, P., Gupta, N., & Kochupillai, N. (2006). Endocrine regulation in asymmetric intrauterine fetal growth retardation. *Journal of Maternal & Fetal Neonatal Medicine, 19,* 615–623.

Maier, S. E., & West, J. R. (2001). Drinking patterns and alcohol-related birth defects. *Alcohol Research and Health, 25,* 168–174.

Malaspina, D., Corcoran, C., Fahim, C., Berman, A., Harkavy-Friedman, J., Yale, S., et al. (2002). Paternal age and sporadic schizophrenia: Evidence for de novo mutations. *American Journal of Medical Genetics, 114,* 299–303.

Malaspina, D., Harlap, S., Fennig, S., Heiman, D., Nahon, D., Feldman, D., et al. (2001). Advancing paternal age and the risk of schizophrenia. *Archives of General Psychiatry, 58,* 361–367.

Malaspina, D., Reichenberg, A., Weiser, M., Fennig, S., Davidson, M., Harlap, S., et al. (2005). Paternal age and intelligence: Implications for age-related genomic changes in male germ cells. *Psychiatry and Genetics, 15,* 117–125.

Manning, F. A., Morrison, I., Lange, I. R., & Harman, C. (1982). Antepartum determination of fetal health: Composite biophysical profile scoring. *Clinics in Perinatology, 9,* 285–296.

March of Dimes Peristats. Retrieved February 22, 2007, from http://www.marchofdimes.com/peristats

Markestad, T., Kaaresen, P. I., Ronnestad, A., Reigstad, H., Lossius, K., & Medbo, S. (2005). Early death, morbidity, and need of treatment among extremely-low-birth-weight infants. *Pediatrics, 115,* 1289–1298.

Marlow, M. N., Greenough, A., Peacock, J. L., Marston, L., Limb, E. S., Johnson, A. H., et al. (2006). Randomised trial of high frequency oscillatory ventilation or conventional ventilation in babies of gestational age 28 weeks or less: Respiratory and neurological outcomes at 2 years. *Archives of Disease in Childhood: Fetal and Neonatal Edition, 91,* F320–326.

Marshall, D. D., Kotelchuck, M., Young, T. E., Bose, C. L., Kruyer, L., & O'Shea, T. M. (1999). Risk factors for chronic lung disease in the surfactant era: A North Carolina population-based study of very-low-birth-weight infants. *Pediatrics, 104,* 1345–1350.

Martin, J. A., Hamilton, B. E., Ventura, S. J., Menocker, F., Park, M. M., & Sutton, P. D. (2002). Births: Final data for 2001. *National Vital Statistics Report, 51,* 1–102.

Mattson, S. N., & Riley, E. P. (1998). A review of the neurobehavioral deficits in children with fetal alcohol syndrome or prenatal exposure to alcohol. *Alcoholism: Clinical and Experimental Research, 22,* 279–294.

Mattson, S. N., Schoenfeld, A. M., & Riley, E. P. (2001). Teratogenic effects of alcohol on brain and behavior. *Alcohol Research and Health, 25,* 185–191.

May, P. A., & Gossage, J. P. (2001). Estimating the prevalence of fetal alcohol syndrome. A summary. *Alcohol Research and Health, 25,* 159–167.

May, P. A., Gossage, J. P., White-Country, M., Goodhart, K., Decoteau, S., Trujillo, P. M., et al. (2004). Alcohol consumption and other maternal risk factors for fetal alcohol syndrome among three distinct samples of women before, during, and after pregnancy: The risk is relative. *American Journal of Medical Genetics, 127C*(1), 10–20.

Mazor, M., Hagay, Z. J., Leiberman, J., Biale, Y., & Insler, V. (1985). Fetal abnormalities associated with breech delivery. *Journal of Reproductive Medicine, 30,* 884–886.

Mazzocco, M. M., Singh Bhatia, N., & Lesniak-Karpiak, K. (2006). Visuospatial skills and their association with math performance in girls with fragile X or Turner syndrome. *Child Neuropsychology, 12,* 87–110.

McBrien, D. M., Mattheis, P. J., & Van Dyke, D. C. (1996). Down syndrome. In M. L. Wolraich (Ed.), *Disorders of development and learning: A practical guide to assessment and management* (2nd ed., pp. 316–345). Boston: Mosby.

McConnell, M. S., Byers, R. H., Frederick, T., Peters, V. B., Dominguez, K. L., Sukalac, T., et al. (2005). Trends in antiretroviral therapy use and survival rates for a large cohort of HIV-infected children and adolescents in the United States, 1989–2001. *Journal of Acquired Immune Deficiency Syndromes, 38,* 488–494.

McLeod, L., & Ray, J. G. (2002). Prevention and detection of diabetic embryopathy. *Community Genetics, 5,* 33–39.

Mecham, M. J. (1996). *Cerebral palsy* (3rd ed.). Austin, TX: PRO-ED.

Meyer, U., Nyffeler, M., Engler, A., Urwyler, A., Schedlowski, M., Knuesel, I., et al. (2006). The time of prenatal immune challenge determines the specificity of inflammation-mediated brain and behavioral pathology. *The Journal of Neuroscience, 26,* 4752–4762.

Milner, A. D., Marsh, M. J., Ingraham, D. M., Fox, G. F., & Susiva, C. (1999). Effects of smoking in pregnancy on neonatal lung function [Fetal neonatal edition]. *Archives of Disease in Childhood, 80,* F8–F14.

Miotti, P. G., Taha, T. E., Kumwenda, N. I., Broadhead, R., Mtimavalye, L. A., Van der Hoeven, L., et al. (1999). HIV transmission through breastfeeding: A study in Malawi. *Journal of the American Medical Association, 282,* 744–749.

Miyake, Y., Sasaki, S., Tanaka, K., Yokoyama, T., Ohya, Y., Fukushima, W., et al. (2006). Dietary folate and vitamins B-sub-1-sub2, B-sub-6, and B-sub-2 intake and the risk of postpartum depression in Japan: The Osaka Maternal and Child Health Study. *Journal of Affective Disorders, 96,* 133–138.

Moehler, E., Brunner, R., Wiebel, A., Reck, C., & Resch, F. (2006). Maternal depressive symptoms in the postnatal period are associated with long-term impairment of mother-child bonding. *Archives of Women's Mental Health,* 9, 273–278.

Molina, J., Chotro, M., & Dominguez, H. (1995). Fetal alcohol learning resulting from contamination of the prenatal environment. In J. P. LeCanue, W. Fifer, N. Krasnegor, & W. Smotherman (Eds.), *Fetal development: A psychobiological perspective* (pp. 419–438). Hillsdale, NJ: Erlbaum.

Moore, K. L. L., & Persaud, T. V. N., & Torchia, M. G. (2007). *The developing human: Clinically oriented embryology with student consult online status (8th ed.).* New York: Elsevier Health Sciences.

Morrow, C. E., Culbertson, J. L., Accornero, V. H., Xue, L., Anthony, J. C., & Bandstra, E. S. (2006). Learning disabilities and intellectual functioning in school-aged children with prenatal cocaine exposure. *Developmental Neuropsychology, 30,* 905–931.

Morrow, C. E., Vogel, A. L., Anthony, J. C., Ofir, A. Y., Dausa, A. T., & Bandstra, E. S. (2004). Expressive and receptive language functioning in preschool children with prenatal cocaine exposure. *Journal of Pediatric Psychology, 29,* 543–554.

Morten, K., Field, P., Ashley, N., Williams, K. A., Harris, D., Hartley, M., et al. (2005). Fetal and neonatal exposure of mice to AZY and low-protein diet affects glucose homeostasis: A model with implications for AIDS prevention. *American Journal of Physiology and Endocrinological Metabolism, 289,* E1115–E1118.

Moses, R. G., Luebcke, M., Davis, W. S., Coleman, K. J., Tapsell, L. C., Petocz, P., et al. (2006). Effect of a low-glycemic-index diet during pregnancy on obstetric outcomes. *American Journal of Clinical Nutrition, 84,* 807–812.

Moshin, M., Wong, F., Bauman, A., & Bai, J. (2003). Maternal and neonatal factors influencing premature birth and low birth weight in Australia. *Journal of Biosocial Science, 35,* 161–174.

Murkoff, H. E., Eisenberg, A., & Hathaway, S. E. (2002). *What to expect when you're expecting* (3rd ed.). New York: Workman Publishing Company.

Murray, A. D., Dolby, R. M., Nation, R. L., & Thomas, D. B. (1981). Effects of epidural anesthesia on newborns and their mothers. *Child Development, 52,* 71.

Myers, S. A., Torrente, S., Hinthorn, D., & Clark, P. L. (2005). Life-threatening maternal and fetal macrocytic anemia from antiretroviral therapy. *Obstetric Gynecology, 106,* 1189–1191.

Nathanielsz, P. W. (1995). The role of basic science in preventing low birth weight. *The Future of Children, 5,* 57–70.

National Clearinghouse for Alcohol and Drug Information. (1995). *Making the link: Alcohol, tobacco and other drugs & pregnancy and parenthood.* Washington, DC: Author.

National Organization on Fetal Alcohol Syndrome. (2007). Facts about FAS/FASD. Washington, DC: Author.

National Research Council, Committee on Maternal Nutrition/Food and Nutrition Board. (1970). *Maternal nutrition during the course of pregnancy: A summary report.* Washington, DC: U.S. Government Printing Office.

Newburn-Cook, C. V., & Onyskiw, J. E. (2005). Is older maternal age a risk factor for preterm birth and fetal growth restriction? A systematic review. *Health Care for Women International, 26,* 852–875.

Nieburg, O., Marks, J. S., McLaren, N. M., & Remington, P. L. (1985). The fetal tobacco syndrome. *Journal of the American Medical Association, 253,* 2998–2999.

Nilsen, R. M., Vollset, S. E., Gjessing, H. K., Magnus, P., Meltzer, H. M., Haugen, M., et al. (2006). Patterns and predictors of folic acid supplement use among pregnant women: The Norwegian Mother and Child Cohort Study. *American Journal of Clinical Nutrition, 84,* 1134–1141.

Noland, J. S., Singer, L. T., Short, E. J., Minnes, S., Arendt, R. E., Kirchner, H. L., et al. (2005). Prenatal drug exposure and selective attention in preschoolers. *Neurotoxicological Teratology, 27,* 429–438.

Oberlander, T. F., Warburton, W., Misri, S., Aghajanian, J., & Hertzman, C. (2006). Neonatal outcomes after prenatal exposure to selective serotonin reuptake inhibitor antidepressants and maternal depression using population-based linked health data. *Archives of General Psychiatry, 63,* 898–906.

O'Connor, T. G., Ben-Shlomo, Y., Heron, J., Golding, J., Adams, D., & Glover, V. (2005). Prenatal anxiety predicts individual differences in cortisol in pre-adolescent children. *Biological Psychiatry, 58,* 211–217.

Olsen, E. M., Petersen, J., Skovgaard, A. M., Weile, B., Jorgensen, T., & Wright, C. M. (2007). Failure to thrive: The prevalence and concurrence of anthropometric criteria in a general infant population. *Archives of Disease in Childhood, 92,* 109–114.

Omori, Y., Minei, S., Testuo, T., Nemoto, K., Shimizu, M., & Sanaka, M. (1994). Current status of pregnancy in diabetic women. A comparison of pregnancy in IDDM and NIDDM mothers. *Diabetes Research and Clinical Practice, 24* (Supplement), 273.

O'Rahilly, R., & Muller, F. (1996). *Human embryology and teratology* (2nd ed.). New York: John Wiley & Sons, Inc.

Ornoy, A., Ratzon, N., Greenbaum, C., Wolf, A., & Dulitzky, M. (2001). School-age children born to diabetic mothers and to mothers with gestational diabetes exhibit a high rate of inattention and fine and gross motor impairment. *Journal of Pediatric Endocrinology and Metabolism, 14* (Supplement 1), 681–689.

O'Shea, T. M., Goldstein, D. J., deRegnier, R., Sheaffer, C. I., Roberts, D. D., & Dillard, R. G. (1996). Outcome at 4 to 5 years of age in children recovered from neonatal chronic lung disease. *Developmental Medicine and Child Neurology, 38,* 830–839.

Perek-Polnik, M., Filipek, I., Dembowska-Baginska, B., Owsik, A., Drogosiewicz, M., Jurkiewicz, E., et al. (2006). Children with neurofibromatosis type 1 treated in the Children's Memorial Health Institute. *Med Wieku Rozwoj, 10,* 699–709.

Pesonen, A., Räikkönen, K., Heinonen, K., Järvenpää, A., & Strandberg, T. E. (2006). Depressive vulnerability in parents and their 5-year-old child's temperament: A family systems perspective. *Journal of Family Psychology, 20,* 648–655.

Peterson, J., Taylor, H. G., Minich, N., Klein, N., & Hack, M. (2006). Subnormal head circumference in very-low-birth-weight children: Neonatal correlates and school-age consequences. *Early Human Development, 82,* 325–334.

Petry, C. J., & Hales, C. N. (2000). Long-term effects on offspring of intrauterine exposure to deficits in nutrition. *Human Reproduction Update, 6,* 578–586.

Pfefferbaum, A., Mathalon, D. H., Sullivan, E. V., Rawles, J. M., Zipursky, R. B., & Lim, K. O. (1994). A quantitative magnetic resonance imaging study of changes in brain morphology from infancy to late adulthood. *Archives of Neurology, 51,* 874–887.

Platt, M. J., Johnson, A., Surman, G., Topp, M., Torrioli, M. G., & Krageloh-Mann, I. (2007). Trends in cerebral palsy among infants of very low birthweight (<1500g) or born prematurely (<32 weeks) in European centres: A database study. *Lancet, 369,* 43–50.

Poustie, V. J., & Rutherford, P. (2000). Dietary interventions for phenlyketonuria. *The Cochrane Library* (Issue 1). Oxford: Update Software.

Puckett, M. B., & Black, J. K. (2004). *The young child: Development from prebirth through age eight* (4th ed.). Upper Saddle River, NJ: Prentice Hall.

Rahman, A., Iqbal, Z., Bunn, J., Lovel, H., & Harrington, R. (2004). The impact of maternal depression on infant nutritional status and illness. *Archives of General Psychiatry, 61,* 946–952.

Rasmussen, C. (2005). Executive functioning and working memory in fetal alcohol spectrum disorder. *Alcoholism: Clinical and Experimental Research, 29,* 1359–1367.

Reddy, U. M., Ko, C., & Willinger, M. (2006). Maternal age and the risk of stillbirth throughout pregnancy in the United States. *American Journal of Obstetrics and Gynecology, 195,* 764–770.

Reichenberg, A., Gross, R., Weiser, M., Bresnahan, M., Silverman, J., Harlap, S., et al. (2006). Advancing paternal age and autism. *Archives of General Psychiatry, 63,* 1026–1032.

Resta, R. G. (2005). Changing demographics of advanced maternal age (AMA) and the impact on the predicted incidence of Down syndrome in the United States. *American Journal of Medical Genetics, 133a,* 31–36.

Rice, D., & Barone, S. (2000). Critical periods of vulnerability for the developing nervous system: Evidence from human and animal models. *Environmental Health Perspectives, 108* (Supplement 3), 511–533.

Richardson, G. A., Hamel, S. C., Goldschmidt, L., & Day, N. L. (1999). Growth of infants prenatally exposed to cocaine/crack: Comparison of a prenatal care and no prenatal care sample. *Pediatrics, 104,* E18.

Richter, L., & Richter, D. M. (2001). Exposure to parental tobacco and alcohol use: Effects on children's health and development. *American Journal of Orthopsychiatry, 71,* 182–203.

Riley, E. P., McGee, C. L., & Sowell, E. R. (2004). Teratogenic effects of alcohol: A decade of brain imaging. *American Journal of Medical Genetics, 127C,* 35–41.

Robins, L. N., & Mills, J. L. (Eds.). (1993). Effects of in-utero exposure to street drugs. *Journal of Public Health, 83* (Supplement), 8–32.

Robinson, J. R., Drotar, D., Boutry, M. (2001). Problem-solving abilities among mothers of infants with failure to thrive. *Journal of Pediatric Psychology, 26,* 21–32.

Rosenberg, D. A., & Krugman, R. D. (1991). Epidemiology and outcome of child abuse. *Annual Review of Medicine, 42,* 217–224.

Russell, D. L., Keil, M. F., Bonat, S. H., Uwaifo, G. L., Nicholson, J. C., McDuffie, J. R., et al. (2001). The relation between skeletal maturation and adiposity in African American and Caucasian children. *Journal of Pediatrics, 139,* 844–848.

Rush, D., & Callahan, K. R. (1989). Exposure to passive cigarette smoking and child development. *Annals of New York Academy of Sciences, 562,* 74–100.

Salihu, H. M., Aliyu, M. H., Kirby, R. S., & Alexander, R. S. (2004). Effect of advanced maternal age on early mortality among quadruplets and quintuplets. *American Journal of Obstetrics and Gynecology, 190,* 383–388.

Savva, G. M., Morris, J. K., Mutton, D. E., & Alberman, E. (2006). Maternal age-specific fetal loss rates in Down syndrome pregnancies. *Prenatal Diagnosis, 26,* 499–504.

Scholl, T. O., Hediger, M. L., Schall, J. I., Khoo, C., & Fischer, R. L. (1996). Dietary and serum folate: Their influence on the outcome of pregnancy. *American Journal of Clinical Nutrition, 63*, 520–525.

Scholl, T. O., Sowers, M., Chen, X., & Lenders, C. (2001). Maternal glucose concentration influences fetal growth, gestation, and pregnancy complications. *American Journal of Epidemiology, 154*, 514–520.

Schuler, M. E., & Nair, P. (1999). Brief report: Frequency of maternal cocaine use during pregnancy and infant neurobehavioral outcome. *Journal of Pediatric Psychology, 24*, 511–514.

Schuster, C. S. (1992). Antenatal development. In C. S. Schuster & S. S. Ashburn (Eds.), *The process of human development: A holistic life-span approach* (3rd ed.). Philadelphia: J. B. Lippincott.

Schwartz, R. M., Luby, A. M., Scanlon, J. W., & Kellogg, R. J. (1994). Effects of surfactant on morbidity, mortality, and resource use in newborn infants weighing 500 to 1,500 g. *New England Journal of Medicine, 330*, 1476–1489.

Scott, G. B., Hutto, C., Makuch, R. W., Mastrucci, M. T., O'Connor, T., Mitchell, C. D., et al. (1989). Survival in children with perinatally acquired human immunodeficiency virus type I infection. *New England Journal of Medicine, 321*, 1791–1796.

Seoud, M. A., Nassar, A. H., Usta, I. M., Melhem, Z., Kazma, A., & Khalil, A. M. (2002). Impact of advanced maternal age on pregnancy outcome. *American Journal of Perinatology, 19*, 1–8.

Shaw, G. M., Lammer, E. J., Wasserman, C. R., & O'Malley, C. D. (1995). Risks of orofacial clefts in children born to women using multivitamins containing folic acid periconceptionally. *Lancet, 346*, 393–396.

Shaw, M., Lawlor, D. A., & Najman, J. M. (2006). Teenage children of teenage mothers: Psychological, behavioural and health outcomes from an Australian prospective longitudinal study. *Social Science & Medicine, 62*, 2526–2539.

Shearer, D. L., Mulvihill, B. A., Klerman, L. V., Wallander, J. L., Houinga, M. E., & Redden, D. T. (2002). Association of early birth and low cognitive ability. *Perspectives on Sexual and Reproductive Health, 34*, 236–243.

Shehata, H. A., & Nelson-Piercy, C. (2001). Drugs in pregnancy. Drugs to avoid. *Best Practices in Research in Clinical Obstetrical Gynecology, 15*, 971–986.

Shi, L., Tu, N., & Patterson, P. H. (2005). Maternal influenza infection is likely to alter fetal brain development indirectly: The virus is not detected in the fetus. *International Journal of Developmental Neuroscience, 23*, 299–305.

Shubert, P. J., & Savage, B. (1994). Smoking, alcohol, and drug abuse. In D. K. James, P. J. Steer, C. P. Weiner, & B. Gonik (Eds.), *High-risk pregnancy: Management options*. Philadelphia: W.B. Saunders.

Sidebotham, P., & Heron, J. (2006). Child maltreatment in the "children of the nineties": A cohort study of risk factors. *Child Abuse and Neglect, 30*, 497–522.

Silverman, B. L., Rizzo, T. A., Cho, N. H., & Metzger, B. E. (1998). Long-term effect of the intrauterine environment. The Northwestern University Diabetes in Pregnancy Center. *Diabetes Care, 21* (Supplement 2), B142–B149.

Singer, L. T., Arendt, R., Minnes, S., Farkas, K., Salvator, A., Kirchner, H. L., et al. (2002). Cognitive and motor outcomes of cocaine-exposed infants. *Journal of the American Medical Association, 287*, 1952–1960.

Singer, L. T., Minnes, S., Short, E. J., Arendt, R. E., Farkas, K., Lewis, B., et al. (2004). Cognitive outcomes of preschool children with prenatal cocaine exposure. *Journal of the American Medical Association, 291*, 2448–2456.

Sirrs, S. M., Laule, C., Madler, B., Brief, E. E., Tahir, S. A., Bishop, C., et al. (2007). Normal-appearing white matter in patients with phenylketonuria: Water content, myelin water fraction, and metabolite concentrations. *Radiology, 242*, 236–243.

Skinner, B. F. (1961). *Cumulative record* (enlarged ed.). New York: Appleton-Century-Crofts.

Skupski, D. W., Eglinton, G. S., Fine, A. D., Hayes, E. B., & O'Leary, D. R. (2006). West Nile Virus during pregnancy: A case study of early second trimester maternal infection. *Fetal Diagnostic Therapy, 21*, 239–295.

Slater, A., von der Schulenbur, C., Brown, E., Badenoch, M., Butterworth, G., Parsons, S., et al. (1998). Newborn infants prefer attractive faces. *Infant Behavior and Development, 21*, 345–354.

Slotkin, T. A. (1998). Fetal nicotine or cocaine exposure: Which one is worse? *Journal of Pharmacological and Experimental Therapies, 285*, 931–945.

Smithells, R. W., Nevin, N. C., Seller, M. J., Sheppard, S., Harris, R., Read, A. P., et al. (1983). Further experience of vitamin supplementation for prevention of neural tube defect recurrences. *Lancet, 1*, 1027–1031.

Sood, B., Delaney-Black, V., Covington, C., Nordstrom-Klee, B., Ager, J., Templin, T., et al. (2001). Prenatal alcohol exposure and childhood behavior at age 6 and 7 years: I. Dose-response effect. *Pediatrics, 108*, E34.

Sowell, E. R., Mattson, S. N., Thompson, P. M., Jernigan, T. L., Riley, E. P., & Toga, A. W. (2001). Mapping callosal morphology and cognitive correlates. *Neurology, 57*, 235–244.

Spinner, M. R., & Siegel, L. (1987). Nonorganic failure to thrive. *Journal of Preventative Psychiatry, 3,* 279–287.

Stein, J., Schettler, T., Wallinga, D., & Valenti, M. (2002). In harm's way: Toxic threats to child development. *Developmental and Behavioral Pediatrics, 23*(1S), S13–S22.

Stephens, R. P., Richardson, A. C., & Lewin, J. S. (1997). Outcome of extremely low-birth-weight infants (500–999 grams) over a 12-year period. *Pediatrics, 99,* 619–622.

Stoler, J. M., & Holmes, L. B. (2004). Recognition of facial features of fetal alcohol syndrome in the newborn. *American Journal of Medical Genetics, 127C,* 21–27.

Strang, R. (1969). *An introduction to child study.* New York: Macmillan.

Strauss, M. E., & Reynolds, K. S. (1983). Psychological characteristics and development of narcotic-addicted infants. *Drug and Alcohol Dependence, 12,* 381–393.

Streissguth, A., & Kanter, J. (Eds.). (1997). *The challenge of fetal alcohol syndrome: Overcoming secondary disabilities.* Seattle: University of Washington Press.

Sturm, L., & Drotar, D. (1989). Prediction of weight-for-height following intervention in three-year-old children with early histories of nonorganic failure to thrive. *Child Abuse and Neglect, 13,* 19.

Sullivan, B. A., Henderson, S. T., & Davis, J. M. (1998). Gestational diabetes. *Journal of the American Pharmacological Association, 38,* 372–373.

Susser, M. (1991). Maternal weight gain, infant birth weight, and diet: Causal sequences. *American Journal of Clinical Nutrition, 53,* 1384–1396.

Swaiman, K. F., Ashwal, S., & Ferrier, D. M. (Eds.). (2006). Pediatric neurology: Principles and practice (4th ed.). Philadelphia: Mosby Elsevier.

Swanson, M. W., Streissguth, A. P., Sampson, P. D., & Olsen, H. C. (1999). Prenatal cocaine and neuromotor outcome at four months: Effect of duration of exposure. *Journal of Developmental and Behavioral Pediatrics, 20,* 325–334.

Tanner, J. M. (1990). *Fetus into man: Physical growth from conception to maturity.* Cambridge, MA: Harvard University Press.

Taylor, H. G., Minich, N., Bangert, B., Filipek, P. A., & Hack, M. (2004). Long-term neuropsychological outcomes of very low birth weight: Associations with early risks for periventricular brain insults. *Journal of the International Neuropsychological Society, 10,* 987–1004.

Tinsley, V. S., & Waters, H. S. (1982). The development of verbal control over motor behavior: A replication and extension of Luria's findings. *Child Development, 53,* 746–753.

Tommiska, V., Heinonen, K., Lehtonen, L., Renlund, M., Saarela, T., Tammela, O., et al. (2007). No improvement in outcome of nationwide extremely low-birth-weight infant populations between 1996–1997 and 1999–2000. *Pediatrics, 119,* 29–36.

Toth, S. L., Rogosch, F. A., & Manly, J. T. (2006). The efficacy of toddler-parent psychotherapy to reorganize attachment in the young offspring of mothers with major depressive disorder: A randomized preventive trial. *Journal of Counseling and Clinical Psychology, 74,* 1006-1016.

Trask, C. L., & Kosofsky, B. E. (2000). Developmental considerations of neurotoxic exposure. *Neurology Clinics, 18,* 541–562.

Tu, M. T., Lupien, S. J., & Walker, C. (2006). Diurnal salivary cortisol levels in postpartum mothers as a function of infant feeding choice and parity. *Psychoneuroendocrinology, 31,* 812–824.

United Nation's Children's Fund (UNICEF). (2006). *The state of the world's children 2006.* New York: Author.

U.S. Department of Health and Human Services, Administration on Children, Youth, and Families. (2006). *Child maltreatment 2004.* Washington, DC: U.S. Government Printing Office.

U.S. General Accounting Office. (2006). *WIC participant and program characteristics report (PC2004).* Washington, DC: Author.

Van Assche, F. A., Holemans, K., & Aerts, L. (2001). Long-term consequences for offspring of diabetes during pregnancy. *British Medical Bulletin, 60,* 173–182.

Van den Bergh, B. R. H., & Marcoen, A. (2004). High antenatal maternal anxiety is related to ADHD symptoms, externalizing problems, and anxiety in 8- and 9-year-olds. *Child Development, 75,* 1085–1097.

Vincer, M. J., Allen, A. C., Joseph, K. S., Stinson, D. A., Scott, H., & Wood, E. (2006). Increasing prevalence of cerebral palsy among very preterm infants: A population-based study. *Pediatrics, 118,* e1621–e1626.

Vogler, G. P., & Kozlowski, L. T. (2002). Differential influence of maternal smoking on infant birth weight: Gene-environment interaction and targeted intervention. *The Journal of the American Medical Association, 287,* 241–242.

Vohr, B. R., Garcia-Coll, C. T., Labato, D., Ynis, K. A., O'Dea, C., & Oh, W. (1991). Neurodevelopmental and medical status of low-birthweight survivors of bronchopulmonary dysplasia at 10–12 years of age. *Developmental Medicine and Child Neurology, 33,* 690–697.

Wakschlag, L. S., Leventhal, B. L., Pine, D. S., Pickett, K. E., & Carter, A. S. (2006). Elucidating early mechanisms of developmental psychopathology: The case of prenatal smoking and disruptive behavior. *Child Development, 77,* 893–906.

Ward, M. J., Lee, S. S., & Lipper, E. G. (2000). Failure-to-thrive is associated with disorganized infant-mother attachment and unresolved maternal attachment. *Infant Mental Health Journal, 21,* 428–442.

Warner, T. D., Behnke, M., Eyler, F. D., Padgett, K., Leonard, C., Hou, W., et al. (2006). Diffusion tensor imaging of frontal white matter and executive functioning in cocaine-exposed children. *Pediatrics, 118,* 2014–2024.

Watson, J. (1924). *Behaviorism.* New York: Norton.

Weber, M. K., Floyd, R. L., Riley, E. P., & Snider, D. E. (2002). National task force on fetal alcohol syndrome and fetal alcohol effect: Defining the national agenda for fetal alcohol syndrome and other prenatal alcohol-related effects. *Morbidity and Mortality Weekly Report, 51,* 9–12.

Weissman, M. M., Warner, V., Wickramarante, P. J., & Kandel, D. B. (1999). Maternal smoking during pregnancy and psychopathology in offspring followed to adulthood. *Journal of the American Academy of Child and Adolescent Psychiatry, 38,* 892–899.

Wentzel, P., Gåreskog, M., & Eriksson, U. J. (2005). Folic acid supplementation diminishes diabetes- and glucose-induced dysmorphogenesis in rat embryos in vivo and in vitro. *Diabetes, 54,* 546–553.

Whitaker, H. A., Bub, D., & Leventer, S. (1981). Neurolinguistic aspects of language acquisition and dulingualism. Annals of the New York Academy of Sciences, 379, 59–74.

White, L. (2004). *Foundations of maternal and pediatric nursing* (2nd ed.). Clifton Park, NY: Thomson Delmar Learning.

Williams, J. H., & Ross, L. (2007). Consequences of prenatal toxin exposure for mental health in children and adolescents: A systematic review. *European Child and Adolescent Psychiatry, 16,* 243–253.

Williams, R. C., & Carta, J. J. (1997). Behavioral outcomes of young children with prenatal exposure to alcohol: Review and analysis of experimental literature. *Infants and Young Children, 8,* 16.

Wilson-Costello, D., Friedman, H., Minich, N., Siner, B., Taylor, G., & Schluchter, M. (2007). Improved neurodevelopmental outcomes for extremely low-birth-weight infants in 2000–2002. *Pediatrics, 119,* 37–45.

Winberg, J., & Porter, R. H. (1998). Olfaction and human behaviour: Clinical implications. *Acta Paediatrica, 87,* 6–10.

Winick, M. (1971). Cellular growth during early malnutrition. *Pediatrics, 47,* 969.

Wisborg, K., Kesmodel, U., Henriksen, T. B., Olsen, S. F., & Secher, N. J. (2001). Exposure to tobacco smoke in utero and the risk of stillbirth and death in the first year of life. *American Journal of Epidemiology, 154,* 322–327.

Wright, A., & Walker, J. (2001). Drugs of abuse in pregnancy. *Best Practice & Research Clinical Obstetrics and Gynaecology, 15,* 987–998.

Wright, D., Sathe, N., & Spagnola, K. (2007). *State estimates of substance abuse from the 2004–2005 National Surveys on Drug Use and Health.* Washington, DC: U.S. Government Office of Applied Studies.

Wu, G., Bazer, F. W., Cudd, T. A., Meininger, C. J., & Spencer, T. E. (2004). Maternal nutrition and fetal development. *Journal of Nutrition, 134,* 2169–2172.

Wu, Y. W., Croen, L. A., Shah, S. J., Newman, T. B., & Najjar, D. V. (2006). Cerebral palsy in a term population: Risk factors and neuroimaging findings. *Pediatrics, 118,* 690–697.

Wyrobek, A. J., Eskenazi, B., Young, S., Arnheim, N., Tiemann-Boege, I., Jabs, E. W., et al. (2006). Advancing age has differential effects on DNA damage, chromatin integrity, gene mutations, and aneuploidies in sperm. *Proceedings of the National Academy of Sciences, 103,* 9601–9606.

Yang, Q., Wen, S. W., Leader, A., Chen, X. K., Lipson, J., & Walker, M. (2007). Paternal age and birth defects: How strong is the association? *Human Reproduction, 22,* 696–701.

Yazigi, R. A., Odem, R. R., & Polakoski, K. L. (1991). Demonstration of specific binding of cocaine to human spermatozoa. *Journal of the American Medical Association, 266,* 1956–1959.

Yehuda, R., Halligan, S. L., & Grossman, R. (2001). Childhood trauma and risk for PTSD: Relationship to intergenerational effects of trauma, parental PTSD, and cortisol excretion. *Development and Psychopathology, 13,* 733–753.

Zeisel, S. H. (2000). Choline: Needed for normal development of memory. *Journal of the American College of Nutrition, 19* (Supplement 5), 528S–531S.

Zeisel, S. H. (2006). The fetal origins of memory: The role of dietary choline in optimal brain development. *The Journal of Pediatrics, 149* (Supplement 1), S131–S136.

Zimmermann, M., & Delange, F. (2004). Iodine supplementation of pregnant women in Europe: A review and recommendations. *European Journal of Clinical Nutrition, 58,* 979–984.

Zolotor, A. J., & Runyan, D. K. (2006). Social capital, family violence, and neglect. *Pediatrics, 117,* e1124–e1131.

PART

II

Developmental Domains

Gross Motor Development

Carole W. Dennis and Kathleen A. Schlough

Chapter Outline

- Theoretical Models of Motor Development
- Stages of Gross Motor Development
- Factors Affecting Gross Motor Development
- Gross Motor Development in Young Children with Special Needs
- Specific Strategies for Assessment of Gross Motor Functioning
- Instructional Methods and Strategies for Intervention
- Assistive Technology for Gross Motor Intervention

Luca

Luca is a 28-month-old child who began receiving early intervention services when he was 12 months old. He was born full term and healthy, and seemed to be developing normally except for problems with nursing and reflux (spitting up food and drink that have been swallowed),which persists. His parents remember that he seemed to enjoy interactions with them, although his hands were fisted and he seemed to be very sensitive to touch. By 4 months of age, he was vocalizing vowel sounds and was visually attentive to people and objects. However, all vocalization ceased by 6 months of age and his parents noted that he wasn't reaching for objects and was uninterested in toys.

At about 9 months of age, he began to exhibit repetitive behaviors, including scratching and flapping his fingers. He became fascinated with water splashing and the movement of shadows. At about the same time, it became clear to his parents that he was not reaching important developmental milestones: He could not yet roll over or sit without assistance. At 12 months of age, he began to sit without support and he started to "drag" his body across the floor at 17 months. When his was 21 months old, he began to crawl on his hands and knees. He finally took his first independent steps at 26 months.

Luca carries a diagnosis of Pervasive Developmental Disorder—Not Otherwise Specified, which is in the autism spectrum. He currently receives intensive early intervention services within his home, including physical therapy (3 hours per week), occupational therapy (2.5 hours per week), speech therapy (4 hours per week), and special instruction (8 hours per week). He seems to learn best when instructions are simple and clear and when toys and food are used as reinforcers. The structure of an applied behavior analysis (ABA) program works well for him. Concerns expressed by his family now include his difficulty becoming satiated when he eats, which leads to temper tantrums when his parents determine he has had enough, and his increasing resistance to demands made of him. In addition, he becomes anxious with unfamiliar people and situations, making visits with friends very challenging.

Luca began to vocalize again at 20 months and now uses some word approximations ("ba" for ball, "ma" for more) and several functional signs (e.g., "eat," "all done," "my turn"). Although Luca is able to walk independently now, safety issues are a concern. His balance is poor and he does not visually attend to where he is walking. He falls frequently and doesn't consistently put his arms out to catch himself. He has a padded helmet, which was purchased to allow him to move without adult guidance, but he does not enjoy wearing it. Now that he has more mobility, it has become clear that he has significant motor planning deficits. He still cannot climb onto the couch or squat to pick up a toy. To learn new motor tasks requires consistent verbal prompts and much repetition. His team members have agreed to use the same prompting sequence for specific skills, such as learning to sit in a chair. If skills are not practiced, he forgets how to do them and he does not generalize skills learned in one activity to other similar activities. His physical therapist is helping Luca to develop muscle control in motor skills, such as learning to get down to the floor without falling and learning how to fall safely. In addition, his efforts to limit his movement to reduce the need for control have resulted in some limitations in joint range of motion, so stretching is part of his therapy.

His motor deficits have been significant for Luca's family, as well, as he has needed to be carried much longer than most children and still isn't safely independent in personal mobility, such as walking and going up and down stairs. His inability to climb, jump, and run is a barrier to his engaging in play with children his age.

Gross motor development represents the child's growing proficiency in controlling posture and movement using the large muscles of the body to produce movements to meet the demands of the physical and social environment. Its significance in the developing child is multifaceted. Through the development of motor skills, the child gains feelings of self-control, competence, and self-esteem. The ability to control one's own body in the immediate physical environment is necessary for the development of feelings of mastery and motivation. Mobility is important for participation in educational, social, and community life. The International Classification of Functioning, Disability and Health (ICF) model proposed by the World Health Organization (WHO, 2001) defines **participation** as the way people live with their health conditions and how these conditions can be improved to achieve a productive, fulfilling life. The child's ability to effectively move and explore his environment is essential for the fulfillment of his life's roles.

In addition, gross motor skills support the development of abilities in the areas of fine motor development, cognition, communication, adaptive skills, and social and emotional competence in the typically developing child. A wonderful example of these phenomena can be found in a body of research surrounding the emergence of creeping on hands and knees (Campos et al., 2000). The experiences provided by this early form of independent mobility herald the development of a host of skills in divergent areas, including the ability to follow a caregiver's gaze or point, to search manually for hidden objects, to be wary of heights, to perceive distance, and to attend to distant objects. This independent mobility leads to changes in mothers' behaviors, which in turn trigger the development of other behaviors by the infant.

Most assessments of cognition, language development, self-care skills, and socialization in the very young child require the demonstration of some type of motor behavior. For example, the behaviors an infant displays that indicate attachment to and separation from the primary caregiver are considered to be important milestones of social and emotional development. These behaviors all require some type of motor output (turning toward, gazing at, and smiling at the caregiver; moving away from the caregiver; and returning to the caregiver for comfort).

Those who work with young children who experience difficulties in gross motor control face several challenges. To help improve such children's motor development, it is important for the early interventionist to understand where delays exist and to hypothesize why they have occurred so that an appropriate intervention plan can be developed. Because motor deficits affect other aspects of development, it is not enough merely to attempt to improve motor skills; it is equally important to consider the impact of adaptation and compensation in relation to task mastery. The use of compensatory techniques for impaired function, adaptation of the environment, provision of specific adaptive equipment, and the modification of activities will have far-reaching implications for the overall development of the child.

:: THEORETICAL MODELS OF MOTOR DEVELOPMENT

Neuromaturational Model

For much of the twentieth century, researchers viewed motor development as the product of maturation of the brain (Adolph, 2002; Thelen, 2000). The early **reflex model,** advocated by Gesell and Amatruda (1947) and Sherrington (1947), proposed that the infant is born with a repertoire of innate movement patterns that serve as the foundation for later movement which progress from primitive, reflexive control to voluntary control of movement (Piper & Darrah, 1995). The **hierarchical model** proposed by Hughlings Jackson (Foerster, 1977) and Rudolf Magnus (Magnus, 1926) expanded upon the reflex model by focusing on the role of the cerebral cortex, the highest level of the central nervous system, on the development of volitional control of movement (Mathiowetz & Haugen, 1994).

The early infant movement patterns observed by these researchers were known as **primitive reflexes.** These are automatic, stereotypical movement patterns that are triggered by sensory stimuli such as touch, stretching of specific muscle groups, the position of the head in relation to the body, and the position of the head in relation to gravity. Primitive reflexes are thought to have a discrete function in development. For example, when an infant's cheek is touched, he turns his head toward the touch in a rooting response, which is necessary for suckling and, consequently, survival among mammals. The **asymmetrical tonic neck reflex** (ATNR) occurs when the infant turns his head to one side. The "face" side arm (and sometimes leg) is in **extension,** and the "skull" side arm (and often the leg) is in **flexion,** in a pose similar to that of a fencer. It has been hypothesized that this reflex supports the coordination of vision and movement necessary for controlled reach and grasp. The stepping response is another reflex that all parents are familiar with. In this reflex, infants make stepping movements when supported in an upright position with their feet touching a surface. Researchers and motor specialists have noted that the primitive reflexes generally disappear by the time an infant is 4 to 6 months of age. Neuromaturational theory suggests that this disappearance is due to maturation of the cortex and the development of volitional movement (Thelen, 2000). Although some vestiges of the primitive reflexes remain throughout life, they are no longer **obligatory** (the response to the stimuli is not always present).

As the developing infant matures, **postural reactions** develop that help to keep the child upright with respect to gravity (righting reactions) and protect him in case of a loss of balance (protective extension and **equilibrium reactions**). These reactions

---

Primitive reflexes are involuntary, automatic, and stereotypical responses to specific sensory stimuli that are typically seen only in infancy.

The asymmetrical tonic neck reflex is a normal response in newborns to turning of the head, in which the arm and leg on the side of the body to which the head is turned extend while the limbs on the opposite side flex. Persistence beyond 3 months of age is considered atypical.

Extension refers to an increased angle at a joint or the straightening of the joint.

Flexion refers to a decreased angle at a joint or bending of the joint.

Obligatory primitive reflexes are automatic, stereotypic movements that always occur (without volitional control) in response to specific sensory stimuli.

Equilibrium reactions are balance/counterbalance responses characterized by muscle tension and movement in response to body movement.

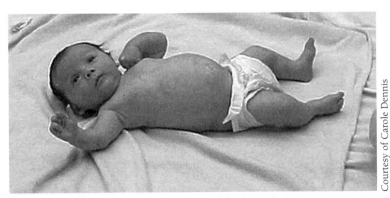

Courtesy of Carole Dennis

The asymmetrical tonic neck reflex (Noah, at corrected age 3½ weeks). Note the extension of the arm on the side of the body where his face is turned, and the flexion of the arm on the skull side of his head.

Protective extension is an automatic reaction that occurs when people reach out to protect themselves from a fall.

The proprioceptive system is a sensory system that provides information through joint and muscle receptors about the body's position in space (i.e., proprioception).

begin to develop during the sixth month of life (just as the primitive reflexes are disappearing) and continue throughout life. Infants first display these reactions as they develop the ability to sit independently. For example, an infant skilled in sitting will be able to reach in all directions toward things of interest because they can compensate for changes in their center of gravity through head and trunk movements. In addition, when they reach too far for these **righting reactions** to be effective, they can break or prevent a fall by reaching out with their arms in a **protective extension** reaction. A similar reaction occurs in an upright position, when a child will take a step or extend a leg in the unstable direction. All of these reactions may happen simultaneously or only one may predominate, depending on the need. Similar reactions involving the whole body are seen in standing and walking.

Neuromaturational theory suggests that early reflexes allow the infant to experience movement without conscious control, thus providing the possibility for use of the movement volitionally in the future. For example, when an infant turns his head to the left side, the ATNR is triggered, which promotes extension of his left arm out to the side of his body. If this movement results in contact with an environmental object, other sensory mechanisms are triggered. The body's **proprioceptive system** registers the position of the limb, the tactile system registers the feel of the object, and the visual system records the optical image of the hand touching the object. As this sequence of movement and feedback is repeated, the infant gradually begins to associate the movement pattern with the sensory rewards just noted and eventually learns to control this pattern volitionally with involvement of higher cortical centers of the central nervous system (Piper & Darrah, 1995). When the infant repeats a volitional movement pattern repeatedly, myelination of the neural connections that imprint the movement pattern occurs, resulting in fast, automatic movement that requires no conscious thought for its execution. **Myelination** is the developmental process whereby nerve fibers are insulated with a fatty sheath (myelin), allowing rapid, efficient neural transmission.

The neuromaturational model embraces several important assumptions: that motor development progresses in a head-to-foot (cephalocaudal) direction, that movement control occurs in a proximal-to-distal sequence (from the center of the body toward the extremities), and that movement occurs in a predictable, sequential pattern among typically developing children (Piper & Darrah, 1995). Although these assumptions still guide much of current therapeutic practice, some important exceptions to the model have been demonstrated. The early domination of reflexive-based movement has been questioned by Touwen (1978), who argued that even neonates have variability of movement, and by Thoman (1987), who demonstrated very early control of body movement in premature neonates. Studies by Thelen and her colleagues (Thelen, 2000) have disputed the explanation offered in the reflex/hierarchical model for the disappearance of primitive reflexes. They found that infant stepping ability is related to leg mass and muscle strength. When the legs of very young infants were weighted to approximate the mass of slightly older infants, the stepping response disappeared. For infants in whom the stepping response had disappeared (explained by this theory as a function of neural maturation), the ability reappeared when these infants were placed on their backs or supported in water. Furthermore, infants who experienced consistent training on a treadmill maintained the stepping reaction longer than expected (Adolph, 2002). These experiments indicated that the disappearance of the reaction is due to changes in leg mass and muscle strength, rather than maturation. In addition, studies indicating that differential acquisition of motor skills may occur because of the type of movement valued in a specific cultural group have caused developmental specialists to question the concept of proximal to distal development of control (Super, 1976). Fetters, Fernandes, and Cermak (1988) have demonstrated through kinematic recordings that infants develop proximal (shoulder girdle) and distal (hand) skills simultaneously when learning to reach for a block. These studies and others led researchers to question basic assumptions of the neuromaturational models and to develop an alternative theory for explaining motor development.

Dynamic Systems Model

Dynamic systems theory acknowledges that maturation of the central nervous system and, hence, neuromaturational theories are insufficient to explain motor development (Adolph, 2002; Thelen, 2000). Motor development is part of an open system that is responsive to factors from within and outside of the body, including the biomechanical properties of the body, properties of the physical environment, perception, motivation, and experience. The dynamic systems model takes into consideration the interaction of constraints of the environment, demands of the task, and self-organization of the body. With a change in any of the three conditions, the movement itself may change (Clark, 1995). For example, a toddler learning to walk may appear to lose his walking ability if the surface (environment) becomes very uneven. If the child wishes to move faster (changing demands of the task), the walking skill may not be sufficient and the child may change from a walk to a toddler's run or revert to a previously learned but faster skill such as **creeping** (on hands and knees). As the child grows and body morphology (body shape and

Creeping is the forward movement of an infant characterized by reciprocal arm and leg movements in the hands-and-knees position. In some texts and in everyday conversation, this movement may also be referred to as "crawling." True crawling is an earlier developmental stage in the prone position where the body is moved forward by pulling with the arms and pushing with the legs.

organization) changes, his center of gravity gradually lowers, helping to make him more stable and allowing for more demanding gross motor skills. Increases in muscle strength and force production, changes in height and weight, improved reactions, and a more efficient cardiorespiratory system also allow for the emergence of higher order skills.

Dynamic systems theory proposes that motor skills are learned through active movement exploration and through the interaction of all systems available to the child within his own body and within the environment. The information from these systems is organized by the child to produce active movement solutions to meet the demands of the environment and the task. Therefore, assessment is directed toward identifying factors within the child, the task, or the environment that may be limiting participation. Treatment is directed toward the accomplishment of functional tasks, with an equal emphasis on problems within the child, the task, and the environment (Ketelaar, Vermeer, Hart, van Petemgen-van Beek, & Helders, 2001; Mahoney, 2004). The importance of involving the parents in all aspects of treatment planning and implementation is stressed. Some clinicians and researchers have proposed that what is normal movement for a typically developing child may not be normal at all for a child whose body structure, sensory, perceptual, and cognitive abilities are very different from those of the typical child. Additionally, current thinking about the importance of movement for informing perception and cognition has led some interventionists to facilitate active exploration with the environment in whatever ways are possible for children with disabilities, even if movement patterns that the child develops are viewed as atypical (Darrah, Law, & Pollock, 2001).

Models of Intervention

Motor specialists who work in early intervention use theory to guide assessment and interventions for children with difficulties in the development of motor skills. The neuromaturational model led to assessments that attempted to place a child at a specific point in the developmental hierarchy. For children who demonstrated delays in the acquisition of specific skills, the neuromaturational model suggested interventions that attempted to replicate normal movement patterns while limiting atypical movement patterns, with the emphasis on correcting problems within the child. Neurodevelopmental treatment (NDT) is one treatment approach that developed within the neuromaturational model. Karel and Berta Bobath developed this approach in the middle of the twentieth century (Howle, 2004). This approach assumes that in children who have suffered specific brain injuries (as occurs in cerebral palsy, tumors of the central nervous system, and traumatic brain injury), the higher systems that are necessary for the development of volitional skilled movement are unable to function due to these brain injuries. The higher centers are unable to override early, primitive reflexes, limiting volitional control and resulting in limited, stereotypical movement. The NDT therapist determines the postural stability, sensory processing, and movement patterns needed to meet movement needs and then uses guided or facilitated movement to promote active movement in the child.

Sensory integration (SI) is another treatment approach from the neuromaturational model. A. Jean Ayres designed the model for children with learning disabilities. Originally, SI assumed that higher functions, such as perception and learning, were dependent on organization of sensory input by lower levels of the central nervous system. Although based on a hierarchical organization of the nervous system, SI views perceptual and motor performance as the result of an interactive system and currently reflects dynamic systems theory. Treatment involves modifying the sensory environment to the sensory demands of the task and using repetition and feedback in a motor learning approach (Fisher, Murray, & Bundy, 2002). Today, SI is used with children with developmental coordination disorder, autism, and similar developmental problems.

Although research on the effectiveness of motor intervention in young children is limited, outcomes have not been promising for traditional NDT or SI. However, these treatment approaches have continued to evolve as a result of newer research findings and both have incorporated dynamic systems theory into current treatment approaches.

:: STAGES OF GROSS MOTOR DEVELOPMENT

In the typically developing infant, motor development follows a predictable course, with expected variations based on individual and environmental differences. Typical development does not occur in every child at the same pace, but rather occurs over a range of time as different infants discover solutions to gain control over their bodies. As Thelen noted, "low energy children with large limbs may have to learn different adaptive strategies than small, wiry, highly energetic ones" (2000, p. 392). Typical motor development in the first several years of life is described here.

Postural control refers to the maintenance of equilibrium and a stable body; changes in postural control are necessary for gross motor development in the infant and young child.

Motor Development: Infancy

Typically developing infants achieve **postural control** along the continuum of control in extension, control in flexion, **coactivation** of both flexion and extension together, which is necessary for postural stability, and **rotation** (the turning of one body part in relation to another). This pattern of development repeats itself at each stage of the developmental sequence (Bly, 1983). The average age of acquisition of infant gross motor **milestones** is provided in Table 3.1.

Rotation is one of the four basic movements allowed by the skeleton; rotation is movement that occurs around the central axis of the body or a limb.

Development of Control in Extension　Typical full-term infants are born in a position of physiological flexion, reflecting the infant's cramped posture in the mother's womb. The infant experiences increasing passive extension (movement away from the body) through the effects of gravity in the supine (face up) position and active extension in the prone (face down) position. Many primitive reflexes (including the Moro reflex and the asymmetrical tonic neck reflex) also support the development of movement and strength in extension.

Developmental milestones are the average ages at which most typically developing children achieve targeted motor skills.

TABLE 3.1	Gross motor skills and age of acquisition in infants.	
Position	**Age of Acquisition***	**Gross Motor Skill**
Prone	Less than 1 month	lifts head momentarily in prone, asymmetrically
	2½ months	bears weight on forearms (elbows ahead of shoulders)
	4½ months	bears weight on hands, arms extended
	6 months	rolls from prone to supine, without rotation
	7½ months	crawls on tummy
	8½ months	creeps on hands and knees, reciprocally
Supine	1 month	balances head in midline in supine
	2½ months	brings hands to midline in supine
	4½ months	brings feet to hands
	5½ months	rolls from supine to prone, without rotation
	6½ months	rolls from supine to prone, with rotation
Sitting	5 months	sits alone briefly
	6½ months	sits alone steadily
	8 months	moves from sitting to four-point (hands and knees)
Standing	8 months	pulls to stand at furniture
	8½ months	pulls to stand through half-kneel position
	10½ months	stands alone momentarily
Walking	9 months	cruises around furniture, without rotation
	11 months	walks independently, five steps
	11½ months	rises from supine to four-point to standing
	12 months	maintains squatting position

*Note: The age of acquisition reflects the age by which 50% of children sampled attained this skill. Most skills were attained by 90% of the infants studied within 2 to 3 months after the mean age.

Source: Data from *Motor Assessment of the Developing Infant* by M. C. Piper & J. Darrah, 1995, Philadelphia: W. B. Saunders. Copyright 1995 by W. B. Saunders.

In prone, the infant lifts his head against gravity to allow breathing and visual exploration. As extensor development continues, the infant raises his upper body from the floor by shifting his weight back toward his pelvis, allowing him to move his arms forward to support himself on his elbows and reach for objects. The infant then learns to push himself up onto extended arms, supporting his weight on his hands, and to pivot in prone to reach for toys that are out of reach.

Development of Control in Flexion   Infants begin to develop contol over flexor muscles in the supine position. Working against gravity, the infant flexes head and neck, and raises his arms to bring hands together at midline, allowing hand-to-mouth play. Continuing development of strength in flexion allows the infant to raise his legs against gravity to kick, and eventually to lift his feet to his mouth in play. By about 6 months of age, the infant is able to roll from the stomach to the back. Shortly thereafter, rolling develops from the back to the stomach. In early rolling, the body moves as a whole; however, as development progresses, segmental rotation occurs at the head, neck, trunk, and pelvis. The improvement in control and increase in muscle strength that infants learn through play on the

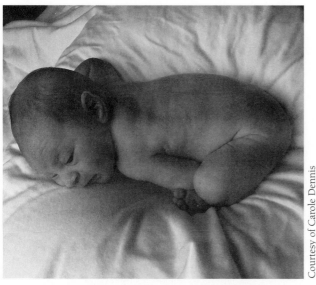

Remy Mae at just four days of age, placed in prone and in supine. The force of gravity results in greater flexion when she is placed on her tummy than when she is on her back.

Courtesy of Carole Dennis

Courtesy of Carole Dennis

floor prepares them for more upright movment against gravity, including sitting independently and creeping on hands and knees.

Back to Sleep, Stomach to Play   Practices relating to prone positioning of very young children have received a great deal of attention in recent years. To decrease the possibility of **sudden infant death syndrome,** the National Institute of Child Health and Human Development and the American Academy of Pediatrics advise caregivers to place the infant in the supine position for sleeping (American Academy of Pediatrics Task Force on Infant Sleep Positions and SIDS, 2002). Although this practice has significantly reduced the occurrence of SIDS (by 40% by 2000; AAP, 2002), studies have found that infants who sleep on their backs attain early motor milestones significantly later than prone sleepers (Davis, Moon, Sacks, & Otolini, 1998; Dewey, Fleming, Golding, & ALSPAC Study Team, 1998). In recognition of the importance of spending time in prone for motor development, in 2000 the AAP revised their guidelines to encourage parents to place infants in prone for play during awake times. Recent studies among 6- and 18 month-old supine sleepers indicate that infants who spend time in prone play have more advanced gross motor development than those with little or no waking experience in prone (Jennings, Sarbaugh, & Payne, 2005; Monson, Deitz, & Kartin, 2003; Salls, Sherman, & Gatty, 2002). The long-term importance of prone play for motor development is not yet clear; at least one study reported that significant

Sudden infant death syndrome (SIDS) is the unexpected and sudden death of an infant during sleep, where no evidence of disease is found by physical examination or autopsy.

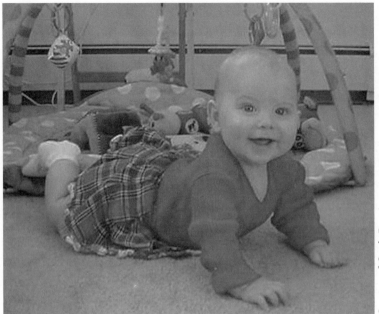

Nena supporting herself on extended arms in the prone position (6 months). Nena is demonstrating good cocontraction in her ability to lift her chest off the floor, and hold her head upright while turning to look at the photographer.

Remy Mae in supine (6 months), demonstrating foot-to-foot play while holding a toy above her body.

differences in locomotor skills persisted beyond infancy (Monson et al., 2003). An additional concern with respect to back sleeping is a marked increase in positional skull flattening (deformational plagiocephaly) since the "back to sleep" campaign (Graham, Gomez, Halberg, Earl, Kreutzman, et al., 2005), with associated torticollis (shortening of muscles in the neck) (de Chalain & Park, 2005; Oregon Health and Science University, Department of Neurosurgery, 2007).

Balanced Control of Extension and Flexion in Sitting   When an infant is first placed in a sitting position, the infant leans forward, working to keep the body upright primarily by extension of the muscles of the back. However, it isn't until he is able to coactivate extension and flexion in the trunk, hips, and legs that he can maintain an upright, balanced position. Usually by the time the infant is between 6 to 9 months of age, he gains control in rotation in sitting and he can turn his head and trunk to reach for toys in the environment. The development of control in sitting allows the child to use both hands to reach for and manipulate objects within the immediate environment.

Development in Four-point   It is from the sitting position that infants first move to the four-point position on hands and knees, usually around 8 months of age. The child may reach toward an object just beyond his reach, fall forward, and catch himself with protective extension of the arms, leaving the infant in the four-point position. From the hands and knees position, the child develops control in flexion and extension of the whole body, so he can move into a sitting position by pushing back with the arms, rock on his hands and knees, and creep (move forward on hands and knees).

The development of creeping allows the child to explore the greater environment and marks a significant event in setting the stage for future cognitive, communicative, and social and emotional development (Campos et al., 2000). However, these new abilities create safety issues and caregivers must safeguard their homes for the exploring child. Some infants may not learn to creep. For example, infants who have experienced abdominal or thoracic surgery may find play in the prone position uncomfortable. They may

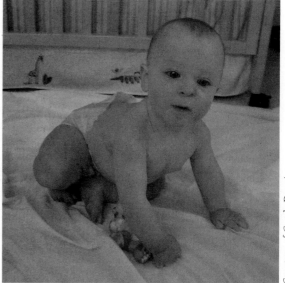

Remy Mae (8 months) moving from sitting to four-point, in preparation for creeping.

Courtesy of Carole Dennis

have weak abdominal control, and often avoid the hands and knees position. They may move about by scooting in a sitting position, and may learn to walk before they are able to move to and from the floor as typical toddlers do.

Most infants first learn to rise to standing from a four-point position, using furniture for support, pulling upward with the arms while extending both legs. Later, the infant learns to bring one leg forward and push up, allowing the other leg to follow. This builds differentiated control in each leg in preparation for cruising or sidestepping along furniture and, finally, walking.

Before infants begin to walk independently, well-meaning parents may encourage the use of a babywalker. However, studies have shown that infants who use babywalkers achieve independent walking at a later age (Burrows & Griffiths, 2002; Garrett, McElroy, & Staines, 2002). Additionally, the use of babywalkers has been associated with serious injuries, such as skull fractures, contusions, lacerations, electrocutions, and burns. These injuries have decreased markedly because of improved safety features (Shields & Smith, 2006), but they are still occurring. Until the United States government bans the sale of babywalkers (as has happened in Canada), parents must be educated about the significant risks of these devices and provided with information about alternatives, such as stationary activity centers.

> The term *degrees of freedom* refers to the possibilities for movement provided by the many muscles, bones, joints, and nerves that contribute to movement. These must be controlled when an individual learns to perform a motor task.

Standing and Walking   During the eleventh and twelfth months, many babies learn to stand independently. When an infant first attains a standing position, strong extension occurs throughout the body to remain upright. A typical child learning to walk uses a **high guard** position, where the arms are held up and away from the body with the elbows bent (see the photo of Luca at the beginning of this chapter). This helps reinforce extension throughout the body and maintain balance. Early walking movements are stiff, with the child swaying the body slightly from side to side ("toddling") to gain initial forward mobility. From a dynamic systems point of view, this stiff body posture is used in an effort to control the child's many **degrees of freedom;** that is, the child must learn to control all the muscles, joints, nerve pathways, and so on to accomplish the task. As he becomes more experienced in standing, he can then "let go" of some of these degrees of freedom and the movement appears smoother, more coordinated, and effortless.

Each time a child (or adult) learns a new motor task, the movement will appear stiff and uncoordinated. With practice, movements become smoother. As the child matures, he will walk with the counter rotation and arm swing that characterize mature walking. With full rotation, as one leg swings forward, the arm on the same side swings backward. During this period, protective extension develops fully so that the child can protect himself when balance is lost by stepping in the direction of fall.

Motor Development: Toddlers and Preschoolers

Once children have mastered the basic movement skills, repetition allows smoother performance of specific motor patterns and combinations of these motor patterns. Preschool children enjoy practicing their skills, challenging themselves and mastering the environment. In the second year of life, children typically explore their environment fully, climbing into containers and onto household furniture. They learn to control their bodies in many different positions, including squatting. Children begin to use these skills in simple social games, such as Duck, Duck, Goose and Tag, in which movements must conform to changing speed and position of the other children playing. Children master more difficult motor skills, such as climbing stairs, jumping, hopping, running, galloping, and skipping. Each of these skills has a predictable pattern of development as well. Table 3.2 provides a list of toddler and preschool gross motor skills and the age at which children typically attain them.

TABLE **3.2**	Gross motor skills and expected ages of acquisition in the toddler and preschooler.

Age of Acquisition	Gross Motor Skill
15 months	creeps up steps
18–23 months	creeps down steps backwards
24–29 months	jumps off floor 2 inches using both feet
2–2½ years	climbs stairs and descends stairs with both feet on each step
2–2½ years	descends stairs with both feet on each step
2½–3 years	climbs stairs, alternating feet
3–3½ years	descends stairs, alternating feet
3–5 years	hops on one foot
4–5 years	gallops
5–6 years	skips, alternating feet
6–7 years	walks four steps on 4-inch balance beam

Sources: Bayley Scales of Infant Development: Second Edition. Copyright © 1993 by The Psychological Corporation. Adapted and reproduced by permission. All rights reserved. "Bayley Scales of Infant Development" is a registered trademark of The Psychological Corporation. Adapted from the *Peabody Developmental Motor Scales,* by M. R. Folio and R. R. Fewell. Copyright by Pro-Ed, Austin, TX.

Nena, "practicing" climbing out of a laundry basket (16 months). This is a complex task, requiring stabilizing with the arms, while supporting herself on one leg while raising the other over the edge of the basket.

Courtesy of Carole Dennis

Nena giving her ducks a bath, demonstrating skill and stability in squatting (21 months).

Courtesy of Carole Dennis

Praxis refers to how a person plans, sequences, and executes a movement or skill.

As movements are sequenced for learning tasks that are more complex, adequate **motor planning,** or **praxis,** is required. Praxis demands adequate sensory capabilities to provide feedback about the correctness of a given motor act and to allow adaptation to environmental demands during execution of the motor plan. Children with poor motor praxis often do not exhibit any motor difficulty until the preschool years, when it becomes apparent that they are unable to learn skills as quickly as their peers. The child may appear clumsy, confused, or uncooperative when, in fact, he cannot process and react to all the information required for the task.

During the preschool years, many gross motor skills are based on core abilities. The ability to stand on one foot while maintaining one's balance is needed to go up and down stairs without holding on, step over obstacles, hop, kick a ball, climb on playground equipment, ride a tricycle, and walk a balance beam. The ability to control total body extension and flexion is needed for age-appropriate skills in activities, such as going down a slide and swinging on a swing.

Courtesy of Carole Dennis

Emilio (3 years 9 months) is just about to enter the "flight" phase of running, when both feet are off the ground. Note the reciprocal pumping of his arms and the rotation through his trunk. Children generally master running between the ages of 2 and 4, gaining control over stopping and starting at age 5 or 6.

:: FACTORS AFFECTING GROSS MOTOR DEVELOPMENT

The failure of a child to attain developmental milestones at the expected age may be cause for concern for parents and professionals. Often, the observant parent, family member, or friend may notice that the child's movements don't look quite right or that he may seem floppy or stiff. In addition to being aware of atypical posture, observers may note that transitions from one position to another are not possible or are accomplished in unusual ways. Figure 3.1 lists movement patterns that may signal motor delays and indicate the need for additional assessment of motor development. Variations in physical and social environments, musculoskeletal development, postural tone, and sensory processing may alter development of motor skills.

Sociocultural Factors   Variability in normal development has been documented in many studies of groups within and outside of the United States. While there is still considerable debate regarding the relative contributions of biological and environmental factors in influencing developmental outcomes, it is clear that sociocultural factors can influence motor skill acquisition in a positive or negative direction. For example, studies of infants facing biological challenges (such as low birth weight and perinatal problems) indicate

PRONE
- newborn assumes position of relative extension, rather than flexion of utero
- infant is unable to lift head off floor by 3 months
- infant maintains a uniform posture; no variety of position or movement in prone
- infant is unable to balance head in a midline position by 5 months
- arms remain pulled into flexion, close to infant's body by 4 months
- infant is unable to assume a position of support on both forearms by 5 months, or on hands by 7 months

SUPINE
- infant is unable to balance head at midline by 4 months
- infant remains in extended position, unable to lift legs from floor, past 6 months
- infant maintains a consistently asymmetrical posture

CREEPING
- infant is unable to crawl on tummy by 8 months
- infant is unable to creep, or utilizes one of the following patterns:
  - commando crawling: pulling self forward on elbows, legs extended
  - bunny creeping: arms and legs move together bilaterally, rather than reciprocally
  - creeps with exaggerated turning of head as arm on same side extends

SITTING
- sits with rounded head, neck, and back past 6 months
- infant is unable to sit independently for extended periods by 9 months
- infant is able to sit, but falls when he or she turns head or reaches for objects past 10 months
- infant is able to sit, but posture is characterized by one of the following:
  - narrow base of support (posterior pelvic tilt, trunk rounded, and head hyperextended)
  - wide base of support (legs spread wide, or habitual sitting in a W pattern)
- infant is unable to prevent falls by extending arms to front, side, and back by 12 months
- infant is unable to move into and out of sitting from other positions by 12 months or uses unusual movement patterns to change position

STANDING AND WALKING
- child is unable to stand independently by 14 months or walk independently by 15 months
- child bears weight on toes, rather than flat on feet
- child stands with significant knee hyperextension or swayback (lordosis) beyond 15 months

TODDLER AND PRESCHOOL SKILLS
- child has met most early milestones, but walking is stiff, unsteady, or met with many falls
- child has difficulty with activities requiring single-limb stability, such as climbing stairs, standing on one foot, and hopping
- child has mastered most basic skills, but has more difficulty than peers when learning new, sequenced motor tasks
- child appears clumsy when compared with typically developing peers

Source: Used with permission of Carole Dennis.

that infants from underprivileged backgrounds tend to experience more developmental problems than infants from advantaged backgrounds. In a study of premature infants from families of low socioeconomic status, Zahr (1999) found that social factors were more highly correlated with motor outcome than biological risk factors. In particular, motor development of African American infants was correlated with maternal education level and days of hospitalization, while for Latino infants, motor development was correlated with qualities of the home environment. A study of 245 Brazilian infants at 12 months of age that examined factors that influenced development found that sociocultural variables (the greatest being poverty) accounted for 19% of the variance in motor development, while biological factors accounted for only 5% of the variance (Lima et al., 2004).

Several studies have identified variations in motor development as a result of ethnicity. McClain, Provost, and Crowe (2000) found that the motor development of a third of their sample of 2-year-old children of Native American background scored at least one standard deviation below the mean. The authors suggested that some biological differences may have played a part in this disparity, but also noted that the children in general were very shy and probably did not give their best performance. A study of children of African American background from birth through 2 years of age achieved gross motor milestones at a significantly earlier age than established norms on developmental assessments (Cohen et al., 1999). An international study reported that black African, black Caribbean, and Indian infants demonstrated significantly less delay in gross motor skills than white infants and that those differences could not be explained by other variables, suggesting an ethnic advantage (Kelly, Sacker, Schoon, & Nazroo, 2006). In a large, multicenter study that examined attainment of early gross motor milestones among children in Ghana, Norway, the United States, Oman, and India, the authors found that development varied significantly based on the country of residence (WHO Multicentre Growth Reference Study, 2006). The greatest differences were seen between infants tested in Ghana (where milestones were met earlier than in other nations) and Norway (where milestones were met later than in the other countries). The authors attributed these differences primarily to child-rearing factors. The Ghanians were noted on field reports to use child-rearing practices that supported the development of motor independence (such as using many different materials to prop infants in sitting), while the Norwegians were reported to wait for the child to spontaneously develop motor skills. Another study examined the functional independence of young Chinese children compared to their counterparts from the United States. Chinese children performed significantly better than U.S. children in self-care and mobility skills (Wong, Wong, Chan, & Wong, 2002). The investigators attributed the differences to the early attendance of the Chinese children in preschool settings where self-care was promoted.

In summary, these apparent differences in motor development for various groups of children must be considered in light of the environment, child-rearing practices, and cultural differences. More studies need to be done describing the contributions of ethnic or cultural differences to motor development in diverse populations of young children before more definitive statements can be made; however, it remains important for these potential differences to be considered when working with young children with special needs and their families.

Prematurity   A premature infant is one born at 37 weeks of gestation or younger. Approximately 11 to 12% of all births in the United States occur before 37 weeks. Recent advances in medicine have greatly decreased the **morbidity** and mortality rates for premature infants; those born as young as 24 weeks' gestation can now survive. However, their gross motor development may diverge from the typical pattern. A recent study of 800 preterm infants from term (the anticipated birth date) through 18 months of age found that motor development scores were significantly lower than those for full-term infants at all age levels tested, even when scores were corrected for prematurity (van Haastert, de Vries, Helders, & Jongmans, 2006). Factors that may affect delayed motor development include impaired brain growth (particularly the cerebellum) and differences in muscle structure, coordination, and strength, resulting in inadequate postural control and control of the body against gravity.

> Morbidity is the state of being diseased or sick.

Infants born at term (37 to 42 weeks) are characteristically in physiological flexion, which means they are in a flexed posture secondary to prolonged positioning in the uterus. Children who are born prematurely do not exhibit physiological flexion and will often exhibit **hypotonicity** (low muscle tone). They demonstrate a classic posture that consists of the head turned to the side and the arms and legs splayed. The arms may fall into a W pattern and the legs are "frogged" (Hunter, 2001). If this is not corrected with therapeutic positioning, even healthy, low-risk, preterm infants may develop deformities that will significantly affect the development of posture and movement (Vaivre-Douret, Ennouri, Jrad, Garrec, & Papiernik, 2004). Typically, developmental specialists will calculate the infant's adjusted or corrected age by subtracting the amount of prematurity from the expected due date and use this "adjusted age" to determine better estimates for ages of acquisition of developmental milestones.

Institutionalized Children   Children raised in situations in which social and environmental interactions are severely restricted may suffer from sensory deprivation. Sensory stimulation is necessary for typical development to occur. Much of an infant's early experiences are sensory in nature, resulting in the formation of neural connections in the brain (Grubb & Thompson, 2004). The consequences of sensory deprivation have been observed in institutionalized children in Eastern Europe, where custodial care was provided but interaction with people and toys was severely limited. Sensory and motor deficits have been well documented in these children (Lin, Cermak, Coster, & Miller, 2005; Sweeney & Bascom, 1995). In a survey of 240 U.S. families with children adopted from China, 68% of adoptive parents reported developmental delays in those children. Of this number, more than 90% were delayed in motor development (Rettig & McCarthy-Rettig, 2005).

Disorders of Postural Tone   Variations in muscle tone are frequently seen in children who show delayed gross motor development. Muscle tone is the degree of tension that exists in a muscle when it is at rest. **Postural tone** (muscle tone response to demands of gravity and movement) may range on a continuum from lower than normal (as is noted in many premature infants and in children with Down syndrome) to greater than normal (as is seen in spastic cerebral palsy), or it may fluctuate. In addition, postural tone may change over time. For example, muscle tone in children with traumatic brain injuries follows a more transitional and dynamic versus static process. Children diagnosed with cerebral palsy or traumatic brain injury may have any type, degree, or distribution of atypical tone, depending on the site and extent of central nervous system dysfunction. The anatomical distribution and impact of hypertonia will be discussed in more detail in the section on cerebral palsy later in this chapter.

Muscle tone that is lower than normal is frequently referred to as hypotonia. **Hypotonia** generally refers to low muscle tone that occurs symmetrically throughout the body. Low muscle tone is characteristic of hypotonic cerebral palsy, prematurity in the first months (Hunter, 2001), myelomeningocele (a form of spina bifida; Hinderer, Hinderer, & Shurtleff, 2000), and many conditions associated with mental retardation including the following syndromes: Down syndrome, Cri du chat syndrome, fragile X syndrome, Prader-Willi syndrome, and early Rett syndrome (McEwen, 2000). Children with hypotonia have difficulty moving against gravity. Parents may describe the quality of such children's tone as "floppy," "double-jointed," or "like that of a rag doll." Excessive range of motion (hypermobility) occurs at the joints. When a child with hypotonia is positioned in supine or prone, the lower extremities exhibit wide hip abduction and external rotation, frequently termed the "frog-leg position." Children with low muscle tone also tend to assume a characteristic posture when standing, with the legs hyperextended or locked at the knees, pelvis rotated forward (anterior pelvic tilt), lumbar spine in lordosis (swayed back), and thoracic spine in kyphosis (rounded back, Figure 3.2). When children with hypotonia and other motor impairments learn to walk, they will often use the high guard position seen in typically developing toddlers to maintain balance. However, this position will persist much longer.

Sensory Registration and Processing Disorders   Sensory difficulties that influence motor skill development may include problems in the registration, discrimination, processing, and organization of sensory stimuli. Skillful execution of motor skills requires sensory input to plan what action needs to occur, as well as sensory feedback to plot the action that has occurred, and to help determine whether that action was successful. Children with cerebral palsy, particularly those with hemiplegia, may have difficulty accurately perceiving their own movement and be unable to identify that the involved extremity has been touched, or they may have difficulty describing the nature of the touch or identifying where on the body it occurred. These phenomena represent problems with registration and discrimination. Difficulties with the processing and organization of sensory stimuli may result in motor incoordination in children with pervasive developmental disorders (e.g., autism), in some children with learning disabilities and attention deficit-hyperactivity disorder (ADHD), and in children raised in situations lacking sufficient sensory stimulation.

Hypotonia refers to decreased tension and resistance to stretch in a muscle. Occupational and physical therapists may use these terms to describe the same condition: *decreased tone, low tone,* or *floppy.*

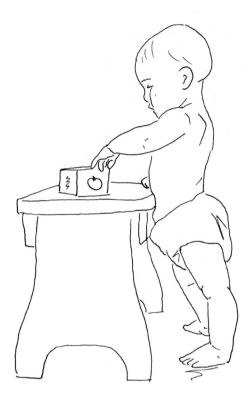

FIGURE 3.2

Supported standing in a toddler with low muscle tone. Note how the child leans into the supporting surface, with locked knees, anterior pelvic tilt, lordosis of lumbar spine, and shoulder instability.

:: GROSS MOTOR DEVELOPMENT IN YOUNG CHILDREN WITH SPECIAL NEEDS

In this section we discuss atypical gross motor development associated with specific diagnoses. We provide information about anticipated developmental problems in each group, and offer some suggestions related to managing the motor problems of these children. It is important to recognize that the diagnostic groups presented here are subsumed under the educational classifications described in chapter 1. For example, Down syndrome typically is included under the classification of intellectual disabilities, whereas cerebral palsy may fit within one of several classifications (e.g., orthopedic impairment or Other Health Impaired).

Cerebral Palsy

Cerebral palsy is a group of non-progressive disorders of movement and posture that result in activity limitations, caused by a disturbance to the developing brain before birth or during infancy (Bax, Goldstein, Rosenbaum, Leviton, & Paneth, 2005). The damage to the developing brain may occur during the prenatal or perinatal period. The prevalence of cerebral palsy in the United States is reported to be 2.0 per 1,000

Dyskinesia is an impairment of the ability to execute voluntary movements. When used with cerebral palsy, this term refers to tonal abnormalities that involve the whole body.

A child often must compensate for atypical muscle tone, posture, or movement by responding with a complementary movement (e.g., if a child sits with the trunk deviated to one side, he must center his balance by deviating his head in the opposite direction).

Hypertonia refers to increased tension and resistance to stretch in a muscle (i.e., "high tone" or "tight").

Spasticity means increased resistance to passive stretch of a muscle or increased muscle tension or tone within the muscle.

Contracture is the loss of motion or fixation at a joint caused by atrophy and shortening of muscle fibers.

(Winter, Autry, Boyle, & Yeargin-Allsopp, 2002). Research indicates that risk is highly related to birth weight. In a European study, the incidence of cerebral palsy among every 1,000 neonatal survivors (infants who survived for at least one month following birth) was 70.6 among infants who weighed less than 1,500 grams (3.3 lbs.) at birth versus 1.2 among infants who weighed more than 2,500 grams (5.5 lbs.) (Surveillance of Cerebral Palsy in Europe Collaborative Group, 2002). Associated problems in cerebral palsy may include sensation, cognition, communication, and perception, as well as possible behavior problems and seizure disorder. Classification of cerebral palsy has historically included the type of postural tone the individual exhibits (spasticity, **dyskinesia**, ataxia, or mixed), as well as the pattern or anatomical distribution (limbs, trunk, etc.) of movement problems (Molnar, 1985; Olney & Wright, 2000). Because of atypical postural tone, children with cerebral palsy do not experience normal movement and develop **compensatory** patterns of movement and posture that may further impede their progress. They also may develop muscular and skeletal anomalies secondary to abnormal muscle pull and poor posture and movement patterns.

Hypertonia refers to tight muscles or **spasticity;** postural tone thus is increased. Hypertonia is characteristic of the spastic and rigid subtypes of cerebral palsy, but the degree of tone can range from mild to severe involvement. Spasticity is the most frequently occurring movement disorder in cerebral palsy and is characterized by stiffness or tightness in the affected limbs. Distribution of hypertonia in the body can vary from child to child. Patterns typically seen include increased tone in one extremity **(monoplegia)**, increased tone primarily in the lower extremities with some mild involvement in the upper extremities **(diplegia)**, increased tone in all extremities **(quadriplegia)** or increased tone or paralysis on one side of the body **(hemiplegia)**, which results in asymmetrical posture and movement. Hypertonia reduces mobility and range of motion (joint flexibility), potentially leading to deformities such as **contractures,** scoliosis (curvature of the spine), or hip dislocation. Hypertonia often results in characteristic problems with posture and movement. When spasticity is present in the lower extremities, the legs tend be adducted (movement of the limbs toward the midline of the body) and internally rotated, with the ankles extended and the feet rotated inward. The hamstring muscles at the back of the upper leg are often tight and tend to rotate the pelvis backward (posterior pelvic tilt), resulting in compensatory rounding of the trunk and extension of the head and neck in sitting.

A child with spastic quadriplegia (the most severe type of cerebral palsy) generally experiences increased extensor tone in the lower extremities with flexor tone predominating in the upper extremities. The persistence of primitive reflexes results in the child being pulled into gravity and, therefore, having great difficulty moving against gravity in the prone and the supine positions. It is usually difficult for the child to raise his head and trunk off the floor when in prone. If rolling is mastered, it is characterized by limited rotation through the trunk ("logrolling") with posturing of the arms in flexion and the legs in extension.

In floor-sitting, the pelvis is pulled into a posterior tilt. Compensatory trunk flexion results in further compensatory neck and head hyperextension to maintain balance in sitting. If the child is able to attain sitting, the legs are often internally rotated with the knees together and the feet out to either side of the body, creating a "W" with the legs (**W sitting**). The child may favor this position because it provides improved stability and frees the arms for use. However, this position is discouraged for several reasons: It may promote dislocation of the hips, it limits trunk rotation in sitting, and it does not require the child to use the lower extremities to assist in maintaining posture, which is necessary for later walking. When the child with spastic quadriplegia crawls, he pulls his body forward with his arms close to the body, whereas the legs usually remain extended and adducted. Some children move on the floor by lying on their backs and pushing with the feet while arching the body into extension.

Children with spastic diplegia (increased tone primarily in the legs) typically creep in a "bunny hop" pattern, with arms and legs moving together in a bilateral, symmetrical pattern rather than reciprocally. When these children walk, the increased extensor tone in the lower extremities results in adduction and internal rotation, with the legs moving in a pattern often termed "scissoring." Often, the ankles are braced to prevent walking on the toes. The upper extremities, though only mildly involved, often pull into a high-guard position because of associated reactions, or overflow.

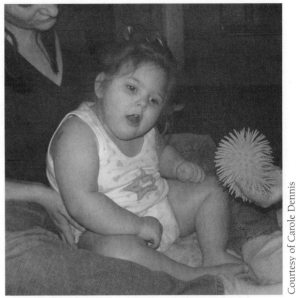

Courtesy of Carole Dennis

Kayla (2 years, 8 months) has mixed and fluctuating muscle tone. In this photo, the posterior pelvic tilt, rounded back, and poor head control are indicative of low tone; however, the fisting of her left hand suggests increased muscle tone. At other times and in other positions, she may exhibit high tone throughout her body.

Many typically developing children use the W sitting position during floor play because it is very stable; however, unlike children with special needs, they are not limited to this position.

| VIGNETTE 3.1 |

EMILY

Emily was diagnosed with cerebral palsy (spastic quadriplegia type) when she was 8 months old. She and her twin brother were born 7 weeks premature by emergency cesarean section. Emily had a prolapsed umbilical cord and, following her birth, she was transferred from the local hospital to the neonatal intensive care unit (NICU) in a nearby city. Emily weighed 4 lb 3 oz and her brother weighed 3 lb 14 oz. Her twin has no apparent side effects from the premature birth and his development has been typical. Emily also has a sister who is 2 years older.

Shortly after her diagnosis of cerebral palsy, Emily was referred for early intervention services. She received an arena assessment, which included an occupational therapist, speech therapist, physical therapist, and developmental psychologist to evaluate her needs. Emily presented with very high muscle tone (spasticity), especially in her calf, hamstring, adductor (muscles that bring the legs together), and her hip flexor muscles. This gave her the typical scissoring posture of the legs, often seen in children with spasticity, when attempting active large motor movement or when standing with support. OT, PT, speech, and special education were recommended in the home. Four different disciplines entering the home several times a week can easily be overwhelming to a family; therefore, specialists in physical therapy and special education were considered the "core" interventionists by the team and were scheduled twice weekly. Occupational and speech therapists consulted with the team and the family on a less frequent basis. Because of Emily's special needs, the team and family decided that the physical therapist and the early childhood educator co-treat during the session to lessen the impact of frequent home visits. Because Emily's physical needs were the greatest concern, the physical therapist would often help move and position her during the therapeutic session while the early childhood educator engaged her in age-appropriate play and cognitive skills. The parents and siblings were present at all sessions and were encouraged to become part of the therapeutic activities.

At the age of 2, Emily attended a private preschool for children with special needs. She attended full time until she was 5 years old, and then was enrolled in a typical classroom in her school district. Parental concerns included her difficulty in mobility, breath support during vocalization, and need for positioning equipment. Intervention in the gross motor area included learning to walk with a walker, propelling her wheelchair, positioning needs, and learning to move in and out of her wheelchair independently.

By the time she was 3 years old, Emily was using a rear walker to walk short distances with supervision. This walking ability was incorporated into her daily classroom routine. She also used a small wheelchair and was able to independently propel it around her preschool classroom, which increased her ability to explore her environment. Her sitting skills were good and no additional trunk support was needed for her wheelchair or adapted chair, which she used in both the classroom and at home. Emily wore ankle-foot orthoses (AFOs) on both feet. They extended from just below her knee to her feet and helped keep her from standing on her toes. They also aided in giving her more stability. Emily also used a stander, especially in the classroom, so that she could stand at various activities like the water table with her peers. She used a specially designed floor sitter to give her stability in sitting during classroom circle time.

The classroom team, which included the OT, PT, SLP, classroom teacher, paraprofessionals, and adapted physical education teacher, met on a regular basis to discuss her progress. The team also met formally several times a year with the family and there was informal communication on a daily basis between the family and at least one member of the team. The entire team (including the family) generated discipline-free goals and objectives for Emily. That is, instead of separate goals for each discipline, the team decided on the most important areas that Emily needed to strengthen and then the objectives were tailored to meet those needs.

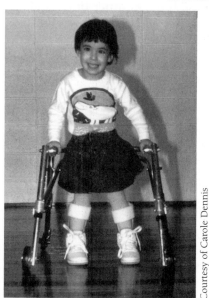

Courtesy of Carole Dennis

Emily using her rear walker (4 years old).

Children with hemiplegia usually have increased tone on one side of the body, resulting in asymmetrical posture and movement. These children typically master the early gross motor developmental milestones and are very mobile. High-level preschool skills are difficult for them, but children with hemiplegia often try to do all that their peers do. The involved ankle is often braced to maintain muscle length to help break up the extensor tone in the leg and to promote walking with the foot flat on the floor.

Children with **athetosis** have fluctuating muscle tone and variable motor capabilities. Some children with athetosis learn to walk independently, but many never advance beyond moving on the floor. Their posture is very unstable and movements are asymmetrical and uncontrolled because the fluctuating tone makes it difficult for them to control flexor and extensor muscles together for coactivation. It is difficult for a child with athetosis to maintain a midline position because of asymmetrical movement and persistence of the asymmetrical tonic neck reflex. This creates difficulty in any activity requiring the maintenance of a midline position, such as eating, writing, reading, or any focused attention directly in front of the child.

Children with **ataxic** cerebral palsy are generally considered very clumsy with poor balance and coordination especially in more upright positions, such as standing. They tend to have difficulty following a straight trajectory when walking and they may have tremors upon movement.

Athetosis is a neuromuscular condition characterized by slow, writhing, continuous, and involuntary movement of the extremities. It is seen in some forms of cerebral palsy, specifically athetoid cerebral palsy.

Ataxia is a condition characterized by impaired ability to coordinate movement, frequently including a staggering gait and postural imbalance.

Traumatic Brain Injury and Brain Tumors

Traumatic brain injury (TBI) is the leading cause of death and disability in children in the United States. The most common causes of TBI in children are motor vehicle accidents, falls, and abuse. In 2003, 1,224,000 children from birth through 4 years of age visited emergency rooms for TBI in the United States. Of these, 290,000 were hospitalized and 51,000 died (Rutland-Brown, Langlois, Thomas, & Xi, 2006). Many of these children are significantly disabled as a result. Depending on the severity, location, and extent of the injury, the child may exhibit a variety of symptoms. Also, the age of the child when the injury occurred will have an impact on the progression of secondary impairments.

In general, the child may experience problems in three different areas: physical, cognitive, and behavioral-emotional. Physical impairments may include problems with muscle tone (spasticity or paralysis), poor balance, speech, vision, and hearing. Cognitive impairments may include short- or long-term memory loss, slowed thinking, and difficulty learning. Behavioral and emotional problems may include lability (i.e., extreme mood swings), agitation, poor emotional control, and depression. Agitation and angry outbursts, in particular, may decrease over time as some healing occurs.

Brain tumors are another type of central nervous system disorder. The incidence of brain tumors in the United States is between 3 and 7 per 100,000, with rates significantly higher among whites than other population groups and among females than among males (National Institute of Health, 2006). Brain and central nervous system tumors make up 21% of all childhood cancers and are the second

The cerebellum is the posterior portion of the brain that primarily coordinates voluntary muscular activity.

The brainstem is a portion of the brain responsible for motor, sensory, and reflexive functions.

Torticollis is an abnormal condition where the head is inclined to one side resulting from a shortening of the muscles on that side of the neck.

Myelomeningocele is a form of spina bifida in which part of the spinal cord protrudes in a cyst, resulting in neurological, motor, and sensory deficits below the level of the cyst.

leading cause of cancer deaths in children. Tumors can occur in a variety of locations in the brain. Clinical signs and symptoms depend on the location and type of tumor. Tumors of the central nervous system may occur in the **cerebellum** (causing ataxia, tremor, **hypotonia,** and poor balance), the **brainstem** (causing problems with gait, **torticollis,** quadriparesis, or hemiparesis), or the cerebral cortex (causing seizures and spasticity; Kerkering & Phillips, 2000).

Gross motor development will vary in infants and young children depending on the severity and extent of the injury or tumor and the age of the child during the onset. Because infants and young children are considered very "plastic" in their musculoskeletal development, care must be taken to avoid secondary problems associated with these systems, such as contractures, decreased range of motion in the joints, and abnormal bone formations. Often, the infant or preschooler who has sustained a TBI also develops spasticity (and sometimes flaccidity or limpness) of the muscles corresponding to the area of the brain that was injured. The clinical signs and symptoms of TBI and brain tumors are similar to those of cerebral palsy; consequently, the physical and occupational therapist may treat the child in a comparable manner.

Spina Bifida (Myelodysplasia)

The National Institute of Neurological Disorders defines spina bifida as a type of neural tube defect that includes an incomplete closure of the fetus's spine during early fetal development. The severity of this defect can range from spina bifida occulta (incomplete closure of the vertebra of the spine with no nerve involvement) to complete avulsion of the spinal cord and meninges (spinal cord's protective covering) into a cyst called a **myelomeningocele.** In the more severe form, the child may have hydrocephalus (excessive cerebral spinal fluid in the brain), be bowel and bladder incontinent, and have partial or full paralysis of the lower extremities (Botto, Moore, Khoury, & Erikson, 1999). It is believed that the incidence of neural tube defects could be decreased by 50 to 70% if women consumed enough folic acid before conception and during the early months of the pregnancy; however, compliance with such guidelines is problematic (Mersereau et al., 2004). Manufacturers have been mandated to fortify breakfast cereals with folic acid since 1998; this mandate has resulted in a 32% decrease in birth prevalence.

Some or all of the muscles of the lower extremities may be paralyzed, causing the growth of muscles and bones to be underdeveloped. Children with spina bifida also may have low muscle tone and some developmental delay. **Hydrocephalus,** an obstruction of cerebrospinal fluid causing increased intracranial pressure, is common in children with myelomeningocele. This pressure on the brain tissue may result in additional central nervous system problems. Children with hydrocephalus often have a shunt surgically implanted, which drains fluid from the brain into the abdominal cavity. Recent efforts in prenatal surgery, largely conducted to relieve the hydrocephalus, also have shown a positive impact on the gross motor development of children with spina bifida (Danzer et al., 2006; Johnson et al., 2006). A malformation on the back of the fetus may be observed with ultrasound and, under the correct circumstances, an early cesarean section may be performed. The lesion is then closed surgically to save some nerve function and, hopefully, decrease the severity of the paralysis.

Therapeutic intervention in the gross motor area may focus on balance, coordination, range of motion, strengthening, and proper positioning. Therapeutic intervention for the affected lower extremities may include positioning, bracing, and range of motion exercises. Briefly standing in a weight-bearing position may be appropriate for the infant. Later, standing either in a special standing frame (a parapodium, which "walks" when the child sways from side to side) or with the assistance of crutches and lower extremity braces may commence when the child is developmentally ready for this position. Depending on the level of the spina bifida, bracing may range from the ankle to the calf using an **ankle/foot orthosis (AFO)**, to the hips using a **hip-knee-ankle orthosis (HKAFO)**, or to the lumbar area (low-back) or thoracic area (mid-back) using a **thoracic-hip-knee-ankle orthosis (THKAFO)**. In some cases, a **reciprocating gait orthosis (RGO)** that extends from the foot to the pelvis, or a parapodium may be used as additional standing and mobility devices. A wheelchair or other rolling device may eventually be the most appropriate and efficient form of mobility for a very high thoracic lesion.

An ankle-foot orthosis (AFO) is a protective external device that can be applied to the ankle area to provide support and prevent deformities.

Generally, care must be taken to prevent deformity of the legs and a possible secondary problem of scoliosis. Lack of sensation in the legs may cause skin breakdown. Obesity is also a concern for this population because of the difficulty in being physically active. As the child ages and has had very little weight bearing in the standing position, he may develop osteoporosis (Quan, Adams, Ekmark, & Bauam, 2003). Stuberg (1992) suggested that a regular standing program would be beneficial to increase bone density in children with developmental disabilities including spina bifida; however, such a program has not been adequately tested to determine effectiveness.

The professional should work closely with the physical and occupational therapist in understanding correct positioning to prevent deformity, osteoporosis, and the possibility of associated fractures. The interventionist also should be aware of signs of shunt dysfunction, which may include fever and malaise, extreme irritability, onset of or increased seizures, and decreased activity levels (Chiafery, 2006). For many years, mobility issues have been felt to be the primary factors related to optimal functioning; however, there is an increasing awareness that cognitive and spatial difficulties may be more important factors in the development of functional independence for individuals with spina bifida (Didelot, 2003).

Degenerative Conditions (Neuromuscular Disorders)

Degenerative diseases are those that cause progressive weakness, muscle atrophy, and increasing disability. Unlike cerebral palsy, spina bifida, Down syndrome, and spinal cord injuries, which are considered static and do not progress, degenerative diseases, including spinal muscular atrophy (SMA) and Duchenne's muscular dystrophy (DMD), pursue a steadily progressive deterioration.

Duchenne's Muscular Dystrophy   DMD is one of the most common forms of muscular dystrophies. It is an X-linked disorder inherited through the mother that affects mostly males. It is a defect of the gene for the protein dystrophin, which is necessary to maintain healthy muscle fibers (Lovering, Porter, & Bloch, 2005). DMD may be detected by the caregiver as early as 3 years or as late as 6 years of age when the child appears to lose motor skills he had previously achieved. The caregiver may note that the child cannot climb the stairs as easily, has more difficulty on the playground equipment, or that the child falls or tires easily. The caregiver may also notice a characteristic maneuver called "Gowers sign" in which the child gets up off the floor by first getting into the all-fours position, straightening the legs, and then using the arms to push on the thighs to stand. Often the calf muscle becomes larger (pseudohypertrophy) as muscle fibers are replaced by increased fibrous connective tissue.

Progressive weakness follows a typical course and, although intervention cannot prevent the eventual loss of muscle strength, it can help prevent secondary problems such as contractures, scoliosis, and decreased respiratory function. Most boys can walk unaided until the age of 6 to 7 years and, by 9 to 10 years, may require assisted ambulation, including the use of AFOs, crutches, or a walker. By 8 to 12 years, most children have lost the ability to walk and require the use of a powered wheelchair for mobility (Lovering et al., 2005). A child with DMD should be allowed to self-limit his activities, especially when he is very young. If a child shows signs of fatigue during the school day, he may be allowed an extra rest period and his school day may be reevaluated to optimize the times when the child has more energy. Evidence is conflicting regarding the amount and type of exercise in which a child with DMD should participate; however, light to moderate exercise has been found to cause no harm in children with DMD and may help to maintain function (Lovering et al., 2005; Toedebusch & LaFontaine, 2005). Contractures of the ankle, knee, and hips are believed to contribute significantly to limitations in walking; therefore, a stretching program is often prescribed. Contractures increase in severity as children lose functional mobility (Gaudreault, Gravel, Nadeau, & Houde, 2005).

Spinal Muscular Atrophy   Spinal muscular atrophy (SMA) may be one of three forms: childhood-onset type I and type II (Werdnig-Hoffmann disease), or juvenile-onset type III (Kugelberg-Welander disease) (Stuberg, 2000). They are all inherited autosomal recessive disorders and affect the anterior horn cell of the spinal cord, which is the area that sends impulses to the muscles. When there are no electrical impulses to the muscles, they eventually atrophy. SMA affects approximately one in every 20,000 children.

Children with the type I SMA are extremely **flaccid** and weak as early as 3 months of age. These children rarely live beyond 3 years of age and often die of complications secondary to respiratory problems. They are considered medically fragile and often require life support. Type II SMA also affects very young babies, but not as severely as the type I form. These children may survive up to early adulthood. One must be cautious when lifting a child with SMA under the arms, because the reflexive tightening of the muscles in the axillary area is very weak and the child may literally "slip" through the hands of the caregiver. Often these children do not learn to walk; they use standing frames to provide stability in a standing position, preferably in a supine stander that supports the head. They may learn to use a motorized wheelchair as early as 18 to 24 months. Contractures, scoliosis, and

Flaccid describes a muscle or limb that is relaxed, having defective or absent muscle tone.

kyphosis are concerns, and careful positioning and range of motion exercises are often part of the gross motor intervention. Although the sensory nerves are not affected, many children complain of increased sensitivity to touch, passive range of motion, and handling. The juvenile form (type III) of SMA may not be diagnosed until later childhood or adolescence (Stuberg, 2000).

Kyphosis is exaggeration of the normal thoracic curve of the spine.

VIGNETTE 3.2

RAMON

Ramon is a bright, curious, and engaging 4-year-old who enjoys his school program and the company of his peers. His motor skills, however, are severely limited by spinal muscular atrophy (type 2), a progressive neuromuscular disorder. He no longer is capable of independent floor mobility and is not able to propel the manual wheelchair that was prescribed when he was 2 years old. Because of his weak neck and back muscles, he requires significant external support and a slightly reclined back to support his head and trunk in order to sit. When his forearms are supported on a smooth surface, he is able to slide his arms from point to point and use his hands quite well in play. However, he does not have sufficient strength to raise his arms off the table.

The preschool team that works in his classroom has carefully considered his capabilities, interests, and needs to design a program that includes him in all classroom activities. He has just received a power wheelchair, which he controls with a joystick. He travels between home and school on a school van with a power lift to accommodate his wheelchair. As in many preschool programs, the day begins with time for free play and toileting. He is capable of controlling bowel and bladder functions and is able to communicate his needs to use the toilet effectively. He uses a special potty chair that supports his trunk and head well and which has a detachable tray to support his arms. Before the structured school program begins each day, he often spends time resting in a side-lying position on a mat placed so that he can reach toys on the bottom shelf in the play area.

When the children gather for circle time, Ramon is positioned in a floor corner seat, which places him at the same level as his classmates when they sit on the floor. This piece of adaptive equipment provides head and trunk control and a tray for arm support. He is able to participate fully in circle time, needing help only to pass materials to the next child in the circle. He uses this same chair later in the day to support him in free play. He enlists his peers to help him get the toys he wants and to play with him. A snack is served at semicircular tables. Ramon is transferred to a fully adjustable classroom chair that fits well under the table. Other than needing help setting up his snack and refilling items as needed, he feeds himself independently. His food is placed on a rimmed plate on top of a raised wooden stand made by the school custodian. His right arm rests on this stand and he is able to control his wrist and fingers well to feed himself finger foods or to scoop food and pivot the spoon to his mouth. His cup has a long plastic straw for liquids; he can slide the cup toward his mouth with his left hand.

When the children go outside to play or walk, Ramon uses his power chair to move through those parts of the play structure that are accessible to wheelchairs. He requires assistance to use most of the outdoor play equipment. When the children engage in water or sand play, Ramon uses a supine stander, which supports his feet, pelvis, trunk, and head in an upright position to play beside his friends. Ramon uses his adapted classroom chair to join his friends in computer games. He controls the computer using a WinMini, a small keyboard that allows him to operate mouse and keyboard functions with his fingers. This keyboard allows him to reach all necessary keys without needing to lift his arms to reposition his hands.

Although this equipment allows Ramon to engage in all classroom activities, it is clear that Ramon needs a well-coordinated team to ensure that his equipment is adjusted correctly and to move him from one piece of equipment to another, as necessary. His team strives to change his position every 30 minutes to ensure his comfort and to maintain skin integrity. A full-time classroom aide assigned to Ramon assists his special education instructor. An occupational therapist and a physical therapist work in the classroom with the special education teacher during one full session a week, where they provide direct services to Ramon and consultation to the other team members. Biweekly meetings are held to carefully coordinate team activities.

Ramon's mother and father are delighted with their son's program. Because of the progressive nature of Ramon's condition, they know that his muscles will continue to grow weaker. They anticipate that his life will be shortened; Ramon's older brother, who also had SMA, died when he was seven years old. Thus, it is tremendously important to them that Ramon be just "one of the kids" for as long as possible.

Spinal Cord Injury and Tumors of the Spinal Cord

Spinal cord injury (SCI) is any injury causing a complete or partial disruption of neural impulses from the spine to the affected muscles, skin, and other organs resulting in complete or partial paralysis. The leading cause for SCI at all ages is trauma from motor vehicle accidents, falls, and violence and abuse (Shakhazizian, Massagli, & Southard, 2000). Depending on the level of the injury, the individual may have paralysis of different areas of the body. Injury to the spinal cord at the cervical level (neck vertebra) may result in quadriplegia or paralysis from the neck down. Injury to the thoracic area (midback) and lumbar area (low back) may result in paraplegia or paralysis from the waist or low-back area continuing down through the legs and feet. There may be full paralysis or partial paralysis depending on the extent of the lesion. Similar clinical findings are found with spinal cord tumors in young children.

The young child with a spinal cord injury or spinal tumor requires special care. The toddler and preschooler may require special devices to learn to sit. A soft back brace may assist the child with sitting balance so that he can use his hands more easily and also to prevent scoliosis (especially if the lesion is high). Preschoolers can use **knee-ankle-foot orthoses (KAFOs)** or long leg braces to learn to walk and also require the use of a walker or crutches. This form of ambulation requires a great deal of energy and the child may eventually prefer to use a wheelchair. A manual wheelchair may be appropriate for a child with a lumbar or low thoracic cord injury in that he still has the strength of the arms and necessary sitting balance needed to propel the wheels. A powered wheelchair may be a better choice for a child with a higher thoracic or cervical cord injury. Many children (and adults) prefer to activate a powered chair with a joystick, but other forms of activation are available for the child with less active movement of the arms. With close supervision, a child as young as 18 to 24 months may be taught to use a wheelchair.

Pressure sores are a problem for children with any level of cord injury because of the loss of sensation in the affected parts. Special wheelchair cushions are available to help alleviate this, but it is important for all caregivers to be aware that the child should be repositioned on a regular basis for pressure relief. Standing frames and other classroom positioning devices are also available for alternative positioning.

Down Syndrome

Down syndrome is a genetic disorder that results from a chromosomal abnormality causing a number of physical and cognitive anomalies (Blackman, 1997). Children with Down syndrome typically have low muscle tone (hypotonia), short stature, and intellectual disability. A number of health problems may accompany this disorder such as congenital heart disease, visual deficits, and lowered resistance to infection. Instability between the first two cervical vertebrae, called **atlantoaxial subluxation,** occurs in 10 to 12% of children with Down syndrome; however, only 1 to 2% display symptoms (Ali, Al-Bustan, Al-Busairi, Al-Mulla, & Esbaita, 2006). X-rays of the neck are often recommended to rule out this condition because, in rare instances, pressure on the head and neck may result in damage to the spinal cord (Blackman, 1997).

Although gross motor delays are typical in children with mental retardation, the degree of delay is greater in Down syndrome than in retardation due to other factors (Fidler, Hepburn, Mankin, & Rogers, 2005). The impact of these delays on the child is great. In a study of 5- to 7-year-old children with Down syndrome, Volman, Visser, and Lensvelt-Mulders (2007) found that motor ability was a much better predictor of functional performance than mental ability. Typically developing children begin to walk without support anywhere from 9 to 15 months; children with Down syndrome begin to walk on average about a year later than typically developing children (Ulrich, Ulrich, Angulo-Kinzler, & Yun, 2001). In general, the age of acquisition of developmental milestones is late and the range of ages in which skills may be acquired is broad (Vicari, 2006). The gap between the age of acquisition of skills between children with Down syndrome and typically developing children becomes greater as motor complexity increases: Children with Down syndrome require more time to learn complex tasks (Palisano et al., 2001).

Lack of trunk rotation, variability, and poor balance characterize the quality of movement in children with Down syndrome. It is felt that these problems are caused by low muscle tone and limited coactivation around the joints (Lauteslager,

Vermeer, & Helders, 1998), resulting in poor stability at the shoulders and hips and leading to limited ability to shift weight. In infancy, resistance against gravity is minimal and range of motion is greater than in typically developing children. Children with Down syndrome tend to use atypical posture in static positions, such as sitting, in which the legs tend to be widely abducted providing a wide base and eliminating the need for weight shift. In sitting, children with Down syndrome tend to avoid rotating the trunk to retrieve objects; instead, they may lean far forward with a rigid trunk or scoot in the sitting position to move toward a desired object.

Atypical movement patterns are often observed when these children move from one position to another. Movement often occurs in straight planes, with limited trunk rotation. For example, whereas the typical child moves from sitting to a modified side-sitting position to the hands-and-knees position, a child with Down syndrome is more likely to vault straight forward over the legs into the hands-and-knees position (Lauteslager et al., 1998; Vicari, 2006). In walking, children with Down syndrome are more likely to have their legs widely abducted and use lateral trunk movements to achieve weight shift for much longer periods than typically developing children do. Few children with Down syndrome develop the mature counterrotation and arm swing present in most typically developing 6-year-old children.

It may be hypothesized that although the movement patterns of young children with Down syndrome are efficient based on their musculoskeletal features, the stereotypical movement patterns they display may result in further delays in the future. For example, when typically developing children move from sitting to hands and knees,

Courtesy of Carole Dennis

Isabella has Down syndrome. Her hypotonia makes it difficult for her to hold her head and trunk up against gravity when placed on her tummy. Compare her position to Nena's on p.124.

they get practice with trunk rotation and have better developed equilibrium reactions, more strength, and more variability of movement to prepare them for higher level skills, such as walking. Children with Down syndrome often do not have the same range of experiences in sitting and do not gain the same degree of control before learning to walk; therefore, the walking pattern is more restricted. To allow the child to experience greater variability of movement, intervention is often focused on tone building and facilitation of coactivation, weight shift, and rotation in movement activities.

Disorders of Motor Coordination

For many years, researchers and experts in child development have used various terms to describe children who exhibit difficulty with motor coordination, including *minimal brain dysfunction, developmental apraxia (dyspraxia),* and *sensory integration disorder (somatodyspraxia)* (Cermak, Gubbay, & Larkin, 2002; David, 2000; Reeves & Cermak, 2002). Within the last 15 years, the term **developmental coordination disorder (DCD)** has been used more frequently to describe motor deficits in children whose incoordination is not associated with primary cognitive, sensory, or known neurological impairment (American Psychiatric Association, 2000; Magalhaes, Missiuna, & Wong, 2006). These motor deficits include significant delays in achieving typical motor milestones (development is below cognitive levels), clumsiness in the execution of motor skills, difficulty with handwriting tasks, and poor performance in sports. The motor impairment must significantly impede functional self-care activities and academic achievement. DCD often coexists with learning disabilities and attention deficit-hyperactivity disorder (Dewey, 2002).

> Developmental coordination disorder (DCD) is poor motor coordination that is not related to primary cognitive, sensory, or neurological impairment.

   Children with DCD may have difficulty with motor planning or with motor execution (Dewey, 2002). Children with motor planning problems may be described as having *developmental dyspraxia,* a term used widely by occupational therapists, neuropsychologists, and neurologists (Cermak et al., 2002). Developmental dyspraxia refers to clumsiness resulting from impairment in the ability to plan nonhabitual motor tasks. Problems with motor planning may be the result of difficulty integrating sensory information from the body or from difficulty with sequencing motor tasks. Children with DCD have been found to have deficits in neuromuscular control and balance and to use less efficient strategies for maintaining balance than typically developing children (Williams, 2002). In addition, they tend to walk with faster, smaller steps than other children and tend to tilt their upper bodies forward to compensate for poor control (Deconinck et al., 2006). The difficulty these children have with motor coordination may affect their self-esteem and social adaptation (Missiuna, Moll, King, King, & Law, 2007). While a skilled observer often can recognize problems in the preschool years, typically the disorder is not identified until the first, second, or third grade, when demands on time, organization, and participation increase (Cermak, 1991). This causes a delay in intervention and increases the risk for positive psychosocial adjustment. Certainly, identification in the preschool years is crucial, but most assessments used for children at this age typically do not examine the qualitative deficits that are the issues in children with DCD (Missiuna, Rivard, & Bartlett, 2006).

Autism

The identifying features of autism and other pervasive developmental disorders have historically been related to qualitative deficits in communication and social interaction. These areas of function have been heavily researched in this population. However, in recent years researchers have identified significant sensory and motor problems as being hallmarks of this population, as well. Parents have reported many sensory issues with children, including hypersensitivity to sound, an aversion to social touch, avoidance of eye contact with others, and specific food preferences, that are frequently paired with a fascination with specific types of sensory stimuli, such as enjoying spinning, watching spinning objects, or rubbing or licking objects. Luca (the child discussed at the beginning of this chapter) demonstrates several of these behaviors.

Kern has conducted several studies of children and adults with autism that investigated their ability to process sensory stimuli (Kern, 2006, 2007). She found that, as a group, individuals with autism have global idiosyncrasies in processing sensory information that encompass auditory, visual, tactile, and oral hypo- and hypersensitivity. Baranek (2002), in a review of the literature, indicated that studies have reported that between 44 and 82% of older children with autism demonstrate unusual response to sensory events, with particular problems identified in auditory processing. Kern's study found that sensory processing difficulties were greatest in her younger participants, suggesting that problems may decrease as individuals age (2006).

Some researchers believe that the ability to integrate sensory information from one's own body and from the environment are crucial to adaptive functioning. They suspect that the sensory problems displayed by many children with autism may reflect a central problem and may influence other aspects of function in autistic children, including communication, social interaction, stereotypic movements, and motor coordination (Rinehart et al., 2006). Motor deficits in children with autism have been found to be widespread, although research in this area is still new and a pattern of motor deficits has not yet emerged (Watson, Baranek, & DiLavore, 2003). Indeed, for many years researchers considered motor skills to be an area of relative success for children with autism (Berkeley, Zittel, Pitney, & Nichols, 2001). Problems with imitation were among the earliest motor deficits examined in children with pervasive developmental disorders (Watson et al., 2003). The ability of children with autism to gather accurate information about their own bodies through proprioception and the bodies of others through visual perception—both of which are required for imitation of motor movement—is in question. Young children with autism are notably poor at imitating the behavior of others, which some feel may account for the problems of socialization and communication inherent in children with autism (Meltzoff & Gopnik, 1993). Newer research suggests that children with autism may have a general motor planning (praxis) deficit, that goes beyond problems with imitation to include problems with preparing for movement, planning movement, and using objects as tools (Mostofsky et al., 2006).

Although in the past researchers felt that poor motor function was present only in low-functioning children with autism, recent research has found that high functioning children with autism and with Asperger syndrome also demonstrate significant weaknesses in motor performance compared to typically developing children in locomotor tasks (Berkeley et al., 2001) and on motor neurological testing (Jansiewicz et al., 2006). A stiff and awkward gait with limited arm swing is characteristic of children with autism and Asperger syndrome (Rinehart, Bradshaw, Brereton, & Tonge, 2002). In addition, research has indicated that children with autism are less coordinated in walking, demonstrating reduced smoothness, variation in stride length, and greater difficulty walking along a straight line than typically developing children (Rinehart et al., 2006). Other gross motor problems that have been identified in children with autism include clumsiness and poor postural control (Minshew, Sung, Jones, & Furman, 2004; Rinehart et al., 2002). In addition to the motor deficits noted here, children with autism frequently have poor visual attention, which results in diminished success with motor tasks.

Luca's motor difficulties (see Luca's story at the beginning of this chapter) are consistent with many of the research findings reported here. He demonstrates poor postural control, difficulty learning new motor tasks (and repeating learned motor tasks), and poor visual attention, all factors that have been reported in children with pervasive developmental disorders.

:: SPECIFIC STRATEGIES FOR ASSESSMENT OF GROSS MOTOR FUNCTIONING

Assessment serves a number of functions in the intervention of young children with motor limitation. Perhaps the first function most families experience is the use of assessment to identify the degree of motor impairment in their child. This type of assessment usually examines those motor skills and activities that a child can and cannot accomplish, and then compares the child's performance to the performance of typically developing children. Identification of those who may benefit from motor intervention is the first step when services are sought under early intervention and preschool legislation. The need for intervention is frequently established by ascertaining a discrepancy between age-expected performance and actual performance, based on standards determined by the state of residence. However, the assessment should do more than merely identify disparity. The assessment also should provide the evaluation team with sufficient information to establish functional goals and objectives to facilitate motor development. In addition, it should allow the team to identify suspected causes of the motor delays. This will help the team determine what type of intervention would be best for the child and what model of service delivery would most effectively meet the needs of the child. The assessment may also provide information that will help to explain other areas of delay (see chapter 8).

Another very important purpose of assessment is to identify the outcomes of early intervention services. This type of assessment helps the team to determine whether the child continues to require motor intervention and, if so, whether the current program is appropriate. Outcomes assessment also provides the team with information to decide whether the methods of intervention are yielding an appropriate rate of progress or if a different method of intervention should be considered.

Assessment of outcomes is generally focused less on reduction of specific impairments and more on improvement in activities or participation. For example, is the child better able to perform motor activities necessary for self-care, socialization, play, and learning, or is the child more able to participate in activities appropriate to his age and interests? While Ramon's motor abilities are expected to deteriorate over time (see vignette on page 141), good intervention will result in his improved participation in daily life.

The assessment of gross motor skills must include both a quantitative and a qualitative evaluation of motor performance. A very young child may be meeting developmental milestones, but a careful examination of the quality of posture and movement may provide information that will identify the probability of future delay. For example, a child with low muscle tone may roll and sit when expected, but his posture in sitting will be qualitatively different from that of a typically developing child. The experienced therapist may help parents and educators understand how the hypotonia may limit the ability to move in and out of sitting, to creep, to pull to stand, and to walk in a normal fashion. In addition, the therapist may be able to suggest therapeutic activities that will minimize potential future problems with motor skills. Assessment results should be interpreted in light of the physical, social, and cultural context of the child, as well as the child's cognitive, communicative, psychosocial, self-care, and fine motor skill development. Children who have difficulty performing motor tasks at a level with their peers may experience decreased self-esteem, may avoid physical activity, or may be fearful of situations that require gross motor control.

Gross motor assessment may occur as part of an interdisciplinary team-based assessment or may occur as a "specialty" evaluation. In the case of the interdisciplinary team, a group of professionals, each assuming responsibility for specific areas of function, may conduct the evaluation. Depending on the child's perceived needs, the age of the child, and the regulations of the state in which the child lives, the format of the evaluation may differ. The evaluation may occur in an arena format (many disciplines evaluate the child, usually during the same appointment, as was the case for Emily), a core format (professionals from key disciplines evaluate the child, usually in the case of an initial evaluation for early intervention), or with separate appointments by one discipline in the home, school, or clinic. If, following an initial evaluation, the team decides that another discipline is needed to do a more thorough assessment in a particular domain, a discipline-specific evaluation is done. Many early intervention and preschool programs prefer that the examination be conducted in the child's home or another natural environment with the primary caregivers present. When children are assessed in unfamiliar environments, they may be constrained in their willingness to explore and move.

Professionals who perform core or initial evaluations use measures that allow assessment across five domains of function which include adaptive (self-care), motor (both fine and gross), cognition, communication (expressive and receptive) and social-emotional skills. Not every assessment tool looks at all five domains of function, and care should be taken by the team to decide which tool is the most appropriate to use for the initial evaluation. There are a number of such measures for young children, including the *Bayley-III* and the *Bayley-III Screening Test*

(Bayley, 2005a; Bayley, 2005b) for children from 1 to 42 months, the *Battelle Developmental Inventory*, for children from birth through eight years (Newborg, 2005), and the *Infant-Toddler Developmental Assessment* (IDA) for children from birth through 36 months (Provence, Erikson, Vater, & Palmeri, 1995). The *Developmental Assessment of Young Children* (DAY-C) was developed for children from 0 to 5 years (Voress & Maddox, 1998). The *Early Learning Accomplishment Profile* (E-LAP) (Hardin & Peisner-Feinberg, 2001) was designed for assessment and program planning for children from birth to three years, and the *Learning Accomplishment Profile—Diagnostic* (LAP–D) (third edition; Hardin, Peisner-Feinberg, E. S., & Weeks, 2005) was developed for children from 30–72 months. The *Hawaii Early Learning Profile* (HELP) *Checklist* (Furuno, 2004) was developed for children from 0 to 3 years of age, and the *HELP for Preschoolers Assessment Strands, Charts, and Checklists* (VORT Corporation, 1995–1999) were designed for children 3 to 6 years of age. These assessments provide information about a child's functioning in self-care, gross motor, fine motor, cognitive, and social and emotional development. The *Ages and Stages Questionnaire* (Bricker & Squires, 1995), which is written in terms easily understood by caregivers, can be completed by parents.

The context in which a child develops is extremely important in the function of the child. An excellent measure for assessing self-care, mobility, and social function in context, which may not meet the needs of educational teams related to eligibility for services, is the *Pediatric Evaluation of Disability Inventory* (PEDI) (Haley, Coster, Ludlow, Haltiwanger, & Andrellos, 1992). In some settings in which a transdisciplinary approach is used and **discipline-free goals** are developed, a team-based contextual evaluation may be preferred, such as the *Transdisciplinary Play-Based Assessment* (Linder, 2007). Discipline-free goals are becoming more favored in the provision of early intervention services and for older children with multiple disabilities (see Emily's vignette). Some teams may conduct an ecological assessment, where a child is observed in the context of the natural environment, engaged in typical daily activities, to determine specific areas of intervention that will have a strong impact on participation. This was particularly helpful with Ramon to help prioritize goals. When specific concerns exist in the gross motor areas, the motor specialist on the team may conduct a more in-depth supplemental evaluation. Some assessments designed specifically to measure development of gross and fine motor skills include the *Peabody Developmental Motor Scales II* for children from birth through 5 years (Folio & Fewell, 2000), the *Toddler and Infant Motor Evaluation* (Miller & Roid, 2002), the *Motor Assessment Battery of Children* for children as young as 4 (MABC; Henderson & Sudgen, 1992), and the *Bruininks-Oseretsky Test of Motor Proficiency* (BOT–2; second edition), which is useful only with children who are at least 4½ years of age (Bruininks & Bruininks, 2005). An instrument designed to measure change in gross motor activity and participation in children with cerebral palsy is the *Gross Motor Function Measure* (GMFM) (Russell, Rosenbaum, & Avery, 2002). This assessment was designed for use by physical and occupational therapists to assess lower-level skills, such as lying and rolling, to higher-level gross motor skills, such as running and jumping, and is suitable for children with cerebral palsy, Down syndrome, and other conditions that affect motor performance.

In addition to using assessments that measure gross motor performance, occupational and physical therapists occasionally use standardized and criterion-referenced assessment tools and qualitative measures to assess *components* of motor skills and sensory processing. A clinical evaluation by the therapist will identify contributing factors that may have an impact on motor functioning, such as reflexive development, atypical postural tone, decreased or increased range of motion, atypical movement patterns and components, poor musculoskeletal integrity, inadequate positioning for function, and disorders in sensory registration, discrimination, and tolerance. There are a number of measures designed primarily to gather information about a child's ability to process sensory information. These provide supplemental information and do not take the place of an assessment of gross motor performance. The *Infant/Toddler Sensory Profile* (Dunn, 2002) and the *Sensory Profile* (Dunn, 1999), for children age 3 and above, use a questionnaire format to provide information about a child's sensory performance. The *DeGangi-Berk Test of Sensory Integration* (DeGangi & Berk, 1983) is designed to measure postural control, bilateral motor integration, and reflex development in children from 3 to 5 years of age. The *Sensory Integration and Praxis Test* (Ayres, 1989) measures visual, tactile, and kinesthetic perception, as well as motor performance in children from 4 to 8 years of age.

In addition to standardized assessment tools, a physical or occupational therapist also will assess impairments that may contribute to the functional performance of the child. These impairment areas include range of motion, muscle tone, strength, sensory and perceptual abilities, pain, skeletal alignment, contractures and quality of movement. The results of the gross motor assessment should be considered together with information about the child's function in other developmental areas as well as family information and concerns to develop appropriate intervention plans that consider the whole child.

:: INSTRUCTIONAL METHODS AND STRATEGIES FOR INTERVENTION

Motor Intervention: Maximizing Participation

Motor intervention for young children requires a comprehensive view of the factors that result in disability. The ICF Model (International Classification of Functioning, Disability, and Health) developed by the World Health Organization (2001) recognizes that a disability may involve dysfunction at the level of impairment (of body function or structure), activity, or participation in a life situation. It further proposes that reducing the severity of disability can occur through two important mechanisms: by improving the functional capacity of the person and by improving performance through modification of the physical and social environment. Comprehensive intervention must consider each of these factors.

Primary impairments may be a focus for intervention when they are believed to be changeable, such as weakness or limited joint flexibility (Missiuna et al., 2006). However, many impairments are not easily changed and improvement of changeable impairment does not automatically result in improved activity performance and involvement in life activities. Sometimes, another focus of intervention will be the prevention of secondary impairments that may be caused by primary impairments. Activity and participation limitations are more frequently the focus of intervention; improvement in these areas generally reflects successful outcomes of intervention. Improvement in the activity area focuses on completing typical tasks that are necessary and important to the child, thus optimizing participation in life situations. Participation, in turn, is heavily influenced by the physical and the social context in which the child functions. This influence is reflected in the concept of family-centered care.

Luca's case illustrates how the ICF model can guide intervention. Poor motor planning, poor balance, and weakness are primary impairments that limit Luca's motor function. As a consequence of the lack of postural stability caused by these impairments, Luca does not move his body through a full range of motion in motor activities, resulting in limitations in range of motion (a secondary impairment). There are many activities that are difficult for Luca, including walking with safety, going up and down stairs, squatting and rising from squatting, getting up from the floor, climbing on furniture, and seating himself in a child's sized seat. These activity limitations constrain his participation in exploring his environment, interacting with his family, and playing with peers in the community. His therapist has addressed his limited range of motion directly through stretching, but his other

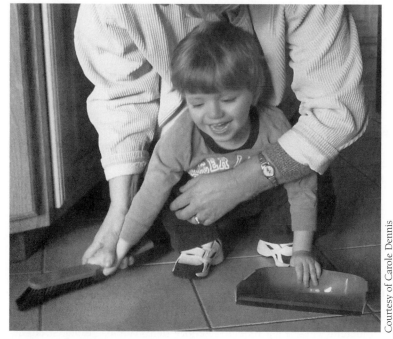

Courtesy of Carole Dennis

Luca's physical therapist has incorporated a functional task (using a dustpan) into therapy designed to address Luca's weakness and instability.

impairments are addressed through intervention focused on the activity and context. Luca practices functional activities that involve squatting, which requires both motor planning and strength. Specific activities, such as seating himself in a chair, are rehearsed using the same sequence and verbal prompts by family and service-providers, thus manipulating the social environment to facilitate function.

His difficulty walking safely is addressed by arranging the furniture in the family room in a circle, thus keeping the distance from one piece of furniture to another short and providing furniture all around his play space to limit falling. During therapy, objects are placed on the floor, requiring Luca to visually attend to them and walk around them. This is an example of the dynamic systems approach, which was discussed as a theory of motor development earlier in this chapter. Luca's abilities and limitations are considered and the environment is manipulated to allow him to explore movement options with freedom and safety to solve motor problems as he plays (Darrah et al., 2001; Ketelaar et al., 2001; Mahoney, 2004).

Theoretical Frameworks for Intervention

Physical and occupational therapists often use several theoretical frameworks from which they base their treatment approaches. They may adhere strictly to one approach or borrow from several approaches depending on the needs and response of the child to the environment and the activity. For example, when Luca was learning to walk, the therapist first needed to address the fact that his hips were held in external rotation and abduction and his feet were very pronated (legs turned out and apart with feet flat). Because it is very difficult for anyone to stand in this manner, stretching to his hips was done with appropriate muscle strengthening, and soft inserts were added to his shoes to improve his overall body alignment. Next, he needed to work on core strengthening of his trunk muscles. This was best done on a therapy ball (he loves balls and music) utilizing many of the techniques typically associated with the NDT approach. Learning to stand unaided and walk without support was best addressed by using the dynamic systems model, which challenged his system to not rely on external stabilization in order to maintain an upright position. The sessions gradually incorporated a variety of toys and activities that motivated and challenged him to walk toward them. Because Luca was fearful of falling, sessions also included safe falling techniques. The approaches used included direct intervention on the impairment level and the activity level and will eventually focus more on his participation level.

Models of Service Delivery for Meeting Gross Motor Needs

Meeting the needs of children with gross motor impairment can be accomplished in a number of different ways. Each model of service delivery has specific strengths that, depending on the needs of the child, the skills of team members, and the nature of the organization providing services, may be considered most appropriate for the individual child. For children younger than 3 years, federal legislation mandates a family-centered approach in early intervention, which recognizes that infants and toddlers are part of an integrated family system where each individual influences the behavior of all other individuals. The family makes decisions about intervention with the early intervention team providing information and support in this process. Although this approach is not mandated for children older than 3, the family is still tremendously important. It behooves the team to include parents and support their wishes as much as is possible in assessment, intervention, and program planning. Parents who become empowered through their child's early intervention program tend to expect to be involved in making decisions about their child's educational experiences at age 3. Suggestions on motor interventions should support the role of the parent and be tailored to the parent's desires, interests, and capabilities.

The needs of the child and the family are considered in light of community and agency resources to determine a service program to meet the needs of the child. When a child has specific motor needs, the appropriate specialist from the team (e.g., the occupational or physical therapist) collaborates with other professionals to determine how services should be provided. The **occupational therapist** views the child within his physical, social, and cultural environment, examining how the environment influences the child's performance in such areas as self-care, play, and schoolwork. The occupational therapist addresses issues related to feeding, dressing, positioning, handwriting, and psychosocial needs, and often is helpful in adapting tasks and the environment for optimal function. Occupational therapists must be certified by the American Occupational Therapy Association in order to practice; in addition, many states also require a professional license. The certified occupational therapy assistant, who works under the supervision of an occupational therapist, holds a certificate or associate's degree.

The **physical therapist** is concerned with children's function related to posture and movement. Physical therapists address issues related to mobility and gross motor skill acquisition and often provide adaptive equipment to support these functions. The majority of physical therapy schools now award a Doctor of Physical Therapy degree (DPT), and all schools have been mandated to award a DPT by the year 2020 (American Physical Therapy Association, 2007). A physical therapy assistant holds an associate's degree. Physical therapists and assistants must be licensed by the state in which they practice. Physical and occupational therapists practicing today may hold either a bachelor's, master's, or doctoral degree in their respective discipline. However, in both fields, anyone entering practice today must receive a minimum of a master's degree in order to be licensed by the appropriate association.

It should be noted that, under early intervention legislation, occupational and physical therapists may provide a "primary" service to the child and family. These therapists, in fact, may represent the only service a child receives if that service is all that is deemed necessary by the early intervention team. It is, however, more typical for the therapist to collaborate with other professionals in meeting the needs of the child in early intervention. When working with preschool and school-aged children, however, occupational and physical therapists are "related" service providers. These services are considered necessary in order for a particular child to benefit from the special education program. In this case, the therapist always works as part of a team to meet the child's educational needs.

Discipline-free goals focus on a child's needs within a given context, rather than upon skills within a specific service provider's domain.

An occupational therapist is a professional who helps individuals participate in those activities (or occupations) that are meaningful and purposeful for them, through remediation of individual skills or modification of the task or environment.

The physical therapist is a professional who focuses on managing a patient's movement system by evaluating and treating the musculoskeletal and neuromotor system.

For school-aged children, physical education is a mandated service (rather than a related service), and children with disabilities should receive physical education or adaptive physical education services as frequently as children without disabilities. Adaptive (or special) physical education is a specialty area within physical education designed to serve children with special needs. Adaptive physical education is provided when the student needs "additional or modified learning opportunities to be successful in physical education or when the student needs a different physical education curriculum" (Shapiro & Sayers, 2003, p. 37). Such teachers may be involved in adapting physical education activities for students or providing programs that foster development of fitness and gross motor skills or that help to correct specific problems related to posture and body movement.

Intervention by the physical or occupational therapist may be provided through direct therapy, supervised therapy, consultation, or a combination of these models (Dunn, 2000), as occurred with Emily. However, decisions should be made based upon a careful analysis of the child, family, and school situation rather than on staff availability or what has been done in the past (Palisano, Campbell, & Harris, 2000).

Direct Therapy   Intervention that is individually designed and carried out by the therapist with one child or a group of children is referred to as *direct therapy*. This model is used when the child or children require very specialized therapy techniques that others cannot be trained to provide. It may occur within a natural environment, such as the child's home, the educational classroom, or the cafeteria, or it may occur in an isolated environment, such as a therapy room. Isolated therapy in a school setting should be provided only when the service the child requires is inappropriate in the natural environment.

Supervised Therapy   When the motor specialist designs a service plan to meet a child's needs, but another person (such as a parent, teacher, classroom aide, or physical or occupational therapy assistant) is trained to carry out the activities, the specialist remains responsible for the implementation of the plan. This is accomplished through monitoring whereby the therapist maintains contact with the child and modifies the intervention as necessary.

Consultation   In the consultation model, the motor specialist provides expertise to another person or program to address concerns identified by that person. In this model, the specialist no longer assumes responsibility for the intervention plan. For example, the occupational or physical therapist may consult with the physical educator in the school to best enhance the student's gross motor performance during physical education class.

Positioning the Child

Regardless of how treatment is conducted, postural control is central to the development of most sensorimotor skills and often represents the initial consideration in intervention. For very young children who have problems with postural tone, simple environmental modifications may promote successful interaction with the environment and may help prevent the development of atypical posture and movement. For example, placing rolled towels under the head and extremities of an infant with hypotonia in supine will facilitate bringing the head, hands, and legs toward midline. This will support the child's visual and tactile exploration of his own body in midline, which many consider to be the first position of learning. For the child with hypertonia, primitive reflexes often dominate the prone and supine positions, making volitional movement difficult. Placement in the side-lying position may eliminate the influence of tonic reflexes by minimizing the effects of gravity on postural tone, allowing the child to move with greater freedom and control.

For children who need postural control at higher levels of functioning, adaptations to infant seats, strollers, highchairs, classroom tables and chairs, toilet seats, bicycles, and even swings may greatly improve the child's functional success. Washington, Deitz, White, and Schwartz (2002) studied the effects of using a home-made foam positioning device in commercially available high chairs on four infants from 9 to 18 months of age. They found that the device improved postural alignment in all four children. In addition, each of their mothers reported that the device increased independence in functional tasks such as play, hand use, and social interaction for their children. Mothers also noted that the positioning device yielded benefits for themselves by better supporting the children, thus freeing the mothers for other tasks. Considerations for fostering posture and mobility through technology are discussed later in this chapter.

Postural Control

When **postural control** is significantly impaired, the physical or occupational therapist may develop a treatment program keyed to the specific needs of the individual child. Treatment programs may include activities to promote more normal muscle tone, to maintain range of motion, and to improve the ability to use protective and equilibrium reactions in functional activities. Because different underlying mechanisms may cause postural deficits in children, the special education teacher should not implement a motor program without guidance from these professionals.

When a young child is not able to move about independently, parents and professionals must do their best to provide the child with as much control as possible over his environment. For example, promoting and responding to communicative attempts by young children with significant motor impairment will maximize their ability to direct others to move them through the environment or to bring the environment to them. In addition, it is important to position these children on a level with peers to foster social interaction and to make the environment as accessible to them as possible.

Improving Gross Motor Skills

As noted above, when a child has difficulties with a necessary gross motor task, the interventionist should consider whether to remediate an impairment in the child, alter the physical or social environment, or modify the task to promote skill. While the importance of modifying the task is often very obvious to interventionists when working with children with severe disabilities, it is important to realize the importance of modifying activities to lessen motor demands may be particularly helpful for children with mild to moderate motor impairments, such as those with developmental motor disorders. Children who have problems with motor coordination are often cognizant of their difficulties and see their performance in motor activities as inferior to those of their peers. They may avoid engaging in activities with other children because of fear of failure and, therefore, limit their own opportunities to improve motor skills performance, and further limiting their experience interacting with other children. Children with motor incoordination may find relative success in activities that provide the opportunity for practice and that do not require constant interaction with changing environmental conditions. The adaptive or special physical educator, the physical therapist, or the occupational therapist may be especially helpful to classroom teachers in finding ways to modify motor tasks for success.

The interventionist also should consider how to help children *learn* motor tasks. For example, children benefit from feedback regarding their performance. However, research on typically developing children has demonstrated that frequent feedback is less effective in fostering motor learning than relatively infrequent feedback. This encourages children to assess their own performance, rather than always relying on others for feedback. While practice is known to improve performance, practicing the same task repeatedly is less effective than varying practice among several different tasks (VanSant, 2003).

For children with specific medical diagnoses, such as cerebral palsy, spina bifida, and juvenile rheumatoid arthritis, it is important to consult with the physical and occupational therapists before instituting a motor program. This is because there are often contraindications for movement that must be considered. For children with mild-to-moderate motor impairment, the most important consideration in improving skills is a firm understanding of the present motor, sensory, and cognitive capabilities of the child. When the goal of an activity is motor performance, the activity should be structured so that it represents the "*just-right challenge,*" or the point at which the task is just difficult enough to entice the child to try to succeed, but not so difficult so as to result in frustration, poor performance, or failure (Koomar & Bundy, 2002).

:: ASSISTIVE TECHNOLOGY FOR GROSS MOTOR INTERVENTION

As noted earlier in this chapter, the ICF model (International Classification of Functioning, Disability, and Health; World Health Organization, 2001) explains individual functioning as a product of the person and the physical and social environment. Assistive technology serves to modify a child's interaction with the environment to reduce limitations in activity and encourage participation. Assistive technology supports function in the areas of mobility, self-care, and social function. The benefits of assistive technology were demonstrated in a study of young children with cerebral palsy (Ostensjo, Carlberg, & Volestad, 2005). Over half of parents reported that mobility aids (including devices such as walkers, seating equipment, and wheelchairs) had a moderate to very large effect on their children's functioning. Two thirds of parents reported similar effects on the need for caregiver assistance.

Low-tech supports include simple seating modifications that may provide better posture and comfort for the child while allowing improved visual regard, arm/hand function, and eye/hand coordination. In general, therapists use such devices to provide control of proximal parts of the body, such as the pelvis and the trunk, allowing freer movement of more distal body parts, such as the arms and hands. The use of seating devices may reduce the degrees of freedom the child must control in order to allow voluntary movement of other parts of the body. Some typical modifications in the preschool classroom for children with motor limitations might include seat belts, back inserts to reduce seat depth, footrests, and a cut-out table, to allow children to support themselves more easily with their forearms and to bring materials closer to them. Modifications such as these are often sufficient for children with mild to moderate motor deficits.

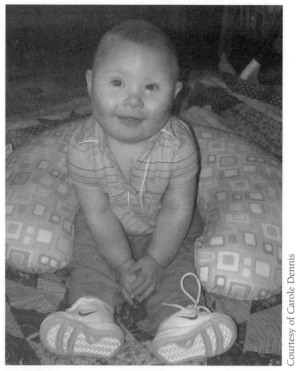

Courtesy of Carole Dennis

Isabella's low tone makes it difficult for her to sit without support. This crescent-shaped pillow helps provide stability.

When homemade adaptations are not practical or sufficient to support the child adequately, special adaptive equipment may be purchased commercially. There are many adaptive seating devices on the market, including floor sitters (to allow children to play with their peers or to participate in floor-time activities that are embedded in many preschool classrooms), **corner seats**, and various special classroom chairs. Children with severe motor impairments often use wheelchairs for postural support and mobility. The options available in wheelchair seating are many and costly, so it is imperative that, when a child needs a wheelchair, the team considers all of the needs of the child. The team must answer many questions regarding the child's **positioning** needs for comfort, function, and socialization. For example, what are the child's mobility needs? What environments must the child travel in? What are the child's capabilities related to controlling the wheelchair? How will the child transfer into and out of the wheelchair? Does the wheelchair need to accommodate communication or special medical devices? How should the child be positioned to support feeding and fine motor activities? Family concerns must be considered, as well. Family members may benefit from a lightweight wheelchair that they can carry in their car and can get into their home. Depending on the services available and the problems that must be addressed, the assistive technology team may include the developmental pediatrician, the physical and occupational therapists,

A corner seat, or floor sitter, is a chair whose back is fashioned in a right angle, or corner, providing postural support to young children so that they can sit on the floor with their peers.

Positioning children at the level of their peers will foster social interactions and make their surroundings more accessible.

the speech-language pathologist, the orthopedist, the rehabilitation technology supplier, the education specialist, and the family. The experienced supplier of specific wheelchairs can be extremely helpful in knowing the products well and ensuring that all needs expressed by the team can be met by the equipment provided.

The interventionist should be knowledgeable about how to handle children when placing them in and out of adapted positioning devices to reduce the influence of atypical tone or primitive reflexes, if these are present. The interventionist also should know about the correct application of seating accessories for wheelchairs such as anterior chest supports, lap trays, and headrests. The best-designed equipment cannot function well unless caregivers and service providers are able to consistently position the child well in the equipment. Team communication is very important here, because sometimes the reasons for specific adjustments and adaptations on wheelchairs are not obvious and team members might decide to change something and unwittingly negate a potential benefit of the equipment. Ramon's case provides a good example of the necessity of providing both high- and low-technology assistive technology to allow him to participate as fully as possible in daily activities. The necessity of team work in determining equipment needs and using assistive technology is very clear.

More physically involved children who cannot stand without support may require a specialized stander. These may provide an opportunity for children to engage in classroom activities in a standing position with classmates and may promote body awareness and self-image in children who cannot stand without support. In addition, standers are provided to support medical and developmental needs such as bone development, circulation, or respiration. There are several different types of standers available: supine, prone, box, or floor standers. The **supine stander** is helpful for the most severely involved child who requires support for the whole body, including the head, neck, and trunk. The stander is positioned horizontally, and the child lies on it while positioning devices and safety straps are adjusted. Then the stander is moved into an upright position. Children with SMA, severe cerebral palsy, high-level spina bifida, or a spinal cord injury may use a supine stander. A **prone stander** supports the front of a child's body, allowing him to lean forward. The child must use some neck and upper back muscles to keep head and shoulders erect, as the stander provides support only through chest level. Often children with less involved cerebral palsy or lower level spina bifida use this type of stander. **Box standers** are used infrequently; better positioning may be available with different types of standers. A **floor stander** is often provided for those who have good trunk, neck, and head control, but who cannot independently stand and maintain balance. It has a wide base of support so the child cannot tip it over, and bars and straps are available for correct trunk, hip, leg, and foot alignment. Floor standers are especially useful to allow more children to play with peers at the sand or water table or to paint or draw at an easel.

A rear walker is a device to support walking in which the horizontal bar is positioned behind the person.

Different types of walkers are available to support independent mobility in children. Therapists generally favor the **backward (or reverse) walker,** which has the wheels and the bar in the back (see the photo of Emily using her rear walker on page 136). This device allows the child to stand up straighter than a walker positioned at the front of the child. There are many different types of orthoses (or

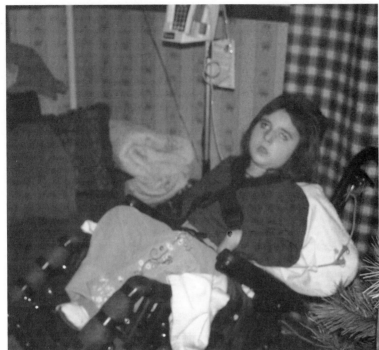

Courtesy of Carole Dennis

Emily's (four years, five months) wheelchair was designed to meet her many needs. It has a tilt-in-space feature that allows her chair to recline when she is tired or when she is being tube-fed.

braces) to support the child's body for better positioning and function. Ankle-foot orthoses (AFOs) were described earlier in this chapter. Additionally, some children may require more or less lower leg control. The hip-knee-ankle-foot orthoses (HKAFO) may be used by a child with very high spina bifida, spinal cord injury, or advanced Duchenne's muscular dystrophy. Children needing less support, including those with mild cerebral palsy, sacral-level spina bifida, and Down syndrome, may use a lower-cut AFO or SMO **(supramalleolar orthoses)**. In a study involving young children with Down syndrome, SMOs provided immediate and long-term improvement in postural stability, as reflected in standing, walking, running, and jumping measures (Martin, 2004).

Powered mobility devices represent high-tech options for children with significant motor impairment; children who are as young as 18 to 24 months may safely operate them. Powered mobility devices that resemble children's toys may be accepted more readily by parents and may promote peer play in children with significant motor impairment (Deitz, 1998). Carlson and Ramsey (2000) provide a concise review of the developmental benefits of power wheelchair provision to young children with disabilities, which include increased communication and peer interaction, increased interaction with objects in the environment, increased motivation for independent mobility, and decreased family perceptions of the child's helplessness. Scull (1996) discusses additional benefits of powered mobility for children as young as 2 years of age. The assistive technology team, the child, and the family determine the best method to access the power wheelchair, depending on the child's physical and cognitive readiness. Powered wheelchairs can be controlled by any part of the body. Options include, but are not limited to, pushing a joystick with the hand or extremities, pressing switch controls mounted on a headrest with the head, moving a chin cup, or blowing into a sip-and-puff control.

Computer programs are often used to foster the development of young children with special needs in many areas, but relatively little exists in this area for improving gross motor skills. However, a number of virtual reality applications have been used with special needs children in experimental situations, with goals including improving gross motor control in children with cerebral palsy (Bryanton et al., 2006; You et al., 2005). While these applications are not feasible for general use at this time, they may provide alternatives for treatment in the future.

SUMMARY

This chapter has presented information on typical and atypical gross motor development in infants and young children, including the acquisition of postural and gross motor skills. Some of the situations and conditions that may result in atypical gross motor development were described and guidelines to help the early interventionist determine when motor development is not following the expected path were provided. Some suggestions for intervention with children who have gross motor deficits were given, with indications of when the help of a motor specialist is needed.

Early interventionists are often the first to observe motor deficits, particularly in children with mild-to-moderate impairment, because they have the benefit of seeing the child with other children of the same age. When an early interventionist has concerns regarding the gross motor development of a child, careful observation of the child is required

in order to clearly articulate the reason for concern. A discussion of these concerns with the intervention team will help the early interventionist determine when additional evaluation is necessary and who should perform the evaluation.

It is important for the early interventionist to gather as much information from the motor specialists on the team as possible so that they have a good understanding of the gross motor needs of the child. It is equally important for the early interventionist to inform the motor specialist (therapist or special physical educator) about the child's function in the home and classroom to aid the motor specialist in understanding the skills the child needs to be able to perform successfully. Only when there is the opportunity for open and ongoing communication among the family, early interventionist, and motor specialist can the benefits of gross motor intervention be optimized.

REVIEW QUESTIONS AND DISCUSSION POINTS

1. Discuss the importance of gross motor development in relationship to the development of skills in communication, cognition, and social-emotional function.

2. Why does a child appear to "toddle" from side to side when he first learns to walk?

3. How does muscle tone influence posture and movement in young children? How does atypical

muscle tone affect young children with special needs?

4. Describe how you would plan assessment and intervention to increase participation for a young child with motor limitations.

5. How could a young child with spastic cerebral palsy who uses a wheelchair or walker be included in activities such as a field trip to the park?

RECOMMENDED RESOURCES

Organizations

American Occupational Therapy Association
4720 Montgomery Lane
PO Box 31220
Bethesda, MD 20824-1220
301-652-2682
http://www.aota.org

Section on Pediatrics—American Physical Therapy Association
111 N. Fairfax St.
Alexandria, VA 22314-1488
800-999-2782, ext. 3254
http://www.PediatricAPTA.org

Brain Injury Association of America
8201 Greensboro Drive
Suite 611
McLean, VA 22102
Telephone: 703-761-0750
http://www.biausa.org

The National Early Childhood Technical Assistance Center
Campus Box 8040, UNC–CH
Chapel Hill, NC 27599-8040
919-962-2001
http://www.nectas.unc.edu

National Institute of Child Health and Human Development
Bldg. 31, Room 2A32, MSC 2425
31 Center Dr.
Bethesda, MD 20892-2425
800-370-2943
http://www.nichd.nih.gov

Resources and Products

Abilitations
PO Box 922668
Norcross, GA 30010-2668
1-800-850-8602
http://abilitations.com

ABLEDATA
8630 Fenton Street, Suite 930
Silver Spring, MD 20910
800-227-0216
www.abledata.com

Achievement Products for Children
PO Box 9033
Canton, Ohio 44711
1-800-766-4303
http://www.specialkidszone.com

Otto Bock HealthCare
Two Carlson Parkway North, Suite 100
Minneapolis, MN 55447
http://www.ottobockus.com

Rifton Equipment
PO Box 260
Rifton, NY 12471-0260
1-800-571-8198
http://rifton.com

Sportime
PO Box 922668
Norcross, GA 30020-2668
1-800-281-5700
http://www.sportime.com

REFERENCES

Adolph, K. E. (2002). Babies' steps make giant strides toward a science of development. *Infant Behavior and Development, 25*(1), 86–90.

Ali, F. A., Al-Bustan, M. A., Al-Busairi, W. A., Al-Mulla, F. A., & Esbaita, E. Y. (2006). Cervical spine abnormalities associated with Down syndrome. *International Orthopaedics, 30*(4), 284–289.

American Academy of Pediatrics Task Force on Infant Sleep Positions and SIDS. (2002). Changing concepts of sudden infant death syndrome: Implications for infant sleeping environment and sleep positions. *Pediatrics, 105,* 650–656,

American Physical Therapy Association. (2007). *Vision 2020.* Retrieved April 22, 2007, from http://www.apta. org/AM/Template.cfm?Section=Vision_20201&Template=/TaggedPage/TaggedPageDisplay.cfm&TPLID=285&ContentID=32061.

American Psychiatric Association. (2000). *Diagnostic and statistical manual of mental disorders* (4th ed.). Washington, DC: Author.

Ayres, A. J. (1989). *Sensory Integration and Praxis Tests.* Los Angeles: Western Psychological Services.

Baranek, G. T. (2002). Efficacy of sensory and motor interventions for children with autism. *Journal of Autism and Developmental Disorders, 32*(5), 1–27.

Bax, M., Goldstein, M., Rosenbaum, P., Leviton, A., & Paneth, N. (2005). Proposed definition and classification of cerebral palsy, April 2005. *Developmental Medicine & Child Neurology, 47,* 571–576.

Bayley, N. (2005a). *Bayley Scales of Infant Development* (3rd ed.). San Antonio, TX: Harcourt Assessment.

Bayley, N. (2005b). *Bayley III Screening Test.* San Antonio, TX: Harcourt Assessment.

Berkeley, S., Zittel, L. L., Pitney, V., & Nichols, S. E. (2001). Motor and object control skills in children diagnosed with autism. *Adapted Physical Education Quarterly, 18,* 405–416.

Blackman, J. A. (1997). *Medical aspects of developmental disabilities in children birth to three* (3rd ed.). Gaithersburg, MD: Aspen.

Bly, L. (1983). *The components of normal movement during the first year of life.* Chicago: Neuro-Developmental Treatment Association, Inc.

Botto, L. D., Moore, C. A., Khoury, M. J., & Erickson, J. D. (1999). Neural tube defects. *New England Journal of Medicine, 341,* 1509–1510.

Bricker, D., & Squires, J. (1995). *The ages and stages questionnaire.* Baltimore, MD: Brookes.

Bruininks, R. H., & Bruininks, B. D. (2005). *Bruininks-Oseretsky Test of Motor Proficiency* (2nd ed.). Circle Pines, MN: American Guidance Service.

Bryanton, C., Bosse, J., Brien, M., McLean, J., McCormick, A., & Sveistrup, H. (2006). Feasibility, motivation, and selective motor control: Virtual reality compared to conventional home exercise in children with cerebral palsy. *CyberPsychology & Behavior, 9*(2), 123–128.

Burrows, P., & Griffiths, P. (2002). Do baby walkers delay onset of walking in young children? *British Journal of Community Nursing, 7*(11), 581–586.

Campos, J. J., Anderson, D. I., Barbu-Roth, M. A., Hubbard, E. M., Hertenstein, M. J., Witherington, D. (2000). Travel broadens the mind. *Infancy, 1,* 149–219.

Carlson, S. J., & Ramsey, C. (2000). Assistive technology. In S. K. Campbell, D. W. Vander Linden, & R. J. Palisano (Eds.), *Physical therapy for children* (2nd ed., pp. 671–708). Philadelphia: W. B. Saunders.

Cermak, S. (1991). Somatodyspraxia. In A. Fisher, E. Murray, & A. Bundy (Eds.), *Sensory integration: Theory and practice* (pp. 137–168). Philadelphia: Davis.

Cermak, S. A., Gubbay, S. S., & Larkin, D. (2002). What is developmental coordination disorder? In S. A. Cermak & D. Larkin (Eds.), *Developmental coordination disorder* (pp. 2–22). Albany, NY: Delmar.

Chiafery, M. (2006). Care and management of the child with shunted hydrocephalus. *Pediatric Nursing, 32*(3), 222–225.

Clark, J. E. (1995). On becoming skillful: Patterns and constraints. *Rehabilitation Quarterly, 66,* 173–183.

Cohen, E., Boettcher, K., Maher, T., Phillips, A., Terrel, L., Nixon-Cave, K., et al. (1999). Evaluation of the Peabody Developmental Gross Motor Scales for young children of African American and Hispanic ethnic backgrounds. *Pediatric Physical Therapy, 11*(4), 191–197.

Danzer, E., Adzick, S., Gerdes, M., Bebbington, M., Sutton, L., Melcheonni, J., et al. (2006). Lower extremity neuro-motor function following in utero myelomeningocele repair. *American Journal of Obstetrics and Gynecology, 195*(6), S22.

Darrah, J., Law, M., & Pollock, N. (2001). Family-centered functional therapy—A choice for children with motor dysfunction. *Infants and Young Children, 13*(4), 79–87.

David, K. S. (2000). Developmental coordination disorders. In S. K. Campbell, D. W. Vander Linden, & A. J. Palisano (Eds.), *Physical therapy for children* (2nd ed., pp. 471–501). Philadelphia: Saunders.

Davis, R. E., Moon, R. Y., Sachs, I., & Otolini, M. C. (1998). Effects of sleep position on infant motor development. *Pediatrics, 102,* 1135–1140.

de Chalain, T. M., & Park, S. (2005). Torticollis associated with positional plagiocephaly: A growing epidemic. *Journal of Craniofacial Surgery, 16*(3), 411–418.

Deconinck, F. J. A., De Clercq, D., Savelsberg, G. J. P., Van Coster, R., Oostra, A., Dewitte, G., et al. (2006). Differences in gait between children with and without developmental coordination disorder. *Motor Control, 10,* 125–142.

DeGangi, G. A., & Berk, R. A. (1983). *The DeGangi-Berk Test of Sensory Integration.* San Antonio, TX: Psychological Corporation.

Deitz, J. C. (1998). Pediatric augmented mobility. In D. B. Gray, L. A. Quatrano, & M. L. Lieberman (Eds.), *Designing and using assistive technology: The human perspective* (pp. 269–284). Baltimore: Brookes.

Dewey, C., Fleming, P., Golding, J., & ALSPAC Study Team. (1998). Does the supine sleeping position have any adverse effects on the child? II. Development in the first 18 months. *Pediatrics, 101*(1), p. e5. Retrieved from http://www.pediatrics.org/cgi/content/full/101/1/e5.

Dewey, D. (2002). Subtypes of developmental coordination disorder. In S. Cermak & D. Larkin (Eds.), *Developmental coordination disorder* (pp. 40–53). Albany, NY: Delmar.

Didelot, W. P. (2003). Current concepts in myelomeningocele. *Current Opinion in Orthopaedics, 14*(6), 398–402.

Dunn, W. (1999). *Sensory Profile: User's Manual.* San Antonio, TX: Psychological Corporation.

Dunn, W. (2000). *Best practice occupational therapy.* Thorofare, NJ: Slack.

Fetters, L., Fernandes, B., & Cermak, S. (1988). The relationship of proximal and distal components in the development of reaching. *Physical Therapy, 68,* 839–845.

Fidler, D. J., Hepburn, S. L., Mankin, G., & Rogers, S. J. (2005). Praxis skills in young children with Down syndrome, other developmental disabilities, and typically developing children. *American Journal of Occupational Therapy, 59*(2), 129–138.

Fisher, A. G., Murray, E. A., & Bundy, A. C. (2002). *Sensory integration: Theory and practice.* Philadelphia, PA: F. A. Davis.

Foerster O. (1977). The motor cortex in man in the light of Hughlings Jackson's Doctrines. In O. D. Payton, S. Hirt, & R. Newman (Eds.), *Scientific basis for neurophysiologic approaches to therapeutic exercise* (pp. 13–18). Philadelphia: Davis.

Folio, M. R., & Fewell, R. R. (2000). *Peabody Developmental Motor Scales, Second* (2nd ed.). San Antonio, TX: Psychological Corporation.

Furuno, S. (2004). *HELP checklist (0–3).* Palo Alto, CA: VORT Corporation.

Garrett, M., McElroy, A. M., & Staines, A. (2002). Locomotor milestones and babywalkers: Cross sectional study. *British Medical Journal, 324,* 1494.

Gaudreault, N., Gravel, D., Nadeau, S., & Houde, S. (2005). Motor function in Duchenne muscular dystrophy children: A review of the literature. *Critical Reviews in Physical and Rehabilitation Medicine, 17*(3), 231–248.

Gesell, A., & Amatruda, C. (1947). *Developmental diagnosis* (2nd ed.). New York: Harper & Row.

Graham, J. M., Gomez, M., Halberg, A., Earl, D. L., Kreutzman, J. T., Cui, J., et al. (2005). Management of deformational plagiocephaly: Repositioning versus orthotic therapy. *The Journal of Pediatrics, 146*(2), 258–262.

Grubb, M. S., & Thompson, I. D. (2004). The influence of early experience on the development of sensory systems. *Current Opinion in Neurobiology, 14*(4), 503–512.

Haley, S. M., Coster, W. J., Ludlow, L. H., Haltiwanger, J. T., & Andrellos P. J. (1992). *Pediatric Evaluation of Disability Inventory.* San Antonio, TX: Psychological Corporation.

Hardin, B. J., & Peisner-Feinberg. (2001). *The Early Learning Accomplishment Profile.* Chapel Hill, NC: Kaplan Early Learning.

Hardin, B. J., Peisner-Feinberg, E. S., & Weeks, S. W. (2005). *Learning Accomplishment Profile—Diagnostics* (3rd ed.). Chapel Hill, NC: Kaplan Early Learning.

Henderson, S. E., & Sugden, D. A. (1992). *The Movement Assessment Battery of Children.* San Antonio, TX: Psychological Corporation.

Hinderer, K. A., Hinderer, S. R., & Shurtleff, D. B. (2000). Myelodysplasia. In S. K. Campbell, D. W. Vander Linden, & R. J. Palisano (Eds.), *Physical therapy for children* (2nd ed, pp. 621–670). Philadelphia: Saunders.

Howle, J. M. (2004). *Neuro-developmental treatment approach: Theoretical foundations and principles of clinical practice.* Laguna Beach, CA: Neuro-developmental Treatment Association.

Hunter, J. G. (2001). The neonatal intensive care unit. In J. Case-Smith (Ed.), *Occupational therapy for children* (4th ed., pp. 636–707). St. Louis: Mosby.

Jansiewicz, E. M., Goldberg, M. C., Newschaffer, C. J., Denckla, M. B., Landa, R., & Mostofsky, S. H. (2006). Motor signs distinguish children with high functioning autism and Asperger's syndrome from controls. *Journal of Autism and Developmental Disorders, 36*(5), 613–621.

Jennings, J. T., Sarbaugh, B. G., & Payne, N. S. (2005). Conveying the message about optimal infant positions. *Physical and Occupational Therapy in Pediatrics, 25*(3), 3–18.

Johnson, M. P., Gerdes, M., Rintoul, N., Pasquariello, P., Melchionni, J., Sutton, L. N., et al. (2006). Maternal-fetal surgery for myelomeningocele: Neurodevelopmental outcomes at 2 years of age. *American Journal of Obstetrics and Gynecology, 194*(4), 1145–1150.

Kelly, Y., Sacker, A., Schoon, I., & Nazroo, J. (2006). Ethnic differences in achievement of developmental milestones by 9 months of age: The Millennium Cohort Study. *Developmental Medicine and Child Neurology, 48*(10), 825–830.

Kerkering, G. A., & Phillips, W. E. (2000). Brain injuries: Traumatic brain injuries, near-drowning, and brain tumors.

In S. K. Campbell, D. W. Vander Linden, & R. J. Palisano (Eds.), *Physical therapy for children* (2nd ed., pp. 597–620). Philadelphia: Saunders.

Kern, J. K. (2006). The pattern of sensory processing abnormalities in autism. *Autism, 10*(5), 480–494.

Kern, J. K. (2007). Sensory correlations in autism. *Autism, 11*(2), 123–134.

Ketelaar, M., Vermeer, A., Hart, H., van Petegem-van Beek, E., & Helders, P. J. M. (2001). Effects of a functional therapy program on motor abilities of children with cerebral palsy. *Physical Therapy, 81*(9), 1534–1545.

Koomar, J. A., & Bundy, A. C. (2002). The art and science of creating direct intervention from theory. In A. Bundy, S. Lane, & E. Murray (Eds.), *Sensory integration: Theory and practice* (2nd ed., pp. 251–314). Philadelphia: Davis.

Lauteslager, P. E. M., Vermeer, A., & Helders, P. J. M. (1998). Disturbances in the motor behavior of children with Down's syndrome: The need for a theoretical framework. *Physiotherapy, 84*(1), 5–13.

Lima, M. C., Eickmann, S. H., Lima, A. V. C., Guerra, M. Q., Lira, P. I. C., Huttly, S. R. K., et al. (2004). Determinants of mental and motor development at 12 months in a low income population: A cohort study in Northeast Brazil. *Acta Paediatrica, 93*, 969–975.

Lin, S. H., Cermak, S., Coster, S. J., & Miller, L. (2005). The relation between length of institutionalization and sensory integration in children adopted from Eastern Europe. *American Journal of Occupational Therapy, 59*(2), 139–147.

Linder, T. W. (2001). *Transdisciplinary play-based assessment* (2nd ed.). Baltimore: Brookes.

Lovering, R. M., Porter, N. C., & Bloch, R. J. (2005). The muscular dystrophies: From genes to therapies. *Physical Therapy, 85*(12), 1372–1388.

Magalhaes, L. C., Missiuna, C., & Wong, S. (2006). Terminology used in research reports of developmental coordination disorder. *Developmental Medicine and Child Neurology, 48*(11), 937–941.

Magnus, R. (1926). Some results of studies in the physiology of posture. *Lancet, 2*, 531–585.

Mahoney, G. (2004). Early motor intervention: The need for new treatment paradigms. *Infants and Young Children, 17*(4), 291–300.

Martin, K. (2004). Effects of supramalleolar orthoses on postural stability in children with Down syndrome. *Developmental Medicine and Child Neurology, 46*(6), 406–411.

Mathiowetz, V., & Haugen, J. B. (1994). Motor behavior research: Implications for therapeutic approaches to central nervous system dysfunction. *American Journal of Occupational Therapy, 48*, 733–745.

McClain, C., Provost, B., & Crowe, T. K. (2000). Motor development of two-year-old typically developing Native American children on the *Bayley Scales of Infant Development II Motor Scale. Pediatric Physical Therapy, 12*, 108–113.

McEwen, I. (2000). Children with cognitive impairments. In S. K. Campbell, D. W. Vander Linden, & R. J. Palisano (Eds.), *Physical therapy for children* (2nd ed., pp. 502–532). Philadelphia: Saunders.

Meltzoff, A., & Gopnik, A. (1993). The role of imitation in understanding persons and developing a theory of mind. In S. Baron-Cohen, H. Tager-Flusberg, & D. J. Cohen (Eds.), *Understanding other minds: Perspectives from autism* (pp. 335–366). New York: Oxford University Press.

Mersereau, P., Kilker, K., Carter, H., Fasset, A., Williams, F., Flores, A., et al. (2004). Spina bifida and anencephaly before and after folic acid mandate—United States, 1995–1996 and 1999–2000. *Morbidity and Mortality Weekly Report, 53*(17), 362–265.

Miller, L. J., & Roid, G. H. (2002). *The T.I.M.E. ® Toddler and Infant Motor Evaluation.* San Antonio, TX: Psychological Corporation.

Minshew, N. J., Sung, K., Jones, B. L., & Furman, J. M. (2004). Underdevelopment of the postural control system in autism. *Neurology 63*(11), 2056–2061.

Missiuna, C., Moll, S., King, S., King, G., & Law, M. (2007). A trajectory of troubles: Parents' impressions of the impact of developmental coordination disorder. *Physical and Occupational Therapy in Pediatrics, 27*(1), 81–101.

Missiuna, C., Rivard, L., & Bartlett, D. (2006). Exploring assessment tools and the target of intervention for children with developmental coordination disorder. *Physical and Occupational Therapy in Pediatrics, 26*(1/2), 71–89.

Molnar, G. E. (1985). *Pediatric rehabilitation.* Baltimore: Williams and Wilkins.

Monson, R. M., Deitz, J., & Kartin, D. (2003). The relationship between awake positioning and motor performance among infants who slept supine. *Pediatric Physical Therapy, 15*(4), 196–203.

Mostofsky, S. H., Dubey, P., Jerath, V. K., Jansiewicz, E. M., Goldberg, M. C., & Denckla, M. B. (2006). Developmental dyspraxia is not limited to imitation in children with autism spectrum disorders. *Journal of the International Neuropsychological Society, 12*(3), 314–326.

National Institute of Health. (2006). *A snapshot of brain and central nervous system cancers.* Retrieved April 4, 2006, from http://searchosp1.nci.nih.gov/disease/Brain-Snapshot.pdf.

Newborg, J. (2005). *Battelle Developmental Inventory* (2nd ed.). Chicago: Riverside.

Olney, S. J., & Wright, M. J. (2000). Cerebral palsy. In S. K. Campbell, D. W. Vander Linden, & R. J. Palisano (Eds.), *Physical therapy for children* (2nd ed., pp. 533–570). Philadelphia: Saunders.

Oregon Health and Science University, Department of Neurosurgery. (2007). Patient information—pediatric positional skull deformity. Retrieved April 22, 2007, from http://www.ohsu.edu/neurosurgery/conditions/positional_skull_deformities.shtml

Ostensjo, S., Carlberg, E. B., & Volestad, N. (2005). The use and impact of assistive devices and other environmental modifications on everyday activities and care in young children with cerebral palsy. *Disability and Rehabilitation, 27*(14), 849–861.

Palisano, R. J., Campbell, S. K., & Harris, S. R. (2000). Clinical decision making in pediatric physical therapy. In S. K. Campbell, D. W. Vander Linden, & R. J. Palisano (Eds.), *Physical therapy for children* (2nd ed., pp. 198–224). Philadelphia: Saunders.

Palisano, R. J., Walter, S. D., Russel, D. J., Rosenbaum, P. L., Gemus, M., Galuppi, B. E., et al. (2001). Gross motor function of children with Down syndrome: Creation of motor growth curves. *Archives of Physical Medicine and Rehabilitation, 82*(4), 494–500.

Piper, M. C., & Darrah, J. (1995). *Motor assessment of the developing infant.* Philadelphia: Saunders.

Provence, S., Erikson, J., Vater, S., & Palmeri, S. (1995). *Infant-Toddler Developmental Assessment.* Itasca, IL: Riverside.

Quan, A., Adams, R., Ekmark, E., & Baum, M. (2003). Bone mineral density in children with myelomeningocele: Effect of hydrochlorothiazide. *Pediatric Nephrology, 18*(9), 929–993.

Reeves, G. D., & Cermak, S. A. (2002). Disorders of praxis. In A. Bundy, S. Lane, & E. Murray (Eds.), *Sensory integration: Theory and practice* (2nd ed., pp. 71–100). Philadelphia: Davis.

Rettig, M. A., & McCarthy-Rettig, K. (2005). A survey of the health, sleep, and development of children adopted from China. *Health and Social Work, 31*(3), 201–207.

Rinehart, N. J., Bradshaw, J. L., Brereton, A. V., & Tonge, B. J. (2002). A clinical and neurobehavioral review of high-functioning autism and Asperger's disorder. *Australian and New Zealand Journal of Psychiatry, 36,* 762–770.

Rinehart, N. J., Tonge, B. J., Iansek, R., McGinley, J., Brereton, A. V., Enticott, P. G., et al. (2006). Gait function in newly diagnosed children with autism: Cerebellar and basal ganglia related motor disorder. *Developmental Medicine & Child Neurology, 48*(10), 819–824.

Russell, D. J., Rosenbaum, L. M., & Avery, M. J. (2002). *Gross Motor Function Measure (GMFM-66 and GMFM-88): User's Manual.* Malden, MA: Blackwell.

Rutland-Brown, W., Langlois, J. A., Thomas, K. E., & Xi, Y. L. (2006). Incidence of traumatic brain injury in the United States, 2003. *Journal of Head Trauma Rehabilitation, 21*(6), 544–548.

Salls, J. S., Sherman, L. N., & Gatty, C. M. (2002). The relationship of infant sleep and play positioning to motor milestone achievement. *American Journal of Occupational Therapy, 56*(5), 577–580.

Scull, S. A. (1996). Mobility and ambulation. In L. A. Kurtz, P. W. Dowrick, S. E. Levy, & M. L. Batshaw (Eds.), *Handbook of developmental disabilities* (pp. 269–326). Gaithersburg, MD: Aspen.

Shapiro, D. K., & Sayers, L. K. (2003). Who does what on the interdisciplinary team regarding physical education for students with disabilities? *Teaching Exceptional Children, 35*(6), 32–28.

Shakhazizian, K. A., Massagli, T. L., & Southard, T. L. (2000). Spinal cord injury. In S. K. Campbell, D. W. Vander Linden, & R. J. Palisano (Eds.), *Physical therapy for children* (2nd ed., pp. 571–596). Philadelphia: Saunders.

Sherrington, C. S. (1947). *The integrative action of the nervous system.* New Haven, CT: Yale University Press.

Shields, B. J., & Smith, G. A. (2006). Success in the prevention of infant walker-related injuries: An analysis of national data, 1990–2001. *Pediatrics, 117*(3), 452–459.

Stuberg, W. A. (1992). Considerations related to weight-bearing programs in children with developmental disabilities. *Physical Therapy, 72,* 35–40.

Stuberg, W. A. (2000). Muscular dystrophy and spinal muscular atrophy. In S. K. Campbell, D. W. Vander Linden, & R. J. Palisano (Eds.), *Physical therapy for children* (2nd ed., pp. 339–368). Philadelphia: Saunders.

Super, C. M. (1976). Environmental effects on motor development: The case of African precocity. *Developmental Medicine and Child Neurology, 18,* 561–567.

Surveillance of Cerebral Palsy in Europe Collaborative Group (2002). Prevalence and Characteristics of Children with cerebral palsy in Europe. *Developmental Medicine and Child Neurology, 44,* 633–640.

Sweeney, J. K., & Bascom, B. B. (1995). Motor development and self-stimulatory movement in institutionalized Romanian children. *Pediatric Physical Therapy, 7,* 124–132.

Thelen, E. (2000). Motor development as foundation and future of developmental psychology. *International Journal of Behavioral Development, 24*(4), 385–397.

Thoman, E. (1987). Self-regulation of stimulation by prematures with a breathing blue bear. In J. J. Gallagher & C. T. Ramey (Eds.), *The malleability of children*. Baltimore: Brookes.

Toedebusch, B., & LaFontaine, T. (2005). Strength and conditioning for persons with muscular dystrophy. *Strength and Conditioning Journal, 27*(3), 39–41.

Touwen, B. C. L. (1978). Variability and stereotypy in normal and deviant development. In C. Apley (Ed.), *Care of the handicapped child* (pp. 99–110). Series title: *Clinics in Developmental Medicine*, No. 67. Philadelphia: Lippincott.

Ulrich, D. A., Ulrich, B. A., Angulo-Kinzler, R. M., & Yun, J. (2001). Treadmill training of infants with Down syndrome: Evidence-based developmental outcomes. *Pediatrics, 108*(5), E84–E84.

Vaivre-Douret, L., Ennouri, K., Jrad, I., Garrec, C., & Papiernik, E. (2004). Effect of positioning on the incidence of abnormalities of muscle tone in low-risk, preterm infants. *European Journal of Paediatric Neurology, 8*(1), 21–34.

Van Haastert, I. C., deVries, L. S., Helders, P. J. M., & Jongmans, M. J. (2006). Early gross motor development of preterm infants according to the Alberta Infant Motor Scale. *The Journal of Pediatrics, 149*(5), 617–622.

VanSant, A. F. (2003). Motor control, motor learning, and motor development. In P. C. Montgomery & B. H. Connolly (Eds.), *Clinical applications of motor control.* (pp. 25–52). Thorofare, NJ: Slack.

Vicari, S. (2006). Motor development and neuropsychologic patterns in persons with Down syndrome. *Behavior Genetics, 36*(3), 355–362.

Volman, M., Visser, J., & Lensvelt-Mulders, G. (2007). Functional status in 5- to 7-year-old children with Down syndrome in relation to motor ability and performance mental ability. *Disability and Rehabilitation, 29*(1), 25–31.

Voress, J. K., & Maddox, T. (1998). *Developmental assessment of young children*. Los Angeles: Western Psychological Services.

VORT Corporation. (1995–1999). *HELP for preschoolers*. Palo Alto, CA: Author.

Washington, K., Deitz, J. C., White, O. R., & Schwartz, I. S. (2002). The effects of a contoured foam seat on postural alignment and upper-extremity function in infants with neuromotor impairments. *Physical Therapy, 82*(11), 1064–1076.

Watson, L. R., Baranek, G., & DiLavore, P. C. (2003). Toddlers with autism. *Infants and Young Children, 16*(3), 201–214.

WHO Multicentre Growth Reference Study. (2006). Assessment of sex differences and heterogeneity in motor milestone attainment among populations in the WHO Multicentre Growth Reference Study by Group. *Acta Paediatrica, 95*(3), 66–75.

Williams, H. G. (2002). Motor control in children with developmental coordination disorder. In S. A. Cermak & D. Larkin (Eds.), *Developmental coordination disorder* (pp. 117–137). Albany, NY: Delmar.

Winter, S., Autry, A., Boyle, C., & Yeargin-Allsopp, M. (2002). Trends in the prevalence of cerebral palsy in the population-based study. *Pediatrics, 110*, 1120–1225.

Wong, V., Wong, S., Chan, K., & Wong, W. (2002). Functional Independence Measure (WeeFIM) for Chinese children: Hong Kong cohort. *Pediatrics, 109*, 317–319.

World Health Organization. (2001). *The international classification of functioning, disability and health (ICF)*. Geneva: World Health Organization.

You, S. H., Jang, S. H., Kim, Y., Kwon, Y., Barrow, I., & Hallett, M. (2005). Cortical reorganization induced by virtual reality therapy in a child with hemiparetic cerebral palsy. *Developmental Medicine and Child Neurology, 47*(9), 628–635.

Zahr, L. K. (1999). Predictors of development in premature infants from low-income families: African Americans and Hispanics. *Journal of Perinatology, 19*(4), 284–289.

Fine Motor, Oral Motor, and Self-Care Development

Jean A. Patz and Rose M. Messina

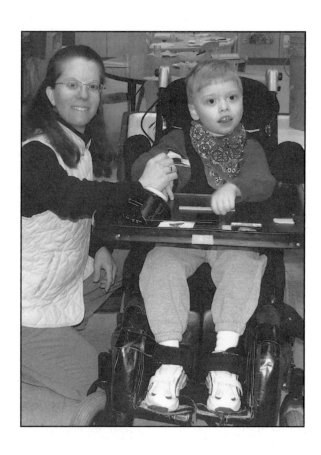

Chapter Outline

Lily

Lily, a 17-month-old fraternal twin, was delivered at 30 weeks with a birth weight of 2 lb 3 oz. The mother indicated that at 27 weeks gestation, Lily developed intrauterine growth retardation. At 1 year of age, Lily manifested delayed motor skills. Her twin sister had learned to crawl and speak, whereas Lily could only roll over and make basic vowel sounds. Lily was initially diagnosed with hypotonia (low muscle tone) of unknown cause. She has signs of hypertonia (high muscle tone) in her extremities as well, which interferes with her ability to manipulate toys and objects, chew or drink effectively from a cup, sit or move in her environment, and participate fully in age-appropriate self-care skills.

Despite her physical limitations, her parents report that Lily is a happy, bright, and healthy child. Lily started seeing a physical therapist (PT) when she was 7 months old, an occupational therapist (OT) when she was 10 months old, and an early intervention teacher when she was 14 months old. The OT addresses issues related to fine motor, oral motor, and self-care skills. In the fine motor area, Lily needs assistance with reach, grasp, release, and manipulation of toys. Her parents want help with her eating because she thrusts her tongue during meals, making it difficult to eat food textures appropriate for her age level. She now eats soft foods such as bread, macaroni and cheese, and pasta, as well as mashed and pureed items. Also, Lily needs additional postural support during play, eating, and transportation due to her inability to sit independently. Lily will be referred to throughout this chapter to exemplify early intervention approaches and considerations that relate to fine motor, oral motor, and self-care development.

This chapter examines development, evaluation, and intervention in the areas of fine motor, oral motor, and self-care skills. **Fine motor skills** reflect a child's ability to manipulate and control objects and tools through control of the upper extremities and small muscle movements of the hands. **Oral motor** refers to movement of the tongue, jaw, lips, and cheeks during sucking, swallowing, munching, chewing, spoon-feeding, and drinking from a bottle or cup. **Self-care skills** refer to basic activities such as dressing, toileting, bathing, grooming, eating, sleeping, and functional mobility (American Occupational Therapy Association, 2002). Other terms used to address the same domain include *self-help, adaptive skills*, or *activities of daily living (ADLs)*.

Fine motor development provides the means by which children interact with and learn about the world around them. A child learns about the perceptual features of objects in the environment by holding objects, bringing them to the mouth, and manipulating them so that what is felt can be paired with what is seen. It is through the hands that a child can experiment with cognitive concepts such as object permanence, cause and effect, classification, and conservation. It is through the development of fine motor skills that the child learns how to connect with and have an effect upon her world. In fact, it is through the hands that a child can demonstrate what she has learned. Most measures of cognitive function rely on the child's ability to control objects with the hands. Clearly, fine motor skills are important for children to fully participate in activities that form much of the curriculum in early childhood learning environments. In second grade classrooms, 50% of the time is devoted to fine motor tasks (McHale & Cermak, 1992).

Oral motor, fine motor, and self-care skills have several common attributes. Each requires the coordination of movement with sensory processes, which includes **tactile** sensation, proprioception, and vision. In addition, each is dependent to some degree on gross motor and postural skills, which provide the scaffold upon which fine motor, oral motor, and self-care skills develop.

> The term *tactile* refers to the child's ability to perceive touch to the skin.

:: THEORIES OF DEVELOPMENT

Current views of the development of fine motor control reflect the theoretical models for motor development described in chapter 3. The neuromaturational model has influenced most descriptions of motor development in very young children. The earliest voluntary movements of newborns appear to be random and lacking in coordination. Postural and motor reflexes provide the very young infant with ways of interacting with the environment (Case-Smith, 2005). As noted in chapter 3, the earliest reflexes, also known as *primitive reflexes,* are stereotypic, predictable movement patterns triggered by specific sensory stimuli. Many of the reflexes observed in very young children have a function in development of necessary components needed for voluntary control of movement. When an object is placed in the palm of a month-old infant, the hand will close around the object in the **grasp reflex**. These gross responses gradually become more differentiated as the infant matures. By 6 months of age, only the fingers that are in contact with an object will flex and the hand will begin to move in the direction of the tactile stimulus. At about this same time, infants can use information from both the tactile and visual systems to reach toward an object and open the hand to grasp an object, representing a transition from reflexive grasp to purposeful, voluntary grasp. This transition from reflexive to voluntary movement is representative of a shift in motor control from lower centers of the central nervous system to higher, cortical control. Practice in reach and grasp results in a smoother motor pattern through structural changes in the brain brought about by learning.

Current views of motor development reflect how motor behavior changes in response to the demands of the situation. Development and motor learning occur through a number of different internal and external dynamic systems (Thelen, 2002). Motor learning is no longer viewed as an isolated event developing in a pure developmental progression. It must be viewed within the context of perceptual, cognitive, and motor processes and environmental factors (Shumway-Cook & Woollacott, 2007). Studies suggest that factors including internal dynamics, intention, preferential movement patterns, differences in body size, as well as object properties will yield different patterns for reach and grasp (Thelen, Corbetta, Kamm, & Spencer, 1993). This supports a dynamic systems view of motor development wherein motor control is a more dynamic process that responds to properties and constraints of the body and the environment. Treatment approaches developed from the neuromaturational model including **neurodevelopmental treatment (NDT)** and sensory-based interventions such as **sensory integration (SI)** have evolved to incorporate this dynamic process. NDT intervention currently addresses not only quality of movement but also how movement and the interplay of other factors such as the environment impact functional tasks (Connolly & Montgomery, 2003). Sensory integration therapy considers the motivation of the child and the meaningfulness of the task as essential parameters of treatment (Reeves & Cermak, 2002).

> Neurodevelopmental treatment (NDT) therapeutic practices are used for children with neurological involvement to facilitate improved posture and movement for functional tasks. NDT uses key points of control through specific handling techniques and the forces of gravity to stimulate improved movement.

The theories used to describe gross and fine motor development can apply to oral motor development as well. Certainly, some therapeutic approaches to swallowing and feeding disorders follow a neurodevelopmental framework, which is consistent with a neuromaturational model of motor control. A number of primitive oral reflexes in the neonate support feeding. For example, when the caregiver places a finger in the infant's mouth, the infant loosely closes the mouth around the finger and initiates sucking. This early **sucking reflex** allows the infant to attach to the nipple when nursing, a function that is later replaced by volitional control. Using the neuromaturational model, the evaluator might address muscle tone, presence of atypical oral reflexes, and physiological state during an oral motor assessment. In addition, the evaluator including a dynamic systems model might address factors such as the type of nipple and bottle, temperature of the liquid, interaction between and experience of the feeder and child, and sensory conditions of the environment. Traditional therapeutic approaches to problems with oral motor control have followed a neurodevelopmental framework. In fact, the most common models of practice employed when children present with impaired oral motor control due to neuromotor dysfunction is neurodevelopmental treatment. Sensory-based intervention techniques may be used with children whose eating problems seem to be related to the inability to process sensory information, as seen in children with autism as described in vignette 4.1.

> Sensory integration (SI) is the ability of the child to process and organize basic sensory information including tactile (touch), proprioceptive (perception of body and joint movement), vestibular (tone and posture), visual (sight), auditory (hearing), olfactory (smell), and gustatory (taste) in order to make a functional and adaptive response to environmental demands.

:: STAGES OF TYPICAL DEVELOPMENT

Fine Motor Development

Fine motor skills are comprised of precise movements of the hands and fingers, supported by the dynamic **stability** of the trunk and control of the shoulder girdle and arms. The skilled, preferred use of one hand (**hand preference**), the ability to use two hands together, and the ability to perform different tasks with each hand are also needed for children to carry out complex movements. In addition to motor

> Stability is the ability to maintain a posture against gravity.

Sensory processing is the way a child receives (sensory registration), regulates (sensory modulation), and habituates to incoming sensory information.

control, fine motor skills require adequate cognition and **sensory processing** of tactile, proprioceptive, and visual information (Mulligan, 2002).

Fine motor control is defined as a child's ability to functionally reach, grasp, and release objects for purposeful manipulation of toys and tools. Development in each of these areas is supported by a child's increasing control in flexion, extension, coactivation, and rotation of the shoulder girdle, forearm, and hand. The foundational components of reach, grasp, and release mature within the first 2 years, allowing for development of higher-level manipulative skills in the toddler and preschool-aged child.

Reach   Reaching is the movement of the arm toward an object. Components for the development of reach are mature by approximately 6 months in supine, 7 months in prone, and 12 months in sitting (Erhardt, 1994b). The development of reach patterns is outlined in Table 4.1.

In prone, the infant progresses from bearing weight on forearms to pushing up on extended arms, which helps to develop stability in the shoulder girdle for reach. The ability to free an arm for reaching occurs when the infant can stabilize the pelvis and shift weight toward one side, thus freeing an arm for reach.

Arm movements of the newborn in supine are random and disorganized and the ability to look at hands has not yet developed. At 2 months of age, when the infant turns her head to one side, the arm on that same side extends while the opposite extremities flex as a result of the influence of the asymmetrical tonic neck reflex. This action provides the first visual connection between the eyes and the arm. Swiping with one hand occurs, as the infant is able to look at interesting faces and objects. Reach progresses from this random swiping to purposeful reaching with both arms together. Two-handed reaching is replaced as the infant matures by the use of one arm in a direct approach toward an object. This movement demonstrates the ability to differentiate one arm from the other. Further refinement occurs when the infant is able to supinate the forearm while reaching (Erhardt, 1994a). **Supination,** which is a critical component of controlled use of the thumb and fingers, is the ability to rotate the forearm so that the thumb moves in an upward direction and the object within the hand is clearly visible to the infant.

Grasp   Grasp is the attainment of an object with the hand. Grasp is usually described according to the placement of the object held within the hand. Grasp on an object is reflexive during the first 2 to 3 months. A primitive squeeze grasp is the child's first attempt to grasp smaller objects against the palm; the thumb is not actively used with this grasp (Erhardt, 1994b). Over the next few months, grasp of small objects progresses from the ulnar or little finger side of the hand, to the middle of the palm **(palmar grasp),** to the radial or thumb side of the hand **(radial palmar grasp),** and finally to the thumb and digits **(radial digital grasp)** (Erhardt 1994b; Gesell & Amatruda, 1947). For tiny objects, such as a pellet, very young children attempt to rake the object with the fingers and trap it against the palm. Next the child grasps an object on the side of the index finger with the thumb **(scissors grasp)** (Gesell & Amatruda, 1947). A **fine pincer grasp** (Erhardt, 1994b) reflects the ability to pick up a small, pellet-sized object between the tips of the index finger and

TABLE 4.1 Development of reach, grasp, and release.

Developmental Domain	Age in Months								
Fine Motor	1–2	3	4	5	6	7	8	9	10–12
Reach	Arms activate upon sight of object	Swipes at objects	Hands to midline; bilateral reach; contacts object in midline	Under-reaches for object; reaches in prone on forearms	Over-reaches for object; circular reach in sitting with one arm	Reaches in prone on extended arms	Direct reach in sitting with one arm		Forearm supination with reach
Grasp on cube	Hands mostly fisted, grasp reflex	Hands mostly open; loosely closed in supine, fisted in prone; grasp reflex diminishes; brief grasp with ulnar digits	Primitive squeeze grasp	Palmar grasp	Radial Palmar grasp		Radial digital grasp; active palmar arches		
Grasp on pellet					Raking grasp	Inferior scissors grasp	Scissors grasp	Inferior pincer grasp	Fine pincer grasp
Release	Immediate involuntary release of objects after brief retaining	Involuntary release of objects after sustained grasp		Beginning direct transfer of object from hand-to-hand		Successful hand-to-hand transfer; releases objects against a surface; object permanence		Controlled release into large container	Precise release with cube; minimal finger extension; begins graded hand opening; begins to stack blocks

	Age in Years						
	1 yr	1.25 yrs	2.5–3 yrs	3–4 yrs	4–5 yrs	5–6 yrs	6–7 yrs
Grasp on crayon, pencil, utensil	Palmar grasp on crayon; fisted grasp on spoon	Pincer grasp with ulnar fingers curled	Begin digital pronate on crayon	Adult grasp on spoon begins	Uses transitional grips on pencil (cross-thumb, four-finger, lateral tripod); static tripod grasp on pencil; mature grasp on fork	Dynamic tripod grasp on pencil	Able to hold knife effectively to spread

Source: Adapted from R. Erhardt (1994). *Developmental Hand Dysfunction: Theory, Assessment, and Treatment* (2nd ed.). San Antonio, TX: Therapy Skill Builders. Adapted by permission. Also adapted from C. Schneck & A. Henderson (1990). Descriptive analysis of the developmental progression of grip position for pencil and crayon control in nondysfunctional children. *The American Journal of Occupational Therapy, 44,* 893–900.

thumb, forming an open web space with the other fingers flexed and the wrist held in slight extension (Figure 4.1). A mature pincer grasp indicates that the child has developed the ability to use one side of the hand actively while the other side is quiet. The development of grasp patterns is outlined in Table 4.1.

Regarding grips on writing and drawing tools, initially, a child uses an immature palmar grasp on a crayon. The shoulder is stable while the entire arm moves as a unit when scribbling (Erhardt, 1994b). Immature grasp on a tool includes holding the object in the palm of the hand with the fingers flexed around the shaft and with the forearm turned in **pronation** or supination.

Movement is initiated from the hand and forearm in a **transitional grasp.** The **dynamic tripod grasp,** (Figure 4.2) the most commonly used mature grasp, incorporates dynamic and precise alternating movements of the index finger, middle finger, and thumb during writing, with the ring finger and little finger stabilized in flexion (Long, Conrad, Hall, & Furler, 1970; Rosenbloom & Horton, 1971). The wrist is stable, and the space between the thumb and index finger is rounded, forming an open web space. Young children tend to hold a pencil in the middle of the shaft, whereas mature finger placement is closer to the tip of the pencil.

Release   Release is the purposeful letting go of an object held within the hand. Voluntary release begins when the infant mouths toys, transferring objects from hand to mouth and back to hand. At this stage, the infant releases toys by stabiliz-

The term *pronation* refers to the movement of the forearm in a direction toward the body, resulting in the palm turning downward.

A transitional grasp evidences a "transition" from immature grasps to mature patterns.

FIGURE 4.1

Pincer grasp in a typically developing 2-year-old child. Note the tip-to-tip prehension and open web space.

Source: Used by permission of Jean Patz.

Courtesy of Jean Patz.

FIGURE 4.2

A typically developing child demonstrates a mature tripod grasp on a marker with slight forearm supination, wrist extension, thumb and finger opposition, an open web space, and engagement of the nonpreferred hand.

ing the object in the mouth and pulling it with the opposite hand or releasing it against a surface. Direct transfer from hand to hand occurs by approximately 7 months (Erhardt, 1994b). Active release occurs by 10 to 11 months, along with the development of object permanence as the child purposefully drops objects from the highchair, using full arm, wrist, and finger extension (Case-Smith, 2006).

Erhardt (1994b) indicates that controlled release of a cube and pellet into a small opening develops by 12 months and 15 months, respectively. As control of release continues, the child is able to place objects into small containers, build towers, and release a ball. The development of voluntary release is outlined in Table 4.1.

Manipulation   This section addresses how young children combine reach, grasp, and release to perform functional tasks, such as those involved in play, prewriting, and cutting with scissors. The focus is on tasks that often are problematic for young children with special needs, including the poor use of both hands to manipulate objects, the lack of development of a hand preference, and the inability to move an object within the hand.

Bilateral Development   Development of **bilateral hand skills** is the ability to use the hands together during functional tasks. Asymmetry is noted in an infant's arm movements during the first few months of life. Then, the infant begins to move her arms together at approximately 3 months of age when the hands are brought to the chest in midline. Bilateral activities include reaching with two hands at 4 to 5 months, transferring from hand to hand by 6 to 8 months, and clapping hands or banging objects together by the end of the first year. By 10 months of age, the child uses one hand for manipulation and the other for stabilization (Exner, 2005) (e.g., stabilizing a bowl while scooping with a spoon). The ability to use opposing hand and arm movements for highly differentiated activities emerges at approximately 18 to 24 months and matures by 2 to 3 years of age (Exner, 2005). Stringing beads and cutting with scissors are examples of the complementary use of both hands. By $3^1/_2$ to 4 years of age, a child can hold scissors correctly and rotate the forearm to guide the scissors; the child is able to move the paper in coordination with cutting by 6 years of age (Lopez, 1986).

Hand Preference   Development of hand preference allows the child success with precise control of one hand for skilled tasks. Right- or left-handedness is noticed around 18 months (Pellegrino, 2002) and a clear hand preference becomes apparent during the preschool years (Gesell & Ames, 1947; Harris & Carlson, 1988; McManus et al., 1988; Tan, 1985). A history of a persistent and strong hand preference under 1 year of age may be indicative of a motor deficit.

In-Hand Manipulation   Whereas grasp patterns capture children's abilities to statically hold objects and to use objects efficiently in many daily tasks, children must be able to move objects within the hand. For example, a child who is given several coins will pick them up with the pads of the fingertips and thumb and transfer them to a palm one at a time **(finger-to-palm translation)** and move the coin from the palm to a piggy bank **(palm-to-finger translation),** which is a more difficult task requiring isolated control of the thumb (Exner, 2005). When stringing beads, a child needs to move the end of the string in the fingers in a linear fashion for more accurate placement **(shift)** and, when using a key, a child may need to rotate the key in a key hole **(simple rotation)** or within a hand so that the correct end faces the keyhole **(complex rotation).** Exner (2005) proposes that these "in-hand manipulation skills" represent a higher level of fine motor skills than grasp alone. These skills begin to emerge between 12 and 15 months of age. A key time for development is from 2 to 4 years of age, with increasing speed, efficiency, and refinement of in-hand manipulation skills occurring through 12 years of age. See Box 4.1 to learn about fine motor empathy exercises.

Oral Motor Development

Oral motor development incorporates coordinated movements of the jaw, tongue, lips, and cheeks during sucking, swallowing, munching, chewing, spoon-feeding, and cup drinking. In addition to the motor control necessary for eating, it is important to consider positioning of the child's head in relationship to the body and to gravity; positioning of the person feeding the child in relationship to the child; positioning of the bottle, cup, or spoon; and the selection of types and textures of

BOX 4.1   FINE MOTOR EMPATHY EXERCISES

■ Cut with a pair of scissors. Note the positions and mobility of your forearm during cutting. Now pronate your forearm (thumb points down toward the floor as in a child with increased postural tone). Keep your forearm in that position while cutting. What do you experience?

■ Grasp your pencil and write your name, noting the position of your fourth and fifth fingers. Now write your name again with those same fingers extended instead of flexed and hold your arm up off the table surface. What happens to the qual-

ity of your writing? This exercise points out the need to stabilize the arm and the nonworking side of the hand during coloring and writing.

■ Pick up several coins, one at a time, and store them in your palm. This skill is finger-to-palm translation with stabilization. Now pretend you have increased postural tone. Pull your thumb in toward your palm and hold your wrist slightly bent and try the same task. Imagine a child with spastic cerebral palsy trying to pick up small objects in a timely manner.

food that are suitable for the developmental level of the child. Intact sensory processing skills are also necessary so the child can respond appropriately to the texture, temperature, taste, color, and smell of foods and liquids. Higher **textured foods** provide the sensory stimulus for the development of more mature oral motor skills. Developmental eating milestones from birth through 2 years of age are listed in Table 4.2.

Textured foods may present a challenge for a child with oral motor difficulties.

Positioning During Meals   Typically, an infant enjoys being held in a semi-reclined position during feedings. By the age of 7 months, most infants can sit independently in a highchair with support provided by a seat belt or tray. Most children can sit in a small chair by 18 months of age (Morris & Klein, 2000). These positions parallel the development of oral structures as well as oral motor skills. Typically developing infants can safely be fed in a semi-reclined position because the relationship of the oral structures to one another makes it unlikely that **aspiration,** the passage of liquids or food into the lungs, will occur.

Aspiration is the passage of liquid or food during swallowing into the trachea and lungs.

As an infant approaches 12 months of age, however, the throat elongates and additional space is created between the base of the tongue and the epiglottis, which

TABLE 4.2	Stages of typical oral motor development.			
Age	Infancy	By 6 months	7–12 months	12–24 months
Oral Motor Skills	Caregiver holds infant during bottle or breast-feeding	Infant may be introduced to new food textures (baby cereals, strained or pureed baby food, soft crackers that melt in the mouth), and utensils (cup and spoon), depending on cultural expectations and medical advice	Child may be gradually introduced to higher textured foods (mashed or soft cooked table food) as chewing skills develop	Child progresses from eating chopped table food to meats and uncooked vegetables; also develops skill in drinking from a straw and cup

covers the trachea during swallowing. This growth change provides a greater opportunity for aspiration to occur when a child is in a reclined position because of the effect of gravity on foods (Case-Smith & Humphrey, 2005). Thus, by this age, children should be in a more upright position that facilitates the ability to handle solid foods safely, to chew, and to drink from a cup.

Sucking   The **rooting reflex,** which the newborn exhibits from birth to 3 months of age, enables the child to locate the source of food. The infant's head turns toward the stimulus and she opens her mouth when touched around the oral area. Reflexive swallowing occurs with the **suck-swallow reflex,** which diminishes around 2 to 4 months of age. A healthy, full-term infant has the ability to initiate suckling, maintain a strong grasp on the nipple using an extension-retraction pattern of the tongue, and ingest the required amount of liquid efficiently within 20–30 minutes (Morris & Klein, 2000). According to Morris and Klein, the mature sucking pattern emerges around 6 to 9 months of age. This action involves a cupped tongue around the nipple, up-and-down tongue movements creating negative intra-oral pressure, smaller movements of the jaw and complete lip closure around the nipple. Children with motor difficulties may thrust their tongue, resulting in an inefficient suck pattern with liquid loss.

> Within about 20 to 30 minutes after birth, a healthy, full-term infant will begin sucking effectively.

Swallowing   Initially, the child uses tongue extension-retraction during swallowing and sucking with a swallow occurring after every second or third suck; tongue movements change at 6 to 8 months of age from slight protrusion to an up-and-down pattern and finally tongue-tip elevation around 2 years of age (Morris & Klein, 2000). The mouth is closed at the point of swallow. This is important to know because many children with oral motor dysfunction do not have mouth closure when swallowing, which can interfere with safe eating and swallowing. The pharyngeal phase of swallow begins when the bolus moves through the pharynx, triggering the **swallow reflex;** the final phase involves passage of liquid or food through the esophagus into the stomach (Brodsky & Arvedson, 2002).

Protective mechanisms to prevent aspiration of liquid or food include elevation of the soft palate to close off the nasal cavities and the backward movement of the epiglottis to cover the airway. A sphincter at the top of the stomach prevents **reflux** (i.e., the back-up of food contents into the esophagus and into the pharynx).

Munching and Chewing   In infancy, a **biting reflex** occurs when a finger is placed on an infant's gum. The infant will open and close the mouth repetitively on the finger. Munching occurs around 5 to 6 months of age as food is simply mashed against the palate with vertical tongue and jaw movements (Morris & Klein, 2000). Tongue lateralization and circular or rotary jaw movements, which are needed to carry food to the side of the mouth and pulverize it for chewing, begin around 7 to 8 months, with mature chewing abilities developing by 2 years of age (Morris & Klein, 2000). Timelines for the introduction of solid foods vary according to pediatricians' recommendations and a family's culture, beliefs, and past experiences. According to Morris and Klein, children are introduced to cereals and pureed or strained baby foods around 4 to 6 months of age; ground or mashed table foods, referred to as "lumpy solids," by approximately 8 months; then coarsely chopped table food around 1 year of age. Most meat and some raw vegetables are appropriate for an 18-month-old.

Spoon-Feeding   The ability to quiet the tongue and jaw upon seeing the spoon approach occurs around 6 months of age (Morris & Klein, 2000). This resting posture of the tongue and jaw is important for preparing the mouth to receive food. Another important milestone during spoon-feeding is the child's ability to actively use the upper lip to clear food from the spoon and keep the bottom lip stable. This actively begins around 7 to 8 months of age (Morris & Klein, 2000).

Cup Drinking   Cup drinking generally begins around 4 to 6 months of age as the mother holds a cup to the child's mouth for a taste. The child drinks with the head in a normal resting posture, slightly flexed. The infant initially uses a suck-swallow pattern. The parent may offer cups with spouted lids to avoid spillage and the child will use more of a sucking pattern when drinking from this type of cup. Gradually, jaw stabilization develops, allowing closure of the lips on a regular cup rim. Jaw stability progresses from wide vertical jaw movements to biting on the cup rim at 15 to 18 months, and the child achieves mature internal jaw stability at approximately 24 months (Morris & Klein, 2000). Movement of the tongue changes from the up-and-down pattern noted in sucking to a simple tongue protrusion pattern during the first year, followed by mature elevation of the tip of the tongue by 2 years (Morris & Klein, 2000). Initially, the child takes individual sips; however, continuous swallowing, or taking several sips in succession, indicates a more mature swallowing pattern. The child generally can drink successfully from a cup held by the feeder by 12 to 15 months of age and will do so with no liquid loss by 2 years of age. See Box 4.2 to learn about oral motor empathy exercises.

BOX 4.2   ORAL MOTOR EMPATHY EXERCISES

- Take a drink and notice what your jaw does at the point of swallowing. Does your jaw totally close? How much? Now swallow with your mouth slightly open (similar to what children do who have oral motor dysfunction). What happens to your tongue during swallowing if the mouth is slightly open? Was it difficult to swallow this way? Take a drink and describe movements of your tongue from the time the liquid enters your mouth to the time you swallow. Now thrust your tongue out of your mouth while drinking (tongue thrust).
- Hyperextend your head slightly by looking upward (similar to positioning seen in children with motor disabilities) and *carefully* swallow a small amount of water. How does it feel? How do you think a child with oral motor dysfunction would feel if someone fed her in this position?
- Take a bite of a cracker and chew normally, paying close attention to your tongue movements. Does your tongue move to the side when chewing (tongue lateralization)? Take another bite and notice your jaw movements. Does your jaw move straight up and down, diagonally, or in a circular movement? All are needed for mature chewing.

A child with oral motor dysfunction is at risk for potential aspiration if swallowing occurs while her head is in hyperextension.

⠠⠠ SELF-CARE DEVELOPMENT

Stages in the development of self-care skills are outlined in Table 4.3.

Stages of Self-Feeding Development

Drinking from a Bottle   Self-feeding with a bottle consists of the child independently holding and drinking from the bottle with two hands beginning at about 4 to 5 months of age. The child progresses to a one-handed grasp on the bottle. The majority of typically developing children will give up the bottle by 2 years according to Morris and Klein (2000).

Finger Feeding   Finger feeding typically occurs by 9–12 months of age (Haley, Coster, Ludlow, Haltiwanger, & Andrellos, 1992; Parks, 2006). Initially, the child picks up a large object, such as a cracker, using a **palmar grasp** then progresses to a smaller object, such as a Cheerio, when a **pincer grasp** (thumb and index finger) develops.

Use of a Spoon   Appropriate use occurs when the child holds the spoon first with a palmar grasp, dipping the spoon into the food. The spoon turns upside down upon approach because the forearm is turned downward (pronated). Scooping sticky food independently and bringing it to the mouth with some spilling occurs between 18 to 24 months (Haley et al., 1992; Parks, 2006). As forearm supination develops by 2 years of age, spoon insertion without turning and minimal spilling generally occur (Haley et al., 1992). More successful spoon-feeding occurs by 24 to 30 months of age (Parks, 2006) with development of a mature grasp, wrist rotation, and forearm supination.

Use of a Fork   Stabbing with a fork requires some strength to push through the food. This skill develops at about 2 to $2^{1}/_{2}$ years, independence by $2^{1}/_{2}$ to 3 years (Parks, 2006), and a mature grasp on a fork by approximately $4^{1}/_{2}$ years.

> The functional use of a spoon, fork, and knife evolves from about 2 years to 8 years of age in most children.

Use of a Knife   Spreading with a knife requires bilateral coordination. The child stabilizes the bread with one hand and spreads with the other. Rotation of the forearm and wrist are prerequisites needed to spread effectively. Spreading is accomplished between $4^{1}/_{2}$ and $5^{1}/_{2}$ years (Haley et al., 1992; Parks, 2006). The ability to cut through soft food, like a sandwich, develops around 5 to $5^{1}/_{2}$ years (Haley et al., 1992), to use a knife and fork by $5^{1}/_{2}$ to $6^{1}/_{2}$ years (Parks, 2006), and to cut meat by 7 to 8 years.

Drinking from a Cup   Generally, a child is exposed to cup drinking by 6 months of age. A parent holds a cup to the child's lips, giving a sip while using a bib. By approximately 12 months, the child is able to hold a cup and drink with some spilling. The child progresses to holding a small cup in one hand with minimal spillage by 2 years of age (Morris & Klein, 2000).

Straw Drinking   Hunt, Lewis, Reisel, Waldrup, and Adam-Wooster (2000) found successful straw drinking in a majority of a small sample of children between 8 and 12 months of age. Morris and Klein (2000) attribute early development of this skill to earlier exposure to straw drinking, i.e. eating at fast-food restaurants.

TABLE 4.3 Stages of typical self-care development.

Typical Development

Self-Care	Age in Months							
	0–3	6–12	12–18	18–24	24–36	36–48	48–60	60–72
Self-Feeding		Holds own bottle, finger feeds, plays with spoon, holds spoon with poor control, takes sip from cup held by parent, shows an interest	Uses spoon, spills, holds spoon with pronated grasp, inserts spoon in dish, fills spoon poorly, brings cup to mouth with two hands, spills, sucks from straw	Turns spoon before arriving at mouth, scoops food, some spill, holds cup but some spill	Feeds self with little spilling, holds spoon independently, pours from small container, holds cup in one hand, releases cup without spilling	Begins adult grasp on utensils, pours from pitcher, stabs with a fork, spreads with a knife, eats independently with minimal to no spilling	Cuts soft foods with a knife, chooses menu	Assists in making simple foods
Dressing		Cooperates, holds out arms and legs, removes hat, socks, shoes, mittens, puts on hat, attempts to put on shoes, unsnaps in front	Removes coat, dress, and pants; puts shoes on wrong feet, moves large zipper	Undresses with no help, removes pullover and dress, unbuttons, buttons one large front button, puts on shorts, front opening shirt, and pants with help	Unties bow, unbuckles belt, unzips front zipper, unsnaps in back, buttons large buttons, puts on coat, dress, pullover shirt, boots, and socks correctly, dresses completely with supervision	Unzips back zipper, buttons front shirt or coat, zips front zipper, laces and is able to Velcro shoes, puts shoes on correct feet, buckles belt, knows front from back and right from wrong side, can turn inside out	Ties shoes, zips back zipper	
Toileting		Wears diapers	Indicates when wet, has regular bowel movements by 1 year	Indicates need	Expresses verbal anticipation, uses control during the day, some accidents, needs reminders, helps with clothes	Has bladder control at night, attempts wiping but may need help, manages clothing during toileting, helps with fasteners, goes to bathroom independently	Maintains full independence, has volitional control of bladder	Majority of children have day and night bladder control, wipes self well
Sleeping	Sleeps 16 to 17 hours per 24-hour day, 3 to 4 hours at a time	Sleeps 13 to 14 hours, takes several naps	Sleeps 12 to 13 hours per 24-hour day, may take one or two naps per day (1 hour each), may transition out of crib	Sleeps 12 to 13 hours per 24-hour day, may take one nap per day, may sleep 11 hours at night	From 2 to 5 years of age, may sleep 11 to 13 hours per 24-hour day, may not need afternoon nap			Sleeps 9 to 11 hours per 24-hour day
Bathing and Grooming			Opens mouth to brush teeth	Attempts to wash body and blow nose, performs incomplete toothbrushing	Incomplete tooth brushing, wipes nose when told, combs hair with supervision	Washes hands and body well, wipes nose without being told	Brushes teeth	Washes face well

Sources: Adapted from Eisenberg, Murkoff, & Hathaway (1994); Haley, Coster, Ludlow, Haltiwanger, & Andrellos (1992); Henderson (1995); Hunt, Lewis, Reisel, Waldrup, & Adam-Wooster (2000); Morris, & Klein (2000); Shepherd (2005).

Stages of Dressing Development

Prerequisites for independent dressing are the ability to sit or stand without assistance, to use the hands in a coordinated fashion, to sequence complex tasks, and to organize clothing spatially. Children typically learn to undress before they can dress and undo fasteners before they can close them. The child begins assisting the caregiver with undressing when less than a year old by pulling the arm or leg from garments partially removed by the caregiver. At about 12 months of age, the child is able to hold out arms or feet for dressing (Finnie, 1997). Independent undressing begins at about 18 months of age, when the child can purposely pull off hat or socks. Between 2 and 3 years of age the child can usually remove all clothing that does not require the control of closures (buttons, snaps, etc.). The child can complete all dressing (including orienting clothing correctly), except for closures, between 3 and 4 years of age. Control of fasteners begins at about 2 years of age with opening large buttons and continues through 6 years of age, when tying is finally mastered (Shepherd, 2005). Stages of normal dressing are detailed in Table 4.3.

Dressing and undressing are not typically mastered until age 5 years.

Stages of Toileting Development

The age when a child becomes independent in toileting depends on cultural and environmental expectations, the physical and emotional readiness of the child, and parental knowledge of and persistence with toilet learning practices (Shepherd, 2005). Stages of development are listed in Table 4.3. Readiness signs include the ability to indicate in some manner when wet, stay dry for at least 1 to 2 hours at a time, regulate bowel movements, desire to be dry and wear underpants, follow simple commands, show an interest in toileting, and understand toileting concepts such as wet and dry (Eisenberg, Murkoff, & Hathaway, 1994). There also is pressure on the child and family to accomplish bowel and bladder control for entry into school and community programs.

:: FACTORS AFFECTING DEVELOPMENT

Sensory Processing Disorders

Vestibular functions relate to structures in the inner ear that are involved in posture and balance maintenance.

A. Jean Ayres pioneered the theory of sensory integration (SI) (Ayres, 1972, 1979, & 2005). Children with problems in SI have difficulty organizing and interpreting sensory information, for example, auditory, tactile, proprioception, **vestibular**, visual, gustatory, and olfactory. This occurs during central processing; the peripheral sensory receptors are intact. Sensory processing disorder (SPD) is the current umbrella term used synonymously with sensory integration dysfunction in the literature. The term SPD was proposed in order to: distinguish the condition (disorder) from the theory (sensory integration), assessment, and intervention; to more clearly identify SPD subtypes for research purposes and treatment planning; and to communicate more effectively with other professionals (Miller, 2006; Miller, Anzalone, Lane, Cermak, & Osten, 2007; Miller, Cermak, Lane, Anzalone & Koomar, 2004).

The incidence of sensory processing disorders has been reported to range between 5% and 13% in a large sample of kindergartners identified by the *Short Sensory Profile*, a screening device for SPD (Ahn, Miller, Milberger, & McIntosh, 2004). Davies and Gavin (2007) provide further validation of SPD through the use of EEG technology; this study found that children with SPD could be discriminated from those without disorders with 86% accuracy. Children identified with SPD on the *Short Sensory Profile* were more apt to show problems with ADLs (White, Mulligan, Merrill, & Wright, 2007) as measured by the *Assessment of Motor and Process Skills* (Fisher, 2003). SPD can co-exist with other conditions such as autism spectrum disorder (Mailloux, 2001), cerebral palsy (Blanche & Nakasuji, 2001), and fragile X syndrome (Hickman, 2001). There are three primary categories of sensory processing disorders: sensory modulation disorder, sensory discrimination disorder, and sensory-based motor disorder (Miller, 2006; Miller et al., 2007). Sensory processing disorders in selected populations will be further discussed in the section concerned with development in young children with special needs.

Sensory Modulation Disorder (SMD)

The process of **modulation** occurs at various levels within the nervous system. The hypothesized purpose of modulation is survival; it protects us from harm while allowing us to explore, learn, and make adaptive responses. The ability to modulate sensory input is an important underlying mechanism for regulation of behavior. Children with modulation disorders may be underresponsive and/or overresponsive to sensory stimuli. A defensive reaction (e.g., tactile defensiveness) is an overresponsive reaction of great intensity to a common sensory input that is interpreted as noxious, painful, or life-threatening. Children who are overresponsive to stimuli may be very sensitive to lights, sound, touch, or movement. They may demonstrate overarousal and have significant difficulty with interacting appropriately with peers and adults and in focusing attention to the task at hand. Problems in self-care areas may develop. For example, the child may not tolerate the echoing sounds of a flushing toilet or the loudness of a hairdryer. Emotional responses often appear excessive. A child with difficulty regulating tactile stimuli, for example, may avoid certain types of clothing, toys, and foods, thus limiting experiences. The child may find the touch of another person irritating, and may strike out when touched accidentally by a child, or avoid being hugged by their parents. Studies have found that moderate to severe regulatory difficulties in infancy are highly predictive of perceptual, language, sensory integrative, and behavioral and emotional problems at the preschool ages (DeGangi, Breinbauer, Roosevelt, Porges, & Greenspan, 2000; Gutman, McCreedy, & Heisler, 2002).

Conversely, children who are underresponsive may require greater amounts of sensory input in order to sustain attention and arousal. They may require more repetition and greater intensity of input in order to be engaged in an activity. The attention or arousal level of the child can appear to fluctuate. At one point the child may appear happy and engaged, but she might quickly become overexcited or stop interacting and appear distressed for no apparent reason. Optimal arousal may not be a linear continuum (overarousal/underarousal). Various hypotheses within sensory integration theory have attempted to explain this phenomenon and why some children show a consistent pattern while others seem to fluctuate. Most important to the educator is careful observation and documentation of the child's behavior with an attempt to identify antecedent sensory events. This will enable better communication with the OT to promote improved understanding and treatment of the child.

Sensory Discrimination Disorder (SDD)

The ability to use sensory information in order to distinguish specific messages is important in refining our responses to learning tasks. We are usually not aware of all the fine discriminations we are making at every moment. As with other sensory processing deficits, problems in discrimination can occur in any of the sensory systems. The child with poor tactile discrimination will have difficulties such as finding a toy using touch. The child who has auditory discrimination problems may be unable to distinguish her name being called through the clamor of other children playing. Problems in visual discrimination may interfere with the ability to notice important details in a picture.

Sensory-Based Motor Disorders (SBMD)

Dyspraxia   As noted in chapter 3, some children with developmental dyspraxia and developmental coordination disorder cannot effectively integrate sensory information provided by their own bodies and their environment. **Dyspraxia**, an impairment in the ability to conceptualize and plan nonhabitual motor tasks, results in poor execution of those tasks (Ayres, 1985). This is usually not a problem with motor execution but with the planning (Reeves & Cermak, 2002) and cannot be explained by other factors such as weakness, incoordination, or medical issues (Giuffrida, 2001, Schumway-Cook & Woolacott, 2007). Children with sensory-based dyspraxia may have difficulty integrating sensory information, and often they cannot adapt their motor behavior to changing environmental demands (Reeves & Cermak, 2002). These children have problems with complex fine motor tasks across developmental stages. A toddler might find it hard to plan building a block tower, manipulating an unfamiliar toy, or using tools such as a crayon or spoon. During the preschool years, poor motor planning would be evident in such fine motor tasks as coloring, drawing, cutting with scissors, putting puzzles together, working with small manipulatives (such as beads and Legos®), and manipulating fasteners on clothing (Reeves & Cermak, 2002). Teachers should consider poor motor planning as a possible reason when a child who has intact motor skills cannot sequence the movements when given verbal directions or novel tasks.

These children have minimal oral motor problems related to feeding; oral problems are more commonly associated with oral dyspraxia. Poor motor planning may affect self-feeding skills, for example, by causing difficulty in using utensils. Reliance on finger feeding may therefore persist for an extended period to avoid frustration with utensils.

Early motor milestones such as crawling and walking are reported as age appropriate for children with dyspraxia, but they have difficulty with tasks such as skipping, which involves bilateral coordination. Unfortunately, many children with these deficits are not referred to occupational therapy until they demonstrate problems keeping up with their peers in school, which can result in significant problems with self-esteem (Missiuna & Polatajko, 1995). A skilled observer often can recognize problems in the preschool years, but typically the disorder is not identified until the early school years, when demands on time, organization, and participation increase (Reeves & Cermak, 2002). Early diagnosis that leads to treatment can help prevent some of the difficulties and frustration these children may encounter, such as poor self-esteem, isolation from peer groups, and teasing. Incorporating variable practice sessions are more effective in learning and remembering movements needed for novel motor activities (Schmidt & Lee, 2005).

Postural Disorder   The child with a sensory-based postural disorder may appear weak with poor endurance, have trouble maintaining upright sitting, and exhibit difficulty coordinating bilateral movements. For example, the child may be able to consciously sit up straight momentarily, but quickly assumes a slumped posture. The underlying problem is a combination of poor postural tone and reduced core strength and endurance. This disorder may be seen with other aspects of sensory processing problems such as underresponsivity or visual perceptual difficulties.

:: PSYCHOSOCIAL ASPECTS OF CHILDREN WITH SPECIAL NEEDS

Teachers working with children who have learning disabilities, sensory processing problems, perceptual-motor, or self-regulation difficulties will be more involved in identifying teaching strategies specific to the individual child. Parents may have much more difficulty addressing the behavioral issues associated with these disabilities. Most teachers working with children who have special needs are trained in behavior management techniques. Learning which behaviors are associated with specific conditions will assist the teacher in identifying antecedents and shape safe and effective interventions. Issues of trust, self-confidence, social competence, self-control, and acceptance of change are often challenges that children face when sensory and motor systems are not typically developing.

Observable behaviors often seen with a variety of special needs include overresponsivity or underresponsivity to a variety of sensory messages (noise, touch, vision, taste, temperature, and texture). For example, the act of bathing and dressing may become laden with fear as a result of the child's inability to accommodate to changes in noise levels in the echoing bathroom. Children with spina bifida or cerebral palsy may not have typical neural function when giving feedback about being wet or having a full bladder.

Overexcitability may be seen in the child who has atypical responses to gravitational (movement) changes. Children with attention deficit may seem disinterested or overly focused on some irrelevant detail of an activity because of problems in shifting focus or gaze.

A child who has auditory processing problems may appear to be ignoring verbal cues or speak in too loud a voice. These problems might be interpreted as willful or intrusive by parents or peers. Providing more processing time and reducing the complexity of language and slowing down the interaction may provide support for the child to react with a more thoughtful, mature response.

Unsafe, risk-taking behaviors can often be seen in children who have spatial-organization problems. Conversely, children who have reduced ability to plan movements may avoid tasks they perceive to be too difficult, such as joining sports activities on the playground.

The early interventionist must teach impulse control and increase the individual's ability to cope with frustration. Part of this process includes reading and understanding nonspoken social cues that comprise a large part of communication. Although the child may be speaking, she must also be able to appraise the meaning of words and movement in social context.

Designing effective interventions must include acceptance of the child's unique sensory and motor needs. The foundations of a safe, trusting interaction are built on helping children learn alternative coping strategies that incrementally build self-confidence and more open approaches to facing change. The intrinsic value of accomplishing a challenge at the "just right" level is potentially more rewarding than external rewards (Gutman, McCreedy, & Heisler, 2002).

▓▓ ATYPICAL FINE MOTOR

When considering atypical fine motor development, it may be helpful to conceptualize three distinct areas of concern. The first is the ability to use the body as a stable base or a foundation for arm use. The second is the development of the basic components of reach, grasp, and release. The third is the combined use of these components for object manipulation in functional activities such as play and self-feeding with greater complexity as perceptual skills and cognition develop.

Although problems may exist in postural control in addition to reach, grasp, and release, fine motor difficulties may not be identified until the child demonstrates problems integrating these skills for object manipulation. Parents may find they have difficulty selecting toys for the child because the child is unable to play with age-appropriate items. They may note problems when the child is expected to use two hands together to manipulate toys or to use objects as tools.

Fine motor difficulties may result from a variety of factors such as neurological problems, including atypical postural tone, persistent primitive reflexes, and lack of refinement (differentiation) in early reflexive patterning; structural limitations such as limb deficiencies; sensory processing deficits; poor motor planning; perceptual difficulties; behavioral issues; environmental limitations; and cognitive delay. Red flags suggestive of fine motor problems (see Figure 4.3) can alert a teacher to potential difficulties in postural control, reach, grasp, release, and manipulation. Atypical postural tone, persistent primitive reflexes, and sensory processing deficits will be discussed in detail in the young children with special needs section.

FIGURE 4.3	Red flags suggestive of fine motor problems.

REACH

- Inability to bring the hands to midline after 4 months of age
- Inability or lack of interest in reaching for objects by 6 months of age
- Tremors upon reach
- Inaccurate or indirect reaching after 9 months of age
- Inability to cross midline of the body

GRASP

- Continual fisting of the hands with thumb in palm beyond 3 months of age; hands are typically open by 3 months
- Lack of variety of grasp patterns to accommodate size and shape of objects
- Lack of ability to isolate the index finger for pointing after 10–12 months of age
- Persistence of a palmar grasp beyond 12 months of age
- Lack of supination of the forearm after 12 months
- Lack of development of a pincer grasp by 15 months of age
- Awkward grasp on the pencil during writing or drawing; thumb wrapped around pencil; presses too hard when writing
- Refusal to use eating utensils during preschool years

RELEASE

- Excessive dropping of objects
- Over- or undershooting target on release
- Inability to actively transfer (coordinate grasp and release) after 6–7 months
- Unable to stack a few blocks after 15–18 months

MANIPULATION

- Strong preferred use of one hand under 1 year of age (hand preference is generally not seen before 12 months of age)
- Poor visual attention to toys
- Inability or unwillingness to manipulate toys; cannot play with age/developmentally appropriate toys
- Extreme difficulty learning how to manipulate scissors by age 3–4 years or later; inability to coordinate after instruction (dependent on exposure)
- Lack of a hand preference by first grade; continual switching of hands while eating or using a pencil

PARENTAL CONCERNS

- Difficulty choosing toys for the child

Source: Used by permission of Jean Patz.

:: ATYPICAL ORAL MOTOR

Many issues can interfere with oral motor development including medical, structural, motor, sensory, behavioral, environmental, and/or neurological problems. Atypical oral motor development may occur when there are problems with postural tone. Hypertonia found in children with spastic cerebral palsy can cause restriction in oral movements (e.g., difficulty opening the mouth) that interfere with eating. Oral asymmetry and atypical oral motor patterns can include tongue thrust, **jaw thrust,** tonic bite reflex, and lip retraction, leading to lengthy feeding time and poor food and liquid intake. Mature oral movements such as isolated, lateral tongue movement needed in chewing may not develop.

Hypotonia in the oral area may cause sluggish oral movements seen in children with Down syndrome and hypotonic or ataxic cerebral palsy. An open-mouth posture prevents a good lip seal on a nipple, cup, or spoon and results in drooling and food and liquid loss. The child with hypotonia may remain on lower textured foods well beyond the expected range of development. Tongue protrusion and tongue thrust interfere with food intake and channeling liquid and solids for swallowing.

Jaw thrust is an atypical, forceful, downward thrusting of the lower jaw that interferes with mouth closure needed for food intake (Morris & Klein, 2000).

A child with variable or fluctuating tone, as in athetoid cerebral palsy, may exhibit involuntary, uncontrolled, extraneous oral movements. The child has difficulty sustaining movements such as maintaining lip closure on a nipple or cup rim. Stability of the head and trunk is lacking, making it difficult for the child to keep her body quiet and still for feeding. A greater degree of tongue thrust or jaw thrust occurs as a result of **involuntary movements**.

Sensitivity to texture and temperature also may result in resistance to eating or difficulties coping with different foods. For some children, prematurity, illness, **gastroesophageal reflux (GER)**, or surgical intervention can result in an interruption of normal feeding procedures. For these children, the discomfort associated with alternative feeding methods such as **nasogastric** and **gastrostomy tube feedings** and lack of appropriate oral stimulation may result in complicated behavioral issues related to feeding. In addition, parents and interventionists should keep in mind that some medical conditions and medications may result in diminished appetite. Any of these problems can contribute to poor intake and low weight gain. Figure 4.4 summarizes indicators suggestive of oral motor problems.

:: FINE MOTOR DEVELOPMENT IN YOUNG CHILDREN WITH SPECIAL NEEDS

In this section, sensory and motor characteristics related to selected diagnostic categories are discussed. It is important to recognize that the common concerns presented here are subsumed under the educational classifications described in chapter 1. For example, Down syndrome typically is included under the classification of mental retardation, whereas cerebral palsy may fit within one of several classifications (e.g., orthopedic impairment, neuromotor disorder).

Cerebral Palsy

Fine motor dysfunction in children with cerebral palsy may be caused by tonal abnormalities, existence of primitive postural reflexes, and sensory deficits.

Atypical Postural Tone

Reach.   Hypertonia restricts the range of motion available during reach. A child with hypertonia may sit with a posterior pelvic tilt, resulting in a rounded trunk and limited ability to raise the arms. Although Lily shows low tone in her trunk muscles, increased tone in her arms reduces her ability to reach directly for desired toys. The child may compensate by elevating shoulders and leaning forward when reaching for objects, rather than extending the arm, as a result of decreased range of motion. In addition, shoulder retraction and elevation (pulling back and raising the shoulders) may limit her ability to bring the hands to midline to manipulate objects. Hypotonia, on the other hand, may prevent lifting the arms up against gravity to meet in the midline or to reach for objects. Hypotonia in the trunk interferes with upright sitting, which limits the range available to reach forward. If trunk rotation has not

FIGURE 4.4	Red flags suggestive of oral motor problems.

POSITIONING

- Caregiver has difficulty holding or positioning the child in a chair during meals
- Child is extremely fussy when held
- Child has trouble sitting independently during meals as a result of poor postural control after 6–8 months of age

SUCKING

- Persistent difficulty initiating sucking and maintaining suck when hungry and alert
- Poor intake
- Consistently takes too long to complete a bottle when hungry and alert—more than 40–60 minutes
- Frequent choking or gagging when drinking from bottle or breast
- Tongue pushes nipple out of mouth involuntarily
- Persistent, involuntary biting on the nipple
- Caregiver feels the need to cut a hole in the bottle nipple to increase intake
- Caregiver has difficulty finding a nipple that the child will consistently use

SWALLOWING

- Coughing during or after eating and drinking
- History of aspiration pneumonia
- Gurgly voice
- Frequent vomiting
- Persistent drooling beyond the teething phase of 6 to 18 months
- Open mouth posture; excessive loss of liquid

CHEWING

- Persists on baby food (strained, pureed, or mashed) beyond 12–15 months
- Negative reaction to solid foods, such as crying or spitting; "picky eater"
- Lack of tongue lateralization; therefore, food stays in the front of the mouth after the first year; food loss
- Persistent choking or gagging on solid food
- Consistent asymmetry of the tongue, jaw, and lips during chewing, crying, or smiling

SPOON-FEEDING

- Persistent, involuntary biting or clamping down on the spoon
- Tongue involuntarily and forcefully pushes spoon out of the mouth on a consistent basis
- Persistent choking or gagging when being spoonfed
- Inability to clear or wipe thickened food off the spoon with the upper lip after 9–12 months of age

CUP DRINKING

- Excessive liquid loss beyond 1 year of age when drinking from a cup held by the caregiver
- Coughing during or after drinking thin liquids from a cup
- Difficulty transitioning from the bottle to a cup at a developmentally appropriate age
- Inability to get enough liquid in by cup; history of dehydration
- Report from the parent that cup drinking is stressful
- Inability of a child over 1 year of age with at least 2 months of cup-drinking experience to take consecutive sips

Source: Used by permission of Jean Patz.

developed as a result of poor proximal stability, reach across the midline will be affected. The child subsequently is forced to reach inefficiently with the hand closest to the object. A child who has variable or fluctuating postural tone, as in athetoid cerebral palsy, demonstrates difficulty in grading movements for reach. The child will attempt to minimize involuntary movements by elevating the shoulders to stabilize the head for eye-hand coordination during reach, locking the elbows in **hyperextension,** or adducting and internally rotating the arms, making it difficult to engage in fine motor activities.

Hyperextension is excessive or unnatural movement in the direction of extension.

Grasp. Children with spastic cerebral palsy frequently demonstrate an atypical arm and grasp pattern (Figure 4.5) that interferes with fine motor control consist-

FIGURE 4.5

Child with spastic quadriplegic cerebral palsy with similar atypical positioning in both arms resulting from increased tone. Note elbow flexion, forearm pronation, wrist flexion, and ulnar deviation upon grasp with a built-up handled spoon and scoop dish.

Source: Used by permission of Jean Patz.

ing of forearm pronation, wrist flexion, hyperextended proximal finger joints, and a thumb flexed and adducted (Erhardt & Lindlons, 2000). Thumb adduction into the palm, a pattern seen in children with more severe neuromotor problems, prevents any oppositional use of the thumb. The lack of forearm rotation in supination makes it difficult for the child to mechanically use mature grasps and to see and learn about the object grasped, as the palm faces downward and hides the object held. Also, limited rotation in the proximal joints of the fingers, particularly the thumb, interrupts the finger-to-thumb opposition needed to grasp small objects or a pencil.

Inability to isolate the index finger to point (in a child who is cognitively ready for this skill) may be a red flag indicating poorly differentiated movements; the child may not have the motor ability to separate one finger from the others.

A child with hypotonia will have difficulty with finger stability in the fine pincer grasp as a result of increased mobility in the joints. Primitive grasp patterns such as the palmar grasp are used for stabilization. Because of the hypotonia or poor sensation in the hand, the child may grip a pencil by wrapping the thumb tightly over the pencil shaft instead of opposing the tips of the thumb and index finger on the pencil. The teacher might observe heavy markings with occasional tearing of the paper during pencil use because of the tight and immature grip.

Release.   Persistence of a primitive grasp pattern, fisting of the hand, exaggerated wrist flexion, limited thumb extension, or lack of forearm supination may all interfere with controlled release. Fisting of the hand, typically seen in children with spastic cerebral palsy, prevents voluntary opening of the hand for release. The inability to bring the hands to the midline will inhibit direct hand-to-hand transfer of an object, the first stage of release. Poor proximal stability of the wrist and lack of forearm supination prevent control in mid-position for precise release. Low tone will cause the child to use a surface to release an object because the surface, whether that is a table or the child's own body, provides stability and sensory feedback.

Manipulation. During the toddler and preschool years, a child may demonstrate continued resistance to using age-appropriate tools such as scissors, a pencil, or a spoon and instead prefer direct contact with her hands, or a child may prefer to play with the toys of younger children. A child who has difficulty manipulating objects within one hand will use compensatory patterns rather than in-hand manipulation skills. Common compensatory substitution patterns include assistance in object manipulation by supporting the object with the other hand, the chest, or a table surface. These children frequently drop objects. Frustration and lack of persistence in practice can interfere with the child's skill development. Tremors may be a red flag indicating the possibility of specific **neuromotor dysfunction** or generalized weakness.

Neuromotor dysfunction is a condition characterized by atypical muscle function, tone, or movement.

Bilateral (two-handed) activities. A child with spastic hemiplegia displays asymmetry in movement as a result of both motor and sensory involvement. As a child with spastic hemiplegia manipulates objects with the noninvolved hand, overflow or associated reactions may be noted in the involved extremity (Figure 4.6). Typically, the child disregards or neglects the involved upper extremity because of poor sensory awareness in that arm, motor planning problems, or inability to initiate movement. Additionally, restricted active movement and posturing of the involved side behind the noninvolved side reinforces this neglect. Exaggerated movements may eventually develop in the noninvolved extremity because of overuse of compensatory patterns with that arm. A child with hemiplegia may not tolerate being touched on the involved arm and will resist any attempts to integrate that arm into fine motor activities.

Children with spastic diplegia usually demonstrate fairly intact fine motor skills or subtle motor involvement. However issues related to perceptual dysfunction may interfere in conceptual development. For example problems perceiving spatial relationships would interfere with the ability to demonstrate sequencing skills (Blanche & Nakasuji, 2001).

Persistence of Primitive Reflexes. If there is persistence of primitive reflexes such as the asymmetrical tonic neck reflex (ATNR) due to delayed integration, turning the head to the side dictates increased tone in the extremities on the face side and increased flexion on the skull side. This persistent primitive reflex makes it difficult for the child to bring her hands together or maintain visual attention to the hand engaged in an activity that requires elbow flexion, such as bringing a cup to the mouth (Erhardt, 1994a).

Sensory Processing Deficits. SPD may exist in children with cerebral palsy. These are difficult to identify but may include, for example, motor planning problems in children with spastic hemiplegia, poor registration of sensory input in

FIGURE 4.6

Atypical posturing in a preschool-aged child with left spastic hemiplegic cerebral palsy. The effort of work with the right hand further increases muscle tone in the left extremity, causing the left arm to pull toward the body with elbow flexion, deviation of the wrist, and fisting of the hand. These patterns interfere with bilateral activities.

Source: Used by permission of Jean Patz.

children with spastic quadriplegia, gravitational insecurity in children with spastic diplegia, or sensory defensiveness in children with hypotonia (Blanche & Nakasuji, 2001).

Down Syndrome

Hypermobility is defined as excessive mobility or range of motion in joints.

As in gross motor skills development, the child with Down syndrome is likely to use bilateral, symmetrical movements of the upper extremities instead of differentiated movements, with minimal use of trunk rotation to support efficient reach. Low muscle tone results in **hypermobility** in the proximal finger and thumb joints that interferes with grasp. Grasp patterns may be immature, with continued use of palmar grasps instead of thumb and index finger opposition, poor differentiation of finger use (Latash, Kang, & Patterson, 2002), and poor pre-positioning of the hand for grasp. Cognitive limitations also affect fine motor skill development. Children with Down syndrome have small, slender bones with poor calcification, low-set thumbs, short fingers, small hands, and delayed development of the carpal bones causing initial instability in the hand (Benda, 1969). Spano et al. (1999) found that fine motor skills in a sample of 5-year-old children with Down syndrome were significantly delayed, and these difficulties were more limiting than delays in gross motor skills. Bruni (2006) provides a good overview of development and intervention strategies to use with children who have Down syndrome.

Some researchers have suggested that children with Down syndrome may have deficits in receiving sensory information. Cole, Abbs, and Turner (1988) found that children with Down syndrome displayed an inability to adapt grip forces to objects and this was unrelated to hypotonia. In addition, the skin of children with Down syndrome may be thick and dry, possibly impairing sensation as age increases (Edwards & Lafreniere, 1995). Sensory processing difficulties have been identified in this population (Brandt, 1996); however, these problems are not the main cause of their developmental disability.

Autism Spectrum Disorders (ASD)

VIGNETTE 4.1

JAKE

Jake is a 3¹/₂-year-old child diagnosed with autism. He was referred to his county's early education program. Occupational therapy, speech therapy, special education, and psychological services were involved in the evaluation process. Following the evaluation, he was found to be eligible for special education services with an educational disability of autism. The OT used the Hawaii Early Learning Profile *(Parks, 2006). Information was gathered from the family regarding Jake's response to movement, sound, vision, and touch as well as oral sensory processing using the* Sensory Profile *(Dunn, 1999).*

An individualized education plan (IEP) was developed with goals in the areas of communication, social-emotional, self-help, sensory-motor, and cognition. It was recommended that Jake be placed in a full-day preschool program where he would receive special education, speech and language services, with the related service of occupational therapy. During observation and evaluation, Jake exhibited a number of behaviors that most likely related to sensory defensiveness in oral motor, auditory, and tactile areas. He preferred letter and number puzzles, would run aimlessly around a room, and swing for long periods of time. Interference with his behaviors usually resulted in temper tantrums. In addition, he would remove his clothing at inappropriate times and would crash into walls and floors. He constantly put toys in his mouth. He covered his ears when he heard a vacuum cleaner or a lawnmower. Jake watched other children and family members at play, but preferred to observe rather than to interact with them. Attempts to toilet train Jake had been difficult. He was overly sensitive to the sound of the flushing toilet and the bright lights in the bathroom. He had difficulty processing verbal commands associated with toileting and did not respond to social praise.

*Parents reported that he did not seem to perceive when he was wet. Strategies in-
cluded using visual cues instead of verbal, gradual introduction of bathroom routines, use of charts, and monitoring sensory responses to the bathroom
environment.*

*As a result of these sensitivities, Jake had a limited diet consisting of "beige"
crunchy foods, reduced play with toys, and difficulty interacting and communicating
with family and peers. The OT assisted the teacher in developing objectives to
increase the variety of his food intake, expand his play skills, and improve his
response to sensory input.*

*Sensory-based interventions were designed by the OT to increase Jake's tol-
erance to light touch, decrease his need for strong proprioceptive input, rechannel
his strong need for movement, and increase the variety of his food intake. Modifications and techniques were introduced one at a time in order to evaluate the
effectiveness of the various sensory interventions that consisted of tactile, proprioceptive, and vestibular activities. This program was explained to the parents and
educational team and was integrated into the classroom routine. For example,
suggestions included Jake sitting on a special movable cushion during circle and
work time in order to better attend to his work and give him opportunities for
movement. Also, an OT created a new feeding program that was carried out daily
at snack and lunch.*

Children with autism and other pervasive developmental disorders frequently demonstrate difficulties responding appropriately to sensory stimuli. A
number of anomalies involving registration, modulation, and response to sensory
stimuli have been described in children with autism. Tomchek and Dunn (2007)
found that the prevalence of SPD in a sample of 3- to 6-year-old children with
ASD was as high as 95% as measured by the *Short Sensory Profile* (SSP) (McIntosh,
Miller, & Shyu, 1999), a screening tool for identifying sensory processing difficulties. More specifically, 83.6% showed scores in the "definite difference" range
as compared to 3.2% of typically developing children. The most salient interfering behaviors, seen within a range of 50 to 79% of the time in children with ASD,
included: tactile defensiveness while grooming; picky eating due to sensitivity to
certain food textures and tastes; sensory-seeking behaviors due to hyporespon-
siveness (e.g., craving movement, noise, and touching objects and people); and
poor auditory processing as exhibited by lack of response when name is called,
disregard when being spoken to, aversion to unexpected loud noises, and difficulty paying attention in a noisy environment (Tomchek & Dunn, 2007). Jake's
parents found it difficult to eat as a family as a result of his extreme sensitivity to
a varied diet, and they were constantly challenged to provide him with appropriate nutrition. Jake's avoidance of social interaction discouraged them from having
friends over for dinner.

Miller, Reisman, McIntosh, and Simon (2001) reported hyporeactive physiological responses to sensory information, yet severe hyperreactive behavioral
responses to tactile, taste, smell, movement, visual, and auditory sensations in a

small sample of children with autism. Volkmar, Cohen, and Paul (1986) reported that most parents described their young children with autism as being hyporeactive to sound and pain stimulation, yet hyperreactive to visual, tactile, and auditory stimuli. The apparent contradiction in responsivity to auditory stimuli may be explained by reports that children with autism may not respond to verbal commands and may have difficulty processing auditory information, but they may become very upset at the presence of specific environmental sounds or loud or unusual auditory stimuli (e.g., a vacuum cleaner, door bell). Other frequent sensory manifestations are a fascination with some visual stimuli (e.g., rotating fans and moving lights), an apparent insensitivity to pain, a tendency to lick or smell objects, and an aversion to specific foods (Rapin, 1988). Differences in tactile processing may be seen in avoidance or obsession with specific textures of objects or foods or the avoidance of touch to particular body parts. Kern, Trivedi, Grannemann, Garver, Johnson, Andrews et al. (2007) showed patterns of sensory processing in individuals with autism improved with age; sensitivity to oral, visual, and auditory input declined with minimal change noted in tactile sensitivity.

Gross and fine motor development in young children with autism, although often the most successful area of development (Cox, 1993), is nonetheless often significantly delayed (Watson & Marcus, 1986). These children may appear to be physically agile and often do quite well in activities such as completing puzzles and block designs, but they may have difficulties in tasks requiring the planning and sequencing of movement (e.g., pedaling a tricycle, drawing, folding a paper). The ability of children with autism to gather accurate information about their own bodies through proprioception and through visual perception, both of which are required for imitation of motor movement, is questionable. Young children with autism are notably poor at imitating the behavior of others, which may be primary to the problems of socialization and communication inherent in children with autism (Meltzoff & Gopnik, 1993).

Provost, Lopez, and Heimerl (2007) found that 60% of a sample of 56 children diagnosed with ASD, 21–41 months of age, demonstrated significant delays in motor skills; 84% scored below two standard deviations on the Motor Scale of the *Bayley Scales of Infant Development* (Bayley, 1993) and 16 to 26% of the same sample scored below two S.D. on the *Peabody Developmental Motor Scales* (Folio & Fewell, 2000). The extent of the delay could qualify them for early intervention services based solely on their motor delays (Provost, Lopez, & Heimerl, 2007). This finding is supported by other studies of infants later diagnosed with autism who had motor delays under 3 years of age (Adrien et al., 1993; Baranek, 1999; & Teitelbaum et al., 2004).

Specific deficits related to motor development that have been noted in children with autism include decreased postural tone, toe walking, drooling, clumsiness, delayed onset of walking (Rapin, 1988), decreased balance, incoordination, and poor finger-to-thumb movements (Jones & Prior, 1985). Stereotypic movements are commonly seen among children with autism. These behaviors may involve hand and arm flapping, finger flicking, rocking, and body spinning. There are two divergent schools of thought regarding the function of these behaviors. Lovaas, Newsom, and Hickman (1987) state that stereotypic movements represent the child's attempt to achieve a state of optimum arousal. King and Grandin (1990), on the other hand, speculate that these behaviors serve the function of calming an overaroused system. Although self-injurious behavior, which is not uncommon in children with autism, has been described as an attempt at communication or as a response to frustration (Van Bourgondien, 1993), it might also represent an inability to cope with intense sensory discomfort. Grandin (1995), in her description of sensory problems in individuals with autism, explains that severe sensory processing problems may result in great bodily discomfort. Deep pressure stimulation has been reported to be effective in dealing with overarousal in children and adults with autism (Grandin, 1995; Nelson, 1984).

Because of the sensory processing difficulties often present in children with autism, **sensory integrative therapy,** which is a method of improving registration, modulation, and adaptation to sensory input (Ayres, 1979, 2005), has been suggested as an intervention approach (Grandin, 1995; Mailloux & Roley, 2001; Siegel, 1996; Williamson & Anzalone, 1997). Efficacy studies have supported the use of SI intervention in children with autism (Case-Smith & Bryan, 1999; Ray, King, & Grandin, 1988). Case-Smith and Bryan found a decrease in nonengaged behavior and an increase in goal-directed play in preschool children with autism who received SI intervention.

Indirect sensory integrative therapy for the child with a sensory processing disorder includes explaining behavior to parents and teachers, thus building better interaction, and modifying the environment to allow optimal function (Williamson & Anzalone, 1997). Direct approaches to intervention may include providing graded, specific sensory input to the child in a supportive environment. Stimuli may be designed to improve arousal and attention, or it may be designed to help calm the child. The goal is always for the child to respond appropriately to the sensory input by demonstrating improved self-regulating responses or to participate in goal-directed play or work experiences. Jake did not have playmates and this was very stressful for the parents. Attempts to arrange play times with neighborhood children often ended in tears due to his avoidance of social interactions and unusual sensory behaviors. The team identified Jake's sensory needs and designed the environment and fostered interactions to support play.

The reader is referred to Baranek (2002) for a complete explanation and summary of efficacy studies related to motor and sensory interventions for children with ASD including sensory integration therapy, sensory diet, the Alert Program, deep pressure (massage, joint pressure, Hug Machine, pressure garments, weighted vests), vestibular stimulation, auditory integration training (AIT), visual therapies (oculomotor exercises, colored filters, ambient prism lenses), sensorimotor handling techniques, and physical exercise.

Janzen (2003) addresses a variety of other recognized intervention strategies for working with children with ASD, such as applied behavioral analysis for teaching skills, the use of the Picture Exchange Communication System (PECS), sign language systems, discrete trial training, floor-time model, and the use of social stories.

:: ORAL MOTOR DEVELOPMENT IN YOUNG CHILDREN WITH SPECIAL NEEDS

VIGNETTE 4.2

A N N

Ann was first seen at 11 months of age by a developmental pediatrician; she was diagnosed with spastic cerebral palsy, mental retardation, and failure to thrive during the initial evaluation. She was referred for early intervention services. The early interventionist, occupational therapist, physical therapist, speech-language therapist, and parents conducted an arena assessment to determine Ann's strengths and areas of difficulty. In addition, she was referred for a videofluoro-scopic swallow study to rule out aspiration and gastroesophageal reflux and to determine the need for more intensified interventions to ensure safety.

The parents were concerned because it was difficult to feed, hold, and console their daughter. Ann had poor weight gain. Her mother reported that it took "forever" to complete a bottle—more than 45 minutes for each feeding. Ann's "tongue was in the way" when her mother inserted the nipple, which resulted in poor initiation of a suck. The parents tried several shapes, sizes, and textures of nipples and finally resorted to cutting a larger hole in the nipple. By report, Ann would periodically "stiffen up" when fed on her mother's lap, and the parents interpreted this behavior as rejection. The mother was the most successful in feeding her daughter; Ann did not tolerate being fed by other family members. Transition to solid foods was not smooth; Ann gagged and coughed on lumpy textured foods. The mother reported difficulty inserting a spoon because Ann would bite down on the spoon, have difficulty letting go, and lose about 50% of each spoonful. Periodically she would cough while swallowing.

Ann sat in a jumper seat that the parents padded with towels during spoon-feeding because she would fall to the side. Ann "stiffened" when bouncing in this seat, and the increased tone interfered with her eating.

It was difficult for Ann to grasp toys because her hands would fist during reach. She was unable to bring her hands to the midline and one arm was noticeably tighter than the other. This asymmetry was noted at less than 1 year of age. It was difficult to find toys that she could manipulate.

As the mother diapered Ann, the child's legs would cross due to hypertoni-city, making it hard to open her legs. Her stiff arms were difficult to insert into a sleeve when dressing. She could not sit independently in a tub, so bathing was challenging.

The occupational therapist assisted in developing goals for feeding, fine motor, play, and self-care areas. Goals included proper positioning for seating and carrying; adaptive equipment for eating, bathing, and play; oral motor handling techniques; neurodevelopmental treatment techniques to address postural issues that affected functional skills; and family education. The PT and OT taught the early interventionist

Adapted positioning devices or methods are designed or prescribed by a team to foster optimal positioning during functional activities.

about **adapted positioning** of Ann in a chair and on the parents' laps to decrease the influence of the atypical postural tone. The use of the bouncy seat during meals was discontinued because it set off atypical postural reflexes and increased overall postural tone, which adversely affected eating.

Results of the videoflourosopy indicated that it was safe to orally feed Ann. An adapted spoon was recommended because Ann had a tonic bite reflex. Feeders were discouraged from using metal or plastic utensils that might hurt Ann or break off in her mouth. A cut-out cup with thickened liquid was recommended to avoid hyperextension of the head while drinking. The bottle was discontinued gradually and cup drinking was introduced because bottle drinking encouraged tongue thrusting. The nutritionist was consulted during this transition to ensure adequate fluid and caloric intake.

Successful oral motor handling techniques were demonstrated to the parents and early interventionist. The parents were given resource materials along with explanations of the impact of cerebral palsy on a young child. The goal was to give the parents as much information as possible so they could independently understand why their child reacted negatively to touch, movement, and sound. In this way, it was hoped they would understand that her "pushing away" was actually spasticity and not a rejection of their parenting.

Adapted positioning, such as playing in sidelying, allowed Ann better use of her hands in midline and counteracted the influence of her asymmetrical tonic neck reflex. The parents were shown how they could affect her tone by speaking softly and moving slowly.

An adapted bath seat with head cushion and reclining back was suggested to provide safety in the tub and to avoid back strain for the parents. A home program was specifically designed to address the family's daily routine. Written instructions with illustrations were given to the parents to share with other family members so they could participate in helping Ann become more functional in her environment.

After several therapy sessions and home visits, the parents stated that mealtimes were getting easier. Ann's irritability diminished and her eating improved as well. The father was able to feed her, giving the mother some much needed respite. The family was less stressed about mealtimes in general.

Cerebral Palsy

Children with cerebral palsy often exhibit a number of characteristics that may interfere with voluntary and involuntary motor control necessary for eating. These characteristics may include atypical postural and oral tone; atypical movement; persistent primitive postural reflexes (e.g., asymmetrical tonic neck reflex) and oral reflexes (e.g., gag, rooting, and sucking reflexes); sensory deficits (hyposensitivity or hypersensitivity); pharyngeal involvement (which can cause aspiration); or esophageal involvement leading to reflux.

Positioning   Poor positioning due to atypical postural tone can have a considerable impact on all feeding functions. These problems may be reflected in an infant who is consistently difficult to hold, seems extremely fussy when held, or prefers being left alone. Caregivers may report that the child's body feels limp or stiff and that they do not have enough hands to support the child during eating. A child's need for additional support in sitting upright beyond the 8- to 12-month level is cause for concern because independent sitting generally develops by 6 to 8 months. Ann's tendency to stiffen when being held interfered with giving her proper nutrition and reduced her ability to interact with other family members during mealtimes.

Poor postural alignment is not conducive to swallowing. Head hyperextension tends to place the oral structures in a position incompatible with normal swallowing. The **atypical posture** mechanically opens the airway, placing a child at risk for aspirating.

Atypical posture can place a child at risk for aspirating.

Sucking   Many factors can interfere with normal sucking including structural deformities, weakness resulting from poor health, poor oral motor control resulting from central nervous system dysfunction, and behavioral issues stemming from inadequate sensory processing. Absent or weak oral reflexes can impede the sucking process. **Tongue thrust,** a forceful protrusion of the tongue seen in some children with cerebral palsy, interferes with sucking because the tongue is either bunched as a result of increased tone, or flat as a result of low tone (Morris & Klein, 2000). This makes it difficult for the tongue to wrap around the nipple to assist in channeling the liquid back into the mouth for swallowing. In short, the thrusting motion of the tongue may push the nipple out of the mouth and the presence of an atypical **tonic bite reflex** sets off a biting-versus-sucking response on the nipple. A tonic bite reflex, which is an atypical clamping of the jaw in response to stimulation on the gums or teeth (Morris & Klein, 2000), is an abnormality seen in children with more severe neuromotor dysfunction. Increased tone can create retraction of the upper lip, making it difficult to achieve lip closure around the nipple. An open mouth posture, resulting from hypertonia or hypotonia, prevents jaw and lip approximation around the nipple. All of these factors can increase feeding times and decrease liquid intake.

Swallowing   Children with neuromotor dysfunction are at risk at all stages of swallowing. Poor oral motor control, resulting from atypical tone, makes it difficult for a child to collect the bolus and time the swallow. Problems may also occur in the pharyngeal and esophageal phases of swallow. Coughing may be a sign of direct or indirect aspiration of food or liquid into the airway. Aspiration without coughing is termed **silent aspiration.** Frequent burping or vomiting may be an indication of reflux. Delayed or atypical oral motor control can contribute to an open mouth posture that fosters drooling. A persistently soaked bib, beyond the time when teething occurs, can indicate oral motor dysfunction.

Chewing   A child's inability or refusal to progress from pureed or strained baby food to more highly textured food beyond the 12- to 15-month level, after repeated introductions of solids, warrants further investigation. A child manipulates food between the molar surface when chewing; inefficient chewing would be suspected if food remained in the front of the mouth. Consistent choking when solids are given after the expected developmental range also is cause for concern. Poor oral motor control, such as that evidenced by tongue thrusting in children with cerebral palsy or

Down syndrome, may appear to be purposeful spitting when, in fact, it is an involuntary tongue protrusion that expels food from the mouth. A child's difficulty carrying food back in the mouth to swallow combined with forward protrusion of the tongue can cause excessive food loss. Tongue thrusting interferes with development of more mature oral movements such as tongue lateralization needed for chewing and tongue cupping needed to channel liquid when swallowing.

A child may not have the oral motor capabilities to maneuver food laterally between the molars for chewing and then back for swallowing. Persistent gagging may indicate a hyperactive gag reflex seen in some children with central nervous system dysfunction. Persistent negative responses to chunky or solid foods (e.g., crying, turning the head away, or spitting) may indicate a strong food preference. However, the resistance may be accounted for by a more serious condition, such as oral hypersensitivity, which occurs when a child is unable to tolerate the tactile qualities of the food, or oral motor dysfunction. Asymmetry in oral movements may be a symptom of motor dysfunction on one side of the body, as in spastic hemiplegia. Signs include an uneven smile, asymmetrical mouth posture when crying, and persistent pocketing of food on one side of the mouth. Another indicator of oral motor problems is the level of stress exhibited by the child and parent.

Spoon-Feeding   Consistently biting down on a spoon with clenched jaws may be a sign of a **tonic bite reflex,** which is a form of tactile hypersensitivity (Morris & Klein, 2000). A tonic bite reflex is a strong bite set off by touch to the gums or teeth that is difficult to release; this atypical reflex interferes with eating. A parent may unknowingly stimulate the tonic bite again by attempting to pull the spoon out of the child's clenched mouth. Lack of development of lip closure due to delayed maturation or neurological impairment can interfere with removing food from a spoon with the upper lip.

When drinking from a cup, excessive fluid loss beyond the first year may be suggestive of an oral-motor problem.

Cup Drinking   Various factors that cause difficulties with cup drinking include: oral motor delay, which can cause a primitive sucking pattern on the cup; atypical tone, which can result in poor oral motor control; and abnormalities in sensory processing, which can lead to oral hypersensitivity (Morris & Klein, 2000). Typically, a child loses liquid when she begins to drink from a cup. Excessive loss beyond the first year may indicate poor development of jaw stability, tongue control, or lip closure. A persistent cough while drinking may indicate aspiration of fluid into the lungs. Oral motor dysfunction, oral hypersensitivity, delayed development, or behavioral resistance might be suspected if the cup has been introduced in the typical developmental time frame, the child repeatedly refuses to drink from a cup, and the parent expresses concern. Further investigation is warranted by an occupational therapist or speech and language pathologist to evaluate what might be causing these problems.

Down Syndrome

The child with Down syndrome has delays from mental retardation, hypotonia, and oral hyposensitivity. Inadequate postural control may result in head hyperextension, which can interfere with safety in swallowing. Infants may exhibit a poor suck resulting from the hypotonia or general weakness from other medical conditions such as associated heart abnormalities. An open-mouth posture and tongue thrusting lead to excessive drooling and poor oral intake. As the child matures, delayed chewing with a lack of progression to more highly textured food, as well as poor spoon-feeding and cup-drinking skills, may become more apparent.

Autism

The diet of children with autism may be limited to particular foods and food textures as a result of atypical tactile, gustatory, or olfactory processing. Children with autism may have hypersensitivity to temperature, smell, touch, taste, sound, and movement (Kientz & Dunn, 1997) that can interfere with mealtime.

Sensory overload during feeding may produce tantrums, stereotypical behaviors, or a withdrawal of attention. Poor communication during mealtime might include nonresponsiveness to the caregiver, limited turn-taking vocalizations, poor communication of needs, and lack of ability to engage the caregiver. Deficits in motor planning can make it difficult for these children to learn how to use utensils. **Pica,** the consumption of inedible substances, is common in autism and may be due to impaired taste perception in children with autism (Van Bourgondien, 1993).

Cleft Lip or Palate

Children with a cleft lip or palate may have difficulty with sucking due to poor oral pressure from an open cleft. Nasal regurgitation, air swallowing, choking, and vomiting may occur until surgical repairs of the cleft are completed.

Low Vision

Children with impaired vision may exhibit behavioral problems during meals as they may not feel in control (e.g., not seeing when a caregiver is approaching with a spoon). There may be resistance to new foods that cannot be seen. Self-feeding may be delayed due to difficulty locating utensils or food on their plate.

Myelomeningocele

Poor oral control in children with myelomeningocele may occur when an accompanying brain anomaly called **Arnold-Chiari malformation** is present. This deviation results from a herniation of the brainstem that can result in delayed swallowing and choking (Liptak, 2002) and vomiting (Morris & Klein, 2000).

Congenital Acquired Immunity Deficiency Syndrome (AIDS)

Children with AIDS may exhibit recurrent, chronic diarrhea; failure to thrive; poor weight gain; progressive and dysfunctional oral motor control similar to neurological problems described under cerebral palsy; and oral thrush.

Learning Disability

Some children with learning disabilities exhibit minor oral motor problems during mealtimes, particularly oral dyspraxia. Poor motor planning may affect self-feeding skills because it will be difficult for the child to hold and coordinate use of utensils. Extended use of fingers occurs to avoid use of utensils. Parents may report sloppiness during mealtimes and poor attention.

:: SELF-CARE DEVELOPMENT IN YOUNG CHILDREN WITH SPECIAL NEEDS

A variety of factors can negatively impact the self-care development of young children with special needs. When one or any combination of factors is present, there are a number of behaviors that can indicate a problem with self-care development. Figure 4.7 provides a list of some of these key behaviors. Specific functional areas of interest include self-feeding, dressing, and toileting.

Self-Feeding

Separating one side of the hand from the other to finger feed can be a difficult task for children with neuromotor dysfunction. For example, a child with spastic cerebral palsy may have a fisted hand due to increased postural tone in the flexors, making it difficult to open the hand, rotate the forearm in pronation and supination, or release the finger food once grasped.

Sensory integrative dysfunction is an inability to organize and process sensory information in the absence of known neurological or sensory receptor abnormality. *Sensory processing disorder* is another term used to represent sensory integrative dysfunction.

Use of a spoon requires motor planning and dexterity. A child with a weak grasp due to atypical postural tone from cerebral palsy may have trouble holding and maintaining grasp on the spoon. For example, a child with athetoid cerebral palsy will have trouble maintaining grasp on a utensil and inserting it into the mouth due to involuntary movement. The child's body is in constant motion, making the mouth a moving target. A child with a learning disability and dyspraxia may have difficulty motor planning use of a utensil and resort to using her fingers well beyond a socially acceptable age. Lack of a hand preference seen in some children with **sensory integrative dysfunction** can make it difficult to develop skilled tool use as the child switches from hand to hand. Limited cognitive abilities in a child with mental retardation may delay understanding the use of utensils.

Dressing

Atypical postural tone may interfere with positioning for dressing; the child may not tolerate or be able to be positioned to help in dressing. One side of the body may be tighter, as in hemiplegia, making it difficult for the child to independently dress with the involved side. Poor fine motor control may prevent manipulation of fasteners. Increased postural tone may make it difficult to insert a tonically extended foot into a shoe or a tightly fisted hand into a glove. Children with poor motor plan-

FIGURE 4.7	Red flags suggestive of self-care problems.

Self-Feeding	Poor postural control that interferes with self-feeding
	Lack of finger feeding beyond 12 months of age
	Poor use of utensils (extended use of an immature grasp pattern, poor bilateral hand use)
	Refusal to use utensils by the appropriate developmental age
	Overly messy or sloppy eater
	Inability to sit still for a meal
	Extreme resistance to finger feeding certain textures of food
Dressing	Poor postural control that interferes with dressing
	Delayed dressing skills beyond expected age
	Poor fine motor skills (unable to button, zip, snap by the expected developmental age)
	Intolerance to certain clothing textures
	Parental report indicating that it took "forever" to teach dressing skills such as tying shoes
Bathing	Inability to independently sit in a bathing device after 8 months of age
	Parental concern about lifting child in and out of the bathtub
	Extreme resistance to washing hair
	Inability to maneuver in and out of the bathtub by the expected age
Toileting	Difficulty opening legs of a child when diapering
	Cannot sit independently on toilet when developmentally appropriate
	Lack of independence in managing clothing after the expected developmental age
	Delayed bowel and bladder control
Grooming	Poor fine motor skills to manage grooming tools such as comb, toothbrush, washcloth, and soap
	"Hates" having hair cut
Sleep	Persistent tantrums at bedtime
	Frequent waking at night beyond infancy
	Absence of or excessive bedtime rituals
	Muscles do not relax during sleep

ning abilities may have difficulty figuring out how to tie shoes or distinguish front from back or right from left. A child who has a sensory impairment may resist wearing certain types and textures of clothing because the sensation of the material is uncomfortable.

Toileting

A child with spina bifida may have a flaccid bladder. Toilet learning may not be possible. The term toilet *learning* versus *training* emphasizes that any approach needs to be a child-centered learning experience (Eisenberg et al., 1994; Mack, 1978). Intervention can be beneficial if the lesion is above the lumbar region (Shepherd, 2005).

Spina bifida occulta, a less severe form of spina bifida, also can cause delayed bladder control, and a toileting program can be successful with this population (Maizels, Rosenbaum, & Keating, 1999).

Children with motor impairment may have problems due to atypical postural tone and limited movement. As was noted earlier, an infant with abnormally tight musculature in the legs due to spastic cerebral palsy may be unable to open the legs for diapering. A child with neurological impairment may have unstable posture due to atypical tone that will make it difficult to independently sit on a toilet in a relaxed manner. The child may not feel safe due to the postural instability. Weakness or decreased range of motion in the arms can impede use of fasteners during toileting.

Functional performance was measured in a cross-sectional study of 5-year-old children with Down syndrome. Of the three areas covered, mobility issues were the most functional while self-care, primarily tasks related to toileting, were the least developed and caused major concern for the parents due to the amount of caregiver assistance needed, social stigma, and lack of readiness for starting school (Dolva, Coster, & Lilja, 2004).

A child with autism may exhibit resistance to change that can interfere with the transition to independence in toileting. Poor social interaction can make social rewards, often used in toileting programs, ineffective. Sensory defensiveness to sensations in the bathroom such as noises, lights, or colors can create an avoidance response to toilet training. Difficulty comprehending language can interfere with the child following toileting directions.

Inappropriate parental expectations also can lead to frustration with their child's accidents and resistance to toilet learning practices. The early interventionist can have a positive impact here by addressing parental frustration and by providing information to help adjust parental expectations.

∷ SPECIFIC STRATEGIES FOR ASSESSMENT

Fine Motor Assessment

Keen observation of the child performing fine motor tasks within her own environment along with input from the parents provide useful information regarding the child's level of independence. The information gathered from medical and educational records, history from the caregivers, educators, and child, and direct observations in the child's environment are analyzed to give a functional picture of the child's level of mastery. The evaluator will want to ask the following questions: Are there developmentally appropriate toys and materials available in the child's environment? What structural barriers interfere with a child's mobility at home, school, or on the playground? What are the child's favorite toys? Do the parents have difficulty choosing toys for their child? Does the child dislike touching objects of different textures?

The cultural background of the family must be considered as well. The parents' concerns guide the evaluation when dealing with infants and toddlers. Baseline data on functional fine motor performance is collected prior to initiation of intervention in order to evaluate effectiveness. The OT assists the teacher by interpreting results of fine motor testing, critically analyzing how sensory, motor, physical, psychosocial, behavioral, and environmental issues affect performance. Integrating information from medical and cognitive assessments is essential for program planning. An evaluation is incomplete if the only areas considered are range of motion, strength, postural tone, and attention. The overall picture of the child's **occupational role** within the home, school, and community needs to be addressed.

Fine motor evaluation is often performed by an OT for children with sensory and neuromotor dysfunction and includes clinical observations of the degree and distribution of postural tone, symmetry, range of motion, existence of primitive reflexes, righting and equilibrium reactions, and quality of movement. The level of mastery and independence in reach, grasp, release, manipulation, bilateral skills, and in-hand manipulation are evaluated during functional activities such as manipulating toys, cutting with scissors, or accessing a computer. Parent and teacher interviews are conducted to gather valuable information about the environments in which the child functions, materials available, and social and cultural issues. Assessment tools are chosen dependent on the overall needs of the child and family; see the following sections for brief descriptions of selected assessment tools.

The *Manual Ability Classification System* (MACS) is a scale used to classify how children with cerebral palsy use their hands during daily functional, age-related, fine motor activities; the five-level scale addresses level of independence and typical versus best performance (Eliasson et al., 2006). The *Toddler and Infant Motor Evaluation* (Miller & Roid, 1994) is a comprehensive standardized assessment to identify quality of movement and motor organization in infants and toddlers. Training in neurodevelopmental treatment (NDT) is recommended in order to adequately analyze test results. The *Erhardt Developmental Prehension Assessment* (EDPA)–Second Edition (Erhardt, 1994b) is a criterion-referenced test that addresses the presence of primitive reflexes and basic components of prehension, including reach, grasp, release, manipulation, and prewriting for children with developmental disabilities or neurological impairments. The *Peabody Developmental Motor Scales II* (Folio & Fewell, 2000) is a standardized, norm-, and criterion-referenced test that evaluates both fine and gross motor abilities in children from birth through 5 years of age. The *Bruininks-Oseretsky Test of Motor Proficiency*–BOT-2 (Bruininks & Bruininks, 2005) is a norm-referenced test that covers upper limb, fine motor, and gross motor abilities in children 4 to 21 years of age.

Broad-based developmental assessments such as the *Hawaii Early Learning Profile* (HELP) (Parks, 2006), the *HELP for Preschoolers* (VORT Corporation, 1999), and the *Learning Accomplishment Profile–Diagnostic 3rd Edition* (LAP–D) (Kaplan Press and Chapel Hill Training Outreach Project, 2005) include sections on fine motor development. The LAP–D divides the fine motor section into two subtests: manipulation and writing. These curriculum-based assessments cover the period from birth to 6 years of age (HELP) and 3 to 6 years (LAP–D).

Play is a primary occupation of a child and the early intervention professional will evaluate play skills through observation of spontaneous play preferably in a

The term *occupational role* refers to the daily activities a child performs, such as playing, dressing, bathing, or writing, within the context of her environment.

natural environment, interaction with peers during play, and choice and availability of appropriate toys for the child's developmental, motor, and sensory needs. Examples of assessment tools that evaluate various aspects of play are the *Test of Playfulness*, which addresses intrinsic motivation, internal control, and the ability to suspend reality (Bundy, 1997), the *Preschool Play Scale* (Bledsoe & Shepherd, 1982; Knox, 1997), and the *Transdisciplinary Play-Based Assessment*, which addresses cognitive, language, motor, physical, and naturalistic play in children birth through 6 years of age (Linder, 1993).

Sensory Processing Assessment

Early identification of children with sensory processing disorders is important to allow intervention by parents and professionals. An OT usually makes the determination of sensory processing disorders after the analysis of results from clinical observations, pertinent historical information, parent/teacher interviews, and standardized testing. The early interventionist assists in the evaluation process by participating in responding to questionnaires related to sensory processing problems such as the *Infant/Toddler Sensory Profile* (Dunn, 2002), the *Sensory Profile* for children ages 3 and older (Dunn, 1999), and the *Sensory Processing Measure* (SPM) (Parham, Ecker, Miller Kuhaneck, Henry, & Glennon, 2007), which measures sensory processing, praxis, and social participation in elementary school-age children. The *Sensory Integration and Praxis Tests* (SIPT; Ayres, 1989a & 1989b) is a standardized assessment tool that measures sensory integration and praxis functions in children 4 to 8.11 years of age; specialized training is required for administration of this test. For further information in this area, the reader can refer to resources detailed in the reference section.

Intervention for sensory-based dyspraxia is based on the hypothesized etiology and the involved sensory systems. For example, if poor coordination is believed to be due to problems with sensory processing within the vestibular and proprioceptive systems, intervention will involve providing rich, graded sensory experiences emphasizing head position, body position/awareness, movement (often rotary), and pushing, pulling, and lifting tasks to provide the child with more information about the environment and the child's own body. Sensory integrative therapy would also structure the environment to promote an adaptive performance. This is often referred to as a "just right challenge" because it is new, more difficult, but attainable by the child. An SI approach emphasizes self-direction and initiation of sensory input by the child, whereas sensory stimulation implies that the child is a "passive recipient of environmentally imposed stimuli" (Spitzer & Roley, 2001, p. 8). During treatment, active sensory input is organized and followed by an adaptive (usually motor) response.

Oral motor problems are evaluated by professionals in occupational therapy and speech-language pathology.

Oral Motor Assessment

The parents and early interventionists are typically the first to suspect oral motor problems. In such cases, they would refer a child for evaluation. Occupational therapists or speech-language pathologists who have training in typical and atypical oral motor development evaluate oral motor problems. Videofluoroscopic swallow studies are done in radiology to rule out problems such as aspiration and gastroesophageal reflux. Other critical team members in the evaluation of swallowing disorders include a developmental pediatrician, gastroenterologist, neurologist, nutritionist/dietitian, otolaryngologist, physical therapist, pediatric surgeon, psychologist, pulmonologist, radiologist, nurse, and social worker (Arvedson & Brodsky, 2002).

Pre-assessment information is gathered from medical and nutritional records. An extensive interview is conducted with the primary caregivers and teachers about concerns related to the child's eating abilities. During the oral motor evaluation, the therapist observes the parent or teacher feeding the child, noting the method of feeding, communication between caregiver and child, positioning, and types of utensils, equipment, and food textures used. The therapist may then feed the child, evaluating typical and atypical sensory and motor aspects of sucking, swallowing, chewing, spoon-feeding, and cup drinking. Behavior during meals is noted. Samples of assessment tools available to guide evaluation of oral motor skills include the *Clinical Feeding Evaluation of Infants* (Wolf & Glass, 1992), *WeeFIM-Functional Independence Measure for Children* (Hamilton & Granger, 2000), *Mealtime Assessment Guide and the Developmental Pre-feeding Checklist* (Morris & Klein, 2000), and the *Schedule for Oral Motor Assessment: SOMA* (Reilly, Skuse, & Wolke, 2000). The therapist develops a treatment plan once the evaluation is completed, together with the child, parents, educational staff, and feeding team. The plan addresses quality of oral motor skills and needs within the child's eating environment.

Self-Care Assessment

Self-care assessment addresses a child's level of development and independence in self-feeding (finger feeding, use of utensils, use of bottle or cup); dressing (undressing, dressing, fasteners, and directionality); toileting (bowel and bladder control); bathing (washing hands, face, and body); grooming (brushing teeth, combing hair); and sleeping.

The early interventionist will collaborate with the OT when postural and sensory problems interfere with self-care tasks and there is a need for adaptive equipment. For example, how can a child with limited range of motion reach the soap in the bathroom to independently wash her hands? Can adapted equipment, such as a wheelchair, fit through the bathroom door and around the classroom? What adaptive equipment is needed to help the child be more independent in self-care skills? How do sensory components, such as tactile properties of clothes or food, noise level, lighting, and smells within the environment, affect self-care performance in a child with **sensory defensiveness?**

Assessment is performed within a cultural context that may be revealed through answers to the following questions: When are solid foods typically introduced into an infant's diet? What foods are restricted? What type of socialization is expected during meals? What level of independence is deemed appropriate at various ages? What type of clothing does the child wear that may be different from that expected by the

> Sensory defensiveness is the hypersensitivity to normal sensations (i.e., the child reacts defensively rather than discriminately to sensory input).

evaluator? When and how is toilet learning addressed in the child's culture? What utensils are used at the meal? (Planning intervention to address manipulation of a spoon or fork is pointless if the child typically uses chopsticks.) The evaluator observes the child within her own environment and integrates the family and educational staff into the assessment process as much as possible.

The following are selected assessment tools that evaluate self-care skills in young children. The *Functional Independence Measure for Children* (WeeFIM) (Hamilton & Granger, 2000) is appropriate for children with physical disabilities functioning within the age range of 6 months to 6 years. The self-care section includes eating, dressing, grooming, bathing, toileting, and bowel and bladder control.

The *Hawaii Early Learning Profile* (HELP) (Parks, 2006) is a curriculum-based, criterion-referenced, interdisciplinary assessment tool. The HELP for infants and toddlers is family-centered, covering birth to 3 years of age. *HELP for Preschoolers* (VORT, 2004) continues up to age 6. Content of the test includes cognition, language, gross motor, fine motor, social-emotional, and self-help. The self-help area addresses oral motor development, dressing, independent feeding, sleep patterns and behaviors, grooming and hygiene, toileting, and household independence/responsibility. Results are reported in developmental age levels.

The *Battelle Developmental Inventory* (BDI–2) covers activities of daily living including eating, dressing, toileting, and grooming; it addresses the birth- to 8-year population (Newborg, 2004).

The *Pediatric Evaluation of Disability Inventory* (PEDI), developed by Haley and colleagues (1992), is a structured interview-judgment-based standardized evaluation given to parents or clinicians familiar with the child. It measures three domains (self-care, mobility, and social function) in children with moderate to severe motor impairment between 6 months and 7 years. The PEDI also addresses the level of assistance and modifications needed. The self-care domain includes 73 items, such as adaptability to food texture; use of utensils; use of drinking containers; toothbrushing; hair brushing; nose care; hand, body, and face washing; maneuvering pullover garments, fasteners, pants, shoes and socks; toileting; and managing bowel and bladder.

:: USE OF TECHNOLOGY IN ASSESSMENT AND INTERVENTION

Technology provides opportunities for children who have significant motor impairment to have a degree of personal control over activities that would otherwise be impossible. An interdisciplinary team knowledgeable in assistive technology evaluates the appropriateness of the devices considering the environmental, cultural, financial, motoric, and sensory needs of the child and family. Most states have lending libraries (often provided through United Cerebral Palsy or Easter Seals, or the local education agency) that provide free loans of assistive technology devices. Local special education departments or teachers and therapists with experience providing services to children with significant motor impairment should be able to supply information about these sources of equipment. Sources also can be found through a Web search (keyed to an assistive technology lending library in the city or state of interest). It is best practice to test these devices before purchase because mistakes can be costly. Some states have provided guidelines to help in assessment procedures for determining most appropriate technology for a given child.

High-tech solutions generally involve the use of electronics, especially the use of computerized devices. Some examples of low-tech options for children with motor impairment might include using Dycem® to prevent a toy from sliding, a pencil grip to allow efficient grasp of a writing implement, or a battery interrupter in a toy to allow single switch use. The ability to activate a single switch (Figure 4.8) with any reliable body movement can allow the child to turn on and off battery-operated toys and electrical devices (such as tape players or, in this case, an electric mixer) directly. With the addition of devices such as the Single Switch Latch and Timer for battery-operated toys or the PowerLink for electrical devices (both by AbleNet, Inc.), single switches can be used in several different modes. A wide range of switches can meet specific motor and sensory needs. Switches vary in size and composition; they may be hard, soft, or cushioned, and may be activated by pressing, squeezing, or altering body position. They may vibrate, light up, or produce sound upon activation. One- or two-switch activation is used for scanning software. For example, a child may be able to use a twitch switch controlled by slight movement of the head and tongue.

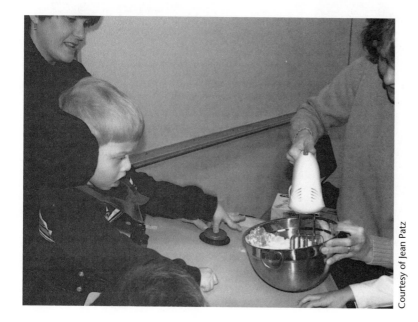

Courtesy of Jean Patz

FIGURE 4.8

A 5-year-old child with spastic quadriplegic cerebral palsy participates in a fun cooking activity in the preschool classroom by activating a mixer with his direct selection switch. The Jelly Bean switch is connected to the mixer with a PowerLink® control unit, both by Ablenet. The teacher places the materials directly in his midline while the OT evaluates best placement of the switch for success.

With the appropriate software and hardware, single switches can be used with computer games, interactive "books," and touch screens to control the cursor. Switches can be used to teach a wide variety of activities such as play exploration, concept development, social interaction, or motor control. Direct selection is the option of choice whenever possible. It is the fastest and most efficient method for activation. Some examples of direct-selection alternatives include the Touch Window™ by Edmark; the Touch-Free™ switch by Riverdeep, which is a "no-touch" input option activated by any part of the body; use of alternative trackballs and keyboards such as IntelliKeys by IntelliTools (Figure 4.9), or the WinMini by Tash Inc.; head pointers or mouth sticks for typing; switches with head array to access computer controls; expanded, enlarged key pads on keyboards or small keyboards; keyguards; keyboard emulators; screen enlargers; one- or three-finger typing; adjustable height table and chair; portable keyboards; and laptop computers (Struck, 1996). The child shown in Figure 4.10 demonstrates appropriate positioning, use of a joy stick, and software appropriate to his perceptual needs.

Adaptive equipment may be necessary when a child has a physical impairment. Equipment is prescribed with consideration for the child's chronological and developmental age as well as the environment in which the equipment will be used.

FIGURE 4.9

The Intellikeys® keyboard provides an array of options ranging from one to multiple key activations depending on the child's abilities.

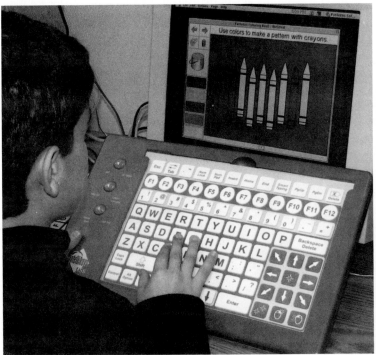

Courtesy of Jean Patz

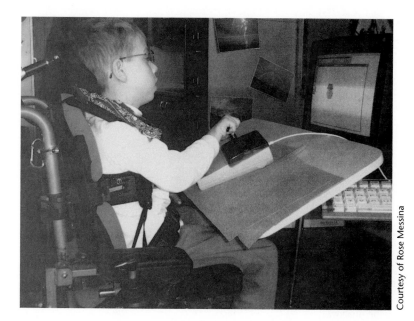

Courtesy of Rose Messina

FIGURE 4.10

This child is accessing a computer game intended to help with spatial manipulation through use of a joy stick while supported in his adapted wheelchair with head and lateral trunk supports, seatbelt for pelvic control, and foot rests. The screen is placed at eye level and in his midline, while the joy stick is supported on a slanted surface for ease of access.

Selected adaptive equipment such as adapted eating utensils or **adapted toilet seats** for the self-care domains are presented in Figure 4.11.

Use of Technology in Toileting

Some typically developing children independently learn toileting quickly whereas others, to the parents' distress, take much longer. Children with disabilities have added disadvantages that can make toilet learning all the more difficult. Some examples of adapted equipment used to enhance independence in toileting are listed in Figure 4.11 and shown in Figure 4.12. An **enuresis alarm** is one aspect of a multidimensional approach for children diagnosed with **nocturnal enuresis** (i.e., urinating during the night due to deep sleep patterns). Other methods may be indicated for children with special needs. A thorough evaluation is conducted to determine if wetting is due to issues such as deep sleep, small bladder size, neurological problems, overproduction of urine, stress in the family, or food sensitivities (Maizels et al., 1999). The alarm is used only when the child has been diagnosed with enuresis. It is not appropriate for a child with **incontinence**. Incontinence indicates that the child does not have a typically functioning urinary tract. The alarm sounds when the child wets during the night. The device includes a moisture sensor that is attached to the outer part of the child's underwear and an alarm that is attached near the shoulder on the child's pajamas. The comprehensive program generally shows success within a matter of months if used consistently (Maizels et al., 1999).

An adapted toilet seat with accessories (e.g., tray, harness, back pad, footrest) provides extra trunk and head support during toileting.

SELF-FEEDING

Bottles

Angled-neck bottles to decrease hyperextension of the head and air swallowing

Specially shaped bottles, grips, or adapted rings added to the bottles to allow for two-handed use

Spoons

Swivel spoons to accommodate lack of arm position and movement

Weighted spoons for children with tremor, athetosis, or sensory disorders

Right-or left-handed curved spoons

Coated spoons to protect the teeth if the child has a tonic bite reflex or sensitivity to temperature

Flexible utensils that can be adjusted to fit the child's changing needs

Various sized and shaped spoons (narrow, wide, shallow, deep) to accommodate the child's needs and the feeder's comfort

Cups

Cut-out cups used to prevent head hyperextension and foster more normal swallowing

Spouted cups to make transition to a regular cup easier. Spouted cups are discouraged if a child has a tongue thrust

Easy-grip and two-handled cups for manageability
Weighted cups for those needing sensory feedback and added stability

Dishes

Scoop dishes with a nonskid bottom and a higher, rounded edge to help the child scoop

Plates with suction cups so they do not move while scooping

Straws of various widths, lengths, and thickness to provide added oral stability

Other: Handles on utensils to enhance grip; built-up handles for weak grasp; long-handled utensils for limited reach; Universal cuff for child with minimal to no grasp; sandwich holders

DRESSING

Buttons

Velcro in place of buttons
Button hook for limited bilateral control
Larger buttons for ease in handling

Zippers

Zipper pull to accommodate a poor grasp
Button hook with zipper pull

Laces

Elastic or coiled laces for poor dexterity

Lace locks for one-handed child

Clothing

Pullover shirts to eliminate the need for fasteners

Velcro or slip-on shoes/sock aid

Elastic waistbands on pants

Other

Lightweight reacher for dressing

Mittens with no thumbs and Velcro cuffs

BATHING

Reclining chair with adjustable seat and back angle with removable mesh fabric that comes in various sizes and includes a chest strap, hip strap, leg strap, and head support

Wraparound bath support that is height adjustable, used for less-involved children needing extra support for safety

Optional shower stands/long-handled shower spray

Tub transfer seat

TOILETING

Toilet reducer ring with splash guard

Toilet support—adjustable, wraparound trunk, or high-back toilet support that attaches to existing toilet

Adapted toilet seats with attachments

Toilet safety frame

Portable, pediatric commodes with chest strap

Raised toilet seats

Available from: Sammons Preston (2007). *Pediatrics Catalog: Special needs products for schools and clinics.* Bolingbrook, IL: An Ability One Corporation. (1-800-323-5547)

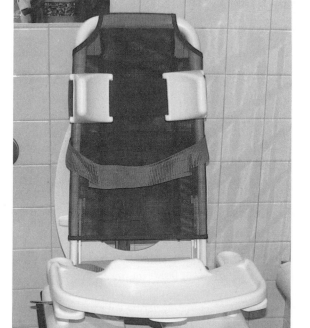

Courtesy of Jean Patz

FIGURE **4.12**

Adapted toilet seat used for children with severe motor involvement.

:: SELECTED STRATEGIES FOR FINE MOTOR INTERVENTION

When considering intervention for the young child with fine motor or sensory needs, the most efficient approach is to first address that which will make the greatest difference in the functional performance of the child. The concept of "zone of proximal development" (Vygotsky, 1978) presented in chapter 5, is useful to the teacher in prioritizing goals. The child will present with a range of skills from dependent to emerging and finally to independent. Skills that are almost independent would be considered in the zone of proximal development. Support targeted at this level would enhance development more efficiently. Skills that the child is dependent in may require adaptations. Often, for example, better performance will result simply by improving the child's posture using adapted seating devices (Exner, 2006). The objects used in performance of the task and the nature of the task itself need to be examined. The use of different objects scaled to the child's hand size or different placement of objects may result in better success. Perhaps the task could be done in a simpler way. When these options have been considered but problems still persist, the interventionist needs to systematically plan how to foster improved development of fine motor skills. A process suggested for assisting in choosing interventions might include the following: (1) Determine major factors interfering with the child's learning process; (2) Consult with the child's therapists regarding the foundational skills missing and needed in order for the child to progress; (3) Prioritize skills according to which will have the greatest impact, taking into account the child's conceptual level, interests, and learning style; and (4) Provide adaptations or supports for lacking components in the sequence if the skill won't be developed soon but is necessary to the task.

The child's sensory needs are as important to address as motor needs. Infants, toddlers, and preschoolers who have sensory processing disorders may need special accommodations at home or in the classroom. Often a child's perceived behavior problem is actually a response to inadequate sensory processing. The early interventionist, knowledgeable about sensory integration methods, can support a child with a sensory processing problem by providing alternative methods to address her sensory needs. The OT can assist the early interventionist by identifying a sensory processing problem and consulting about intervention.

Examples of accommodations might include the use of sensory preparatory activities prior to engaging in fine motor skills, addressing the child's level of arousal before expecting functional performance within the classroom, giving the child who is slow in processing sensory information extra time for completion of tasks, or allowing the use of movable equipment within the classroom for children who crave movement. Equipment within the classroom can be provided or adapted to allow the child to choose what can fulfill her sensory needs. For example, a child can sit on a movable, dynamic surface while doing table top activities to help with arousal. Push toys with added weight provide proprioceptive feedback that can be organizing for the child. Toys with various tactile properties can address tactile needs for those who are overresponsive or underresponsive to touch. Most early learning centers provide sensory tables used for water, beans, buttons, and other materials to encourage sensory explorations and fine motor skills. Bean bag chairs can be used for sitting or building. Once children have their sensory needs met, they may have a better chance of interacting effectively within their environment.

Positioning the Child

It is important to consider specific ways to carry, move, or position children with atypical postural tone during their daily routines because this can influence fine motor functioning. Finnie (1997) addresses methods to position and carry children with cerebral palsy according to their atypical postural tone. For example, the parent or teacher can actively use her body as a positioning support for a young child who cannot sit independently due to poor postural tone and persistent primitive reflexes. Carrying the child in a manner to foster head and trunk control, with arms toward midline, and facing the child forward allows her to take in the environment. During floor sitting, the child's head, trunk, arms, and legs could be supported by the adult's body to enhance fine motor functioning. The team working with Ann taught her parents key points of control when carrying, holding, and positioning her to prevent thrusting of her head, shoulders, and pelvis. The team suggested the use of an elasticized orthotic undergarment with customized strapping system to provide dynamic postural support when Ann is not in therapy.

An **adapted chair** (see Figure 4.10) including such features as a solid back and seat insert, **seat belt,** lateral trunk and pelvic supports, anterior chest support, or **lap tray** may be indicated for a child who cannot sit independently because of poor trunk control.

Working on sitting with stability and hand skills simultaneously is counterproductive for a child with poor trunk control. Depending on the child's degree of involvement, appropriate positioning during fine motor tasks may include sidelying, prone or supine lying, sitting, or standing. Adaptations can be evaluated for each of these positions to achieve optimal postural control.

In the older child who is embarking on prewriting or writing skills, ideal positioning includes a chair height that allows the child to place her feet firmly on the floor, hips and knees bent at 90 degrees, and a desk height approximately 2 inches above the child's bent elbow at 90 degrees when the child is seated symmetrically and erect (Benbow, 1990) (Figure 4.13). A child may lean into the table if the surface is too low; a table that is too high tends to turn the arms inward and thumbs downward, resulting in poor control and opposition of the thumb and index finger (Exner, 2006). The seat depth and height of school chairs are often too large for the students. Smith-Zuzovsky and Exner (2004) measured the effect of positioning on fine motor performance in 6- and 7-year-old typically developing children. Results indicated that those seated optimally, as described above, in chairs appropriate for their size scored significantly higher on tasks requiring complex hand skills. It is important for the early interventionist to recognize the impact appropriate seating can have on fine motor function.

An adapted chair is a homemade or commercially available chair with added supports to provide optimal positioning for a child.

A seatbelt is the simplest means of stabilizing the pelvis. The line of pull should be in a posterior, inferior direction (45 degrees) and inferior to the anterior-superior iliac spine (ASIS).

A lap tray is a wooden or clear plastic tray attached to a wheelchair that provides a working surface as well as some trunk support. Accessories can include padded top, easel, hand dowel, and activity bar.

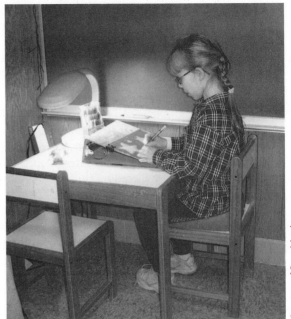

FIGURE 4.13

Simple adaptations make prewriting activities more effective for a child with fine motor difficulties. She is seated in a chair that is the appropriate height with her feet flat on the floor, table surface supporting the arms, three-ring binder used as a slant board to foster more wrist extension and upright head positioning, use of a pencil grip for better stability, and a seating cushion to encourage upright sitting. In this case, the cushion is intended to help with pelvic positioning. It could also be used by a child who has difficulty attending.

Positioning of Objects

The term *chin jut* refers to the atypical position of the head in which the chin juts forward due to atypical tone. If high tone, the head is pulled into hyperextension; if low tone, the head reacts to gravity and falls into hyperextension.

The term *chin tuck* refers to the normal resting posture of the head in which the chin is in a neutral position and the neck is elongated.

How an object is presented to the child can make a difference in arm, hand, and finger positioning and postural control. If a child demonstrates atypical head hyperextension with a **chin jut** when sitting (Figure 4.14), for example, the early interventionist can present objects closer to the child below chin level to promote active head flexion with a **chin tuck** (Figure 4.15). Lily typically would reach for toys with her arm turned inward (pronation), making it difficult to effectively reach and grasp a toy. Placing objects at the child's midline is important, particularly for children with central nervous system dysfunction, to minimize the influence of persistent primitive reflexes such as the asymmetrical tonic neck reflex. Optimal placement of the paper during writing tasks can be determined by having the child grasp her hands in the midline while resting on the desktop and pre-positioning the paper under the writing arm so it slants parallel to that arm (Benbow, 1990). A study by Yakimishyn and Magill-Evans (2002) supports the use of short crayons used in a vertical plane to facilitate a more mature tripod grip.

It is important to evaluate the **ergonomics** for computer use because many younger children are using computers for longer periods of time (National Center for Education Statistics, 2000). For children who require assistive technology in order to demonstrate their knowledge it is even more important. Musculoskeletal problems and eye strain can cause problems for a child who is inappropriately positioned while using the computer at home and in school. An OT can assist with

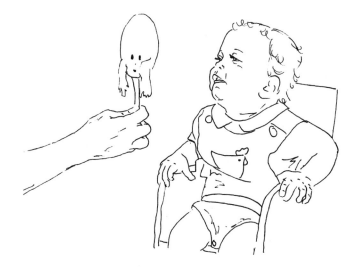

FIGURE 4.14

Inappropriate object presentation to toddler with spastic diplegic cerebral palsy.

Source: Used by permission of Jean Patz.

FIGURE 4.15

Improved presentation of object below eye level, fostering appropriate head (chin tuck), trunk, and upper extremity control.

Source: Used by permission of Jean Patz.

positioning a child to facilitate use of the computer. Positioning at the computer to prevent injury in children includes: lower back and foot support with hips, knees, and ankles at 90 degrees; monitor at eye level and directly in front of the child, about an arm's length away to prevent neck strain; arms close to the side with elbows at 90 degrees or greater; the keyboard placed for a neutral wrist position; and child-sized keyboard and mouse (Healthy Computing for Kids, n.d.). Children who have visual-perceptual problems interfering with form and letter discrimination may benefit from software that uses picture sequences and auditory feedback.

Fine Motor Materials

Larger toys may assist the child who has a poor or weak grasp. Large lacing beads, easy-grip pegs, and **knobbed puzzles** are available commercially and from special-order catalogs. Lily was cognitively ready and interested in grasping and manipulating toys, but she had difficulty maintaining grasp on toys due to her motor involvement. She is able to complete a puzzle by using puzzle pieces that have a knob with a 1-inch clearance for ease in grasp (Figure 4.16). A variety of beginner puzzles have single shapes with vegetables, fruits, animals, geometric figures, or flowers. Switch-activated toys are particularly useful for children with restricted arm use. Switches can be activated with any part of the body such as the head, arm, foot, or knee.

In adapting activities for children with special needs, one should consider the array of variables that can be changed in order to enhance the learning process. These variables may include changing the type of seating or body position, the materials used, the placement of materials (horizontal to vertical), the visual parameters (lighting, brilliant colors) and the weight, texture and size of materials; using another body part to perform an activity; constraining or enlarging the space in which the activity occurs; adjusting timing parameters (fast/slow); and combining or reducing variables to increase or decrease the complexity of any activity. See Figure 4.13 for some examples.

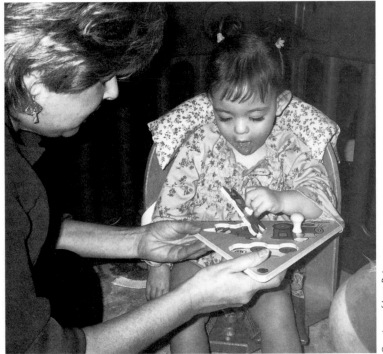

FIGURE 4.16

Lily uses a puzzle with knobs to assist in grasping. She is positioned in an adapted corner chair for added support in sitting so that her hands are free to manipulate toys. The early interventionist can position material in various planes to foster more mature movement patterns.

Courtesy of Jean Patz.

Foundational Skills for Handwriting

Sufficient repeated practice in a number of skills in the early years will help lay the foundations for legible hand writing in the early grades. Requisite skills to be considered include a preferred handedness for writing tools, ability to sustain upright head and trunk control in order to stabilize the extremities for movement, ability to maintain attention to the task, and motivation to learn controlled movement of a writing tool. Right or left hand preference can be seen by ages 3 to 4 (McManus et al., 1988). The concepts of directional components such as on/under/top/bottom/ side and crossing the perceptual midline are required for following verbal directions. Motoric control needed includes the ability to touch the thumb to each finger, to translate objects from finger to palm and palm to fingers, and use of both arms in a coordinated fashion (one to control a tool, the other to stabilize materials). An efficient grip with control from the fingers and thumb (dynamic tripod grip) will evolve with consistent instruction and practice.

Readiness for handwriting varies from child to child, and beginning of formal instruction varies from school to school because there are no national standards for instruction in handwriting in the United States (Amundson, 2005). Beery, Buktenical, and Beery (2005) suggest that the accurate completion of the first nine forms (vertical and horizontal line, circle, cross, right and left oblique line, square, oblique cross, and triangle) on the *Test of Visual-Motor Integration* (VMI) is a good indicator of the child's perceptual and motoric readiness to receive direct instruction in formal handwriting skills. These prerequisite skills are usually present by the later part of the second semester of kindergarten (Daly, Kelley, & Krauss, 2003). In the years before kindergarten, there are several prewriting skills found to be important perceptual and motor prerequisites or foundations critical to the development of written language skills. Cornhill and Case-Smith (1996) identified three areas of sensory and motor performance that separated children with poor handwriting from those with good handwriting as assessed by teachers. Eye-hand coordination, visual-motor integration, and in-hand manipulation were major areas of difficulty for children who had problems with writing. Later studies (Hammerschmidt & Sudsawad, 2004) identified correct letter formation, directionality, and proper spacing as factors determining legibility by teachers.

The reader is directed to the reference section for more detailed information on readings and Web sites related to assistive technology that enables the development of foundational skills for handwriting. It is worth noting that some current catalogues have started providing valuable information on how to use their equipment in creative ways.

Prewriting Adaptations

Adaptations may be needed to assist the child in holding a pencil in a more mature pattern. An OT can fabricate splints to assist fine motor functioning at home and within the classroom.

FIGURE 4.17

A child uses a large bulb-shaped pencil grip for improved grasp, a Handi-Writer™ for correct angle of the pencil, and raised-line paper. The small side of the pencil grip is positioned toward the tip of the pencil, and the letters *R* or *L* on the grip help the child position the thumb correctly.

Pencil grips come in a variety of shapes, sizes, and textures, such as pear-shaped grips, to guide placement of the index finger and thumb and prevent cramping, Super-Grips® for large $^1/_2$-inch-diameter pencils, triangular pen grips, round rubber or soft foam grips, bulb-design built-up grips (Figure 4.17), Grotto grip, similar to the bulb grip, with an end piece for better finger placement, and Stetro™ grips. Choice of the grip depends on the child's needs and comfort. The Handi-Writer™ (see Figure 4.17) is a device that can assist with correct pencil angle and stabilization of the lateral fingers. The child holds a plastic charm attached to the Handi-Writer™ within the fourth and fifth fingers for stabilization. The loop encourages appropriate angle of the pencil resting within the web space and pointing back toward the shoulder. Adjustable-angle tabletops can assist the child in maintaining a more upright posture during prewriting or writing activities. Nonslip mats may be used to stabilize a child's writing paper, or self-adhesive strips can be wrapped around utensils or other tools for a better hold.

Prewriting Programs

A number of resources can assist the interventionist in developing a prewriting program for preschool-aged children. For example, Klein's (1990a) illustrated book describes typical prewriting development, the necessary prerequisite skills, and suggestions for intervention. Witt and Klein (1990) have compiled activities that address kinesthetic and sensory awareness needed for the development of writing and school readiness, and Levine (1995) has developed a visual analysis of the normal components necessary for prewriting as well as scissor skills from birth to 6 years of age.

Scissors Skills

Equipment for Scissor Skills   Appropriate scissors should be selected to address the child's needs (Klein, 1990b). For children who have not developed handedness, scissors for use with either the right or left hand are indicated to avoid frustration. Fiskar® scissors for preschoolers require the child to squeeze while cutting, but open automatically, helping a child who has difficulty with the opening action. A child with poor or weak grasp can easily squeeze loop scissors that consist of one large, flexible loop. Benbow (2006) has developed scissors designed especially for a child's hand that are only $3\frac{1}{2}$ inches in length with small loops to encourage isolated use of the index and thumb while cutting. Kraus (2006) suggests that even when tools are designed for right or left handedness, there continues to be a bias toward right hand tool design as seen in how the blades of a scissors cross and may block vision for left hand use.

Care should be taken to select scissors that cut well; many standard scissors sold for children's use do not. **Four-loop training scissors** have an extra pair of loops placed adjacent to the child's loops; the interventionist places a hand over the child's for extra guidance. Another type of training scissors, **double-loop scissors,** have an extra pair of loops placed vertically to the child's loops. The interventionist holds the distal loops while the child holds the proximal loops. This procedure can be useful for a child who is tactually defensive to the interventionist's hand touching hers or for one who finds touch uncomfortable (Klein, 1990b).

Pre-scissor Programs   An illustrated workbook is available to foster pre-scissor skills for preschool and school-aged children (Klein, 1990b). Schneck and Battaglia (1992) suggest precutting activities to develop eye-hand coordination, hand strength, and fine motor dexterity in children who are not ready to use scissors. Activities include modeling clay for building strength and manipulating squeeze toys or squirt guns for opening and closing the hand, as well as bilateral activities such as snapping and unsnapping pop beads, sewing cards, or stringing beads. If the child has poor coordination because of tremors or jerkiness, the interventionist can provide external stabilization to the shoulder, arm, forearm, or wrist while cutting. This support can be gradually reduced. When the child begins cutting, Schneck and Battaglia suggest using long, narrow strips of paper, increasing the width as the child's skills develop, and grading the thickness of paper from thick paper to thin followed by non-paper items.

In summary, the fine motor domain consists of the motor and sensory aspects of reach, grasp, release, manipulation, and bilateral control. It is important to examine how the child puts these components together to perform functional tasks within her daily routine. Environmental issues such as materials and toys available to the child, cultural values, or parental and school expectations play a major role in the child's development of these skills. Intervention addresses the child's needs, her participation in skills development, and adaptations or adjustments to her environment.

:: SELECTED STRATEGIES FOR ORAL MOTOR INTERVENTION

When providing intervention for a child with poor oral motor control that affects eating, the early intervention team includes the parents, physician, early interventionist, occupational therapist or speech-language pathologist, nutritionist, and nurse. The oral motor specialists will address positioning of the child, the caregiver, and equipment; functional eating tasks including sucking, swallowing, chewing, spoon-feeding, and cup drinking; diet texture modifications; and provision of adapted equipment when indicated. Consultation from appropriate professionals regarding possible food allergies and swallowing irregularities also may be necessary.

Positioning the Child   If the infant must be held for feeding, she should be held in as upright a position as possible, with the head slightly flexed. The arms should be supported forward and the hips bent at approximately 90 degrees (Figure 4.18). The person feeding the infant cradles the infant's head in the crook of an elbow in order

FIGURE 4.18

A grandfather holding his grandson for feeding, supporting the child's head with his arm while maintaining the child's arms forward and supporting the child's hips in flexion. The child has severe spastic quadriplegic cerebral palsy.

Source: Used by permission of Jean Patz.

to actively move that arm to counteract tonic head hyperextension in a child with increased postural tone due to spastic cerebral palsy. The feeder may cross his leg to create a seat for the infant, which bends the hips in flexion and counteracts the atypical extension.

Positioning of the Feeder   Positioning of the feeder is important as well, particularly for children with cerebral palsy. Generally, the feeder needs to sit directly in front of the child, not to the side, and at eye level to foster symmetry and more typical postural tone and to decrease the influence of atypical primitive reflexes for better success with eating. The plate of food is placed on the side of the feeder's dominant hand for efficiency when feeding. The person feeding the child should ensure her own comfort in a suitable chair.

Sucking   Medical issues must be ruled out prior to initiation of any program addressing sucking problems in infants. Intervention may address the type of equipment used to foster more efficient sucking from a bottle. Characteristics of nipples such as type, configuration, size, and ease of flow should be evaluated. Various choices of bottles are available. For example, angled-neck bottles, available commercially, allow the child to be fed in a more upright position, thus reducing air intake and decreasing head hyperextension. Special positioning may be indicated to enhance a neutral or slightly forward flexion of the head needed for sucking from the breast or bottle. Oral facilitation techniques such as jaw support (Figure 4.19) may be warranted to provide better oral stability during sucking.

Swallowing   Intervention for swallowing dysfunction should be addressed by professionals skilled in oral motor evaluation and intervention. For a child who aspirates fluids, intervention can range from thickening the child's food or liquid texture to gastrostomy feeding. Whatever type of problem the child has, early interventionists

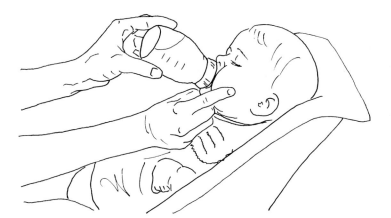

FIGURE 4.19

Jaw support provided to an infant with a weak suck. The lateral surface of the middle finger supports the jaw, while the index finger and thumb support the infant's cheeks.

Source: Used by permission of Jean Patz.

should be familiar with modifications. Johnson and Scott (1993) have developed a resource guide addressing assessment and intervention for management of drooling.

Chewing   Children can easily choke on small pieces of food; therefore, caution is required when developmentally young children are given higher textured foods. Consultation with a professional trained in oral motor assessment and intervention is recommended. Chewing requires coordinated movements of the tongue, jaw, lips, and cheeks. Given the complexity of chewing, children with severe oral motor problems may not acquire this skill, thus necessitating adjustments to the type of food given. Intervention addresses factors that interfere with normal chewing, such as tongue thrust, tongue retraction, jaw thrust, tonic bite reflex, lip retraction, jaw instability, and oral hypersensitivity (Morris & Klein, 2000).

A change in food texture may foster chewing development. The child may move from low-textured foods, such as cereals and strained or ground foods that do not require chewing, to foods thickened with baby cereals, rice cereal, dehydrated fruit flakes, and lumpy, soft foods (Morris & Klein, 2000). Foods that melt in the mouth, such as graham crackers, are used when the child has progressed to the stage of beginning to orally manipulate small pieces. Foods that make noise when they are crunched, such as cereal bits, can be fun for the child; however, these foods can present a choking hazard depending on the size. Special handling techniques may be necessary to assist the child who has oral motor difficulties accept and manipulate more highly textured foods. Particularly for children who exhibit oral hypersensitivity, tolerating more highly textured foods will be a major challenge.

The therapist can assist in training the interventionist and parents in oral motor techniques. The feeder must be aware of the sensory and proprioceptive components of feeding and positioning. The feeder should maintain a relaxed position with good support and be sensitive to the temperature of his own hand when touching the child as well as to how much pressure he is exerting, for example, when applying oral control techniques. A cold hand may startle the child. A light touch can be noxious to a child who has overly sensitive responses to touch, whereas too firm a touch might restrict necessary jaw movements. Therefore, moderation is recommended.

Diet Texture   The primary goal related to diet texture is that the child can experience and accept developmentally appropriate food textures. The primary goal for parents is that they can prepare appropriately textured foods to accommodate their child's oral motor capabilities. Adjusting food texture and liquid consistency for a child with special needs is the responsibility of an occupational therapist or speech pathologist who has performed a thorough oral motor and pharyngeal evaluation. The therapist often will consult with the pediatrician and nutritionist prior to making recommendations. The interventionist should know what texture has been recommended for the child. For the child with sensory processing issues as seen in autism, temperature and taste should also be addressed as some children will have specific sensitivities with these variables. Grading the texture as the child's processing improves should be planned in increments to avoid gagging and choking responses. Preparation prior to feeding the child can include facial massage to reduce aversive or startle responses when approaching the face.

Spoon-Feeding   A proper approach with the spoon can promote a more normal head position and easier swallowing. When spoon-feeding a child, the feeder should sit in front of the child at eye level to encourage midline positioning of the head and to discourage head/neck hyperextension. When the feeder approaches with the spoon from below chin level, the child looks slightly down, creating a chin tuck. Also, it is important to bring the spoon close enough to the child so that she actively tucks the chin instead of jutting the chin forward to approach a spoon offered too far away. The feeder waits for the child to actively flex the head slightly (chin tuck) to clear food from the spoon. The spoon is inserted and removed in a horizontal fashion to encourage lip closure instead of wiping the spoon in an upward fashion, which negates the need for active lip closure on the spoon.

This method is also helpful for a child with cerebral palsy who has a tonic bite reflex because the approach avoids stimulating the gums or teeth upon spoon removal. The feeder should avoid pulling the spoon out of the child's mouth once the tonic bite reflex has been elicited because this will further strengthen the response. Instead, the feeder should wait for the child to relax. The therapist can show the feeder effective methods to help reduce overall postural tone to address this problem. A calm and quiet feeding environment is also helpful because these children overrespond to sensory stimulation. Coated spoons are recommended to protect the child's teeth and provide a soft biting surface. Many types of spoons are available from medical supply companies to meet the needs of children with feeding problems. These include coated spoons, shallow-bowled spoons, built-up-handled spoons, weighted spoons, adjustable-angle spoons, swivel spoons, and spoons with horizontal or vertical palm grips. A universal cuff may provide a means to hold different utensils; this is a strap wrapped around the palm of the hand with a pocket to hold utensils in place.

Cup Drinking   Introduction of a cup into play situations prior to initiation of a cup drinking program is recommended so that the child will have seen and handled a cup. General principles can be applied to teaching cup-drinking skills. Positioning the cup appropriately ensures that the child does not have to wait too long to drink, which could set off tongue thrusting. The feeder tips the cup enough so that the liquid is close to the rim prior to bringing the cup to the mouth. **Cut-out cups** are often recommended to foster a more normal head position. Lily is given liquids from a cut-out cup because she has a tendency to hyperextend her head during drinking, which would put her at risk for aspiration (Figure 4.20). The cut-out portion allows space for her nose when the cup is tipped up, preventing head hyperextension.

A cut-out cup is a therapeutically designed cup with a portion of the rim cut away to allow space for the nose when tipping the cup during drinking. It prevents head hyperextension during drinking.

FIGURE 4.20

A cut-out cup is placed on Lily's lower lip while providing chin support. Note the cut-out portion of the cup is positioned to avoid hitting her nose.

Product available from Sammons Preston (2007). Pediatrics Catalog: Special needs products for school and clinics. Bolingbrook, IL: An Ability One Corporation.

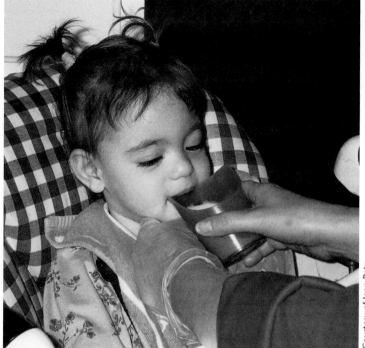

Courtesy of Jean Patz

Thickened liquids may be used initially to slow the flow for ease in swallowing. Age-appropriate foods, such as strained baby fruit, rice cereal, mashed bananas, and yogurt, can be mixed with the liquid. It is important for the caregiver to prepare the recommended thickness of liquid and consult with the physician or nutritionist regarding fluid intake.

Handling techniques to provide jaw support can be used when recommended if the difficulty is an open-mouth posture, as noted in Lily's case. The feeder approaches the child slowly with the cup to avoid eliciting any jaw thrust or atypical oral movements. The uncut side of the cup, opposite the cut-out portion, is placed on the midsection of the lower lip, not between the teeth. A small amount of liquid is poured slowly into the child's mouth to encourage one sip at a time when the child is first learning the skill; the amount is increased gradually to foster consecutive swallowing. If jaw support is recommended, the feeder maintains the jaw control until the child swallows the liquid. The child's reactions should be observed continuously to monitor what she can handle.

The goals for those feeding a child with oral motor concerns are that they will (1) understand the oral motor strengths and needs of the child; (2) solve feeding problems that may arise outside of the intervention sessions; (3) know where to find resources regarding eating; (4) teach others how to skillfully feed the child; (5) use adapted equipment appropriately and in the most efficient manner; (6) offer or prepare appropriate textured foods that are consistent with the child's oral motor capabilities; (7) integrate the oral motor intervention into the daily routine; and (8) identify safety issues in the feeding process. Vignette 4.2 illustrates oral motor development in a child with severe spastic cerebral palsy.

:: SELECTED STRATEGIES FOR SELF-CARE INTERVENTION

Intervention for development of self-care skills in children utilizes developmental, remedial, compensatory, and educational approaches (Shepherd, 2005). These approaches can be used in isolation or combination. In the developmental approach, tasks are taught in a developmental sequence. A child's chronological and developmental age are used as guidelines for progression of skills. This approach is most useful for children with mild disabilities. The remedial approach focuses on direct intervention to address missing components that interfere with acquisition of self-care skills. The OT or PT will use **neurodevelopmental treatment techniques** (NDT), for example, to modify atypical postural tone or **sensory processing approaches** to modify sensory integrative dysfunction for functional skill development. For example, Lily wanted to help with undressing, yet she was unable to accomplish this because she could not sit independently and her atypical postural tone prevented her hands from coming to the midline to reach and grasp effectively. The therapist consulted with the parents and early interventionist about special handling techniques to diminish the atypical tone and movement so that Lily could participate in undressing.

The **compensatory approach** includes the use of adaptive equipment (see Figures 4.10, 4.11, 4.12, 4.13, and 4.14) to compensate for missing skills. In addition, Shepherd (2005) discusses how to grade activities through task analysis, personal assistance, partial participation, backward and forward chaining, and verbal, gestural, or physical prompts to modify a task.

The **educational approach** is a component of all the other intervention methods. The interventionist collaborates with the family, child, and educational staff to disseminate information in a manner that addresses the best learning style of each child. The interventionist uses open dialogue, modeling, and clear and concise written information that may include pictures. Additional resources are suggested to the parents for further reading or specific assistance in an area of need.

Early intervention service providers target the family's concerns as a priority during evaluation and intervention. Goals are determined together with the parents. Team members analyze the barriers to independence. Cultural values and practices are considered as well. The program that is developed should be consistent with daily family and school routines.

Selective dorsal rhizotomy is a surgical procedure to reduce lower extremity spasticity by cutting sensory dorsal nerve rootlets that cause the atypical increased tone.

Baclofen is a medication for muscle relaxation that is used to reduce spasticity in children with cerebral palsy. Intrathecal baclofen pump is a method to deliver baclofen; the pump dispenses medication into the spinal fluid.

Other Interventions

Botulinum toxin (Botox) is a bacterial toxin used to decrease dystonia and spasticity; it is injected into muscles and treatment is repeated at approximately 3 to 4 months.

Dystonia is defined as sustained muscle contractions resulting in atypical postures consisting of twisting and repetitive movements; secondary dystonia is found with CP (Fahn, 1988).

Interventions frequently change. The early interventionist needs to be aware of current surgical and medical approaches such as **selective rhizotomy, intrathecal baclofen,** and **Botulinum toxin** (Botox) used along with occupational therapy and physical therapy intervention to improve levels of functioning in children with spasticity. Children with spastic cerebral palsy improved significantly in fine motor abilities (Mittal et al., 2002a) and self-care skills (Mittal et al., 2002b) following selective posterior rhizotomy, a surgical procedure for children with spasticity. Long-term gains were more significant in the mildly involved children. Albright, Barry, Shafron, & Ferson (2001) found an increase in quality of life and ease of caregiving following use of intrathecal bacolfen in 86% of a sample of 3–4 year old individuals with severe generalized **dystonia;** 71% of the participants had dystonia associated with cerebral palsy. Benefits were sustained over a mean of 29 months in 92% of the participants with a baclofen pump. Botulinum toxin, injected directly into spastic muscles, can affect functional performance significantly as noted in a sample of 2- to 12-year-old children with cerebral palsy (Wallen, O'Flaherty, & Waugh, 2004); this medication must be readministered for continued effects.

SUMMARY

Early postural control and gross motor skills provide the child with the necessary tools to become independent from caregivers. Development of a sense of "self," however, comes from an ability to do many things for oneself. Fine motor and self-care competence helps to build self-esteem in the young child.

Intervention in the areas of fine motor, oral motor, and self-care skills may be implemented by a number of specialists. The occupational therapist may be the most knowledgeable member of the team regarding fine motor dysfunction. The occupational therapist or the speech-language pathologist may be best able to address assessment and program planning for oral motor skills. However, it is the early interventionist who most often introduces the child to fine motor and self-care tasks, working closely with the parents and other professionals. In order to have a successful program, good communication and mutual respect among all team members are imperative.

REVIEW QUESTIONS AND DISCUSSION POINTS

1. Name three interfering factors that would prevent a child with cerebral palsy, Down syndrome, and autism from grasping a toy accurately.
2. Describe five elements important in designing an activity to teach prewriting skills to a child with neuromotor dysfunction.
3. Identify two important factors in positioning critical to the health and safety of a child with poor tone during feeding.
4. Discuss ways that a teacher can design a classroom to address the needs of children who have sensory processing problems.
5. What prerequisites would you look for in a child before initiating a toileting program?

RECOMMENDED RESOURCES

Autism

Janzen, J. (2003). *Understanding the nature of autism: A guide to the Autism Spectrum Disorders* (2nd ed.). Austin, TX: Hammill Institute on Disabilities.

Larkey, S. (2006). *Practical sensory programmes for students with autism spectrum disorder and other special needs.* London: Jessica Kingsley Publishers.

Tanguay, P. (2000). *Nonverbal learning disabilities at home: A parent's guide.* London: Jessica Kingsley.

Dressing

Klein, M. (1983). *Pre-dressing skills.* San Antonio, TX: Therapy Skill Builders.

Cerebral Palsy

Finnie, N. (1997). *Handling the young child with cerebral palsy at home* (3rd ed.). Woburn, MA: Butterworth-Heinemann.

Geralis, E. (Ed.). (1998). *Children with cerebral palsy: A parents' guide* (2nd ed.). Bethesda, MD: Woodbine House.

Miller, F. (2005). *Cerebral palsy.* New York: Springer.

Sensory Integration / Sensory Processing Resources

Auer, C., & Blumberg, S. (2006). *Parenting a child with sensory processing disorder: A family guide to understanding and supporting your sensory-sensitive child.* Oakland, CA: New Harbinger Publications.

Ayres, A. (2005). *Sensory integration and the child.* Los Angeles: Western Psychological Services.

Biel, L., & Peske, N. (2005). *Raising a sensory smart child: The definitive handbook for helping your child with sensory integration issues.* New York: Penguin Books.

Emmons, P., & Anderson, L. (2006). *Understanding sensory dysfunction: Learning, development and sensory dysfunction in autism spectrum disorders, ADHD, learning disabilities and bipolar disorder.* London: Jessica Kingsley.

Janzen, J. (2003). *Understanding the nature of autism: A guide to the autism spectrum disorders* (2nd ed.). Austin, TX: Hammill Institute on Disabilities. Janzen presents a good foundation for understanding autism spectrum disorders. She incorporates parental roles for partnership with professionals in development of interventions. She provides an effective framework for decision making and presents a wide array of recognized intervention strategies.

Kranowitz, C. (2005). *The out-of-sync child: Recognizing and coping with sensory processing disorder* (Rev. ed.). Perigee Trade or Berkley Pub Group.

Toileting

Gomi, T. (2001). *Everyone poops.* La Jolla, CA: Kane/Miller Book Publishers.

Maizels, M., Rosenbaum, D., & Keating, B. (1999). *Getting to dry: How to help your child overcome bedwetting.* Boston: The Harvard Common Press.

Mack, A. (1983). *Toilet learning: The picture book technique for children and parents.* Boston: Little, Brown.

Websites

Assistive Technology
AbleNet: *http://www.ablenetinc.com.* 1-800-322-0956

Don Johnston
http://www.donjohnston.com. 1-800-999-4660

Enabling Devices
http://enablingdevices.com. 1-800-832-8697

IntelliTools
www.intellitools.com. 1-800-899-6687

Tash Inc.
http://www.tachinc.com. 1-800-463-5685

Equipment for Special Needs
Abilitations (special needs-mobility, positioning, visual motor/play, sensory, communication, fine motor): *www.abilitations. com.* 1-800-850-8602

Achievement Products for Children: *www.specialkidszone. com.* 1-800-373-4699

Beyond Play (early interventions products): *www.beyondplay. com.* 1-877-428-1244

Equipment Shop (therapy balls, seating/positioning equipment, ADL & eating aids): *http://equipmentshop.com/*

Integrations (sensory processing equipment): *www. integrationscatalog.com*

Mealtime Catalog (a resource for oral motor, feeding, and mealtime programs): Faber, VA: New Visions *http://www. necom*

Pocket Full of Therapy (writing resources, seating, ball equipment, sensory items, oral motor equipment, computer products): *http://pfot.com*

Sammons Preston–Pediatrics (special needs products): *www.sammonspreston.com.* 1-800-323-5547

SenseAbilities (assessments, books, oral motor, toys): *www.senseabilities.com.au/*

Sensory Processing Disorder Resource Center (symptoms, picky eaters, treatment activities, sensory equipment, parent/teacher resource): *http://sensory-processing-disorder.com/index.html*

Sensory Resources (books, CDs, videos, tapes for therapists, teachers and parents on sensory processing): *www.Sensory Resources.com.* 1-888-357-5867

Southpaw Enterprises (developmental and sensory integration products): *www.southpawenterprises.com* 1-800-228-1698

Southpawei (early intervention products): *www.southpawei.com* 1-866-848-6460

TheraTogs™ (elasticized orthotic undergarments with customized strapping system to provide dynamic postural support): *www.theratogs.com* 1-888-634-0495

Ergonomics and Computer Use

http://ergo.human.cornell.edu/cuweguideline.htm
http://www.kidstation.com/ergonomics/index.shtml
http://www.healthycomputing.com/kids/computers.html
http://www.askergoworks.com/cart_ergo_kids.asp

Prewriting and Handwriting

Callirobics (prewriting information): *www.callirobics.com*
Handwriting Without Tears: *www.hwtears.com*
Zaner-Bloser Handwriting: *www.zaner-bloser*

REFERENCES

Adrien, J. L., Lenoir, P., Martineau, J., Perrot, A., Hameury, L., Larmande, C., & Sauvage, D. (1993). Blind ratings of early symptoms of autism based upon family home movies. *Journal of the American Academy of Child and Adolescent Psychiatry, 32,* 617–626.

Ahn, R., Miller, L. J., Milberger, S., & McIntosh, D. (2004). Prevalence of parents' perceptions of sensory processing disorders among kindergarten children. *American Journal of Occupational Therapy, 58,* 287–293.

Albright, A. L., Barry, M., Shafron, D., & Ferson, S. (2001). Intrathecal baclofen for generalized dystonia. *Developmental Medicine & Child Neurology, 43,* 652–657.

Amundson, S. (2005). Prewriting and handwriting skills. In J. Case-Smith (Ed.), *Occupational therapy for children* (5th ed., pp. 587–610). St. Louis: Elsevier Mosby.

Arvedson, J., & Brodsky, L. (2002). *Pediatric swallowing and feeding: Assessment and management* (2nd ed., pp. 3–11). Albany, NY: Thomson.

Ayres, A. J. (1972). *Sensory integration and learning disorders.* Los Angeles: Western Psychological Services.

Ayres, A. J. (1979). *Sensory integration and the child.* Los Angeles: Western Psychological Services.

Ayres, A. J. (1985). *Developmental dyspraxia and adult-onset apraxia.* Torrance, CA: Sensory Integration International.

Ayres, A. J. (1989a). *Sensory Integration and Praxis Tests.* Los Angeles: Western Psychological Services.

Ayres, A. J. (1989b). *Sensory Integration and Praxis Tests manual.* Los Angeles: Western Psychological Services.

Ayres, A. J. (2005). *Sensory integration and the child: Understanding hidden sensory challenges* (25th anniversary ed.). Los Angeles: Western Psychological Services.

Baranek, G. (2002). Efficacy of sensory and motor interventions for children with autism. *Journal of Autism and Developmental Disorders, 32,* 397–422.

Baranek, G. T. (1999). Autism during infancy: A retrospective video analysis of sensory-motor and social behaviors at 9–12 months of age. *Journal of Autism and Developmental Disorders, 29,* 213–224.

Beery, K. E., & Buktenica, N. A., & Beery, N. A. (2005). Beery-Buktenica Developmental Test of Visual-Motor Integration, 5th ed. Bloomington, MN: Pearson Education, Inc.

Benbow, M. (1990). *Loops and other groups: A kinesthetic writing system.* San Antonio, TX: Therapy Skill Builders.

Benbow, M. (2006). Principles and practices of teaching handwriting. In A. Henderson & C. Pehoski (Eds.), *Hand function in the child: Foundations for remediation* (2nd ed., pp. 338–340). St. Louis, MO: Mosby Elsevier.

Benda, C. D. (1969). *Down syndrome: Mongolism and its management.* New York: Grune & Stratton.

Blanche, E., & Nakasuji, B. (2001). Sensory integration and the child with cerebral palsy. In S. Roley, E. Blanche, & R. Schaaf (Eds.), *Understanding the nature of sensory integration with diverse populations* (pp. 345–364). San Antonio, TX: Therapy Skill Builders.

Bledsoe, N., & Shepherd, J. (1982). A study of reliability and validity of a preschool play scale. *The American Journal of Occupational Therapy, 36,* 783–788.

Brandt, B. R. (1996). Impaired tactual perception in children with Down's syndrome. *Scandinavian Journal of Psychology, 37,* 12–16.

Brodsky, L., & Arvedson, J. (2002). Anatomy, embryology, physiology, and normal development. In J. Arvedson and L. Brodsky (Eds.), *Pediatric swallowing and feeding: Assessment and management* (pp. 13–79). Albany, NY: Thomson Delmar Learning.

Bruininks, R., & Bruininks, B. (2005). BOT-2: *Bruininks-Oseretsky Test of Motor Proficiency Manual* (2nd ed.). Circle Pines, MN: AGS Publishing.

Bruni, M. (2006). *Fine motor skills for children with Down syndrome: A guide for parents and professionals* (2nd ed.). Bethesda, MD: Woodbine House.

Bundy, A. C. (1997). Play and playfulness: What to look for. In L. D. Parham & L. S. Fazio (Eds.), *Play in occupational therapy for children* (pp. 52–66). Baltimore: Mosby.

Case-Smith, J. (2005). Development of childhood occupations. In J. Case-Smith (Ed.), *Occupational therapy for children* (5th ed., pp. 88–116). St. Louis, MO: Mosby.

Case-Smith, J. (2006). Hand skill development in the context of infants' play: Birth to 2 years. In A. Henderson & C. Pehoski (Eds.), *Hand function in the child: Foundations for remediation* (2nd ed., pp. 117–141). St. Louis, MO: Mosby Elsevier.

Case-Smith, J., & Bryan, T. (1999). The effects of occupational therapy with sensory integration emphasis on preschool-age children with autism. *The American Journal of Occupational Therapy, 53,* 489–497.

Case-Smith, J., & Humphrey, R. (2005). Feeding intervention. In J. Case-Smith (Ed.), *Occupational therapy for children* (5th ed., pp. 481–520). St. Louis, MO: Elsevier Mosby.

Cole, K., Abbs, J., & Turner, G. (1988). Deficits in the production of grip forces in Down syndrome. *Developmental Medicine & Child Neurology, 30,* 752–758.

Connolly, B., & Montgomery, P. (2003). A framework for examination, evaluation, and intervention. In P. Montgomery & B. Connolly (Eds.), *Clinical applications for motor control* (pp. 5–6). Thorofare, NJ: Slack.

Cornhill, H., & Case-Smith, J. (1996). Factors that relate to good and poor handwriting. *American Journal of Occupational Therapy, 50,* 732–739.

Cox, R. D. (1993). Normal childhood development from birth to five years. In E. Schopler, M. E. Van Bourgondien, & M. M. Bristol (Eds.), *Preschool issues in autism* (pp. 39–57). New York: Plenum Press.

Daly, C. J., Kelley, G. T., & Krauss, A. (2003). Relationship between visual motor integration and handwriting skills of children in kindergarten: A modified replication study. *American Journal of Occupational Therapy, 57,* 459–462.

Davies, P., & Gavin, W. (2007). Validating the diagnosis of sensory processing disorders using EEG technology. *American Journal of Occupational Therapy, 61,* 176–189.

DeGangi, G. A., Breinbauer, C., Roosevelt, J. D., Porges, S., & Greenspan, S. (2000). Prediction of childhood problems at three years in children experiencing disorders of regulation during infancy. *Infant Mental Health Journal, 21,* 156–176.

Dolva, A., Coster, W., & Lilja, M. (2004). Functional performance in children with Down syndrome. *American Journal of Occupational Therapy, 58,* 621–629.

Dunn, W. (1999). *Sensory Profile.* San Antonio, TX: Psychological Corporation.

Dunn, W. (2002). *The Infant/Toddler Sensory Profile.* San Antonio, TX: Psychological Corporation.

Edwards, S., & Lafreniere, M. (1995). Hand function in the Down syndrome population. In A. Henderson & C. Pehoski (Eds.), *Hand function in the child: Foundations for remediation* (pp. 299–311). St. Louis, MO: Mosby.

Eisenberg, A., Murkoff, H., & Hathaway, S. (1994). *What to expect: The toddler years.* New York: Workman.

Eliasson, A., Krumlinde-Sundholm, L., Rösblad, B., Beckung, E., Arner, M., Öhrvall, A., et al., (2006). The Manual Ability Classification System (MACS) for children with cerebral palsy: Scale development and evidence of validity and reliability. *Developmental Medicine & Child Neurology, 48,* 549–554.

Erhardt, R. (1994a). *Developmental hand dysfunction: Theory, assessment, and treatment* (2nd ed.). San Antonio, TX: Therapy Skill Builders.

Erhardt, R. (1994b). *Erhardt Developmental Prehension Assessment* (EDPA), Revised. Tucson, AZ: Therapy Skill Builders.

Exner, C. (2005). Development of hand skills. In J. Case-Smith (Ed.), *Occupational therapy for children* (5th ed., pp. 304–355). St. Louis, MO: Elsevier Mosby.

Exner, C. (2006). Intervention for children with hand skill problems. In A. Henderson and C. Pehoski (Eds.), *Hand function in the child* (2nd ed., pp. 239–266). St. Louis, MO: Mosby Elsevier.

Finnie, N. (1997). *Handling the young child with cerebral palsy at home* (3rd ed.). Woburn, MA: Butterworth-Heinemann.

Fisher, A. G. (2003). *The Assessment of Motor and Processing Skills* (5th ed.). Fort Collins, CO: Three Star Press.

Folio, M. R., & Fewell, R. R. (2000). *Peabody Developmental Motor Scales* (2nd ed.). Chicago: Riverside.

Gesell, A., & Amatruda, C. (1947). *Developmental diagnosis.* New York: Harper & Row.

Gesell, A., & Ames, L. E. (1947). The development of handedness. *The Journal of Genetic Psychology, 70,* 155–175.

Giuffrida, C. (2001). Praxis, motor planning, and motor learning. In S. Roley, E. Blanche, & R. Schaaf (Eds.), *Understanding the nature of sensory integration with diverse populations* (pp. 133–161). San Antonio, TX: Therapy Skill Builders.

Grandin, T. (1995). *Thinking in pictures.* New York: Doubleday.

Gutman, S., McCreedy, P., & Heisler, P. (April, 2002). The psychosocial deficits of children with regulatory disorders. *OT Practice, 7,* 1–7.

Haley, S. M., Coster, W. L., Ludlow, L. H., Haltiwanger, J. T., & Andrellos, P. J. (1992). *Pediatric Evaluation of Disability Inventory.* Boston: New England Medical Center Hospital Inc., and PEDI Research Group.

Hamilton, B., & Granger, C. (2000). *Functional Independence Measure for Children (WeeFIM-II).* Buffalo: Research Foundation of the State University of New York.

Hammerschmidt, S., & Sudsawad, P. (2004). Teachers survey on problems with handwriting: Referral, evaluation, and outcomes. *American Journal of Occupational Therapy, 58,* 185–192.

Harris, L. J., & Carlson, D. F. (1988). Pathological left-handedness: An analysis of theories and evidence. In D. L. Molfese & S. J. Segalowitz (Eds.), *Brain lateralization in children: Developmental implications* (pp. 289–372). New York: Guilford Press.

Healthy Computing for Kids. (n.d.). Ergonomics for kids: Computers. Retrieved March 7, 2007, from *http://healthycomputing.com/kids/computers.html*

Henderson, A. (1995). Self-care and hand skill. In A. Henderson & C. Pehoski (Eds.), *Hand function in the child: Foundations for remediation* (pp. 164–183). St. Louis, MO: Mosby.

Hickman, L. (2001). Sensory integration and fragile X syndrome. In S. Smith Roley, E. Blanche, & R. Schaaf (Eds.), *Understanding the nature of sensory integration with diverse populations* (pp. 410–420). San Antonio, TX: Therapy Skill Builders.

Hunt, L., Lewis, D., Reisel, S., Waldrup, L., & Adam-Wooster, D. (2000). Age norms for straw-drinking ability. *The Transdisciplinary Journal, 10,* 1–8.

Johnson, H., & Scott, A. (1993). *A practical approach to saliva control.* Tucson, AZ: Therapy Skill Builders.

Jones, V., & Prior, M. R. (1985). Motor imitation abilities and neurological signs in autistic children. *Journal of Autism and Developmental Disorders, 15,* 37–46.

Kaplan Press and Chapel Hill Training Outreach Project. (2005). *Learning Accomplishment Profile-Diagnostic Standardized Assessment* (3rd ed.). Lewisville, NC: Kaplan Press.

Kern, J. K., Trivedi, M. H., Grannemann, B. D., Garver, C. R., Johnson, D. G., Andrews, A. A., et al. (2007), *Sensory Correlations in Autisim. Autisim, 11,* 123–134.

Kientz, M., & Dunn, W. (1997). A comparison of the performance of children with and without autism on the *Sensory Profile. American Journal of Occupational Therapy, 51,* 530–537.

King, L. J., & Grandin, T. (1990). *Attention deficits in learning disorder and autism: A sensory integrative treatment approach.* Workshop presented at the Conference Proceedings of the Continuing Education Programs of America, Milwaukee, WI.

Klein, M. (1990a). *Pre-writing skills* (Rev. ed.). San Antonio, TX: Therapy Skill Builders.

Klein, M. (1990b). *Pre-scissor skills* (3rd ed.). San Antonio, TX: Therapy Skill Builders.

Knox, S. (1997). Development and current use of the *Knox Preschool Play Scale.* In L. D. Parham & L. S. Fazio (Eds.), *Play in occupational therapy* (pp. 35–51). St. Louis, MO: Mosby.

Kraus, E. (2006). Handedness in children. In A. Henderson & C. Pehoski (Eds.), *Hand function in the child: Foundations for remediation* (pp. 161–191). St. Louis, MO: Mosby Elsevier.

Latash, M., Kang, N., & Patterson, D. (2002). Finger coordination in persons with Down syndrome: Atypical patterns of coordination and the effects of practice. *Experimental Brain Research, 146,* 345–355.

Levine, K. (1995). *Development of pre-writing and scissor skills: A visual analysis* [Videocassette]. San Antonio, TX: Therapy Skill Builders.

Linder, T. W. (1993). *Transdisciplinary play-based assessment: A functional approach to working with young children* (Rev. ed.). Baltimore: Brookes.

Liptak, G. (2002). Neural tube defects. In M. Batshaw (Ed.), *Children with disabilities* (5th ed., p. 474). Baltimore: Brookes.

Long, C., Conrad, P., Hall, E., & Furler, S. (1970). Intrinsic-extrinsic muscle control of the hand in power and precision handling. *Journal of Bone and Joint Surgery, 52–A,* 853–867.

Lopez, M. (1986). *Developmental sequence of the skill of cutting with scissors in normal children 2 to 6 years old.* Unpublished master's thesis, Boston University.

Lovaas, O. I., Newsom, C., & Hickman, C. (1987). Self-stimulatory behavior and perceptual reinforcement. *Journal of Applied Behavior Analysis, 20,* 45–68.

Mack, A. (1978). *Toilet learning: The picture book technique for children and parents.* Boston: Little, Brown.

Mailloux, Z. (2001). Sensory integrative principles in intervention with children with autistic disorder. In S. Roley, E. Blanche, & R. Schaaf (Eds.), *Understanding the nature of sensory integration with diverse populations* (pp. 365–384). San Antonio, TX: Therapy Skill Builders.

Mailloux, Z., & Roley, S. S. (2001). Sensory integration. In H. M. Miller-Kuhaneck (Ed.), *Autism: A comprehensive occupational therapy approach* (pp. 101–132). Bethesda, MD: American Occupational Therapy Association.

Maizels, M., Rosenbaum, D., & Keating, B. (1999). *Getting to dry: How to help your child overcome bedwetting.* Boston, MA: Harvard Common Press.

McHale, K., & Cermak, S. A. (1992). Fine motor activities in elementary school: Preliminary findings and provisional implications for children with fine motor problems. *American Journal of Occupational Therapy, 45,* 701–706.

McIntosh, D., Miller, L., & Shyu, V. (1999). Development and validation of the *Short Sensory Profile.* In W. Dunn (Ed.), *Sensory Profile Manual* (pp. 59–73). San Antonio, TX: Psychological Corporation.

McManus, I. C., Ski, G., Cole, D. R., Mellon, A. F., Wong, J., & Kloss, J. (1988). The development of handedness in children. *British Journal of Psychology, 6,* 257–273.

Meltzoff, A., & Gopnik, A. (1993). The role of imitation in understanding persons and developing a theory of mind. In S. Baron-Cohen, H. Tager-Flusberg, & D. J. Cohen (Eds.), *Understanding other minds: Perspectives from autism* (pp. 335–366). New York: Oxford University Press.

Miller, L. J. (2006). *Sensational kids: Hope and help for children with sensory processing disorder (SPD).* New York: G. P. Putnam's Sons.

Miller, L. J., Anzalone, M., Lane, S., Cermak, S., & Osten, E. (2007). Concept evolution in sensory integration: A proposed nosology for diagnosis. *American Journal of Occupational Therapy, 61,* 135–140.

Miller, L. J., Cermak, S., Lane, S., Anzalone, M., & Koomar, J. (2004). Position statement on terminology related to sensory integration dysfunction. *S.I. Focus, 6*–8.

Miller, L. J., Reisman, J., McIntosh, D., & Simon, J. (2001). An ecological model of sensory modulation: Performance of children with Fragile X syndrome, autistic disorder, attention-deficit/hyperactivity disorder, and sensory modulation dysfunction. In S. Smith Roley, E. Blanche, & R. Schaaf (Eds.), *Understanding the nature of sensory integration with diverse populations* (pp. 57–79). San Antonio, TX: Therapy Skill Builders.

Miller, L. J., & Roid, G. H. (1994). *Toddler and Infant Motor Evaluation (TIME).* San Antonio, TX: Psychological Corporation.

Missiuna, C., & Polatajko, H. (1995). Developmental dyspraxia by any other name: Are they all just clumsy children? *The American Journal of Occupational Therapy, 49,* 619–627.

Mittal, S., Farmer, J. P., Al-Atassi, B., Montpetit, K., Gervais, N., Poulin, C., et al. (2002a). Impact of selective posterior rhizotomy on fine motor skills: Long-term results using a validated evaluative measure. *Pediatric Neurosurgery, 36,* 133–141.

Mittal S., Farmer, J. P., Al-Atassi, B., Montpetit, K., Gervais, N., Poulin, C., et al. (2002b). Functional performance following selective posterior rhizotomy: Long-term results determined using a validated evaluative measure. *Journal of Neurosurgery, 97,* 510–518.

Morris, S., & Klein, M. (2000). *Pre-feeding skills: A comprehensive resource for mealtime development.* San Antonio, TX: Therapy Skill Builders.

Mulligan, S. (2002). Advances in sensory integration research. In A. Bundy, S. Lane, & E. Murray (Eds.), *Sensory integration theory and practice* (2nd ed., pp. 400–401). Philadelphia: F. A. Davis.

National Center for Education Statistics. (2000). *Internet access in public schools and classrooms: 1994–99.* Washington, DC: U.S. Department of Education, Office of Educational Research and Improvement.

Nelson, D. L. (1984). *Children with autism.* Thorofare, NJ: Slack.

Newborg, J. (2004). *The Battelle Developmental Inventory—BDI–2* (2nd ed.). Rolling Meadows, IL: Riverside.

Parham, L. D., Ecker, C., Miller Kuhaneck, H., Henry, D., & Glennon, T. J. (2007). *Sensory Processing Measure (SPM) Manual.* Los Angeles: Western Psychological Services.

Parks, S. (2006). *Inside HELP: Administration and reference manual for the* Hawaii Early Learning Profile (HELP). Palo Alto, CA: VORT Corporation.

Pellegrino, L. (2002). Cerebral palsy. In M. Batshaw (Ed.), *Children with disabilities* (5th ed., p. 447). Baltimore: Brookes.

Provost, B., Lopez, B., & Heimerl, S. (2007). A comparison of motor delays in young children: Autism spectrum disorder, developmental delay, and developmental concerns. *Journal of Autism and Developmental Disorders, 37,* 321–328.

Rapin, I. (1988). Disorders of higher cerebral function in preschool children. Part II: Autistic spectrum disorder. *American Journal of Diseases of Children, 142,* 1178–1182.

Ray, T., King, L., & Grandin, T. (1988). The effectiveness of self-initiated vestibular stimulation in producing speech sounds in an autistic child. *Occupational Therapy Journal of Research, 8,* 186–190.

Reeves, G. D., & Cermak, S. A. (2002). Disorders of praxis. In A. Bundy, S. Lane, & E. Murray (Eds.), *Sensory integration: Theory and practice* (2nd ed., pp. 71–95). Philadelphia: F. A. Davis.

Reilly, S., Skuse, D., & Wolke, D. (2000). *SOMA: Schedule for Oral Motor Assessment.* Eastgardens, New South Wales: Whurr.

Rosenbloom, L., & Horton, M. (1971). The maturation of fine prehension in young children. *Developmental Medicine & Child Neurology, 13,* 3–8.

Schmidt, R. A., & Lee, T. D. (2005). *Motor control and learning: A behavioral emphasis.* Champaign, IL: Human Kinetics.

Schneck, C., & Battaglia, C. (1992). Developing scissor skills in young children. In J. Case-Smith & C. Pehoski (Eds.), *Development of hand skills in the child* (pp. 79–89). Rockville, MD: American Occupational Therapy Association.

Schneck, C., & Henderson, A. (1990). Descriptive analysis of the developmental progression of grip position for pencil and crayon control in nondysfunctional children. *The American Journal of Occupational Therapy, 44,* 890–893.

Shepherd, J. (2005). Activities of daily living and adaptations for independent living. In J. Case-Smith (Ed.), *Occupational therapy for children* (5th ed., pp. 521–570). St. Louis, MO: Elsevier Mosby.

Shumway-Cook, A., & Woollacott, M. H. (2007). *Motor control: Translating research into clinical practice* (3rd ed.). Philadelphia: Lippincott Williams & Wilkins.

Siegel, B. (1996). *The world of the autistic child.* New York: Oxford University Press.

Smith-Zuzovsky, N., & Exner, C. (2004). The effect of seated positioning quality on typical 6- and 7-year-old children's object manipulation skills. *The American Journal of Occupational Therapy, 58,* 380–388.

Spano, M., Mercuri, E., Rando, T., Panto, T., Gagliano, A., Henderson, S., et al. (1999). Motor and perceptual-motor competence in children with Down's syndrome: Variation in performance with age. *European Journal of Pediatric Neurology, 3,* 7–14.

Spitzer, S., & Roley, S. (2001). Sensory integration revisited: A philosophy of practice. In S. Smith Roley, E. Blanche, & R. Schaaf (Eds.), *Understanding the nature of sensory integration with diverse populations* (pp. 3–27). Tucson, AZ: Therapy Skill Builders.

Struck, M. (1996). *Assistive technology in the schools: AOTA self-paced clinical course.* Rockville, MD: American Occupational Therapy Association.

Tan, L. E. (1985). Laterality and motor skills in four-year-olds. *Child Development, 56,* 119–124.

Teitelbaum, O., Benton, T., Shah, P. K., Prince, A., Kelly, J. L., & Teitelbaum, P. (2004). Eshkol-Wachman movement notation in diagnosis: The early detection of Asperger's syndrome. *Proceedings of the National Academy of Sciences of the United States of America, 101,* 11909–11914.

Thelen, E. (2002). Self-organization in developmental processes: Can systems approaches work? In M. Johnson & Y. Munakata (Eds.), *Brain development and cognition: A reader* (2nd ed., pp. 544–557). Malden, MA: Blackwell.

Thelen, E., Corbetta, D., Kamm, K., & Spencer, J. (1993). The transition to reaching: Mapping intention and intrinsic dynamics. *Child Development, 64,* 1058–1098.

Tomchek, S. D., & Dunn, W. (2007). Sensory processing in children with and without autism: A comparative study using the *Short Sensory Profile. American Journal of Occupational Therapy, 61,* 190–200.

Van Bourgondien, M. E. (1993). Behavior management in the preschool years. In E. Schopler, M. E. Van Bourgondien, M. M. Bristol (Eds.), *Preschool issues in autism* (pp. 129–145). New York: Plenum Press.

Volkmar, F. R., Cohen, D. J., & Paul, R. (1986). Classification and diagnosis of childhood autism. *Journal of the American Academy of Child & Adolescent Psychiatry, 25,* 190–197.

VORT Corporation. (1999). *HELP for Preschoolers Assessment & Curriculum Guide.* Palo Alto, CA: Author.

VORT Corporation. (2004). *HELP for Preschoolers Assessment Strands.* Palo Alto, CA: Author.

Vygotsky, L. (1978). *Mind in society: The development of higher psychological process.* Cambridge, MA: Harvard University Press.

Wallen, M. A., O'Flaherty, S. J., & Waugh, M. C. (2004). Functional outcomes of intramuscular botulinum toxin type A in the upper limbs of children with cerebral palsy: A phase II trial. *Archives of Physical Medicine and Rehabilitation, 85,* 192–200.

Watson, L. R., & Marcus, L. M. (1986). Diagnosis and assessment of preschool children. In E. Schopler & G. Mesibov

(Eds.), *Social behavior in autism* (pp. 285–303). New York: Plenum Press.

White, B., Mulligan, S., Merrill, K., & Wright, J. (2007). An examination of the relationships between motor and process skills and scores on the *Sensory Profile. American Journal of Occupational Therapy, 61,* 154–160.

Williamson, G. G., & Anzalone, M. (1997). Sensory integration: A key component of the evaluation and treatment of young children with severe difficulties in relating and communicating. *ZERO TO THREE, 17,* 29–36.

Witt, B., & Klein, M. (1990). *Prepare: An interdisciplinary approach to perceptual-motor readiness.* San Antonio, TX: Therapy Skill Builders.

Yakimishyn, J. E., & Magill-Evans, J. (2002). Comparisons among tools, surface orientation, and pencil grasp for children 23 months of age. *American Journal of Occupational Therapy, 56,* 564–572.

We would like to thank the children, their families, and teachers for sharing their wonderful stories. We would also like to thank Betsy Cohen for her expertise related to the case studies and Sandra Phelps for her help in locating current and valuable resources.

Cognitive Development

Warren Umansky

Chapter Outline

- The Range of Cognitive Skills
- Piaget's Theory of Cognitive Development
- Piaget's Stages of Development
- Other Theories of Development
- Relationships Between Developmental and Cognitive Processing Models
- Factors That Affect Cognitive Development
- Cognitive Development and the Child with Special Needs
- Strategies for Assessment of Cognitive Development
- Facilitating Cognitive Development
- Technology in Assessment and Intervention

Carrie

Carrie, a 4-year-old child with cerebral palsy, participates in an inclusive preschool class at a local synagogue. Her teacher has set up a classroom with a multisensory flavor. Children learn by doing and by experiencing the consequences of learning activities.

The painting center has cardboard boxes of different sizes that children have the opportunity to paint. The boxes then will become storage space for each child's belongings or mobiles that hang from the ceiling.

Carrie is having a grand time painting with blue and yellow paint. In some places on the carton the colors have mixed, producing a vivid green color. "What color is that?" the teacher asks. "It's green," Carrie responds. "Where did you get green paint?" the teacher asks with a smile. Carrie looks at her containers of blue and yellow paint and her bright eyes reflect the thoughtful activity taking place behind them.

The casual observer of a 4-year-old child hard at play may be mystified by the intensity and variety of the child's behavior. Objects seem to take on life, simple problems evoke interesting attempts at solutions, and newly discovered skills are repeated and applied in different ways. The newborn presents quite another picture—that of a child whose day is spent mostly asleep, whose movements appear to be spontaneous and random, and whose communication repertoire consists only of crying and silence.

The transitions that occur in the typical child during the early years are as exciting to behold as a well-performed ballet is. The acquisition and refinement of skills are evidence that the higher levels of the brain are establishing control and that the child is developing into a cognitive being.

Cognition is difficult to define other than in terms of the many processes it encompasses. The word describes mental activity and other behaviors that allow us to understand and participate in events around us. Fundamental to cognitive development is a person's ability to translate objects and events into a symbolic form that can be stored in the brain. The developing thinker is able to store increasingly complex and abstract information and is able to manipulate the information in a variety of ways. The facility of a child to acquire, store, and manipulate information also is intimately related to development of language, social competence, and purposeful motor skills. For this reason, children who score low on intelligence tests that purport to measure levels of cognition frequently show delays in other areas of development as well.

This chapter examines the development of cognitive processes in young children and the impact that disabling conditions may have on cognition. By understanding how a child's overt behaviors reflect the unfolding of mental processes, one is better able to interpret a child's performance and thereby plan a developmentally appropriate program. The chapter concludes with suggestions and principles for providing experiences to children to facilitate cognitive development.

:: THE RANGE OF COGNITIVE SKILLS

Perception is the link between our senses and our experiences.

We receive information through five senses: vision, hearing, taste, smell, and touch. Relating that information to what we have accumulated from past experiences is called **perception.** Perception, then, is sensation with meaning. At yet a higher level of cognitive development, **logical thought** (the ability to use meaningful information to make decisions and solve problems) emerges. This marks the appearance of conceptual skills.

Even in a newborn, the foundations of cognition are apparent. At birth, a child reveals a varied repertoire of perceptual skills that expands rapidly during the early weeks and months of life. Soon after birth, infants fix briefly on visual stimuli (often the mother's eyes and face because of an attraction to forms with sharp contrasts) and even track moving objects over short distances. They turn away from strong odors, change their sucking patterns for fluids with different tastes, and become quiet in response to certain patterns of sound. Table 5.1 presents an array of perceptual skills present in most typical children during the early years of development.

One must be impressed by the capabilities of a young child, who progresses in about 9 months from the fusion of two cells to a complex and skilled organism. In 9

TABLE **5.1**	Typical perceptual skills.			
Visual	**Auditory**	**Tactile**	**Olfactory**	**Gustatory**
Fixing	Localization	Discrimination	Localization	Discrimination
Tracking	Auditory memory	Form	Discrimination	
		Temperature		
		Texture		
		Pressure		
Depth perception	Discrimination:			
	Sound			
	Speech			
Discrimination:				
Pattern				
Color				
Form				
Size				
Visual memory				
Figure ground				

more months, the child is able to discriminate among information in the environment and remember a few meaningful experiences. He seems to recognize his caregivers, anticipate feeding, and show definite preferences for types and textures of food. During the third 9 months, the child remembers more experiences and begins attaching labels to people and things, permitting finer distinctions among similar stimuli and forming the basis for spoken language. For example, the 18-month-old child is unable to name colors, but he has internal labels for different colors that allow him to distinguish one color from another. The inner language represented by this labeling system is described by Vygotsky (1986) and Mirolli and Parisi (2005). It is the means by which a child manipulates information in more and more complex ways. No longer controlled by the physical characteristics of things, a child suspects that the staunch-looking refrigerator carton might be empty and offer an excellent place to play. He indicates a grasp of temporal concepts by wanting something now rather than later. He anticipates the arrival of his mother from work when the sun begins to set. His spatial awareness and ability to pull together numerous bits of old and new information permit him to think through possible ways to get to the cookie jar on the refrigerator and to try only the solution he thinks is most likely to work. This is quite a change from the infant for whom time and space were dimensions too abstract to understand. A child who attaches the label "book" to all varieties of books, who knows that there are many kinds of four-legged animals, and who can sort blocks by color or shape or texture also demonstrates a grasp of classification concepts, reflecting another step on the ladder of cognitive skills.

As a child gets older, perceptual skills are refined and integrated into higher-level thought processes. Random scribbling on paper, for example, develops into drawings that reflect a similarity to the model. Piaget and Inhelder (1969) have described children's unique efforts at this stage of emerging conceptual development:

> A face seen in profile will have a second eye because a man has two eyes, or a horseman, in addition to his visible leg, will have a leg which can be seen through the horse. Similarly, one will see potatoes in the ground, if that is where they are, or in a man's stomach. (pp. 64–65)

A child's developing language is also indicative of the expanding range of cognitive skills. He must first sort out the meaningful sounds in his environment. He also must use sound differences to identify and store words for later recognition and speech production (Carroll, Snowling, Hulme, & Stevenson, 2003). Initial words tend to be names for people, very familiar objects, and function forms, such as *there, stop, gone,* and *more*. This vocabulary dominates a child's spoken language from approximately 12 to 18 months. When, in the second half of the second year, a child strings words together, it is a demonstration of his capacity to represent relationships between objects and events. There is support for the belief that a child at the stage of one-word utterances actually knows considerably more about sentence structure than he is able to demonstrate. He is prevented from exercising his knowledge by a limited short-term memory and oral-motor control.

In many areas, young children appear capable of processing more complex information than they are able to demonstrate.

Length and complexity of a child's utterances increase within a speaking environment that provides a rich variety of language samples. A child's choice of words in speech then becomes a means to express the ways in which he thinks. Piaget based much of his theory of cognitive development on talks he had with children.

Courtesy of Jean Patz

The facility of the child to acquire, store, and manipulate information is intimately related to the development of language, social competence, and purposeful motor skills.

:: PIAGET'S THEORY OF COGNITIVE DEVELOPMENT

Jean Piaget contributed the most comprehensive theory of how cognitive development progresses in children. He viewed development as an unfolding of ever more complex skills as children modify their mental structures to deal with new experiences.

Development is a continuous process that may vary in the rate at which it occurs in different children, but it always progresses in the same sequence. As with a house, for which the foundation first must be laid, then the outside structures, the wiring, the plumbing, and finally the interior walls, so cognitive development follows an orderly, unchanging progression. Substantial research on children with disabilities has documented the slower rate of development of children with disabilities compared with children who do not have disabilities; however, the same sequence of development as that which typically developing children have has been documented in children with visual impairments (Celeste, 2002; Maurer, Lewis, &

Development progresses in the same sequence for all children, but the rate may vary.

Mondlich, 2005), mental retardation (Walker & Johnson, 2006), and hearing impairments (Lauwerier, de Chouly de Lenclave, & Bailly, 2003).

Piaget gave the name **schemata** to the cognitive structures responsible for maintaining a child's internal representations of objects and experiences. As a child engages in different experiences, receives novel sensory input, and is called upon to respond in new ways, new schemata are formed or old ones are modified. A child organizes his experiences, as he develops, into more complex mental structures. By coordinating schemata, for example, he is capable of generalizing behaviors to new situations. Reaching for an interesting-looking toy might be viewed as the coordination of the schemata of vision, reaching, and wanting a familiar object.

Piaget described two processes by which a child adapts to new or unique demands from the environment. In **assimilation,** a child interprets new experiences only in terms of schemata that he already has. If, for example, his schema for flying things includes only birds, he may inaccurately identify all flying things as birds. All four-legged animals may be "horses" if someone has once identified a specific four-legged animal for him as a horse. These overgeneralizations that children make are a reflection of how they perceive the world based on a limited store of experiences and information. A second process helps them bring their perspectives more in line with reality. Through **accommodation,** a child's schemata are modified with experience. By being shown a kite or a plane or by having the differences among a kite, a plane, and a bird described, the child expands his schema for flying things to include the new information. He also may begin to expand his store of information about birds to include different types of birds.

Interactions with the environment almost always involve assimilation and accommodation. In the former, it appears that children change the world by fitting new experiences into their understanding. In the latter, the world changes children by altering their understanding to conform to reality. The continuous changing of cognitive structures, or schemata, occurs throughout life.

Young children identify characteristics of the world based on physical attributes. That is, they cannot comprehend that a large box may be full or empty; they can perceive it based upon its surface qualities only. These percepts often provide erroneous information to a child. As he interacts more with his environment, he may be bound less and less to physical attributes. He may formulate concepts based on how things are used and of what they are made, and he uses more discrete differences among objects and experiences to solve problems and make logical decisions.

> Assimilation is a process by which the child interprets new information in terms of current schemata.

> In accommodation, the child modifies current schemata in light of information from new experiences.

Organization of Development

Qualitative changes mark the development of cognitive abilities in children. Piaget described the **principle of equilibrium** as one of the mechanisms that facilitates change as a child seeks balance in his interactions with the environment. With organization of and adaptation to new experiences through assimilation and accommodation, he achieves stability, or equilibrium.

Piaget presented the significant developmental accomplishments of children in terms of periods and stages. Again, he emphasized the sequence of changes more than the specific ages at which they occur. This explains why we frequently find

> Through the principle of equilibrium, the child modifies his understanding of experiences in the world to achieve balance.

Anne Vega/Merrill

In the early stages of cognitive development, a child is drawn to the surface characteristics of objects. Later, objects become meaningful for what they do or represent.

children with disabilities experiencing a period of cognitive development associated with much younger children. Awareness of this developmental pattern provides valuable direction in program planning for the cognitively young child.

The first two periods of cognitive development—**sensorimotor** and **preoperational thought**—describe a child's progress through a mental age of about 7 or 8 years. The periods of **concrete operations** and **formal operations** describe mental processes of older children. Discussion of the latter two developmental periods is beyond the scope of this book; however, the interested reader is referred to some of the original works of Piaget (e.g., Piaget, 1952; Piaget, 1954; Piaget & Inhelder, 1969) and newer interpretations of his work (Bornstein, Lamb, & Teti, 2002; Lee, 2000).

:: PIAGET'S STAGES OF DEVELOPMENT
Sensorimotor Period

A child's earliest behaviors are reflexive in nature; the child gives the same motor response to the same types of stimuli with little understanding of what is happening. A loud noise or sudden movement elicits a startle. Stimulation of the area around the mouth elicits a rooting or suck-swallow response. During the sensorimotor period, mental operations go through a transition from being exclusively overt and motoric to being partially internalized. The child makes more effort at understanding the world. He begins to reflect on sensory information and selects a response from a number of alternatives. He can categorize many stimuli appropriately. Experiences provide the opportunity for the child to recognize the uniqueness of certain stimuli through accommodation. During this period, then, certain people and objects take on greater importance in the child's life.

A child also recognizes his ability to make things happen. He may throw his spoon on the floor and watch its descent intently. He may repeat this over and over, thrilled at his power over matter and at the responses he elicits from his parents.

One of the most significant changes during this period is the development of **object permanence,** the knowledge that an object continues to exist even though it is out of sight (Moore & Meltzoff, 2004; Schutte & Spencer, 2002). A keen observer notes that when a very young child drops a rattle out of his crib, he may cry briefly, but does not search for it. At about 12 months, however, he looks for it where he thinks it fell. A child's remembering the existence of an object after it is out of sight indicates that the child has internalized a symbolic representation of the object. The symbolic image is maintained by the child in the absence of the sensory image. This mental operation is a most significant milestone in a child's development of cognition. The gradual unfolding of object permanence occurs sequentially during the sensorimotor period, as shown in Table 5.2.

> Object permanence requires that a child maintain a symbolic representation of the object in memory so that it continues to exist although out of sight.

Reflexive Stage   Cognitive development begins in a child as a group of invariant reflex behaviors. The cerebral cortex is still immature, permitting lower centers of the central nervous system to maintain dominance over sensorimotor performance. A child sucks, roots, grasps, and startles almost indiscriminately, and often in the absence of a stimulus. A child will suck, for example, even when a nipple is not present. Piaget observed that when a schema of particular importance is present, there is a tendency to exercise it. This process, called **functional assimilation,** allows a child to refine the behavior and to begin extending it to other situations. Thumb sucking, which has been observed even in utero, is one such extension of a schema. **Recognitive assimilation** also appears early, as the child begins to discriminate among objects to which a schema applies and those to which it does not. A child selects a nipple over other suckable objects when he is hungry, for example.

TABLE 5.2	Stages in attainment of object permanence.
Age	**Behavior**
0–4 months	Does not actively search for objects that have moved out of sight
4–8 months	Searches for partially concealed objects
	Anticipates the destination of a moving object that is lost from sight
8–12 months	Searches for objects seen being hidden
12–18 months	Searches for objects hidden in visible changes of location
18–24 months	Searches for objects in hidden displacements by recreating the sequence

Infants enter the world prepared to receive and distinguish a variety of sensory information. Refinement of skills occurs quickly. A newborn's explorations and interactions with the environment reflect primitive behaviors, an immature nervous system, and schemata that assure the child's survival. These experiences provide the foundation for building more complex cognitive structures and prepare the child to become more directed in his actions.

Primary Circular Reactions   This stage in a child's development of cognition is characterized by attempts to repeat an action that has been done reflexively or by chance. These actions are described as **primary** because they are limited to basic actions involving a child's own body, and as **circular** because they are repeated. An infant cannot yet initiate new actions. If, by chance, he brought his thumb to his mouth, he might try to repeat the event. By positioning his hand and head appropriately he may accomplish the task after a number of misses. Through accommodation a child modifies his schemata until he becomes more precise in repeating actions.

A child at this stage also begins to show anticipatory behavior. Whereas a newborn begins purposeful sucking when his lips are in contact with a nipple, a child now may begin to suck when he is placed in a position that he associates with feeding.

Several other important signs appear at this stage indicating a child's growing alertness to stimuli in his surroundings. At approximately 3 months of age, a typical child begins to look in the direction of a sound. He also responds differentially to various visual stimuli. Novel and complex objects or pictures are likely to draw a more lengthy and intent gaze than do things familiar to the child. Continued exploration of novel stimuli in the environment through gross coordination of the senses enables an infant to begin developing schemata for the structure of the environment. This then becomes the foundation for relating new information to former experiences and further modifying schemata. This process is the basis for cognitive functioning and is refined during the third stage of the sensorimotor period.

Secondary Circular Reactions   Many parents claim that the most enjoyable stage in infancy comes at about 4 to 8 months of age. By this time, a baby focuses his attention on objects rather than on his own body. He reaches and grasps, providing himself greater freedom in manipulating and exploring objects. His random movements may cause his hand or foot to strike the mobile above the crib, and he begins to refine these movements until he is able to keep the mobile going with purposeful swipes. A child also begins responding in the same way to objects that appear the same to him. This type of primitive classification system develops through recognitive assimilation. A child will swipe at another mobile or something that looks like a mobile until he discovers a more appropriate way to approach the new object. Observing this type of activity and the perception of sameness in his daughter, Lucienne, prompted Piaget's belief that actions are the precursors of thought processes.

The child becomes interested in and begins interacting with objects in the secondary circular reactions stage.

Rattles are interesting toys for children at this age who are able to reach, grasp, and shake them, and who find the sound pleasing. The significance of specific objects and people signals the development of **object concept,** upon which Piaget put great emphasis. In the first stages of development of object concept, infants perceive an object only in terms of themselves; that is, something to suck, hold, or drop. During this later stage, however, objects begin to gain importance in relation to other objects. They become something with which to learn about spatial relationships and the stability of the universe. Related to this is the concept of object permanence. During the early phase of object permanence, children show a fascination for hide-and-seek games. They can find partially hidden objects, and when a toy is moved under a blanket in a predictable trajectory, they may anticipate where it will reappear. The search for hidden objects is likely to be brief, however, perhaps as a function of infants' short memory span and attention (Moore & Meltzoff, 2004). Nevertheless, as they develop, the images of objects and experiences beyond their immediate surroundings become more permanent residents of their schemata (Bremner, et al, 2005; Mareschal, Plunkett, & Harris, 1999).

A child's ability to sit independently at this stage and the appearance of teeth afford him a new perspective. Sights, sounds, smells, tastes, and tactile information are likely to increase in quantity and diversity, permitting the child to further refine his schemata for the environment. A child can make finer distinctions between the people and objects nearby. He can distinguish a familiar person or toy from others and can recognize them in different positions or when they are partially hidden from view.

> Sitting in an upright position enhances a child's view of his world.

Coordination of Secondary Schemata   This stage is marked by three important characteristics: **intention, imitation,** and **anticipation.** A child applies old schemata in new situations to attain a goal. For example, he uses a hitting action for the first time to move a barrier out of his path to get to a toy. He moves his parent's hand to a container that he cannot open himself. This intentional behavior is reflective of the child's beginning awareness of **causality,** the concept that people and things around him can cause change.

> The child's emerging understanding of how the world works is reflected in behaviors that are intentional, imitative, and anticipatory.

A child at this stage also begins to imitate on two planes: verbal and gestural. At earlier stages, the child tried to imitate sounds that he made and that were repeated by someone else. Now, through approximations of his own sounds and then sounds he hears, the child begins to refine his verbal imitation skills. The first imitations to appear are the most closely related to sounds already in the child's repertoire. The same progression is seen in gestural skills. A child first attempts to repeat movements already in his repertoire and then modifies his movements to approximate those of someone else. One of the earliest gestural imitations seen in children is waving bye-bye, which is a modification of children's schemata for reaching, grasping, and releasing.

Children of approximately 10 months of age show rather sophisticated anticipatory behavior. They may begin to cry when adults put on their coats, in anticipation of the adults' departure, or when food is placed before them that they do not like. It is not necessary at this stage for the parents to actually depart or for the child to taste the food in order for the child to cry; he can anticipate the outcome.

Also at this stage, the function of objects assumes greater importance to a child than does merely their appearance. The child is most interested in objects that can be manipulated in different ways, that make sounds, and that have visual fascination when they are explored. The child no longer perceives an object merely by its surface characteristics. He is able to hypothesize what things do by looking at them and, in play, uses the objects in purposeful ways.

Tertiary Circular Reactions   Primary reactions involve the child's own body. Secondary reactions involve simple exploration with objects. In the stage of tertiary circular reactions, the child approaches objects with an attitude that can be characterized as curiosity. He will repeat the same behavior, then experiment with variations. A child in a high chair might drop his spoon on the tray in the same way several times. He might then begin to drop it from different heights, letting it fall straight or allowing it to spin. The child also begins to use a spoon and can drink from a cup at about this time. Spilling milk on the floor or tossing food across the kitchen is part of a child's exploration. The child may participate in this trial-and-error experimentation until he finds one strategy that is particularly satisfying or effective. In the same way, a child engages other objects in similar unsystematic explorations and continues to broaden his understanding of relationships in his universe.

There is good evidence that, in this stage, **decentration** evolves on the action level, wherein the child learns that events take place in the universe without his involvement or control. He is still limited in interpreting cause–effect relationships for actions, but enjoys watching an activity in which he does not participate. When a child watches someone hide an object and then move it to another hiding place, he searches for the object where it has been moved. Formerly, he would have looked in its original position.

Because a typically developing child usually stands and walks during this stage, his ability to explore sights and sounds in the environment increases dramatically. He can classify objects by function or action in addition to shape. After a child has an opportunity to manipulate the objects, however, he classifies them by action or function.

Invention of New Means Through Mental Combinations   Near 2 years of age, a typical child no longer is tied to his actions, but can think through solutions to simple problems without the need for acting them out. The development of symbolic function marks the transition from the sensorimotor to the preoperational period.

The earliest symbols used by a child are probably internal images derived from his perceptual actions. That is, he retains the memory of an experience in some symbolic form. This allows for what Piaget called **deferred imitation.** A child can watch an action, store the image of the action in memory, and repeat it at a later time. A child's ability to imitate also improves because he is able to work through an action internally before acting it out.

A child's internal symbolic representations are also expressed in his understanding that pictures represent objects. He enjoys looking through a storybook and touching pictures of familiar objects. A child's language also may be a reflection of the experiences he considers most important. **Action terms** predominate in early language, as do names for objects that children associate with action (Bernstein, Loftus, & Meltzoff, 2005).

At the end of this stage, a child perceives objects as permanent and independent. He understands that if an object is out of sight, it may be in one of several other places and he may seek it out in a more systematic way. He recognizes spatial relationships among objects, as when he places forms in a form board correctly or holds a chip in his hand to drop it through a slit in the top of a can.

Decentration is the process through which the child realizes that events occur in the world in which he is not involved and has no control.

By the end of the sensorimotor period, the child has internalized images of objects and experiences, but makes many errors.

During the first 2 years of life, then, a child has learned about the physical properties of his environment. Initially, all behavior is overt and related to the child's body. Gradually, the child becomes more interested in other objects and actions and is able to translate these into symbols that he internalizes. More complex manipulations of symbolic representations characterize the next period of cognitive development.

Preoperational Period

As a child enters this period in cognitive development, thought processes are still immature. A child often is misled by his perceptions of the environment. The broad changes that take place on the action level during the sensorimotor period are matched by similar changes on the level of representational thought during the preoperational period.

Piaget began formulating his theory relating to this period by talking with and observing many different children. He focused on children's egocentrism in relation to communication skills, morality, and reasoning. He later refined his method and gave children specific problems to solve. He then described their thought processes based on their approaches to problem solving. He called their first attempts at constructing ideas or notions **preconcepts** to signify that children's conceptualization of the universe is still perceptually dominant.

Marked changes take place during the preoperational period. These are presented in the following paragraphs.

Egocentrism   An egocentric child is unable to view things from another perspective. On the three-mountain problem used by Piaget (see Figure 5.1), a child is asked to indicate what a doll would see by looking at the scene from different sides of the table. Not being able to imagine that someone can have a different viewpoint, the child chooses his own point of view.

Children's language also reflects egocentricism. Piaget's daughter Jacqueline, for example, defined *daddy* as "a man who has lots of Jacquelines" (Piaget, 1951). The three forms of egocentric speech are **monologue, collective monologue,** and

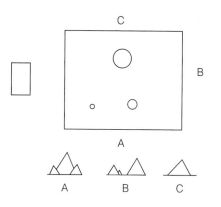

Piaget's three-mountain problem.

A child in the preoperational period cannot yet view things from another's perspective or consider multiple attributes of an object at one time.

repetition (echolalia). In the first, a child talks continuously while working or playing, apparently practicing the synthesis of action, language, and thought. Collective monologue takes place in a group situation. A child speaks with no apparent connection to what another child is saying. Although the social setting is different, the reasons for collective monologue appear to be the same as for simple monologue. Repetition is the third form of egocentric speech. A child repeats what another child has said, but presents it as if it were a unique contribution.

A child in the preoperational period is unable to anticipate the strategies that another will use in game-playing or problem-solving situations, yet he assumes that others know what he is thinking. In relating a story, for example, he may present it disjointedly or leave out parts, yet believe that the listener understands as he does (Girbau, 2001).

Centration   Successful problem solving requires that a child attend to many attributes of an object at one time. A preoperational child shows centration in thinking. He is unable to consider multiple attributes simultaneously, which causes errors in problem solving. If a child watches while a ball of clay is rolled into a snake, returned to its original form, and rolled again, he focuses on only one dimension when telling why the ball and snake are not equal. One child may say the ball is taller; another may say the snake is longer. Their inability to see the reciprocal changes in dimensions interferes with logical thinking and problem solving. The following problem provides another example of centration.

Given a group of red blocks and blue blocks that are all the same size and shape, a child has little difficulty putting together the blocks that are alike because they differ in only one attribute. However, if the child is given a group of red and blue blocks and red and blue disks, he will be confused. He tends to focus on one attribute at a time; therefore, he may group them all into two piles, or his attention may shift to another attribute during sorting and he may produce a conglomerate of piles.

Similarly, if a child is given seven blue and three white wooden beads, he will correctly name the color of the majority of the beads. But the child will be confused if he is asked whether there are more blue or white beads. Again, the child cannot focus on multiple attributes of the whole and its parts.

Irreversibility and Focus on Successive States   A preoperational child does not see that all logical operations are reversible. This is apparent in different types of problems. A child does not understand that if a ball of clay is rolled into a snake, it can just as easily be returned to its original form. Similarly, a child who is asked whether he has a brother may say "yes," but when he is asked whether his brother has a brother, he says "no."

This process also is associated with a child's focusing on successive stages of change rather than on the smooth transformation from one state to another. Piaget referred to a child's thought as being like a sequence of individual frames on a film. A child's view of changed states is exemplified in the difficulty he has arranging a series of pictures to reconstruct the movement of a stick falling from a vertical to a horizontal position.

Conservation problems require that a child be able to focus on the transformation from state to state in relation to mass, length, number, volume, and area. Figure 5.2 presents some simple tests of conservation. Conservation of number is

FIGURE 5.2 Simple tests of conservation.

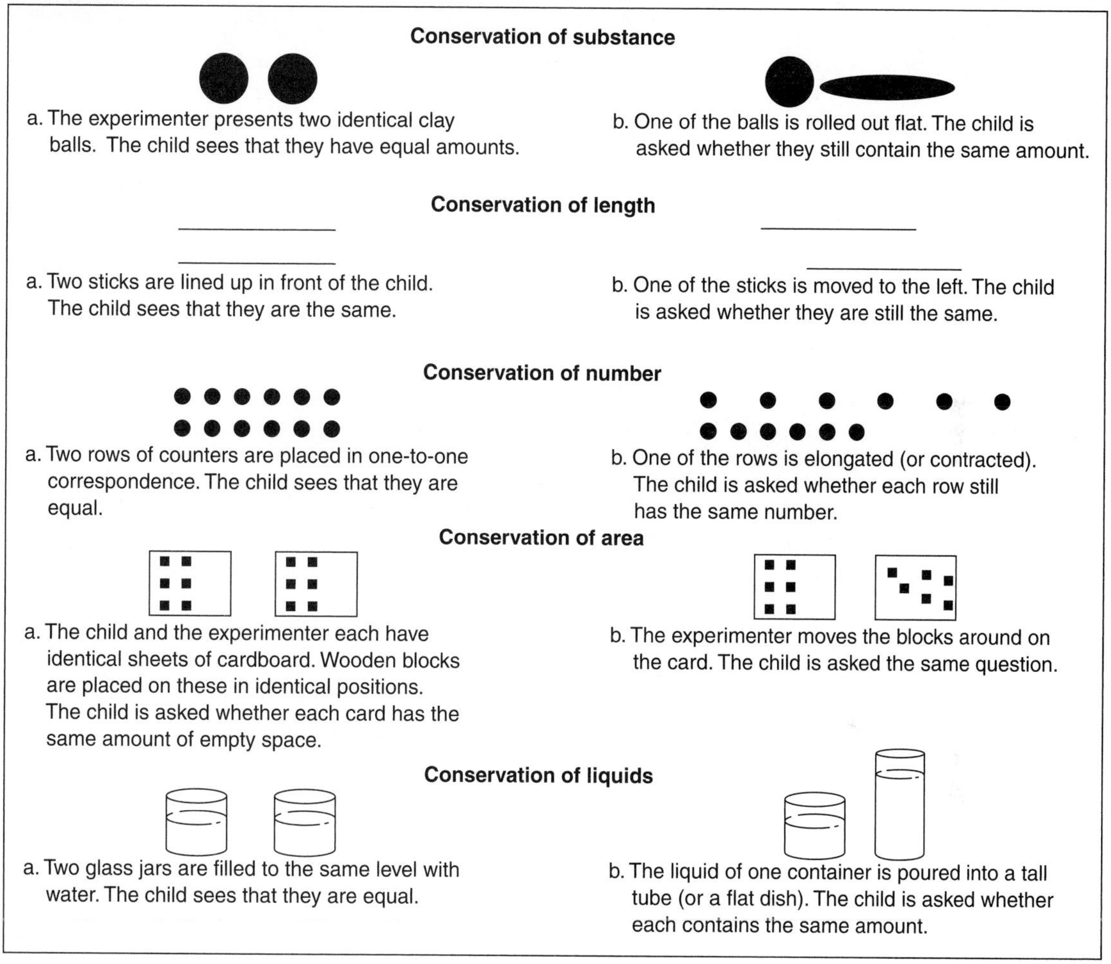

Conservation of substance

a. The experimenter presents two identical clay balls. The child sees that they have equal amounts.

b. One of the balls is rolled out flat. The child is asked whether they still contain the same amount.

Conservation of length

a. Two sticks are lined up in front of the child. The child sees that they are the same.

b. One of the sticks is moved to the left. The child is asked whether they are still the same.

Conservation of number

a. Two rows of counters are placed in one-to-one correspondence. The child sees that they are equal.

b. One of the rows is elongated (or contracted). The child is asked whether each row still has the same number.

Conservation of area

a. The child and the experimenter each have identical sheets of cardboard. Wooden blocks are placed on these in identical positions. The child is asked whether each card has the same amount of empty space.

b. The experimenter moves the blocks around on the card. The child is asked the same question.

Conservation of liquids

a. Two glass jars are filled to the same level with water. The child sees that they are equal.

b. The liquid of one container is poured into a tall tube (or a flat dish). The child is asked whether each contains the same amount.

usually achieved by age 6. By age 7, a child attains conservation of mass and length; by age 9, weight; and volume after age 11.

Transductive Reasoning Logical reasoning requires induction and deduction. In inductive reasoning, one generalizes from specific cases. In deductive reasoning, one applies general rules to specific cases. These processes require a child to recognize the stability of attributes despite changing circumstances and differences among attributes under the same circumstances. A preoperational child is not capable of deductive or inductive reasoning. Birds remain birds whether they are perched in a tree in the park or flying in the air. There are distinctive differences between the birds in the two cases. Yet the child who uses transductive reasoning assumes that the two birds he sees are one and the same. He sees relationships at a perceptual level without considering the possibility of higher order relationships.

> In conservation problems, the child must be able to recognize transformations from one state to another.

TABLE 5.3	Development of simple classification, space and number, and seriation concepts.	
Classification	**Space and Numbers**	**Seriation**
Simple sorting: Groups according to single perceptual attribute	*One-to-one correspondence:* Establishes equality between two sets of objects that visually correspond	*Orders objects* according to one property
True classification: Abstracts common property in group of objects; finds some property in other objects in group	*One-to-one correspondence in absence of physical correspondence:* Recognizes equality in absence of spatial equivalence	*Orders two inversely related series:* Arranges two series at once in inverse order
Multiplicative classification: Classifies by more than one attribute at a time; sees that object can belong to several classes at same time	*Conservation of quantity:* Quantity does not vary even when it occupies a different space	*Seriation and visual representation:* Draws a picture of objects he arranged in series, then draws in advance of ordering
All-some relation: Distinguishes classes based on property of all members and subclasses based on property of some members	*Conservation of the whole:* The whole does not vary even when divided into parts	*Seriation of geometric shapes:* Orders shapes based on area or number of sides
Class-inclusion relation: Forms subclasses of objects and includes subclasses in larger class	*Conservation of area:* Area is conserved even if appearance is changed	
	Transformation of perspective: Pictures objects from different perspective when they are moved	

Source: From *Piaget's Theory Applied to an Early Childhood Curriculum*, by C. S. Lavatelli, 1973, Nashua, NH: Delta Education, Inc. Copyright © 1973 by Delta Education, Inc. Reprinted by permission.

The Beginning of Concept Formation   The emergence of logical thought in a child is manifested in problem-solving and decision-making abilities. He begins to put things and events into some type of order. Objects show similarities and differences in their physical attributes, in their functions, and in their relationships to other objects. The child begins to group what he sees into classes and subclasses. Lavatelli (1973) provides the best summary of the logical processes of classification, space and number, and seriation as they develop in a young child. These processes are presented in Table 5.3.

Problem-solving and decision-making abilities signal the emergence of logical thought.

:: OTHER THEORIES OF DEVELOPMENT
Vygotsky's Theory

Whereas Piaget focused on the natural laws of intellectual development, Russian psychologist **Lev Vygotsky** (1978) concentrated on the role of language and culture, describing the roles of instruction, play, help, and learning. He explained cognitive development in terms of social systems comprised of productive interactions between the child and caregiver. Not unlike Piaget, he saw a responsive environment as the key to intellectual development.

Vygotsky used the term **zone of proximal development** to describe the distance between actual and potential development. **Actual development** is measured by watching a child's independent problem solving. **Potential development** is what the child does with help or guidance, and it becomes actual development through the mechanism of **internalization.** This mechanism describes the developmental progression of a child from other-regulation, wherein another individual (an adult or more advanced child) guides the child's activities, to self-regulation, wherein the child initiates purposeful action with other available individuals who provide necessary support only. The successful negotiation of this shift toward greater independence and control requires **intersubjectivity.**

According to Rochat (2005), intersubjectivity occurs when both parties share an understanding of the purpose of a given task and each recognizes this of the other. For a productive interaction to occur between an adult and child, there must be a shared social reality such that both are working on the same problem. When shared understanding does not exist, some negotiation between the two parties must occur, requiring communicative interaction or semiotic mediation. There is a **primary intersubjectivity** present at birth between an infant and his caregiver. At 7 to 8 months of age, the infant enters a period of **secondary intersubjectivity.** At this point, the child and caregiver can share meanings at a higher cognitive level (Fivaz-Depeursinge, Favez, & Frascarolo, 2005). Although Vygotsky stressed the language component of mediation, mechanisms such as joint eye gaze, following others' pointings, and catching other people's attention by using gestures and pointing also can be successful in the formulation of intersubjectivity. The adult can strive for a new level of intersubjectivity by representing objects and events in different ways, thereby stimulating cognitive development in the infant.

Vygotsky also proposed a sociocultural theory of disability in which compensation comes from cultural enlightment and socialization. He offered a comprehensive and practical approach to educating children with special needs. The foundation of this **theory of disontogenesis,** or distorted development, is that children have two classes of defects. Organic impairments (primary defects) result from both endogenous and exogenous biological causes. Children also experience distortions of higher psychological functions (secondary defects) as a result of social factors. Vygotsky's view was that the development of a child with a disability is determined by the social implications of the organic impairment, but that social support systems can overcome the obstacles imposed by that impairment.

The main objective of special education and, especially, early intervention, is the application of the principles just described to the development of the child's higher psychological functions by capitalizing on the child's current abilities and by providing meaning to new experiences. Children with caregivers who offer verbal and nonverbal support and who seek a shared understanding with the child of the task to be accomplished, for example, appear to be more motivated to persist with other challenging tasks on their own (Hauser-Cram, Warfield, Shonkoff, & Krauss, 2001). The objective of early intervention, therefore, must be the identification of a child from the point of strength rather than disability (Gindis, 2003). Social support systems can help children with disabilities overcome obstacles as they evolve processes to adapt to environmental demands.

> The term *zone of proximal development* describes the gap between what the child can currently do on his own and what he can do with help or guidance.

> Vygotsky emphasizes the importance of social support systems in bringing children with disabilities to higher levels of skill.

Behavioral Theories

In spite of the fact that new brain imaging techniques have provided clear evidence of specific changes in the cortex of the brain that parallel changes in developmental skills (Casey, Tottenham, Liston, & Durston, 2005; Gogtay et al., 2004), not everyone endorses the theory that cognition evolves through developmental changes in the organization of mental structures or that these changes are reflected in children's behavior in learning situations. There are numerous theories about how children learn or how they ascend to adulthood with growing sophistication in their ability to relate to their environment. From the behaviorist perspective, cognitive development is the result of the method and amount of learning children gain from their surroundings. Although most theories of development emphasize predictable and measurable changes in behavior that are governed by interactions with the environment, the classical research behind the development of these theories took place in the laboratory. The results of these laboratory studies have been applied in natural settings to study particular processes related to learning and the development of cognitive skills.

Cognitive development requires that a child be able to attend to the critical details in his environment.

Attention   Attention often is considered the foundation for cognitive and neuropsychological processes. A developing child is exposed to a large and diverse group of stimuli at any given time: the sound of a car in the street; the clothes dryer rumbling its tune in the next room; the radio playing; the brightly colored wallpaper; the toys, books, and magazines scattered around the room; the soup and roast cooking in the kitchen; and the family talking.

Very young children sustain attention for only brief periods. When they do attend, it is likely to be to the most intense stimuli in the environment—bright objects, loud noises, and strong smells. As children develop, they begin to concentrate on stimuli with the greatest functional value to the task at hand (Huang-Pollock, Carr, & Nigg, 2002). They are less apt to be distracted by irrelevant and incidental attributes, and more apt to focus on the relevant details of an object or situation. Neurological changes contribute to a child's improved attention over time (Booth et al., 2003). Attention theory is considered to be the critical factor for developmental transitions in perception, memory, thought, and problem solving. Children must be able to focus on the meaningful stimuli in their surroundings and ignore nonmeaningful stimuli for normal development and efficient learning to occur (Colombo, Shaddy, Richman, Maikranz, & Blaga, 2004).

Perception   Children differ in how they interpret sensory information. They may perceive the same situation in different ways depending upon their dominant sensory mode and dimension preferences. A newborn may give the same response for many types of stimuli but, as he develops, fewer stimuli elicit the same response. In addition, at different ages an infant shows shifts in the sensory mode he prefers for receiving information. Infants are more tactually attuned to the environment. As they get older, their explorations of the environment shift toward a more visual orientation.

Predictable shifts also occur in a child's preference for characteristics of stimuli during a problem-solving task. For example, a dimension is a category that includes all the variations of an attribute. Whereas color comprises numerous qualities, it is considered a single dimension. Similarly, shape and size are other dimensions in the visual mode. The earliest preference for a stimulus dimension occurs at about age 2, when the child attempts to solve a choice problem by continually selecting the stimulus on the same side (left or right). Older children select stimuli based first on color or size, then based on shape at about 6 years of age.

A child also becomes better able to distinguish among stimuli as he develops. This is described by **differentiation theory,** which proposes that, through a child's rich experiences with stimuli, he learns to differentiate attributes of objects and situations and then selects those that are relevant (Gibson & Pick, 2003). In addition to becoming aware that different objects and events have different characteristics, he learns through experiences that some attributes are invariant. His toy car is the same whether it is in his hand or across the room, where it appears to be smaller. Similarly, it is the same toy car whether it is viewed from the front, the back, or the side.

Memory   The neurological basis for memory is becoming more clearly understood thanks to brain imaging techniques (Buckner, 2003; Rajah & McIntosh, 2005). Specific areas of the brain play primary roles in information storage and communication of stored memory to other areas of the brain. The distinction between perception and conception is often characterized by the quantity of information stored in the brain's data bank and the extent to which a child can take new information and make associations with past knowledge. A child becomes more of a conceptual thinker when the data bank is full of verbal labels for objects and events and there are clusters of related information or symbols to be drawn upon.

> Conceptual thinking requires a rich bank of symbolic labels to be stored in memory.

Children's retention of information for short and long periods follows different paths of development (Carver & Bauer, 2001). The capacity of short-term memory is small. If we tell a child what to order at a quick-serve restaurant, he is likely to forget unless he uses the information immediately. Even then, if the phrase or word string is too long or has little meaning as a whole, he will probably forget it quickly. A 3-year-old child can repeat a string of three numbers presented to him orally; a 7-year-old can recall five numbers. To put this in perspective, most adults do not have a much greater capacity in **short-term memory** (seven numbers). Short-term memory also allows a child to look for an object that moves out of sight (i.e., object permanence) and facilitates manipulation of information in problem solving later in the preschool years (i.e., **working memory**).

Long-term memory has a greater storage capacity and shows greater differences among ages. It is likely that increased memory capacity over time is a result of a richer abundance of material already in the brain's data bank to which new information can be related. The more meaningful new information is, the easier it is to memorize. Retention of new material also appears to be related to an ability to disregard irrelevant information and to the speed of processing incoming information.

Three strategies used to memorize new information appear to be applied often by new learners. These strategies relate to the ability to group stimuli on the basis of more complex perceptual and conceptual attributes. The first strategy is memory through **rehearsal,** which is used more with increasing age. For example, when children are shown a series of pictures and asked to recall the order in which the examiner points to them, children who say the words for the pictures to themselves have much better recall. This use of verbal mediation increases with age. The inability to produce the verbal mediators may be a hindrance in certain memory tasks. The acquisition and use of verbal labels appear to account for age changes in memory capacity. In preverbal children, active manipulation of stimuli may facilitate memory.

Imagery is a second strategy for committing new information to memory. It entails superimposing mental images of one or more stimuli upon each other so that the association of each with the other aids recall. For example, if a child is shown pictures of a dog, a wagon, a toothbrush, and a key, the child might formulate the image of a dog riding in a wagon with a toothbrush in one paw and a key in the other. Although imagery is more effective with concrete stimuli, abstractions may be incorporated into a mental image if they are paired with a concrete object, such as a large orange.

The third strategy reflects some of the more interesting data on developmental progressions. **Organization** of stimuli into meaningful clusters appears to contribute to their acquisition and recall; however, children organize information in different ways at different ages. For example, 2-year-olds tend to cluster together words that rhyme; 3-year-olds cluster words that have syntactic meaning (such as *eat—apple* and *men—work*); 4-year-olds cluster words by functional similarity (such as *hand—leg* and *peach—apple*); and 5-year-olds recall words most often in the order in which they hear them. Clustering based on more and more complex factors is consistent with what we have already learned about cognitive processes.

Hypothesis Testing   Children under 6 years of age do little systematic testing of hypotheses. Trying to guess the answer in a game of I'm Thinking of Something, a young child's questions are not likely to reflect strategy: "Is it a horse?" "Is it something to eat?" "Is it something I like?" As the child gets older, however, he uses a strategy that involves asking questions that gradually focus on the answer: "Does it move?" "Does it have wheels?" "Does someone drive it?" "Is it a car?"

Complex techniques of hypothesis testing may not be attained until adulthood. Even then, the problem-solving strategies used may be insufficient or ineffective in producing the correct answer.

:: RELATIONSHIPS BETWEEN DEVELOPMENTAL AND COGNITIVE PROCESSING MODELS

It is important to keep in mind that the differences among the theories of cognitive development are not great. Piaget, representing a developmental approach, focused on the gradual organization of cognitive structures that permits a child to solve problems and perform logical operations. According to Piaget, cognition provides a means to adapt to environmental demands by assimilating new information and modifying cognitive structures—schemata—that are already present. Even a newborn has a basis for interacting with the environment in a motoric, reflexive way.

Cognition provides a means to adapt to environmental demands.

Proponents of behavioral models focus on the operations involved in receiving, storing, and recalling information. Although they do not disavow recognition of internal processes, behaviorists believe that "it is not profitable to speculate about these internal processes since they cannot be directly observed or controlled"

(Maccoby & Zellner, 1970, p. 34). They believe that behavior is controlled by stimuli and that development progresses as behaviors are modified to the demands of stimuli. On the other hand, developmental theorists offer examples that cannot be explained sufficiently by behavioral models. For example, in the situation involving blue and white wooden beads described in the earlier section on centration, Piaget's theory explains that 4-year-olds do not have the ability to consider a part of a class (i.e., only the blue beads) and the whole class (all wooden beads) at the same time. Once they think about a part, the whole no longer exists. By 8 years of age, however, children are able to separate the whole into parts and put them back together as an internal operation. Developmental theorists contend that behavioral models do not explain the development of these types of logical operations. Furthermore, developmental theorists assert that forcing development to occur by selectively reinforcing behaviors that are chronologically age-appropriate for a child is probably wasteful— if not harmful. Such is the case when children are expected to learn to read because they are 5 years old. If they do not yet have the cognitive structures to assimilate the new information, reading becomes a meaningless exercise for them. To memorize something without understanding it epitomizes teaching without learning. In addition, if a child is force-fed information that his cognitive perspective of the universe says is wrong, it may cause future conflicts in his perspective of reality.

Behaviorism may be viewed as a complement to certain aspects of developmental theory. When the cognitive structures for simple number concepts have developed, for example, repetition is the best way to learn counting and basic skills in arithmetic. Similar strategies from behavioral theory are effective for learning the alphabet and sight words.

> Behaviorism can nicely complement selected aspects of developmental theory.

:: FACTORS THAT AFFECT COGNITIVE DEVELOPMENT

Cognition unfolds gradually and in a consistent sequence as a function of maturation. Skills are modified and refined, however, in response to the demands of the environment.

Many factors can interfere with the processes involved in the typical cognitive development of a child. Those factors that may affect the developing fetus were discussed in chapter 2. These include the age of the parents, number of pregnancies, maternal substance use, illness, and nutrition, exposure to infection and toxins, and chromosomal and genetic abnormalities. One or more of these factors may influence brain development by compromising the structural integrity of the organ or the functioning of brain chemicals that allow for efficient and accurate processing of information. These prenatal factors also may impair a child's ability to receive (e.g., see or hear) or respond to (e.g., speak or move) information. The next section addresses those environmental factors that also may influence cognitive development of the young child.

Cognition and the Environment

It has been a continuing challenge to determine when a child's development deviates from typical to atypical and what caused this deviation. Numerous models and theories have been proposed (Simeonsson, 2006). In 1961, Pasamanick and Knobloch made the classic proposal that children are susceptible to a continuum of damage as a result of reproductive complications. The damage may range from minor and undetectable trauma to significant serious disabilities affecting one's mental, physical, and emotional capacities. The researchers called this a **continuum of reproductive casualty** and identified five disorders related to reproductive casualty: epilepsy, behavior disorders, cerebral palsy, mental retardation, and reading disabilities (Pasamanick & Knobloch, 1966). Several years later, Sameroff and Chandler (1975) presented their **continuum of caretaking casualty**. They emphasized that a poor caretaking environment may similarly yield a range of deviant developmental outcomes for children. In fact, the influence of the environment on a child and the transactional nature of a child's relationship with those in the environment may be more potent and expansive than biological factors in determining how a child will develop. Reports of several longitudinal studies (Gray & Sanson, 2005; Mulligan & Flanagan, 2006; NICHD Early Child Care Research Network, 2005; Poland & Legge, 2005; Smyke, Dumitrescu, & Zeanah, 2002) that followed large cohorts of children revealed that outcome was not related to a single factor of socioeconomic status. Rather, children who grow up in poverty are exposed to numerous environmental inequities that include less education of the parent(s), a greater likelihood of a single parent and a less stable home, fewer educational materials in the child's environment, less involvement of the parent(s) in the child's education, more crowded and noisy homes, and more dangerous neighborhoods (Evans, 2004).

> The continuum of reproductive casualty and the continuum of caretaking casualty explain the outcomes of children with disabilities.

A substantive body of research now exists that documents the positive influences on cognitive development when the environment is made more stimulating for the child (Campbell, Pungello, Miller-Johnson, Burchinal, & Ramey, 2001; Reynolds, Ou, & Topitzes, 2004). Children moved from poor institutional settings into adoptive homes showed significant developmental gains, with the best outcomes for children who spent the least time in the institution (Beckett et al., 2006; Dalen, 2001). For children with organic (biological) impairments, the results are more equivocal. For example, a large group of children who were of very low birth weight and premature and who subsequently received early intervention showed no greater developmental gains at age 18 than the "no intervention" control group. The heavier low-birth-weight group, however, showed significant gains from intervention compared to the control group (McCormick et al., 2006). Similar mixed results were reported for other children with disabilities (Bailey et al., 2005; Bono et al., 2005).

A child is not a passive learner. A parent's approval and nurturing of the exploratory behavior of a child experimenting with his surroundings facilitate typical cognitive development in the child. With the exception of children who have severe disabilities, a child's early social environment appears to be a better predictor of how development will progress than are biological factors at birth (Luthar, 2003; Sameroff, McDonough, & Rosenblum, 2005). From the first visual and physical contact a child has with his parent(s), he asserts his influence on the parent(s). If the child shows extremes in temperament that conflict with the parent's personality, it creates a more adverse relationship between parent and child. A variety of other family and environmental characteristics also may cause stresses in the home (see,

---

BOX 5.1 SLEEP AND THE YOUNG CHILD WITH SPECIAL NEEDS

Most young children go through periods when they have a difficult time falling asleep or wake up one or more times during the night, with varying degrees of difficulty falling back asleep. For young children with special needs, sleep difficulties tend to be more common and can wreak havoc on the child, his family, and every other person and environment with which the child comes in contact.

A growing body of research indicates that children who have sleep problems, whether due to sleep apnea (very short periods of cessation of breathing during the night) or other organic problems, perform poorly during the daytime hours. They are less focused and less able to perform daily tasks (Chervin et al., 2006; Fallone, Acebo, Seifer, & Carskadon, 2001; Halbower et al., 2006; Hiscock, Caterford, Ukoumunne, & Wake, 2007). What is explored less in this regard is the impact on the parents. College students who have ever pulled all-nighters, once the adrenalin rush is over

following the exam or handing in the term paper the next day, know the dreadful feeling of fatigue. Parents of young children with special needs who face this night after night are ill-equipped to perform parenting or work functions in an effective manner. Everyone suffers: The sleep-deprived child is less able to benefit from early intervention activities. The sleep-deprived parents are too tired to be emotionally involved with the child or carry out prescribed early intervention activities. The child care facility must try to work with a child who is sleepy, behaves unpredictably, and has difficulty focusing on learning activities.

Many physicians believe sleep is a critical process in a child's life that requires medical attention, when necessary. The early interventionist would do well to question parents about their child's sleep pattern and suggest they talk with their physician if the child shows the characteristics described above and if there is a poor sleep pattern.

---

for example, Kim-Cohen, Caspi, Rutter, Tomas, & Moffitt, 2006). The traditional nature of parent-child relationships (i.e., the child and caregiver influencing and being influenced by the other) increases the likelihood that a single stress will lead to others. Cognitive competence during the early years depends as much for its continuity on the unfolding of innate capacities as on environmental constraints (Rutter, Moffitt, & Caspi, 2006).

Kearsley (1979) observed that some children might learn to be cognitively incompetent. He used the term **iatrogenic retardation** to describe children who have the potential for typical development—that is, who are structurally normal but "whose development [has] taken place in an environment characterized by prolonged parental anxiety and inappropriate caretaking practices" (p. 155). For the past several decades, professionals concerned with early intervention have directed their efforts toward refining procedures and materials for stimulating the development of these children and others who are likely to have disabilities later in life. These efforts have generated programs for applying numerous theoretical and conceptual models that explain how infants develop and learn. The presumption upon which many of the approaches were founded was that the quality of the caregiver (parent or teacher) and the quality of the environment contribute to facilitating development and learning. By improving the input the infant received, the thinking

> Cognitive competence depends on the unfolding of innate capacities *and* on environmental constraints.

went, development would be maximized within the biological and genetic limits of the child. This thinking led to a plethora of curricula dedicated to this stimulus-based (or stimulation-oriented) approach.

Recently, there have been challenges to what had become the traditional approach to intervention with young children who are developmentally disabled. With the proposal of greater emphasis on **co-occurrences** in relation to young children's development—that is, the detection by children that two events occurring together or in close temporal proximity are associated—a new conceptual framework for intervention has evolved (Rodrigo et al., 2006; Smith & Gasser, 2005).

> Co-occurrences describe events that take place together or close to each other and are perceived by the child as being related.

Piaget (1952) viewed the influence of co-occurrences on a child as having four aspects: They orient the child to aspects of the environment; they arouse the child and help to modulate his state; their detection provides satisfaction and confidence; and they exercise memory processes as the foundation for development of more complex mental structures. These influences are most easily viewed within the context of parent-child interactions and, particularly, maternal responsiveness to a child's actions and cues. Studies, for example, provide evidence that in infants through 2 years of age, maternal responsiveness is significantly related to a child's later development (Paavola, Kunnan, & Moilanen, 2005; Smith, Landry, & Swank, 2006; Tamis-LeMonda, Bornstein, & Baumwell, 2001) and significantly more related to development than is maternal stimulation (Landry, Swank, Assel, Smith, & Vellet, 2001). In addition, the *quality of responsiveness* rather than the *quantity of interaction* is related to an infant's development. Quantity is related to *stimulation,* which is time the mother spends smiling at, holding, and talking to the child. On the other hand, *responsiveness* is the frequency of time the mother performs these behaviors immediately following the infant's actions. Quality is related to the type of responsiveness. Proximal responsiveness (touching, holding, and rocking) is positively correlated with measures of cognitive development in the youngest children. This relationship lessens as a child gets older, when the relationship between distal responsiveness of the mother (talking to, looking at, and smiling at) and measures of cognitive development increase.

Similar results were found in studies of fathers and interactions with their young children. Outcomes for the child were related to the level of responsiveness of the father (Vogel, Bradley, Raikes, Boller, & Shears, 2006). In an effort to understand the underlying basis of the importance of parental support to development, Ryan, Martin, and Brooks-Gunn (2006) studied families with one, two, and no responsive parents in the home. They found that children with two supportive parents did best and those with no supportive parents were particularly disadvantaged.

Although the relationship between a child's development and parental responsiveness has not been shown to be causal in nature, a contingent environment facilitates important aspects of a child's cognitive development. Piaget's emphasis on a child's discovery of the environment during the sensorimotor period is founded on this concept. In the intact child, circular reactions provide the child with information about the nature of objects in the environment and his influence on them. In children with developmental problems, detection of these simple relationships and more complex relationships may be more fleeting and less available (Dunst, 2003; Hutto, 2003).

An unresponsive or stressful environment or one in which the expectations for a child are low may contribute to generalized retardation of cognitive development. An unknown but very large number of children with cognitive impairments probably fall into this category.

:: COGNITIVE DEVELOPMENT AND THE CHILD WITH SPECIAL NEEDS

It is beneficial to consider, from time to time, the amazing ascent of a human being from the union of egg and sperm to a mature, cognitive being. With this perspective, we are better able to appreciate the plight of individuals with disabilities, who must function in a world that makes the same demands upon them as upon intact persons. Imagine a child who is congenitally blind trying to understand what an airplane is or what colors are. Consider how much worldly learning a child who is deaf misses or the social learning opportunities a child with physical disabilities never gets because he cannot participate in games and sports. Developmental theorists look upon the limitations in sensory experiences as restricting the growth and refinement of schemata. Cognitive learning advocates view the same limitations as restricting opportunities for appropriate behaviors to be reinforced, practiced, built upon, and generalized to other situations. From either perspective, a child with an impairment that limits his ability to receive, process, or respond to sensory information is likely to demonstrate delays or gaps in cognitive development.

Considerable research has investigated the effects of various disabilities on cognitive development. However, it contributes little to our understanding of children when they are described in broad categorical terms, such as "retarded" or "delayed." The following discussion therefore looks at the state of our knowledge regarding specific aspects of cognition in young children with disabilities.

Intellectual Disability

As noted in chapter 1, the term *intellectual disability* implies cognitive deficits. Much evidence points to key problems in memory and attention being responsible for the atypical performance of a child with an intellectual disability when compared to that of his typical peers. Differences in the brain structure of children with disabilities underlie these performance deficits.

Several theories have been proposed to explain memory deficits. Broadbent's (1958) **limited buffer theory** suggests that individuals with mental retardation have a smaller-than-normal capacity to store information, and that the addition of new information requires the purging of "old" information. The **"bottleneck" theory** was proposed by Tulving (1968). Slamecka (1968), in his elaboration of this theory, asserted that memory is impaired by the inability of a child to retrieve information, not by a limited storage capacity. This theory is supported by the superiority of our recognition memory skills over our recall skills. For example, consider a child who is shown a card with eight pictures on it and told to try to remember all the pictures. When the card is removed, the child will remember more pictures if he is given an opportunity to tell whether a certain

> Children with intellectual disabilities might have a smaller memory capacity, difficulty acquiring and storing information, or a decreased ability to retrieve stored information.

picture was present or not (recognition memory) than if he must name the pictures he saw (recall memory). Numerous other theories regarding memory skills have been proposed over the years (Neath & Surprenant, 2003). For children with Down syndrome, short-term memory for verbal information appears to be more impaired than for visual and spatial material (Jarrold & Baddeley, 2001; Purser & Jarrold, 2005), but deficits increase with age for all types of memory (Chapman & Hesketh, 2001). Vicari and others studied the memory skills of children with various conditions notable for intellectual disabilities (e.g., Down syndrome and Williams syndrome). Different patterns of memory skills appear to be present in children with different conditions (Vicari, 2004; Vicari, Bellucci, & Carlesimo, 2005). It is likely that these differences in various memory skills (recognition vs. recall, auditory vs. visual vs. spatial, for example) are due to abnormal development or functioning of different parts of the brain as a consequence of the specific disability (Curtis, 2004); that is, a number of brain structures have been implicated in various types of memory skills. As a consequence of damage to genes and chromosomes, as a consequence of the cut-off of oxygen to the brain prior to or during delivery, or due to infectious or toxic agents, one or more of those parts of the brain may be damaged and interfere with specific types of memory skills. Furthermore, the damage may influence the storage of information and/or the retrieval of information.

Another important component of the acquisition of information that appears to distinguish typically-developing children from those with intellectual disabilities is attention to relevant stimuli. "Attention refers to a complex set of physiological and behavioural responses to environmental stimuli. The purpose of attention is to direct cognitive resources to events or situations with the intention of gathering information about the event" (Choudhury & Gorman, 2000, p. 128) and is divided into stimulus orienting and sustained attention. The child orients to a stimulus when he detects change or becomes aware of a particular stimulus in the environment. The child must be able to make a decision at this point whether to disengage or maintain attention to the stimulus. It is during sustained attention that processing of information and learning take place. Some children who are severely impaired may be unaware of their surroundings and, consequently, be unable to benefit from the stimulating qualities of their environment. Environments of children from low-income families, on the other hand, may be abundant in stimuli, but they often are ambiguous or excessive. The inability of a child to orient and sustain attention to relevant stimuli in such environments, particularly if they are complex or demanding, has been implicated as a cause for the poor performance of children from low-income families on cognitive tasks (NICHD Early Child Care Research Network, 2003), of infants born prematurely (Lawson & Ruff, 2004), and of infants exposed to cocaine (Sheinkopf, Mundy, Claussen, & Willoughby, 2004) and lead (Davis, Chang, Burns, Robinson, & Dossett, 2004; Ris, Dietrich, Succop, Berger, & Bornschein, 2004). It is likely, however, that early intervention can minimize the impact of these factors.

Similar deficits appear to be inherent in children with mental retardation. From a Piagetian perspective, a child orients to a stimulus through arousal of one or more of the senses. He then compares the input with schemata for similar sensory information. The inability of a child with intellectual deficits to retain or recall numerous or complex representations restricts the meaningful interpretation of new stimuli. Consequently, there is no motivation to sustain attention to that stimulus.

Visual Impairments

Piaget and Inhelder (1969) observed a hierarchy of deficits in the cognitive development of children who were blind from birth. Departures from typical development were most obvious during the third stage of the sensorimotor period, when children who were blind failed to reach for objects. Limitations in visual sensory experiences prevented these children from forming basic sensorimotor schemata. This affected their acquisition of higher-level cognitive skills.

Obviously, children who are blind and partially sighted do not gain the same perceptions of the nature of their environment as do children with sight. Their inability to be lured by objects that promote sustained attention and require them to change their physical position or to judge positions in space delays the development of object concept (Miles, 2003). Reaching for and attaining an object that makes sound may not occur until late in the second year. Only then does a child begin mobility that facilitates his construction of the environment. Furthermore, pretend play occurs infrequently in children who are blind before 18 months of age, whereas it is common for their sighted peers. Langley (1980) noted the following:

> Limited in independent mobility until approximately 19 months, the blind child is not able to explore various rooms of the house, to touch objects of interest, and to have them labeled. Unless the blind child is taught systematic scanning and exploration strategies, the similarities between objects and the ability to make generalizations may not develop. The absence of visual opportunities to associate tactual properties with auditory input often leads to meaningless rote verbalization. (p. 18)

Object concept appears from 1 to 3 years late in children who are blind. Consequently, the lack of knowledge of the permanence of objects in space and critical relationships hinders progress in these children's cognitive development (Bigelow, 2003). A child who is unable to use vision to integrate auditory and tactile cues learns much later than sighted children how to maintain contact with his environment. Even very limited vision significantly alters how a child perceives and interacts with the world.

Still, there is evidence that children who are and who are not visually impaired show approximate equivalence in certain concepts (Brekke, Williams, & Tait, 1974; Friedman & Pasnak, 1973). Reynell (1978) indicated that parallel development is most likely to appear at about 3 or 4 years of age, when logical thought begins to replace visual perception as the major learning process. Certainly, the abilities of people such as Helen Keller and Stevie Wonder show that visual impairments from early in life need not limit development of abstract thought. Children who are impaired from birth may develop complex cognitive skills if they are taught to make maximal use of action learning (Piaget & Inhelder, 1969).

Object concept appears 1 to 3 years later in children who are blind.

Vision allows a child to be more mobile and to explore his environment, thus facilitating cognitive development.

Hearing Impairments

Children with hearing impairments are more often identified by their failure to exhibit appropriate language milestones than by difficulties in sensorimotor or preconceptual abilities. This suggests that cognitive development can progress normally in the absence of hearing.

Much of the alienation from the environment of a child with a hearing impairment results from the influence of the impairment on language reception and production. Unfortunately, many tests of intelligence rely on language. Children with hearing impairments, therefore, may be erroneously identified as retarded. Improved training of testing personnel may alleviate this problem. Nevertheless, the negative reinforcement a child receives based on the lower expectations people have for him as a "retarded" child may contribute to a poorer performance, as well. Children with hearing impairments also have the greatest difficulties with tasks for which instructions cannot be easily conveyed with gestures. The widening gap between the performance of children who do and do not have hearing impairments that occurs as they get older may result, in part, from the increasing complexity of instructions required for tasks at older ages. It is possible that the cumulative effect of decreased cognitive stimulation and poor interpersonal relations contributes to poorer demonstrated performance by children with hearing impairments. Schorr, Fox, van Wassenhove, and Knudsen (2005) emphasize the importance of integrating auditory and visual modalities to accurately interpret the environment. They found, for example, that, when hearing impaired children received cochlear implants prior to $2\frac{1}{2}$ years of age, which allowed them to process auditory information, they could interpret their communicative environment at almost the same level as their hearing peers and better than children who received the implants at older ages. Leybaert and D'Hondt (2003) explain the process from a neurophysiological perspective. They suggest that, in the absence of early stimulation, deaf children do not develop specialization of the left brain hemisphere necessary for typical language development.

Hearing impaired children who are raised by deaf parents (less than 10% of hearing impaired children) exhibit normal patterns of cognitive, social, and linguistic development compared to their normal peers (Marschark, 2000). This is likely due to compensations parents make knowing their child is hearing impaired and to a common means of communication between hearing impaired parents and their child. Hearing parents might be able to make the same compensations if they knew their young child was hearing impaired, but they often are not aware of the hearing impairment until a later age. At least in expressing important concepts such as the nature and direction of motion events, Zheng and Goldin-Meadow (2002) found that deaf children of non-signing parents develop their own gestural communication systems. Nevertheless, this might not be adequate to help the child integrate successfully and to meet the cognitive demands of a hearing world.

Can we develop thought processes without language? Piaget (1952) and Vygotsky (1986) believed that the two develop along parallel and independent courses. At least at the earliest stages of development, however, certain cognitive structures must be present for the initiation of language. According to Mandler (2004):

> Recent research in infant cognitive development shows that at least by 9 months of age infants have developed a conceptual system sufficiently rich to allow language to begin. Evidence for this system is shown by categorization of objects above and beyond their perceptual appearance, problem-solving, long-term recall of events, and inductive inferences. (p. 508)

If the environment is contingently responsive, cognitive development can progress normally in a child with a hearing impairment.

Furthermore, Boucher (1998) concludes that the evidence "argues against . . . strong theories of either the independence, or the inseparability, of language and thought" (p. 74).

An interesting line of research with hearing impaired and typical children addresses what developmental psychologists call Theory of Mind, which has its foundation in Piagetian theory. As noted earlier, very young children are egocentric thinkers. As children mature, "[t]hey come to understand that what they think or believe may be different from what another person thinks and believes" (Schick, deVilliers, deVilliers, & Hoffmeister, 2002, p. 1). Mature thinkers are always testing the truth or falseness of what they see. Flavell (2004) provides the following example: "After children discover that a cookie box actually contains pencils instead of cookies, they are asked what another child who has not looked inside the box will think the box contains. Younger preschoolers say pencils; older ones, with a better understanding of belief, say cookies" (p. 275). Differences have been found, however, in Theory of Mind development and understanding of false beliefs of hearing impaired children compared to typically developing children along similar lines to those discussed earlier. That is, children with hearing impairments whose mothers had a communication system with them had Theory of Mind development more similar to typical children than to hearing impaired children with hearing parents (Courtin & Melot, 2005; Moeller & Schick, 2006). Schick et al. (2002) conclude that "the language delays that are typically observed in children who are deaf are causally related to delays in major aspects of cognitive development" (p. 5).

Physical Impairments and Chronic Illnesses

Children who have a condition in this category often experience cognitive deficits. The deficits may be specific to a particular type of illness, reflecting the disease process, to generalized restrictions on the child's interactions with his environment, or to lowered expectations for the child by the caregivers or professionals who work with the child. For example, cognitive deficits have been reported in children with epilepsy (Henkin et al., 2005; Oostrom, vanTeeseling, Smeets-Schouten, Peters, & Jenneken-Schinkel, 2005), with sickle cell disease (Schatz, 2004), those who were born very low birth weight (Hack et al., 2005; Seitz et al., 2006), with cancer (Raymond-Speden, Tripp, Lawrence, & Holdaway, 2000), and with failure to thrive syndrome (Corbett & Drewett, 2004). Long periods in the hospital, lack of motivation, and negative feedback from environmental interactions likely account for at least some of the cognitive deficits.

A child's first years are ones in which he formulates a perception of the universe through action. Similar to a child with a visual impairment, a child with a physical impairment or chronic illness who is unable to move freely or interact freely with his environment is at a great disadvantage. He may miss the opportunity to see his arms and legs move about—at first, erratically, then in predictable, voluntary ways. He may be unable to manipulate objects or recognize his influence on the universe. He may be unable or reluctant to change position in order to view his surroundings from different perspectives. These children may perceive their universe differently than a typical child because of the limitations or uniqueness in how they interact with their surroundings.

Severe language problems combined with limited movement create an atmosphere whereby we perceive children as being more intellectually disabled than they are because of their inability to communicate or perform appropriately. The insufficiency of traditional test instruments to assess cognitive functioning in the absence of adequate language and movement has led to inaccurate and sometimes harmful judgments about children. Some efforts have been made toward forming more objective determinations about the cognitive functioning of children with severe physical impairments.

For example, numerous researchers (Brian, Landry, Szatmari, Niccols, & Bryson, 2003; Colombo et al., 2004; Courage, Reynolds, & Richards, 2006; Wellman, Phillips, Dunphy-Lelii, & LaLonde, 2004) used an attention paradigm to test children who were unable to respond to test items in traditional ways. **Habituation** is the term for the decrement in an individual's response to a repeatedly presented stimulus. When one is presented with a new or novel stimulus, attention to the stimulus and one's heart rate increase. After repeated presentations, attention wanes and heart rate decreases as one learns to anticipate the event. Monitoring attention and heart rate in children during repeated presentations of the same stimulus, followed by the introduction of a subtle variation and then a return to the original stimulus, enables the examiner to estimate a child's cognitive processing skills. Cognitive level is a function of the speed with which a child habituates to the original stimulus, recognizes and dishabituates to the variation (evidenced by increased attention and heart rate), and recognizes the original stimulus when it is presented again by habituating more quickly.

Additional research has helped to specify the influence of physical impairment on various perceptual and cognitive tasks. Visual and auditory perception problems appear in children with various types of disabilities, including hydrocephalus and myelomeningocele (Lindquist, Carlsson, Persson, & Uvebrant, 2005) and cerebral palsy (Stiers et al., 2002). These children have difficulties discriminating among various shapes and organizing their spatial environment, for example. Poor visual and auditory perceptual skills of children with cerebral palsy have been attributed to the absence of the motor skills that train the visual and auditory systems. Rolling elicits visual pursuit, fusion, and accommodation of the lens to focus on objects at various distances and from different perspectives. Poor muscle stability in the neck may inhibit visual fixation; poor stability in the shoulders and arms may cause poor reaching patterns.

> Care should be taken not to assume the presence of cognitive deficiencies in a young child with motor and/or language problems.

> Habituation paradigms have been used to measure cognitive levels of young children and children with disabilities, but few normative standards have been established.

Autism Spectrum Disorders

Children with autism pose an interesting puzzle of perceptual and conceptual skill development. They have difficulty processing sensory input and, as a consequence, may show exaggerated responses or no response to stimuli. They may show no response even to intense auditory or visual stimuli, yet they may engage in rubbing textures, spinning objects, or scratching surfaces. The earliest behaviors that parents recall from the first year of life of their child who later is diagnosed with autism are extremes in temperament (from marked irritability to frightening passivity), poor eye contact, and a lack of response to the parent's voice or attempts to engage in interactions (Zwaigenbaum et al., 2007). By 3 years of age, more definitive impairments are apparent in language, social reciprocity, communication, and restricted or repetitive interests.

It is unclear whether the cognitive impairments of children with autism represent a single brain abnormality or a combination of factors (Happé, 2003). Recent evidence based on brain studies has found specific structural brain differences in children with autism. Most notably, brain volume shows abnormal enlargement during infancy, with those differences diminishing during late childhood and adolescence. Other brain differences have been identified, as well (DiCicco-Bloom et al., 2006). These early-appearing brain differences probably account for the social, communicative, and cognitive patterns that appear to be unique to children with autism and are the focus of considerable research to relate specific unique behavior patterns to nerve pathways in the brain that may be compromised by the abnormal brain structures.

Several researchers have identified early behaviors that distinguish children who will be identified with autism from their typical peers. These include decreased synchrony (turn-taking) during interactions with their mothers at 4 months of age (Yirmiya et al., 2006), less eye contact, poorer visual tracking, poor orienting to name, inconsistent imitation (Zwaigenbaum, Bryson, Roberts, Brian, & Szatmari, 2005), and an overfocused pattern of sensation and attention, marked by overreactivity to stimuli, perseverative behavior and interests, overfocused attention, and unusually keen memory (Liss, Saulnier, Fein, & Kinsbourne, 2006). Joint attention, an important milestone following Vygotsky's theory of development, also appears to be impaired in dyads of adult and child with autism. Schertz and Odom (2004) define joint attention as "coordinating attention to an event or object with another individual, sharing interest and social engagement, and showing an understanding that the partner is sharing the same focus" (p. 42).

It is easy to understand, based on the characteristics described above, why children with autism might learn less than children who can interact in more typical ways with a stimulating environment. In a comparison of infants who were at high risk for autism (i.e., having a sibling with autism places a child at higher risk) and low risk (Landa & Garrett-Mayer, 2006), performance was evaluated at 6, 14, and 24 months on various measures of early learning. No significant differences were noted at 6 months. At 14 months, the high-risk group did worse on all scales except visual recognition. At 24 months, the high-risk group did more poorly on all measures. The second year of life appears to be particularly vulnerable to disruptions in developmental progress.

Executive functions have been proposed as a core problem in individuals with autism. These functions are controlled by specific structures in the frontal area of the brain and include planning, working memory, impulse control, inhibition of responses, flexibility of thinking, and prioritization, initiation, and monitoring of actions. Children with autism show deficits in some of these functions (e.g., poor memory for complex visual and verbal information and spatial working memory vs. verbal working memory and recognition memory), based on the limited tests available to assess performance (Williams, Goldstein, & Minshew, 2006). The limits to our current knowledge about specific performance of children with autism on executive function led Hill (2004) to conclude that "more detailed research is needed to fractionate the executive system in autism by assessing a wide range of executive functions as well as their neuroanatomical correlates in the same individuals across the lifespan" (p. 26).

:: STRATEGIES FOR ASSESSMENT OF COGNITIVE DEVELOPMENT

The systematic collection of data on young children with special needs is driven by several factors. First, special education laws require that children meet certain criteria to be eligible for special education services in the intellectual disability or developmental delay categories. These criteria are discussed in chapter 1 and, at least in part, require measurable and standardized information. Furthermore, IDEA provides for periodic formal reassessment to determine the need for modifying goals and objectives and to determine a child's continued eligibility for special education services.

Second, evidence-based practice demands that the professional and program be accountable for demonstrating that intervention is effective. By collecting baseline data (i.e., assessing prior to the start of intervention), and then assessing periodically during the course of intervention, one can demonstrate the child's longitudinal progress. (Note that, in the absence of a control group—that is, a similar group of children that receives no intervention—there is no definitive proof that progress is not due to maturation rather than to intervention.) Frequent informal assessment (e.g., review of lesson outcomes) allows the interventionist to change strategies to maximize child outcomes.

Additional benefits of formal and informal assessment are discussed in chapter 8.

Types of Cognitive Assessment

Useful information about a child's level of cognitive development can be collected through a number of useful and acceptable approaches.

Developmental Assessment   These types of instruments compare a child against a number of accepted developmental milestones. These instruments most often are used for screening purposes rather than to clearly define areas of cognitive strength and weakness. In most cases, cognition is but one of several developmental domains assessed. The *Gesell Developmental Schedule* was one of the first of these types of instruments. Others in common use include the *Denver Developmental Screening Test* and the *Early Screening Inventory.*

Standardized Cognitive Assessment   These instruments are administered under well-controlled conditions and results are compared to a normative group. Unfortunately, the performance of young children is strongly influenced by emotional state and recent experiences, which may contribute to unstable scores. In addition, these instruments rarely include children in the normative group who share the same specific disabilities and characteristics as the children who are being tested. These instruments also are founded on a theoretical model of what constitutes cognition. Examples of standardized cognitive instruments are the *Stanford-Binet Intelligence Scale*, the *Bayley Scales of Infant Development II*, and the *Wechsler Preschool and Primary Scale of Intelligence III*.

Dynamic Assessment   This approach grows out of Vygotsky's theory. Specific learning experiences are embedded within the assessment process and the child's response to the experiences is measured. What is actually being measured, following this model, is the efficiency and speed with which the child learns how to learn. This procedure is described nicely by Tzuriel (2000).

Curriculum-Based Assessment   Macy, Bricker, & Squires (2005) support the use of this approach to determine eligibility of children for special services. The main benefit of this type of assessment (often called *authentic assessment*) is that children's skill repertoires are assessed in familiar environments and performance is linked to programmatic efforts. Many early childhood curricula have been developed that include an assessment component for cognitive skills. Some of these are the *Hawaii Early Learning Profile* (HELP), the *Assessment, Evaluation, and Programming System* (AEPS), and the *Carolina Curriculum* series. The reader is referred to Volume 28(1) of the *Journal of Early Intervention* for a comprehensive discussion of this type of testing.

Play-Based Assessment   This type of assessment involves structured play settings during which young children engage with a number of specifically selected materials. Play-based assessment may be considered a subset of **ecological assessment** or **naturalistic observation**. The former approach examines the interrelationships among the child, the family, and the environment in order to plan interventions that will enhance or normalize these interrelationships. The latter approach, compared to testing a child in an isolated or contrived setting, is based on observation of the child in a number of settings familiar to him. The observer might, for example, be looking at how the child learns from experiences, at problem-solving skills, and at the level of activities and objects that the child selects or with which he interacts.

Other Assessment Approaches   Joint attention has been discussed earlier as an important cognitive milestone for young children. Its presence or absence is significant from a diagnostic perspective. For a more comprehensive discussion of joint attention, see the special issue (Volume 8) of *Triad Research Reader* (available at *www. TRIADatVanderbilt.com*) or Campbell (2002). Many Piagetian practitioners advocate the use of tests of conservation or the three-mountain problem as ways to assess cognitive development. While still in the experimental phase, a habituation paradigm has been used to demonstrate visual processing abilities of infants. Using this model, infants are exposed repeatedly to a visual stimulus. There is a decrease in attention (habituation measured by gaze and heart rate) with repeated presentations. A modification of the stimulus is then presented. An increase in attention and faster heart rate indicate that the infant recognized differences between the new stimulus and the original stimulus. This dishabituation response is thought to reflect maturity and integrity of the visual processing mechanism and a measure of cognitive ability.

:: FACILITATING COGNITIVE DEVELOPMENT

Children are born to learn. From their first noisy expression of hearty crying, they are storing and using information to make simple decisions. It is only when new information is no longer available in a form the child can use that cognitive development slows. This may represent an attitude of neglect on the part of the caregiver, for the nature of all children is to take advantage of the learning opportunities in their environment. Infants explore tactual stimuli with their hands, feet, and mouths, and slow their movements to listen to new sounds. Children with visual impairments gravitate toward auditory stimuli and children with hearing impairments toward those visual and tactile cues in their environment that carry new information. Children with mental retardation attend to complex stimuli around them when the input is simplified and clarified. In all situations in which a child is in an environment where he is unable to participate independently, the abilities of the teacher and caregiver grow in importance.

Many early intervention programs are founded on the belief that, if children are busy, they are learning. Paper and crayons, puzzles, pegboards, and shape boxes are placed before a child to stimulate learning. The teacher returns periodically to see whether the child has finished the task. When the paper is full of crayon marks, the puzzle pieces are in place, a peg fills each hole, or the shapes rest securely in the container, the child is praised for having learned. Has the teacher missed valuable opportunities to facilitate learning? Unquestionably!

With all young children, but particularly with those who are disabled, learning cannot be left to chance. We know, by studying children who are disadvantaged, that undesirable consequences result from poor caregiving strategies and a disorganized environment. We also know the benefits of a sound home environment. The distinctions between high and low quality in a child's home life also can be made in an educational program. As goes the parent, so goes the quality of the child's home life. Similarly, as goes the teacher, so goes the quality of the child's educational program. Fancy facilities and elaborate equipment may enhance a good program, but they cannot create one. An orientation toward the *way* a child does something rather than *what* he does is the basic approach that provides a cognitively stimulating environment.

In light of the glut of educational materials on the market today—some of which are promoted particularly for young children with disabilities—it is easy to conclude that equipment and curricular materials are the most important factors in facilitating cognition. But such is not the case. Materials are not as important to the early interventionist as sound guidance and a rock-solid understanding of development.

The early interventionist must be proficient in understanding cognitive development.

Focusing on the Process

Although there are dozens of manuals on the market that contain teaching-learning activities for young children with special needs, they are of limited value to a limited audience. They may be helpful to educational technicians who lack the flexibility or the authority to tailor their approach to individual children's needs. They also may be useful for interventionists seeking ideas around which to develop their own activities. Restricting themselves to teaching by the numbers, however, may mean that their focus is on accomplishing an activity rather than on how children process information as the activity is presented.

Education is often more concerned with the product than with the process of learning. Is it any wonder, then, that children have difficulty applying concepts and skills in different appropriate situations? In the vignette at the beginning of the chapter, Carrie would have produced a very colorful carton that she might have used for storage or that might have been hung from the ceiling as a mobile. She then would have gone on to another activity. With the minimal intervention of the teacher in the learning process, however, it is more likely that Carrie will now experiment with mixing other colors of paint. She may mix them in different proportions and begin to experiment with controlling color shades and tones. She may even extend the concept to mixing fluids or different colors of sand, thereby learning other principles about the attributes of matter.

Skills of the Interventionist

Good interventionists and caregivers are notable for their consistent and nurturing approach with children. Beyond that, however, they exhibit specific skills that are particularly effective in facilitating cognitive development. These skills are useful with all children, but their application may differ when the child is disabled.

Good intervention begins with discovery of the child's assets. Box 5.2 provides a sample of a "discovery activity." Such activities help the caregiver learn about how the young and developmentally young child receives and responds to different types of stimuli. (Additional activities are included at the end of the chapter in Appendix A.) This process involves a number of factors that turns observation into prescriptive intervention for optimal cognitive development.

Use Materials and Activities That Catch and Sustain a Child's Interest As discussed earlier, attention is a prerequisite for learning. To attract a child's attention to a specific object or task, we must win the competition with many other stimuli in the environment that are also vying for the child's attention. The primary consideration is appropriate positioning of the child. Equipment should be modified or created to place the child in a position in which he is most free to move and most in contact with his surroundings. Stimuli can then be modified to maximize the child's awareness.

With very young children and children with severe disabilities, increasing the intensity of a stimulus may be sufficient to draw their attention. Loud sounds may improve auditory attention, bright colors and lights may attract visual attention, and

---

BOX 5.2   SAMPLE DISCOVERY ACTIVITIES

Objective: To Find Ways Your Baby Uses Her Hearing.

Most babies like to listen. How does *your* baby use her hearing? Do these activities to find out . . .

1. Use a rattle, bell, or some other noise maker (see Objective 2B, Activity 2 for ideas on making rattles).
   A. Hold the rattle out of your baby's sight, but far from her ear (your arm's length). Shake it, sometimes loud and sometimes gently. What does your baby do? Check as many as you see.
   — Baby looks away or pulls back   — Baby makes faces   — Baby yawns
   — Doesn't seem to hear;   — Baby gets still   — Baby moves more
      no change in activity
   — Baby looks for the sound   — Baby smiles   — Baby fusses
   B. Now move it closer to your baby's ear (6″ to 12″). Again, shake it loudly sometimes and gently sometimes. What does your baby do? Check as many as you see.
   — Baby looks away or pulls back   — Baby makes faces   — Baby yawns
   — Doesn't seem to hear;   — Baby gets still   — Baby moves more
      no change in activity
   — Baby looks for the sound   — Baby smiles   — Baby fusses
   C. Now move it right next to your baby's ear. Again, shake it loudly sometimes and gently sometimes. What does your baby do? Check as many as you see.
   — Baby looks away or pulls back   — Baby makes faces   — Baby yawns
   — Doesn't seem to hear;   — Baby gets still   — Baby moves more
      no change in activity
   — Baby looks for the sound   — Baby smiles   — Baby fusses

Does your baby seem to hear better when things are:
__ far __ close (6″ to 12″) __ very close (right next to ear)
How can you tell? _____
_____

Do *you* like a loud noise in your ear? Probably not.
Did your baby like it when you made a loud noise right next to her ear? __ Yes __ No

Adapted from: Sanders, W. S., Baskin, C. H., & Umansky, W. (1987). Discovering your baby: Activities for the new parent. Authors: Athens, GA.

varied textures may enhance attention for grasping and manipulation. With older children and children who are less severely disabled, novel variations of familiar activities are most likely to hold their interest. The hazard in using the same familiar tasks over and over is that, although children may retain the skill longer as a result of overlearning, responses reach only the very basic rote level of cognition. There are decreasing incentive and challenge to apply skills in new ways to accomplish the same task. When an activity is changed slightly during subsequent presentations, benefits may include accelerated cognitive development and better generalization of skills to varied situations. Play at a sand table becomes even more exciting and stimulating when new measuring devices and containers are substituted for the familiar ones. The listening center holds a child's interest when there are new sounds and pictures to match. A new puppet that requires finer manipulations than the old ones do may visit the dress-up area and stimulate many new skills and concepts.

Select Activities with Intrinsic Termination Points One interventionist prided herself on integrating prevocational skills into her preschool classroom. She had the children sand a block of wood for 10 minutes each day, after which they punched holes in soft leather for 5 minutes. The utter futility of the task would be obvious if one watched the children's attention meander the entire time. The teacher made two fatal errors. First, she provided a task totally out of context to what is meaningful to children. Had she shown the children a toy wagon or a set of blocks that would result from their efforts, the activity might have had some merit. Her second error was not building in a point of successful termination. Time, an extraneous element in the activity, is not an appropriate reason for ending a task. What logic is there for a child when, working through a task, the teacher says that time is up? Each task should be in the form of a problem or challenge for which the child must find a resolution. An activity should not be ended until there is resolution and the child is aware of it. With the sanding task, the teacher could have colored an area on the block with a marker. The children could then have sanded until the marker's color was no longer visible. With the hole punching, she could have outlined holes in geometric patterns, numbers, or letters, and the children could have stopped when the pattern was complete.

In teaching children to control their own behavior, it is desirable that they rely on the teacher as little as possible for continuous directions. Even though it is a good teaching strategy to provide guidance, feedback, and reinforcement to each child, it is equally important to offer developmentally appropriate activities that provide the child with feedback from his own performance and the knowledge of when he has solved the problem. This best occurs, of course, with activities of the self-testing variety. With these, a child knows whether he has performed the task correctly and, if not, he can try another approach immediately. During this phase and at the completion of the task, the teacher can investigate the cognitive processes leading to the child's solution. This is a difficult but necessary skill for interventionists to master.

Use Language as a Cognitive Tool A substantial body of literature supports the close link between language and thought. For a child to perceive relationships and attain development of concepts, he must have labels to represent objects, people, and feelings. The teacher must provide these word labels for the child until he is able to use them to synthesize thoughts and to solve problems. The interventionist who names new objects for a child, describes what that child or other children are doing, gives names to feelings, and discusses the relationships among things and events in the child's environment is contributing to language competence in the child and, therefore, to development of cognitive skills.

Ask the Child Questions That Provide Challenge and Satisfaction   When a child has created a clay structure or paste-up and the teacher responds with "What's that?" it gives the child a clear message. What the child thought to be a realistic imitation of an object or person is not good enough to be identified as such by the teacher. A more reinforcing and thought-provoking response, whether the teacher recognizes the child's creation or not, is "I like what you made. Tell me about it." This approach gives the child a feeling of worth, while allowing the teacher to investigate the development of the child's skills.

The master teacher acknowledges a child's efforts and extracts the child's problem-solving strategy.

The key ingredients in a good teacher's response to a child's task are acknowledgement of the child's efforts and extraction of the child's problem-solving strategy. Was it just luck that allowed a child with a visual impairment to place the round shape in the round slot and not the square or triangular slot, or did the child use a particular strategy to place it correctly? "Good, Joan. Why does that round shape go where you put it?" the teacher should ask.

With children who are nonverbal, the challenge to the teacher is greater. In these cases, the teacher may verbalize through the problem-solving process and demonstrate the strategies leading to a correct response. For example: "Good. This pile has pictures of things we eat and this pile has pictures of things we eat with." Or, "Let's do it again so that one pile has things we eat and another pile has things we eat with. I'll do the first ones; now you do the rest."

Questions should be nonjudgmental and purposeful—not "Why did you do it like that?" but rather "Why do you think those go together?" Put yourself in the place of a child. Given a task to perform, consider the logic involved and the variety of ways to perform the task. Then try to determine the child's approach to performing the task by asking questions that reveal the child's strategy.

Allow for Learning Through Discovery and for the Child to Choose Learning Tasks   In European schools, one rarely finds materials stored away in cabinets or on high shelves. The Montessori approach, begun in Italy, advocates the availability and accessibility of materials to children in the classroom. Through exploration and teacher guidance, children learn what materials are on and off limits to them, how to use new materials, and how to select materials of interest to them.

Discovery is important in the development of cognitive skills. Through exploration, children assimilate information about the order of their surroundings. In many programs, teachers demonstrate how to use new and challenging pieces of equipment, such as graded cylinders or matrix puzzles. They give children an opportunity to work on the task with guidance and then place it in an accessible location so the children may use it at other times. This move toward nurturing independence can work very well with young children with disabilities. However, when interventionists tell children what to do or give them every task to perform, they deprive the children of the rich developmental opportunities that discovery and independent decision making provide.

Some children have difficulty selecting tasks. The following progression indicates how children at different developmental levels can be challenged to participate in activity selection.

Barbara Schwartz/Merrill

Children learn more quickly and retain information better when a multisensory approach is used—one combining two or more senses in the learning activity.

1. Let's paint. (noncommunicative child)
2. Do you want to paint? (verbal or nonverbal response acceptable)
3. Do you want to paint or play at the sand table? (verbal, imitative response; the list of choices can be expanded)
4. Show me what you would like to do now. (nonverbal, open-ended response)
5. Tell me what you would like to do now. (verbal, open-ended response)

Children at any level of development can be included in the scheme of selecting and discovering through their own initiative. For this to occur, they must feel secure moving about in their environment (aided by consistency of objects' locations), and materials must be accessible to them. Finally, the interventionist can help children to discover how materials are used, where they are located, and what pleasures they hold. For example, children with visual impairments should be able to expect that their tactual materials are arranged on specific shelves, with the least difficult items on the lower shelves. Similar patterns may be established for children with other disabilities.

Identify and Use Each Child's Primary Input Mode   All learners show a differential preference for receiving and processing information; some learn more effectively from auditory input, and others from tactile or visual input. Children with disabilities are not excluded from this learning characteristic, but if the preferential input mode is the locus of the impairment, learning may be considerably more difficult. The adaptability of young children makes it incumbent upon the interventionist to take advantage of input channels through which accurate information is likely to be received and to nurture and stimulate the secondary input channels that are the site of the impairment.

Young children and children with severe disabilities learn initially through movement. The kinesthetic stimulation of one's arms and legs moving in space, along with watching them move and hearing the sounds of objects they touch or strike, offers the initial learning experiences for a child. Physical movement remains an important mode of learning throughout life.

Education tends to become more and more auditory as a child progresses through formal schooling. Many children discover that they learn more from textbooks or field trips than they do from lectures. Children with disabilities show the same individual differences in how they learn. Consequently, interventionists must be flexible in their approaches. One child may learn a task quickly with a verbal explanation. Another child may require demonstration as well as verbal explanation or may have to be moved through the task, hand-over-hand. Interventionists should, therefore, give careful consideration to how children process different forms of input and use this information in their instructional strategies.

Structuring the Curriculum

The most important criterion for program success is a staff made up of people who know how to teach. Nevertheless, interventionists also must be able to organize the educational program so that it includes aspects that are most beneficial to children's intellectual growth. A program should help children progress from a concrete to a symbolic level in classification, space and number, and seriation operations, from which all concepts are constructed. These may be used as the focus for activities in early intervention programs. The teacher also can organize materials based on the same principles. Puzzles can be ordered by difficulty based not only on the number of pieces, but also on the spatial complexities of the position of pieces. Different groups of objects and pictures can be available for children to sort or classify. Some groups can contain objects that are very different and other groups can have objects or pictures with only subtle differences. Children can be given dolls to hold that are progressively bigger in size or can be asked to draw another one that is smaller, and then one that's even smaller. Containers at the water table can be color-coded to correspond with the daily color of the water to which food dye has been added. An infant can be given different-sized bottles from which to drink his milk.

> The structure and application of a curriculum are critical to a young child's cognitive development— but the most important element is good teaching!

If activities are considered in terms of the cognitive processes they require or nurture, program planning can yield more individualization and challenge for children. Chapter 9 provides suggestions for specific curriculum resources.

:: TECHNOLOGY IN ASSESSMENT AND INTERVENTION

Using technology is a cognitive task. The child's awareness that pushing a button causes something to happen is an indicator of understanding cause-effect relationships. This technology has been adapted using microswitches to determine cognitive skills of children with various disabilities. Schweigert (1989) found that a deaf-blind child who was severely orthopedically impaired and who had previously shown no contingent awareness of the environment achieved the targeted behavior of activating a switch to receive a reward. Fell et al. (1994) used this approach with a pad that had pressure switches linked to a computer. In a preliminary study with a 5-month-old infant with hydrocephalus, club feet, and poor muscle tone, the infant increased the frequency of head-rolling, leg-lifting, and kicking to produce digitized sounds and in response to his mother's voice. The use of this technology aided in assessing the child's understanding of cause and effect. Furthermore, it revealed an ability of the child to control the environment in positive ways, which is a developmental task of infancy and an important goal of early intervention.

Beyond the simple application of the very complex technology described above, there is an endless array of proprietary software and hardware to evaluate knowledge of and teach the breadth and depth of cognitive skills from simple to complex. Add the capabilities of a touch-screen and spoken instructions and the child can respond to "Touch red" or "Touch the green triangle" or "Show where the dog sleeps." With spoken feedback (i.e., "Good, that's the green triangle" or "Try again") and repetition, the child has endless opportunities to succeed. Following principles of computer-assisted instruction, many computer programs will move a child along to new skills once one is mastered, or continue with novel presentations to teach a skill that is very challenging for a child. The presentation of tasks is based on the child's level of learning: acquisition, proficiency or fluency, maintenance, generalization, or application (Heller, 2004). An excellent example of this type of software with touchscreen technology is *The Discrete Trial Trainer* (see *www.DTTrainer.com* for further information on the latest version), which offers many options for presentation of visual and auditory stimuli, types of prompts and reinforcers, the order of training sequences, and ways for determining skill level and evaluating progress.

Technology provides the opportunity for heightened motivation of the learner and, often, for self-guided instruction. With greater access to home computers and decreasing costs of hardware and software (some programs are free on the Internet!), many more families can extend the structured part of learning time for their child. As a consequence, young children with special needs have the potential to learn more and at earlier ages than their cohorts of just a decade ago. This will prepare them to address the challenges of their future with greater security and competence.

SUMMARY

For all children, the road to understanding and using complex concepts is quite similar. Children first learn about their worlds by their looks, smells, sounds, tastes, and feel. By seeing how different people and objects in their environments interact, children begin to formulate basic constructs of their worlds based on the simple relationships they perceive. As they add word labels to their experiences and observations, their understanding of the world increases significantly.

A disability may interrupt the cognitive process in four ways: It may interfere with a child's ability to attend to a stimulus, as in a neurological or sensory impairment; it may impede reception of potentially valuable stimuli, as in a visual or hearing impairment; it may disrupt the storage and processing of information, as in brain damage associated with mental retardation; and it may interfere with a child's ability to express his cognitive abilities, as in speech disorders and orthopedic impairments. A Piagetian framework was emphasized in this chapter because it helps us to interpret children's cognitive development even in light of these extreme differences. Furthermore, it provides the interventionist with a foundation from which to plan a program based on a child's current level of performance rather than on his chronological age.

The skills that have been described are caregiver skills and cannot be considered the province of the interventionist alone. Through home visits, parent participation in the classroom, and other broad strategies that include all of the caregivers, the child will be the beneficiary of an environment that has the potential to maximize intellectual development.

REVIEW QUESTIONS AND DISCUSSION POINTS

1. Discuss Piaget's theory of development and its relationship to young children with special needs.
2. How does each type of disability potentially influence cognitive development of the young child?

3. Compare three theories of development discussed in this chapter in relation to young children with special needs.
4. What factors contribute to development of cognitive skills in an early intervention program?

RECOMMENDED RESOURCES

Websites

Cognitive Development in Young Children with Down Syndrome: Developmental Strengths, Developmental Weaknesses (Riverbend Down Syndrome Parent Support Group)
http://altonweb.com/cs/downsyndrome/index.html

Cognitive Development Theories
http://www.education.indiana.edu/~p540/webcourse/develop.html

Publications and Other Media

Bybee, R. W., & Sund, R. B. (1990). *Piaget for educators* (2nd ed.). Prospect Heights, IL: Waveland Press.

High/Scope Educational Research Foundation (2008). *High/Scope preschool curriculum.* (600 North River Street, Ypsilanti, MI 48198.)

Johnson-Martin, N. M., Jens, K. G., Attermeier, S. M., & Hacker, B. J. (1991). *The Carolina curriculum for infants and toddlers with special needs* (2nd ed.). Baltimore: Brookes.

Kamii, C., & Ewing, J. K. (1996). Basing teaching on Piaget's constructivism. *Childhood Education, 72,* 260–264.

Leong, D. J., & Bedrova, E. (1996). *Tools of the mind: A Vygotskian approach to early childhood education.* Upper Saddle River, NJ: Merrill/Prentice Hall.

Singer, D. G., & Ravenson, T. (1996). *A Piaget primer: How a child thinks.* New York: Plume Books.

REFERENCES

Bailey, D. B., Hebbeler, K., Spiker, D., Scarborough, A., Mallik, S., & Nelson, L. (2005). Thirty-six-month outcomes for families of children who have disabilities and participated in early intervention. *Pediatrics, 116*(6), 1346–1352.

Beckett, C., Maughan, B., Rutter, M., Castle, J., Colvert, E., Groothues, et al. (2006). Do the effects of early severe deprivation on cognition persist into adolescence?: Findings from the English and Romanian adoptees study. *Child Development, 77*(3), 696–711.

Bernstein, D. M., Loftus, G. R., & Meltzoff, A. N. (2005). Object identification in preschool children and adults. *Developmental Science, 8,* 151–161.

Bigelow, A. E. (2003). The development of joint attention in blind infants. *Developmental Psychopathology, 15*(2), 259–275.

Bono, K. E., Bolzani-Dinehart, L. H., Claussen, A. H., Scott, K. G., Mundy, P. C., & Katz, L. F. (2005). Early intervention with children prenatally exposed to cocaine: Expansion with multiple cohorts. *Journal of Early Intervention, 27*(4), 268–284.

Booth, J. R., Burman, D. D., Meyer, J. R., Lei, Z., Trommer, B. L., Davenport, N. D., et al. (2003). Neural development of selective attention and response inhibition. *Neuro-Image, 20,* 737–751.

Bornstein, M. H., Lamb, M. E., & Teti, D. M. (2002). *Development in infancy: An introduction.* Mahwah, NJ: Lawrence Erlbaum Associates.

Boucher, J. (1998). The prerequisites for language acquisition: evidence from cases of anomalous language development. In P. Carruthers & J. Boucher (Eds.), *Language and thought: Interdisciplinary themes* (pp. 55–75). Cambridge: Cambridge University Press.

Brekke, B., Williams, J. E., & Tait, P. (1974). The acquisition of conservation of weight by visually impaired children. *Journal of Genetic Psychology, 125,* 89–97.

Bremner, J. G., Johnson, S. P., Slater, A., Mason, U., Foster, K., Cheshire, A., et al. (2005). Conditions for young infants' perception of object trajectories. *Child Development, 76*(5), 1029–1043.

Brian, J. A., Landry, R., Szatmari, P., Niccols, A., & Bryson, S. (2003). Habituation in high-risk infants: Reliability and patterns of responding. *Infant and Child Development, 12*(4), 387–394.

Broadbent, D. (1958). *Perception and communication.* London: Pergamon Press.

Buckner, R. L. (2003). Functional-anatomic correlates of control processes in memory. *The Journal of Neuroscience, 23*(10), 3999–4004.

Campbell, F. A., Pungello, E. P., Miller-Johnson, S., Burchinal, M., & Ramey, C.T. (2001). The development of cognitive and academic abilities: Growth curves from an early childhood educational experiment. *Developmental Psychology, 37,* 231–242.

Campbell, J. (2002). *Reference and consciousness.* Oxford: Oxford University Press.

Carroll, J. M., Snowling, M. J., Hulme, C., & Stevenson, J. (2003). The development of phonological awareness in preschool children. *Developmental Psychology, 39*(5), 913–923.

Carver, L. J., & Bauer, P. J. (2001). Memory in infants: The emergence of long- and short-term explicit memory in infancy. *Journal of Experimental Psychology (General), 130,* 726–747.

Casey, B. J., Tottenham, N., Liston, C., & Durston, S. (2005). Imaging the developing brain: What have we learned about cognitive development? *Trends in Cognitive Sciences, 9*(3), 104–110.

Celeste, M. (2002). A survey of motor development for infants and young children with visual impairments. *Journal of Visual Impairment & Blindness, 96,* 169–175.

Chapman, R. S., & Hesketh, L. J. (2001). Language, cognition, and short-term memory in individuals with Down syndrome. *Down Syndrome Research and Practice, 7*(1), 1–7.

Chervin, R. D., Rizicka, D. L., Giordani, B. J., Weatherly, R. A., Dillon, J. E., Hodes, E. K., et al. (2006). Sleep-disordered breathing, behavior, and cognition in children before and after adenotonsillectomy. *Pediatrics, 117*(4), 769–778.

Choudhury, N., & Gorman, K. S. (2000). The relationship between sustained attention and cognitive performance in 17–24-month old toddlers. *Infant and Child Development, 9,* 127–146.

Colombo, J., Shaddy, D. J, Richman, W. A., Maikranz, J. M., & Blaga, O. M. (2004). The developmental course of habituation in infancy and preschool outcome. *Infancy, 5*(1), 1–38.

Corbett, S. S., & Drewett, R. F. (2004). To what extent is failure to thrive in infancy associated with poorer cognitive development? A review and meta-analysis. *Journal of Child Psychology and Psychiatry, 45*(3), 641–654.

Courage, M. L., Reynolds, G. D., & Richards, J. E. (2006). Infants' attention to patterned stimuli: Developmental change from 3 to 12 months of age. *Child Development, 77*(3), 680–695.

Courtin, C., & Melot, A. M. (2005). Metacognitive development of deaf children: Lessons from the appearance-reality and false belief tasks. *Developmental Science, 8*(1), 16–25.

Curtis, M. (2004). Down link. *Dartmouth Medicine.* Winter edition.

Dalen, M. (2001). The state of knowledge of foreign adoptions. Retrieved February 7, 2007, from *http://www.community.com/adoption/adopt/research.html*

Davis, D. W., Chang, F., Burns, B. M., Robinson, J., & Dossett, D. (2004). Low lead levels and attention regulation in children from Head Start. *Development Medicine and Child Neurology, 46,* 825–831.

DiCicco-Bloom, E., Lord, C., Zwaigenbaum, L., Couchesne, E., Dager, S. R., Schmitz, C., et al. (2006). The developmental neurophysiology of autism spectrum disorder. *The Journal of Neuroscience, 26*(26), 6897–6906.

Dunst, C. J. (2003). Social-emotional consequences of response-contingent learning opportunities. *Bridges, 1*(1), 1–17.

Evans, G. W. (2004). The environment of childhood poverty. *American Psychologist, 59*(2), 77–92.

Fallone, G., Acebo, C., Seifer, R., & Carskadon, M. A. (2001). Effects of acute sleep restriction on behavior, sustained attention, and response inhibition in children. *Perceptual and Motor Skills, 93*, 213–229.

Fivaz-Depeursinge, E., Favez, N., & Frascarolo, F. (2005). Threesome intersubjectivity in infancy: A contribution to the development of self-awareness. *Psyche, 11*(6), 24–34.

Flavell, J. H. (2004). Theory-of-mind development: Retrospect and prospect. *Merrill-Palmer Quarterly, 50*(3), 274–290.

Friedman, J., & Pasnak, S. (1973). Attainment of classification and seriation concepts by blind children. *Education of the Visually Handicapped, 5*, 55–62.

Gibson, E. J., & Pick, A. D. (2003). *An ecological approach to perceptual learning and development.* New York: Oxford University Press.

Gindis, B. (2003). Remediation through education: Socio/cultural theory and children with special needs. In A. Kozulin, B. Gindis, V. S. Ageyez, & S. M. Miller (Eds.), *Vygotsky's educational theory in cultural context.* (pp. 200–222). Cambridge: Cambridge University Press.

Girbau, D. (2001). Children's referential communication failure. *Journal of Language and Social Psychology, 20*, 81–90.

Gogtay, N., Giedd, J. N., Lusk, L., Hayashi, K. M., Greenstein, D., Vaituzis, A. C., et al. (2004). Dynamic mapping of human cortical development during childhood through early adulthood. *Proceedings of the National Academy of Science, 101*, 8174–8179.

Gray, M., & Sanson, A. (2005). Growing up in Australia: The longitudinal study of Australian children. *Family Matters, 72*, 4–9.

Hack, M., Taylor, H. G., Drotar, D., Schlucter, M., Cartar, L., Andreias, L., et al. (2005). Chronic conditions, functional limitations, and special health care needs of school-age children born with extremely low-birth-weight in the 1990s. *Journal of the American Medical Association, 294*(3), 318–325.

Halbower, A. C., Degaonkar, M., Barker, P. B., Earley, C. J., Marcus, C. L., Smith, P. L., et al. (2006). Childhood obstructive sleep apnea associates with neuropsychological deficits and neuronal brain injury. *PLoS Medicine, 3*(8): e301 DOI: 10.1371/journal.pmend.0030301.

Happé, F. (2003). Cognition in autism: One defect or many? *Novartis Foundation Symposiums, 251*, 198–207.

Hauser-Cram, P., Warfield, M., Shonkoff, J. P., & Krauss, M. W. (2001). Children with disabilities: A longitudinal study of child development and parent well-being. *Monographs of the Society for Research in Child Development, 66*(3) (Serial No. 266).

Heller, K. W. (2004). Technology for assessment and intervention. In S. R. Hooper & W. Umansky (Eds.)., *Young children with special needs* (4th ed.) (pp. 188–223). Upper Saddle River, NJ: Pearson Education.

Henkin, Y., Sadeh, M., Kivity, S., Shabtai, E., Kishon-Rabin, L., & Gadoth, N. (2005). Cognitive function in idiopathic generalized epilepsy of childhood. *Developmental Medicine & Child Neurology, 47*, 126–132.

Hill, E. L. (2004). Executive dysfunction in autism. *Trends in Cognitive Science, 8*(1), 26–32.

Hiscock, H., Caterford, L., Ukoumunne, O. C., & Wake, M. (2007). Adverse associations of sleep problems in Australian preschoolers: National Population Study. *Pediatrics, 119*(1), 86–93.

Huang-Pollock, C. L., Carr, T. H., & Nigg, J. T. (2002). Development of selective attention: Perceptual load influences early versus late attentional selection in children and adults. *Developmental Psychology, 38*, 363–375.

Hutto, M. D. (2003). Latency to learn in contingency studies of young children with disabilities or developmental delays. *Bridges, 1*(2), 1–16.

Jarrold, C., & Baddeley, A. D. (2001). Short-term memory in Down syndrome: Applying the working memory model. *Down Syndrome Research and Practice, 7*(1), 17–23.

Kearsley, R. B. (1979). Iatrogenic retardation: A syndrome of learned incompetence. In R. B. Kearsley & I. E. Sigel (Eds.), *Infants at risk: Assessment of cognitive functioning.* (pp. 153–180) Hillsdale, NJ: Erlbaum.

Kim-Cohen, J., Caspi, A., Rutter, M., Tomas, M. P., & Moffitt, T. E. (2006). The caregiving environments provided to children by depressed mothers with or without an antisocial history. *American Journal of Psychiatry, 163*(6), 951–953.

Landa, R., & Garrett-Mayer, E. (2006). Development in infants with autism spectrum disorders: A prospective study. *Journal of Child Psychology and Psychiatry, 47*(6), 629–638.

Landry, S. H., Swank, P. R., Assel, M. A., Smith, K. E., & Vellet, S. (2001). Does early responsive parenting have a special importance for children's development or is consistency across early childhood necessary? *Developmental Psychology, 37*, 387–403.

Langley, M. B. (1980). *The teachable moment and the handicapped infant.* Reston, VA: ERIC Clearinghouse on Handicapped and Gifted Children.

Lauwerier, L., de Chouly de Lenclave, M. B., & Bailly, D. (2003). Hearing impairment and cognitive development. *Archives in Pediatrics, 10*(2), 140–146.

Lavatelli C. S. (1973). *Piaget's theory applied to an early childhood curriculum.* Nashua, NH: Delta Education, Inc.

Lawson, K. R., & Ruff, H. A. (2004). Early focused attention predicts outcome for children born prematurely. *Journal of Developmental and Behavioral Pediatrics, 25*(6), 399–406.

Lee, K. (2000). *Childhood cognitive development: The essential readings.* Oxford: Blackwell.

Leybaert, J., & D'Hondt, M. (2003). Neurolinguistic development in deaf children: The effect of early language experience. *International Journal of Audiology, 4* (Supplement 1), 34–40.

Lindquist, B., Carlsson, G., Persson, E. K., & Uvebrant, P. (2005). Learning disabilities in a population-based group of children with hydrocephalus. *Acta Paediatrica, 94*(7), 878–883.

Liss, M., Saulnier, C., Fein, D., & Kinsbourne, M. (2006). Sensory and attention abnormalities in autistic spectrum disorders. *Autism, 10*(2), 155–172.

Luthar, S. S. (2003). *Resilience and vulnerability: Adaptation in the context of childhood adversities.* New York: Cambridge University Press.

Maccoby, E. E., & Zellner, M. (1970). *Experiments in primary education: Aspects of Project Follow-Through.* New York: Harcourt Brace Jovanovich.

Macy, M. G., Bricker, D. D., & Squires, J. K. (2005). Validity and reliability of a curriculum-based assessment approach to determine eligibility for part C services. *Journal of Early Intervention, 28*(1), 1–16.

Mandler, J. M. (2004). Thought before language. *Trends in Cognitive Sciences, 8*(11), 508–513.

Mareschal, D., Plunkett, K., & Harris, P. (1999). A computational and neuropsychological account of object-oriented behaviors in infancy. *Developmental Science, 2,* 306–317.

Marschark, M. (2000). *Psychological development of deaf children.* Gloucestershire, England: Forest Books.

Maurer, D., Lewis, T. L., & Mondlich, C. J. (2005). Missing sights. Consequences for visual cognitive development. *Trends in Cognitive Science, 9*(3), 144–151.

Miles, B. (2003). Talking the language of the hands to the hands. *DB-Link.* Available online at *www.dblink.org/lib/hands.htm*

Mirolli, M., & Parisi, D. (2005). Language as an aid to categorization: A neural network model of language acquisition. In A. Cangelosi, G. Bugmann, & R. Borisyuk (Eds.), *Modeling language, cognition and action* (pp. 97–106). Singapore: World Scientific.

Moeller, M. P., & Schick, B. (2006). Relations between maternal input and theory of mind understanding in deaf children. *Child Development, 77*(3), 751–766.

Moore, M. K., & Meltzoff, A. N. (2004). Object permanence after a 24-hr delay and leaving the locale of disappearance:

The role of memory, space, and identity. *Developmental Psychology, 40*(4), 606–620.

Mulligan, G. M., & Flanagan, K. D. (2006). Age 2: Findings from the 2-year-old follow-up of the Early Childhood Longitudinal Study, birth cohort (ECLS-B). Available online at *http://nces.ed.gov/pubsearch/pubsinfo.asp?pubid =2006043*

Neath, I., & Surprenant, A. (2003). *Human memory.* Belmont, CA: Thomson Learning.

NICHD Early Child Care Research Network. (2003). Do children's attention processes mediate the link between family predictors and school readiness? *Developmental Psychology, 39*(3), 581–593.

NICHD Early Child Care Research Network. (2005). Predicting individual differences in attention, memory, and planning in first graders from experiences at home, child care, and school. *Developmental Psychology, 41*(1), 99–114

Oostrom, K. J., vanTeeseling, H., Smeets-Schouten, A., Peters, A. C. B., & Jenneken-Schinkel, A. (2005). Three to four years after diagnosis: Cognition and behavior in children with 'epilepsy only.' A prospective, controlled study. *Brain, 128*(7), 1546–1555.

Paavola, L., Kunnan, S., & Moilanen, I. (2005). Maternal responsiveness and infant intentional communication: Implications for the early communicative and linguistic development. *Child: Care, Health, and Development, 31*(6), 727–735.

Pasamanick, B., & Knobloch, H. (1966). Retrospective studies on the epidemiology of reproductive casualty: Old and new. *Merrill-Palmer Quarterly, 12,* 7–26.

Piaget, J. (1951). *Play, dreams and imitation in childhood.* New York: Norton.

Piaget, J. (1952). *The origins of intelligence in children.* New York: International Universities Press.

Piaget, J. (1954). *The construction of reality in the child.* New York: Basic Books.

Piaget, J., & Inhelder, B. (1969). *The psychology of the child.* New York: Basic Books.

Poland, M., & Legge, J. (2005). *Review of New Zealand longitudinal studies.* New Zealand: Families Commission.

Purser, H. R., & Jarrold, C. (2005). Impaired verbal short-term memory in Down syndrome reflects a capacity limitation rather than atypically rapid forgetting. *Journal of Experimental Child Psychology, 91*(1), 1–23.

Rajah, M. N., & McIntosh, A. R. (2005). Overlap in the functional neural systems involved in semantic and episodic memory retrieval. *Journal of Cognitive Neuroscience, 17,* 470–482.

Raymond-Speden, E., Tripp, G., Lawrence, B., & Holdaway, D. (2000). Intellectual, neuropsychological, and academic functioning in long-term survivors of leukemia. *Journal of Pediatric Psychology, 25*(2), 59–68.

Reynell, J. (1978). Developmental patterns of visually handicapped children. *Child: Care, Health, and Development, 4,* 291–303.

Reynolds, A. J., Ou, S., & Topitzes, J. D. (2004). Paths of effects of early childhood intervention on educational attainment and delinquency: A confirmatory analysis of the Chicago Child-Parent Centers. *Child Development, 75*(5), 1299–1338.

Ris, M. D., Dietrich, K. N., Succop, P. A., Berger, O. G., & Bornschein, R. L. (2004). Early exposure to lead and neuropsychological outcome in adolescence. *Journal of the International Neuropsychological Society, 10,* 261–270.

Rochat, P. R. (2005). The emergence of self-awareness as *co-awareness* in early child development. *Psyche, 11*(6), 3–23.

Rodrigo, M. J., Gonzalez, A., Ato, M., Rodriguez, G., deVega, M., & Muneton, M. (2006). Co-development of child-mother gestures over the second and the third years. *Infant and Child Development, 15*(1), 1–17.

Rutter, M., Moffitt, T. E., & Caspi, A. (2006). Gene-environment interplay and psychopathology: Multiple varieties but real effects. *Journal of Child Psychology and Psychiatry, 47*(3–4), 226–261.

Ryan, R. M., Martin, A., & Brooks-Gunn, J. (2006). Is one good parent good enough? Patterns of mother and father parenting and child cognitive outcomes at 24 and 36 months. *Parenting, 6*(2–3), 211–228.

Sameroff, A. J., & Chandler, M. J. (1975). Reproductive risk and the continuum of caretaking casualty. In F. D. Horowitz, M. Hetherington, S. Scarr-Salapetek, & G. Siegel (Eds.), *Review of child development research* (Vol. 4, pp. 187–244). Chicago: University of Chicago Press.

Sameroff, A. J., McDonough, S. C., & Rosenblum, K. L. (Eds.) (2005). *Treating parent-infant relationship problems: Strategies for intervention.* New York: Guilford Publications.

Schatz, J. (2004). Brief report: Academic attainment in children with sickle cell disease. *Journal of Pediatric Psychology, 29*(8), 627–633.

Schertz, H. H., & Odom, S. L. (2004). Joint attention and early intervention with autism: A conceptual framework and promising approaches. *Journal of Early Intervention, 27*(1), 42–54.

Schick, B., deVilliers, J., deVilliers, P., & Hoffmeister, B. (2002). Theory of mind: Language and cognition in deaf children. *The ASHA Leader Online.* Retrieved February 7, 2007, from *www.asha.org/about/publications/leader-online/archives/2002/q4/f021203.htm*

Schorr, E. A., Fox, N. A., van Wassenhove, V., & Knudsen, E. I. (2005). Auditory-visual fusion in speech perception in children with cochlear implants. *Proceedings of the National Academy of Sciences of the United States of America, 102*(51), 18748–18750.

Schutte, A. R., & Spencer, J. P. (2002). Generalizing the dynamic field theory of the A-and-B error beyond infancy: Three-year-olds' delay- and experience-dependent location memory biases. *Child Development, 73,* 377–404.

Schweigert, P. (1989). Use of microswitch technology to facilitate social contingency awareness as a basis for early communication skills. *Augmentative & Alternative Communication, 5*(3), 192–198.

Seitz, J., Jenni, O. G., Molinari, L., Caflisch, J., Largo, R. H., & Latal Hajnal, B. (2006). Correlations between motor performance and cognitive functions in children born <125 g. at school age. *Neuropediatrics, 37*(1), 6–12.

Sheinkopf, S., Mundy, P., Claussen, A., & Willoughby, J. (2004). Infant joint attention and 36-month behavioral outcome in cocaine-exposed infants. *Development and Psychopathology, 16,* 273–293.

Simeonsson, R. J. (2006). Defining and classifying disability in children (Appendix C). *Workshop on disability in America: A new look—summary and background papers,* pp. 67–87. Washington, DC: The National Academy of Sciences.

Slamecka, N. (1968). An examination of trace storage in free recall. *Journal of Experimental Psychology, 76,* 504–513.

Smith, K. E., Landry, S. H., & Swank, P. R. (2006). The role of early maternal responsiveness in supporting school-aged cognitive development for children who vary in birth status. *Pediatrics, 117*(5), 1608–1617.

Smith, L. B., & Gasser, M. (2005). The development of embodied cognition: Six lessons from babies. *Artificial Life, 11,* 13–30.

Smyke, A. T., Dumitrescu, B. A., & Zeanah, C. H. (2002). Attachment disturbances in young children. I. The continuum of caretaking casualty. *Journal of the American Academy of Child and Adolescent Psychiatry, 41*(8), 972–982.

Stiers, P., Vanderkelen, R., Vanneste, G., Coene, S., DeRammelaere, M., & Vandenbussche, E. (2002). Visual-perceptual impairment in a random sample of children with cerebral palsy. *Developmental Medicine & Child Neurology, 44*(6), 370–382.

Tamis-LeMonda, C. S., Bornstein, M. H., & Baumwell, L. (2001). Maternal responsiveness and children's achievement of language milestones. *Child Development, 72*(3), 748–767.

Tulving, E. (1968). Theoretical issues in free recall. In T. Dixon & D. Horton (Eds.), *Verbal behavior and general behavior theory* (pp. 2–36). Upper Saddle River, NJ: Prentice Hall.

Tzuriel, D. (2000). Dynamic assessment of young children: Educational and intervention perspectives. *Educational Psychology Review, 12*(4), 385–435.

Vicari, S. (2004). Memory development and intellectual disabilities. *Acta Paediatrica Supplement, 93*(445), 60–63.

Vicari, S., Belluci, S., & Carlesimo, G. A. (2005). Visual and spatial long-term memory: Differential pattern of impairments in Williams and Down syndromes. *Developmental Medicine & Child Neurology, 47*(5), 305–311.

Vogel, C. A., Bradley, R. H., Raikes, H. H., Boller, K., & Shears, J. K. (2006). Relation between father connectedness and child outcomes. *Parenting, 6*(2–3), 189–209.

Vygotsky, L. S. (1978). *Mind in society: The development of higher psychological process.* Cambridge, MA: Harvard University Press.

Vygotsky, L. S. (1986). *Thought and language.* (Rev. ed.). Cambridge, MA: MIT Press.

Walker, W. O., & Johnson, C. P. (2006). Mental retardation: Overview and diagnosis. *Pediatrics in Review, 27*(6), 204–212.

Wellman, H. M., Phillips, A. T., Dunphy-Lelii, S., & LaLonde, N. (2004). Infant understanding of persons predicts preschool social cognition. *Developmental Science, 7*(3), 283–288.

Williams, D. L., Goldstein, G., & Minshew, N. J. (2006). The profile of memory function in children with autism. *Neuropsychology, 20*(1), 21–29.

Yirmiya, N., Gamliel, I., Pilowsky, T., Feldman, R., Baron-Cohen, S., & Sigman, M. (2006). The development of siblings of children with autism at 4 and 14 months: Social engagement, communication and cognition. *Journal of Child Psychology and Psychiatry, 47,* 511–523.

Zheng, M., & Goldin-Meadow, S. (2002). Thought before language: How deaf and hearing children express motion events across cultures. *Cognition, 85,* 145–175.

Zwaigenbaum, L., Bryson, T., Roberts, W., Brian, J., & Szatmari, P. (2005). Behavioral manifestations of autism in the first year of life. *International Journal of Developmental Neuroscience, 23*(2–3), 143–152.

Zwaigenbaum, L., Thurm, A., Stone, W., Baranek, G., Bryson, S. E., Iverson, J., et al. (2007). Studying the emergence of autism spectrum disorders in high risk infants: Methodological and practical issues. *Journal of Autism and Developmental Disorders, 37,* 466–480.

Sample Discovery Activities for Young and Developmentally Young Children*

*Adapted from *Discovering your baby: Activities for the new parent.* Available from Children's Clinic, P.O. Box 15516, Augusta, GA 30919 (706. 736.8500). Used with permission from W. Umansky.

FINDING WAYS MY BABY USES HER EYES

How does your baby use her eyes? Complete these activities to find out.

1. Find a bright ball, shiny spoon, a mirror, or any toy your baby likes. Hold it close to the baby. What does she do? Check as many as you see.

2. Now move it far away from the baby (the length of your arm). Now what does she do? Check as many as you see.

3. Now, hold it very close to the baby's face (1 to 2 inches, right at her face). What does she do? Check as many as you see.

☐ Gets still	☐ Gets still	☐ Gets still
☐ Eyes get bigger	☐ Eyes get bigger	☐ Eyes get bigger
☐ Gets quiet	☐ Gets quiet	☐ Gets quiet
☐ Looks at it while you count to 3	☐ Looks at it while you count to 3	☐ Looks at it while you count to 3
☐ Doesn't really look at it; looks around	☐ Doesn't really look at it; looks around	☐ Doesn't really look at it; looks around
☐ Keeps moving	☐ Keeps moving	☐ Keeps moving
☐ Keeps making sounds	☐ Keeps making sounds	☐ Keeps making sounds
☐ Fusses	☐ Fusses	☐ Fusses
☐ Looks away, pulls back	☐ Looks away, pulls back	☐ Looks away, pulls back
☐ Yawns	☐ Yawns	☐ Yawns
☐ Makes faces	☐ Makes faces	☐ Makes faces

Get two pieces of white paper. On one of them, draw bright red circles in the shape of a bull's eye—like this.
(See last page for printed tear-out.)

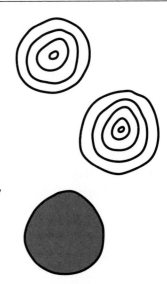

On the other piece, draw a big circle and fill it in with a lighter softer color (pink, yellow, peach, etc.). Hold them up together, close enough for your baby to see. Hold them far enough apart from each other so you can tell which one your baby looks at. Notice:

1. Does your baby look at each of them? ☐ Yes ☐ No

2. Does your baby look at one of them more than the other?
☐ Yes ☐ No

3. If so, which one? _____

4. Which one do you think your baby likes best? _____

_____

5. How can you tell? _____

_____

_____

_____

_____

GIVING MY BABY A CHANCE TO SEE HIS WORLD

Now that you know how your baby can use his eyes, be sure you give him lots of practice. Fill in this chart with things you have learned and tried with your baby.

What I learned about how my baby uses his eyes.	What can I do to help him use his eyes?	When I helped my baby do it.
		Time _____ Place _____ How long _____
		Time _____ Place _____ How long _____
		Time _____ Place _____ How long _____

Hold your baby in your lap, lay him on the bed with you, or put him in an infant seat. Hold different toys and objects close enough for him to see. Move them slowly side to side, or up and down, and see if your baby follows them around. If he doesn't follow them, try moving the objects more slowly, or use brighter or larger objects. Do this at least five times.

Place _____ Time _____

How long did you play? _____

List three different things you used. _____

_____

_____

_____

Which one(s) did your baby seem most interested in? _____

_____

_____

_____

_____

How could you tell? _____

_____

_____

_____

_____

Take your baby on a "tour" of your room. Tell him what he is seeing while you show him some of your favorite things (pictures, make-up, perfume, records, tapes, clothes). Be sure to hold things close enough or hold your baby where he can see things.

Time _____ Place _____

How long did you tour? _____

List five things you showed to your baby. _____

_____

_____

_____

_____

Did your baby like doing this? ☐ Yes ☐ No

How could you tell? _____

_____

_____

_____

_____

These are other places your baby may spend time. Fill in the checklist about them. Are these places bright and interesting to look at? What can you do to make them that way?

Place	What's there now?	What can I put there?
Car Seat	*Ceiling of car is blue, back seat is blue.*	*Tape paper plates there with bright shapes colored on them.*
Playpen		
Quilt (on the floor)		
Infant Seat		
Car Seat		
_____ (Other)		
_____ (Other)		

NOISE CHECKLIST

Too much loud noise is not good for your baby and may make her feel uncomfortable. How noisy is **your** house? Fill out the "noise checklist" to find out.

Room	Which letter goes with this room? N–Noisy all the time O–Always quiet S–Sometimes noisy Sometimes quiet	Noisy times (can be all day or part of the day)	A quiet place to take baby
Living Room	~~EXAMPLE~~ S (people watch TV and talk)	3:00, dinner, after dinner, bedtime	my bedroom
Kitchen			
Living Room			
Dining Room			
Bathroom			
Family Room			
Your Room			
Baby's Bedroom			

What baby does	Rattle	My talking	My singing	_____	_____
Baby doesn't seem to listen; no change in activity.					
Baby gets still.					
Baby moves more.					
Baby looks for sound.					
Baby smiles.					
Baby frowns or makes a face.					
Baby yawns.					
Baby cries or fusses.					

FINDING WAYS MY BABY CAN BECOME A GOOD LISTENER

Now that you know how your baby can use his ears, be sure you give him lots of practice. Fill in this chart with things you have learned and tried with your baby.

What I learned about how my baby listens.	What can I do to help my baby become a good listener?	When I helped my baby do it.
		Time _____ Place _____ How long _____
		Time _____ Place _____ How long _____
		Time _____ Place _____ How long _____

There is something else your baby likes to hear—his own voice! Sometimes when you talk to your baby and look at him, he begins to make his **own** sounds. What sounds does **your** baby make? Check the one you hear.

☐ "AH"

☐ "OO"

☐ "EE"

☐ "LA LA"

Does your baby like this game?

☐ Yes ☐ No

How can you tell? _____

_____

_____

_____

_____

_____

When your baby makes sounds, look at him and smile. Now, make the same sounds. What does he do? Check as many as you see or hear.

☐ Baby smiles.

☐ Baby makes more sounds.

☐ Baby looks at you.

☐ Baby moves arms and legs.

☐ Baby turns away.

☐ Baby fusses.

Does your baby like this game?

☐ Yes ☐ No

How can you tell? _____

_____

_____

_____

_____

Pick two of your favorite songs. Sing them to your baby—not too loud! And don't be shy. Your baby needs to hear your voice. Sing from start to finish. If you forget the words, hum.

Time _____ How long _____

Place _____

Songs I sang _____

_____

_____

Does your baby like to hear singing? ☐ Yes ☐ No

How can you tell? _____

_____

_____

_____

_____

Now pick a lullaby. That's a song to sing to your baby while he's falling asleep, like "Rockabye, Baby." You can ask your friend, your mother, or your aunt to teach you a good song.

Name of song _____

Sing it softly to your baby while he's falling asleep.

Time _____ Place _____

What are some other songs you can sing to your baby? Think of three.

1. _____

2. _____

3. _____

If your bady likes music, sing to him as often as you like. What does your baby do if he's tired of listening or if the sound is too loud? Check as many as fit your baby.

☐ Smiles ☐ Looks at you ☐ Yawns ☐ Fusses ☐ Gets very still
☐ Turns away from you

R • E • M • E • M • B • E • R

Baby might need a break from listening. How can you tell? _____
_____
_____

LEARNING HOW MY BABY TRIES TO TELL ME THINGS

1. Check all the things **your** baby does to let you know she's hungry.

☐ Yawns

☐ Frets or fusses

☐ Smiles

☐ Coos

☐ Cries

☐ Sucks her hand

☐ Doesn't eat

☐ Looks at your face

☐ Turns her head away from you

☐ Moves her arms and legs a lot

☐ Gets very quiet and still

☐ Sleeps more than usual

2. Check all the things **your** baby does to let you know she's wet.

☐ Yawns

☐ Frets or fusses

☐ Smiles

☐ Coos

☐ Cries

☐ Sucks her hand

☐ Doesn't eat

☐ Looks at your face

☐ Turns her head away from you

☐ Moves her arms and legs a lot

☐ Gets very quiet and still

☐ Sleeps more than usual

3. Check all the things **your** baby does to tell you she's sleepy.

☐ Yawns

☐ Frets or fusses

☐ Smiles

☐ Coos

☐ Cries

☐ Sucks her hand

☐ Doesn't eat

☐ Looks at your face

☐ Turns her head away from you

☐ Moves her arms and legs a lot

☐ Gets very quiet and still

☐ Sleeps more than usual

1. Check all the things **your** baby does to tell you she's ready to play.

☐ Turns her head away from you

☐ Moves her arms and legs

☐ Coos

☐ Frets or fusses

☐ Smiles

☐ Looks at your face

☐ Gets very quiet and still

☐ Eyes get wider

2. Check all the things **your** baby does to tell you she needs a break.

☐ Turns her head away from you

☐ Sucks her hand

☐ Fusses or cries

☐ Yawns

☐ Smiles

☐ Pulls away from you

☐ Looks at your face

RESPONDING WHEN MY BABY TELLS ME THINGS

Choose three times during the day to watch your baby: once in the morning, once in the afternoon, and once in the evening. At each of these times, watch your baby for 10 minutes. What does she look at? Does she move her arms and legs? Does she make noises? Does she have different facial expressions?

List five words or short phrases to describe what she is doing. Remember: Your description may be different from other babies because **your** baby is special!

Morning	Afternoon	Evening
Time 8:30 AM 5 things that describe my baby 1. followed me around the room with her eyes 2. moved arms & legs (EXAMPLE) 3. smiled 4. made noises 5. looked at her hands	Time _____ 5 things that describe my baby 1. 2. 3. 4. 5.	Time _____ 5 things that describe my baby 1. 2. 3. 4. 5.
Time _____ 5 things that describe my baby 1. 2. 3. 4. 5.	Time _____ 5 things that describe my baby 1. 2. 3. 4. 5.	Time _____ 5 things that describe my baby 1. 2. 3. 4. 5.

Look at the things you just listed. What do you think **your** baby was trying to tell you each of the three times.

Morning _____

_____

How did you respond to her? _____

_____

_____

What might you have done differently? _____

_____

_____

Afternoon _____

_____

How did you respond to her? _____

_____

_____

What might you have done differently? _____

_____

_____

Evening _____

_____

How did you respond to her? _____

_____

_____

What might you have done differently? _____

_____

_____

Choose a time when your baby is upset and fussy but does not seem to be hungry. Pick her up and try this: Jiggle or **lightly** bounce her on your lap to calm her down. What does she do?

☐ Gets quiet
☐ Smiles and coos
☐ Stops crying

☐ Gets tense and stiff
☐ Gets more upset
☐ Cries harder

Now try this: Hold her close to you, pat or rub her back lightly, and rock her gently. What does she do?

☐ Cries more
☐ Cuddles up to me
☐ Relaxes

☐ Gets tense and stiff
☐ Stops crying
☐ Smiles and coos

Which of these things calms your baby?

☐ Being held close and
   gently rocked
☐ Being jiggled and bounced

☐ Neither

How can you tell? _____

_____

When my baby is fussy and upset, I should _____

_____

I should do this because _____

_____

_____

FINDING WAYS MY BABY USES HIS BODY

Take something small, like the handle on a rattle or your finger, and press it against the inside of your baby's hand. What happens? (Check as many as you see.)

☐ He turns away.   ☐ He closes his hand
☐ He moves his arms and legs.   around the object.
☐ He cries.   ☐ Nothing happens.

If your baby closes his hand around the object, it is called the **grasping reflex.**

Lay your baby on his back in a safe and quiet place, like the bed or his infant seat. Make a loud noise close to your baby. (For example, clap your hands together, drop a book down on the floor, or slam a door or drawer.) What happens?

☐ He cries.   ☐ He gets very quiet.
☐ His arms and legs jerk.   ☐ He holds his breath.
☐ His eyes blink.   ☐ He stays very still.

If your baby jerked, cried, or blinked, it is called the **startle reflex.** This is normal for babies. The startle reflex does not completely disappear. We adults can also be startled by a loud noise or by something surprising us. It is our body's way of protecting us by telling us to pay attention to what is happening.

Take one finger and lightly touch the corner of your baby's mouth. What happens? (Check as many as you see.)

☐ He turns away.   ☐ He turns toward my finger.
☐ He moves around a lot.   ☐ Nothing happens.

If your baby turns toward your finger, it is called the **rooting reflex.** Now try these activities to learn more about your baby's body.

Put your baby on his back on a soft surface (for example, the bed or the sofa). Bend over him and hold his hands in yours. **Very slowly** pull him up so that his head is off the bed a few inches and then **gently** put him back down on the bed. **Be careful** not to bump his head.

What did your baby do with his head when you pulled him up?

☐ He turned it to one side.   ☐ He dropped his head back.
☐ He raised his head up.   ☐ Nothing.

As your baby gets older and his neck and stomach muscles get stronger, he will hold his head straighter and help pull to a sitting position.

Place your baby on his stomach on the bed, the sofa, or a soft blanket on the floor. Call his name, gently shake a rattle near him, or try to get him to look at a shiny object.

Watch your baby's head and what he does with it. Does he:

☐ Turn his head side to side?
☐ Lift his head up a little?
☐ Lift his head up all the way?

☐ Do nothing?
☐ Lift his head up and
turn it to one side?

As your baby gets stronger, he will be able to hold his head up to look at toys and he will also learn to prop himself up on his arms.

Hold your baby in an upright supported sitting position or on a firm surface—your lap, the sofa, or a table. Watch your baby (especially his back and head) and check all of the things you see.

☐ His head is wobbly and falls a little to the front.
☐ He is able to balance himself a little.
☐ He cannot balance himself at all and I have to support him completely.
☐ His back and shoulders are rounded over a lot.
☐ His back and shoulders are rounded over a little.
☐ He can hold his head up all the way most of the time and it does not wobble.

R • E • M • E • M • B • E • R
Your baby needs lots of practice in order to grow strong.

GIVING MY BABY CHANCES TO GROW STRONGER

Now that you've discovered how your baby uses her body, give her lots of chances to exercise and grow strong!

Make a pad on the floor with some quilts and baby blankets. Make sure it is thick enough for your baby to feel comfortable and warm. Let your baby spend 15–30 minutes every day on the pad, moving her body and playing. Be sure you watch her so she can't move off the pad.

Put your baby on the pad on his tummy. Now get down on the floor so your baby can see you if he lifts his head. Make gentle sounds in the three ways listed below, and watch what your baby does. Put a check beside each thing your baby does when he hears each noise.

1. Talk to your baby. Say his name and ask him to look at you. What does your baby do?

   ☐ He moves his head from side to side.

   ☐ He raises his head up.

   ☐ He raises his head up and looks at me.

   ☐ He raises his head up and looks around.

2. Gently shake a rattle several inches in front of your baby's head. What does your baby do?

   ☐ He moves his head from side to side.

   ☐ He raises his head up.

   ☐ He raises his head up and looks at the rattle.

   ☐ He raises his head up and looks around.

3. Hold a musical toy several inches in front of your baby's head while the music plays. What does your baby do?

   ☐ He moves his head from side to side.

   ☐ He raises his head up.

   ☐ He raises his head up and looks at the toy.

   ☐ He raises his head up and looks around.

Which sound did your baby work hardest to find? _____

_____

How could you tell? _____

_____

Use that sound every day when you play with your baby on the pad. As he gets older, try new toys or sing to him. The sounds he likes the most are the ones he will work hardest to find, and his muscles will grow strong.

Put your baby on her back on the pad. Find a rattle or some other noisy toy that is small enough for her to hold. Give her the toy and let her practice holding it. If she drops it, put it back in her hand. As she gets older, she may be able to: hold the rattle for a longer time, hold the rattle while she shakes it, hold the rattle while she brings it to her mouth.

Play this game every day. It helps her arms and hands get stronger.

Put your baby on the pad on his tummy. Get his attention with a toy he really likes. While he looks at the toy, put it on the pad where he can see it but can't reach it. As he gets older, he may be able to: look at the toy for a long time with his head up, reach for the toy, try to move to get the toy, but be unable to, move to the toy and get it.

Play this game every day. Tell your baby all about the toy. When he works hard to try to get it, remember to tell him how proud you are!

R • E • M • E • M • B • E • R

Talk to your baby and smile at her while she plays.

Tell about one "special time" you had with your baby that wasn't a scheduled time. Tell what you and your baby did, and how you felt.

_____

_____

_____

_____

It's nice to spend special time playing with your baby every day. Look back at the diary pages in this section. What is the best time every day to **play** with your baby?

   Turn to the next page and read the suggestions for things to do with your baby. Then pick two of these activities and do them during one of your playtimes. Fill in the chart to tell about doing them.

Date:	Time:	Place:	
What we did	Did your baby like it?	How could you tell?	Did you like it?

PLAYTIME IDEAS

Try to spend 10 minutes **each day** playing at this special time. Here are some suggestions for things to do.

1. Give your baby a massage. First warm your hands. Gently rub her tummy, legs, arms, and back. Talk to her and name her body parts while you rub her. Put baby lotion or baby powder on your hands.

2. Stroke your baby's skin with things that feel different. Try:

    A cotton ball   A feather   A piece of soft cloth

3. Sing to your baby.

4. Talk to your baby, and "play around" with your voice. Make it slow and fast, high and low. If your baby smiles at you and makes sounds ("ah" or cooing noises) you should smile back and make the same noises.

5. Brush your baby's hair.

6. Get out pictures of your family, your friends, and yourself. Tell your baby about the people in the pictures—who they are, what they do, and how you know them. Your baby won't understand everything you say, but she should enjoy hearing your voice and seeing the pictures.

7. Find a mirror in your house that you can get close to. Hold your baby so that she can see you **and** herself in the mirror. Tell your baby about you and herself: "There you are. Mama's holding you. See your pretty eyes? And there's your nose. . . . "

Communication Development

Susan R. Easterbrooks and Tanya L. Parker

Chapter Outline

- Definitional Issues
- Stages of Normal Language Acquisition
- Theoretical Models
- Factors Affecting Communication Development
- Communication Development in Young Children with Special Needs
- Specific Strategies for Assessment of Communication Functioning
- Instructional Methods and Strategies for Intervention
- Technology in Assessment and Intervention

Ian

Ian is a 12-month-old boy whose hearing loss was identified while he was in the newborn nursery as a result of laws regarding universal newborn hearing screening. Because there were some problems with the equipment, screening results were questioned. He was retested, but the second set of equipment also malfunctioned. This led his parents to assume that all was well. Subsequent testing revealed that there was a severe loss in one ear and a moderately severe loss in the other. Additional testing revealed genetics to be the cause of the loss.

A professional in the field suggested cochlear implants, which are devices implanted in the inner ear, but because Ian had usable residual hearing, his parents opted for a different treatment. Ian received the latest digital hearing aids at 10 months of age. He has been attending a private auditory verbal program weekly, where his mother receives instruction in assisting him to learn to listen and use spoken language. A parent-infant adviser available through his state's parent-infant program also sees him twice monthly. Ian babbles consistently when wearing his hearing aids. He is able to match sounds to objects, such as "brrrmm, brrrmm" to an airplane. He is progressing very well.

The ability to understand and use language is a distinctly human trait. Language permits us to express our basic needs, provides a vehicle through which we learn about the world, and fosters social interactions. Children who are delayed in communication, for whatever reason, are at risk within a world that primarily conveys its demands and changes through language.

Listening to typically developing toddler language is a charming experience. The errors that infants and toddlers make during the language development process are a constant source of delight to adults. The preschool years are those during which language acquisition unfolds. By the time children enter school, they are using all the sentence types produced by adults (Owens, 2004). According to Chomsky (1957), the critical period for language acquisition is before the age of 5. Youngsters whose parents have recognized their special needs early in childhood are fortunate because intervention can be initiated before these precious years of learning have passed. This chapter reviews theories and stages of language development, factors that affect communication development, and intervention approaches.

DEFINITIONAL ISSUES

Communication

Communication is the exchange of information and ideas.

The term **communication** refers to an exchange of information and ideas. This broad definition requires that we view communication as occurring vocally, nonvocally, gesturally, pictorially, through sign language, through written language, or through any number of representational systems such as those used with communication boards.

Speech

The term *speech* refers to the acoustic-articulatory code by which spoken languages are conveyed.

Speech refers to the auditory-articulatory code by which we represent spoken languages. Speech includes phonation and articulation of the specific **phonemes** (the sounds of letters and letter combinations) of a language. Disorders of speech include but are not limited to articulation, dysfluency (stuttering), and voice disorders such as hoarseness or harshness. However, speech is not the only means by which we represent language.

Language

Language represents a culture-based code of arbitrary symbols used to communicate.

Language, as defined by Bloom and Lahey (1978), is a "code whereby ideas about the world are represented through a conventional system of arbitrary signals for communication" (p. 4). In spoken language, we represent this code through numerous conventional systems including phonology, morphology, syntax, semantics, and pragmatics. Some children have difficulty mastering a first language because of problems with these systems. Others have difficulty because the language spoken at home differs from the language spoken at school or by the larger community. Other children must learn signed or coded forms of English (e.g., Signing Exact English or Cued Speech); still others must learn American Sign Language, which is a distinctly separate language from signed forms of English.

Form, Content, and Use

Language is a subject that has both perplexed and fascinated scholars. It has been studied from many perspectives. Bloom and Lahey (1978) proposed that communication could be organized into three aspects, and that language competence was dependent on interactions among these aspects. They saw language as being comprised of elements of **form, content,** and **use.** The form of language is comprised of phonology, morphology, and syntax; the content of language is often referred to as *semantics*; and the use of language includes functions and contexts, or *pragmatics*.

Table 6.1 identifies some of the basic components of form, content, and use elements in the language of young children. For example, here is a conversation between a mother and her baby that demonstrates aspects of form, content, and use.

Mother: Good morning, honey. Time to get up.
Baby: (Reaching for mother) Up?

> *Mother:*   That's my girl. Are you hungry? Are you ready for breakfast?
> *Baby:*   Want eat.
> *Mother:*   Good. I'm glad you're hungry, but let me change you first.
> *Baby:*   (Crying) No! No! Want eat, want eat. Want eat!

Regarding form, this child is at the presyntactic stage, combining words into two-word utterances. The baby is not demonstrating any of the morphological elements such as word endings that convey tense and number, but we still get the message. Content is illustrated by the baby being able to understand and talk about concepts in

TABLE 6.1   Elements of Form, Content, and Use in Young Children.

Aspect	Linguistic Categories	Components	
Form	Morphology and Syntax	Declarative, imperative, and question sentence types Simple sentences: one subject, one verb, simple verb tense Simple transformations: passive voice, negation, conjunction, complements, *there* as sentence starter Questions forms: *Wh-* questions, yes/no, *What . . . do*, tag questions, subject-auxiliary inversion questions Complex sentences: dependent and independent clauses, relative clauses, complementation, verbs requiring special consideration, advanced verb tense	
Content	Semantics	Agent Entity Object/Patient Recipient Action 　Transitive verb 　Intransitive verb Process 　Transitive verb 　Intransitive verb Stative verb Possessor Vocative Existence Nonexistence	Recurrence Disappearance Denial Rejection Attribute Location/Position Manner Time Frequency Duration Purpose Intensifier Inclusion Question forms
Use	Pragmatics	Mutual Repair of failed message Ritualized gestures Mutuality Reciprocity Synchronicity Turn taking Whispering Hints Opens conversation Sustains topic Changes topic	Closes conversation Communicative intention Attention seeking Requesting Protesting Commenting Greeting Answering Teasing, taunting Knowledge of context Knowledge of audience

Sources: Bloom & Lahey, 1978; Coggins & Carpenter, 1981; Owens, 2004.

her daily experience. She has certain semantic categories such as action (eat) and rejection (no change). Use is demonstrated by the child's mastering early pragmatic uses of her communication, such as mutuality and protesting.

Now recall Ian, our young friend who is deaf, in the opening vignette. In terms of form, he is communicating at the one-word, presyntactic level and is expressing declarative, imperative, and question forms through facial expression and voice intonation. Content-wise, he understands some vocabulary items in the categories of object and agent (see Table 6.1) because he will look for a toy or for his mother when someone asks, "Where's Mama?" He also uses the category of rejection, using grunts, whines, and gestures to let others know when he does not want something. Pragmatically, he uses his communication to seek attention, request, protest, and greet, albeit vocally, but not necessarily verbally.

Phonology

The term *phonology* refers to the study of sound units of speech.

Chomsky and Halle (1968) studied the phonological components of language, which are the sound patterns of speech, or the articulatory-acoustic properties that allow us to represent our thoughts. **Phonology** is the study of speech sounds. Jakobson (1968) proposed that the phonemes of any language (i.e., the basic units of speech sounds) could be classified in terms of their articulatory and acoustic properties, and that these features were universal. See chapter 2 for the ages by which most children acquire specific use of phonemes. Knowledge of the expected sequence of development is crucial in determining appropriate intervention goals. Babies develop the ability to use speech through distinct stages.

Morphology

Morphology is the study of grammatical units of words.

Morphology is the study of the smallest meaningful units of language, such as *-ed*, *-s*, and *un-*. Berko (1958), in one of the original studies on morphology, devised a task for eliciting grammatical morphemes using nonsensical sentences and pictures. For example, in one task, a researcher first showed a child a picture of a bird-like creature, and then said, "This is a wug." Next she showed a picture of two of the bird-like creatures and said, "Here are two _____," requiring the child to supply the missing word. Examiners refer to this task as the **cloze** procedure. Other tasks based on the cloze procedure were used to study a number of grammatical morphemes and to chart the children's developmental sequences. Brown (1973) added to the basic understanding of morphology in young children and proposed the **mean length of utterance (MLU)**, or the average number of morphemes in an utterance, as a way of quantifying language. The MLU is considered a good predictor of the rate of acquisition of language (Rice, Wexler, & Hershberger, 1998) up to the 5–MLU level. (See Owens, 2004, for the rules of calculating MLU.)

Syntax

Syntax is the grammatical organization of sentences.

Syntax is that aspect of language pertaining to the organizational rules of sentences. Syntax and morphology combine to form what is called *grammar* and include

phrase structure rules (e.g., basic sentence patterns), **transformational operations** (e.g., passive voice and conjoining), and **morphological rules** (e.g., pluralization and noun–verb agreement).

Lenneberg (1967) postulated that individuals possess an **innate language acquisition device (LAD)**. The LAD codes information two ways: first, as the deep structure of an utterance, which carries meaning; and second, as the surface structure of an utterance, which can take many forms. For example, although "Buddy hit Billy" is the deep structure, one might instead say, "Billy was hit by Buddy" on the surface. Language becomes the process of moving from meaning (deep structure) to increasingly sophisticated forms of expression (surface structure). Once an individual has internalized the associated language rules, she is able to generate an infinite number of utterances.

Semantics

Semantics is the study of meaning and content; that is, what one is talking about. Researchers call the object, event, or interaction to which we refer the **referent** (Bates, Camaioni, & Volterra, 1975; Bloom & Lahey, 1978; Gray, 2004), and referents, or ideas to which a word refers, are related to one another in specific ways. Important adults in a child's life play a significant role in how their child labels things. During normal conversations, adults typically label objects, events, and relationships that form the child's **lexicon,** or vocabulary (Thompson, 2006). A rich base of experiences with the world is essential to the language acquisition process. Without experiencing objects and events and how they relate, a child has nothing to which a marker or lexical item can be attached (see chapter 5). Semantic study is especially pertinent to the fields of preschool development and special education; thus, the early interventionist should become familiar with this subject.

Semantics is defined as the study of the development and changes in the meanings of words, phrases, sentences, and discourse.

Pragmatics

The term **pragmatics** refers to the social contexts around which we learn and use language. Language develops in a social context (Muma & Teller, 2001); thus the culture of the family as well as the broader culture have a significant influence on what a child learns. Early researchers (Bates, 1976; Dore, 1974; Halliday, 1975) developed taxonomies of pragmatic skills that identified the components of pragmatics. Once a child is involved in a social context where communication is fostered, pragmatic skills evolve into those rules that determine when and where to use language.

The psychosocial and cultural dynamics around which we develop and use communication are referred to as pragmatics.

The **speech act** is considered to be the basic unit of pragmatics (Garcia, 2004), just as the morpheme is the basic unit of morphology and syntax. Several theorists have suggested outlines for common speech acts. In addition, Halliday (1975) grouped the uses of language into three categories that emerge between 18 and 24 months of age: interpersonal (or pragmatic), intrapersonal (or mathetic), and ideational (problem solving). Between 2 and 3 years of age, children begin to use contingent queries to clarify the meaning of what someone has said, and they engage in rapid topic change (Shulman, 1985). The 3-year-old is very competent

A speech act is an utterance containing meaning and function.

Discourse consists of any extended utterance beyond a single unit, and includes monologues and dialogues.

A set of communicative turns is called an adjacency pair.

Canonical babbling consists of reduplicated consonant-vowel combinations.

at **code switching** (Conboy & Mills, 2006), produces contingent queries to maintain conversations (Ferrier, Dunham, & Dunham, 2000), and is temporarily able to assume the perspective of another person through language (Moll & Tomasello, 2006).

Conducting a conversation, or engaging in **discourse**, although seemingly effortless, actually requires a complex set of practical skills. The first of these is **turn taking.** Before any kind of conversation takes place, the speakers must agree to certain characteristics of an interchange that result in orderliness. If these rules are violated, orderliness ceases and the communication breaks down. Each set of communicative turns is referred to as an **adjacency pair.** Common, early adjacency pairs include opening question–answer, greeting–greeting, offer–acceptance/rejection, assertion–acknowledgement, compliment–acceptance/rejection, request–grant, summon–answer, and closing–closing.

:: STAGES OF NORMAL LANGUAGE ACQUISITION

No matter what language you are referring to, a child's ability to use that language develops through a series of characteristic patterns (Brownlee, 1998; Tomasello, 1992). These forms emerge best when they are developed from a rich base of experiences. A child must experience the world for language to hold any meaning.

Courtesy of Dr. Susan Easterbrooks

Language development is influenced by early communication experiences.

Prelinguistic and Babbling Stage

Long before they utter their first words, infants refer to the world around them through their bodies (Bates et al., 1975). Prelinguistic communication has two components: perlocutionary and illocutionary acts (Bates, 1976). **Perlocutionary acts** are nonverbal means of communication such as gazing, crying, touching, smiling, laughing, grasping, and sucking. **Illocutionary acts** are vocal means of expression such as the use of vocalizations, intonation, and grunts and nonverbal acts including giving, pointing, and showing. The amount of communication acts an infant uses is a good predictor of later language ability (Paavola, Kunnari, & Moilanen, 2005). Studying an infant's perlocutionary and illocutionary skills may be helpful in determining any need for intervention.

A baby goes through several stages of **canonical babbling**, referred to as precanonical, canonical, and postcanonical babbling (Oller, 1980; Stoel-Gammon, 1998). **Precanonical vocalizations** occur from birth to 6 months and include gruntlike vocalizations, squeals, quasiresonated vowels, raspberries, clicks, cries, and laughter that lack the form of true syllables. **Canonical vocalizations** emerge from 6 to 10 months when the child combines vowels (V) and consonants (C) into true syllables that sound very speechlike. **Postcanonical vocalizations** emerge from 10 to 18 months and include closed syllables (CVC) and open (CV) syllables. Babies also acquire greater articulatory control. Spencer (1993) found that the rate at which a child with a hearing loss produces canonical babblings is predictive of her spoken language production at 18 months, indicating that, at least in children with a hearing loss, canonical babbling may be a useful diagnostic indicator.

A later stage of prelinguistic development is the **jargon stage**, which overlaps babbling stages and may begin as early as 9 months. In this stage, children continue to develop strings of utterances that carry the stress and intonational patterns of adult speech (deBoysson-Bardies, Sagart, & Durand, 1984; Morgan, 1996). They appear to be talking but say no distinguishable words. Jargoning overlaps into the **one-word** and **combined-words stages,** when children often produce strings of inflected babbling with a real word included. Jargon usually disappears by 2 years of age (Trantham & Pedersen, 1976).

> Jargon is babbling that contains the intonation of adult speech.

One-Word Stage

Children utter recognizable words somewhere around their first birthday (Owens, 2004; Veneziano, Sinclair & Berthoud, 1990). A child who uses one-word utterances, or **holophrases**, is said to be in the holophrastic stage. During this phase a child uses one word to represent a whole phrase, and context is needed to understand what the child means. For example, the word *ball* might mean "I want the ball," "I have the ball," or "The dog is chasing the ball." As every parent knows who has experienced a child screaming "Ball! Ball! Ball!," context and intonation are not always enough to make meaning apparent.

> Holophrases are single words representing whole phrases.

Vocabulary during the one-word stage must be able to assist a child in causing change (Nelson, 1973). Words such as *bush* and *table* are not very common in early vocabularies because a child's use of these words is not likely to bring about much change. However, the use of words such as *milk, blanket,* and *ball* are likely to result in some kind of action. Also in this stage, children engage in **overextensions**. When a child does not know the specific word for a particular referent, she uses familiar words as substitutes, thus overextending the actual meaning of that particular marker (Mandler, 2004). For example, the word *mama* may refer to all females, especially female caregivers. Children often apply concepts of shape when referring to something for which they have no label (Clark & Clark, 1977). For example, the word *ball* may be applied to a toy, an orange, or the moon. Other concepts that form the basis for overextensions are movement, size, sound, texture, and taste. Shortly after children label objects, they begin to use spatial prepositions and adjectives. If a child experiences disruptions in perception of location in space, spatial terminology will be extremely problematic (Lucas, 1980).

> The term *overextension* refers to the application of a word (*ball*) to an object whose label is unknown (*moon*) based on a similar feature or trait of that object (*roundness*).

At this time the child enters into a stage of rapid vocabulary development called **rapid-mapping**, where she maps meaning to new words with only a few examples of the word (Lederberg, Prezbindowski, & Spencer, 2000; Rice, Buhr, & Nemeth, 1990).

> Once the child utters her first word, her expressive vocabulary increases exponentially, reaching approximately 50 words by 16 to 18 months of age (Dromi, 1999; Fenson et al., 1994).

Early Word Combinations

Before young children start to put words together, they combine a word with the pointing gesture (Iverson, Volterra, Pizzuto, & Capirci, 1994). Initially the pointing gesture is a repeat of the word, but just prior to two-word combinations, it represents a different function "apparently signaling a cognitive readiness for the expression of relations between symbolic elements" (Spencer & Lederberg, 1997, p. 222). Soon after children enter the period of accelerated vocabulary growth, multiword combinations emerge.

As young children learn to put words together, they leave out such extraneous language as verb tense but preserve nouns and verbs. Children also leave out verb expansions and the determiner system (e.g., *a* and *the*) and say, for example, "Baby fall" or "Puppy jump." The auxiliary system develops during the period from 18 months to 3 years. Early word combinations generally are in the form of **semantic-syntactic pairs,** such as agent-action ("Kitty jump") or notice-object ("There shoe").

Multiword Combinations

The term *overgeneralization* refers to the application of a regular grammatical feature (*-ed*) to a word requiring an irregular form (*runned*).

Overlapping the stages from single words to adult grammar is a period during which children use **overgeneralizations** of the grammar they have just learned (Gershkoff-Stowe, Connell, & Smith, 2006). For example, although children begin to use specific irregular verbs at a very young age, they often overgeneralize the use of the regular marker *-ed*, as in "runned" for *ran*, and "hided" for *hid*, and even add an *-ed* to some irregular forms, thereby producing "satted" for *sat* and "sawed" for *saw*. Children also overgeneralize plural forms, as in "foots," "mouses," and "mans."

Simple Sentence Structure

Following the development of all semantic categories and the verb and auxiliary systems, children move into higher-order transformations of basic sentence patterns. Children produce basic transitive sentences (e.g., "He cried"), intransitive sentences (e.g., "He ate the ice cream"), predicate nominative sentences using linking verbs (e.g., "He is a fireman"), predicate adjective sentences using linking verbs (e.g., "He is tired"), and sentences where linking verbs tie the subject to adverbial complements (e.g., "He is in the treehouse"). These basic forms and later transformations (e.g., questions, negation, passive voice, etc.) complete children's journeys toward the use of adult forms.

The rapid development of normal communication in such a brief period is truly remarkable. Never again does a child learn a skill of such magnitude in so little time. All the areas of language are closely intertwined such that a deficit in one area can lead to a deficit in another. Careful analysis of each component is essential in identifying deficits and planning appropriate remediation.

:: THEORETICAL MODELS

As in all avenues of study, various theories have developed to explain the phenomenon of communication development. Although each theory has had its heyday, in fact, children may benefit from various aspects of each as they attempt the formidable task of learning to communicate. The four major theories of language acquisition are the behavioral theory, the innatist theory, the cognitive theory, and the social interaction theory.

Behavioral Theory

The behavioral theory, associated most notably with Skinner (1957), holds that language is a subset of learned behaviors and, as such, is learned through a process of reinforcement. Ogletree and Oren (2001) identified a set of language instructional principles, paraphrased below. These include:

- **Stimulus control**—the provision of certain antecedent behaviors that serve as a cue for other behaviors; for example, showing a picture as a stimulus to assist a child to learn pronouns.
- **Responses**—the child's behaviors after receiving a stimulus; for example, saying "cats" when shown a picture of more than one cat.
- **Consequences**—the direct results of a child's response to a stimulus; for example, receiving a toy to play with after correctly identifying the toy.
- **Positive reinforcement**—the functional relationship between two events that increases a behavior; for example, a child's receiving praise every time she makes a correct response.
- **Extinction**—the elimination of a behavior where reinforcement is no longer needed; for example, when a child no longer uses false starts to an utterance.
- **Negative reinforcement**—the functional relationship between two events that increases a behavior when a stimulus is removed; for example, modifying an intimidating situation so that a communication act can occur.
- **Punishment**—the functional relationship between two events that decreases a behavior; for example, placing a child in time-out after a tantrum.

Applied behavior analysis principles are commonly used with students with severe disabilities such as autism or severe retardation (Durand & Merges, 2001) and include such techniques as prompting, chaining, modeling, and cuing.

Innatist Theory

The innatist theory has been described under many labels—psycholinguistic theory, syntactic theory, and biological theory among them. Attributed to Chomsky (1957) and Lenneberg (1967), among others, the innatist theory holds that there is a biological basis for language acquisition, and that all humans are prewired to learn language because of the existence of a **language acquisition device**; it is just a matter of what aspect and at what rate language skills develop. Language is processed as a culturally determined set of rules, which is developmentally organized, and all infants pass through this developmental sequence in the same order, albeit at differing rates. The fact that all children go through the developmental sequence appropriate for the language of their cultures is cited as evidence of the existence of the language acquisition device. Although this theory fails to consider the importance of meaning and context in language development, it does provide great insight into how we process sentences.

Recently, there has been a resurgence of interest in the biological basis of language (Stromswold, 2006) as genetic research continues to bring us closer and closer to an understanding of the **human sentence processing mechanism** (HSPM) (Crago & Gopnik, 1994; Dale et al., 1998). Such a mechanism may be responsible for our ability to process sentences and may be genetically predetermined. Clarification of the existence of such a mechanism would have implications for therapy.

Cognitive Theory

Alternately known as psycholinguistic/semantic theory, case grammar theory, and information processing theory, cognitive theory argues that language development is based on meaning, or semantics, rather than on syntax. Bloom (1970) argued that there is a set of presyntactic, semantic relationships that precede true syntax. The order of their development reflects the order of development of cognitive structures (Bloom, 1973; Brown, 1973). For example, children develop the cognitive skill of object permanence before they talk about the appearance or disappearance of objects.

The semantic/cognitive theory has contributed significantly to our understanding of what young children talk about, when, and why. It explains language within the overall context of child development and forms the basis for models of intervention that stress active involvement of children with their environment.

Social Interaction Theory

The social interaction theory focuses on the social and personal purposes for which we use language. Social interaction theorists (Bruner, 1981; Prutting, 1979) see language as culturally driven and based on the human need to communicate. Children learn to communicate within the context of their environment under the guidance of an important adult caregiver (Matychuck, 2005). The need to communicate springs from the need for human interaction. Social interaction theorists feel that the naturalistic environment is a key element in early intervention (Noonan & McCormick, 2006). Play-based intervention, multidisciplinary teaming, and parent involvement are all components of instruction in naturalistic environments.

▪▪ FACTORS AFFECTING COMMUNICATION DEVELOPMENT

The process of acquiring language is extremely complex and requires an intact individual in an intact environment. Certain prerequisite systems are functioning in the typically developing youngster, and when they are delayed, defective, or absent, they have a significant impact on this acquisition process. Inefficient neurophysiological systems, damaged sensory systems, limited intellectual potential, and high-risk medical and social environments significantly influence communication development. This section discusses the relationships of hearing, vision, intelligence, memory, and attention to language development.

Hearing

A hearing loss represents one of the most serious of all deterrents to spoken language development. We talk because we hear. When a child does not have normal hearing, she struggles to learn every sound, every concept, every word, and every grammatical structure of spoken language. Youngsters are surrounded by a world that is constantly being labeled, described, and defined by adults. Parents of a child with normal hearing unconsciously revise their language to meet the child's needs (Jung & Short, 2004). They naturally babble and repeat intonational patterns in a fashion that will support a youngster's comprehension. When hearing is deficient, the natural interaction between adults and infant breaks down and the typical developmental sequence is disrupted.

> Even a minor or temporary hearing loss can disrupt language development in the first 3 years of life.

So much occurs linguistically in the first 3 years of life that even a minor or temporary hearing loss can be very disruptive. When young children experience mild fluctuating losses that result from colds and ear infections, their normal language acquisition is impeded (Zeisel & Roberts, 2003). This interference with language development may never be overcome. Referring a child with chronic colds, allergies, and ear infections to an otologist may save that child needless problems in developing language as a preschooler and in learning core (pre)academic skills. For children who are learning language, a mild **conductive loss** (i.e., a loss caused by problems with the outer or middle ear) places them under great stress. A high percentage of students with learning disabilities have past histories of middle ear medical problems as well as fluctuating hearing losses (Lindsay, Tomazic, Whitman, & Accardo, 1999).

> Universal newborn hearing screening and intervention (UNHSI) is the process of screening the hearing of all infants before they leave the hospital and instituting services for those who need them.

One innovation that holds potential for alleviating the impact of a hearing loss is **universal newborn hearing screening and intervention** (UNHSI). Every day, 33 babies (or 12,000 each year) are born in the United States with permanent hearing loss. With 3 of every 1,000 newborns having a hearing loss, it is the most frequently occurring birth defect (National Center for Hearing Assessment & Management, 2002). In 1993 the National Institutes of Health recommended the initiation of universal newborn hearing screening and intervention. Prior to that time, only about 30% to 50% of those children born with significant hearing loss were identified early, with the remaining children identified by 3 years of age. Screening technology, such as **Auditory Brain Response** (ABR) and **Transient Otoacoustic Emissions** (OAE), is rapid, reliable, sensitive, and easily administered (National Institutes of Health, 1993). However, universal newborn screening is not a replacement for vigilance during the developmental years because 20% to 30% of children acquire hearing loss during early childhood.

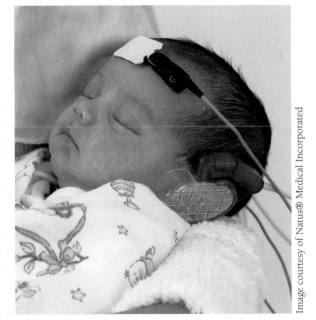

Image courtesy of Natus® Medical Incorporated

Universal newborn hearing screening is important for identifying hearing loss early in life.

Although universal screening is essential, it must go hand-in-hand with early intervention.

Children with hearing loss, who begin early intervention programs before the age of 6 months, show significantly more progress in language acquisition than do their peers who begin early intervention programs after 6 months of age (Yoshinaga-Itano & Apuzzo, 1998). New resources and new tools are becoming available more and more rapidly to assist states in implementing appropriate services to infants and toddlers who are deaf and hard of hearing. Yet, without concerted efforts toward the development of appropriate services that would be available to all parents, this potential may not be realized.

Vision

The role of vision in language learning is often discussed in terms of the higher linguistic functions of reading and writing. Visual disorders of perception, discrimination, memory, and the like have been associated with the inability to read and write; however, the impact of visual impairment becomes far more significant in reviewing the stages of language development in infants.

One of the first significant developments in language is **joint attending.** In joint attending, the caregiver and child view the same object, and the caregiver provides the label, thus helping to organize the child's world. Joint attending for a child with vision problems requires a more deliberate action; the caregiver must bring the object to the child's tactile and auditory awareness. At around 9 to 12 months of age, infants develop a gestural system by which they communicate to adults. The assumption is that the adult will see the child's gesture or gaze, follow the direction of the gaze or gesture, and see the object or event that the child intends to share. Infants who have never been able to see and who have no language skills are unaware that adults *can* see, so they do not engage in communicative gazing and gesturing in the same fashion as do children who are sighted. Thus, the language acquisition process for children who are blind is different from that of children who are sighted (Wakefield, Homewood, & Taylor, 2006).

Even a slight deficiency in vision can influence language learning. Being able to see does not necessarily mean that children are able to look at or to make sense out of what they are viewing. Problems with depth perception, color blindness, uncorrected near- or farsightedness, nystagmus, and astigmatism interfere with how children perceive and interpret what they see. Whereas hearing is primarily used to detect temporal aspects and changes, vision is primarily used to detect spatial aspects and changes (Zarfaty, Nunes, & Bryant, 2004). The sense of touch is not as effective as the eye in dealing with spatial information. Spatial adjectives and prepositions present a challenge to a child with vision impairment.

Intelligence

The role of intelligence in language has been explored for many years (Piaget, 1952; Vygotsky, 1962), yet the relationship is still not fully understood. Language and thought are not synonymous. A complex relationship between intelligence and language exists, and they may be bidirectional in their influence. Environmental factors, social pressures, inadequate sensory experiences, or perceptual problems may diminish the experiences of a youngster and cause poor test performance. This is because all tests, whether they purport to measure intelligence, aptitude, or achievement, measure what a child has learned (Sattler, 2001). Difficulty in receiving information does not necessarily mean low intelligence. Further, children can develop near-normal ability in some areas of intelligence yet be quite deficient in others.

All other things being equal, language delays become more prevalent as mental age becomes more negatively disparate from chronological age (Seung & Chapman, 2004), and children with diminished capacity appear to make gains in language more slowly than those with normal capacity (Iverson, Longobardi, & Caselli, 2003). However, the variety of factors and their interrelationships are so numerous and complex that one cannot assume a one-to-one correspondence between intelligence and language.

Memory

Memory plays a significant role in the acquisition of language. Children must formulate and hold a visual image in memory so that the auditory symbol used to represent what they saw will have a point of reference. The process of **categorization** is extremely important to learning in general and to learning language in particular (Donohue, 2006). Children need help seeing likenesses and differences in the world around them in order to organize their worlds. Efficient organization of experiences assists in the memory and retrieval processes.

Youngsters who are developing language rehearse that language both out loud and in their heads. Language **rehearsal** plays an important role in memory. Children with language problems often have difficulty with language rehearsal (Montgomery, 2000). Further, information that is taken in by a faulty sensory system or interpreted by a faulty perceptual system will be coded in the fashion in which it is experienced. Inaccurate, poorly rehearsed, or incomplete concepts of language are stored in that fashion, and when retrieved for use, they will be employed in inaccurate and incomplete ways.

Attention

Children at risk for attention disorders often have difficulty with language development (Warner-Rogers, Taylor, Taylor, & Sandberg, 2000). Attention is a neurobiological process, and attention deficits are real. They are not a result of poor parenting, lack of motivation, or ignorance; however, they are difficult to diagnose in preschool children.

Attention implies the ability to focus actively on a stimulus. Sometimes we are required to focus by choice. In order for children to attend, they must consciously take in specific information while inhibiting a whole array of competing messages. Selection and inhibition require a judgment on the part of the child that a particular piece of information is worthy of attention. Children with problems in selective attention often have problems with language and its influence on interpersonal relationships (Spira & Fischel, 2005). For children who have not matured neurologically in their ability to inhibit competing stimuli, or for those who have specific neurochemical dysfunctions, it is important that the interventionist assist in the selection and inhibition process by making information more readily accessible, and focusing on specific, salient aspects. Factors such as pitch, voice quality, loudness, spatial localization, and time of onset affect attending abilities. Further, the interventionist must assist in the judgment process by making what is to be learned meaningful and worthwhile to the child. To do this, the interventionist must have a good understanding of what is interesting to youngsters at different mental ages and of how to make linguistic information more auditorily and visually salient.

Separating vision, hearing, attention, memory, and intelligence for discussion purposes may be appropriate, but to think of them as individual blocks, stacked neatly one upon the other, is an inaccurate view of the learning process. These aspects are interdependent and, thus, mutually influential.

Children from Culturally and Linguistically Diverse Backgrounds

Children from culturally diverse backgrounds represent about one-third of the students served by speech-language pathologists.

A survey conducted by the American Speech-Language-Hearing Association (ASHA, 1998) revealed that approximately one-third of the students on the caseload of speech-language pathologists nationwide were comprised of children from culturally and linguistically diverse (CLD) backgrounds, and that the percentage of CLD students is on the rise. This means that a large portion of the early interventionist's caseload will consist of families who are nonspeakers or new learners of English.

Moore-Brown and Montgomery (2001) identified several factors that must be considered in designing services for CLD children. These include:

- Selecting a language of instruction
- Knowledge of the child's facility with each language
- Knowledge of when and how to use interpreters, or not to use interpreters
- Awareness of accents and dialects within languages
- Cultural factors that must be taken into consideration prior to intervention

This population will continue to change the face of instruction over the next several decades.

∷ COMMUNICATION DEVELOPMENT IN YOUNG CHILDREN WITH SPECIAL NEEDS

When a child's sensory, cognitive, motor, or social-affective systems are compromised, language development may be impaired. This next section describes the impact of various disabilities on the development of communication in children.

Mental Retardation/Intellectual Disabilities

Mental retardation, or intellectual disability, appears to influence language learning, with greater degrees of retardation accounting for greater problems with communication (Facon, Facon-Bollengier, & Grubar, 2002; Mar & Sall, 1999). Disorders of grammar and vocabulary influencing both receptive and expressive skills have been noted. In addition, speech delays are typically found in children with mental retardation. In fact, mental retardation accounts for more than 50% of all cases with speech delay (Leung & Kao, 1999).

Children with mental retardation learn all the morphological components of language but do so at a slower rate. Similarly, delays in syntax, semantics, and vocabulary are highly prevalent in children with mental retardation (Facon et al., 2002). In summary, children with mild to moderate mental retardation have global language delays, but they also exhibit poor adaptive skills and possible gross and fine motor delays (Downey et al., 2002).

With the present emphasis on including children with disabilities in regular school classes, interest in pragmatic language skills has increased. Because language develops more quickly in children with mental retardation when it is intended for highly functional purposes, pragmatic issues must be specifically addressed in classrooms with preschool-age children. Environmental approaches that stress the inclusion of a child's natural communication partners seem most effective in enhancing development (Owens, 2004).

Learning Disabilities

Although highly heterogeneous and painfully obvious in school-age children, learning disabilities are difficult to diagnose in preschool-aged children and are rarely identified as such; however, a look at the histories of older children who have learning disabilities indicates language problems in the preschool years. Learning disabilities are neurologically based, and children whose families have a history of learning disorders often have language learning problems (Lyytinen, Poikkeus, Laaks, Eklund, & Lyytinen, 2001). Although children with learning disabilities may have normal vision and hearing, their brains have difficulty interpreting what they hear or see. These processing deficits may result in problems with spatial orientation, sequencing, discrimination, and memory. People with language-based learning disabilities often experience word retrieval problems (Rubin & Johnson, 2002; Wiig & Semel, 1984). To carry on a conversation, one must be able to pull words from one's memory bank on demand. Inefficiency in this area interferes with communicative interaction essential to the language learning process and creates frustration in social situations.

Children with learning disabilities may have inefficient or inadequately developed neurophysiological systems (Collins & Rourke, 2003). To pay attention to what others say as well as to one's own thoughts, one's body must cooperate. The bodies of children who have learning disabilities do not cooperate with them, and they may exhibit poor listening skills (Bradlow, Kraus, & Hayes, 2003), hyper- or hypoactivity, distractibility, perseveration, disinhibition, problems with phonological processing, and other qualities. These may evolve into significant problems later. Many children with learning disabilities need extra time to master the basics of oral language before they are ready to handle the kindergarten curriculum. Many will always have language-based problems, and these will contribute to later problems with reading, math, writing, and perhaps social-behavioral functioning. The semantic and pragmatic aspects of language are often problematic as well.

Behavior Disorders

There are numerous reasons why some children have behavior disorders. For example, when children have not matured neurologically to the point where they can inhibit their responses to stimuli, they may act out. Inability to inhibit a language response may result in a child's blurting out information at inappropriate times. Many children have undetected hearing and vision problems that result in behavioral manifestations and concomitant language problems. Often, a youngster with a learning disability or intellectual disability who does not have the cognitive, motor, speech, or language abilities to interact with the world appears to have a behavior disorder because her responses to language and nonlanguage events are inappropriate. Children who have received no supervision or have had inappropriate role models may say and do unexpected things. These children need a highly structured, organized environment in which expectations are made clear and natural consequences to actions are meted out firmly but fairly. It also is essential to provide a structured language environment in which words make sense and are consistently applied to experiences.

Specific Speech Disorders

There are many forms of disordered speech. Each disability impacts speech development in its own way. However, three categories are recognized as common among children with speech disorders. These are disorders of fluency, articulation, and voice. Physical disabilities such as cleft palate and other anomalies may also be found.

Fluency is defined as the natural flow of the breath stream and vocalization during speech.

Fluency   Fluency involves the forward flow of speech. A child whose speech is dysfluent (i.e., to a greater degree than is typical of preschoolers) used to be referred to as a stutterer. More males are dysfluent than females, and the onset of dysfluency usually occurs between the ages of 3 and 5. Dysfluency cannot be picked up by the imitation of speech patterns of another child. It is often hereditary and may be found in combination with other problems. It almost always influences a child's social and emotional status (Treon, Dempster, & Blaesing, 2006). Problems of fluency require intensive intervention to overcome, and the **speech-language pathologist** and parent must work as a team.

The term *articulation* refers to the correct placement of the articulators (teeth, tongue, lips, jaw, etc.) during speech.

Articulation   Young children typically make **articulation** errors that adults find charming (e.g., *yap* for *lap*), but when baby talk is not outgrown, parents may become concerned. It is necessary to be clear about which articulation errors are typical and which are the results of a delay. Table 1.2 shows the average rate of acquisition of phonemes and provides a standard against which to judge articulation development. When articulation is severely delayed, professional assistance from a speech-language pathologist is needed.

Voice disorders consist of problems with duration, intensity, pitch, and voice quality.

Voice Disorders   Voice disorders include problems with pitch, such as when the voice register is too high or too low, and with loudness, such as when a child is unable to monitor the loudness or softness of her voice. Voice quality features such as harshness, hoarseness, breathiness, hyper- or hyponasality, and problems of resonance may occur in young children with speech disorders. These require professional intervention.

Cleft Palate and Other Craniofacial Anomalies Cleft palate and other craniofacial anomalies are medical conditions that require specialized care. Often, surgery is involved and, for many newborns, even the act of sucking is affected. Children with cleft palates may be hesitant to speak, resulting in delayed production. Those with severe impairments may have limited social contacts as a result of either increased illnesses and hospitalizations or fear of rejection by the child or parent. The teacher, parent, and medical professional must work together closely to develop and carry out a program to meet the child's comprehensive needs.

Specific Language Impairment

Language impairments may occur secondary to hearing loss, mental retardation, autism, emotional conflict, learning disabilities, physical disabilities, and lack of English in the home environment. Still, when all these are ruled out, there remains a population of children whose language problems are of an unknown source. They are said to have **specific language impairment**. Leonard (2000, 2003) defines specific language impairment (SLI) as a problem in the comprehension and/or expression of language with other areas of development being relatively intact. Children with SLI lag behind their peers in word acquisition (Nash & Donaldson, 2005) and initial grammatical skills (Hamann et al., 2003). There is evidence that young children with SLI have family histories of the same (Tallal et al., 2001), that SLI influences later reading and academic success, and that SLI may continue into adulthood (Crago & Gopnik, 1994). When assessing a preschooler for the presence of SLI, it is helpful to determine if a family history exists. A distinguishing characteristic of the SLI population is that development among language components occurs differentially, with "moderate levels of difficulty with several linguistic domains, such as the lexicon, in conjunction with significant and long-lasting problems with grammatical morphology" (Watkins, 1997, p. 173). It is this discrepancy among the child's proficiency with various components of language that is the hallmark of SLI.

> Specific language impairment results from problems with language comprehension and production unaccounted for by intellectual, social, emotional, or experiential factors.

Hearing Loss

The majority of children who are deaf and have parents who can hear remain significantly delayed in communication throughout their lives, whether the comparison is to children and parents who can hear or children and parents who are deaf (Bandurski & Galkowski, 2004). Language development, whether spoken or signed, is dependent on the opportunities a child has for uptake of the language (Lederberg & Spencer, 2001). Many children who are deaf and hard of hearing and have parents who can hear grow up linguistically impoverished. Spencer and Lederberg (1997) and Lederberg and Prezbindowski (2000) summarized the literature on the interactions of mothers who could hear with their babies who were deaf and found that the mothers missed their children's signals or cues. When a mother

Courtesy of Dr. Susan Easterbrooks

The responsiveness of a caring adult is critical to early communication development.

For children with hearing loss, how and when intervention begins is more important to the child's communicative abilities than whether or not the parents use spoken language or signed language.

misses these, she misses a prime opportunity to provide language stimulation. Although mothers with normal hearing tend to lack natural skills in visual communication, mothers who are deaf understand how to maintain their child's attention. Communication development is based on shared attention, which in turn depends on the responsiveness of a caring adult with whom the child routinely interacts (Sass-Lehrer, 1999). Jung and Short (2004) noted that mothers who are deaf clarify communication for their preschoolers who are deaf and willingly produce ungrammatical (i.e., baby talk) utterances in an effort to make their messages clear.

Of great concern in the instruction of children with hearing loss is the need to provide a coherent, consistent model of natural language as early as possible. However, this rarely occurs because families tend to change communication modes over time (Lederberg & Spencer, 2001). Typically, prompted by various professionals, families first choose an oral approach (Meadow, 2005), and often switch to a signing approach at a later date. Fathers who can hear tend to have poorer signing skills than do mothers who can hear (Gregory, 1995), further limiting available communication in the home. Although there are few studies with large numbers of children that compare signed to spoken language development, the case and small-group studies available consistently report positive benefits for language development in the presence of sign (Preisler & Ahlstroem, 1997; Wilbur, 2000). Whether a hearing loss is mild or profound, it significantly affects the language learning process.

Vision Loss

Although the grammar of children with vision loss is not significantly different from that of sighted children (Matsuda, 1984), differences are found in how their language is acquired. Impairment in vision results in an absence of the early gestural language that occurs between a mother and an infant. Further, a child with vision impairment lacks mobility, resulting in fewer experiences with the environment. Limiting direct experiences results in a child's forming concepts based on insufficient or incomplete perceptual clues that, in turn, result in only partial understanding of experiences (House & Davidson, 2000). According to Santin and Simmons (1977), the "early language of the blind child does not seem to mirror his developing knowledge of the world, but rather his knowledge of the language of others" (p. 427).

The preschool teacher must assume a number of roles in relation to the developing language of a child who is visually impaired. In particular, the teacher must be aware of helping the child overcome **verbalisms**. First, the teacher must make words as richly meaningful as possible so that they hold semantic loads as close as possible to normal. Second, the teacher must help keep the child in touch with the environment. Because much communication is gestural, children who are blind miss out on many aspects of a daily routine. For example, children who are sighted see the teacher putting away his materials and know it is time to go to the music circle. They see the juice tray rolled into the room and know it is snack time. Children who are visually impaired must be told that these events are occurring. The teacher must maintain a running dialogue with a child who is blind, describing each event that occurs in the room to give the child an opportunity to interact more naturally with the environment. Keeping a running commentary going can be very tiring, but it is absolutely essential. If aides or parents are in the classroom, rotating turns will keep the child in touch while giving the speaker a rest.

> Verbalisms are words used for which the speaker has no experiential base.

Cerebral Palsy

The language of a young child with cerebral palsy may be restricted by neuromuscular involvement. There are multiple challenges to serving a preschooler with cerebral palsy who also has language deficits. Olswang and Pinder (1995) found that as children with cerebral palsy improved in their ability to engage in coordinated looking, or joint attending, with an adult to an object, their sophistication in play behaviors increased. Restricted mobility may limit a child's interaction with the environment, resulting in a sparser meaning to the language that the child understands and produces. Pragmatically, the child may not have the opportunity to interact with the world in the same fashion as her peers with no motor problems; hence, some of the functions of language may be overused whereas others are delayed in developing. Children with cerebral palsy must learn to compensate for structural differences.

> As many as 80% of babies with cerebral palsy may have some form of speech or language impairment (Odding, Roebroeck, & Stam, 2006).

Other Health Impairments and Neurological Problems

The category of other health impairments and neurological problems is so extensive that it cannot be treated adequately in this chapter. Several of the more pervasive problems, however, are described briefly.

Substance Abuse   As noted in chapter 2, maternal ingestion of chemical substances such as alcohol, tobacco, tranquilizers, cocaine, and marijuana can cause disabilities in newborns. In fact, ingestion of a chemical often is taking place before a mother knows she is pregnant (Floyd, Ebrahim, Tsai, O'Connor, & Sokol, 2006), and within the drug-addicted population, there is significantly less prenatal care (Behnke, Eyler, Woods, Wobie, & Conlon, 1997). For example, infants with fetal alcohol syndrome (FAS) have distinct physical features and behavior manifestations, including characteristics of attention deficit disorder, memory problems, and language delays. Children with FAS can be difficult to manage because, due to language delays, they are unresponsive to verbal cautions (Coggins, Timler, & Olswang, 2007), exhibit poor impulse control, have difficulty relating behavior to consequences, possess poor short-term memory, have an inconsistent knowledge base, have difficulty grasping abstract concepts, have difficulty managing anger, have rapid mood swings, possess poor judgment, and have unusual physiological responses (Hoyme et al., 2005; McCreight, 1997). These problems interfere with language acquisition as well as with social interactions.

AIDS/HIV   Approximately 75% of children who are infected with HIV are born to mothers who are intravenous drug users or who were infected through sexual activity (Crites, Fischer, McNeish-Stengel, & Seigel, 1992). Children born with HIV/AIDS have multiple insults associated not only with the disease, but also with the drug used, the poor nutrition usually found in drug users, and the prematurity of infants born to drug users. Prematurity and poor nutrition influence all aspects of a child's development, including the development of communication.

Autism Spectrum Disorder

Among the most challenging of preschool children are those with autism spectrum disorders (ASD), which occur in between 4 to almost 60 per 10,000 children (Prior, 2003). Disorders along the continuum include autism, Asperger's disorder, pervasive developmental disorder (PDD), childhood disintegrative disorder, and Rett syndrome (American Psychiatric Association, 1995). The absence or delay of communication skills is a common characteristic of children along the autism spectrum and is a diagnostic criterion of ASD (Ralabate, 2006). Because ASD exists along a spectrum, behavior, and thus communication intervention, are highly individualized (Moes & Frea, 2002). Moore-Brown and Montgomery (2001) reported the existence of a variety of methods for communication intervention. The decision regarding which method to use is best made by interdisciplinary teams of professionals which include the parents. The perspective on language often associated with ASD is that individuals have severe deficits in joint attention initiation (MacDonald et al., 2006), which requires the ability to focus on the same thing as the communicative partner. Language development may be impaired because joint attending (intersubjectivity) is a key component to language development.

Bernard-Opitz (1982) discovered that the pragmatic behavior of her subjects varied across communicative settings and partners, but was stable within settings and with partners. **Communicative intent** is difficult to understand in children with autism. Even individuals who are very familiar with a child may have difficulty understanding what various actions mean (Keen, Sigafoos, & Woodyatt, 2005); however, pragmatic study may prove to be useful in elucidating the needs of these children. Such information suggests that there may be a base of abilities from which to work with children who have autism.

Attention Deficit-Hyperactivity Disorder

Many of the characteristics of children with **central auditory processing disorders** (CAPD)—that is, difficulties in perceiving and understanding language not associated with hearing loss, intelligence, or specific language impairment—are similar in nature to the characteristics of children who have attention deficit-hyperactivity disorder (ADHD), although assessment and intervention for these two disorders differ (Riccio, Cohen, Garrison, & Smith, 2005). Some of these shared characteristics include inappropriate verbal responses, distraction in the presence of background noise, difficulty in sustaining attention for verbal instruction over a period, inattention, and difficulty completing multistep tasks. An evaluation of a child with ADHD should include information about her auditory processing skills. This includes assessment of the child's ability to make fine auditory discriminations, to retain and recall auditory sequences, and to focus on an auditory figure against a distracting background.

:: SPECIFIC STRATEGIES FOR ASSESSMENT OF COMMUNICATIVE FUNCTIONING

Assessing speech and language is an intensive and time-consuming process. Numerous test instruments provide a quick survey of skills; however, quick surveys offer little direction for formulating the necessary remediation strategies. Communication assessment should be ongoing. A variety of strategies should be used, from language sampling and formal tests to observations of the child's behaviors in natural settings. All areas of development should be considered as they relate to communication acquisition. Parents and/or primary caregivers should be involved actively in the process. Assessment should be tailored to specific communication objectives rather than being determined by a score, and application to intervention should always be considered (Sigafoos, Arthur-Kelly, & Butterfield, 2006). Screening assessments and diagnostic assessments must be conducted on young children, and information from these assessments must be shared at a team meeting with different disciplines present.

A few particularly noteworthy tests for preschoolers are presented in Table 6.2. Because new tests appear on the market often and because of the unique needs of young children, it is wise to consult a speech-language pathologist to determine how best to assess current communication skills. Further, a strong knowledge base in the development of speech and language skills will make the evaluator or interventionist a more astute consumer.

| TABLE **6.2**   Commonly used tests of preschool communication development. |||
Test	Author/Publisher	Description
Receptive-Expressive Emergent Language Test (3rd ed.)	Bzoch, K., League, R., & Brown, V. (2003). Austin, TX: PRO-ED.	The REEL–2 is a revision of an earlier tool. Designed for use in early intervention programs, it assesses both receptive and expressive language via parent interviews of infants and toddlers.
Boehm Test of Basic Concepts 3–Preschool Version	Boehm, A. (2001). New York: Psychological Corporation.	The *Boehm Preschool Version* assesses the knowledge in children aged 3 to 5 years of 26 basic relational concepts necessary to begin school.
Sequenced Inventory of Communication Development (Rev. ed.)	Hendrick, D., Prather, E., & Tobin, A. (1984). Austin, TX: PRO-ED.	The SICD–R is a diagnostic battery useful with children whose functional levels range from 4 months to 4 years. The kit includes engaging materials designed to hold even the youngest child's attention.
Test of Early Language Development–(3rd ed.)	Hresko, W., Reid, D. K., & Hammill, D. (1999). New York: Psychological Corporation.	The TELD–3 is a diagnostic language test for use with children from 2.0 to 7.11 years of age. It provides data on receptive and expressive language systems and syntactic/semantic language features.
Preschool Language Scale (4th ed.) and *Preschool Language Scale*–Spanish Edition	Zimmerman, I., Steiner, V., & Pond, R. (2002). New York: Psychological Corporation.	The PLS–4 assesses auditory comprehension and expressive communication in children from 2 weeks of age to 6 years 11 months.
Clinical Evaluation of Language Fundamentals–Preschool (2nd ed.)	Wiig, E. H., Secord, W., & Semel, E. M. (2004). New York: Psychological Corporation.	Measures a broad range of receptive and expressive language skills in children aged 3 to 6.

∷ INSTRUCTIONAL METHODS AND STRATEGIES FOR INTERVENTION

Early intervention is the key to communication development in children who are not progressing at normal developmental rates (Calderon & Naidu, 2000; Talay-Ongan, 2001; Yoshinaga-Itano, 1999). The age at which intervention begins has such a critical influence on a child's development that IDEA requires states to provide preschool services to all children with disabilities. Early intervention encourages family members to incorporate appropriate interactions into their daily routines and develop a supportive communication environment without which a child's communication development may be permanently delayed. Without a foundation of early intervention, the child may not have the foundation upon which to build later education.

Intervention approaches and practices have changed over the years to reflect the changes in linguistic theory described earlier in this chapter. A discussion of general theories of intervention and some guiding principles for intervention follow.

Collaboration

Early interventionists are required to understand a variety of intervention procedures across an array of service options to meet the needs of a diverse population. In order to bring into play the best expertise, **collaboration** is often necessary. "Collaboration is a style in which two co-equal parties engage voluntarily in shared decision making as they work toward a common goal. It involves shared participation, resources ownership, accountability, and rewards" (Secord, 1999, p. 7). Sharing problems, resources, and solutions to enhance outcomes for children is the key to this approach. Collaboration must occur during every facet of intervention, from identification and assessment through goal and objective setting to service provision.

With regard to the youngest children, the early interventionist, the parents, and related personnel become the collaborators. Because the parents have such a central role in the application of information, they must by necessity become the focal point. Parents should be recognized for their expertise. They know their children better than anyone else does, and they know their family's lifestyle better than anyone else does. Mutual respect fosters trust, and trust is the key to involvement. The only way to make a real impact on the life of a child within the context of the family is to be involved with that family. A spirit of openness, sharing of information, and a mutual effort to bring about positive change and growth are the hallmarks of collaborative consultation.

Didactic and Child-Directed Approaches

Didactic approaches are those that involve direct teaching of a communication goal in a highly structured manner (McConkey-Robbins, 1998). Techniques such as reinforcement, shaping, chaining, fading, and prompting are used as well as modeling, imitation, and expansion (Angeliki, 2006). Many of these techniques are based in behavioral theories and can be found in resources describing behavioral principles and applied behavior analysis (ABA) strategies (Angeliki, 2006).

Caregiver-Child Interactions and Naturalistic Environments

Parents are a child's first language teachers. When a child has an obvious disability or when language is not developing as expected, some parents begin to doubt their effectiveness in guiding their youngsters through the communication environment. However, parents *can* learn strategies to develop communication in their children (Kashinath, Woods, & Goldstein, 2006). Instruction for the parents in the home, or for caregivers in a child-care environment outside the home, can build confidence in both the parent or caregiver and child (Gallagher, Easterbrooks, & Malone, 2006).

Influence of Preschool Inclusion on Language Intervention

The early education classroom can be an excellent environment for assisting children in developing communication skills. For a young child with even the most severe disability, the social environment of a preschool can provide opportunities to learn new ways to communicate and to practice developing skills. Interaction is the key ingredient to communication development, and most children are often full of ideas and desires that they can share more easily with their peers.

Principles of Intervention

It is a rewarding challenge to help young children learn to communicate. Consider the following principles and practices when designing communication interventions:

1. *Use comprehensive assessment results.* Interventionists should base language goals and objectives on a sound assessment of a child's current and unique status. Assessment based on a good understanding of developmental sequences in form, content, and use of language is essential. Chronological and mental ages can give only gross approximations of a child's needs and abilities.

2. *Develop activities that focus on interaction within a social context.* This means that language should be worked on in the context of communication with others. Computer-assisted instruction, picture cards, and sentence-building cards are useful for reinforcement, but they cannot take the place of human interaction while new forms and uses of language are developing.

3. *Make activities purposeful.* Language must be meaningful and purposeful, not rote and sterile, if a child is to achieve maximum gains. Involving teachers, classmates, parents, siblings, and all possible intervention agents in the interactive process is essential. Create the need to communicate.

4. *Use natural situations.* Language should be taught naturally. Asking the child to repeat "The spoon is in the box" is unrealistic because one rarely places a spoon in a shoe box in real life. Encouraging language in naturalistic settings does not, however, mean that the choice of skills to be taught should be left up to chance occurrence in the communicative exchange. Specific language goals should be outlined, and appropriate situations that allow for the development of these should be fostered. Table 6.3 provides some suggestions for encouraging communication at different ages in the natural setting.

5. *Allow for variability of development.* Language does not develop in a linear fashion. Some processes develop rapidly whereas others develop more slowly; growth in one area affects growth in another. Children tend to learn language in spurts. The early interventionist must account for these spurts and pace intervention to a child's rhythm, not to what a particular checklist or convention dictates.

6. *Take advantage of spontaneous opportunities.* Although programming decisions must be based on a firm knowledge of the developmental processes, this does not preclude the need to take advantage of vicarious, incidental, and spontaneous learning experiences. For example, if someone knocks on their door, Ian's mother might call his attention to the sound and ask, "Who is that? Who

Communication problems represent critical components in the diagnosis of ASD.

Language does not develop in a linear fashion.

TABLE 6.3	Helpful suggestions for encouraging communication at different ages.
Age	**What You Can Do**
Birth to 3 months	Sing. Talk, talk, talk. Listen to music. Imitate baby's cooing sounds back to her.
3 to 6 months	Get eye contact, then talk, smile, and sing. Imitate baby's precanonical babblings back to her. Touch baby and move her arms and legs rhythmically to a sing-songy voice. Talk, talk, talk.
6 to 9 months	Move baby's hands to play peek-a-boo and pat-a-cake. Play silly voice games. Present child with a variety of toys and other familiar objects. Describe these. Use lots of intonation and inflection. Play "Where's the _____? There's the _____." Point out the location of the object in question. Play with baby's name. Search around and say, "Where's _____? There you are. I see _____!" Play same game in front of mirror. Look at what child is looking at and label it. Talk, talk, talk. Show child picture books that she can chew and touch. Describe the objects.
9 to 12 months	Sing. Talk, talk, talk. Wave baby's hand "bye-bye" when someone leaves. Start other scripting activities. Play "Where's your nose? There's your nose. Where's Mommy's nose? There's Mommy's nose." Attach a familiar sound to a set of objects, such as *brrrr-brrrr-brrr* to a toy car, *wooo-wooo* to a toy train, and *mooooo* to a toy cow. Roll balls back and forth saying, "Roll the ball." Engage in repetitive activities where you say a word multiple times, such as *rock-rock, rock-rock* or *washy-wash, washy-wash*. Imitate her babblings. Show child picture books that she can manipulate. Watch what child is pointing to and comment about it.
12 to 15 months	Label objects in the environment and describe them. Read stories to child and talk about the pictures. Ask child to label familiar objects in the pictures. Engage in fingerplays. Sing. Script interactions such as, "Say, 'Please.' Say, 'Thank you.' Say 'Night-night, Daddy.'" Tell your child nursery rhymes. Express great enthusiasm when your child produces words. Do activities over and over again. Children of this age love repetition and familiarity. When child gives you an object, talk about it. Label objects and actions associated with daily routines.
15 to 18 months	Allow child time to express herself. When she pulls you somewhere, go along and talk about what she has led you to. Ask questions about objects and actions associated with daily routines, such as "Which cup do you want today? The blue cup or the red cup?"

(Continued)

TABLE **6.3** (Continued)	
Age	**What You Can Do**
	Introduce "sabotage," where you place an object in an unusual situation. For example, put child's sock on your head and say, "Sock, sock, where are you, sock?" or give her a serving spoon to eat with, then say, "Uh-oh. That's too big. You need a smaller spoon." Engage in pretend play with dolls, cars, stuffed animals, etc.
	Expand scripting to social routines, such as, "Say, 'Don't hit me.'" Or "Say, 'I want some.'"
	Expand on child's language. Repeat what she has said, then add a little bit more grammar or a little bit more information. Read stories with evident sequences. Reread multiple times.
18 to 24 months	Encourage child to do activities where she must follow directions, such as bringing her shoe or throwing away her napkin. Read, read, read. Teach child lots of nursery rhymes. Expand pretend play to include actions that occur outside the home. Expand scripting to community routines, such as, "Tell the mailman, 'Here's a letter.'" Or "Tell the grocery store lady, 'See you tomorrow.'"
2 to 3 years	Language is growing by leaps and bounds. Continue to provide a model of good grammar, good speech, and good manners. Continue to model and expand child's language. Engage in imaginary play extensively. Teach child her first and last name. Expand descriptions of objects and actions in the environment by using descriptive adjectives. Read and reread favorite books. Go to storytime at the local library. Be sure that Dad reads to child as well. Continue to develop a repertoire of nursery rhymes and fingerplays. Ask lots of questions about everything. Answer all her questions. Set aside some quiet time where you and child can sing, read, talk, or just be quiet with each other.

Sources: Adapted from Estabrooks, 1994; Hulit & Howard, 2001; Morrisset-Huebner & Lines, 1994.

is that? Let's see. Open the door. Oh! It's Grandma!" If they are at the park and someone accidentally loses some balloons, she could call Ian's attention to the balloons and say, "Uh-oh. The balloons are loose. Look. I see a red balloon. I see a green balloon. Up, up, up. They're going up."

7. *Develop new information within the context of old information.* Children need a means of classifying and categorizing what they are learning. They accomplish this most easily when interventionists attach new information to old. New syntax structure should develop within the context of known experiences and known vocabulary (e.g., When teaching Ian "my," his mother would make sure Ian knows the name for the articles they are identifying, such as my shoe/your shoe, my socks/your socks.). New vocabulary should develop within the context of known syntax. For example, when teaching color words, Ian's mother should make sure that he already knows the "description-object" form, such as "big ball" or "little dog." Then she can easily help him master "red ball" or

"brown dog." Children need to have their auditory environment organized and consistent in order for it to make sense.

8. *Teach vocabulary in depth.* Teach all contexts and meanings of a word. Using one word in all its contexts and functions is better than using a number of words in a limited context and more closely approximates natural language development. Initially children put most of their efforts into labeling objects and actions, but they rapidly try them out in new situations as if they were testing their hypotheses about language. If interventionists are too concerned about adding greater numbers of words to children's vocabularies, children may stay at the labeling stage far longer than is natural. This does not give children the opportunity to test and expand the language skills that they have acquired. Conversely, a core lexicon of 50 vocabulary items is required for **novel-mapping**. Novel-mapping refers to the child's ability to map unknown words onto new objects, and it provides an important gateway into multiword use.

9. *Make language experiences fun.* Often, what an adult thinks is fun is entirely different from what a child thinks is fun. Knowledge of what children find enjoyable at different ages is essential.

10. *Be aware of developmentally appropriate intervention.* There are significant differences between how a baby learns and how a toddler learns. Intervene as is developmentally appropriate.

VIGNETTE 6.1

IAN

Ian, the little boy in this chapter's opening vignette, is now 3 years old and eligible for preschool services from his local school system. In preparation for his transition to the new setting, his parents and intervention specialist meet to develop an appropriate program plan. Although he has made considerable progress, he is still approximately one year behind his peers in language development. In particular, his sentence structure is limited as evidenced by his scores on the Sequenced Inventory of Communication Development–Revised and the Test of Early Language Development–3, and he does not routinely use repair strategies to correct miscommunications. He also has difficulty with "where" and "when" questions. The team agrees that these would be appropriate instructional objectives for Ian. They agree that language support should be a focus of the social and play activities that the teacher will develop and use. Ian is in for a very fun year.

:: TECHNOLOGY IN ASSESSMENT AND INTERVENTION

IDEA defines **assistive technology** (AT) as "any item, piece of equipment, or product system, whether acquired commercially off the shelf, modified, or customized, that is used to increase, maintain, or improve functional capabilities of a child with a disability"

The term *assistive technology* refers to any of a variety of technologies that assist individuals with disabilities.

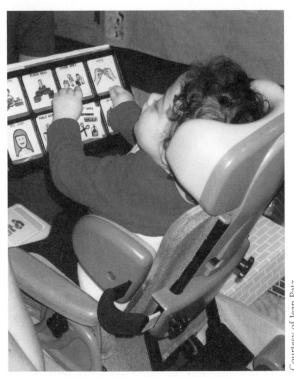

Alternative communication technology can assist children with communication across different settings.

Augmentative communication is a process of assisting individuals to communicate through the use of high-tech or low-tech devices.

Typically developing babies of about 9 to 13 months of age rely heavily on communicative gesturing and develop a pseudosign system to express their wishes and needs.

(34 C.F.D. Sec. 300.5), and includes such things as hearing aids, other assistive listening devices, tape recorders, closed-circuit televisions, and computer programs. **Augmentative** and **alternative communication** (AAC) devices are AT tools that assist students specifically in the area of communication. For children with severe mental and motor impairments, oral communication may not be a realistic goal; yet, given appropriate tools, these children may be able to communicate their needs and wishes.

Augmentative communication is the use of symbols, aided or unaided, to support individuals with difficulties in communication (Hetzroni, 2004). Usually, the use of aided symbols "is applied by assistive technology" (p. 1306). They include (a) the communication device or technique, (b) the representational symbol set or system, and (c) the communication skills necessary for effective use of the system" (p. 429). They include such products as communication boards, picture exchange communication systems, speech-to-speech telephone access, speech output augmentation devices, and assistive listening devices (Moore-Brown & Montgomery, 2001).

When assessing which AT or AAC option to choose, team members should take several factors into account. First, an evaluation of the student's communication skills and needs must be conducted. Second, training and technical assistance for the device must be secured. Third, procedures for acquiring and using the device must be undertaken. Fourth, procedures for maintaining and troubleshooting the device must be established. In addition, there must be procedures in place to coordinate training for users and managers of the device (Moore-Brown & Montgomery, 2001). The use of AT and AAC devices is a dynamic process, not a static one, and continued monitoring of the child's skills is essential as her communication skills likely will change over the course of her development, and the AAC needs will change in tandem. Finally, although AT and AAC devices can be of significant value, they are useless if no one knows how to fix them when they break or whom to turn to for assistance. Consequently, ongoing **developmental surveillance** is a must.

An alternative communication system that has been used successfully with a wide array of communication problems is **sign language.** It has been used with such disabilities as autism (Bondy & Frost, 2002) and mental retardation (Grove & Dockrell, 2000). Sign language is an appropriate tool because it can be used by individuals at very young mental ages. We have long known that children as young as 8 months of age who have a hearing disability are able to use sign language (Schlesinger & Meadow, 1972). In fact, in typical development, babies of about 9 to 13 months of age rely heavily on communicative gesturing and develop a pseudosign system to express their wishes and needs (Rodrigo et al., 2006). This tool allows them to communicate long before they are developmentally ready to utter their first words. Therefore, until a child with a disability is developmentally ready to produce words orally, the use of signs may provide the same kind of bridge between understanding and orally communicating as does communicative gesturing in the typically developing child.

> Collaboration entails calling upon the expertise of a variety of individuals to understand and provide for the needs of an individual child.

SUMMARY

The acquisition of a system of communication is an achievement of monumental proportion; yet, good communication is so central to our existence that we are barely aware of it. Only when communication is delayed does the complexity of its nature become apparent. This chapter discussed development, assessment, disorders, and intervention within the domain of communication. Current communication theory points to the need on the part of interventionists to understand the complex nature of communication. Communication is multifaceted and tends to develop in a common sequence; however, it does not develop in a linear fashion. Indeed, different processes undergo spurts at different times. Delays or growth in one area affect delays or growth in

another. By 4 years of age, the average youngster has mastered the basics of adult language. If remediation is not available to children with communication problems before they reach school age, they may never completely catch up on all their delayed skills.

Assessment of communication in children is the first step toward remediation. Depending on the cause of the deficit, different intervention strategies may be appropriate. In some cases, alternative communication devices may be recommended for a child. Collaboration among professionals and caregivers is always an essential ingredient. The importance of communication in our society demands that its development be a high priority in programs for young children with special needs.

REVIEW QUESTIONS AND DISCUSSION POINTS

1. What are the important features of development around the one-word stage that lead to a child's acquisition of word combinations?
2. Why is newborn hearing screening so important?
3. Describe how the following influence language development: hearing loss, vision loss, diminished

   intellectual capacity, and linguistic and cultural diversity.
4. Reread the opening vignette. How would you relate the issue of naturalistic environment to Ian's case?
5. Language develops within a cultural context. Explain what this means.

RECOMMENDED RESOURCES

Recommended Reading

Journal of Early Intervention

Young Exceptional Children

Hemmeter, M. L., Joseph, G. E., Smith, B. J., & Sandall, S. (Eds.). (2001). *DEC recommended practices program assessment: Improving practices for young children with special*

needs and their families. Denver, CO: Division for Early Childhood. Order online at *http://www.sopriswest.com*

Sandall, S., McLean, M., Smith, B. (Eds.). (2000). *DEC recommended practices in early intervention/early childhood special education.* Denver, CO: Division for Early Childhood. Order online at *http://sopriswest.com*

Professional Associations

American Association of Homebased Early
  Interventionists (AAHBEI) AAHBEI serves parents and
  those who work in the field of early home intervention
  with infants, toddlers, and preschoolers with special
  needs. (*www.aahbei.org*)

Division for Communicative Disabilities and Deafness
  (DCDD) DCDD is the division of the Council for
  Exceptional Children that focuses on issues
  pertaining to communication. Its Constituent
  Committee on Infants, Toddlers, and Preschoolers
  addresses early intervention. (*http://education.gsu.edu/
  dcdd*)

Division for Early Childhood (DEC) of the Council for
  Exceptional Children (CEC) The Division for Early
  Childhood promotes polices and advances evidence-
  based practices that support families and enhance the
  optimal development of young children who have or
  are at risk for developmental delays and disabilities.
  (*http://www.dec-sped.org*)

Websites

American Speech-Language-Hearing Association
http://www.asha.org

Boystown National Research Hospital
http://www.babyhearing.org

Head Start Bureau
http://www.acf.dhhs.gov/programs/hsb/

***National Center for Hearing
Assessment Management***
http://www.infanthearing.org

National Childcare Information Center
http://ericps.crc.uiuc.edu/nccic/

***National Association for the Education
of Young Children (NAEYC)***
http://www.naeyc.org

Zero to Three National Training Institute
http://www.zerotothree.org/

REFERENCES

American Psychiatric Association. (1995). *Diagnostic and statistical manual of mental disorders* (4th ed.). Washington,
DC: Author.

American Speech-Language-Hearing Association. (1998).
*Survey of speech-language pathology services in school-based
settings* [Final report]. Rockville, MD: Author.

Angeliki, G. (2006). The effects of prompting and social reinforcement on establishing social interactions with peers
during the inclusion of four children with autism in preschool. *International Journal of Psychology, 41*(6), 541–554.

Bandurski, M., & Galkowski, T. (2004). The development of
analogical reasoning in deaf children and their parents'
communication mode. *Journal of Deaf Studies and Deaf
Education, 9*(2), 153–175.

Bates, E. (1976). *Language and context: The acquisition of pragmatics.* New York: Academic Press.

Bates, E., Camaioni, L., & Volterra, V. (1975). The acquisition of performatives prior to speech. *Merrill-Palmer
Quarterly, 21,* 205–226.

Behnke, M., Eyler, F., Woods, N., Wobie, K., & Conlon, M.
(1997). Rural pregnant cocaine users: An in-depth

sociodemographic comparison. *Journal of Drug Issues,
27*(3), 501–524.

Berko, J. (1958). The child's learning of English morphology.
Word, 14, 150–177.

Bernard-Opitz, V. (1982). Pragmatic analysis of the communicative behavior of an autistic child. *Journal of Speech
and Hearing Disorders, 47,* 96–99.

Bloom, L. (1970). *Language development: Form and function in
emerging grammars.* Cambridge, MA: MIT Press.

Bloom, L. (1973). *One word at a time: The use of single-
word utterances before syntax.* The Hague, Netherlands:
Mouton.

Bloom, L., & Lahey, M. (1978). *Language development and
language disorders.* New York: Wiley.

Boehm, A. (2001). *Boehm test of basic concepts–Preschool version.* New York: Psychological Corporation.

Bondy, A., & Frost, L. (2002). *A picture's worth: PECS and
other visual communication strategies in autism.* Topics in
Autism. Bethesda, MD: Woodbine House.

Bradlow, A., Kraus, N., & Hayes, E. (2003). Speaking clearly
for children with learning disabilities: Sentence percep-

tion in noise. *Journal of Speech, Language, and Hearing Research, 46*(1), 80–97.

Brown, R. (1973). *A first language: The early stages.* Cambridge, MA: Harvard University Press.

Brownlee, S. (1998, June 15). Baby talk. *U.S. News & World Report, 124*(23), 48–50.

Bruner, J. (1981). The social context of language acquisition. *Language and Communication, 1,* 155–178.

Bzoch, K., & League, R. (2003). *Receptive-expressive emergent language test* (3rd ed.). Austin, TX: PRO-ED.

Calderon, R., & Naidu, S. (2000). Further support of the benefits of early identification and intervention with children with hearing loss. *The Volta Review, 100,* 53–84.

Chomsky, N. (1957). *Syntactic structures.* The Hague, Netherlands: Mouton.

Chomsky, N., & Halle, M. (1968). *The sound pattern of English.* New York: Harper and Row.

Clark, H., & Clark, E. (1977). *Psychology and language.* New York: Harcourt Brace Jovanovich.

Coggins, R., & Carpenter, R. (1981). The *communicative intention inventory*: A system for coding children's early intentional communication. *Applied Psycholinguistics, 2,* 235–252.

Coggins, T. E., Timler, G. R., & Olswang, L. B. (2007). A state of double jeopardy: Impact of prenatal alcohol exposure and adverse environments on the social communicative abilities of school-age children with fetal alcohol spectrum disorder. *Language, Speech, and Hearing Services in Schools, 38,* 117–127.

Collins, D., & Rourke, B. (2003). Learning-disabled brains: A review of literature. *Journal of Clinical and Experimental Neuropsychology, 25*(7), 1011–1034.

Conboy, B. T., & Mills, D. L. (2006). Two languages, one developing brain: Event-related potentials to words in bilingual toddlers. *Developmental Science, 9*(1), F1–F12.

Crago, M. B., & Gopnik, M. (1994). From families to phenotypes: Theoretical and clinical implications of research into the genetic basis of specific language impairment. In R. Watkins & M. Rice (Eds.), *Specific language impairment in children.* Baltimore: Brookes.

Crites, L., Fischer, K., McNeish-Stengel, M., & Seigel, C. (1992). Working with families of drug-exposed children: Three model programs. In L. Rosetti (Ed.), *Developmental problems of drug-exposed infants.* San Diego, CA: Singular.

Dale, P., Simonoff, E., Bishop, D., Eley, T., Oliver, B., Price, T., et al. (1998). Genetic influence on language delay in two-year-old children. *Nature Neuroscience, 1,* 324–328.

deBoysson-Bardies, B., Sagart, L., & Durand, C. (1984). Discernible differences in the babbling of infants according to target language. *Journal of Child Language, 11,* 1–15.

Donohue, M. (2006). Classification and human language. *Theory, Culture, & Society, 23*(2/3), 40–42.

Dore, J. (1974). A pragmatic description of early development. *Journal of Psycholinguistic Research, 3,* 343–350.

Dromi, E. (1999). Early lexical development. In M. Barrett (Ed.), *The development of language: Studies in developmental psychology* (pp. 99–131). Philadelphia: Psychology Press.

Downey, D., Mraz, R., Knott, J., Knutson, C., Hotte, L., Van Dyke, D. (2002). Diagnosis and evaluation of children who are not talking. *Infants and Young Children, 15,* 38–48.

Durand, V. M., & Merges, E. (2001). Functional communication training: A contemporary behavior analytic intervention for problem behaviors. *Focus on Autism and Other Developmental Disabilities, 16,* 110–119.

Estabrooks, W. (1994). *Auditory-verbal therapy for parents and professionals.* Washington, DC: AG Bell Association.

Facon, B., Facon-Bollengier, T., & Grubar, J. (2002). Chronological age, receptive vocabulary, and syntax comprehension in children and adolescents with mental retardation. *American Journal on Mental Retardation, 107,* 91–98.

Fenson, L., Dale, P. S., Reznick, J. S., Bates, E., Thal, D. J., & Pethick, S. J. (1994). Variability in early communicative development. *Monographs of the Society for Research in Child Development, 59*(5), (Serial No. 242).

Ferrier, S., Dunham, P., & Dunham, F. (2000). The confused robot: Two-year-olds' responses to breakdowns in conversation. *Social Development, 9*(3), 337–347.

Floyd, R., Ebrahim, S., Tsai, J., O'Connor, M., & Sokol, R. (2006). Strategies to reduce alcohol-exposed pregnancies. *Maternal Health Journal, 10,* 5149–5151.

Gallagher, P. A., Easterbrooks, S., & Malone, D. G. (2006). Universal newborn hearing screening and intervention. *Infants & Young Children: An Interdisciplinary Journal of Special Care Practices, 19*(1), 59–71.

Garcia, P. (2004). Developmental differences in speech act recognition: A pragmatic awareness study. *Language Awareness, 13*(2), 96–115.

Gershkoff-Stowe, L., Connell, B., & Smith, L. (2006). Priming overgeneralizations in two- and four-year-old children. *Journal of Child Language, 33*(3), 461–486.

Gray, S. (2004). Word learning by preschoolers with specific language impairment: Predictors and poor learners. *Journal of Speech, Language, and Hearing Research, 45*(5), 1117.

Gregory, S. (1995). *Deaf children and their families.* Cambridge, England: Cambridge University Press.

Grove, N., & Dockrell, J. (2000). Multisign combinations by children with intellectual impairments: An analysis of language skills. *Journal of Speech, Language, and Hearing Research, 43*, 309–323.

Halliday, M. (1975). *Learning how to mean: Explorations in the development of language*. London: Edward Arnold.

Hamann, C., Ohayon, S., Dube, S., Fraunfelder, U. H., Rizzi, L., Starke, M., & Zesiger, P. (2003). Aspects of grammatical development in young French children with SLI. *Developmental Science, 6*(2), 151–158.

Hendrick, D., Prather, E., & Tobin, A. (1984). *Sequenced inventory of communication development* (Rev. ed.). Austin, TX: PRO-ED.

Hetzroni, O. E. (2004). AAC and literacy. *Disability and Rehabilitation, 26*(21/22), 1305–1312.

House, S., & Davidson, R. (2000). Increasing language development through orientation and mobility instruction. *Re:View, 31*(4), 149–152.

Hoyme, H., May, P., Kalberg, W., Kodituwakku, P., Gossage, J., Trujillo, P., et al. (2005). A practical clinical approach to diagnosis of fetal alcohol spectrum disorders: Clarification of the 1996 Institute of Medicine criteria. *Pediatrics, 115*(1), 39–47.

Hresko, W., Reid, D. K., & Hammill, D. (1999). *Test of early language development* (3rd ed.). Austin, TX: PRO-ED.

Hulit, L. M., & Howard, M. R. (2001). *Born to talk* (3rd ed.). Upper Saddle River, NJ: Merrill/Prentice Hall.

Iverson, J. M., Longobardi, E., & Caselli, M. C. (2003). Relationship between gestures and words in children with Down's syndrome and typically developing children in the early stages of communicative development. *International Journal of Language & Communication Disorders, 38*(2), 179.

Iverson, J., Volterra, V., Pizzuto, E., & Capirici, O. (1994, June). *The role of communicative gestures in the transition to the two-word stage*. Poster presented at International Conference of Infant Development, Paris, France.

Jakobson, R. (1968). *Child language, aphasia, and phonological universals*. The Hague, Netherlands: Mouton.

Jung, V., & Short, R. (2004). Organization of successive events during social-emotional interactions between infants who are deaf or hard of hearing and caretakers: Implications for learning syntax. *The Volta Review, 104*(2), 69–92.

Kashinath, S., Woods, J., & Goldstein, H. (2006). Enhancing generalized teaching strategy use in daily routines by parents of children with autism. *Journal of Speech, Language, and Hearing Research, 49*(3), 466–485.

Keen, D., Sigafoos, J., & Woodyatt, G. (2005). Teacher responses to the communicative attempts of children with autism. *Journal of Developmental & Physical Disabilities, 17*(1), 19–33.

Lederberg, A. R., & Prezbindowski, A. K. (2000). Impact of child deafness on mother-toddler interaction: Strengths and weaknesses. In P. Spencer, C. Erting, & M. Marschark (Eds.), *The deaf child in the family and at school: Essays in honor of Kathryn P. Meadow-Orlans* (pp. 73–92). Mahwah, NJ: Lawrence Erlbaum Associates.

Lederberg, A. R., Prezbindowski, A. K., & Spencer, P. E. (2000). Word learning skills of deaf preschoolers: The development of novel mapping and rapid word learning strategies. *Child Development, 71*, 1571–1585.

Lederberg, A. R., & Spencer, P. E. (2001). Vocabulary development of young deaf and hard of hearing children. In M. D. Clark, M. Marschark, & M. Karchmer (Eds.), *Context, cognition, and deafness* (pp. 88–112). Washington, DC: Gallaudet University Press.

Lenneberg, E. (1967). *Biological foundations of language*. New York: Wiley.

Leonard, L. B. (2000). *Children with specific language impairment*. Cambridge, MA.: MIT Press.

Leonard, L. B. (2003). Specific Language Impairment: Characterizing the deficit. In Y. Levy & J. C. Shaeffer (Eds.), *Language competence across populations. Toward a definition of Specific Language Impairment* (pp. 209–231). Mahwah, NJ: Lawrence Erlbaum.

Leung, A. K. C., & Kao, C. P. (1999). Evaluation and management of the child with speech delays. American Family Physician, 59, 3121–3127.

Lindsay, R., Tomazic, T., Whitman, B., & Accardo, P. (1999). Early ear problems and developmental problems at school age. *Clinical Pediatrics, 38*(3), 123–132.

Lucas, E. V. (1980). *Semantic and pragmatic language: Assessment and remediation*. Rockville, MD: Aspen.

Lyytinen, P., Poikkeus, A., Laaks, M., Eklund, K., & Lyytinen, H. (2001). Language development and symbolic play in children with and without familial risk for dyslexia. *Journal of Speech, Language, and Hearing Research, 44*, 873–885.

MacDonald, R., Anderson, J., Dube, W., Geckeler, A., Green, G., Holcomb, W., et al. (2006). Behavioral assessment on joint attention: A methodological report. *Research in Developmental Disabilities, 27*(2), 138–150.

Mandler, J. M. (2004). Thought before language. *Trends in Cognitive Sciences, 8*(11), 508–513.

Mar, H. H., & Sall, N. (1999). Profiles of the expressive communication skills of children and adolescents with severe cognitive disabilities. *Education and Training in Mental Retardation and Developmental Disabilities, 34*, 77–89.

Matsuda, M. M. (1984). Comparative analysis of blind and sighted children's communication skills. *Journal of Visual Impairment and Blindness, 78*, 1–5.

Matychuck, P. (2005). The role of child-directed speech in language acquisition: A case study. *Language Sciences, 27*(3), 301–379.

McConkey-Robbins, P. (1998). Two paths of auditory development for children with cochlear implants. *Loud and Clear Newsletter, 1*(1), 1.

McCreight, B. (1997). *Recognizing and managing children with fetal alcohol syndrome/fetal alcohol effects: A guidebook.* Washington, DC: Child Welfare League of America, Inc.

Meadow, K. P. (2005). Early manual communication in relation to the deaf child's intellectual, social, and communicative functioning. *Journal of Deaf Studies and Deaf Education, 10*(4), 321–329.

Moes, D., & Frea, W. (2002). Contextualized behavior support in early intervention for children with autism and their families. *Journal of Autism and Developmental Disorders, 32*(6), 519–533.

Moll, H., & Tomasello, M. (2006). Level 1 perspective-taking at 24 months of age. *British Journal of Developmental Psychology, 24*(3), 603–613.

Montgomery, J. (2000). Verbal working memory and sentence comprehension in children with specific language impairment. *Journal of Speech, Language, and Hearing Research, 43*, 293–308.

Moore-Brown, B. J., & Montgomery, J. (2001). *Making a difference for America's children: Speech-language pathologists in public schools.* Eau Claire, WI: Thinking Publications.

Morgan, J. L. (1996). Prosody and the roots of parsing. *Language and Cognitive Processes, 11*, 69–106.

Morrisset-Huebner, C. E., & Lines, P. (1994). *Learning link: Helping your baby learn to talk.* Washington, DC: U.S. Department of Education, Office of Educational Research and Improvement.

Muma, J., & Teller, H. (2001). Developments in cognitive socialization: Implications for deaf education. *American Annals of the Deaf, 146*(1), 31–38.

Nash, M., & Donaldson, M. (2005). Word learning in children with vocabulary deficits. *Journal of Speech, Language and Hearing Research, 48*(2), 439–459.

National Center for Hearing Assessment & Management. (2002). *Early hearing detection and intervention information & resource center.* Retrieved September 1, 2002, from http://www.infanthearing.org/ehdi.html

National Institutes of Health. (1993). Early identification of hearing impairment in infants and young children. *NIH Consensus Statement, 11*, 1–24.

Nelson, I. (1973). Structure and strategy in learning to talk. *Monographs of the Society for Research in Child Development, 38*, (Serial No. 149).

Noonan, M., & McCormick, L. (2006). *Young children with disabilities in natural environments: Methods and procedures.* Baltimore: Brooks Publishing Company.

Ogletree, B. T., & Oren, T. (2001). Application of ABA principles to general communication instruction. *Focus on Autism and Other Developmental Disabilities, 16*, 102–109.

Oller, K. D. (1980). The emergence of the sounds of speech in infancy. In G. Yeni-Komshian, J. Kavanaugh, & C. Ferguson (Eds.), *Child phonology* (pp. 93–112). New York: Academic Press.

Olswang, L. B., & Pinder, G. L. (1995). Preverbal functional communication and the role of object play in children with cerebral palsy. *Infant-Toddler Intervention: The Transdisciplinary Journal, 5*, 277–299.

Owens, R. (2004). *Language development: An introduction* (6th ed.). Boston: Allyn & Bacon.

Paavola, L., Kunnari, S., & Moilanen, I. (2005). Maternal responsiveness and infant intentional communication: Implications for the early communicative and linguistic development. *Child Care, Health and Development, 31*(6), 727–735.

Preisler, G. M., & Ahlstroem, M. (1997). Sign language for hard of hearing children: A hidrance or a benefit for their development? *European Journal of Psychology and Education, 12*(4), 465–477.

Prior, M. (2003). Is there an increase in the prevalence of autism spectrum disorders? *Journal of Paediatrics and Child Health, 39*(2), 81–82.

Prutting, C. (1979). Process: The action of moving forward progressively from one point to another on the way to completion. *Journal of Speech and Hearing Disorders, 44*, 1–20.

Ralabate, P. (2006). The puzzle of autism. Washington, DC: National Education Association.

Riccio, C. A., Cohen, M. J., Garrison, T., & Smith, B. (2005). Auditory processing measures: Correlation with neuropsychological measures of attention, memory, and behavior. *Child Neuropsychology, 11*, 363–372.

Rice, M. L., Buhr, J. C., & Nemeth, M. (1990). Fast mapping word learning abilities of language-delayed preschoolers. *Journal of Speech and Hearing Research, 55*, 33–42.

Rice, M., Wexler, K., & Hershberger, S. (1998). Tense over time: The longitudinal course of tense acquisition in children with specific language impairment. *Journal of Speech, Language, and Hearing Research, 41*(6), 1412–1431.

Rodrigo, J. M., González, A., Ato, M., Rodriguez, G., de Vega, M., & Muñetón, Y.M. (2006). Co-development of child-mother gestures over the second and third years. *Infant and Child Development, 15*(1), 1–17.

Rubin, S., & Johnson, C. (2002). Lexical access in college students with learning disabilities: An electrophysiological and performance-based investigation. *Journal of Learning Disabilities, 35*(3), 257–267.

Santin, S., & Simmons, J. N. (1977). Problems in the construction of reality in congenitally blind children. *Journal of Visual Impairment or Blindness, 71,* 425–429.

Sass-Lehrer, M. (1999). Techniques for infants and toddlers who are deaf or hard of hearing. In S. Raver (Ed.), *Strategies for infants and toddlers with special needs: A team approach* (2nd ed., pp. 259–297). New York: Prentice Hall.

Sattler, J. (2001). *Assessment of children: Cognitive applications* (4th ed.). San Diego: Author.

Schlesinger, H., & Meadow, K. (1972). *Sound and sign.* Los Angeles: University of California Press.

Secord, W. A. (1999). *School consultation: Concepts, models, and procedures.* Flagstaff: Northern Arizona University.

Seung, H. K., & Chapman, R. (2004). Sentence memory of individuals with Down's syndrome and typically developing children. *Journal of Intellectual Disability Research, 48*(2), 160–171.

Shulman, B. (1985). *Using play behavior to describe young children's conversational abilities.* Paper presented at the annual meeting of the National Association for the Education of Young Children, Los Angeles, CA.

Sigafoos, J., Arthur-Kelly, M., & Butterfield, N. (2006). *Enhancing everyday communication for children with disabilities.* Baltimore: Brookes Publishing Company.

Skinner, B. F. (1957). *Verbal behavior.* Acton, MA: Copley Publishing Group.

Spencer, P. (1993). Communication behaviors of infants with hearing loss and their hearing mothers. *Journal of Speech and Hearing Research, 36,* 311–321.

Spira, E., & Fischel, J. (2005). The impact of preschool inattention, hyperactivity, and impulsivity on social and academic development: A review. *Journal of Child Psychology and Psychiatry, 46*(7), 755–773.

Stoel-Gammon, C. (1998). Role of babbling and phonology in early linguistic development. In A. M. Wetherby, S. F. Warren, & J. Reichle (Eds.), *Transitions in prelinguistic communication* (pp. 87–110). Baltimore: Brookes.

Stromswold, K. (2006). Why aren't identical twins linguistically identical? Genetic, prenatal, and postnatal factors. *Cognition, 101,* 333–384.

Talay-Ongan, A. (2001). Early intervention: Critical roles of early childhood service providers. *International Journal of Early Years Education, 9,* 221–228.

Tallal, P., Hirsch, L. S., Realpe-Bonilla, T., Miller, S., Brzustowicz, L. M., Bartlett, C., et al. (2001). Familial aggregation in specific language impairment. *Journal of Speech, Language, and Hearing Research, 44,* 1172–1182.

Tomasello, M. (1992). *First verbs: A case study of early grammatical development.* New York: Cambridge University Press.

Trantham, C. R., & Pedersen, J. K. (1976). *Normal language development.* Baltimore: Williams & Wilkins.

Treon, M., Dempster, L., & Blaesing, K. (2006). MMPI-2/A Assessed personality differences in people who do, and do not, stutter. *Social Behavior and Personality: An International Journal, 34*(3), 271–293.

Veneziano, E., Sinclair, H., & Berthoud, I. (1990). From one to two words: Repetition patterns on the way to structured speech. *Journal of Child Language, 17,* 633–650.

Vygotsky, L. (1962). *Thought and language.* Cambridge, MA: MIT Press.

Wakefield, C., Homewood, J., & Taylor, A. (2006). Early blindness may be associated with changes in performance on verbal fluency tasks. *Journal of Visual Impairment & Blindness, 100*(5), 306–310.

Warner-Rogers, J., Taylor, A., Taylor, E., & Sandberg, S. (2000). Inattentive behavior in childhood: Epidemiology and implications for development. *Journal of Learning Disabilities, 33,* 520–536.

Watkins, R. (1997). The linguistic profile of SLI. In L. B. Adamson & M. A. Romski (Eds.), *Communication and language acquisition: Discoveries from atypical development* (pp. 161–185). Baltimore: Brookes.

Wiig, E. H., & Semel, E. M. (1984). *Language assessment and intervention for the learning disabled* (2nd ed.). Upper Saddle River, NJ: Merrill/Prentice Hall.

Wilbur, R. B. (2000). The use of ASL to support the development of English and literacy. *Journal of Deaf Studies and Deaf Education, 5*(1), 81–104.

Yoshinaga-Itano, C. (1999). Development of audition and speech: Implications for early intervention with infants who are deaf or hard of hearing. *Volta Review, 100*(5), 213–234.

Yoshinaga-Itano, C., & Apuzzo, M. L. (1998). Identification of hearing loss after 18 months is not early enough. *American Annals of the Deaf, 143*(5), 380–387.

Zarfaty, Y., Nunes, T., & Bryant, P. (2004). The performance of young deaf children in spatial and temporal number tasks. *Journal of Deaf Studies and Deaf Education, 9*(3), 315–326.

Zeisel, S., & Roberts, J. (2003). Otitis media in young children with disabilities. *Infants and Young Children, 16*(2), 106–119.

Zimmerman, I., Steiner, V., & Pond, R. (2002). *Preschool language scale–4.* New York: Psychological Corporation.

Social and Emotional Development

Joan Lieber[*]

[*] Warren Umansky contributed to this chapter.

Chapter Outline

- Definitional Issues
- Theories of Social and Emotional Development
- Factors Affecting Social and Emotional Development
- Social and Emotional Development in Children with Special Needs
- Specific Strategies for Assessment of Social-Emotional Functioning
- Types of Assessment and Assessment Instruments
- Intervention Strategies to Promote Social and Emotional Development
- Technology in Assessment and Intervention

Adam

Mrs. Glenn is a teacher at Brookfield, an inclusive childcare program. She has 15 children in her classroom ranging in age from 3 years to almost 5 years. About a month ago, a new child, Adam, started the program. He has Down syndrome and he's having a hard time getting used to the classroom routine and particularly to the other children. When Adam's mom brought him to the program on his first day, he had a hard time separating from his mother. He clung to her and became teary-eyed. But Mrs. Glenn knew that Adam really liked trains, so she asked Adam's mom to make sure Adam brought his favorite engine with him. When Adam noticed the train track that was on the floor in the block area, he brought his engine over and added it to the trains on the track. At that point, Adam's mom was able to leave.

In the month that Adam has been at Brookfield, Mrs. Glenn has spent some time observing him as he participates in the daily routine. Although Adam now engages in most of the teacher-led activities, Mrs. Glenn has noticed that Adam doesn't pay much attention to the other children. There are many times during the day when children have the opportunity to interact: circle time, choice time, snack time, and outside time. The 45-minute choice time gives him the opportunity to initiate whatever activity he wants and to be with other children. But Mrs. Glenn has observed that Adam spends his time wandering around the room, taking toys off the shelves, and watching other children. If another child approaches him, Adam might smile, but he hasn't joined the play of the other children. Mrs. Glenn knows that Adam has been at Brookfield only a month, but she's concerned that he doesn't have even one friend. Mrs. Glenn has concerns about Adam's social and emotional development.

:: DEFINITIONAL ISSUES

Social and emotional development in children is a particularly rich and complex topic. These areas not only encompass the development of abilities in the individual himself, but how he uses these abilities to engage others. Emotions evolve from simple physiological responses to more complex responses. These include a cognitive component that is necessary to understand one's own emotions as well as those of others. Social behavior also starts out simply, with overtures toward others that can be as straightforward as a smile. Social responses quickly become more complex and soon children are engaged in friendships.

When we study social and emotional behavior, partner and setting are important considerations. Children interact quite differently with different partners such as their parents, teachers, and peers. Children's behaviors vary in different settings as well: at home, at school, and on the playground, for example.

Emotional Development

Emotion involves the expression of feelings, needs, and desires accompanied by specific physiological responses. Because emotions are biologically based, they are "one of the most ancient and enduring features of human functioning" (Shonkoff & Phillips, 2000, pp. 106–107).

As children grow, they develop **emotional competence.** According to Denham and Burton (2003), emotional competence has three components: expression, understanding, and regulation.

Emotional Expression   Children show emotion in reaction to an event that happens (e.g., a loud noise) or in reaction to what other people do (Denham & Burton, 2003). What children do in reaction to the emotions they feel is termed **emotional expression.** Children express basic emotions like happiness and sadness, as well as more sophisticated ones like pride, shame, and empathy.

Emotional Understanding   As infants and toddlers become preschoolers, their cognitive and language abilities mature and they become better equipped to understand their own emotions and those of others. According to Denham and Burton (2003), preschool children base their emotional understanding on others' expressions as well as situations. Young children tend to understand happy situations better than those that are negative, and are even capable of using language to describe emotions they have experienced.

Emotional Regulation   It is difficult to separate children's emotional development from their ability to regulate emotions so that they can function adequately in social interactions (Shonkoff & Phillips, 2000). Emotional regulation is needed when "the experience and expression of emotion become too much or too little . . . for the child and/or his social partners" (Denham & Burton, 2003, p. 110). For example, children spend 15 minutes chasing each other on the playground during outside time at their preschool. They grow more and more excited, but then their teacher abruptly tells them it is time to come in and get ready for story time. They need to use emotional regulation to switch their expression of excitement to calmness for both themselves and for their teacher. At another time during the preschool day, a child learns to regulate his anger at a peer who knocks down an elaborately constructed block structure. He expresses his anger through words rather than by hitting or having a tantrum.

Emotion involves the expression of feelings, needs, and desires accompanied by specific physiological responses.

Emotional competence has three components: expression, understanding, and regulation.

What children do in reaction to the emotions they feel is termed emotional expression.

Emotional understanding is the ability to understand one's own emotions and the emotions of others.

Emotional regulation is necessary when the presence or absence of emotional expression and experience interfere with a person's goals.

Denham and Burton (2003) suggest that children go through three steps when confronted with an emotion that needs regulation. In the first step, they take notice of their emotion. Second, they consider what the emotion means to them. Finally, they choose a specific response: "Given this feeling, what can I *do* about it?" (p. 111). This response is not necessarily an overt behavior. Children can cope emotionally, cognitively, or behaviorally. For example, the child who gets angry because someone knocks down the block structure he was building might glare at his peer rather than hit him, thereby coping through modulating his response. The child whose mother will not take him to the movies might cope cognitively by saying to himself, "I didn't want to go anyway." The child who is confronted with a snarling dog might cope behaviorally by seeking protection from his mother.

So, for young children, the emotions that begin as mere feelings during infancy combine with developing cognition and language during early childhood to become quite sophisticated. As the variety of emotions increases, emotions often may be kept hidden from others. A normal part of the child's growth process is increasing control over emotional expression, resulting in his ability to self-soothe without the need for adult intervention.

> Children go through three steps when confronted with an emotion that needs regulation.

Social Competence with Peers

Children who are socially competent can "form positive, successful social relationships" (Fabes, Gaertner, & Popp, 2006, p. 299). According to Fabes et al., socially competent children play with other children, enjoy social interactions, and are sought out by their peers.

> Socially competent children form successful social relationships.

The development of social competence begins with children showing an interest in their peers through individual social behaviors. Children as young as 6 months look, smile, and vocalize to another child, and although there seems to be no negative intent, young children also pull hair and poke a finger into another child's eye (Vandell, Nenide, & Van Winkle, 2006). Those individual behaviors develop into social interactions when one child directs a social behavior to another child who responds with a social behavior of his own (Vandell et al., 2006).

> Social interactions occur when one child directs a social behavior to another child who, in turn, responds with a social behavior.

During the preschool years, children interact with their peers with greater frequency and complexity. In an influential study conducted over 70 years ago, Parten (1932) proposed categories to describe how children's social participation changes over the preschool years. Her categories were the following:

> During the preschool years, children interact with their peers with greater frequency and complexity.

- unoccupied behavior
- solitary play
- onlooker behavior
- parallel play, in which children play next to each other but do not interact
- associative play, in which children play and share with others
- cooperative play, in which children coordinate their efforts

Preschool children also are able to combine social play with pretend play (Goncu, Patt, & Kouba, 2002). Children may play together in the "housekeeping" area of a classroom, with one child assuming the role of mother and the other the role of father. The ability to coordinate pretend play with another child is more

In social pretend play, children engage in pretense, interact with others, and coordinate these two activities.

difficult and occurs later than solitary pretend play. **Social pretend play** is considered more complex than other forms of social play because the child must not only be able to engage in pretense and interact with others, but must also coordinate these two activities. Although Adam is a preschooler, his social interactions with his peers are not sophisticated. They are limited to watching his peers play and giving simple responses to their overtures.

Friendship

Friendships are special social relationships; children can engage in both positive and negative social interactions without having friends.

Friendships are special social relationships; children can engage in both positive and negative social interactions without having friends. Craig (2000) describes the distinction. First, friendships are reciprocal. Both partners must share the feeling. Second, the partners feel affection toward their friend. They seek each other out, not because of what they can do for each other, but rather because of what they feel for each other. Third, friendship is voluntary; friendships cannot be mandated.

Friendship is a special social relationship that is reciprocal, affectionate, and voluntary.

Children as young as 2 years of age form friendships, and preferences for some children over others continue into the preschool years and beyond. Children select friends who are similar to them in age, sex, or behavior; and once they select these friends, their social interactions with them are different from social interactions with nonfriends. Play with friends is more positive and more complex. Friends also have more conflicts with each other; but once these conflicts are resolved, they continue to play near each other and engage in interactions (Vandell et al., 2006).

:: THEORIES OF SOCIAL AND EMOTIONAL DEVELOPMENT

Many theories have contributed to our understanding of how children develop emotionally and socially in their first five years. Some theories emphasize the role of nature and suggest that children are born with particular emotional and social tendencies. Others emphasize nurture. In these theories, the environment plays the more important role in children's social and emotional development. Some of those theories and the research traditions that have developed from them are discussed below.

Attachment Theory

Children's attachment to their caregivers not only explains that primary relationship, but it also influences children's relationships with their peers.

Attachment theory is one of the most well-known and well-researched theories to explain children's relationships with their caregivers. Children's attachment to their caregivers not only explains that primary relationship, but it also influences children's relationships with their peers.

Attachment theory was first described by John Bowlby in the 1940s and 1950s. Mary Ainsworth, who worked with Bowlby, was also a major contributor to the theory (Belsky, 2006). According to Bowlby, **attachment** is an evolutionary process through which infants form bonds with their caregivers so that they have a secure base from which to explore their environment (Belsky, 2006). Infants exhibit attachment behaviors, like approaching, crying, and seeking contact, when they want comfort and reassurance. Depending on the infant's perception of how the caregiver responds to these behaviors, an attachment relationship may be formed.

Ainsworth et al. (1978) developed the **"Strange Situation Procedure"** to assess the quality of the attachment relationship between the infant and his caregiver. Solomon and George (1999) explain that during this assessment, which takes about 20 minutes, a parent and an infant (between 12 and 20 months) are put into a room. After the infant has had a few minutes to explore, a stranger enters the room and attempts to play with the infant. Then both the parent and the stranger leave the room. The parent returns and then leaves again. Next, the stranger enters the room. Finally, the parent returns and the stranger leaves. During all these comings and goings, the infant's reactions are observed.

Based on his responses, the infant's attachment with his caregiver is categorized into a pattern of attachment: secure, insecure–resistant, or insecure–avoidant. Infants who are securely attached "use their mother as a secure base from which to explore, reduce their exploration and may be distressed in her absence, but greet her positively on her return, and then return to exploration" (Belsky, 2006, p. 55). In contrast, infants who are insecure–resistant are reluctant to move away from their mother and do not explore their environment. Finally, infants who are insecure–avoidant do not base their exploration on their mother's behavior, are not distressed if their mother leaves, and ignore her when she returns. This theory has spawned hundreds of empirical studies on topics from how attachment changes from infancy through adulthood to how children who are avoidant or ambivalent may become hostile, aggressive, and antisocial to cross-cultural studies of attachment.

There also have been a series of studies of attachment with children with disabilities including Down syndrome (Atkinson et al., 1999), cerebral palsy, and autism (Pipp-Siegel, Siegel, & Dean, 1999). These studies reveal that children with severe disabilities often show atypical attachment patterns. In interpreting these findings, Barnett, Butler and Vondra (1999) concluded that children with Down syndrome may be delayed in their ability to exhibit attachment-related behaviors (e.g., smiling, approaching, vocalizations) and their mothers may have difficulty in interpreting their signals. On the other hand, children with cerebral palsy may have difficulty because they have "damage to the systems that underlie movement" (p. 176). Barnett et al. suggest that children with disabilities may behave differently than typically developing children in the "Strange Situation" used for assessment purposes, but that difference may be one of form rather than function. That is, the children may have the cognitive intent, but are unable to carry out attachment behaviors as a result of their disability.

Emotional Intelligence

Along with a renewed interest in the physiology of emotions, the concept of emotional intelligence has been proposed. The model was first proposed by Salovey and Mayer (1990). In Salovey and Mayer's view, intelligence includes more than the cognitive and linguistic components measured by standardized IQ tests. They suggest that intelligence includes an emotional component that is part of social intelligence. It is the "ability to monitor one's own and others' feelings and emotions, to discriminate among them, and to use this information to guide one's thinking and actions" (Salovey & Mayer, 1990, p. 189). **Emotional intelligence** allows people to live and work well with others. According to Salovey and Mayer, emotional intelligence has several distinct components:

- knowing and expressing emotions
- regulating emotions
- recognizing emotions in others and responding to them in empathetic ways
- using emotions in adaptive ways

Social Learning Theory

Learning theory emphasizes the role of the environment in the development of personality and specific behaviors. Bijou and Baer (1979) place great emphasis on interpreting a child's current behaviors based on his history of interactions with the environment. **Socialization,** then, is viewed as a child's range of experiences from which he develops his personality and learns appropriate behaviors.

Bandura (1977) provided the foundation for explaining social learning theory and for distinguishing it from behavioral theory. Whereas the latter emphasizes the role of reinforcement in maintaining or halting certain behaviors, Bandura proposed that most learning occurs when children observe, model, and imitate people in their environment. Consequently, an organized and carefully structured environment helps children achieve desired goals. As applied to development of social and emotional skills, sound models and situations that encourage the display of prosocial behaviors are those that facilitate the most normal development.

A Developmental Biopsychosocial Model: The Developmental, Individual Differences, Relationship-Based (DIR) Approach

Greenspan and Wieder (2006) suggest that development comes about as a result of three influences: (1) the child's genetic inheritance, (2) the child's social environment, including his family and culture, and (3) the interaction between heredity and environment.

Using these influences, Greenspan and Wiedner developed their DIR approach to assess and work with children who have developmental problems.

First, they evaluate a child's functional emotional development (D) to see "how the child uses everyday functioning to integrate all capacities to carry out emotionally meaningful goals" (Greenspan & Wiedner, 2006, p. 4). These areas of development include the following:

- the ability to stay calm while receiving sensory experiences
- interaction with familiar caregivers
- having interactions that include two-way communication and problem solving
- giving meaning to symbols
- linking two or more ideas

Although each child progresses through each of these stages of development, there are individual differences (I) among children. Children differ in their ability to modulate sensory input; in the way they process language, auditory and visual input, and emotions; and in their muscle tone, motor planning, and sequencing. Finally, children develop within a unique family, community, and culture (R).

:: FACTORS AFFECTING SOCIAL AND EMOTIONAL DEVELOPMENT

Young children often show unique behaviors in their interactions with others or when they are confronted with overwhelming emotions. Yet, the range of typical behavior is broad. Children's behaviors and reactions can be attributed to factors that are within and outside themselves.

Temperament

Theorists and researchers who emphasize the role of nature in development believe that every child is born with a set of personality characteristics that Thomas and Chess (1977) call **temperament.** These characteristics play an important role in shaping the responses of a child's caregivers and, ultimately, in molding the child's future personality. There has been enormous interest in temperament since researchers first studied it in the 1920s. Since those early investigations, the concept of temperament has evolved. For example, Thomas and Chess originally identified nine dimensions of temperament. Because their dimensions were not independent, other researchers combined them into three dimensions. Sanson, Hemphill, and Smart (2002) call the first dimension *negative emotionality,* and include irritability, negative mood, inflexibility, and high intensity as negative reactions. *Self-regulation* is the second dimension, and includes persistence, nondistractibility, and emotional control. The third dimension, *approach/withdrawal, inhibition, or sociability* includes both approaching new situations and people or withdrawing from them.

These attributes of temperament combine to characterize differences between children and how they respond to their caregivers (Thomas & Chess, 1977). The **easy child,** for example, is very adaptable, playful, and responsive to adults. This type of child is likely to receive a great deal of adult attention during the early years because interactions are so pleasant and reinforcing. The **difficult child,** on the other hand, provides little positive feedback to adults. He is fussy, difficult to soothe, and has problems sleeping and eating. Finally, the temperament of the **slow-to-warm-up child** is characterized by slow adaptability. Adults who sustain contact with this type of child are usually rewarded by the positive behaviors found in the easy child, but it takes considerably longer to elicit them.

Although there is some evidence that temperament is stable over time, there are some factors that affect some types of temperament. Martin and Fox (2006) suggest that these factors include the sex of the child (e.g., inhibited girls are more likely to change than inhibited boys), children's participation in out-of-the-home care (e.g., children who receive outside child care become less inhibited over time), and parental characteristics

> Attributes of temperament combine to characterize differences among children and how they respond to their caregivers.

(e.g., parents who are overcontrolling have children who remain inhibited over time). Limited research has examined the role of cultural differences on temperament; this research largely has been conducted with older children (Sanson et al., 2002).

Gender

One of the more widely reported gender differences in social and emotional development is that boys exhibit more aggression than girls. Although there seems to be little difference in the rate of aggression in infancy, by the time children enter preschool, boys engage in more conflict and in more verbally and physically aggressive acts than girls. According to Underwood (2002), this gender difference holds across socioeconomic groups and across cultures. Males tend to be more vulnerable to family and life stresses than females (Patterson, DeBaryshe, & Ramsey, 2000). It has been postulated, however, that males are reinforced for more aggressive and competitive behavior by family members and peers, which accounts for increasing differences in their social patterns as they develop (Coie & Jacobs, 2000).

Although the rate of **overt aggression** is much higher among boys, **relational aggression** is higher among girls. Relational aggression "harms others through manipulation or control of relationships" (Crick, 2000, p. 310). Crick and her colleagues designed teacher and peer rating scales to measure relational aggression in preschool children. Behaviors that reflected relational aggression included not inviting a classmate or peer to a birthday party, not letting a peer play in the group, and not listening to a peer or other person because of feelings of anger toward that individual. These behaviors contrasted with those that reflected overt aggression such as pushing and shoving and throwing objects at others in response to frustration. Crick and her colleagues found that teachers particularly rated preschool-aged girls as more relationally aggressive and less overtly aggressive than preschool-aged boys. They also found that children who showed either type of aggression were rejected by their peers more often than those who were not aggressive.

> Children who show overt or relational aggression are rejected by their peers more often than children who do not.

Stress

The formation of a child's personality is closely related to the types of stress to which he is subjected in his early years and to how he deals with that stress. A child who lives in poverty, has multiple hospital stays, or comes from a dysfunctional home is at risk for long-lasting psychosocial disorder. Still, some resilient children handle stress better than others do and many progress through adverse early years relatively undamaged (Masten & Gerwitz, 2006). Those resilient children benefit from adults in both their family and their community who are competent and caring (Masten, 2001).

Sibling Relationships

Researchers have speculated that children's social interactions with peers are affected by the relationships they have with their siblings. This makes intuitive sense for a number of reasons. First, children spend a lot of time with siblings—more time than they spend with either their parents or, when they are young, with their peers. Second, siblings give children the opportunity to practice social skills. They have

Courtesy of Jean Patz

Siblings can affect children's relationships with their peers.

the opportunity to engage in positive social exchanges and to resolve conflict with partners who, unlike parents, have a similar level of sophistication. Although researchers have hypothesized that there is a link between children's interactions with siblings and with peers, little empirical evidence for that link exists (Dunn, 2002).

There is particularly limited research on the nature of sibling relationships in minority communities and in non-Western cultures (Dunn, 2002). The nature of sibling relationships outside of the United States may differ because, in a number of cultures, siblings often function as caregivers from an early age and may serve to socialize children for parenthood (Dunn, 2002).

Parental Style

Baumrind (1973) speculated that parents' style of interacting with their child would have an impact on that child's later development. He described parents as authoritative, authoritarian, or permissive.

The **authoritative parent** is firm and willing to set limits, but not intrusive. Authoritative parents encourage their children to explore their environments and gain interpersonal competence. In contrast, the **authoritarian parent** is harsh, rigid, and unresponsive to her child. The third type of parent, the **permissive parent**, is affectionate toward her child but lax and inconsistent with her discipline. As a consequence, her child is uncontrolled and may show impulsive behavior (Parke & Buriel, 1998).

Parke and Buriel (1998) found a number of problems with Baumrind's conceptualization of parental style. First, a distinction can be drawn between style (or parental attitudes) and parental practices. Second, as noted by Sameroff and his colleagues (Sameroff & Chandler, 1975; Sameroff & Fiese, 1990), the direction of effects is as likely to be from the child to the parent as the reverse. Finally, the scheme may not be universal. It may not apply to parents from different socioeconomic backgrounds or to parents from diverse cultures. For example, Russell, Mize, and Bissaker (2002) note that some research has shown that, in African American families, harsh discipline co-exists with warm and nurturing relationships more often than in white families.

According to Parke et al. (2002), parents do indeed affect their children's social and emotional development through three different routes: (1) they interact directly with their children; (2) they instruct, teaching their children about what constitutes important social behavior; and (3) they provide their children with opportunities for social experiences.

Parke et al. (2002) assert that children's social relationships extend beyond the immediate family to the extended family, the neighborhood and school, and places of worship. Because children have so many chances to interact with others and form relationships, parents can enhance children's relationships by actively managing these opportunities. For example, parents can supervise their children's choice of activities and friends, they can initiate and arrange play dates for their children, and they can enroll their child in organized activities like religious (pre)school.

Both mothers and fathers influence children's social and emotional development. Research does not make clear whether the relationships that children have with mothers and fathers is more similar than different; however, there is some evidence that interaction with fathers is more often focused on play and recreation, while interactions with mothers tend to revolve around caregiving (Russell et al., 2002).

> Because children have so many chances to interact with others and form relationships, parents can enhance children's relationships by actively managing these opportunities.

:: SOCIAL AND EMOTIONAL DEVELOPMENT IN CHILDREN WITH SPECIAL NEEDS

A spectrum of disabilities can affect children's development in the areas of emotion and emotional regulation, social skills, social competence, and friendship formation. Establishing successful relationships with peers is a complex process that proves difficult for many children. Asher (1990) noted that as many as 10% of children in elementary school are rejected by their peers. These numbers are even higher for some groups of children, particularly those with disabilities.

> Establishing successful relationships with peers is a complex process that proves difficult for many children.

Children with Autism

According to the National Research Council (2001), children with autism have major difficulties in both their social and emotional relationships in a number of areas.

- They have low rates of social initiation with and response to peers.
- They show little nonverbal communication. Gesturing and emotional expression may be absent.
- They pay less attention to others' emotional displays than do their typical peers.
- They show less empathy or shared emotion.

One particularly important social deficit in children with autism is that they fail to develop **joint attention** skills. According to Mundy and Stella (2000), joint attention is the "tendency to use eye contact, affect, and gestures for the singularly social purpose of sharing experiences with others" (p. 55).

The majority of children with autism show differences in emotional understanding as well. Sigman and her colleagues (1992, 1999) found that children with autism were less responsive to adults who pretended to injure themselves. They spent less time looking at the injured adult and were rated as showing less empathy than either typically developing children or children with Down syndrome. Sigman and Ruskin (1999) concluded that children with autism generally show a lack of social attention and are particularly deficient in attending to the faces of other people.

Children with autism also have particular difficulty in their social relationships with peers. When Sigman and Ruskin (1999) compared children with autism to children with developmental delays, they found that the children with autism played in isolation significantly more often. When these children were at recess, much of their time was spent in self-stimulatory activities rather than in play with others. Although they sometimes attempted to interact with other children, they initiated contact and responded to contact less frequently than children with other disabilities. When children with autism did participate in social activities with other children and made social bids, those bids were accepted as frequently as those of other children. Once they began social interchanges, they lasted as long as those of other children.

Children with Developmental Delays

Sigman and Ruskin (1999) conducted a series of studies examining the emotional development of children with Down syndrome and other developmental delays. In contrast to the children with autism, when confronted with an experimenter who showed distress, the children with developmental delays looked frequently at the experimenter's face. They also were rated as showing greater empathy than the children with autism and were rated similarly to the typically developing children in the sample.

Substantial research has documented the social interactions and social competence of young children with developmental delays. Guralnick (2001) found that, in comparison to typically developing peers, children with developmental delays generally show more solitary play, are more negative with their partners during play, and have less success with peers when they make social bids. Hestenes and Carroll (2000) found similar results. The preschool children with disabilities that they studied spent more of their time in solitary and onlooker play than their peers. They did, however, spend about 30% of their play time in cooperative play.

Children with Communication Disabilities

It might be expected that children with communication disabilities would have difficulty developing successful relationships with their peers. These children may have difficulty with any of a number of areas of communication, including articulation, syntax, semantics, and pragmatics. These disabilities may affect children's expressive abilities, which in turn may influence their ability to be understood by their peers as well as their peers' subsequent willingness to participate in a social interchange.

Guralnick, Connor, Hammond, Gottman, & Kinnish (1996) used play groups of children with communication disabilities and typically developing children to evaluate the social interactions and the social competence of both groups. They evaluated children's play for the proportion of solitary, parallel, and group play, as well as the amount of time spent unoccupied, as onlookers, and in other activities, such as reading and interacting with an adult. They also observed children's peer-related behavior in other categories, such as using peers as resources, expressing affection, imitating a peer, joining a peer's play, and expressing hostility. Finally, each child was rated by the other children as someone they really liked to play with, someone they "kinda" liked to play with, or someone they do not like to play with—a measure of popularity.

Children with communication disorders were similar to their typically developing peers in a number of areas. Neither group of children had much unoccupied time and there were no differences in acceptance in the two groups. However, children with communication disorders engaged in fewer conversations than their typical peers, had lower rates of positive social behavior, and were less successful when they made social overtures to their peers.

> Children with communication disorders engaged in fewer conversations, had lower rates of positive social behavior, and were less successful when they made social overtures to their peers.

Children with Sensory Impairments

Visual Impairments   There has been little research on how young children with limited sight interact with their peers. There are a number of reasons why research has been so limited. Children with vision impairments make up a diverse group. There are children who are completely blind and those with functional vision. In addition, children with visual impairments often have other disabilities as well, so it is difficult to attribute results to the visual impairment alone. Finally, visual impairments are a very low incidence disability; consequently, the number of children who are affected is small (Diamond, 2002). In spite of these limitations, we do know something about the social development of children who are blind.

It is logical to assume that the social development of children with visual impairments would be affected by their loss of sight. Vision is important in our social interchanges because a major part of these interchanges involves the observation of others. Children who have visual impairments may have difficulty in social relationships because their poor vision prevents them from interpreting subtle social cues, because they cannot see how others respond to their behavior, and

> Vision is important in our social interchanges.

because their understanding of play activities, social rules, and social conventions may be limited or distorted by their lack of sight (Diamond, 2002, p. 581).

Children who are typically developing provide challenges to children who are blind, too. Young children—particularly those who play without using much language—may be unpredictable in their movements around children who are blind (Zanandra, 1998). They may expect quick responses to their social overtures and may move quickly from one activity to another. Expectations for a quick response and transitions from one play activity to another present problems for children who are blind (Zanandra, 1998).

Diamond (2002) reports that studies that do describe the social interactions of children with visual impairments show that they interact more with adults than peers, and that they participate more in solitary activities than would be expected for their age. However, McGaha and Farran (2001) compared the social behaviors of children who were visually impaired or sighted and who attended an inclusive pre-school program. Both groups of children spent most of their time near children who were sighted, but there was no difference between the groups in interaction with other children. In an interesting finding, McGaha and Farran (2001) found that children with visual impairments participated in more interactive play when they were indoors and more parallel play when they were outdoors. They speculated that children who have visual impairments are challenged to engage in interactions when confronted by the large space of a playground and children's tendency to be mobile.

Hearing Impairments Children who have limited hearing share the problems and frustrations in social interaction experienced by children with other sensory impairments. This disability limits children's social experiences and feelings of social competence (Brown, Remine, Prescott, & Rickards, 2000). On the other hand, Vandell and George (1981) reported examples of consistent social competence by children with hearing impairments in their interactions with hearing children. They were persistent initiators of interactions and, in the absence of language, developed alternate communication strategies. Hearing children did not do as well in modifying their communication strategies (i.e., they still used verbal modes), but their social interactions were positive. The implications of these findings support the position that children with hearing impairments can benefit from opportunities for independence and interactions with their environment at an early age.

Researchers have also investigated how children who are deaf or hard of hearing enter and maintain play episodes with their peers. Brown and her colleagues (2000) compared entry strategies to dramatic play and nonplay activities of kindergarteners with profound hearing losses and those with normal hearing. They found both similarities and differences between these two groups. Both groups used utterances or actions that were related to the group activity to gain entry to sociodramatic play and nonplay activities. Both groups were equally successful in gaining entry to the group. However, children with normal hearing showed a greater range of entry behaviors. For example, these children were more likely than children with hearing loss to survey the ongoing play activity and then choose an entry behavior that was related to the play. Children with normal hearing also used entry behaviors that brought attention to themselves and that provided information about themselves to the other play partners.

Children who have limited hearing share the problems and frustrations in social interaction experienced by children with other sensory impairments.

It is important to note that there may be differences between children who are deaf and born to deaf parents compared to children who are deaf and born to hearing parents. Children who are deaf and born to deaf parents may have different opportunities to learn language from their parents and may have the opportunity to interact with peers who share their language system (Brinton & Fujiki, 2002). There is limited research on this important topic, however.

Children with Challenging Behaviors

Many different terms are used to describe and categorize children who exhibit problematic behavior. However, it remains unclear how the available classification systems apply to young children, particularly when normal developmental variations are taken into consideration. There are no norms to help us determine, for example, what constitutes normal activity level, patience, or attention during the preschool years. Additionally, children who have difficulty expressing themselves with words may attempt to resolve their conflicts physically. There is agreement, however, that "it's not the presence of specific problem behaviors that differentiates 'normal' from 'abnormal,' but their frequency, intensity, chronicity, constellation, and social context" (Campbell, 1988, p. 60).

> There are no norms to help us determine what constitutes normal activity level, patience, or attention during the preschool years.

Despite the relative lack of data on their application to preschool children, a number of classification systems exist and are used to diagnose and describe specific emotional and behavioral problems in children. It is important for professionals working with young children with special needs to be familiar with these systems, particularly because some of these systems have measurement devices that may need to be completed by teachers as part of the diagnostic evaluation process.

One of the most commonly recognized systems for classifying child psychopathology is the *Diagnostic and Statistical Manual* (DSM) of the American Psychiatric Association (2000). Now in its fourth edition, this system provides a multidimensional framework for conceptualizing problem behaviors. The current version of the DSM has more specific diagnoses for children than any previous version and requires greater specification for a professional to assign a specific diagnosis. This is the diagnostic system that typically is used by most mental health professionals in the United States.

Regardless of the classification system used, there is a very high prevalence of young children in whom parents and teachers report challenging behaviors. According to Rockhill, Collett, McClellan, and Speltz (2006), 2 to 3% of children fit the criteria for a clinical diagnosis of oppositional defiant disorder (ODD). Among other behaviors, these children exhibit anger, defiance, and noncompliance. About 25 to 50% of the children who are diagnosed with ODD also have attention deficit–hyperactivity disorder (ADHD) (Rockhill et al., 2006). Moreover, children with ODD may also have depressive or anxiety disorders. It is important to note, however, that because of problems with how symptoms are defined for these disorders, we cannot be sure how often they actually co-occur (Rockhill et al., 2006).

> One way of classifying challenging behaviors is by considering those children who have problems with externalizing versus internalizing behaviors.

One way of classifying challenging behaviors is by considering those children who have problems with **externalizing** versus **internalizing** behaviors. Children who exhibit externalizing behaviors show high rates of hyperactivity, impulsivity, aggression, defiance, and noncompliance. These children show undercontrol; their behaviors are often annoying and can cause hurt to others (Campbell, 1990, p. 66). Externalizing behaviors are directed outwardly toward people or objects.

In contrast, children who have internalizing behaviors are fearful, depressed, and withdrawn (Rockhill et al., 2006). Internalizing behaviors are directed inward by the child. Both parents and teachers have more difficulty with children with externalizing behaviors, and those behaviors are remarkably stable over time. Campbell (2002) found that over half of the children who had moderate to severe externalizing behaviors in preschool still showed those behaviors in elementary school, with 67% of these children diagnosed with attention deficit–hyperactivity disorder, oppositional defiant disorder, or a conduct disorder at age 9.

It is not clear what causes children to have behavior problems at such an early age, but researchers have suggested that both organic and environmental factors may put them at risk. For example, children with delays in social, communication, or cognitive development and children who experience poor home or school environments are more likely to exhibit challenging behaviors (Conroy & Davis, 2000).

> Children with delays in social, communication, or cognitive development and children who experience poor home or school environments are more likely to exhibit challenging behaviors.

Children with Attention Deficits

Attention deficit disorders are neurologically based problems causing a child to manifest inattention, distractibility, and impulsivity, and may occur with hyperactivity as well. In fact, it is often the hyperactivity component that contributes to the earlier identification of the problem in young children. For children who do not exhibit the impulsive/hyperactivity component, diagnosis frequently is delayed until the child is in an academic setting.

It is difficult to diagnose ADHD in preschool children for several reasons. First, most of the diagnostic efforts have been with children from 6 to 12 years of age. Second, children may have other disabilities (e.g., language disorders or developmental delays) that lead them to exhibit inattention or an inability to comply with directions. Finally, some of the symptoms of ADHD may be appropriate behaviors for young children. For example, many young children have difficulty sitting still and paying attention (Steinhoff et al., 2006). In spite of the difficulties, it is important to diagnose and treat children with ADHD early, and preschool children should receive a comprehensive evaluation and be followed closely during that developmental period.

For many children with ADHD, effective treatment begins with parent training and a consistent behavior management program. When that alone is not successful, medication may be considered (Steinhoff et al., 2006). While most ADHD medications are not approved for children under 6 years of age, experience from the Preschool ADHD Treatment Study (Greenhill, Kollins, & Abikoff, 2006) indicates that ADHD medications are effective and safe with preschoolers as well as older children and adults.

The classroom teacher often is part of a team consisting of a physician, therapists, the child's parents, and other professionals who help decide on the best course of treatment and intervention for young children with ADHD. With early treatment, social and academic outcomes can be positive.

Social Acceptance and Rejection

Many children with disabilities have successful social relationships with their typically developing peers.

Although there is agreement that children without disabilities interact more often with others without disabilities than they do with those who have disabilities (Hestenes & Carroll, 2000), many children with disabilities have successful social relationships with their typically developing peers. Odom et al. (2002) suggested that, if we look only at the frequency of interactions for children with disabilities, we are not getting a complete view of their social relationships. They also suggested that we should broaden our perspective and use a multimethod approach. In their work, they combined observations of children's interactions with peers, peers' ratings of how much they like to play with others in their classrooms, and teachers' and parents' descriptions of friendships to develop indices of children who were socially accepted and socially rejected. Although children with disabilities were rejected more than their typically developing peers, about one-third of the children in their sample of 80 were well accepted by their peers. Those well-accepted children had a number of characteristics and abilities in common. They had effective social skills, had at least one friend, could communicate with and show affection toward others, could engage in pretend play, and were interested in interacting with their peers. Children who were rejected had a number of characteristics in common as well. These children lacked effective communication and social skills, were disruptive, came into conflict with other children, and were often physically aggressive.

Friendship in Children with Disabilities

Friendship provides children with the potential for enhanced cognitive and language development as well as social and emotional benefits.

Although the social behaviors and social interactions of young children with disabilities have been widely studied, fewer researchers have specifically examined friendship. Having at least one friend is important for children with disabilities for several reasons. According to Buysse (2002), friendship provides children with the potential for enhanced cognitive and language development as well as social and emotional benefits. Buysse (2002) noted that these benefits are "an increased capacity for understanding another's perspective, the ability to regulate one's emotions, and a general feeling of well-being and happiness" (p. 18).

Buysse, Goldman, and Skinner (2002) investigated the friendships of 120 children with disabilities who attended either inclusive child care programs, where a majority of children were typically developing, or specialized programs, where a majority of children had disabilities. Children had a variety of disabilities, with about 40% having severe disabilities. They found that, as a group, 28% of the children with disabilities had no friends, according to their teachers. However, children with disabilities in the inclusive child care programs were almost twice as likely to have at least one friend than the children in specialized programs. In addition, they found that, in child care settings, the children with disabilities were more likely to have a friend who was typically developing.

:: SPECIFIC STRATEGIES FOR ASSESSMENT OF SOCIAL-EMOTIONAL FUNCTIONING

Social skills and emotions are perhaps the most difficult areas of human development to understand. They are situational in nature; that is, a child may be aggressive in one situation and passive in another. He may cry when confronted with some strangers and befriend others. He may engage in complex imaginary play at the babysitter's house but not at home. How, then, is one to gain an understanding of this complex of behaviors? Systematic assessment of the child may provide some answers.

Multimethod Assessment

The behavior of young children is extremely variable depending upon the setting, the time of day, who is present, and other factors. As a result, there has been a shift away from using a single instrument or observation to document a child's behavior. It is important to evaluate children's behavior over time and in a variety of settings. A multimethod approach uses a combination of strategies for collecting information and often includes systematic observations in various settings and at different times of day, interviews, and rating scales.

It is important to evaluate children's behavior over time and in a variety of settings.

Direct observation of a child in different settings may be the most desirable means to evaluate developmental characteristics, because the farther one strays from direct measurements of behavior, the less reliable the results are likely to be. However, in considering the behavior of a young child, observation can be enhanced by including information from those individuals who spend the most time with him (e.g., parents, babysitters, and teachers). There are plusses and minuses when parent reporting is used. Yarrow (1963), for example, examined the value of the interview as an assessment technique and found that information gathered by interviewing parents tends to follow a pattern of idealized expectations and cultural stereotypes. Parents may confuse a child with siblings or feel obligated to respond to questions in spite of vague recollections.

Others, however, have found parental reports to be quite valid. Rothbart and Bates (1998) noted that researchers have determined the accuracy of parental reports by correlating parent ratings with those of an independent rater. When correlations are low, people assume that it is the parents who are less accurate than independent raters. However, it may actually be the independent raters who are not accurate. They may not be familiar with the child and may not see all the behaviors that the parent sees. Additionally, the parents are likely to be aware of children's behaviors that occur infrequently, but may greatly influence ratings.

The skill of the interviewer also affects parents' responses. Parents may not understand exactly what information the interviewer wants. The validity of information gathered in this way may be improved when the parent is requested to recall recent events, when the behaviors to be recalled are clearly defined, and when response choices are specific and easily quantified.

Interviews with children—a technique that Piaget utilized to discover how they process information—are limited by a child's verbal skills. However, the technique does offer an opportunity for the evaluator to establish a relationship with the child that can be helpful throughout the assessment process. With older and typically developing children, interviews may provide valuable information about social and emotional development.

What Is Normal?

A basic problem arises with the issue of assessment of social and emotional development. Although we have discussed characteristics of normal development in these areas, it is quite difficult to assign expected ages to significant social and emotional milestones. There appears to be some consensus about what abnormal behavior is, so that an observer can identify a child exhibiting inappropriate behavior. It is considerably more difficult to be precise about what behaviors children should be displaying in various situations and at different ages since, at young ages, the range of what is considered typical behavior is quite broad. Newer assessment instruments have increased our ability to make comparisons among children and among different situations for a single child.

Assessments Related to Emotional Competence

There has been a long history of assessing social behavior in young children. Parten (1932), for example, developed her observation system for levels of play and social interaction in the 1930s. There has been less history of assessing young children's emotional competence. According to Denham and Burton (2003), however, researchers are now developing assessments to evaluate young children's emotional expressiveness, emotional knowledge, and emotional regulation.

:: TYPES OF ASSESSMENT AND ASSESSMENT INSTRUMENTS
Systematic Observation

The most reliable information about a child can be gathered by observing him in a familiar setting. For most children, that setting can be the home or classroom. In the vignette at the beginning of this chapter, Adam's teacher, Mrs. Glenn, relied on observation to evaluate Adam's behavior. Several principles guide this type of assessment. Observations across many settings may be necessary to get a complete impression of how a child interacts with others, how he interacts with objects, and how he deals with challenging situations or conflicts. Moreover, if the child is not familiar with the observer, it is important to establish rapport with the child before the observation begins.

Finally, the assessor must have defined specific behaviors to observe and have an objective way of recording her observations. Many electronic coding devices have been developed to record time and frequency data, but sophistication is necessary to record information reflecting a child's abilities.

Direct observation is valuable to document the frequency of individual social behaviors as well as social interactions among groups of children.

Direct observation is valuable to document the frequency of individual social behaviors as well as social interactions among groups of children. When a child's social behaviors are observed, the assessor typically notes the frequency and duration of particular behaviors, as well as their quality (Gresham, 2001; McClelland & Scalzo, 2006). One observation system that can be used is the *Individual Social Behavior Scale* designed by Guralnick et al. (1996). With this scale, the frequency is recorded of 19 different behaviors a child directs toward a peer. These behaviors include seeking attention, using a peer as a resource, leading peer activities, imitating a peer, observing a peer, joining a peer, showing pride, competing with a peer for adult attention, expressing affection, showing empathy, showing hostility, taking an unoffered object, defending property, and seeking agreement. Given that this is a complicated system, it requires a lot of practice to observe all of these behaviors reliably. However, once proficiency is achieved with this system, a great deal of information about a child's social behavior with peers is revealed.

Other observational measures go beyond the individual social behaviors of a child and capture the child's participation within a group. One measure that is used extensively was initially described by Parten (1932), wherein observers decide if the target child is engaging in solitary, parallel, or group play as well as determining if there is functional, constructive, or sociodramatic play. Rubin, Coplan, Fox, and Calkins (1995) expanded this system even further to capture behaviors of extremely withdrawn or extremely aggressive children.

Denham (1986) developed the *FOCAL Observation System* to evaluate a child's emotional expressiveness during play. Emotions include happiness, sadness, anger, fear, and several others. Observers document the frequency and duration of these emotionally expressive types of behaviors.

These observational systems give early interventionists valuable information that can be used to make decisions about children's eligibility for special education services, to plan interventions, and to evaluate children's progress. They do have a downside, however, in that they require a great deal of time to administer.

There are other general developmental assessments that include measures of social and emotional development and rely on observation or a combination of observation and interviews with the parent. The *AEPS Test—Birth to Three Years and Three to Six Years* (Bricker, Capt, & Pretti-Frontczak, 2002) includes a social domain among other developmental domains. The assessor uses a combination of observation, parent report, and direct testing to measure children's interactions with others and with the environment, and their knowledge of self and others.

Another popular assessment that is appropriate for children from birth through age six is the *Transdisciplinary Play-Based Assessment* (Linder, 1993). A child's social-emotional development is assessed primarily through observation. This assessment is unique in that each child is systematically observed with a variety of partners including the parent, the facilitator, and peers. In addition, the observer rates a child's temperament, mastery motivation, humor, and use of social conventions.

Interviews and Questionnaires

Most assessment batteries now include a social and family history in the form of an interview or questionnaire protocol. For example, The *DIAL 3* (Mardell-Czudnowski & Goldenberg, 1998), a developmental screening instrument, includes a questionnaire that the parent completes before the child's motor, concepts, and language abilities are screened. The questionnaire includes items about a child's social development and behavior.

A questionnaire also has been devised for early interventionists to assess children's friendships. In *Playmates and Friends* (Goldman & Buysse, 2002), teachers list a child's playmates and how often the child plays with each playmate. The teacher also lists the child's special friends and characteristics of those special friends including age, sex of the friend, whether the friend is also a classmate, how long the children have been friends, and whether the friend has a disability.

Squires, Bricker and Twombly (2002) developed the *Ages and Stages Questionnaires: Social-Emotional* specifically to identify young children who may need further assessment and intervention to address their social-emotional problems. The questionnaire uses a parent report to identify the child's social-emotional competence as well as problem behaviors. Parents report on their child's behavior in the areas of self-regulation, compliance, communication, adaptive behaviors, autonomy, affect, and interactions with people. Some of the questions that parents respond to are: "When upset, can your child calm down within 15 minutes?" and "Does your child try to hurt other children, adults, or animals?" This instrument is appropriate for children from 3 to 63 months of age.

Rating Scales

Approximately 30 years ago, O'Leary and Johnson (1979) indicated that rating scales were very popular for assessing social development. They suggested four strategies to maximize the reliability and validity of a scale: (1) Use raters who know the child very well, (2) use as many raters as possible, (3) use clearly defined points on the scale, and (4) use scales that have several response alternatives. For example, yes–no responses offer little information in assessing a child's aggressiveness, while a range of 5 to 7 points along a scale makes the rating more meaningful. Even earlier, Lorr and McNair (1965) suggested that a rating for a single characteristic should range from "no appearance of the behavior" to "maximum appearance."

There are a number of rating scales that parents and teachers can use to evaluate a child's emotional and social development. Some rating scales cover all developmental domains and some target only social and emotional development.

One rating scale that specifically targets social and emotional development is the *Devereux Early Childhood Assessment–Clinical Form* (LaBuffe & Naglieri, 2003). This scale is one of the few norm-referenced instruments with a focus on social and emotional development. It can be used by both parents and teachers, and it asks them to rate a child's behavior over the past month. It has seven subscales that rate a child's initiative, self-control, and attachment (combined to form a total score for protective factors), and withdrawal/depression, emotional control problems, attention problems, and aggression (combined to form a total score for behavior concerns).

Another widely used measure is the *Child Behavior Checklist* (CBCL) (Achenbach, 2000), whose scales combine to define children with externalizing and internalizing behaviors. The CBCL has numerous other scales that help raters to identify children who are emotionally reactive, anxious/depressed, withdrawn, have somatic complaints, or who manifest aggressive behaviors or attention problems. These scales are appropriate for children from $1\frac{1}{2}$ to 5 years of age.

Sociometric Measures

Children's popularity and how well they are accepted by their peers are measured using sociometric measures. One example of a sociometric assessment is a peer rating measure developed by Asher, Singleton, Tinsley, and Hymel (1979). A child is shown a picture of every other child in his class. He then puts each picture into a box. One box is for children he likes to play with a lot, a second is for children he likes to play with a little, and a third is for children with whom he doesn't like to play. Average peer ratings are then computed for each child. Children who receive ratings close to 3 ("play with a lot") are considered well-accepted by their peers; those who receive ratings close to 1 ("don't like to play with") are considered rejected by their peers. These measures have been used reliably with preschool children who have first been trained in the sorting procedure using pictures of toys and food.

In summary, the state of the art in assessment of social and emotional development emphasizes systematic observation of quantifiable behaviors. It is not sufficient to say that "the child is very active." One should be able to specify a relative level of activity. In addition, information from parents and other good reporters should be integrated with observational data to identify the child's needs in terms of his interactions with others and his responses to various new and challenging situations.

> Children's popularity and how well they are accepted by their peers are measured using sociometric measures.

:: INTERVENTION STRATEGIES TO PROMOTE SOCIAL AND EMOTIONAL DEVELOPMENT

The need for external controls is important for maintaining order in one's life and in society. That is the fundamental reason for having laws and rules that govern society and its institutions. But external controls do not obviate each individual's need to control his impulses and make independent decisions about his own behavior. Children with special needs often have a particularly difficult time with this responsibility. However, whether they have a cognitive deficit that limits problem-solving and decision-making skills, or a sensory or physical impairment that limits the quality of their interactions with the environment, children can learn to be more socially and emotionally competent individuals.

Trivette (2003) recommends ways to promote social interaction and emotional development for young children with special needs and their families. She suggests that interventions for infants and toddlers should focus on helping the caregivers be responsive to the child's behavior in a way that is "sensitive and appropriate to the child's developmental level" (p. 1). The focus of interventions for preschoolers should be on social interaction with peers, development of secure peer relationships,

> Interventions for infants and toddlers should focus on helping caregivers to be responsive to the child's behavior.

and specific social skills. According to Denham and Burton (2003), preschoolers can become more effective socially if they understand their emotions and learn to regulate them.

Family-Focused Interventions

For infants and toddlers with disabilities, IDEA stipulates that interventions take place in the child's natural environment. Further, interventions for these youngest children should be family-focused rather than child-focused. According to Bailey et al. (1998), focusing on the family optimizes outcomes for children for a number of reasons. First, outcomes for children are affected by the quality of the interactions they have with their parents. Second, because infants and toddlers are with their parents more than any other adults, parents have the greatest influence on young children's development. Finally, parents often face special challenges as caregivers of children with disabilities. If interventionists can help parents with these challenges, the children will benefit.

Skills of the Caregiver

Consistency of Care   A very young child develops trust in a relationship when his needs are met and he gains satisfaction. Subsequently, he begins to feel secure enough to explore the environment and take small risks with new experiences. Caregivers who are consistent in meeting a child's biological needs (e.g., feeding, changing diapers, and attending to scrapes), and subsequent needs for support in his explorations (e.g., through confidence-building hugs and positive words), are likely to find the child becoming confident in his own abilities and secure in relationships with new people.

With a child who has disabilities, the caregiver may require help in determining the child's needs and how to meet them. The interventionist may find that enhancing the confidence and observation skills of the caregiver are of primary importance. Some caregivers overrespond to a child's cues, never giving the child an opportunity to respond or causing the child to become overstimulated and withdraw (Greenspan & Wieder, 2006). The child may be expressing his needs plainly, but the caregiver expects something different from a child with special needs. Further, when interactions between caregiver and child are not fun, or at least reinforcing, the caregiver may become less responsive to the child. The interventionist may choose to spend considerable time with the caregiver, at least initially, observing the child and helping the caregiver interpret the different ways the child expresses his wants and feelings.

Providing High-quality Interactions   The ways in which caregivers and children interact have been the subject of extensive study (Haney & Klein, 1993; Wasserman, Lennon, Allen, & Shilansky, 1987) and the importance of verbal and nonverbal communication between the two is universally acknowledged. Face-to-face interaction helps to establish eye contact and attentional skills in a young child. When tied to supportive verbalizations by the caregiver (e.g., "What a nice smile" and "I'm going to kiss you on the nose"), the child is encouraged to experiment with vocal play. Later, the caregiver provides words for feelings and for important objects in the child's environment. The child is then better able to communicate his own thoughts and feelings without being totally dependent on adult interpretation. The interventionist should model appropriate ways to interact with a child, observe the caregiver doing it, and provide feedback. For a child with disabilities, assistance may be needed to identify the child's signaling system or to help the child develop a consistent way to communicate (Roper & Dunst, 2003). Principles of behavior theory (e.g., shaping of successive approximations, prompting, and reinforcement) may be utilized to shape the responses of a child with a severe disability so that the caregiver can more easily interpret the messages that the child is conveying.

Providing Diverse Learning Experiences   As Dunst and his colleagues note, "children's everyday lives include many different kinds of learning experiences and opportunities" (Dunst, Bruder, Trivette, Raab, & McLean, 2001, p. 19). The interventionist may be able to help a caregiver plan a way to take a child along to the grocery store rather than leave him home with an older child. The local park may not have been utilized before by the family, but the interventionist can show the caregiver how the child and family can enjoy and benefit from a periodic outing. She also may be in a position to bring a group of caregivers and children together regularly for play groups. The interventionist need not be present at these and, in fact, may choose to be absent in order to facilitate spontaneous sharing by the caregivers. The interventionist can help the family see the neighborhood and the larger community as places where the young child can learn to interact socially with a variety of partners.

Barbara Schwartz/Merrill

The interventionist should facilitate social activities outside of the classroom setting.

Dunst et al. (2001) suggest that the interventionist help the child's parents identify appropriate learning environments in the community by asking the following questions.

- What gets the child excited?
- What makes the child laugh and smile?
- What does the child especially work hard at doing?
- What activities does the child enjoy doing?
- What gets and keeps the child's attention?

For a child who likes water, a good learning environment might be the community pool; for a child who likes the feel of sand, the local school playground might provide both a sandbox and other toddlers. Dunst et al. (2001) list a wide variety of other locations that may be available to parents and children including shopping malls, the library, a church or temple Sunday school, the beach, a local recreation center, and even the post office.

Skills of the Interventionist

Early intervention has changed since its advent with the passage of Public Law 99–457 in 1986. Our field has come a long way from "the initial notion of parent involvement, which said that parents should participate in the activities that professionals deemed important" (McWilliam, Tocci, & Harbin, 1998, p. 206). Now interventionists seek to establish a collaborative relationship with families (Dunst, 2002).

Interventionists seek to establish a collaborative relationship with families.

Working in a home setting demands that an interventionist be able to modify strategies quickly, be sensitive to and an excellent observer of family dynamics, and know how to suggest and model, while letting the caregiver assume responsibility for interactions with the child. Little is gained from working with a child in the home if the interventionist is not absolutely sure that the caregiver has benefited and that the child will receive those benefits in her absence.

Family-Focused Intervention Example

Greenspan and Wieder (2006) developed the Developmental, Individual-Difference, Relationship (DIR) model which has "floortime" as its central component. The goal during floortime is to "promote shared attention, engagement, and intentional back-and-forth signaling by following the child's lead and giving attention to individual sensory differences" (Schertz & Odom, 2004, p. 49). An example of a floortime activity follows.

> *The Funny Sound, Face, and Feeling Game:* Notice the sounds and facial expressions the baby naturally uses when he's expressing joy, annoyance, surprise or any other feeling, and mirror these sounds and facial expressions back to him in a playful way. See if you can get a back-and-forth going (Greenspan & Wieder, 2006, p. 350).

Child-Focused Interventions

The classroom provides its own challenges to the teacher of young children with special needs. Not the least of these is attempting to meet the individual needs of children in a group setting. The classroom provides the teacher with an opportunity to guide a child's interactions in a minisociety. Although it may be unlike life on the outside, it does offer the child opportunities to learn and practice skills that are transferable to real-world situations and that relate to his success in later school and life experiences (Chandler, Lubek, & Fowler, 1992).

The Classroom Setting

Providing inclusive classrooms in which young children with disabilities learn alongside their typically developing peers has been advocated as a way to improve social outcomes for children with disabilities. Teachers and parents believe that children with disabilities improve their cognitive, linguistic, and social skills through observing, modeling, and interacting with more competent peers (Lieber et al., 1998). Researchers have found, however, that just providing access to inclusive classrooms is not always sufficient to improve children's outcomes (Odom, 2000), so it is important for teachers to be familiar with a range of interventions to foster social and emotional development.

Providing access to inclusive classrooms alone is not always sufficient to improve children's outcomes.

Strategies to Improve Social Relationships

Brown, Odom, and Conroy (2001) outline an intervention hierarchy that classroom teachers can use to foster children's social relationships and friendships. What is valuable about the interventions they include in their hierarchy is that they are ones that teachers can implement easily and that researchers have shown are effective in improving social outcomes. The base of their hierarchy consists of two foundational approaches that can be used with all children. If those basic approaches do not result in improved social outcomes for children with disabilities, then Brown et al. offer two naturalistic interventions. Teachers should be prepared to move up the hierarchy to direct interventions with individual children. Mrs. Glenn, Adam's teacher, can use the intervention hierarchy if, over time, she remains concerned about Adam's social and emotional development.

Foundation One: *Have a high-quality preschool program.* High-quality programs use developmentally appropriate practices. Teachers in these programs plan for activities that are interesting and engaging to children and offer them physical and emotional security (Sandall & Schwartz, 2002). In high-quality programs, teachers ensure that children have plenty of social opportunities. For example, teachers can provide materials that encourage participation by more than one child—like ball games, some outdoor equipment, and learning centers using housekeeping and blocks. Teachers can provide extended time periods that allow children to engage in complex pretend play with other children. In addition, teachers are available to offer encouragement, model play and social behaviors, and provide feedback to children.

Foundation Two: *Promote positive attitudes.* Teachers can provide a variety of activities in their classroom that promote positive attitudes toward children with disabilities. Favazza, LaRoe, Phillipsen, and Kumar (2000) recommend that teachers read positive

FIGURE **7.1**   Intervention hierarchy to foster children's social relationships.

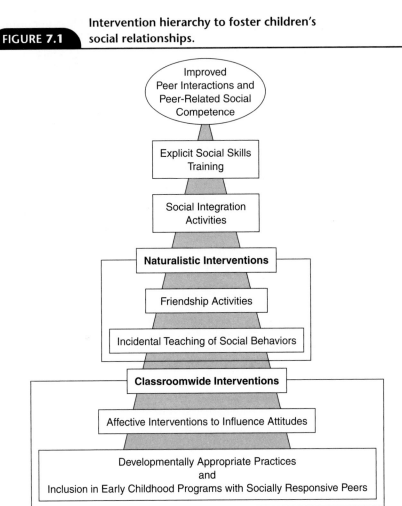

Source: From "An Intervention Hierarchy for Promoting Young Children's Peer Interactions in Natural Environments" by W. H. Brown, S. L. Odom, and M. A. Conroy, *Topics in Early Childhood Special Education* (2001) by Hammill Institute on Disabilities. Reprinted with permission. *Childhood Special Education: Enhancing Professional Development for Providers of Early Care and Intervention, 21,* p. 164.

and realistic stories about children with disabilities, talk about people with disabilities, and have materials that include pictures of people with disabilities available.

Naturalistic Approach One: *Teach social behaviors incidentally.* Incidental teaching opportunities occur when children are involved in an activity and the teacher uses that involvement as an opportunity to zero in on a child's objectives. For example, Mrs. Glenn has noticed that Adam spends his time in the sandbox playing next to other children. Mrs. Glenn might purposely provide only a few materials, then help Adam ask his peers to share the shovel or the dump truck. This helps him initiate a social interchange. In this case, the opportunity to target Adam's social skills emerged from the ongoing activity.

Courtesy of Jean Patz

Some materials are designed to help children work together.

Naturalistic Approach Two: *Plan friendship activities.* Friendship activities have been widely used and are easy for teachers to implement (McEvoy et al., 1988). For these activities, teachers take early childhood songs, games, and other activities and transform them into positive, supportive experiences. They can be as easy as having children exchange "high fives" at the end of circle time (Sandall & Schwartz, 2002).

Individual Intervention One: *Social integration activities.* At the next level of the hierarchy, teachers need to provide more direct opportunities for children to learn social skills and participate in successful social interactions. Brown et al. (2001) describe one way of implementing these activities.

- Teachers select children who have problems with social interactions. They also select responsive peers.
- Teachers select an area of the room for the activity. It might be the block area one day and the housekeeping area another day.
- Children play within that area for 5–15 minutes.
- Teachers plan activities to promote specific social behaviors like sharing, talking, and helping each other.
- Teachers organize and introduce the activity, then monitor children to be sure they are interacting. If they are not, the teacher might suggest an idea, comment on the play, or directly prompt the child to interact.

Individual Intervention Two: *Explicit social skills instruction.* Some children need explicit instruction in social skills to learn how to interact successfully with their peers. If that is true for Adam, Mrs. Glenn could try the buddy-skills training program (English, Goldstein, Shafer, & Kaczmarek, 1997). In this program, Mrs. Glenn would coach a buddy to "stay with [Adam], play with [Adam], and talk with [Adam]" (p. 233) through modeling, guided practice, and independent practice with feedback. She would also set up free play, snack, and large group activities. Adam would also be taught to stay and play.

Interventions That Include Emotional Development

Beginning in the 1970s, researchers developed comprehensive curricula that focused on helping children develop a wide range of emotional skills including the ability to label, recognize, and regulate emotions. Typically, these curricula included instruction in problem-solving skills and positive peer relations. Joseph and Strain (2003) reviewed eight of these curricula and found that two were particularly promising. One promising curriculum is *Incredible Years: Dina Dinosaur's Social, Emotional and Problem-Solving Curriculum* (Webster-Stratton, 1990). The components in the curriculum include:

- school rules
- how to be successful at school
- understanding one's own and others' emotions
- friendship and communication skills
- anger management
- interpersonal problem solving. (Webster-Stratton & Reid, 2003)

Webster-Stratton and Reid (2003) describe how the *Dina Dinosaur* curriculum helps children identify their feelings, identify and understand the emotions of others, and regulate their own emotions. First children learn basic feelings, such as happiness and anger, then more complex feelings, such as frustration and loneliness. They learn to recognize these feelings by monitoring their own bodies, particularly the tension level of their muscles. Next, children learn to identify feelings in others by using cues such as others' facial expressions, their behaviors, or their tone of voice. Finally, children learn how to change negative feelings into more positive feelings through games and activities.

Interventions for Challenging Behaviors

In spite of the comprehensive nature of the social and emotional skills curricula, there are some children who exhibit behaviors that interfere with their learning, are dangerous, or are of tremendous concern to their families. These challenging behaviors often respond well to positive behavior support, a practice that has been used successfully by parents and teachers (Fox, Dunlap, & Cushing, 2002).

Prior to implementing an intervention, the team (e.g., parent, teacher, behavior resource person) meets to plan and conduct a functional behavioral assessment (FBA).

The team uses multiple sources of information, including observations of the child's behavior, interviews with people who interact with the child regularly, and a review of the child's records. The team uses these data to understand what happens before the problem behavior occurs, what the problem behavior looks like, and what happens after the problem behavior occurs.

The team then attempts to determine the purpose of the child's behavior. For example, does the child use his behavior to obtain something or to escape something? (Fox & Duda, n.d.)

Once the intervention team has developed some hypotheses about why the challenging behavior is occurring, it develops a behavior support plan. This plan consists of three steps.

- Strategies are identified to modify the curriculum, the environment, activities, or interactions with the child to prevent the behavior from occurring.
- The child is taught a new skill to use in place of the challenging behavior.
- The plan is evaluated to ensure that the new skills have been learned and the challenging behavior has decreased. (Fox, n.d.)

Like Brown et al. (2001), Hemmeter, Ostrosky, and Fox (2006) use a pyramid to describe their intervention model, which supports young children's social and emotional development and prevents and addresses challenging behavior. They summarize evidence to show that children have improved outcomes when interventionists (1) target relationships among families, classroom staff, and children; (2) provide supportive environments; (3) teach specific social and emotional behaviors; and (4) individualize interventions for young children with challenging behavior.

:: TECHNOLOGY IN ASSESSMENT AND INTERVENTION

As early as the 1980s, computers were found to facilitate social interactions for young children with disabilities. In an early study, Spiegel-McGill, Zippiroli, and Mistrett (1989) observed four young children with disabilities and four children without disabilities paired in three different conditions: a typical free-play condition, a computer condition in which pairs of children had the opportunity to work together using a variety of programs, and a condition in which the children could activate a remote-controlled robot. They found that the children with disabilities, particularly those with more significant impairments, showed more socially directed behaviors when they were working at the computer.

Using a larger sample of children, Howard, Greyrose, Kehr, Espinosa, and Beckwith (1996) found similar results. The social behaviors of groups of two or three toddlers and preschoolers with disabilities who participated in computer activities were compared to those who used toys. Both toddlers and preschoolers on the computer showed more positive affect (e.g., laughter and positive vocalizations) and engaged in more parallel play in which they were aware of the play of other children than those in the non-computer group.

There is some evidence that social behavior between children with disabilities and their peers during computer activities is facilitated when teachers are involved. Lau, Higgins, Gelfer, Hon, and Miller (2005) compared the social behaviors and interactions of 18 dyads of children with and without disabilities who worked together on *Elmo's Art Workshop*. Nine of the dyads' work at the computer was facilitated by their teacher and nine dyads worked alone. The investigators found that when the teacher was present, the dyads showed significantly more positive interactions, higher levels of play, and the children with disabilities initiated more interaction and made more positive responses to their partners. Because of the positive social behavior during the computer activity when the teacher was present, Lau and colleagues concluded that this structured activity provided a good alternative to free play to encourage social behavior among young children with disabilities.

Although some early childhood educators have expressed concern about the effect of technology use on the social skills of children, these concerns seem unwarranted. Hutinger and Johanson (2000) noted that when technology is integrated into a developmentally appropriate curriculum, it can foster children's development in a variety of areas including communication, sharing, turn-taking, and positive social interactions (p. 162). When the researchers evaluated their Early Childhood Comprehensive Technology System (ECCTS), they found that children made progress in all areas of development, but gains were particularly impressive in the social-emotional area. Children's growth rate in this area more than doubled in comparison to growth before the classrooms instituted the technology system.

Technology use is, of course, not limited to children using computers. Young children benefit from having a range of assistive technology (AT) supports available both at home and in the classroom. These supports may be low-tech and commercially available. Mistrett, Lane, and Ruffino (2005) describe a number of AT devices that enhance young children's ability to communicate and interact socially with others. These include LITTLEmack, Say It/Play It, and CheapTalk. Moreover, using switches and adapted battery-operated toys allow children to play cooperatively with siblings and other children (Mistrett et al., 2005).

> Technology that is integrated into a developmentally appropriate curriculum can foster children's development in a variety of areas including communication, sharing, turn taking, and positive social interactions.

SUMMARY

A child's concept of himself and of the world around him is constantly being shaped by every event in his life. For all children, social and emotional development benefits from a loving and secure relationship with caregivers and by having the opportunity to interact and develop relationships with a variety of peers and adults outside the family.

The ability of children with disabilities to form satisfying social and emotional relationships may be affected by aspects of their impairment. Parents, in collaboration with interventionists and teachers, can take steps to mediate the effects of those disabilities.

Social skills and emotions are perhaps the most elusive areas of human development to comprehend. Maladaptive behaviors evolve over many years, yet they change from day to day and from situation to situation. How these behaviors evolve may contribute to great success in life or contribute to misery and frustration—especially without early intervention efforts.

In this chapter, substantial evidence has been provided that reveals the critical components of social and emotional development in young children with special needs. Interventionists can be optimistic that many of the factors that contribute most to a child's outcome can be influenced by their efforts. By including both child and caregiver in the positive educational process, a socially competent and emotionally mature young person can develop.

REVIEW QUESTIONS AND DISCUSSION POINTS

1. Spend time observing pairs of infants, toddlers, and preschoolers. What differences do you see between the children in how they interact with each other?
2. Identify four emotions that you might see in young children. Describe how the ways in which children express these emotions change from infancy to young childhood.
3. How can disabilities affect young children's social competence? Which disabilities are likely to have the greatest effects on the development of social skills?
4. You are a child care provider and are concerned about the behavior of one of the children in your classroom. What assessment methods would you use to evaluate the child's behavior? What are the strengths and weaknesses of each of these methods?
5. Interview a teacher in an inclusive preschool classroom. Ask the teacher what strategies he or she uses to encourage social relationships among the children with and without disabilities in the classroom.

RECOMMENDED RESOURCES

Programs

Fox, L., Jack, S., & Broyles, I. (2005). *Program-wide positive behavior support: Supporting young children's social-emotional development and addressing challenging behavior.* Tampa, FL: University of South Florida, Louis de la Parte Florida Mental Health Institute.

Websites

Research and Training Center on Early Childhood Development

http://www.researchtopractice.info/index.php

Center for Evidence-Based Practice: Young Children with Challenging Behavior

http://challengingbehavior.fmhi.usf.edu/

Center on the Social and Emotional Foundations for Early Learning

http://www.csefel.uiuc.edu/

REFERENCES

Achenbach, T.M. (2000). *The child behavior checklist.* Burlington, VT: Achenbach System of Empirically Based Assessment.

Ainsworth, M. D. S., Blehar, M. C., Waters, E., & Wall, S. (1978). *Patterns of attachment: A psychological study of the strange situation.* Hillsdale, NJ: Erlbaum.

American Psychiatric Association. (2000). *Diagnostic and statistical manual of mental disorders* (4th ed.). Washington, DC: Author.

Asher, S. R., Singleton, L. C., Tinsley, B. R., & Hymel, S. (1979). A reliable sociometric measure for preschool children. *Developmental Psychology, 15,* 443–444.

Atkinson, L., Chisolm, V. C., Scott, B., Goldberg, S., Vaughn, B. E., Blackwell, J., Dickens, S., et al. (1999). Maternal sensitivity, child functional level, and attachment in Down syndrome. *Monographs of the Society for Research in Child Development, 64*(3) (Serial No. 258), 45–66.

Bandura, A. (1977). *Social learning theory.* Upper Saddle River, NJ: Prentice Hall.

Barnett, D., Butler, C. M., & Vondra, J. I. (1999). Atypical patterns of early attachment: Discussion and future directions. *Monographs of the Society for Research in Child Development, 64*(3) (Serial No. 258), 172–192.

Baumrind, D. (1973). The development of instrumental competence through socialization. In A. D. Pick (Ed.), *Minnesota symposium on child psychology* (Vol. 7, pp. 3–46). Minneapolis: University of Minnesota Press.

Belsky, J. (2006). Determinants and consequences of infant-parent attachment. In L. Balter & C. S. Tamis-LeMonda (Eds.), *Child psychology: A handbook of contemporary issues* (2nd ed., pp. 53–77). New York: Psychology Press.

Bijou, S. W., & Baer, D. M, (1979). Child development I: A systematic and empirical theory. In B. G. Suran & V. Rizzo (Eds.), *Special children: An integrative approach.* Glenview, IL: Scott Foresman.

Bricker, D., Capt, B., & Pretti-Frontczak, K. (2002). *AEPS test: Birth to three years and three to six years* (2nd ed.). Baltimore: Brookes.

Brinton, B., & Fujiki, M. (2002). Social development in children with specific language impairment and profound hearing loss. In P. K. Smith & C. H. Hart (Eds.), *Blackwell handbook of childhood social development* (pp. 588–603). Malden, MA: Blackwell Publishers.

Brown, P. M., Remine, M. D., Prescott, S. J., & Rickards, F. W. (2000). Social interactions of preschoolers with and without impaired hearing in integrated kindergarten. *Journal of Early Intervention, 23,* 200–211.

Brown, W. H., Odom, S. L., & Conroy, M. A. (2001). An intervention hierarchy for promoting young children's peer interactions in natural environments. *Topics in Early Childhood Special Education, 21,* 162–175.

Buysse, V. (2002, Winter). Friendship formation. *Early Developments, 6,* 18–19.

Buysse, V., Goldman, B. D., & Skinner, M. L. (2002). Setting effects on friendship formation among young children with and without disabilities. *Exceptional Children, 68,* 503–517.

Campbell, S. B. (2002). *Behavior problems in preschool children: Clinical and developmental issues* (2nd ed.). New York: Guilford Press.

Chandler, L. K., Lubek, R. C., & Fowler, S. A. (1992). Generalization and maintenance of preschool children's social skills: A critical review and analysis. *Journal of Applied Behavior Analysis, 25,* 415–428.

Coie, J. D., & Jacobs, M. R. (2000). The role of social context in the prevention of conduct disorder. In W. Craig (Ed.), *Childhood social development: The essential readings* (pp. 350–371). Malden, MA: Blackwell Publishers.

Conroy, M. A., & Davis, C. A. (2000). Early elementary-aged children with challenging behaviors: Legal and educational issues related to IDEA and assessment. *Preventing School Failure, 44,* 163–171.

Craig, W. (2000). *Childhood social development: The essential readings.* Malden, MA: Blackwell Publishers.

Crick, N. R. (2000). Engagement in gender normative versus nonnormative forms of aggression: Links to social-psychological adjustment. In W. Craig (Ed.), *Childhood social development: The essential readings* (pp. 309–329). Malden, MA: Blackwell Publishers.

Denham, S. A. (1986). Social cognition, social behavior, and emotion in preschoolers: Contextual validation. *Child Development, 57,* 194–201.

Denham, S. A., & Burton, R. (2003). *Social and emotional prevention and intervention programming for preschoolers.* New York: Kluwer Academic/Plenum Publishers.

Diamond, K. E. (2002). The development of social competence in children with disabilities. In P. K. Smith & C. H. Hart (Eds.), *Blackwell handbook of childhood social development* (pp. 571–587). Malden, MA: Blackwell Publishers.

Dunn, J. (2002). Sibling relationships. In P. K. Smith & C. H. Hart (Eds.), *Blackwell handbook of childhood social development* (pp. 223–237). Malden, MA: Blackwell Publishers.

Dunst, C. J. (2002). Family-centered practices: Birth through high school. *Journal of Special Education, 36*(3), 139–147.

Dunst, C. J., Bruder, M. B., Trivette, C. M., Raab, M., & McLean, M. (2001). Natural learning opportunities for infants, toddlers, and preschoolers. *Young Exceptional Children, 4,* 18–25.

English, K., Goldstein, H., Shafer, K., & Kaczmarek, L. (1997). Promoting interactions among preschoolers with and without disabilities: Effects of a buddy-skills training program. *Exceptional Children, 63,* 229–243.

Fabes, R. A., Gaertner, B. M., & Popp, T. K. (2006). Getting along with others: Social competence in early childhood. In K. McCartney & D. Phillips (Eds.), *Blackwell handbook of early childhood development* (pp. 297–316). Malden, MA: Blackwell Publishing.

Favazza, P. C., LaRoe, J., Phillipsen, L., & Kumar, P. (2000). Representing young children with disabilities in classroom environments. *Young Exceptional Children, 3*(3), 2–9.

Fox, L. (n.d.). *Positive behavior support: An individualized approach for addressing challenging behavior.* Center on the Social and Emotional Foundations of Early Learning. Retrieved October 2006 from *http://csefel.uiuc.edu/whatworks.html*

Fox, L., & Duda, M. (n.d.). *What are children trying to tell us? Assessing the function of their behavior.* Center on the Social and Emotional Foundations of Early Learning. Retrieved October 2006 from *http://csefel.uiuc.edu/whatworks.html*

Fox, L., Dunlap, G., & Cushing, L. (2002). Early intervention, positive behavior support, and transition to school.

Journal of Emotional and Behavioral Disorders, 10(3), 149–157.

Goldman, B. D., & Buysse, V. (2002). *Playmates and friends questionnaire for teachers–revised.* Chapel Hill, NC: University of North Carolina, FPG Child Development Institute.

Goncu, A., Patt, M. B., & Kouba, E. (2002). Understanding young children's pretend play in context. In P. K. Smith & C. H. Hart (Eds.), *Blackwell handbook of childhood social development* (pp. 418–437). Malden, MA: Blackwell Publishers.

Greenhill, L., Kollins, S., & Abikoff, H. (2006). Efficacy and safety of immediate-release methylphenidate treatment for preschoolers with ADHD. *Journal of the American Academy of Child & Adolescent Psychiatry, 45*(11), 1284–1293.

Greenspan, S. I., & Wieder, S. (2006). *Infant and early childhood mental health: A comprehensive developmental approach to assessment and intervention.* Washington, DC: American Psychiatric Publishing.

Gresham, F. M. (2001). Assessment of social skills in children and adolescents. In J. J. Andrews, D. H. Saklofske, & H. L. Janzen (Eds.), *Handbook of psychoeducational assessment: Ability, achievement and behavior in children* (pp. 325–355). San Diego, CA: Academic Press.

Guralnick, M. J. (2001). Social competence with peers and early childhood inclusion. In M. J. Guralnick (Ed.), *Early childhood inclusion: Focus on change* (pp. 481–502). Baltimore: Brookes.

Guralnick, M. J., Connor, R. T., Hammond, M. A., Gottman, J. M., & Kinnish, K. (1996). The peer relations of preschool children with communication disorders. *Child Development, 67,* 471–489.

Haney, M., & Klein, D. M. (1993). Impact of a program to facilitate mother-infant communication in high-risk families of high-risk infants. *Journal of Communication Disorders, 15,* 15–22.

Hemmeter, M. L., Ostrosky, M., & Fox, L. (2006). Social and emotional foundation for early learning: A conceptual model for intervention. *School Psychology Review, 35*(4), 583–601.

Hestenes, L. L., & Carroll, D. E. (2000). The play interactions of young children with and without disabilities: Individual and environmental influences. *Early Childhood Research Quarterly, 15,* 229–246.

Howard, J., Greyrose, E., Kehr, K., Espinosa, M., & Beckwith, L. (1996). Teacher-facilitated microcomputer activities: Enhancing social play and affect in young children with disabilities. *Journal of Special Education Technology, 13,* 36–47.

Hutinger, P. L., & Johanson, J. (2000). Implementing and maintaining an effective early childhood comprehensive technology system. *Topics in Early Childhood Special Education, 20,* 159–173.

Joseph, G. E., & Strain, P. S. (2003). Comprehensive evidence-based social-emotional curricula for young children: An analysis of efficacious adoption potential. *Topics in Early Childhood Special Education, 23*(2), 65–76.

LaBuffe, P. A., & Naglieri, J. A. (2003). *The Devereux Early Childhood Assessment–Clinical Form.* Lewisville, NC: Kaplan Early Learning.

Lau, C., Higgins, K., Gelfer, J., Hon, E., & Miller, S. (2005). The effects of teacher facilitation on the social interactions of young children during computer activities. *Topics in Early Childhood Special Education, 25*(4), 208–217.

Lieber, J., Capell, K., Sandall, S. R., Wolfberg, P., Horn, E., & Beckman, P. (1998). Inclusive preschool programs: Teachers' beliefs and practices. *Early Childhood Research Quarterly, 13,* 87–105.

Linder, T. W. (1993). *The Transdisciplinary play-based assessment* (Rev. ed.). Baltimore: Brookes.

Lorr, M., & McNair, D. M. (1965). Expansion of the interpersonal behavior circle. *Journal of Personality and Social Psychology, 2,* 823–830.

Mardell-Czudnowski, C., & Goldenberg, D. S. (1998). *DIAL3: Developmental indicators for the assessment of learning* (3rd ed.). Circle Pines, MN: American Guidance Service.

Martin, J. N., & Fox, N. A. (2006). Temperament. In K. McCartney & D. Phillips (Eds.), *Blackwell handbook of early childhood development* (pp. 126–146). Malden, MA: Blackwell Publishing.

Masten, A. S. (2001). Ordinary magic: Resilience processes in development. *American Psychologist, 56,* 227–238.

Masten, A. S., & Gewirtz, A. H. (2006). Vulnerability and resilience in development. In K. McCartney & D. Phillips (Eds.), *Blackwell handbook of early childhood development* (pp. 22–43). Malden, MA: Blackwell Publishing.

McClelland, M. M., & Scalzo, C. (2006). Social skills deficits. In M. Hersen (Ed.), *Clinician's handbook of child behavioral assessment* (pp. 313–335). Amsterdam: Elsevier.

McEvoy, M. A., Nordquist, V. M., Twardosz, S., Heckaman, K., Wehby, J. H., & Denny, R. K. (1988). Promoting autistic children's peer interaction in an integrated early childhood setting using affection activities. *Journal of Applied Behavior Analysis, 21,* 193–200.

McGaha, C. G., & Farran, D. C. (2001). Interactions in inclusive classrooms: The effects of visual status and setting. *Journal of Visual Impairment & Blindness, 95*(2), 80–94.

McWilliam, R. A., Tocci, L., & Harbin, G. (1998). Family-centered services: Service providers' discourse and behavior. *Topics in Early Childhood Special Education, 18*, 206–221.

Mistrett, S. G., Lane, S. J., & Ruffino, A. G. (2005). Growing and learning through technology: Birth to five. In D. Edyburn, K. Higgins, & R. Boone (Eds.), *Handbook of special education technology: Research and practice* (pp. 273–306). Whitefish Bay, WI: Knowledge by Design.

Mundy, P., & Stella, J. (2000). Joint attention, social orienting and nonverbal communication in autism. In A. M. Wetherby & B. M. Prizant (Eds.), *Autism spectrum disorders: A transactional approach* (pp. 55–77). Baltimore: Brookes.

National Research Council. (2001). *Educating children with autism.* Washington, DC: National Academy Press.

Odom, S. L. (2000). Preschool inclusion: What we know and where we go from here. *Topics in Early Childhood Special Education, 20*, 20–27.

Odom, S. L., Zercher, C., Marquart, J., Li, S., Sandall, S. R., & Wolfberg, P. (2002). Social relationships of children with disabilities and their peers in inclusive preschool classrooms. In S. L. Odom (Ed.), *Widening the circle: Including children with disabilities in preschool programs* (pp. 61–80). New York: Teachers College Press.

O'Leary, K. D., & Johnson, S. B. (1979). Psychological assessment. In H. C. Quay & J. S. Werry (Eds.), *Psychopathological disorders of childhood* (pp. 210–246). New York: Wiley.

Parke, R. D., & Buriel, R. (1998). Socialization in the family: Ethnic and ecological perspectives. In W. Damon (Series Ed.) & N. Eisenberg (Vol. Ed.), *Handbook of child psychology.* Vol 3: *Social, emotional and personality development* (5th ed., pp. 463–552). New York: Wiley.

Parke, R. D., Simpkins, S. D., McDowell, D. J., Kim, M., Killian, C., Dennis, J., et al. (2002). Relative contributions of families and peers to children's social development. In P. K. Smith & C. H. Hart (Eds.), *Blackwell handbook of childhood social development* (pp. 156–177). Malden, MA: Blackwell Publishers.

Parten, M. (1932). Social participation among preschool children. *Journal of Abnormal and Social Psychology, 27*, 243–269.

Patterson, G. R., DeBaryshe, B. D., & Ramsey, E. (2000). A developmental perspective on antisocial behavior. In W. Craig (Ed.), *Childhood social development: The essential readings* (pp. 333–348). Malden, MA: Blackwell Publishers.

Pipp-Siegel, S., Siegel, C. H., & Dean, J. (1999). Neurological aspects of the disorganized/disoriented attachment classification system: Differentiating quality of the attachment relationship from neurological impairment. *Monographs of the Society for Research in Child Development, 64*(3) (Serial No. 258), 25–44.

Rockhill, C. M., Collett, B. R., McClellan, J. M., & Speltz, M. L. (2006). Oppositional defiant disorder. In J. L. Luby (Ed.), *Handbook of preschool mental health: Development, disorders, and treatment* (pp. 80–114). New York: The Guilford Press.

Rothbart, M. K., & Bates, J. E. (1998). Temperament. In W. Damon (Series Ed.) & N. Eisenberg (Vol. Ed.) *Handbook of child psychology.* Vol 3: *Social, emotional and personality development* (5th ed., pp. 105–176). New York: Wiley.

Roper, N., & Dunst, C. J. (2003). Communication intervention in natural learning environments: Guidelines for practice. *Infants and Young Children, 16*(3), 215–226.

Rubin, K. H., Coplan, R. J., Fox, N. A., & Calkins, S. (1995). Emotionality, emotion regulation, and preschoolers' social adaptation. *Development and Psychopathology, 7*, 49–62.

Russell, A., Mize, J., & Bissaker, K. (2002). Parent-child relationships. In P. K. Smith & C. H. Hart (Eds.), *Blackwell handbook of childhood social development* (pp. 205–222). Malden, MA: Blackwell Publishers.

Salovey, P., & Mayer, J. D. (1990). Emotional intelligence. *Imagination, Cognition, and Personality, 9*, 185–211.

Sameroff, A. J., & Chandler, M. J. (1975). Reproductive risk and the continuum of caretaking casualty. In F. D. Horowitz, E. M. Hetherington, S. Scarr-Salapatek, & G. W. Siegel (Eds.), *Review of child development research* (Vol.4). (pp. 187–244). Chicago: University of Chicago Press.

Sameroff, A. J., & Fiese, B. H. (1990). Transactional regulation and early intervention. In S. J. Meisels & J. P. Shonkoff (Eds.), *Handbook of early childhood intervention* (pp. 119–149). New York: Cambridge University Press.

Sandall, S. R., & Schwartz, I. S. (2002). *Building blocks for teaching preschoolers with special needs.* Baltimore: Brookes.

Sanson, A., Hemphill, S. A., & Smart, D. (2002). Temperament and social development. In P. K. Smith & C. H. Hart (Eds.), *Blackwell handbook of childhood social development* (pp. 97–116). Malden, MA: Blackwell Publishers.

Schertz, H. H., & Odom, S. L. (2004). Joint attention and early intervention with autism: A conceptual framework and promising approaches. *Journal of Early Intervention, 27*(1), 42–54.

Shonkoff, J. P., & Phillips, D. A. (Eds.). (2000). *From neurons to neighborhoods: The science of early childhood development.* Washington, DC: National Academy Press.

Sigman, M. D., Kasari, C., Kwon, J. H., & Yirmiya, N. (1992). Responses to the negative emotions of others by autistic, mentally retarded, and normal children. *Child Development, 63,* 796–807.

Sigman, M. D., & Ruskin, E. (1999). Continuity and change in the social competence of children with autism, Down syndrome, and developmental delays. *Monographs of the Society for Research in Child Development, 64* (1, Serial No. 256).

Solomon, J., & George, C. (1999). The measurement of attachment security in infancy and childhood. In J. Cassidy & P. R. Shaver (Eds.), *Handbook of attachment* (pp. 287–316). New York: The Guildford Press.

Spiegel-McGill, P., Zippiroli, S. M., & Mistrett, S. G. (1989). Microcomputers as social facilitators in integrated preschools. *Journal of Early Intervention, 13,* 249–260.

Squires, J., Bricker, D., & Twombly, E. (2002). *Ages and Stages Quesionnaires. Social-Emotional.* Baltimore: Brookes.

Steinhoff, K. W., Lerner, M., Kapilinsky, A., Kotkin, R., Wigal, S., Steinberg-Epstein, R., et al., (2006). Attention-deficit/hyperactivity disorder. In J. L. Luby (Ed.), *Handbook of preschool mental health: Development, disorders, and treatment* (pp. 63–79). New York: The Guilford Press.

Thomas, A., & Chess, S. (1977). *Temperament and development.* New York: Bruner/Mazel.

Trivette, C. M. (2003). Influence of caregiver responsiveness on the development of young children with or at risk for developmental disabilities. *Bridges: Practice-Based-Research Syntheses, 1*(6). Retrieved October 2006 from *http://www.researchtopractice.info/bridges/*

Underwood, M. K. (2002). Sticks and stones and social exclusion: Aggression among girls and boys. In P. K. Smith & C. H. Hart (Eds.), *Blackwell handbook of childhood social development* (pp. 533–548). Malden, MA: Blackwell Publishers.

Vandell, D. L., & George. L. B. (1981). Social interactions in hearing and deaf preschoolers. Successes and failures in initiations. *Child Development, 52,* 627–635.

Vandell, D. L., Nenide, L., & Van Winkle, S. J. (2006). Peer relationships in early childhood. In K. McCartney & D. Phillips (Eds.), *Blackwell handbook of early childhood development* (pp. 455–470). Malden, MA: Blackwell Publishers.

Wasserman, G. A., Lennon, M. C., Allen, R., & Shilansky, M. (1987). Contributors to attachment in normal and physically handicapped infants. *Journal of the American Academy of Child and Adolescent Psychiatry, 26,* 9–15.

Webster-Stratton, C. *Dina Dinosaur's Social, Emotional, and Problem-Solving Curriculum, 1990.* Seattle, WA.

Webster-Stratton, C., & Reid, M. J. (2003). Treating conduct problems and strengthening social and emotional competence in young children: The Dina Dinosaur Treatment Program. *Journal of Emotional and Behavioral Disorders, 11*(3), 130–143.

Yarrow, M. R. (1963). Problems of methods in parent-child research. *Child Development, 34,* 215–226.

Zanandra, M. (1998). Play, social interaction, and motor development: Practical activities for preschoolers with visual impairments. *Journal of Visual Impairment & Blindness, 92,* 176–188.

Principles of Assessment and Intervention

Assessment of Young Children: Standards, Stages, and Approaches

Rebecca Edmondson Pretzel, Jennifer Hiemenz, and Rita Kahng

Chapter Outline

- Current Standards for the Assessment Process
- Stages of Assessment
- Team Approaches and Typologies
- Considerations for the Assessment of Young Children

Evan

As they drove to the meeting with Evan's preschool teacher, Mr. and Mrs. DeCruz could not help but remember the difficult news they had received four months ago at Evan's transition evaluation at the university-based center. That day, they were told that their beautiful 34-month-old child had autism. Although they had known for a long time that Evan was different from their two older children, particularly in his language development and play skills, it was still very hard to hear and accept that he had a lifelong disability. Within a month, however, Mr. and Mrs. DeCruz had read a lot about autism, met several other families who had children with autism, and enrolled Evan in an inclusive preschool setting. He now has a wonderful teacher, Mr. Parker, and receives speech-language and occupational therapy twice a week. Mr. Parker sends daily reports home about Evan's activities and they have had several meetings with him to talk about Evan's adjustment to school. Today, however, is the first time that they will hear about Evan's developmental progress based on his teacher's assessment over the first few months of preschool.

Mr. Parker has been assessing Evan's skill development using an alternative procedure called portfolio assessment. After greeting Mr. and Mrs. DeCruz, he brought a large notebook to the table and began to share information about Evan with them. Mr. and Mrs. DeCruz were impressed with the wide range of materials that documented Evan's progress in different areas of his development. The first section, labeled "Preacademic Skills," contained samples of actual work Evan had completed, such as coloring sheets and artwork involving colors and shapes. Evan had even tried to write an E on the papers to mark his work! In addition, notes and checklists completed by Mr. Parker on a weekly basis provided valuable information regarding the order in which Evan acquired certain preacademic skills and the instructional methods that had benefited him the most. In another section of the notebook, Mr. and Mrs. DeCruz found progress notes and test results compiled by Evan's speech and language therapist, documenting Evan's mastery of various articulation, social, and communication goals.

Perhaps the part of Evan's portfolio that excited Mr. and Mrs. DeCruz the most was the collection of photographs and video clips Mr. Parker had put together showing Evan's progress in developing social skills. Mr. and Mrs. DeCruz recalled the struggles Evan had experienced while transitioning into his preschool program at the beginning of the year. At times, they had wondered if they had made the right decision, but they now felt a sense of joy and relief to see that Evan was able to follow his individualized schedule, participate in group activities for short periods of time, and even imitate classmates during play! They also got some helpful ideas for how to structure Evan's time at home by seeing examples of the visual schedule, transition objects, and pictures Evan had been using in the classroom.

During their conversation with Mr. Parker, Mr. and Mrs. DeCruz had the opportunity to reflect on Evan's achievements, and they felt grateful to his intervention team. At the end of the meeting, they asked if they could take Evan's portfolio home to review again and to share with other members of the family.

Greenspan and Meisels (1996) define **assessment** as

> a process designed to deepen understanding of a child's competencies and resources, and of the caregiving and learning environments most likely to help a child make fullest use of his or her developmental potential. Assessment should be an ongoing, collaborative process of systematic observation and analysis. This process involves formulating questions, gathering information, sharing observations, and making interpretations in order to form new questions. (p. 11)

More specific to the field of early childhood education, assessment is the systematic recording over time of observations about a child's development with respect to functional behaviors occurring in their daily routines with familiar caregivers in natural environments (Bagnato & Ho, 2006). Assessment is a variable process that uses numerous measures and techniques; the assessment format depends on the questions being asked, the type of challenges encountered by the child and family, and a myriad social, developmental, and contextual factors. In this sense, assessment applies to all data collection methods used to facilitate decision-making processes, from the earliest concern about development through the ongoing determination points about a child's progress and program.

This chapter provides an overview of the complex process of early childhood assessment. In addition to discussing current standards that regulate assessment in early childhood, this chapter explores the different stages of the assessment process, including screening and specific components to be considered in a comprehensive evaluation, a variety of assessment approaches, and commonly used assessment techniques and measures. The importance of assessment–intervention linkage is also stressed, particularly in relation to current standards of practice. The chapter concludes with specific considerations for the assessment of young children with special needs. It is beyond the scope of this chapter to provide a comprehensive review of early childhood assessment measures (many of these measures will be described in other chapters); instead, we focus on the standards for assessment and the specific approaches that can be employed. An understanding of these aspects of assessment and of child development across the various domains described in this text is far more useful to the early interventionist than is being able to identify the latest tests.

> Assessment is an ongoing, goal-oriented, problem-solving process.

> The early interventionist must understand the various assessment standards and approaches that are available.

:: CURRENT STANDARDS FOR THE ASSESSMENT PROCESS

Several key pieces of legislation over the past three decades have contributed to the evolution of the assessment process for young children with special needs. Specifically, the Education for All Handicapped Children Act amendments (P.L. 99–457, 1986), later renamed the Individuals with Disabilities Education Act (IDEA, P.L. 102–119, 1998), the 1997 version of IDEA (P.L. 105–17, 1997–1998), the 2001 Elementary and Secondary Education Act (**No Child Left Behind**, P.L. 107–110), and the most recently authorized 2004 version of IDEA (Individuals with Disabilities Education Improvement Act, P.L. 108–446) have all provided critical guidelines

BOX 8.1   NO CHILD LEFT BEHIND

The 2002 Elementary and Secondary Education Act, better known as **No Child Left Behind,** mandates specific academic progress monitoring in reading, writing, and mathematics for students in elementary, middle, and high schools. Formal testing in these areas is required beginning in third grade. While similar regulations have not been enacted at the preschool level, there has been some movement at the federal level to enact similar plans in Head Start programs because of the importance of early intervention. However, there is concern that putting rigid pre-academic standards and assessment programs in place in these settings will not be developmentally appropriate and may reduce the emphasis in early childhood programs to a narrow focus on academic outcomes, rather than broad enrichment and readiness for school (Stipek, 2005).

for the identification, assessment, and treatment of young children with special needs. While, initially, the focus of legislation was to merely identify children in need of early intervention services, there has been an increased emphasis in the most recent legislation (IDEA 2004; NCLB) on looking ahead to school-based services. By specifically examining precursors to reading and mathematics skills, assessment teams are getting a clearer picture of potential academic difficulties and determining which educational interventions may be helpful at the preschool level. While a **Response to Intervention** approach is beginning to be used in the early elementary school years to look at children with specific learning disabilities (IDEA, 2004), it is only beginning to be examined for use at the preschool level (Coleman, Buysse, & Nietzel, 2006). This is a shift that will likely occur within the next decade.

Concurrent with these legal initiatives, several professional organizations have introduced a number of standards for assessment and treatment in the early childhood domain. Organizations such as the American Speech-Language-Hearing

BOX 8.2   RESPONSE TO INTERVENTION

Over the past decade, the **Response to Intervention** (RTI) movement increasingly has been implemented with school-age children to provide assistance and earlier intervention to those who may be struggling in school settings. This approach was introduced as an option for working with students at risk for learning disabilities in the Individuals with Disabilities Education Improvement Act (2004). The basic premise of RTI is that struggling learners benefit from targeted early academic intervention, and that waiting until they fall far enough behind to be eligible for special educational services exacerbates the problem. Key components of an RTI model include systematic screening and progress monitoring, the use of multiple tiers of increasingly intense and individualized interventions, and a problem-solving process to aid in decision making (Coleman, Buysee & Nietzel, 2006).

Association (ASHA, 1990), the National Association of School Psychologists (2005), and the Division for Early Childhood of the Council for Exceptional Children (1993, 2002; Neisworth & Bagnato, 2000) have offered statements pertaining to the assessment of and treatment practices for young children with special needs. Additionally, the National Association for the Education of Young Children and the National Association of Early Childhood Specialists in state departments of education published a joint position statement pertaining to guidelines for the assessment of young children (NAEYC & NAECS/SDE, 2002). Selected principles include the following:

1. Professionals and families collaborate in planning and implementing the multidisciplinary team assessment.
2. Assessment is individualized and both developmentally and culturally appropriate for the child and family.
3. Assessment provides useful information for intervention and leads to benefits for children, families, and programs.
4. Assessment measures must meet accepted professional standards of validity and reliability.
5. Professionals share information in respectful and useful ways.

Specific assessment standards have been recommended for early childhood assessment (Neisworth & Bagnato, 1996; Neisworth & Bagnato, 2001). Although these standards seem quite reasonable and have been promoted for many years, it is likely that they have not yet been fully implemented across all early childhood assessment settings. Several recommended assessment standards are depicted in Table 8.1 and discussed briefly in the following paragraphs.

Treatment Utility

The term *treatment utility* refers to the usefulness of the scale and its findings for intervention planning.

One of the major considerations in the assessment process should be **treatment utility;** that is, the usefulness of the measure or approach to guide intervention and educational planning. Results of the assessment should link directly to curriculum competencies or help identify instructional or therapy goals. Many traditional types

TABLE 8.1	Developmentally appropriate assessment standards.
Utility	Usefulness for intervention
Acceptability	Social worth and agreement
Authenticity	Natural methods and contexts
Equity	Adaptable for special needs
Sensitivity	Fine measure gradations
Convergence	Synthesis of information
Collaboration	Parent-professional teamwork
Congruence	Special design/field validation

Source: Adapted from Bagnato & Neisworth (2001).

of assessment strategies that have been applied to preschool-aged as well as school-aged children have yielded little information useful for program planning and specific treatment strategies (Neisworth & Bagnato, 2004). Although traditional tools, such as formal cognitive measures, might be a component of a child's evaluation in terms of making a diagnosis or establishing eligibility, these should be augmented routinely with other measures that are more sensitive to treatment utility.

Social Validity

The second standard, **social validity,** refers to the perceived value, acceptability, and appropriateness of the assessment. Several key questions should be asked in relation to this standard, such as, "Is the assessment viewed as valuable for the specific situational factors presented by a child and his family?" and "Are the assessment methods acceptable to the participants?" Many of the items found on typical early childhood assessment measures require a child to perform tasks that represent isolated skills, but the tasks themselves have little validity with respect to that child's daily functioning. For example, completing a pegboard may be an important normative finding (i.e., can the child perform this task at the same level as other children of the same age?), but the process may or may not relate to why the child is having trouble with buttoning, zipping, and other functional activities in her daily life. Social validity considerations also may increase the probability that the family and other professionals will become more involved in the assessment, treatment, and monitoring processes.

> The term *social validity* refers to the value and appropriateness of an assessment method.

> Does the assessment task relate to activities within the child's daily routine?

Convergent Assessment

There is a legal mandate that treatment planning not be based on a single assessment procedure. **Convergent assessment** is a process to synthesize information collected across multiple methods, sources, settings, and occasions. The specific methods by which data are gathered are less critical than the importance of involving multiple sources of information from parents, teachers, and others who know the child well. The subsequent pooling of information offers a more comprehensive and valid picture of the child's strengths and needs across settings. As a result, the process provides a firmer foundation upon which to make diagnostic and programmatic decisions and establishes multiple mechanisms for monitoring development. Convergent assessment values and encourages the participation of family members and others throughout this process.

> The term *convergent assessment* refers to the process wherein information is obtained from multiple sources.

Consensual Validity

A final standard, **consensual validity,** reflects the need to reach assessment decisions via collaboration and consensus among the team members. This occasionally is much easier said than done. Although the general intent of multidisciplinary teams is to serve the best interests of the child and family, sometimes this intent can become clouded by issues related to the team's group dynamics. Problems can occur,

> The term *consensual validity* refers to the collaboration of team members to create an assessment plan.

such as one professional not being able to communicate clearly to another professional because of discipline-specific jargon (i.e., no common language), no common assessment purpose or tools (i.e., their "measuring sticks" are different), a lack of clear leadership, or an attempt by one discipline to control or take precedence over others. Each of these problems can interfere with the mission of the team: to determine the child's developmental and educational needs and to link them to an appropriate plan of intervention.

:: STAGES OF ASSESSMENT

Assessment strategies are vital components at each stage of service delivery, although the ultimate goals and objectives at each stage may be different.

As illustrated in the vignette at the beginning of this chapter, assessment is an on-going and continuous process, often utilizing various strategies. In early childhood assessment and intervention, there are four major stages that occur prior to and during the delivery of services. These stages include (1) early identification, (2) comprehensive evaluation, (3) program planning and implementation, and (4) program evaluation. Figure 8.1 illustrates these stages in a decision-point format.

Stage 1: Early Identification

The overarching goal in early intervention is to identify young children who may need services and to provide those services as early as possible in order to obtain the maximum benefit. Identification in early childhood can occur at any point from conception through the first years of formal schooling, and it typically involves any procedure that leads to the identification of a child with special needs. Early identification is mandated by the Individuals with Disabilities Education Act and is usually under the jurisdiction of the designated lead agency, often the public schools. (See Chapter 1 for a list of the lead agencies in each state.) This process includes two major activities: Child Find and screening.

Child Find is the systematic procedure used to locate young children who may qualify for early childhood services.

Child Find   Federal legislation mandates that each state conduct comprehensive and coordinated activities in order to identify as early as possible any children who need early intervention services (Harbin, McWilliam, & Gallagher, 2000; IDEA 2004). **Child Find** is a community-wide effort involving many agencies that have contact with infants and young children and their families. In this regard, one key Child Find function is to increase public awareness of issues related to disability and to encourage individuals to identify potential cases that may be eligible for intervention services.

Public Awareness.   Awareness is one of the initial components of early identification and refers to the various methods (e.g., television, radio, the Internet, pamphlets, newspaper releases) used to alert the public and professional communities about typical and atypical early childhood development. This involves organized efforts to inform and influence the public, especially community leaders and families, about

FIGURE **8.1** Stages of the assessment process.

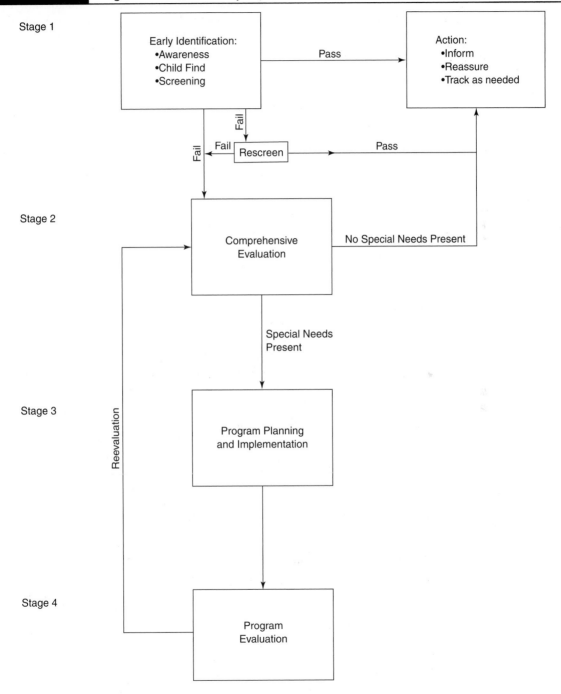

programs for young children who have or are at risk for disabilities. Its purpose is to find children in need of special services and make families and communities aware of the referral procedures to access appropriate programs. Awareness efforts not only promote support for intervention programs, but also encourage close community observation of the quality of these services.

Screening   The second major activity of early intervention is screening. In addition to increasing public awareness, Child Find activities are designed to locate infants, toddlers, and preschool children who will participate in an informal or formal **screening** process. A screening assessment can serve one of several roles. It can be performed to identify children who (a) have a delay or disability that warrants further attention or monitoring, (b) are eligible or "ready" for specific programs, or (c) are in need of a more comprehensive evaluation (Dunst, Trivette, Appl, & Bagnato, 2004). Screening is often the first step in the intervention process when children have been identified as being at risk for experiencing developmental difficulties. The information obtained from screening is not, however, appropriate for making diagnoses or making specific recommendations for intervention or curriculum planning (Slentz, 2004). Screening efforts typically employ brief, relatively inexpensive measures that can be quickly and easily administered by a variety of professionals and paraprofessionals.

Federal legislation has encouraged the implementation of large-scale, early identification screening, or **mass screening,** wherein a program attempts to screen every child in a specified population. Although this type of effort can be expensive, the cost should be viewed within a preventive framework that considers the probable reduction of long-term special education costs if earlier intervention services are received. Widespread screening increases the chances that young children with special needs will not be overlooked; furthermore, there tends to be little or no stigma associated with such screening practices because nearly everyone in the specified population participates. Some programs may elect to engage in **selective screening** rather than mass screening. This approach to screening may target specific high-risk groups of children, such as children with a variety of chronic illnesses or children from poverty-stricken areas, or it might be used at specific developmental points in time, such as just prior to kindergarten entry.

Regardless of the type of screening approach, the basic premise of early childhood services is that early identification and intervention strive to lessen the impact of developmental risks and disabilities on children.

Critical Qualities of Screening Measures.   Given that the focus of screening is to determine which children need further assessment, a key question is whether the decision to refer or not to refer a child for a comprehensive evaluation was accurate. There are several important concepts to consider in this regard: hit rates, sensitivity, specificity, false positives, and false negatives. Overall **hit rates** are important to screening in that they provide an index of the overall accuracy of the screening measure or measures.

As shown in Figure 8.2 there are four basic outcomes from a screening decision: two accurate and two inaccurate. When a screening decision suggests that a child may be at risk for a medical or developmental problem, and the child indeed needs

---

Children are selected for more thorough evaluation through the process of screening.

The cost of widespread screening activities should be viewed within a preventive framework, with consideration given to the probable reduction of long-term special education costs if children and families are identified during early childhood.

Hit rates reflect the degree of accuracy of screening measures.

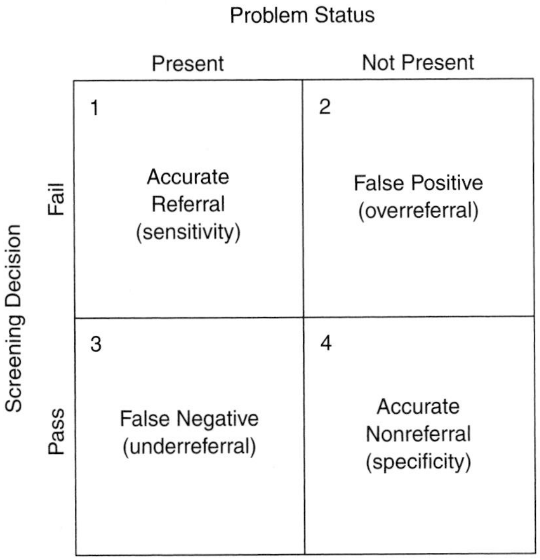

Problem Status

FIGURE 8.2

Types of screening decision outcomes.

special services, then an accurate referral has been made. This is referred to as **sensitivity**. Ideally, a good screening device or program should capture at least 80% of children with problems (Glascoe, 1996). Similarly, when a screening decision indicates that a child is at low risk for having a medical or developmental problem and the child does not have the target problem, then an accurate nonreferral has been made. This is referred to as **specificity**. Glascoe (1996) suggests that this rate should be at least 90% to minimize overreferrals. Accurate decisions are represented in cells 1 and 4 of Figure 8.2.

Sometimes, a screening decision leads to a referral when in fact the child may not have the medical or developmental problem of concern. This leads to what is called a **false positive** and contributes to overreferrals, as shown in cell 2 of Figure 8.2. Additionally, screening decisions can suggest that a specific problem does not exist, but the child actually manifests the target problem. This type of decision-making error is shown in cell 3 of Figure 8.2 and is referred to as a **false negative.** False negatives can result in underreferral of children for specific problems which, in turn, may contribute to a delay in receiving services and subsequent ongoing difficulties for those children and their families. The risk and frequency of false negatives provides a strong rationale for conducting ongoing developmental monitoring, even when a child may not appear to have a problem.

Obviously, the implementation of effective screening is a huge responsibility for a community and an integral part of the early intervention process. When choosing screening tools, it is critical that measures not only have adequate sensitivity and specificity but also have appropriate reliability and validity; these two dimensions are discussed later in this chapter. Further, it is also critical for screening, or developmental monitoring, to take place on a recurrent or periodic basis and include input from a variety of professionals.

The term *sensitivity* refers to accurate identification of a child who needs special services.

The term *specificity* refers to accurate identification of a child who does not need special services.

A false positive occurs when screening suggests special services that are not needed.

A false negative occurs when screening fails to detect a problem that exists.

Formal Screening Procedures As part of the early identification process and intimately related to Child Find, young children with special needs can be identified through formal screening procedures.

Prenatal and Neonatal Screening. The initial identification of a disability often is made by a physician, such as the pediatrician, neonatologist, or the obstetrician, who may become aware of a disability as early as the first few weeks of pregnancy through prenatal diagnostic techniques (e.g., ultrasound). Recent guidelines by the American College of Obstetricians and Gynecologists recommend that all pregnant women be offered screening for Down syndrome before 20 weeks of gestation, which is a significant change from the previous recommendation to offer this screening only to women over 35 years of age (ACOG, 2007). In some cases, early identification also has allowed for surgical correction of congenital problems in utero, such as fetal surgery for spina bifida (Bruner & Tulipan, 2005) or for other life-threatening conditions (Menon & N. Rao, 2005), although these procedures are far from common and are completed in very few academic medical centers (Manning, Jennings, & Madsen, 2000). Some of the more common prenatal screening or diagnostic procedures are presented in Table 8.2. Prenatal diagnosis is now a routine part of obstetric care, especially in the case of high-risk pregnancies.

An obstetrician is often able to recognize factors that can indicate a potential disability at the birth of an infant. These conditions include **anoxia** (lack of oxygen), possibly caused by a twisted or knotted umbilical cord; a prolonged, stressful labor during which the infant may aspirate **meconium** (fetal waste products) into the lungs; and prematurity or very low birth weight (Taylor, Klein, & Hack, 2000; Taylor, Klein, Minich, & Hack, 2001).

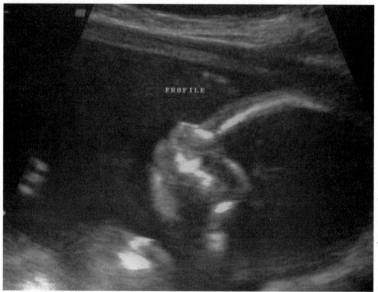

Courtesy of Dr. Jennifer Hiemenz

Ultrasound provides physicians and parents with an early view of the baby.

TABLE 8.2	Common prenatal screening procedures.
Screening Procedure	**Procedures/Utility**
Urine Screen	A special stick is inserted in a urine sample at each prenatal visit to identify gestational diabetes. Low levels of sugar may indicate hypoglycemia, whereas high levels may indicate hyperglycemia. These conditions may affect the developing fetus.
Blood Pressure	Blood pressure is measured with a cuff and stethoscope at each prenatal visit. Abnormal pressure readings may suggest complications such as preeclampsia (maternal hypertension with high levels of protein in the urine and body swelling).
Hemoglobin Screen	Blood is drawn from an arm or finger prick at about 4 months gestation and throughout the pregnancy, as warranted. The blood is examined for iron levels, with low levels indicating the presence of anemia.
Amniocentesis	A hollow needle is inserted through the abdominal wall into the uterus to withdraw a small amount of amniotic fluid. This procedure usually is done in conjunction with an ultrasound to avoid injuring the fetus, umbilical cord, or placenta. It is conducted at about 13 to 18 weeks gestation and typically is performed for high-risk pregnancies (e.g., advanced maternal age and known family history of chromosomal abnormalities). Amniocentesis can provide relatively reliable information about neural tube defects and genetic defects such as Down syndrome. It also can reveal the gender of the fetus. It is essential for this procedure to be conducted in conjunction with ultrasound.
Alpha-Fetoprotein Test (Triple Screen)	Blood from a finger prick is used to screen for neural tube defects between 14 and 18 weeks gestation. A high AFP level is a possible indicator of neural tube defects (e.g., spina bifida and anencephaly), whereas a low level may suggest an increased risk of Down syndrome or other chromosomal problems. Abnormal levels indicate the need for additional AFP testing, a sonogram, and amniocentesis.
Chorionic Villi Sampling	A needle is inserted into the vagina or abdomen, and then into the uterine wall to the edge of the placenta. Chorionic villi (the fetal components of the developing placenta) are withdrawn and examined. This procedure is generally done between 9 and 12 weeks gestation. It can reveal chromosomal and genetic abnormalities (e.g., Down syndrome), Tay-Sachs disease and other inborn errors of metabolism, types of cystic fibrosis, and thalessemia (e.g., sickle cell anemia). Testing for other specific disorders and diseases can be done if the family history warrants it.
Ultrasound (Sonography)	Using sonography to generate a live outline of the fetus in utero, this procedure can reveal orthopedic impairment, problems with major organs, and other physical abnormalities. Recently, the American College of Obstetricians and Gynecologists recommended examining *nuchal translucency* (the thickness at the back of the neck) as a screening marker for Down syndrome. An ultrasound typically is performed between weeks 14 and 20 of the pregnancy.
Magnetic Resonance Imaging (MRI)	This procedure uses a strong magnetic field to create a higher-resolution image of the developing fetus than ultrasound can offer, and is used to assess structural defects in the brain and organs of the fetus. It is not typically performed except as a follow up assessment to concerns noted on ultrasound.

Other predictors of an abnormality may be observed during a routine examination of an infant immediately following birth. This process generally involves blood and urine tests for metabolic disorders such as phenylketonuria (PKU), and the **Apgar rating** (Apgar, 1953) which evaluates heart rate, breathing effort, muscle tone, reflex irritability, and skin tone. More detailed behavioral examinations of a newborn may be accomplished using such tests as the *Brazelton Neonatal Behavioral Assessment Scale* (NBAS) (Brazelton, 1984; Brazelton & Nugent, 1995), and other neurological examinations (Chervenak & Kurjak, 1996; Mindes, Ireton, & Mardell-Czudnowski, 1996). Scales such as the Brazelton NBAS allow a pediatrician or another appropriately trained professional to identify possible abnormalities in the central nervous system and in the sensory abilities of a newborn. According to Bergen and Wright (1994), the NBAS is a more sensitive predictor of later developmental outcomes than is the Apgar score. Further, it offers the opportunity for parents to observe and talk about their baby with a professional rather than to be directly or indirectly taught about general infant behavior.

Early Childhood Screening.   Developmental screening has traditionally been viewed as the role of the physician; however, given the involvement of a variety of agencies in early childhood intervention and service delivery, numerous health care providers (nurse practitioners, pediatric and public health nurses, dentists) and other professionals now participate in Child Find and associated screening efforts.

Most young children receive medical care from a pediatrician or other primary care provider through well-child visits. This system allows the health care provider the opportunity to observe a child's development frequently and over an extended period. A pediatrician may suspect possible disabilities if there is a record of stressful birth events, a history of pediatric illnesses, or a family history of developmental problems. Later, if a child does not achieve major developmental milestones (e.g., walking and talking) at expected times, then the pediatrician or health care provider might determine the need for further examination. A recent policy statement from the Council on Children with Disabilities (2006) suggested that screening tests be administered regularly at the 9-, 18- and 24- or 30-month visits. Primary health care providers often are the main source of guidance when parents believe that their child is not developing as expected or is experiencing difficulties in any area. For Evan (our case study), potential language delays and social-emotional or behavioral differences may have been noticed by his pediatrician through the use of developmental screening tools or discussions with Mr. and Mrs. DeCruz. Additionally, if his pediatrician suspected an autism spectrum disorder, there are available screening measures that target critical areas of development that may suggest autism and the need for a comprehensive evaluation.

Formal screening instruments can be used by health care providers as well as other professionals who are involved in screening. Two instruments that can be used with infants and toddlers are the *Bayley Infant Neurodevelopmental Screener* (BINS) (Aylward, 1995) and the *Denver–II* (Frankenburg et al., 1990). The BINS, developed for children ages 3–24 months, assesses basic neurological functions/intactness, receptive functions, expressive functions, and cognitive processes. Similarly, the *Denver–II* quickly screens a child's gross motor, language, fine motor–adaptive, and personal–social skills in comparison to other children of the same age.

Early interventionists, preschool teachers, and other child care providers also play an important role in the early identification of children with special needs; they have the unique advantage of regular, often daily, observation of a child. Whereas many professionals are primarily concerned with a specific facet of a child's development, an early interventionist or educator observes all aspects of a child's development, thus providing a more holistic view. Other professionals, such as social workers, may also assist in the screening process by providing insight into the family strengths as well as familial and ecological risk factors.

Other popular screening measures that may be used by various professionals include the *Ages and Stages Questionnaires* (ASQ): *A Parent-Completed, Child-Monitoring System, Second Edition* (Squires, Potter, & Bricker, 1999); the *Battelle Developmental Inventory–Second Edition,* (Newborg, 2004); the *Developmental Indicators for the Assessment of Learning–Third Edition* (Mardell-Czudnowski & Goldenberg, 1998); and the *The Early Learning Accomplishment Profile for Developmentally Young Children* (Chapel Hill Training Outreach Project, 2002).

Professional involvement is certainly valuable in the early identification of children with disabilities, but perhaps even more critical is the role of parents. In fact, as discussed in chapters 1 and 10, legislation has mandated that the family be involved as active participants throughout the early intervention process. As the primary observers of their child, parents have firsthand knowledge of their child's total development. If a problem is suspected, the parents may be the first to see evidence of it and subsequently seek advice from one or more professionals. Most parents are in a position to confirm, or at least discuss, the clinical suspicions of any professionals who may have expressed concerns.

> Child care providers and early interventionists often have daily contact with young children, thus allowing them to observe a child's functional abilities in a natural environment.

> The involvement of the family in the early identification process is critical.

Stage 2: Comprehensive Evaluation

Once a child moves into stage 2, the purpose of the assessment changes from early identification of possible needs and concerns to determining whether or not a significant problem exists. Certainly, the primary purpose of a comprehensive evaluation can vary; it can include documentation of a delay, diagnosis of a disability, or the establishment of eligibility for intervention or education services. Moreover, the philosophy underlying the assessment approach can vary (see section on assessment typologies). Regardless, good comprehensive evaluation seeks to (a) advocate for the child, (b) clarify the referral questions and concerns, (c) generate hypotheses regarding what may be going on with the child and gather data using assessment instruments that are psychometrically sound and sensitive to individual differences (e.g., developmental, physical, cultural, and linguistic), (d) synthesize the information that has been collected to provide a better understanding of the child's unique profile of strengths and weaknesses, (e) determine the nature and extent of any problems that might be present, and (f) provide a clear link to stage 3, program planning and implementation, through the generation of recommendations that are practical and relevant to the child's everyday environment. Of course, these goals should be developed in collaboration with caregivers, educators, and other professionals involved in the child's care.

Federal legislation mandates that the assessment of infants and young children with special needs be conducted using a team approach (specific approaches are discussed later in this chapter). An underlying premise of a team evaluation is that it should be comprehensive, covering the important domains of development, thus providing critical information for decision making. Most professionals would agree

In early childhood, it is important to understand and appreciate that a child's development is both integrated and interactive, and takes place within a family and community context.

that several developmental domains should be assessed in a comprehensive evaluation due to the interrelated and integrated skills across these domains. Additionally, many early intervention programs require information about a child's functioning across several areas of development in order to document eligibility for special education services and to plan a child's individualized education plan (IEP) or individualized family service plan (IFSP). Medical and family information also is critical at this stage and should be complementary to information gained from the developmental domains.

Developmental Domains   Five key developmental domains are typically considered in a comprehensive evaluation: cognitive, motor, communication, social/play, and self-care/adaptive skills.

Cognitive skills are those related to mental and intellectual development (see chapter 5). In early childhood, these skills include concepts such as **object permanence**, **imitation**, **means–end** or **causality**, and spatial relationships. As a child reaches preschool age, the assessment of cognitive development includes more pre-academic skills, such as literacy and early quantitative abilities.

Motor skills are related to the use of muscles, joints, and limbs. As discussed in chapters 3 and 4, the assessment of motor skills typically is divided into two areas: gross motor and fine motor. Gross motor skills require the use of large muscles and movements such as walking, running, throwing, jumping, and maintaining balance. Fine motor skills refer to the use of small muscles and more refined movements such as cutting, writing, grasping, and buttoning; these skills often overlap with skills within the self-help or adaptive domain and can be referred to as **activities of daily living** or ADLs.

Communication skills are those that allow a child to give and receive information (see chapter 6). Two areas of communication that are frequently assessed are receptive and expressive language. **Receptive language** refers to a child's ability to understand and comprehend information being presented. **Expressive language** is a child's ability to communicate thoughts, feelings, or ideas to others. A child's speech production and ability to produce sounds and words (articulation) may also be assessed. Communication includes not only the use of words but also gestures, pictures, facial expressions, and augmentative devices.

Social and play skills refer to a child's ability to interact with peers and adults, specific behaviors in social situations, and use of toys. The level of a child's play (i.e., manipulative, symbolic, pretend, constructive) can provide important developmental information. Frequently, a play assessment is conducted in order to understand a child's cognitive, motor, and communication skills as expressed through the medium of play. As noted in chapter 7, these skills are critical to children's social-emotional and academic development.

Self-care or adaptive skills are related to a child's ability to function independently in meeting daily needs such as toileting, feeding, and dressing. Understanding a young child's needs for help or assistance during such daily caretaking activities can provide invaluable information for making decisions about placement and the need for individualized assistance and support. These were discussed in chapter 4.

Courtesy of Rebecca Edmondson Pretzel and Jennifer Hiemenz

Observation of a child in her natural setting can facilitate the assessment process by allowing the child to function in her natural environment.

Medical Issues Because of the complex nature of many early childhood disabilities and conditions, it is imperative that medical issues receive consideration in the evaluation process. In addition to whatever information can be provided from the prenatal history of a child (e.g., findings derived from prenatal tests), a physical examination may help determine the nature or etiology of a child's disability. A thorough physical exam can provide diagnostic (e.g., fragile X syndrome, neurofibromatosis, or epilepsy) and selected prognostic information. Understanding a child's medical condition also can provide information about the need for specialized attention and assistance within the childcare or preschool setting. Medical factors can significantly impact a child's rate and course of development and acquisition of new skills. For example, children with infectious diseases, metabolic disorders, and chronic illnesses require ongoing medical monitoring and perhaps medication or frequent hospitalizations. These factors also may dictate the setting in which services are provided. In Evan's case, autism is sometimes associated with other medical diagnoses such as fragile X syndrome. A thorough medical examination and genetic testing can help his family better understand his condition and also assist them and Evan's siblings with future family planning issues.

Family Issues   The Individuals with Disabilities Education Act requires assessment practices to include an examination of the family's strengths and needs in addition to those of the child. By establishing a collaborative partnership with families, professionals can gain a better understanding of a child's strengths, needs, and overall resources. Parents know their child better than anyone else and most can provide important details about the child's past and current development. For Evan to have received a diagnosis of autism, information about his developmental history as well as his current skills and behaviors would have been provided by his parents and would be a critical component of his diagnostic evaluation. In addition, interviewing a child's parents or having them complete questionnaires can provide pertinent information about their parenting skills and attitudes, their discipline techniques, and their understanding of their child's developmental strengths and challenges. Having the family involved in the assessment process also elicits their input, questions, and cooperation in relation to ongoing developmental surveillance, monitoring, and subsequent intervention.

Stage 3: Program Planning and Implementation

The comprehensive evaluation serves as a prerequisite and foundation for stage 3, program planning and implementation. It provides the information needed to discuss optional settings for a child and to develop relevant goals for an IEP or IFSP (i.e., what and how a child should be taught). This information is then translated into a plan of action for the preschool teacher, related services personnel, early interventionist, and family. Although more detailed information about intervention is provided in other chapters, it is important to note here that assessment does not stop once intervention begins. Rather, assessment should be considered the first step in program planning and should be an ongoing process that informs feasible interventions and monitors intervention progress at different points along a child's developmental path. A core feature of early childhood assessment is that it goes beyond taking a snapshot view of the child, and seeks to understand both protective and risk factors in the context of future development. The rapid and often unpredictable changes that take place across multiple areas of development during early childhood pose unique challenges to both assessment and intervention with this population (Nagle, 2007). However, based on the information that a comprehensive evaluation provides regarding the projected developmental and educational trajectory of the child, the goal of intervention is to facilitate the acquisition of new skills and mastery of key developmental tasks. Because the results of a comprehensive evaluation inform what and how a child should be taught, it is critical that the evaluation be performed in a manner that is ecologically valid for the specific child who has been referred.

Federal regulations now mandate that a child's individual education plan shall include "specific early intervention services based on peer-reviewed research, to the extent practicable," and a "statement of the measurable results or outcomes" (IDEA, 2004). The teacher or early interventionist is required to provide ongoing formal and informal assessment of a child's progress in targeted developmental domains and behaviors, as specified in the IEP or IFSP; assessment information pertaining to preliteracy and language skills is now emphasized as well. From an assessment perspective, criterion-referenced types of measures can be useful for tracking progress frequently and in a developmentally sensitive fashion.

Stage 4: Program Evaluation

This stage involves assessment procedures that measure both the progress of the child and the effectiveness of the intervention plan or program. The overall goals of this stage are (1) to reassess the current developmental levels of a child, (2) to monitor progress related to developmental goals established by the team and family members for the IEP or IFSP, and (3) to determine the need for adjustments and modifications in the child's intervention program. In some instances, a child's developmental gains may have progressed to a point at which they are within age-appropriate levels, and no further services may be needed at that time. On the other hand, follow-up assessment may reveal areas of development that require further monitoring and provide information regarding how a program can be modified to better serve the child's intervention needs.

From an accountability standpoint, this type of evaluation can assist schools and teachers in ensuring that they meet early learning standards. Assessing the quality of a program can also help in justifying why a program should exist and assist in securing available sources of funding. Ultimately, teachers, along with other professionals and caregivers working with a child, should know whether specific interventions actually result in increased learning and development. More recently, there has been a focus on delineating the causal links between specific program components and child outcomes so that there may be a better understanding of the processes by which programs effect change (Nagle, 2007). Therefore, the goal of program evaluation is to determine how much progress, if any, has been made, as well as to identify why change occurred.

:: TEAM APPROACHES AND TYPOLOGIES

A number of approaches and techniques can be employed in the assessment process; indeed, an assessment team may elect to use a combination of these techniques, depending on the nature of the presenting problem and the information they need to gather.

Team Models

IDEA and accepted standards of best practice mandate that assessment strategies involve multiple disciplines as well as the family (McWilliam, 2000). Given the many different challenges faced by children with special needs, and despite the financial costs inherent in bringing a (large) group of professionals together, a team approach clearly is the preferred method of gathering assessment data. The team can include a combination of, but not be limited to, a psychologist, social worker, early interventionist, audiologist, nurse, speech and language pathologist, nutritionist, occupational therapist, physical therapist, pediatrician, and the child's parents. How this team operates, however, can be quite varied. At present, there are at least three commonly recognized versions of the team process: multidisciplinary, interdisciplinary, and transdisciplinary (Nagle, 2007).

Multidisciplinary Team

The multidisciplinary team consists of professionals from various disciplines who conduct independent assessments.

On the **multidisciplinary team**, whose origins are based on the medical model, the number of team members may be set or members may be selected to address the problems presented by the referral source (e.g., one referral problem may demand the presence of a physical therapist whereas another may not). Regardless of the team makeup, each professional on the team has a clearly defined role with specific areas of responsibility. In a multidisciplinary evaluation, each discipline conducts an assessment independently of the others and provides feedback to the parents or referral source, perhaps on different days, without necessarily discussing the findings with other team members. Clearly, due to the inherent lack of collaboration and communication among disciplines, this type of assessment process can result in redundant or potentially conflicting results. Moreover, the practicalities of attending independent assessment and feedback sessions can be quite time-consuming for families. In many instances, despite the fact that a wide range of disciplines has been involved, families or early interventionists may not feel that they have an integrated understanding of the child, particularly when they are presented with contradictory findings from different professionals. Even when a selected professional is deemed responsible for presenting the results from all of the different disciplines involved, concerns may arise related to the comfort of that professional with all of the information being provided and biases can emerge (Nagle, 2007). For example, such a situation could arise when an early childhood professional attempts to interpret the assessment of a geneticist or an occupational therapist.

Interdisciplinary Team

On the interdisciplinary team, although members are from different disciplines, they collaborate and communicate for a more integrated process.

A variant of the multidisciplinary team is the **interdisciplinary team**. The number and type of professionals involved in multidisciplinary and interdisciplinary assessment may be very similar and disciplines typically conduct individual evaluations. Major differences, however, lie in the interdisciplinary team's ongoing communication to develop a more integrated plan for assessment and the sharing of results by team members to ensure that families receive a unified interpretation and set of recommendations. Although the emphasis on ongoing communication may improve the information being provided to families and referral sources, there remain potential problems; for example, one professional may take charge and unnecessarily dominate a team meeting. Also, despite the fact that professionals may have the opportunities to talk to one another about their findings, this does not ensure that they will understand one another or reach consensus on the findings and recommendations.

Transdisciplinary Team

Transdisciplinary team members commit to teaching, learning, and working across disciplinary boundaries to plan and provide integrated services (Garland, McGonigel, Frank, & Buck, 1989).

A third variant of the team model is the **transdisciplinary team**. Using this model, team members meet regularly, share assessment and intervention responsibilities, and always include families as part of the team (Garland, McGonigel, Frank, & Buck, 1989). An assessment approach often associated with this type of team is **arena assessment.** With this data-gathering approach, a team of professionals observes the child in some type of interaction with another professional or facilitator. One way for this process to unfold is for a single professional, such as a psychologist or speech and language pathologist, to begin assessment and to have the other professionals observe and assist in various ways (e.g., "coaching" and taking notes). The basic premise underlying this model is that many of the items used in different assessment instruments across disciplines will overlap or similar behaviors will be elicited. Therefore, rather than having each discipline perform independent assessments, team members often collaborate by either taking turns administering items that fall under their area of expertise or observing the behaviors that are relevant to their domain while another professional works with the child. For example, on a block task, a speech and language pathologist might be interested in whether a child can follow verbal directions necessary to perform a motor task, whereas an occupational therapist may be most concerned with the fine motor capabilities of the child. One major advantage to using the transdisciplinary team approach is that professionals do not have to readminister redundant items, thereby saving time, minimizing practice effects, and preserving the child's stamina for other tasks. This model is particularly beneficial for assessing young children who may have difficulty sustaining their attention and motivation through lengthy assessments. Play-based assessment models that embody the transdisciplinary approach have also been developed over the recent years (Linder, 2007; Athanasiou, 2007).

Transdisciplinary assessment can provide an enormous amount of practical information to clinicians, early interventionists, and parents across all of the key developmental domains of interest. One minor drawback to using a transdisciplinary assessment model, however, is that there are few assessment tools available that can be used well by a transdisciplinary team and that meet the reliability and validity standards of some of the more traditional single-discipline measures. On the other hand, when using "single-discipline" instruments in a transdisciplinary model, standardized procedures are difficult to maintain because the same task may have different specific directions in each of the different measures. For example, the *Bayley Scales of Infant Development–Third Edition* (Bayley, 2005), the *Mullen Scales of Early Learning* (Mullen, 1995), the *Differential Ability Scales–Second Edition* (Elliott, 2006), and the *Denver–II* (Frankenburg et al., 1990) have a block-stacking task, but the blocks themselves, the directions to the child, and the scoring are all different. However, if the goal of this task in the transdisciplinary assessment is to determine whether or not the child can stack blocks, this problem may be relevant only to the scoring of the specific measures used. Obviously, observation of the child's ability and how it relates to daily tasks may be much more relevant to goal setting and program planning.

Another potential drawback to using a transdisciplinary approach (i.e., arena assessment) is that parents and/or the child may feel more comfortable in a one-on-one setting versus being in the presence of multiple professionals. In addition, the degree of coordination required for team members to be available at the same time and the frequency with which they must meet to plan and carry out the evaluation, discuss findings, and meet with the family can be quite time-consuming for professionals.

At the same time, this process generally becomes more efficient as team members adjust to working with one another over time and professionals find that engaging in transdisciplinary practice enhances their competencies (McWilliam, 2000). In addition, this approach to assessment should pose less of a logistical burden on families; parents often appreciate the benefits associated with receiving services under such a collaborative team model.

Assessment Typologies

To gain a comprehensive view of a young child, particularly one with suspected delays or documented disabilities, it is important to choose a multidimensional assessment approach that employs a variety of measures, gathers information from multiple sources, examines several developmental and behavioral domains, and accomplishes a range of goals.

Although the intent of this section is not to review specific tests and procedures in any detail, Benner (1992) provided a framework that remains useful in helping early childhood professionals organize various assessment approaches and techniques across different strands. These include: (1) formal/informal, (2) normative/ criterion-referenced, (3) standardized/adaptive-to-disability, (4) direct/indirect, (5) naturalistic/clinical, and (6) product/process.

Formal/Informal Assessment   In a formal assessment, the primary strategy for data collection involves the use of standardized tests, which are selected by the examiner(s) with a specific purpose in mind (e.g., screening, comprehensive evaluation, or program evaluation), and a specific assessment plan then is set into action.

At the other end of the continuum are more informal assessment strategies, which often involve the use of nonstandardized assessment procedures. Informal assessment tools include behavioral observations, checklists, rating scales, and work samples. An informal data-gathering strategy may indicate the need for and set into motion more formal data collection.

Normative/Criterion-Referenced Assessment   Normative data collection places the primary emphasis on how one child compares with other children of the same chronological age. This is one of the most frequently used strategies in early childhood assessment and is considered a formal approach that employs standardized procedures. Examples of widely used normative-based instruments in early childhood assessment include the *Bayley Scales of Infant Development–Third Edition* (Bayley, 2005) and the *Mullen Scales of Early Learning* (Mullen, 1995). The *Bayley–III* is designed for children aged 1 month to 42 months and assesses cognitive, motor, and language development. Caregivers can also provide information regarding social–emotional functioning and adaptive behavior via questionnaires. Formal scores are derived by comparing the child's performance in each of these developmental domains to the performance of children of similar chronological age in the "reference" or "normative" group. Similarly, the Mullen is a norm-referenced instrument that assesses language, motor, and visual perceptual skills in children from birth to 68 months.

Normative assessment compares a child's performance with that of age-level peers.

Criterion-referenced assessment can help identify specific tasks a child can and cannot do as opposed to comparing her to her peers.

In contrast to **norm-referenced assessment, criterion-referenced measures** focus on the degree to which a child demonstrates certain skills in comparison to a specific performance standard (e.g., identifying basic colors). Although task analyses and many different tests may be necessary to gain meaningful information about individual skills, this type of data-gathering strategy often contributes useful information to a child's IEP or IFSP because it can be directly linked to a developmentally sequenced curriculum (i.e., curriculum-based assessment). Furthermore, this approach can be less formal, as a preschool teacher or early interventionist can create criterion-referenced assessment tools to inform ongoing program planning and evaluation.

Curriculum-based assessment is one of the most representative assessment strategies of the criterion-referenced approach. This type of assessment allows the early childhood professional to assess a child's current skills and to monitor progress according to specific program objectives. Curriculum-based assessment also allows a teacher to delineate skills in the curriculum that a child has not yet mastered and to plan accordingly. One potential weakness of curriculum-based assessment, however, is that the skills assessed are based on a specific curriculum and may not generalize to another program.

> Curriculum-based assessment identifies skills, tasks, and behaviors that are important within a particular curriculum.

Standardized/Adaptive-to-Disability Assessment

In standardized assessment, examiners adhere to a fixed set of specific guidelines regarding test content (e.g., using the test stimuli that are provided), the manner in which to administer each task (e.g., verbatim instructions, starting and stopping points, number of trials to administer, opportunity for teaching trials), scoring criteria (e.g., guidelines for 0-, 1, or 2-point responses), and interpretation of test scores (e.g., what scores constitute "average"). On the one hand, examiners are encouraged to develop rapport and weigh each child's individual factors during test administration and interpretation; however, this is balanced by the desire to make the test content and assessment conditions as uniform and consistent as possible so that error variance explanations of a child's score (e.g., differences in test materials and administration procedures) are minimized and the ability to attribute a child's score to his or her actual knowledge or skill level is maximized (Sattler, 2001).

Adaptive-to-disability data-gathering strategies afford professionals and early childhood teams greater flexibility in attempting to gain a profile of a child's abilities. While many would prefer to use a measure that is designed for use with the specific population at hand when a disability is involved, one strategy may be to modify the properties of the objects and materials used in an assessment. For example, for children with a visual impairment, it may be helpful to make materials larger and brighter or add visual contrast or textured components. For children with language difficulties, it may be helpful to minimize the number and extent of verbal directions or reduce the number of possible response choices available. Bagnato and colleagues (1997) discuss a dynamic modification in which a child might first be tested, then taught the task, and subsequently be retested to gain an estimate of learning rate. Additionally, Sattler (2001) provides a number of suggestions for testing the limits of standardized procedures, particularly for older preschoolers (e.g., eliminating time limits and asking probing questions).

Direct/Indirect Assessment   The direct/indirect continuum refers to *how* examiners or early intervention teams collect information about a child. Most often, a professional works with the child face-to-face in direct assessment; other times, different strategies can be used (e.g., observing a videotape to code a child's behaviors). This direct format of data gathering is likely the most frequently used strategy and is considered an essential component of any early childhood assessment.

The indirect data-gathering strategy involves the collection of information about a child via other assessment techniques. For example, interviewing parents and other caregivers (e.g., preschool teachers) or having them complete rating scales may provide some index of how a child is functioning in various settings. While the focus of indirect assessment is on the child, this strategy can also yield related information that is critical to the child's development, such as information about family resources and parental discipline techniques. One example of an indirect or third-party assessment tool is the early childhood version of the *Child Behavior Checklist* (CBCL) (Achenbach & Rescorla, 2000), a multidimensional parent rating system that presents parents with questions regarding their child's behavior and emotional functioning. In the same family of assessment instruments, the *Caregiver–Teacher Report Form* (Achenbach & Rescorla, 2000) allows teachers to rate their observations of similar behaviors. Another commonly used indirect instrument, the *Behavior Assessment Scale for Children, 2nd Edition* (BASC-2) (Reynolds & Kamphaus, 2004), includes parent and teacher report questionnaires for children ages 2 through 5.

Naturalistic/Clinical Observations   Observational data are critical to all assessment processes. Naturalistic observational strategies require that information be collected in a child's natural environment under routine circumstances. Such strategies can involve observation of the child's overall behavior within a setting or they can focus on more specific types of behaviors (e.g., temper tantrums at home, social skills during group activities, or fine motor skills during an art activity). Naturalistic observations can be one of the most ecologically valid data-gathering strategies because they focus on a child's everyday activities (Bagnato & Ho, 2006). In fact, many of these assessment strategies are intimately linked to play scales such as the *Play Assessment Scale* (PAS) (Fewell, 1991), or play-based assessment such as the *Communication– Symbolic Behaviors Scales–Developmental Profile* (CSBS-DP) (Wetherby & Prizant, 2002). Transdisciplinary play-based assessment (TPBA) (Linder, 2007), a commonly used model of play-based assessment, is a comprehensive tool developed to assess development in infants and children up to 6 years of age in both home- and center-based settings. By observing a range of play sessions (e.g., unstructured, structured, child–parent play, child–peer play), a team of early childhood professionals, working together under a transdisciplinary assessment model, gathers information regarding a child's cognitive, communication, sensorimotor, social, and emotional functions. Parents also have the opportunity to collaborate with the evaluation team by attending team meetings and providing information about the child's development via questionnaires and rating forms. This assessment approach is integrated with a transdisciplinary play-based intervention model (TPBI) (Linder, 2007), allowing the TPBA results to directly inform intervention activities that are specifically designed to address the child's individual needs.

Federal legislation suggests that natural environments are settings that are natural or normal for the child's same-age peers without disabilities.

Interactive and ecological types of naturalistic observations also fall toward this end of the continuum (Athanasiou, 2007). For example, the *Brazelton Neonatal Behavioral Assessment Scale* (Brazelton, 1984; Brazelton & Nugent, 1995) assesses neonatal interactive and organizational behaviors by measuring elements such as states of arousal, habituation, state regulation, and orientation.

Ecological assessment techniques comprise another class of naturalistic observation strategies which examine factors within a child's life that may contribute to developmental status, including the family, home, and classroom characteristics. Two ecological assessment tools that can be employed to examine a child's environments are the *Home Observation for Measurement of the Environment–Third Edition* (HOME) (Caldwell & Bradley, 2001) and the *Early Childhood Environment Rating Scale–Revised Edition* (ECERS) (Harms, Clifford, & Cryer, 1998). More specific measures relating to parenting stress, such as the *Parenting Stress Index* (Abidin, 1995) and other psychosocial factors also are available.

Clinical observation refers to when a child is evaluated in a clinical setting, such as when a pediatrician performs a physical examination or a professional conducts a comprehensive evaluation at a child development center. In this type of strategy, observations of specific behaviors are typically collected over a period of time in a systematic, objective, and quantifiable manner. The focus of systematic observation is on measurable, overt behaviors (e.g., the number of times a child throws a toy) that are often recorded via data sheets or coding systems. Although skilled evaluators can extract reliable and valid behaviors from young children, children often act differently in novel, highly structured settings than they do in their natural environment (Bracken, 2007). Consequently, the use of naturalistic observations is certainly needed to supplement clinical ones for a more accurate picture of a child's overall functional capabilities.

Product-/Process-Oriented Assessment   A product-oriented data-gathering strategy generally involves obtaining a child's performance level on a battery of tests and procedures to establish initial developmental or instructional levels for programming. The main emphasis is on *what* the child does versus *how* the child accomplishes a task. Many commonly used norm-referenced measures such as the *Bayley Scales of Infant Development–Third Edition* (Bayley, 2005) and the *Wechsler Preschool and Primary Scale of Intelligence–Third Edition* (Wechsler, 2002) fall into this category. In addition, certain performance-based strategies, such as collecting samples of a child's work over time, also are included on the product-oriented side of the continuum.

Process-oriented data-gathering strategies, on the other hand, examine *how* a child learns and interacts with the environment. As a result, this approach examines both how a child passes *and* fails selected tasks and items. Piagetian types of measures, such as the *Uzgiris–Hunt Scales* (Uzgiris & Hunt, 1975) and dynamic assessment procedures, such as those advocated by Feuerstein (1979), Vygotsky (1978), and Lidz (2003), are considered process-oriented data-gathering strategies (further discussed later in this section). In some types of process-oriented or dynamic assessments, children may be exposed to a task and then their performance is observed. If children experience difficulties in performing a selected task, they can then be taught and reassessed in a **test-teach-test** format.

While the framework presented above provides a useful tool for thinking about different approaches to early childhood assessment, these strategies often overlap in practice. For example, the terms *formal*, *standardized*, and *norm-referenced* are often used interchangeably in the context of conventional assessment because these approaches are intimately intertwined. Similarly, a specific product- or process-oriented assessment approach may either be formal or informal.

Strengths and Weaknesses of Conventional Assessment   Despite the acceptance and use of standardized tests among many teachers and other professionals, debates have emerged in recent years regarding whether benefits of conventional assessment strategies outweigh their potential shortcomings. One advantage of formal instruments is that they often have excellent psychometric properties due to the rigorous standards associated with test development and administration (Sattler, 2001). In addition, information regarding how a child is developing in relation to same-age peers can often be helpful in establishing cutoffs for determination of a diagnosis or disability as well as eligibility for services. At the present time, documentation of a delay with the use of norm-referenced tests is required for entry into many intervention programs. In Evan's situation, it was helpful for his family to receive a diagnosis of autism so that they could begin to better understand his condition and to make him eligible for the inclusive special preschool program. Quantification of a child's level of functioning also can provide a relatively user-friendly basis for tracking a child's development over time.

Appl (2000) points out that, when used appropriately, norm-referenced instruments can be used to describe a child's functioning in terms of developmental norms, determine diagnostic category, and predict development. Because of these advantages, Sattler (2001) maintains that standardized assessment tools are indispensable to the enterprise of childhood assessment and continue to play an important role. However, others such as Neisworth and Bagnato (2004) have promoted alternative rather than conventional methods of assessment, arguing that they are decontextualized to a child's *"natural developmental ecology."* Perhaps the strongest criticism of standardized assessment is that the information obtained bears little relevance to the child's everyday environment and, therefore, is of limited usefulness when it comes to informing interventions (Lidz, 2003; Neisworth & Bagnato, 2004). More specifically, the skills that are assessed in many conventional early developmental tests (e.g., imitating block formations) and the conditions under which children are tested (e.g., at an evaluation center by a stranger) fail to capture the typical demands of a child's real-life home and school environment. In addition, the skills required in a standardized assessment, such as sitting at a table for lengthy periods of time and completing tasks on demand, may not be developmentally appropriate for young children (Bagnato & Ho, 2006; Bracken, 2007).

Many norm-referenced tests hold limited utility for children with special needs because they have not been developed with those specific populations in mind (Appl, 2000). For example, they usually employ typically developing comparison samples and have fewer items that assess the lower range of developmental functioning, thereby making it difficult to measure baseline skills as well as changes in skills over time. Limitations with **test floors, item gradients**, and **reliability** are particularly problematic in tests used even with typically developing children under the age of four (Nagle, 2007). In addition, standard administration procedures may not be appropriate for children with certain difficulties (e.g., motor or visual impairment). Therefore, although conventional tests may be able to provide information regarding where aspects of a child's development are relative to where they "should" be, parents of children with developmental disabilities may find it disheartening to receive scores that place more of an emphasis on what a child cannot do versus what he or she can do. Furthermore, the lack of sensitivity in these assessment tools at the lower range of functioning may suggest an absence of or very little developmental progress when, in fact, the child has gained a number of skills that have not been measured (Neisworth & Bagnato, 2004).

Alternative Assessment Due to the increasing dissatisfaction with conventional strategies for certain applications of early childhood assessment, there has been a push toward using alternative assessment models (Bagnato & Ho, 2006; Neisworth & Bagnato, 2004). Alternative assessment does not refer to a specific group of tests and procedures but, rather, a philosophy and organizational approach toward describing and measuring a child's behavior. A wide range of assessment procedures falls under the larger umbrella of alternative assessment. The term *alternative* emphasizes that the approach employs strategies other than those used by conventional assessment models. This type of assessment is also referred to as "performance-based," which focuses on the child's actual work (e.g., portfolio); "authentic," which stresses observation of the child in the natural environment; and "curriculum-based,"

Courtesy of Dr. Jennifer Hiemenz

Alternative assessment procedures allow you to gather information about a child's social and play development with peers within natural settings.

which refers to the integration of assessment with curriculum (Linn & Miller, 2005). These assessments employ a range of formal and informal methods; however, most are direct and process-based, as they are just as interested in how a child learns a new skill as they are in knowing what a child can already do (Lidz, 2003; Montgomery, 2001). While these terms are not necessarily interchangeable, there are overlapping features. The family of alternative assessment strategies generally seeks to provide direct links between curriculum, assessment, and intervention by emphasizing the ways in which children learn in their natural environments (Gullo, 2005; Puckett & Black, 2000).

Although a curriculum is typically thought of in relation to a formal educational program, such as a preschool, it also can be used more broadly to represent the content and methods used to promote development in any setting where a child is engaged in activity. The main criticism of traditional assessment measures is that they fail, in large part, to reflect the curricular content and instructional methods used in a child's natural environment. In many instances of standardized assessment, because a child learns under one set of conditions but is then evaluated using a different set of assumptions, the child's performance may not be an accurate representation of her abilities. Alternative assessment strategies, on the other hand, aim to provide a closer match between curriculum and assessment methodology. A strong emphasis is placed on the demonstration of hands-on, "real-life" skills, and, in many instances, the assessment tasks are almost indistinguishable from a child's day-to-day curricular activities (Montgomery, 2001). Therefore, the specific curriculum drives the instrumentation process rather than the other way around (Gullo, 2005).

In an alternative assessment that takes place in a classroom, a teacher might (1) design an assessment battery based on the curriculum content (product) and educational strategies (process) used for a specific child, (2) use the results from this assessment to modify instructional practices, (3) reassess the child to determine which modifications have benefited her, (4) make further refinements in the child's educational plan based on the findings, and (5) repeat these steps in a dynamic fashion as a child progresses through her curriculum-based learning goals. Outside of the classroom, it may be a parent or other caretaker who is very knowledgeable about a child's development who makes systematic observations of the child while she is engaged in natually occuring routines (Bagnato & Ho, 2006). One example of an authentic assessment measure is the *Assessment, Evaluation, and Programming System for Infants and Children–Second Edition* (AEPS) (Bricker, Pretti-Frontczak, Johnson, & Straka, 2002). This activity-based instrument is designed for children from birth to 6 years of age who have disabilities or are at risk for developmental delay. The AEPS links curriculum goals with assessment items in six developmental areas (fine motor, gross motor, cognitive, adaptive, social–communication, and social), and learning goals are generated according to each child's individual profile.

Portfolio-Based Assessment   In portfolio-based assessment, one of the more commonly used performance-based approaches in the classroom, the teacher or examiner collects samples of actual work that has been completed by a child in an organized and systematic manner. Decisions regarding what work to include in a child's portfolio are based on current learning objectives, curriculum content, and teaching strategies, and work samples are chosen to reflect the developmental and educational

Portfolio assessment provides documentation of a child's work over time and can include artwork, journal writing, audiotapes, photos, and other artifacts.

progress of the child (Kubiszyn & Borich, 2003; Linn & Miller, 2005). While one aim of this approach is to identify areas for improvement in a child's performance, the main focus is on the child's capabilities and strengths, which, in turn, helps the child feel a stronger sense of accomplishment and motivation. This approach is viewed by some as more family-friendly than traditional norm-referenced assessment because it provides a better representation of a child's skills and emphasizes a child's individual achievement rather than how the child compares to peers. In addition, proponents of portfolio-based assessment argue that because a child's skills are sampled over time in the natural environment, this type of assessment places less performance pressure and anxiety on the child. Moreover, being able to refer to examples of a child's actual work is likely to facilitate easier communication between teachers and parents about a child's skills, progress, and goals (Montgomery, 2001; Puckett & Black, 2000). For Evan's parents, seeing his actual work samples and the videoclips of him with his classmates was a very positive and encouraging experience. It also provided them with a good idea of "next steps" for Evan to be working on both at home and in the classroom.

In general, portfolio-based assessment is considered most applicable in settings where curricular goals are flexible and individual performance is valued. However, because no specific protocol is specified regarding portfolio content and evaluation criteria, there can be considerable variation in how this approach is employed. Decisions must be made regarding which curriculum areas to cover (e.g., letter and number skills), which work samples to take, how many samples to collect, and the length of time that the portfolio spans. Once the portfolio is complete, criteria for evaluating the child's work as well as the format for reporting the findings must be determined. Scoring systems, or rubrics, which involve ratings of various aspects of the child's performance, are often employed, as are checklists (Kubiszyn & Borich, 2003; Linn & Miller, 2005; Montgomery, 2001; Puckett & Black, 2000). However, a certain level of subjectivity is associated with these evaluation methods, as it is often up to individual teachers to develop the methods necessary for collecting and assessing children's work. Although some portfolio-based assessments are more formal and systematic than others, one challenge in evaluating a child's performance is that multiple skill areas are usually involved in the completion of a single task and, therefore, it can be difficult to isolate the skill of interest (Kubiszyn & Borich, 2003). In addition, teachers may feel inclined to collect only samples of a child's best performance, which may not be the best indicators of the child's overall level of abilities. Moreover, teachers face the practical decisions of how long to keep children's portfolios and where to store them.

The *Work Sampling System* (Meisels, Jablon, Marsden, Dichtelmiller, & Dorfman, 2001) is a curriculum-embedded assessment tool that includes a comprehensive and formal approach to portfolio development. This tool, developed for use with preschoolers up to sixth graders, provides teachers with formal guidelines for sampling and evaluating children's performance in various domains of learning and development (e.g., literacy, social and emotional development, mathematics, and physical health). Criteria for evaluating a child's performance according to age- and grade-specific state and national curriculum-based standards are also provided, and teachers have the ability to generate a summary report of the child's strengths and weaknesses three times a year. Through this process, teachers also can obtain indicators of a child's progress over time as well as suggestions for instructional planning.

Dynamic Assessment   Another form of authentic assessment that has been gaining popularity is dynamic assessment. This approach employs mediated learning experiences to gain information about children's abilities and learning styles. Using a test-intervene-retest design, the teacher or assessor uses activities from a child's actual curriculum, which facilitates the process of the assessment findings informing the next steps in a child's educational and developmental sequence. Tasks are strategically selected to capture a child's **zone of proximal development,** which refers to the zone of learning in which a child requires some assistance to complete a task. By working with a child as she is in the active process of learning a new skill, the teacher is able to determine which types of instruction or intervention strategies benefit the child most (Gullo, 2005; Lidz, 2003). Therefore, a stronger focus is placed on the processes by which a child learns than on the outcome or product(s). Because of its unique features, dynamic assessment offers teachers an opportunity to assess many types of learning that cannot be measured by conventional tests.

Lidz (2003) presents a generic approach to dynamic assessment in which the assessor (1) selects a curriculum task that is within a child's zone of proximal development, (2) performs a process analysis to determine the task demands in different areas of development (e.g., attention, perception, memory, knowledge base, conceptual processing, and metacognition), (3) administers a pretest to determine the child's initial skill level, (4) uses the pretest findings to conduct an intervention that is within the framework of a mediated learning experience, and (5) administers a posttest to gain an estimate of the child's response to intervention. The *Application of Cognitive Functions Scale,* a packaged tool that provides standardized guidelines for using dynamic assessment with children ages 3 to 5 years is also available (Lidz, 2000). This instrument is considered curriculum-based in the sense that the tasks reflect many of the developmental demands of a typical American preschool program.

One limitation that is often cited in reference to dynamic assessment as well as other forms of alternative assessment is that these approaches take a lot of time and resources to plan and execute. In addition, because specific guidelines are not typically available for alternative assessments, the steps involved in developing the content, evaluation criteria, and method of reporting may be overwhelming or intimidating for those who lack some degree of expertise in these techniques. A teacher may also need to generate a number of assessment activities in order to capture an adequate range of a child's abilities. Additionally, because a range of methodology can be employed and a higher level of subjectivity is involved in scoring and interpretation procedures, the psychometric properties (e.g., reliability) of alternative assessments may be weaker than for conventional tests. Lidz (2003) points out, however, that a learning curve is associated with gaining proficiency with any new assessment model. Also, there are situations where the benefits of alternative assessment strategies clearly outweigh their limitations, particularly when traditional assessment tools have limited utility.

Gullo (2005) suggests that an assessment committee can be helpful for schools and other settings that are interested in employing alternative assessment approaches.

Such a committee could develop an assessment philosophy, generate formal guidelines for using specific assessment strategies, and make recommendations for linking assessment with curriculum planning. Despite what appears to be a division between those who align with a conventional versus alternative assessment philosophy, these approaches are not necessarily mutually exclusive, and it certainly is possible to use a combination of strategies in the practice of early childhood assessment. Regardless of the specific approach used, the important factor to consider is that every assessment instrument has its own set of strengths and weaknesses. Accordingly, it is necessary to use informed judgment and caution when selecting an assessment battery (Nagle, 2007).

░ CONSIDERATIONS FOR THE ASSESSMENT OF YOUNG CHILDREN

Several factors must be considered when assessing young children, especially ones who may have special needs. Among these are the selection of approaches and tools that link assessment and intervention, situational constraints, including child and environmental variables, and the involvement of the family.

Selection of Assessment Measures and Methods

Assessment should be a process driven by questions pertinent to a child's development and individual needs and designed for a specific purpose. This process notwithstanding, the selection of assessment methods should be guided by basic canons of science (e.g., reliability and validity), cultural sensitivity, and good old common sense.

> The first step in the assessment process is to define a purpose or posit question to be answered.

Reliability and validity are critical scientific concepts that must be understood when selecting a specific assessment tool for any part of the assessment process (e.g., screening, diagnostic, or program evaluation). Does the test (or procedure) measure what it is supposed to measure in a dependable fashion? Obtaining dependable information from any young child is a challenge; it is critical for examiners to choose tests that have adequate reliability. The test should have adequate **content validity** (Does the test reflect the content it is purportedly measuring?); **concurrent validity** (Does the test correlate with other accepted criteria of performance in each skill area?); **predictive validity** (To what extent do the obtained scores correlate with some criterion for successful performance in the future?); **construct validity** (Does the test address the theoretical constructs upon which it is based?); and **discriminant validity** (Do subtests measure separate and distinct skills?). Additionally, the concept of **developmental validity** (Are the skills being measured developmentally suitable for the child?) is of special importance. Although a detailed discussion of these psychometric issues is beyond the scope of this chapter, the early childhood professional should examine test manuals for such information prior to employing any test for screening, diagnostic, or program evaluation purposes.

> The term *reliability* refers to consistency.

> The term *validity* refers to how well the test measures what it is supposed to measure.

In addition to the basic psychometric aspects of the assessment tools, it is critical that they be nonbiased and nondiscriminatory. These issues have been addressed in court cases (*Diana v. State Board of Education,* 1973; *Larry P. v. Riles,* 1979) and, subsequently, in our federal laws; however, it is the responsibility of each early childhood professional to be highly sensitive to these issues. **Nondiscriminatory assessment** refers to the multicultural nature of society and means that any assessment must be equally fair to all children. It is important to note that the nature of any assessment is discriminatory: its overarching purpose is to distinguish between those who need services and those who do not. But an assessment *unfairly* discriminates if it does not allow for cultural differences. Allowing for cultural differences should include administering tests in a child's native language or other modes of communication and providing experiences that are familiar to the child. Closely related to nondiscriminatory assessment is the concept of **cultural equivalence.** Helms (1992) defined cultural equivalence as whether or not an assessment tool measures the same constructs across various cultural groups. Further, tests used should have functional equivalence (e.g., test scores mean the same thing across groups), conceptual equivalence (e.g., groups are equally familiar with the content of test items), linguistic equivalence (e.g., language used in test items has the same meaning across groups), and psychometric equivalence (e.g., tests measure the same things across groups).

Finally, it is important for the early childhood professional to possess plain old common sense! Although it may seem obvious, it is critical that the tests selected actually assist in answering the referral questions. Will the tests provide and/or assist in the assessment–treatment linkages? If so, how? Further, is the content appropriate for the child? Is the professional administering the test appropriately trained to administer and interpret it? Again, although they are basic, the application of these common-sense considerations lessens the misuse and abuse of assessment tools.

Situational Considerations

Traditional early childhood assessment has been described as "the science of the strange behavior of children with strange adults in strange situations for the briefest period of time" (Bronfenbrenner, 1979). Situational constraints clearly contribute to the "strangeness" of the assessment process, as described by Bronfenbrenner, and can involve any number of concerns that may arise in the assessment process. One of the most common constraints encountered is when a child simply refuses to engage in an activity on request. The child might be frightened, fatigued, slow-to-warm-up to the testing session, or, in the case of an infant, sleeping! Other children may present extreme behavioral difficulties that do not facilitate the assessment process. Further, in assessing young children with special needs, it is of vital importance to take any functional impairments into account when observing behaviors, including possible vision or hearing impairments, motor impairments, or language impairments or differences. Testing materials should be appropriate for the child in terms of language, size, and ability. It is best to use a seating system in which the child is adequately and comfortably supported, and from which the child can interact with the testing materials appropriately. When a typical response modality cannot be used, it may be possible to gather the same information by using another communication system. For example, the child may use an **augmentative**

communication device or a system of pictures, gestures, or eyeblinks to indicate a response. In all of these situations, it is important for the early childhood professional to be familiar with the many different types of data-gathering methods to minimize these situational constraints.

When establishing rapport with the child and family at the outset of the evaluation process, it is important to establish a solid play and work partnership with the child. When working with small children in particular, it is vital to ask, "What's in it for the child?" Some children are extremely motivated by verbal praise and the undivided attention of adults; they are extremely easy to assess and eager to please. Others will require more tangible incentives and rewards—such as stickers, snacks, or toys—in exchange for their efforts. Parents and other familiar caregivers should be partners in eliciting the child's best efforts, confirming if the child's performance is typical of her abilities and suggesting how a task might be presented differently in order to gain greater effort.

At times, it will not be possible to get a child to complete formal testing tasks for one reason or another. For example, when an examiner or team is trying to conduct a formal assessment and a child is noncompliant, it might be useful to shift to more informal (e.g., observation), indirect (e.g., parent ratings or report), and process-oriented (e.g., play) types of data-gathering strategies. If an examiner has a strong background in child development, behavioral guidance, and management strategies, useful information can be gained from observation of the child's play or other naturalistic observations. If the examiner continues to make demands on the child to complete the formal assessment, on the other hand, opportunities to learn more about the adaptive functioning of the child could be lost. It also is helpful to learn about the child's performance in the natural environment. This should include gaining knowledge about the child's childcare center or preschool, teachers, therapists, and the home setting.

Family and Parental Involvement

As discussed earlier in chapter 1 and later in more detail in chapter 10, the importance of the family (and other caregivers) in the assessment process cannot be overemphasized. A critical facet of early childhood assessment is the collaborative, working partnership between parents and professionals. This relationship goes beyond traditional "rapport" and includes respect, reciprocity, and flexibility (Meisels & Atkins-Burnett, 2000). Parents play a vital (and mandated) role in the gathering of information about the child, the family, and the home and community environments. As noted at the beginning of this chapter, family members need to view assessment and intervention as consistent with their perceptions of and expectations for their child as well as with their current familial values and needs. Understanding a family's perspectives and concerns *prior to* initiating any assessment is critical in guiding the assessment process. This contributes to appropriate decisions about where the assessment will take place, what kind of data-gathering approaches will be useful, and which specific tools (if any) may be used. The development of intervention plans in collaboration with the family also can increase the likelihood that the plans will be accepted, implemented, and successful.

It is logical to expect improved outcomes for children when parents and other care providers are actively involved in assessment and intervention planning.

SUMMARY

This chapter provided an overview of the assessment process in early childhood. Definitions of the term *assessment* were provided and contemporary assessment standards were discussed. These included treatment utility, social validity, convergent assessment, and consensual validity, all of which should be applied to any assessment in early childhood to increase the accuracy and utility of the assessment information and to provide for valid and functional intervention plans. The various stages of assessment were detailed with particular emphasis on early identification, including issues related to screening and the major components of a comprehensive assessment. The ongoing process of assessment was highlighted within the intervention and program evaluation phases.

In addition to these aspects of assessment, a number of approaches to assessment were detailed in accordance with a set of strands or typologies. The team approach to assessment in accordance with federal laws was discussed, with a specific emphasis on transdisciplinary teams. Although the focus of this chapter was not on describing the many assessment tools available to the early childhood professional, selected tools were mentioned to illustrate the various strands of assessment. A discussion of some of the issues pertinent to the assessment process, such as test selection, situational constraints, and involvement of the family, also was provided. A good understanding of the assessment process together with a firm grounding in basic child development will allow the early interventionist to address the assessment of young children with special needs in a sensitive, thoughtful, and meaningful fashion.

REVIEW QUESTIONS AND DISCUSSION POINTS

1. Describe current standards related to best practice in early childhood assessment.
2. What are three common assessment team models? Describe the similarities and differences among the three teams.
3. What are some of the advantages and disadvantages of formal, normative-based assessment tools?
4. In a difficult assessment situation in which a child refuses to comply with the testing process, what are some alternative ways to get the same information?
5. How can an evaluation–treatment team maximize the utility of the information gathered during assessment toward developing and evaluating treatment goals?

RECOMMENDED RESOURCES

Bracken, B. A., & Nagle, R. J. (Eds.). (2007). *Psychoeducational assessment of preschool children* (4th ed.). Mahwah, NJ: Lawrence Erlbaum Associates, Inc.

Division for Early Childhood, Council for Exceptional Children. (2002). Assessment strategies. *Young Exceptional Children Monograph* (Series No. 4). Longmont, CO: Sopris West.

Sandall, S., McLean, M. E., & Smith, B. J. (Eds.). (2000). *DEC recommended practices in early intervention/early childhood special education*. Division for Early Childhood, Council for Exceptional Children. Longmont, CO: Sopris West.

Sattler, J. M. (2001). *Assessment of children: Cognitive applications* (4th ed.). La Mesa, CA: Sattler.

Sattler, J. M. (2002). *Assessment of children: Behavioral and clinical applications* (4th ed.). La Mesa, CA: Sattler.

REFERENCES

Abidin, R. (1995). *Parenting stress index.* Odessa: FL: Psychological Assessment Resources.

Achenbach, T. M., & Rescorla, L. A. (2000). *Manual for ASEBA preschool forms & profiles.* Burlington, VT: University of Vermont, Research Center for Children, Youth, & Families.

American College of Obstetricians and Gynecologists. (2007). Practice bulletin number 77: Screening for fetal chromosomal abnormalities. *Obstetrics and Gynecology, 109*(1), 217–227.

American Speech-Language-Hearing Association. (1990). *Guidelines for practices in early intervention.* Rockville, MD: Author.

Apgar, V. (1953). A proposal for a new method of evaluation of the newborn infant. *Current Research in Anesthesia and Analgesia, 32,* 260–267.

Appl, D. J. (2000). Clarifying the preschool assessment process: Traditional practices and alternative approaches. *Early Childhood Education Journal, 27,* 219–225.

Athanasiou, M. S. (2007). Play-based approaches to preschool assessment. In B. A. Bracken & R. J. Nagle (Eds.), *Psychoeducational assessment of preschool children* (4th ed., pp. 219–238). Mahwah, NJ: Lawrence Erlbaum Associates, Inc.

Aylward, G. P. (1995). *Bayley infant neurodevelopmental screener.* San Antonio, TX: Psychological Corporation.

Bagnato, S. J., & Ho, H. Y. (2006). High-stakes testing with preschool children: Violation of professional standards for evidence-based practice in early education intervention. *KEDI Journal of Educational Policy, 3,* 23–43.

Bagnato, S. J., Neisworth, J. T., & Munson, S. M. (1997). *LINKing assessment and early intervention: An authentic curriculum-based approach.* Baltimore: Brookes.

Bayley, N. (2005). *Bayley scales of infant development–Third edition.* San Antonio, TX: Psychological Corporation.

Benner, S. M. (1992). *Assessing young children with special needs: An ecological perspective.* New York: Longman.

Bergen, D., & Wright, M. (1994). Medical assessment perspectives. In D. Bergen (Ed.), *Assessment methods for infants and toddlers: Transdisciplinary team approaches* (pp. 40–56). New York: Teachers College Press.

Bracken, B. A. (2007). Creating the optimal preschool testing situation. In B. A. Bracken & R. J. Nagle (Eds.), *Psychoeducational assessment of preschool children* (4th ed., pp. 137–154). Mahwah, NJ: Lawrence Erlbaum Associates, Inc.

Brazelton, T. B. (1984). *Neonatal assessment scale* (2nd ed.). *Clinics in Developmental Medicine,* No. 88. Philadelphia: Lippincott.

Brazelton, T. B., & Nugent, J. K. (1995). *The neonatal behavioral assessment scale.* Cambridge: Mac Keith Press.

Bricker, B., Pretti-Frontczak, K., Johnson, J., & Straka, E. (Eds.). (2002). *Assessment, evaluation, and programming system for infants and children–Second edition administration guide.* Baltimore, MD: Brookes.

Bronfenbrenner, U. (1979). *The ecology of human development: Experiments by nature and design.* Cambridge, MA: Harvard University Press.

Bruner, J. P., & Tulipan, N. (2005). Intrauterine repair of spina bifida. *Clinical Obstetrics and Gynecology, 48*(4), 942–955.

Caldwell, B. M., & Bradley, R. H. (2001). *HOME inventory.* Little Rock: University of Arkansas.

Chapel Hill Training Outreach Project. (2002). *Early learning accomplishment profile.* Chapel Hill, NC: Author.

Chervenak, F. A., & Kurjak, A. (Eds.). (1996). *The fetus as a patient.* New York: Parthenon.

Coleman, M. R., Buysse, V., & Neitzel, J. (2006). *Recognition and response: An early intervening system for young children at risk for learning disabilities. Executive Summary.* Chapel Hill: The University of North Carolina at Chapel Hill, FPG Child Development Institute.

Council on Children with Disabilities, Section on Developmental Behavioral Pediatrics, Bright Futures Steering Committee and Medical Home Initiatives for Children with Special Needs Project Advisory Committee. (2006). Identifying infants and young children with developmental disorders in the medical home: An algorithm for developmental surveillance and screening. *Pediatrics, 118*(1), 405–420.

Diana v. Board of Education, No. C-70-37 RFP, Consent Decree (N. D. Cal. 1973).

Division for Early Childhood, Council for Exceptional Children. (2002). Assessment strategies. *Young Exceptional Children Monograph* (Series No. 4). Longmont, CO: Sopris West.

Dunst, C. J., Trivette, C. M., Appl, D. J., & Bagnato, S. J. (2004). Framework for investigating child find, referral, early identification and eligibility determination practices. *Tracelines, 1,* 1–11.

Elliott, C. (2006). *Differential ability scales–Second edition.* San Antonio, TX: Psychological Corporation.

Feuerstein, R. (1979). *The dynamic assessment of retarded performers: The learning potential assessment device, theory, instrument, and techniques*. Baltimore: University Park Press.

Fewell, R. R. (1991). *Play assessment scale* (5th rev.). Unpublished document. Miami, FL: University of Miami School of Medicine.

Frankenburg, W. K., Dodds, J., Archer, P., Bresnick, B., Maschka, P., Edelman, N., et al. (1990). *Denver–II*. Denver, CO: Denver Developmental Materials.

Garland, C. G., McGonigel, J. J., Frank, A., & Buck, D. (1989). *The transdisciplinary model of service delivery*. Lightfoot, VA: Child Development Resources.

Glascoe, F. P. (1996). Developmental screening. In M. L. Wolraich (Ed.), *Disorders of development and learning: A practical guide to assessment and management* (2nd ed., pp. 89–128). New York: Mosby.

Greenspan, S. I., & Meisels, S. J. (1996). Toward a new vision for the developmental assessment of infants and young children. In S. J. Meisels & E. Fenichel (Eds.), *New visions for the developmental assessment of infants and young children* (pp. 11–26). Washington, DC: ZERO TO THREE.

Gullo, D. F. (2005). *Understanding assessment and evaluation in early childhood education* (2nd ed.). New York: Teachers College Press.

Harbin, G. L., McWilliam, R. A., & Gallagher, J. J. (2000). Services for young children with disabilities and their families. In J. P. Shonkoff & S. J. Meisels, (Eds.), *Handbook of early childhood intervention* (2nd ed.). New York: Cambridge University Press.

Harms, T., Clifford, R. M., & Cryer, D. (1998). *Early Childhood Environment Rating Scale*. New York: Teachers College Press.

Helms, J. E. (1992). Why is there no study of cultural influence in standardized cognitive ability testing? *American Psychologist, 47*, 1083–1101.

Kubiszyn, T., & Borich, G. (2003). *Educational testing and measurement* (7th ed.). Hoboken, NJ: John Wiley & Sons, Inc.

Larry P. v. Riles, 343 F. Supp. 1306, 502 F.2d 963 (N. D. Cal. 1979).

Lidz, C. S. (2003). *Early childhood assessment*. Hoboken, NJ: John Wiley & Sons, Inc.

Lidz, C. S. (2000). The application of *Cognitive Functions Scale* (ACFS): An example of curriculum-based dynamic assessment. In C. S. Lidz & J. G. Elliott (Eds.), *Dynamic assessment: Prevailing models and applications* (pp. 407–439). Amsterdam: JAI/Elsevier Science.

Linder, T. W. (2007). *Transdisciplinary play-based assessment: A functional approach to working with young children* (Rev. ed.). Baltimore: Brookes.

Linn, R. L., & Miller, M. D. (2005). *Measurement and assessment in teaching* (9th ed.). Upper Saddle River, NJ: Pearson Education, Inc.

Manning, S. M., Jennings, R., & Madsen, J. R. (2000). Pathophysiology, prevention, and potential treatment of neural tube defects. *Mental Retardation and Developmental Disabilities Research Reviews, 6*, 6–14.

Mardell-Czudnowski, C., & Goldenberg, D. S. (1998). *DIAL-3: Developmental indicators for the assessment of learning–Third edition*. Circle Pines, MN: American Guidance Service.

McWilliam, R. A. (2000). Recommended practices in interdisciplinary models. In S. Sandall, M. E. McLean, & B. J. Smith (Eds.), *DEC-recommended practices in early intervention/early childhood special education* (pp. 47–54). Longmont, CO: Sopris West.

Meisels, S. J., & Atkins-Burnett, S. (2000). The elements of early childhood assessment. In J. P. Shonkoff & S. J. Meisels (Eds.), *Handbook of early childhood intervention* (2nd ed.). New York: Cambridge University Press.

Meisels, S. J., Jablon, J. R., Marsden, D. B., Dichtelmiller, M. L., & Dorfman, A. B. (2001). *The work sampling system* (4th ed.). Ann Arbor, MI: Rebus.

Menon, P. N., & Rao, K. L. (2005). Current status of fetal surgery. *Indian Journal of Pediatrics, 72*, 433–436.

Mindes, G., Ireton, H., & Mardell-Czudnowski, C. (1996). *Assessing young children*. Albany, NY: Delmar.

Montgomery, K. (2001). *Authentic assessment: A guide for elementary teachers*. New York: Longman.

Mullen, E. (1995). *Mullen Scales of Early Learning, AGS Edition*. Circle Pines, MN: American Guidance Service.

Nagle, R. J. (2007). Issues in preschool assessment. In B. A. Bracken & R. J. Nagle (Eds.), *Psychoeducational assessment of preschool children* (4th ed., pp. 29–48). Mahwah, NJ: Lawrence Earlbaum Associates, Inc.

National Association for the Education of Young Children, National Association of Early Childhood Specialists in State Departments of Education. (2002). *Early learning standards: Creating the conditions for success* [joint position statement]. Retrieved December 13, 2002, from *http://www.naeyc.org*

National Association of School Psychologists. (2005). Position statement on early childhood assessment. Retrieved February 13, 2007, from *http://www.nasponline.org*

Neisworth, J. T., & Bagnato, S. J. (1996). Assessment for early intervention: Emerging themes and practices. In S. L.

Odom & M. E. McLean (Eds.), *Early intervention/early childhood special education: Recommended practices.* Austin, TX: PRO-ED.

Neisworth, J. T., & Bagnato, S. J. (2000). Recommended practices in assessment. In S. Sandall, M. E. McLean, & B. J. Smith (Eds.), *DEC-recommended practices in early intervention/early childhood special education* (pp. 17–27). Longmont, CO: Sopris West.

Neisworth, J. T., & Bagnato, S. J. (2001). Recommended practices for assessment in early childhood settings (Teleconference held April 11, 2001). Chapel Hill, NC: NECTAS (*http://www.nectac.org*)

Neisworth, J. T., & Bagnato, S. J. (2004). The mismeasure of young children: The authentic assessment alternative. *Infants and Young Children, 17,* 198–212.

Newborg, J. (2004). *Battelle developmental inventory, second edition (BDI-2 screener kit).* Rolling Meadows, IL: Riverside Publishing.

Puckett, M. B., & Black, J. K. (2000). *Authentic assessment of the young child: Celebrating development and learning.* Upper Saddle River, NJ: Merrill/Prentice Hall.

Reynolds, C. R., & Kamphaus, R. W. (2004). *Behavioral assessment system for children–2.* Circle Pines, MN: American Guidance Service.

Sattler, J. M. (2001). *Assessment of children: Cognitive applications* (4th ed.). La Mesa, CA: Sattler.

Slentz, K. (2004). *Early childhood developmental screening: Helping children at home and school II: Handouts for families and educators.* Bethesda, MD: National Association of School Psychologists.

Squires, J., Potter, L., & Bricker, D. (1999). *Ages & stages questionnaires (ASQ): A parent-completed, child-monitoring system* (2nd ed.). Baltimore: Brookes.

Stipek, D. (2005, July/August). Early childhood education at a crossroads. *Harvard Education Letter.* Retrieved May 15, 2007, from *http://www.edletter.org/past/issues/2005-ja/crossroads.shtml*

Taylor, H. G., Klein, N., & Hack, M. (2000). School-age consequences of birth weight less than 750 g: A review and update. *Developmental Neuropsychology, 17*(3), 289–321.

Taylor, H. G., Klein, N., Minich, N. M., & Hack, M. (2001). Long-term family outcomes for children with very low birth weights. *Archives of Pediatric and Adolescent Medicine, 155*(2), 155–161.

Uzgiris, I. C., & Hunt, J. M. (Eds.). (1975). *Assessment in infancy: Ordinal scales of psychological development.* Urbana: University of Illinois Press.

Vygotsky, L. S. (1978). *Mind in society: The development of higher psychological processes.* Cambridge, MA: Harvard University Press.

Wechsler, D. (2002). *Wechsler preschool and primary scale of intelligence* (3rd ed.). San Antonio, TX: Psychological Corporation.

Wetherby, A. M., & Prizant, B. M. (2002). *Communication and symbolic behavior scales–developmental profile* (CSBS-DP). Baltimore: Brookes.

Intervention

Tina M. Smith-Bonahue, Jennifer Harman,
and Tashawna Duncan

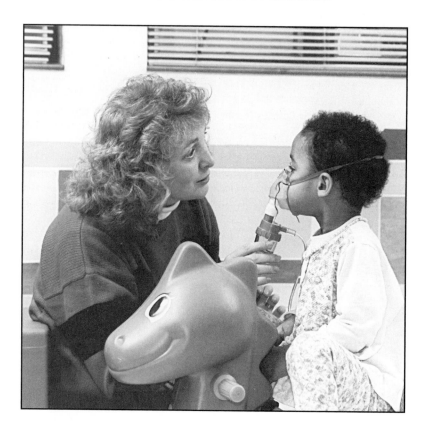

Chapter Outline

- Defining Intervention
- Family-Centered Intervention
- Program Planning

Carla

*F*our-year-old Carla receives early intervention services for developmental delay at Happy Acres Child Care Center. Carla is the youngest of four children. Her pediatrician referred her for an evaluation at age 3 years after her parents expressed concerns that she wasn't talking as well as her siblings had at the same age. Carla's grandparents emigrated to the United States from Puerto Rico and her family speaks mostly Spanish at home. Currently, under Part B of IDEA, Carla receives services from an early childhood special educator and a speech and language therapist.

Carla attends Happy Acres, a regular child care center, along with an older sibling. Her speech and language therapist, Ms. Watkins, visits Happy Acres once a week for 45 minutes. During that time, Ms. Watkins pulls Carla and a few other children into a small group and works with them on language enrichment activities. The activities are based on Carla's needs and she is the focus of them. The other children seem unaware of this and enjoy playing "Miss W's games." Because Ms. Watkins rarely sees Carla's parents at school, she tries to send weekly notes to them describing Carla's progress. Carla's parents sometimes write back, but Ms. Watkins has difficulty understanding their English; she often finds herself wishing she spoke Spanish!

Carla also received special education services at Happy Acres, but Carla is oblivious to the services. Mr. Banks, an early childhood special educator, meets weekly with Carla's regular child care teacher, Ms. Taylor. They talk about Carla's progress and any concerns Ms. Taylor has, and Mr. Banks helps Ms. Taylor modify the curriculum so that Carla can participate in a meaningful way. Mr. Banks also is available as a consultant to Ms. Taylor any time concerns arise. Mr. Banks tries to time his weekly visits to overlap with Carla's parents picking her up or dropping her off. He speaks some Spanish and has had some success establishing a collaborative relationship with Carla's parents. He's offered to work with them on any concerns they have at home, but they always say that they don't have any concerns.

The concept of intervention represents the heart and soul of our work with children. In its broadest sense, intervention includes nearly every interaction that professionals have with children and families. The purpose of this chapter is to discuss intervention as it specifically relates to young children. We begin by offering a general definition of the term *intervention* to put the recent practice of early intervention into a historical context. Next, our discussion turns to more pragmatic aspects specific to early intervention and proceeds through planning, implementing, and evaluating intervention with young children.

:: DEFINING INTERVENTION

Perhaps the most helpful way to begin a discussion of intervention is to define the basic concept. For the professional, a functional definition of the term *intervention* serves three purposes. First, it differentiates intervention from related but different clinical and educational endeavors, such as assessment. Second, a definition provides the framework necessary for formulating individual and program goals. For any field of study to progress, at least some agreement must be reached regarding the goals and objectives. In the words of Yogi Berra, "You have to be very careful when you don't know where you're going, or you might never get there." A functional definition of intervention gives the professional an idea of "how to get there." Finally, a definition provides insight into the assumptions underlying professional practice and research.

A number of educational and psychological theorists have attempted to explicate *intervention*. Rhodes and Tracey (1972) define it as any directed action intended to remedy the ill fit between a child and the environment. Suran and Rizzo (1979) suggest that intervention is any professional effort to facilitate a child's ongoing healthy development. Guralnick and Albertini (2006) and Margalit, A-Yagon, and Kleitman (2006) define *intervention* broadly to include health care and social services in addition to educational goals, adding that early intervention efforts should support the relationship between parents and their children.

These definitions overlap to a considerable degree and any of them may serve as a starting point for understanding intervention. However, each is also insufficient in certain respects. For example, Rhodes and Tracey do not address the outcomes of intervention. Intervention can have a multitude of outcomes, some desirable and some undesirable. Although a strong research base helps suggest what the outcomes of a planned intervention will be, there are always unexpected outcomes as well.

Definitions that consider only problems or disabilities also have limitations. Intervention should not automatically imply the presence of significant problems. While intervention is usually intended to **remediate** a problem or area of need, it also can be used to establish and maintain positive functioning. For example, prevention is a type of intervention used by everyone at some time to avoid a problem. If we understand intervention this broadly, then every person is in need of some form of intervention at some point in development. The essential question is deciding when to intervene, who will be involved in the intervention, and the extent and type of intervention.

Finally, a definition of *intervention* also should account for the environmental influence of social systems beyond the individual and immediate family, such as school and the local community. Intervention is implemented *in environments*, not just *for individuals*. Notably, a person's functioning and development always occur in a given context. For the purposes of this chapter, *intervention* is broadly defined to refer to outcomes (both positive and negative, intentional and unintentional), conditions eliciting intervention (both positive and negative), and a consideration of the multiple systems affecting and affected by intervention (the individual, family, school, and community). Therefore, we offer the following definition of **intervention:**

> Intervention is a directed, purposeful process. It is the intentional application of resources with the aim of developing, improving, changing, or maintaining conditions

within an individual, environment, or interactions between an individual and the environment. Intervention always results in both intended and unexpected outcomes, which may be either positive or negative in nature.

Young children and their families can qualify for early intervention services for various reasons. Recently, a longitudinal study of early intervention services in the United States documented that approximately one-third of individuals receiving early intervention services were low-birth-weight babies. Moreover, the data suggest that individuals who receive early intervention services due to biological or environmental risk factors generally enter into services during their first year of life. Conversely, individuals who receive services due to developmental delays are more likely to begin services as toddlers (Scarborough et al., 2004). Despite why or when individuals begin receiving early intervention services, the services they are provided incorporate families as an integral part of the intervention process.

:: FAMILY-CENTERED INTERVENTION

An important assumption in early intervention for infants and toddlers is that the family is the unit of intervention for services. By taking into account family needs, intervention efforts for infants and toddlers are likely to include goals that go well beyond the educational objectives mandated by special education laws relating to older children. For example, in the case of a family with three children, one of whom has a medical condition that requires constant attention and access to a respirator, one challenge faced by the parents may be how to give the other children the time and attention they need. For this family, one relevant intervention goal would be the provision of respite services for the child with special needs (or providing access to services) so that the parents can spend time with their other children. Such needs can and should be addressed by early intervention. Ideally, parents take an active role in the education and development of their children at all ages. Moreover, Margalit and colleagues (2006) point out that utilizing parental strengths and building upon these strengths within intervention planning and implementation is essential.

Initially, family-centered services consisted of the sole notion of parental involvement. In other words, family-centered services used to simply call for parents to "participate in activities that professionals deemed appropriate" (McWilliam, Tocci, & Harbin, 1998, p. 206). Then, in the 1980s, researchers and early interventionists (e.g., Dunst, 1985; Foster, Berger, & McLean, 1981) began to call for family empowerment. In other words, families were afforded previously denied decision-making power and allotted a say in the development of intervention plans (McWilliam, Tocci, & Harbin, 1998).

The term *family-centered* was coined to express the idea of services meeting the whole family's needs and not just the needs of the individual patient/child/client (McWilliam, Tocci, & Harbin, 1998). According to Dunst (2002),

Family-centeredness characterizes beliefs and practices that treat families with dignity and respect; individualized, flexible, and responsive practices; information sharing so that families can make informed decisions; family choice regarding any number of aspects of program practices and intervention options; parent–professional collaboration and partnerships as a context for family–program relations; and the provision and mobilization of resources and supports necessary for families to care for and rear their children in ways that produce optimal child, parent, and family outcomes. (p. 206)

Family-centered practices are composed of relational and participatory components (Dempsey & Dunst, 2004; Dunst, 2002). The relational component includes the use of clinical skills and the beliefs about and attitudes toward families held by the professional (Dunst, 2002). The participatory component includes "practices (a) that are individualized, flexible, and responsive to family concerns and priorities, and (b) that provide families with opportunities to be actively involved in decisions and choices, family–professional collaboration, and family actions to achieve desired goals and outcomes" (Dunst, 2002, p. 206). Dempsey and Dunst (2006) assert that the use of a relational *and* a participatory help-giving style facilitates family and parent empowerment across different cultural groups.

In the example from the vignette at the beginning of the chapter, Carla first began receiving early intervention services shortly after her third birthday. Based on their evaluation, the multidisciplinary team decided that Carla would benefit from language enrichment. The team also believed that Carla would benefit from participation in a **self-contained class** for preschoolers with disabilities that was housed in public school. Her parents wanted Carla to remain in her current child care placement; one sister currently attended there and her two older brothers had gone there as well. The team pointed out that the teacher in the self-contained classroom was well-trained and certified and could provide intensive intervention. Carla's parents trusted the teachers at Happy Acres and valued Carla's being near her sister and in the care of a known and trusted teacher. As a result, the team agreed to provide consultative speech services to Happy Acres personnel.

Bailey and colleagues (2006) point out that, in determining the effectiveness of early intervention family services, various outcomes should be evaluated. These outcomes include whether (a) the family is aware of their child's strengths, as well as his special needs, (b) the family understands their legal rights and is able to advocate for their child, (c) the family is cognizant of ways to help their child learn, (d) the family is aware of and is able to utilize various support systems, and (e) the family is able to obtain necessary services through their communities.

Carla's family was able to advocate for her. Her family felt it would be most beneficial to have Carla attend an early childhood center where her sister was. Therefore, Carla's family advocated for keeping Carla in a center with which they were familiar. In doing so, early intervention services were able to be provided to Carla at Happy Acres. Carla's family consequently was able to utilize familiar teachers as one support system, and lessen disruption in the family by giving them one less place to go during the week.

BOX 9.1   ROLE OF FAMILIES IN EARLY INTERVENTION

With the inclusion of Part C in P.L. 99–457, Congress acknowledged that families are an integral aspect of a child's life and worthy of intervention services in their own right. While this legislation and its subsequent reauthorizations (e.g, IDEIA, 2004) make clear the mandate to involve families in their children's early intervention, the definition of *family involvement* remains elusive. Bailey (2001) identified three themes related to families and early intervention. First, he points out the importance of individualizing the ways in which parents are in-volved, taking into account cultural diversity, family resources, and family preferences. The second important point is the expectation that families will take an active, decision-making role in the planning and implementation of their children's interventions. Finally and perhaps most importantly, Bailey describes families as "the ultimate decision makers and long-term care providers for their children" (p. 1); therefore, intervention must have as a goal facilitating families' competence and confidence in advocating for their children.

Multiculturalism and Early Intervention

One aspect of family-centered intervention that has become critical is providing services that are culturally sensitive. U.S. society is a diverse, dynamic, and interactive landscape comprised of communities and individuals. In 1970, 12% of the population in the United States under 5 years of age was nonwhite. By 1984, 36% of all babies in the United States were born to nonwhite, non-Anglo parents (Research and Policy Committee of the Committee for Economic Development, 1987). By the 1990s, our nation's growing diversity became even more apparent. For example, the 1990 census recorded that over 380 different languages were actively spoken by U.S. citizens (U. S. Bureau of the Census, 1990). Predictions for the year 2030 are dramatic, projecting a decline of 6.2 million in the population of white, non-Hispanic children. This prediction also means that nearly half of all school-aged children will be nonwhite. As the number of children of color in the general population increases, we can expect a concomitant increase in the number of nonwhite, non-Anglo children requiring early intervention services. However, with so few minorities entering social service professions, the likelihood is that the majority of professionals providing early intervention services will continue to be white.

> Because the United States is ethnically mixed, a respect for the uniqueness of cultural beliefs, values, and practices that encourages newcomers to the United States to retain their cultural identity while simultaneously becoming part of the larger "American" culture, is critical in educational settings.

Current and predicted cultural mismatches between service providers and families offer new challenges for education professionals. Potential conflicts rooted in culture are likely and unfortunate, because both interventionists and families share the same goal of wanting to help children. These potential cultural misunderstandings arise because people are bathed in a culture from birth. Brown and Lenneberg (1965) found that children may establish a cultural identity as early as 5 years of age. Because our primary culture is a deeply set part of our values, attitudes, and behavior, we may easily misinterpret a second culture. In any case, the impact of culture on early intervention is indisputable.

Although many teachers, health care professionals, and psychologists often refer to "cultural issues," little consensus exists regarding a definition of **culture**. There are several formal definitions of the term *culture*, but Turnbull, Turnbull, Shank, and Leal (2002) point out that many different factors shape our views of culture. However, most of us do not rely on textbook definitions. Instead, we operate under the assumption that everyone has an implicit understanding of what is meant by the term *culture;* yet, these connotative definitions frequently lead to disagreement and misunderstanding among professionals and between service providers and families. In his seminal article on understanding culture, Frisby (1992) asserts that the term *culture* means different things to different people:

Culture A refers to differences in clothing, lifestyle, values, and traditions associated with a people's level of technological attainment or geographic location. For example, some anthropologists refer to Western or modern culture when discussing societies of Europe or the Americas.

Culture B is equated with the humanistic achievement of racial or ethnic groups. For example, when school classrooms celebrate Black History Month, administrators and teachers encourage students to explore the fundamentals of "black culture."

Culture C designates common attitudes, values, and beliefs that guide an individual's identification with a particular group. For example, many African American community leaders garner great support because they are able to articulate the "black experience" in the United States.

Culture D refers to the immediate context of an individual. For example, many anthropologists and politicians espouse the ideas of a "culture of poverty" and a "culture of the schools."

Culture E is associated with superficial lifestyle choices. For example, in the late 1970s there was a "punk culture" whose members were easily identified by their music, clothing, and appearance. Teachers and linguists use this meaning of culture when they identify certain patterns of speech as "Black English."

Culture F equates culture with race. This connotative definition of culture is the most superficial and simplistic. Not surprisingly, this definition of culture is also the primary source of misunderstandings between families and professionals. After all, should we assume that a family is culturally different simply because it is racially different?

As early interventionists, one of our primary concerns should be how we will provide an effective and responsible delivery of services that is also sensitive to the needs of families whose language, culture, and experiences are different from our own.

Ethnocentrism: Views that emphasize one's own cultural or ethnic beliefs, attitudes, and traditions without regard for others' backgrounds, often identifying themselves and their own beliefs as "normal."

For example, Harry (2002) points out that what is normal for one group may not be considered normal, or even acceptable, for another. However, that does not mean that one group's views—or beliefs or values—should be considered superior to another's. Therefore, in order to ensure that a family's beliefs and values are being considered, practitioners must be **culturally competent**, as well as able to engage in a collaborative relationship with parents and family members.

BOX 9.2 ANTI-BIAS CURRICULUM

In order for children to develop a healthy self-identity, an educational environment that not only accepts, but respects and affirms their culture of origin is crucial. Increasingly, preschools are examining and modifying curricula to eliminate bias for one culture or group over another. This is often referred to as an **anti-bias curriculum.** The goal within this framework is to ensure that all children feel affirmed and accepted in their educational environment, regardless of their race, ethnicity, religion, gender, socioeconomic status, or disability.

It's important to examine and evaluate every aspect of the environment for bias. For example, there may be posters on the walls that show women and men in traditional gender roles (e.g., male fire fighters, female nurses); these might be replaced with visuals showing people in nontraditional roles. Similarly, the anti-bias curriculum emphasizes that multicultural elements be embedded in resources and activities children encounter in their classroom on a daily basis—not simply on "special" occasions, like holidays.

Ultimately more important than the relatively superficial considerations of classroom decoration and costume is the way in which teachers convey respect and acceptance of difference to children. For example, art activities in which children draw self-portraits are perfect opportunities to model appreciation of differences and help children explore their own uniqueness. Rather than referring to children as "black" or "white," teachers can use more precise language, such as "Justin's skin is a light tan color, with lots of reddish freckles that match his wonderful red hair; Jose's skin is light brown, and he has beautiful dark brown hair and eyes."

Barriers to Effective Family Involvement

Despite the intent of the law and the best efforts of professionals, parents often are inadvertently left out of the early intervention planning process. Part of the difficulty of including parents stems from the way services were provided in the past. Historically, education professionals have focused intervention efforts on the child. With IDEA's mandates for family-centered intervention, however, came a fundamental shift in the way professionals view themselves and families. Bailey, Buysse, Edmondson, and Smith (1992) outline four basic assumptions underlying family-centered practice that radically shift intervention efforts away from the individual child and toward the entire family (p. 299):

1. Children and families are inextricably intertwined. Intentional or not, intervention with children almost invariably influences families; likewise, intervention with and support of families invariably influence children.
2. Interventions involving and supporting families are likely to be more powerful than those focusing exclusively on the child.
3. Family members should be able to choose their level of involvement in program planning, decision making, and service delivery.
4. Professionals should attend to family priorities for goals and services, even when those priorities differ substantially from professional priorities.

In addition to the paradigm shift from child-centered to family-centered intervention, three types of barriers to full family participation have been identified: **family,**

Policy makers are those who determine the policies and procedures that govern intervention services (e.g., school superintendents, elected officials, and state and federal employees charged with overseeing programs and funding).

The term *preservice education* refers to training that individuals receive prior to being certified or employed as an educational professional.

Inservice education is the on-the-job training and professional development opportunities provided for employees after they are certified and employed.

system, and **professional barriers** (Bailey et al., 1992). Family barriers include lack of parental skill (e.g., parents who are themselves developmentally disabled), inadequate resources (e.g., parents are unable to attend meetings because of work demands, lack of child care, or unavailable transportation), and attitudinal problems (e.g., lack of confidence or assertiveness). When these types of barriers exist, it is the responsibility of the professional to help the family overcome them so that fuller and more meaningful participation is possible.

System barriers, perhaps the most frustrating for professionals, are obstacles resulting from the bureaucracy or agencies responsible for service provision. System barriers include such difficulties as lack of time and resources, entrenched bureaucracies that are slow to change policies, and inflexible administrative practices. For example, one difficulty frequently encountered when professionals attempt to accommodate families is an inability to schedule meetings after work or on weekends so that working parents can attend. Although system barriers must be addressed at the administrative level, it is important for parents and professionals at all levels to bring their concerns to the attention of **policy makers.**

Professional barriers result from a lack of knowledge or skills or from attitudinal problems on the part of the interventionist. Knowledge barriers can arise when professionals are not prepared by their **preservice programs** or **inservice training** to work effectively with families or when they lack experience. Professional attitudinal barriers may present an even greater challenge than lack of knowledge or skill because they involve the fundamental assumptions professionals hold about the ability of families to make decisions about their children's needs and to be involved in early intervention services. Sometimes, the social service professional approaches intervention with an **ethnocentric** attitude, using his own culture and experiences as a measure of what is normal, expected, and superior. As one professional reported, "We seem to have the attitude that we know what's best for the child" (Bailey et al., 1992, p. 304).

:: PROGRAM PLANNING

An underlying principle of IDEA is that all children, including young children with disabilities, are entitled to a meaningful educational experience. This principle was further reinforced in the 1997 Amendments to IDEA, and reiterated in the 2004 Reauthorization of IDEA. To ensure the quality and richness of this experience for a child with special needs, the educational program must be based on individualized goals and objectives. IDEA requires that these goals and objectives be written down and that an individualized service plan be created for each child with special needs. This plan is intended to be the blueprint for the child's intervention program. This section of the chapter describes the planning process and the products of this process: the **individualized family service plan** (IFSP) and the **individualized educational plan** (IEP).

Multidisciplinary teams consist of professionals from at least two different disciplines (e.g., speech and language therapists, occupational therapists, early childhood special educators, psychologists).

Step 1: Assessment

The first step in planning an intervention program is to identify areas of strength and need. To a large extent, the success of this process and, ultimately, the intervention itself, is dependent on the success of the first phase; that is, the child's assessment. In early intervention, assessment is always accomplished through a multidisciplinary team or interdisciplinary team evaluation and an in-depth assessment of every aspect of the child's development. By law, professionals from at least two disciplines (e.g., psychology, special education, regular education, physical therapy) must participate in the assessment.

Many assessment experts recommend a transdisciplinary team evaluation as the most thorough and effective means of identifying young children's strengths and needs. As was discussed in chapter 8, in transdisciplinary assessment, a team of professionals from several disciplines reaches consensus regarding the unique combination of methods and procedures necessary to assess a child. In practice, the collaborative, transdisciplinary approach reduces overlap of assessment and intervention services because the focus of the assessment is to collect information specifically for the purpose of writing the child's personalized service plan (Woodruff & Shelton, 2006). For example, in the transdisciplinary model, professionals from different disciplines collaborate to obtain the information necessary to plan the child's services.

> A transdisciplinary team, like a multidisciplinary team, consists of individuals from at least two different disciplines, but these individuals collaborate more closely to the point of sharing assessment and intervention activities.

The transdisciplinary model differs from the more traditional multidisciplinary team assessment in that, in the multidisciplinary model, professionals from each discipline conduct their own assessment independently and without regard for the assessments of other professionals. Because there is naturally occurring overlap among assessment activities across developmental domains (e.g., language, cognition, and motor), there also is overlap in the assessments. For example, a psychologist and a speech-language pathologist would both be interested in a child's ability to respond to the question "What is a cow?" While the speech and language pathologist may be assessing the child's ability to understand language and to express himself verbally, the psychologist is likely to be interested in the maturity of the child's cognitive abilities. Rather than asking the child the question twice, as would occur in a multidisciplinary assessment, within the transdisciplinary model one of these professionals administers the items and the two then work together to interpret the child's responses.

Multicultural Considerations in Assessment Families from diverse cultures pose special challenges at this stage in the intervention process. Many of the tests and procedures commonly used to determine a child's developmental and cognitive abilities have been criticized by families, teachers, and psychologists as being biased against ethnic and minority groups. For example, opponents of intelligence tests frequently invoke the argument that they measure only skills and abilities valued by the dominant, Western culture and, therefore, children from non-Western or nondominant cultures may be at a unique disadvantage. **Test bias** is a complex issue, in part because we cannot clearly define how many and which behaviors and mental processes a specific test might actually be measuring and what factors might confound test performance. For example, in some cultures, children convey respect by behaving in a subdued manner around adults, especially strangers. Thus, when they are tested, these children may hold back meaningful interaction with their examiners. In such instances, the professionals may never obtain a clear idea of these children's potential or areas of need. Other researchers have found that children who are aware that they are being tested perform better than children who are naive to the situational demands of formal testing. Obviously, some cultures—particularly the mainstream culture of the United States—have more experience than others in test situations. Simply stated, a child's cultural experiences may dramatically influence the testing session. Therefore, the early interventionist should ask some difficult but necessary questions. Have children been referred for early intervention because of an objectively determined real need or because of a value judgment on the part of social service professionals? Are screening and assessment instruments appropriate to the child's language and cultural background? Are families included in the assessment procedure or are they excluded? Will testing be done in familiar or unfamiliar settings? Are opportunities provided for re-assessment and developmental surveillance?

Although many service delivery systems still adhere to a one-size-fits-all assessment protocol, a number of researchers and practitioners advocate that assessment be customized to reflect the unique needs, concerns, and priorities of the child and family (Sattler & Hoge, 2006). Customizing assessment communicates to the family that its cultural differences will be recognized and honored throughout the entire intervention process. For example, because Carla's family speaks Spanish at home, it was important that the assessment team include someone fluent in Spanish, both for interviewing the parents as well as for testing Carla. The fact that Carla was referred for language problems exacerbated the need for a native speaker.

Step 2: The Individualized Service Plan

What Are Individualized Service Plans?   Once a child's needs and the family's strengths, concerns, and priorities have been identified, the intervention plan is outlined in detail. The program plan for most children age 3 and older is called an individualized educational plan (IEP). For infants and toddlers, service goals are outlined in an individualized family service plan (IFSP). Although most children older than 3 years receive services based on an IEP, federal law does allow states to use IFSPs for preschoolers or to use IEPs for 2-year-olds who will undergo transitions into preschool programs within the year. IEPs and IFSPs are legal documents required by IDEA, and the law is very specific regarding their contents. The specific elements of IEPs and IFSPs required by IDEA are outlined in Tables 9.1 and 9.2, and the following paragraphs briefly compare and contrast the two types of program plans.

Similarities Between IEPs and IFSPs.   As Tables 9.1 and 9.2 indicate, both IEPs and IFSPs are statements of specific goals and objectives for providing services to children. To this end, both types of plans identify the specific services the child will receive together with criteria and procedures that will be used to evaluate the outcome for each service. Both IEPs and IFSPs specify when the services will begin and how long they are expected to last. In addition, although the wording is somewhat different, both IEPs and IFSPs document the environments in which services will be provided. Emphasis is placed on providing services in the **least restrictive environment** (LRE). Placement in a classroom or clinic specifically for children with special needs occurs only when specialized, one-to-one services are deemed necessary to meet the child's educational needs. This is most clearly delineated in the 1997 Amendments to IDEA and updated in the Individuals with Disabilities Educational Improvement Act

The term *least restrictive environment* refers to the educational placement most like that of typically developing children of the same age as the child with special needs.

(IDEIA, 2004), which require justification when a child does not receive services in a natural setting. Finally, both IEPs and IFSPs contain provisions to facilitate the transition from infant/toddler services to preschool services or from preschool services to school-age services.

Differences Between IEPs and IFSPs.   Although there are many similarities between IEPs and IFSPs, there also are several important differences. Some differences seem minor, but have important implications for the ways services are provided. For example, although both plans contain a statement of the child's current func-

TABLE 9.1	Elements of an individualized family service plan.

1. A statement of the child's current functioning in the following areas:
   a. physical development
   b. cognitive development
   c. language development
   d. psychosocial development
   e. self-help skills or adaptive behavior
2. A description of the family's resources, priorities, and concerns.
3. The outcomes expected to be achieved as a result of intervention for the child and family. This should include the criteria that will be used to determine success, time lines for attaining goals, and whether modifications or revisions of the services or outcomes are needed.
4. The specific services—including frequency, intensity, and methods—that will be used to deliver the early intervention services. Also, the specific date that services will begin and the anticipated length of services should be included.
5. A description of where the intervention will take place, including the "natural environments" (i.e., inclusive environments as opposed to specialized clinic or school settings).
6. The name of the service coordinator who is responsible for overseeing the implementation of the plan and coordinating the efforts of various agencies.
7. Anticipated dates when services will begin and end.
8. A statement of the necessary services for the child's successful transition from an early intervention program to a preschool program (from Title I and Title II).

TABLE 9.2	Elements of an individualized education plan for young children.

1. A description of the current educational performance of the child.
2. Annual goals and short-term instructional objectives.
3. Which specific educational services will be provided to the child.
4. The extent to which the child will be able to participate in regular educational classrooms or activities.
5. When the services will begin, and how long they are expected to last.
6. Objective criteria, evaluation procedures, and schedules for determining whether objectives are being achieved.

tioning, IEPs address only educational performance while IFSPs require a broader statement of the child's overall development. This means that IFSPs address the family's concerns, resources, and priorities, as well as five specific domains of child functioning: physical development, cognitive development, language development, psychosocial development, and self-help skills. Because IEPs place less emphasis on the family, only characteristics describing the individual child are included.

Another difference relates to the way program goals are specified. IEPs must include specific short-term objectives, while IFSPs can be more general, including the outcomes that are expected but not specific goals and objectives. In contrast to IEPs, IFSPs allow early intervention services for infants younger than 3 years to begin before specific details of the program are completed. IFSPs also provide for evaluation of objectives every 6 months rather than annually, as is required for IEPs. These provisions acknowledge the rapid development of infants and the importance of immediate intervention.

Family Involvement in Program Planning.   One important difference between IEPs and IFSPs is that professionals are required by law to address families' resources, strengths, and priorities when they are providing early intervention services (usually based on IFSPs) to children younger than 3 years. The implications of this difference for the way services are provided are substantial and reflect fundamental differences in the underlying philosophies of intervention. While the law allows IEPs to include instruction for parents, such instruction is not mandated or even emphasized. However, because IFSPs focus on the family's resources, strengths, and priorities, the plan should specify goals that are designed to build on the family's strengths in order to maximize the child's functioning.

The investment of the family in the early intervention process highlights the need for the professional to work effectively with family members. An important first step in establishing a family–professional partnership is for the interventionist to learn culture-specific information about the various groups living in the family's immediate community, particularly related to the family's attitudes and beliefs regarding appropriate roles for parents in the education of their children (Wong & Hughes, 2006). With the help of a cultural or community guide, the professional can learn and recognize the family's patterns, beliefs, and practices. Such information is important in discerning which aspects of the family's involvement in the child's intervention result from personal preferences, lack of information, or cultural differences. In fact, what a white parent might regard as passive indifference might be considered active, valid participation by other families and cultures. Further, Wong and Hughes (2006) point out the importance of examining aspects of parent involvement because members of some cultural groups may prioritize certain kinds of involvement (e.g., help with homework) over other kinds (e.g., participating in PTA). However, even if a family is perceived to be totally uninvolved in the planning process, the interventionist should never discount or exclude the family from the decision-making process.

To ensure optimal parental participation during program planning meetings, Lynch and Hanson (1998, 2004) identify several steps.

- Retain an inclusive definition of *family*, recognizing that in many families, extended family members and unofficial family members (e.g., godparents) are heavily involved in the care of and decision making about the child. It is often helpful for families to bring people important to them, including clergy, friends, and relatives, to meetings.
- Adapt the meeting such that its pace is consistent with the preference of family members. For some families, this may mean holding several preliminary meetings to get to know each member of the family and transdisciplinary team.
- Many families are likely to be intimidated by U.S. bureaucracy. In these cases, the professional should meet with the family beforehand and be prepared to present the family's perspective to others on the transdisciplinary team. The professional also should anticipate and answer the questions the family may not even know to ask.
- Goals, objectives, and outcomes should be consistent with the family's culture and should reflect the family's own perceived needs and priorities. Additionally, a language that is family-friendly should be utilized.
- Identify community resources, especially individuals and groups that may share the family's language, unique experiences, and culture, that can be of assistance to the family.

In Carla's case, her parents live next door to her maternal grandparents. Because Carla's grandparents are a very important part of the family's life, her parents invited them to the meeting. As a result of their attending, Carla's grandmother, who had initially been opposed to the evaluation, gained better understanding of Carla's strengths and needs. According to Carla's mother, Carla's grandmother is able to be much more supportive and is less likely to dismiss her own daughter's concerns.

It also is important to note that different families perceive early intervention differently and their attitudes have a direct impact on the level of family involvement. For some families, the very idea of intervention may be foreign or unacceptable. One of the major tacit assumptions of early intervention is that circumstances for the child and family will change for the better. Some families, especially those new to this country, may resist change and perceive intervention efforts as a threat to the integrity of the family unit. Even families who have been in the United States for generations may perceive an early interventionist's well-intended efforts as meddling. If the family has members who are undocumented immigrants, they may even fear the service provider.

Frequently, a family's attitude toward intervention is directly related to its perceptions of handicapping conditions and causation. Hanson, Lynch, and Wayman (1990) found that family perceptions of disabilities fall on a wide continuum, with some families emphasizing the role of fate and other families directly assigning responsibility to family members, essentially blaming themselves for their child's handicap. For example, Vietnamese families may perceive a child's handicap as a stroke of fate and resist intervention as being futile (Green, 1982). Other cultures may view a handicap as punishment for past sins and, in some Native American cultures it is thought that the child makes a prenatal choice to be born disabled. By understanding and honoring such cultural differences, the professional may avoid misunderstandings and engender a positive partnership with the child's most important resource: the family.

Who Writes Individualized Service Plans? Individualized service plans, both IFSPs and IEPs, are developed through a collaboration of a child's parents and at least two early intervention professionals. In addition to these individuals, team members may include other family members (e.g., grandparents or siblings) or individuals designated by the family, a parent advocate, service coordinator, evaluators, and interventionists. For IEPs, the 1997 Amendments to IDEA expanded the number of team members by requiring participation of the special education teacher, the regular education teacher, when appropriate, a person who can interpret the educational implications of evaluation results, and other individuals, at the discretion of the parent or agency, who have expertise relative to the child's needs. For example, a team that is writing a program plan for a child with cerebral palsy would probably include a physical therapist, while an occupational therapist might be needed for a child whose primary problem relates to speech and language or oral motor difficulties. A wide range of disciplines provide services in early intervention and may be involved in writing IEPs and IFSPs. Team members can include, but are not limited to, professionals in the areas of audiology, education, medicine, nursing, nutrition, occupational therapy, physical therapy, psychology, social work, special education, and speech-language therapy. These requirements continue to be present in the 2004 Reauthorization of IDEA.

When Are Individualized Service Plans Written? An IEP or IFSP should be written within 45 days of a child's being referred for services. Typically, the plan is written at a meeting of the child's parents and the professionals who will work with them. This first official meeting can be very important in that it represents the beginning of the child's involvement with the educational system and, as such, sets the tone for later interactions between parents and professionals. The goal of the meeting is for parents and professionals to agree to a plan of services for the next year (or 6 months, for children under 3 years). This agreement is formalized by all members of the planning team—most importantly the parents—when they sign the written document.

How Are Individualized Service Plans Written? An individualized service plan is a very important document in that it determines the nature and level of services that a child will receive. All too often, however, busy professionals view IEPs and IFSPs as nothing more than paperwork to be gotten out of the way. When this attitude is present, the writing of the service plan is not taken seriously, which results in a document with little utility and a program of services that has not been well thought out. Because the writing of the service plan has such important implications for effective intervention, strategies for writing practical goals and objectives are described next.

Linking Assessment and Intervention. Goals and objectives of a service plan are framed from the information gathered from the assessment. Thus, the starting point for writing the service plan is the report from the transdisciplinary team evaluation. When thinking about appropriate goals, the team not only should consider the child's needs or areas of weakness, but also should endeavor to create a document that reflects the child's strengths as well as the family's resources and concerns. As each goal is considered, intervention strategies are generated that build on the child's and family's strengths. Effective service plans contain information that enables the team to identify those strengths and resources that can be used to address deficits.

Writing Goals. Goals are intended to describe in practical detail exactly what a child is expected to accomplish within the next 6 months (for IFSPs) or year (for IEPs). They represent observable, incremental steps to intended outcomes, including the maximal degree of participation in natural environments and in a typical curriculum. Although the process may seem straightforward, many professionals find that writing appropriate, helpful goals is among their most difficult tasks. In many respects, the goals of the IEP and IFSP are identical; that is, the basic sequence for establishing and selecting goals is the same for both documents. The fundamental difference is that goals written for the IFSP include family as well as child-centered outcomes. By asking the following questions, professionals increase the likelihood that the goals they write for any service plan will be accomplished and, hopefully, will result in positive changes for the child and family.

1. *Were the parents involved in a meaningful way in formulating the goal statements?* To ensure optimal parental involvement in program implementation, the goals of the IEP and IFSP must reflect the priorities and concerns of the family. Parents are more likely to participate in early intervention in a meaningful way if the goals of intervention are meaningful to the family.
   Rather than projecting their own values and choices onto the family, professionals should begin by addressing concerns that are identified by the family (Sandall, Hemmeter, Smith, & McLean, 2005). Moreover, goals must consider the unique strengths and limitations of each family member. Child rearing is a complex task and certain aspects of caring for a child with special needs may be particularly difficult for some families. For example, many low socioeconomic status families struggle with a host of day-to-day survival problems stemming from poverty. Such conditions may make some long-range goals of the individualized plan unattainable. If families are struggling to meet basic survival needs, they will be unable to plan for the future. Therefore, family problems, such as unemployment and lack of adequate clothing and food, need to be incorporated into individualized plans.

   Before service plans can target families' needs, professionals and families must work together to identify and prioritize areas for intervention. This process, known in early intervention as **family assessment,** is crucial to the success of intervention. A number of instruments and techniques have been developed to facilitate the assessment of family needs and priorities. Ideally, professionals use several methods of obtaining information about families' needs and priorities, including interviews and questionnaires.

2. *Are the goals functional and age-appropriate?* Goals and objectives always should be embedded in the functional activities within a child's social system and environment; that is, goals and objectives must be useful. After all, the purpose of early intervention is to enhance children's functioning within the context of their family and environment. Therefore, in relation to the goals of intervention, it is important to include only those activities that will lead to improved functioning in the environment. Obviously, this means considering

A naturalistic environment is that setting in which the child would be educated if he or she did not have special needs.

Self-contained settings are specialized settings specifically designed to provide educational or therapeutic services to children with special needs.

Fine motor functions refer to the small movements of the hands and fingers.

a child's overall environment as well as the child's specific characteristics. Further, if a child's disability limits participation in regular educational or social settings, then the intervention plan should be geared toward helping the child move into the most **naturalistic environment** possible. This means helping to ensure that children in **self-contained settings** are working toward moving into regular classrooms.

Functional goals also are designed to help make caring for a child easier for the family. For example, in the case of a young boy with fine motor impairments, one functional goal might address his ability to help dress himself. On the other hand, a nonfunctional goal might involve working to improve the time it takes him to complete a pegboard. While the second goal may serve to increase his experiences in the fine motor domain, it will have at best a remote relationship to the greater goal of helping him learn to function independently. Dunst, Bruder, Trivette, and Hamby (2006) suggest that using everyday activities as learning opportunities is beneficial for children with disabilities, as well as their families.

3. *Are the goals realistic?* Goals must be attainable given the specific strengths of a child and the demands of the environment. Achievable goals serve to increase the autonomy of the child and family by improving the caregiver's sense of self-efficacy. If expectations go unrealized because they were unrealistic, family members may interpret this as evidence of their failure. Worse, if the family of a child with special needs consistently believes that no progress is being made, the family may become either isolated and discouraged about intervention services or, perhaps, overly dependent on them.

One way to avoid setting goals that are unrealistic is to establish long-term goals as well as short-term objectives. Long-term goals acknowledge family members' dreams for their child and can serve to keep intervention efforts in line with the family's priorities across several years. Short-term objectives, on the other hand, act to keep intervention efforts in the present and help keep families and professionals from becoming discouraged or overwhelmed by goals that may require years of effort before they are realized.

The process of breaking a goal into its component parts is called **task analysis.** Once the family and interventionists have identified a child's current level of functioning and their goals, the next step is task analysis. In this step, every skill necessary to accomplish the ultimate goal is identified. If necessary, these skills may be broken into **subskills** until the tasks seem manageable. To gain an appreciation for the process of task analysis, consider a simple activity that you do every day, such as brushing your teeth. Next, think about all the steps involved in this seemingly simple routine. First, you must find and pick up the toothpaste, then unscrew the cap. Next, you may pick up your toothbrush and then squeeze the toothpaste with the other hand, and so on. Most of us can complete such tasks with a minimum of mental and physical effort, but, for a child with fine motor impairment, each step may require intense concentration and practice.

4. *Does the goal account for all levels of learning?* Haring and White have pointed out that the process of learning a new skill has traditionally been

conceptualized as progressing through five phases: acquisition, fluency, maintenance, generalization, and adaptation (as cited in Alberto & Troutman, 2003). **Acquisition** is the most basic level of learning and means that a child can successfully complete the basic requirements of a skill. **Fluency** refers to the child's ability to complete the task smoothly and quickly. **Maintenance** refers to the child's performance of the skill in settings similar to the training situation, while **generalization** refers to the child's ability to perform the skill in settings different from the training situation. **Adaptation** represents the highest level of achievement because it reflects the child's ability to modify the skill to fit environmental demands or conditions. All too often, intervention goals stop at the level of acquisition in that, once a child demonstrates accurate task completion, the goal is considered to have been attained. This, however, does not ensure that the child will be able to use the new skill in other settings or that it will actually improve the child's day-to-day functioning. In fact, more recent evidence suggests that requiring students to master "lower" levels before moving to generalization and adaptation may be counterproductive. New skills taught in natural environments are more likely to be reinforced by naturally occurring events, and therefore may be more lasting and functional (Alberto & Troutman, 2003).

Step 3: Implementation of Intervention

Once goals have been written, they must be implemented. **Implementation** of intervention involves translating goals and intended outcomes into a planned program of activities. Just as service plans are individualized blueprints for service delivery, the implementation process likewise is unique for each child. Two children may have an identical goal, but the implementation of services to achieve this goal will likely be quite different, depending on each child's unique circumstances, the philosophy and resources of the programs providing the services, and the qualities of the interventionist.

Identifying Resources   The first step in implementation is to identify all the resources needed to accomplish the desired goals and outcomes detailed in the service plan. Resources can take many different forms, but always are the tools of the trade for the interventionist. Although the law mandates that a child's needs—not the agency's resources—dictate the services provided, the manner in which a child's needs are addressed is likely to vary according to the resources available.

Family Resources.   The most significant resource for a child is the primary caregiver; as such, the caregiver's resources and priorities must be taken into account as intervention is implemented (Sandall et. al, 2005). For example, if the primary caregiver does not have reliable transportation, intervention involving clinic-based therapy is doomed to failure unless the problem of getting the child to the clinic is addressed. Also, the caregiver's resources should be reassessed periodically as family circumstances change. Many unforeseen events can interfere with or enhance family members' abilities to support or participate in their child's intervention. Negative events (e.g., illness, sudden unemployment, or a car needing repair) may cause a sudden shift in the family's priorities and necessitate a change in the manner in which services are provided to a child. Likewise, positive events (e.g., extended family members moving nearby or a job promotion) may allow the family to assume additional responsibilities.

In identifying the family's resources, it also is important for the interventionist to understand the **family's developmental stage** and its impact on perceptions of the child's special needs (Harry, 2002; Turnbull & Turnbull, 1986). Life-cycle theorists point out that all families go through a series of developmental stages that influence family functioning and needs. Normal life events, such as the birth of a new child or a change in employment, affect in a profound way the family's psychological and material resources. Therefore, it is important for professionals to remain flexible and sensitive to the family's changing needs and resources as they implement intervention.

Professional Resources.   To avoid having services provided to a child in a piecemeal fashion or in isolation, the critical task of implementing professional recommendations and treatment must be coordinated by a single person typically known as the **service coordinator.** The responsibility of the service coordinator is to work with a child's primary caregiver in the integration of intervention services. The importance of a service coordinator is particularly pronounced for children who have multiple needs or whose families are struggling with multiple stressors (Hanson, Morrow, & Bandstra, 2006).

Because program implementation is the most active component of the intervention process, it is also the stage at which a family's cultural differences become most apparent. Any misunderstandings related to the professional–parent collaboration are likely to manifest themselves during implementation. One way to avoid these misunderstandings is through the involvement of **community guides.** Community guides are respected individuals who are familiar with a family's cultural **norms,** attitudes, traditions, and perceptions. They may or may not be members of the transdisciplinary team, depending on the wishes of the family. Community guides may be religious leaders, interpreters, elders, or business leaders. They provide the interventionist insight into community norms and expectations and ensure that resources within a family's community are identified and utilized in a meaningful way.

> Norms are the beliefs shared by a cultural group regarding appropriate behavior of its members.

Next, intervention professionals must be identified and their efforts coordinated with those of the primary caregiver. Depending on the needs of a child, these professional resource people may include psychologists, teachers, speech pathologists, physical and occupational therapists, audiologists, physicians, nutritionists, or social workers. Within the community, professional resource people may be identified through local schools, daycare programs, Head Start, mental health organizations, governmental agencies, or private nonprofit groups. For the purposes of this discussion, four categories of professional resources are considered: medical, allied health, mental health, and educational resources. Members of each of these professional resources may be trained in the implementation of family-centered practices; however, they are likely to be lacking expertise regarding naturalistic environments in early intervention, the development of IFSPs, teaming, and service coordination (Bruder & Dunst, 2005).

Medical Professionals. Most severe or multiple disabilities are associated with medical conditions. Children with these disabilities often are identified at or soon after birth. In some cases, this identification is made prenatally through **amniocentesis,** or other medical techniques (e.g., sonography or alpha-fetoprotein testing). Families of such children find themselves immediately involved with medical professionals. If a child's condition is identified at birth, it is likely that the child's first physician will be a **neonatalogist,** a physician who specializes in the care and treatment of newborns.

For most children, however, the primary health care provider is a **pediatrician** or pediatric nurse practitioner. Depending on a child's particular health care needs, the child may be involved with many types of medical specialists. Some specialists commonly encountered by young children with disabilities include **pulmonologists** (respiratory system), **neurologists** (nervous system), **orthopedists** (skeletal and muscular systems), **cardiologists** (heart and circulatory system), **endocrinologists** (endocrine system), and **ophthalmologists** (eyes). For children with multiple medical needs, pediatricians often assume the role of medical service coordinator. For nonmedical interventionists, such as teachers and psychologists, pediatricians can be an important resource and should be viewed as colleagues in the development of intervention plans for children.

Nurses also are important professional resources for many children with disabilities. A number of medical conditions require around-the-clock care or frequent medical procedures. Because of financial considerations and families' needs to resume their normal lives, many children, particularly those born prematurely, are released from the hospital with ongoing needs for medical intervention, such as feeding tubes, heart monitors, and respirators. These children are likely to receive home-based nursing care. In many instances, the nurse becomes one of the primary care providers and, as such, a vital agent of intervention.

Allied Health Professionals. Included in this category are specialized therapists, including **speech-language pathologists (SLPs), occupational therapists (OTs),** and **physical therapists (PTs).** As their name implies, SLPs are concerned with disorders related to communication and oral motor problems. Many young children with disabilities have difficulties with receptive or expressive language that can be addressed by SLPs. In addition, SLPs work with children who have normal language abilities, but have difficulty communicating because of unclear speech. There also are SLPs who specialize in the oral motor structures involved in speech and eating, and they may be called upon to work with children with feeding difficulties or structural deformities (e.g., cleft palate) that interfere primarily with eating and speaking.

Physical and occupational therapists are similar in that both are concerned with motor abilities. As a general rule, however, the two professionals can be distinguished by the fact that PTs are primarily concerned with large muscle groups or **gross motor** activities, such as walking, sitting, and jumping, while OTs typically address small muscle groups or **fine motor** activities, such as writing and tying

Amniocentesis: A test, usually performed in the first or second trimester of pregnancy, in which a needle is inserted into the uterus in order to sample the amniotic fluid surrounding the fetus. Results from this test provide information that assist in the diagnosis of genetic and developmental disabilities.

shoes. OTs also are called upon to assist with daily living tasks and, along with specially trained SLPs, address feeding problems.

Depending on the specialized needs of a child, the expertise of other allied health professionals also may be required. For example, a child with visual impairments may require services from a vision specialist. Vision specialists typically assess the degree of vision loss and its impact on development, provide early mobility training, and recommend specialized equipment. Similarly, audiologists and specialists in educational programming work with children who are deaf or have various hearing impairments.

Mental Health Professionals.   Families of children with disabilities are likely to encounter a number of mental health professionals as a result of their involvement with early intervention and various forms of social services. **Psychologists** are likely to be involved in the initial assessment of a child and often are called upon to provide estimates of children's cognitive or developmental abilities. Beyond the assessment phase of intervention, psychologists may provide grief counseling services or therapy to address specific problems (e.g., child behavior problems).

Social workers are another type of mental health professional likely to work with families of children with special needs. Social workers' unique understanding of social services and agencies make them a natural choice as service coordinators. Even if social workers are not designated as service coordinators, they often play a vital role in helping a family gain access to social services. Additionally, social workers may provide counseling, parent training, and other mental health services as their training, interests, and job responsibilities permit.

IEPs and IFSPs are developed through collaboration of a child's parents and early intervention professionals.

Todd Yarrington/Merrill

Education Professionals. Perhaps the most common professional resource in early intervention is the early childhood educator. Two distinct types of educators can be identified: **early childhood educators** (ECEs) and **early childhood special educators** (ECSEs). Whether a child is served primarily by an ECE or ECSE depends in large part on the setting in which services are provided. ECEs commonly work with typically developing preschoolers, usually in a classroom-based early childhood setting. ECSEs, on the other hand, specialize in working with infants and young children with disabilities.

In addition to working in different settings, ECEs and ECSEs have historically relied on different educational philosophies and practices (Bredekamp, 1993; Burton, Haines, & Hanline, 1992; Wolery & Wilburs, 1994). ECEs have typically attended teacher training programs that have been grounded in constructivism, while ECSEs have typically attended training programs that have been based largely on behavioral theory (Smith, Miller, & Bredekamp, 1998; Jacobs, 2001; Wolery, Werts, & Holcombe, 1993; Wolery & Wilburs, 1994). Historically, early childhood education and early childhood special education have maintained separate programs and services. Thus, it was possible for ECEs and ECSEs to keep their educational philosophies and practices separate (Smith & Bredekamp, 1998). In recent years, however, more children with special needs are being included in early childhood classrooms via inclusion policies (LaParo, Sexton, & Snyder, 1998; Wolery et al., 1993; Wolery, Holcombe, & Werts, 1994), and this has resulted in educators being called upon to instruct all types of children. Therefore, despite the traditional split among education professionals, as more children with special needs are served in regular educational settings, the differences between ECEs and ECSEs has begun to narrow.

Location of Intervention The place where a child with special needs receives services has become a topic of great interest in the past several years. For many years, children with special needs of all ages received educational and therapeutic services in relative isolation. For example, a young child with cerebral palsy might have received educational services in a separate facility operated by the United Cerebral Palsy agency or, later, in a "preschool class for handicapped children" in a public school. He might have received PT services in the therapist's office, rarely if ever interacting with typically developing peers. In recent years, however, the trend toward serving children with special needs in regular settings has gained momentum. The trend appears to be moving away from center-based services (Buysse, Bernier, & McWilliam, 2002). The continuum of setting options, ranging from clinic- or school-based self-contained classrooms to fully normalized settings, is described next.

Self-Contained Settings. Early efforts to provide early intervention services generally relied on self-contained classrooms based on the assumption that disabilities precluded children from benefiting from standard classrooms and required specialized care. Early intervention efforts now are frequently subsumed under a larger "system" that includes not only programs funded under special education laws, but Head Start and other early prevention programs as well (VanDerHeyden & Snyder, 2006). Similarly, other therapies (e.g., occupational, physical, speech-language therapy) have traditionally been conducted in isolation, often in hospital-based or clinic settings. Within the context of self-contained placements, a technique known as **reverse mainstreaming** has been used to increase contact between children with disabilities and their typically developing peers. With this technique, children without disabilities are brought into the special education classroom or therapy session for varying amounts of time. However, current public policies (e.g., Response-to-Intervention) and position statements from advocacy groups such as the Division for Early Childhood (DEC) call for greater integration of service delivery into normalized settings.

Normalized Settings.   Federal law requires that intervention be provided in the **least restrictive environment** (LRE) possible. For infants and toddlers, this often means that services are provided in the child's home. Home-based intervention consists of an interventionist (e.g., an ECSE, SLP, PT, or OT) visiting a child's home on a weekly or biweekly basis, depending on the child's needs and IFSP or IEP goals, and providing direct therapy to the child and consultation with the care providers.

Depending on a family's needs and the age of a child, early intervention services also may be provided in the context of regular childcare settings, such as preschools or daycare centers. In such cases, an interventionist may assume a number of roles.

For example, an SLP may work with a group of children, only one of whom has a disability, in a daycare classroom. An SLP also may function as a consultant to the regular teachers or assistants. A number of advantages have been identified for this type of service delivery (McWilliam & Bailey, 1994), most notably, by including intervention into a child's regular routine, the child is more likely to generalize the skills to everyday life demands. An additional advantage is that the skills addressed are more likely to be functional in nature. As the most appropriate setting for providing intervention services is determined, however, a number of factors must be taken into account. Within the context of family-centered intervention services, the family's preferences must be accommodated to as great a degree as possible and the decision regarding the setting for service delivery must be made on a case-by-case basis.

Inclusion   Few professionals, parents, or individuals with disabilities would dispute that the overarching goal of early intervention and special education is to enable children with special needs to participate fully in all the settings and environments enjoyed by those without special needs. This principle also is reflected in federal law. Increasingly, parents and professionals in special education and related fields have come to expect full inclusion of all children—including children with significant special needs. Although a range of definitions exists, advocates for **full inclusion** have defined an **inclusive school** as "a place where everybody belongs, is accepted, supports, and is supported by his or her peers and other members of the school community in the course of having his or her educational needs met" (Stainback & Stainback, 1992, p. 3). Further, within such a school, all types of children learn together, without regard for the nature or severity of their disabilities. Stainback and Stainback argue that, because children with special needs receive services from special educators, regular educators have begun to view special education as a dumping ground for "undesirable" children or children with problems. The only way to correct this, they argue, is to abolish special education completely.

The Division of Early Childhood (DEC) of the Council for Exceptional Children (CEC), the major organization devoted to the education of children with special needs, has issued a position statement endorsing inclusion for young children with disabilities.

Developing a Strategy   Once the resources have been identified and the setting selected, the next salient issue is how to use these resources to facilitate the child's optimal development within the framework of the service plan. An instructional, therapeutic strategy is required. Several researchers (Barnett & Carey, 1992; Bricker & Cripe, 1998; Dunst, Hamby, Trivette, Raab, & Bruder, 2000) suggest that a naturalistic, **activity-based approach** is the best strategy for program implementation. Naturalistic intervention incorporates environmental variables into service delivery with training goals embedded in daily routines. Naturalistic, activity-based intervention is preferred for several reasons. First, intervention is most likely to be successful if it is linked to the caregiver's current living situation. Approximately 20 years ago, Bricker (1989) reminded us that "the family situation itself dictates where, when, how, and in what areas to begin intervention" (p. 165), and this holds true to the present. Second, skills acquired in naturalistic settings are most likely to generalize to different environments. Third, naturalistic intervention strategies emphasize the competency and involvement of caregivers. Finally, a naturalistic, activity-based approach ensures that targeted goals and outcomes are likely to be functionally appropriate and valued by the child and family. For the well-trained interventionist, natural family and community settings provide varied and rich opportunities for intervention within the very contexts that matter most to families (Dunst et al., 2000).

> An activity-based approach is a functional approach to instruction that capitalizes on the use of naturally occurring activities as "teachable" opportunities.

Within the structure of naturalistic intervention, short-term, measurable objectives can facilitate the acquisition of new skills. Hanson (1987) advocates task analysis in the teaching of such objectives. Again, in task analysis, a target behavior is first identified and then broken down into a series of smaller tasks required to achieve the target. For example, a target behavior for an infant might be to roll over from his back to his front. The series of behaviors leading to successful completion of the target behavior might be that (a) the infant extends his arm to one side and rolls his shoulders, (b) the infant shifts his leg to align with his shoulders, and (c) the infant completes the roll by turning over to his front. While the primary focus is on the target behavior, task analysis methods also provide the child and family with insight into the process of learning. Moreover, the emphasis on measurable objectives facilitates program evaluation.

Bricker (1989) recommends a combination of home-based and center-based implementation strategies. **Home-based strategies** are frequently used with children up to age 3 years. As described earlier in this chapter, professionals visit the home on a regular basis and help the caregiver implement the selected treatments and activities. The advantages of home-based strategies are obvious: Parental involvement is increased and the interventionist is afforded the opportunity to observe parent–child interaction. In addition, home visits become training sessions for the parent and other family members.

Center-based models, on the other hand, rely on structured classroom activities and are usually employed with children older than age 3. Head Start is an example of an intervention program that uses a center-based strategy. Center-based programs may include only children with special needs (self-contained setting) or children both with and without disabilities (inclusive or mainstreamed setting).

BOX 9.3   SCHOOL READINESS

Educators, policy makers, and researchers have identified the early childhood years as critically important to children's success in school. Head Start has long had as a goal providing quality educational opportunities to children at risk for school failure because of economic disadvantage. In an effort to reach more children, a number of states have begun initiatives designed to provide high-quality preschool experiences to all children. The goal of these projects was derived largely from the National Educational Goals Panel—that all children enter kindergarten cognitively, emotionally, socially, and motorically ready to learn. As additional public funds are spent on early education, the opportunities for children with special needs to receive intervention with their typically developing peers is likely to increase as well.

Although preschools vary in terms of their philosophies, they typically stress the acquisition of developmental, cognitive, social, and self-help skills necessary for success in elementary school.

Center-based models and strategies also afford the child a new setting for practicing skills acquired in the home. A child's ability to generalize skills across settings is crucial for successful transition to new, less-restrictive environments. For the family, center-based models also provide the opportunity to interact with other parents as well as needed respite from the child.

Philosophical Approaches and Developmental Theories   One of the crucial ways in which early intervention programs differ from one another is reflected by differences in their philosophical orientations. Early intervention relies on a rich history of developmental theory. Although no one school or theory is right or wrong, different developmental theories are founded on different models of intervention. In addition, programs may focus on specific areas of development based on their underlying theories.

Anne Vega/Merrill

Whenever possible, children with special needs should participate fully in settings enjoyed by children without special needs.

To be effective, intervention should be based on an underlying developmental theory. Not only are programs guided by the theoretical perspectives on which they are based, but professionals working with children and families also are influenced by their own beliefs about the ways children develop and learn and the best ways to effect change. These beliefs also are influenced by one's theoretical or philosophical perspectives. Given this central role of developmental theory in intervention, the following paragraphs briefly describe three of the most prevalent theoretical models: developmental, behavioral, and contextual.

Developmental Models. Developmental models emphasize a child's biological make-up and maturation and are based largely on the theories of Piaget, Dewey, and Erikson. Intervention based on such models rests on the assumption that development occurs along a natural course internal to a child. As the child encounters new and different experiences, he feels dissatisfied with his current means of solving problems and is motivated to accommodate new information and new ways of thinking.

Interventionists who adhere to developmental models believe that children are internally motivated to explore and master the world around them. For example, Piaget described young children as little scientists who explore the world around them through active manipulation (Rathus, 2006). Further, this model maintains that the best and most efficient way for children to learn is through hands-on experiences and interactions with the material world. The role of the interventionist, then, is to provide experiences and create environments that support and facilitate a child's individual, self-directed growth.

Professionals who adhere to developmental models such as those based on Piaget's theories often refer to their philosophy as **developmentally appropriate practice (DAP).** *Developmental appropriateness* was defined by the National Association for the Education of Young Children (Bredekamp & Copple, 1997) and refers both to age appropriateness (i.e., the predictable pattern and stages of development described by theorists such as Piaget and Erikson) and to an individual child's pattern of development. Montessori programs are often cited as examples of programs for young children that adhere to this definition of DAP. As the name suggests, Montessori programs are based on the work of Maria Montessori, an educator who worked in Rome in the early twentieth century. Montessori methods include ungraded classrooms, instruction individualized to meet each child's unique educational needs, material that is ordered sequentially to reflect stages of development, and an absence of punishment (Richmond & Ayoub, 1993).

Behavioral Models. These models are based on the structured principles of behavioral psychology. Unlike developmental models, behavioral models de-emphasize the internal motivations of the individual. Instead, specific target behaviors are identified and taught using reinforcement, shaping, and modeling. In its simplest form, behavioral theory relies on the principles of reward and punishment: If a child is rewarded for a behavior, the child is likely to repeat the behavior. In contrast, punishing or ignoring a child following a behavior is likely to decrease the chances that the behavior will be repeated. In contrast to programs guided by developmental theories, programs guided by behavioral theory typically rely more heavily on direct, one-on-one instruction.

An adaptation of behavioral theory is social learning theory, an approach emphasizing that children learn through observation and imitation. Within this framework, behavior is believed to be changed because of exposure to models. For example, in the case of a child who cannot play appropriately with other children because of her aggressive behavior, intervention based on social learning theory might include having the child watch other children play together without fighting.

Contextual Models.   Contextual models emphasize the role of the environment in shaping the development of a young child. Within such models, the roles of family and community, as well as the greater society, are considered. Urie Bronfenbrenner's ecological model is widely used as an intervention framework. Bronfenbrenner (1986) suggests that a child, family, community, and larger society can be viewed as concentric circles of influence that all affect the child's development. Similarly, Lev Vygotsky's **sociohistorical theory** has been used widely with students who have disabilities (Brown, Evans, Weed, & Owen, 1987). This model is sometimes called the *functional model* because it emphasizes the importance of social context in the acquisition of domestic, vocational, and communication skills that increase a child's self-sufficiency and independence in daily life. As one might expect, intervention based on this model seeks to facilitate the development of strong, supportive social networks for the family of the target child.

Within the contextual model, Sameroff and Chandler (1975) first described a **transactional approach** that examines the intersection between characteristics of the individual and the environment. Because of its sensitivity to both dynamics, this approach provides a framework that is particularly relevant to early intervention. In the transactional model, Sameroff and Chandler suggest that development results from a cycle of ongoing, dynamic, and reciprocal interactions between a child and his environment, which includes parents and other caregivers. By introducing the notion of reciprocal interactions, the transactional model maintains that a child not only is influenced by his environment, but also influences his environment. For example, consider a child who was born with health problems that have caused him to be irritable and to cry most of the time. Because the mother is unable to soothe the child, the mother begins to feel that she is a bad parent. Further, because of the negative feelings the mother experiences around her crying baby, she begins to avoid interacting with the child. Consequently, because the mother rarely talks to or interacts with the child, the child's language does not develop as rapidly as it otherwise would and, as a preschooler, he is diagnosed with a language delay. Clearly, the child's language delay was not caused by either the mother's or the child's characteristics alone. Instead, the problem resulted from an interaction or from the series of dynamic transactions between the child's characteristics and the mother's feelings and behaviors.

Despite the apparent differences among the three broad kinds of models, all share a single, strong commonality: The thread running through all models of intervention and associated theories is that a child is an active, competent, and social learner. Therefore, although there certainly are biological components to a child's development, there also are interactions between the child and the environment that affect both the child's development and the larger social context. Accordingly, a child's developmental outcome is the result of biological constituents, the environment, and transactions between them.

Developmental theories guide our understanding of intervention with children and families by helping us to answer two fundamental questions: *Why* do children behave the way they do? and *How* do children develop more mature behaviors? Let's return now to Carla, the 4-year-old girl with cerebral palsy who attends Happy Acres Child Care Center. She is having trouble getting along with her peers. This vignette is presented to illustrate the differences among developmental, behavioral, and contextual theories.

VIGNETTE 9.1

CARLA AND HER PEERS

Carla's parents are concerned because she has recently begun to hit other children in her preschool. Her parents have asked three child development experts, each with a different theoretical orientation, to explain why Carla hits other children and to offer solutions for helping her improve her peer relationships.

Jake is a developmental (cognitive) theorist, the first child development expert contacted by Carla's parents. Jake believes that children's behavior is best understood in the context of their level of cognitive maturation. Therefore, in order to explain Carla's behavior, Jake decides to find out more about Carla's development; that is, what does Carla understand about the effects of her behaviors? After spending some time watching Carla and talking with her, her parents, and her teacher, Jake decides that Carla has been hitting other children because she does not understand that it hurts others when she hits them. Thus, Jake concludes that cognitive immaturity, a deficit in the development of her understanding of the environment, explains Carla's poor peer relationships. Jake believes that the best way to help Carla learn more appropriate ways of interacting with her peers is to address this lack of understanding by first helping her learn to take the perspective of her peers. Jake recommends that Carla's parents and teacher talk with Carla about how her choices (hitting versus not hitting) affect others. Additionally, because Jake believes that children learn from their natural interactions with their environment, he also talks with Carla's teacher about the classroom and ways to structure Carla's environment so that she learns how to play appropriately.

Unlike Jake, Karen does not believe that understanding Carla's internal thought processes is very important for explaining or changing her behavior. Karen instead focuses on the actual behavior (hitting others). She believes that Carla hits other children because hitting them is rewarding for Carla in some way. According to Karen, the key to understanding Carla's behaviors is to discover what leads up to and follows her hitting of others. To determine what is causing the hitting behavior, Karen decides to observe Carla playing with her peers at school. After watching Carla for several days and recording what precedes and follows her hitting behavior, Karen decides that Carla hits other children when they try to play with a toy she wants. Carla is rewarded for hitting because, after she hits a child, the child leaves and Carla can play with the toy of her choice. To help Carla learn more appropriate play skills, Karens recommends that Carla be rewarded with a sticker when she shares a toy without hitting other children and that she be sent to time-out when she hits others.

Sara is a contextual theorist, the third child development expert contacted by Carla's parents. Sara believes that the environment shapes the way a child behaves. In order to understand why Carla hits other children, Sara wants to know about Carla's environment and about the interactions between Carla's characteristics and her environment. Not only does Sara want to know about Carla's classroom, she also wants to know about Carla's home life. Sara interviews Carla's parents and teacher, and observes Carla at home and at school. Sara decides that Carla hits others because she hasn't learned social interaction skills from her environment. According to Sara, it is important for all of the people in Carla's social network (e.g., parents, teachers, grandparents, and peers) to help Carla learn more adaptive ways of dealing with conflict. Sara also emphasizes that, if Carla's parents are anxious or overwhelmed by parenting responsibilities, Carla may feel upset and act out at school. Therefore, Sara thinks that an important way for Carla's parents to help Carla is to seek some form of social support.

Courtesy of Tina Smith

Particularly for children with behavior problems or other difficulties interacting with peers, a social skills-based preschool may be an appropriate form of intervention.

Types of Programs   In addition to having different theoretical orientations, center-based early intervention programs focus on different areas of child development. Some programs develop their focus as a result of their theoretical orientations. For example, preschools based on developmental theories are likely to focus on children's play because of the belief that play is the most effective and developmentally appropriate way to encourage children's development. However, other programs focus on one area of development because they are specifically designed to serve children who demonstrate particular problems (e.g., language problems). Some of the most prominent types of preschool programs, including **play-based**, **academically oriented**, **language-based**, and **social skills-based programs**, are described next.

Play-Based Programs.   Regardless of their theoretical orientation, most early interventionists believe in developmentally appropriate practice (e.g., Jalongo & Isenberg, 2008) and, therefore, agree that play should be a vital component of every early childhood program. As the name implies, play-based early intervention programs recognize that children learn best through play. Preschools adhering to this philosophy typically are child-directed, meaning that children are encouraged to select their own activities. By creating a rich learning environment, teachers facilitate development through manipulation of materials and through children's interactions with each other and with adults. Most play-based classrooms are organized around centers (e.g., a housekeeping center, block center, art center, etc.), and children are allowed to rotate among the activities at their own pace.

Academically Oriented Programs.   In contrast to play-based models, there also are traditional, academically oriented preschools. Academically oriented preschools strive to teach preacademic skills and prepare children for school. Rather than being allowed to choose their own activities, as occurs in play-based preschools, children in academically oriented preschools spend most of their time engaged in teacher-directed activities. Often, these activities involve seatwork or circle time, in which the entire class gathers around the teacher for a lesson. Although some preschoolers may be able to cope with the demands of such a structured setting, most experts in child development agree that large-group activities and teacher-directed programming do not reflect developmentally appropriate practice and are not an efficient way to facilitate the cognitive, language, social, or motor development of young children (Jalongo & Isenberg, 2008).

Language-Based Programs.   One of the most important developmental tasks of the preschool years is learning language. Language deficits are among the developmental difficulties most frequently encountered by early intervention professionals. For this reason, many preschools are designed specifically to address language deficits. Language-based preschools employ a number of techniques to encourage the use of language and they often utilize environmental factors, such as the types of toys that are available, to encourage children to use language adaptively. For example, rather than having a large number of toys that encourage solitary play (e.g., puzzles), language-based preschools are likely to contain more social toys (e.g., dramatic play materials and games that require talking or turn-taking). Teachers also may wish to

Language deficits are among the developmental difficulties most frequently encountered by early intervention professionals.

set up language-based classrooms in such a way that children are encouraged to ask for help. For example, the most desirable toys may be kept on out-of-reach shelves so that children are motivated to ask for assistance.

Heward (2005) identified two approaches for systematically promoting language development in the preschool: the **incidental teaching model** (Hart & Risley, 1975) and the **mand model** (Rogers-Warren & Warren, 1980). In the incidental teaching model, the teacher uses naturally occurring opportunities to facilitate language use. Any time that a child wants something from the teacher, the teacher attempts to draw out the conversation. For example, if a child walks up to the teacher on the playground and points to the swings, rather than attempting to anticipate the child's desire to swing, the teacher might say, "Can you say *swing?*" If the child says the word, the teacher assists the child with the swing and gives praise. If the child does not say the word, the teacher still provides assistance without reprimand. In the incidental teaching model, it is very important that the child not perceive interactions with the teacher as punitive or unpleasant. This model assumes that language will be learned most effectively if children frequently initiate language opportunities with their teachers.

In the mand model, the interactions are typically initiated by the teacher. In the context of regular activities, the teacher attempts to elicit a target response from a child, usually by asking a question. Using the example of the child who wants to swing, the teacher might say, "What do you want to do?" If the child does not respond, the teacher "demands" a response by saying something like, "Tell me." The teacher then attempts to elicit a more elaborate response by saying, for example, "Say 'Want to swing.'"

Social Skills-Based Programs.

A developmental task closely associated with language is social interaction. For many children, preschool is their first opportunity to interact with peers. Particularly for children with behavior problems or other difficulties that interfere with interaction with peers, a social skills-based preschool may be an appropriate type of intervention. Many such programs use model children—children who are competent social partners—to encourage appropriate play. As with language-based preschools, the environment can be manipulated to increase interaction opportunities. For example, limiting the number of toys available encourages children to play together, and teachers can intervene to encourage appropriate sharing behavior. **Therapeutic preschools**—programs that incorporate psychological therapy along with educational goals—may be available for young children with severe emotional or behavioral problems.

Recommended Practices in Early Intervention.

To facilitate excellence in program implementation, it helps to have established standards of practice. Such recommended practices provide a benchmark for measuring the overall quality of any intervention program. Apart from the legal criteria mandated by Parts B and C of IDEIA, there are no firmly established standards of practice for early intervention programs. However, several state educational agencies have proposed standards that are believed to be consistent with appropriate practice. Hanson et al. (2006) suggest that best practices in early intervention include the following.

- The range of services offered vary in intensity based on the needs of children.
- Individualized teaching plans consist of goals and objectives based on careful analyses of children's strengths and weaknesses and on skills required for future school and nonschool environments.
- Transdisciplinary assessment is frequent enough to adequately monitor children's progress.
- Instructional approaches are effective, efficient, functional, and normalized.
- Instructional approaches actively engage children and their families.
- Activities strengthen the abilities of families to promote their children's development by increasing opportunities for involvement in the broader community.
- Program managers and workers respect and acknowledge the diversity of patterns and structures within each family and contribute to intervention success.

Carta et al. (1991) and Johnson et al. (1989) also offer the following suggestions for best practices in early intervention.

- Families must be permitted to choose their level of involvement with the IFSP process. To help families with decision making, professionals must be clear and honest in their communications with them. Within the framework provided by parental involvement, professionals must respect families' rights to privacy and confidentiality.
- The program manager should strive to form a partnership and collaboration with a child's family. This relationship is fostered by adopting and adapting service delivery strategies that conform to the family's diversity and structure. Professionals also must be accessible and responsive to the family's questions and requests.
- Early intervention services should be flexible, accessible, and responsive to family-identified needs. To address these needs, the family and intervention team should compose goals and objectives that are functional and representative of the family's choices.
- Early intervention services should be provided according to the normalization principle; that is, families should have access to services that are provided in as normal a fashion and environment as possible and that promote the integration of the child and family within the community.
- Planning and service delivery should incorporate multiple agencies and disciplines. This approach acknowledges that no single agency or discipline can entirely meet the complex needs of young children with special needs and their families.
- Family members should be present for all decision-making opportunities.

Step 4: Evaluation

Evaluation has become increasingly central to education, as recent federal and state legislation (e.g., the No Child Left Behind Act) emphasizes educational accountability and mandates testing across grades in publicly funded schools. Over 15 years ago, Snyder and Sheehan (1993) defined evaluation as "the process of systematically gathering, synthesizing, and interpreting reliable and valid information about programs for the purpose of aiding with decision making" (p. 269). Beyond political requirements for accountability, the bottom line for evaluation is the determination of the overall worth of a program (Bagnato, 2007; Bailey, 2001). In early intervention, program evaluation has two complementary purposes: (1) to examine the effectiveness of a program, and (2) to determine the impact of a program on an individual child and family.

Evaluation is often synonymous with accountability, which can be loosely defined as the systematic activities through which we seek to demonstrate to our stakeholders that our actions have accomplished the desired outcomes. The "stakeholders" of early intervention include all parties with an investment in the early intervention program. The most obvious type of investment is financial. Like all state and federally funded programs, early intervention programs have a social and legal obligation to provide proof of their effectiveness. Because administrators, legislators, and other decision makers must determine which programs will receive funding, program evaluation provides vital information. In addition, by evaluating themselves and their programs, professionals help ensure that they will provide the most effective, evidence-based intervention to the families they serve.

Families who participate in early intervention also have investments of time and personal resources in the program and, as such, should be considered an audience for evaluation efforts (Bagnato, 2007). Program evaluation thus attempts to determine the impact of early intervention on individual children and their families. Accordingly, evaluation provides an index of program success related to three aspects of service implementation:

1. *Efficiency of service delivery:* Was intervention implemented as stated in the IEP or IFSP? Were services rendered in a timely and appropriate manner?
2. *Overall child outcomes:* What changes in the child's behavior occurred and can be demonstrated to be the result of intervention? What was the quality of these changes? Were any unexpected or undesired outcomes observed? To what extent were the desired outcomes of the IEP or IFSP achieved?

    With regard to overall child outcomes, Bruder and her colleagues (2005) list the following competencies as those that early intervention teams should assess: (1) Whether the development of target children is enhanced; (2) Whether the children are safe and healthy; (3) Whether the early intervention has enabled the child to have a smooth transition to elementary school or future services; and (4) Whether the child received early intervention services that were individualized, coordinated, and effective.

    Bagnato (2005) advocates for the use of authentic assessments instead of conventional testing procedures to document the effectiveness of early intervention services for individual children. In fact, authentic assessments should be incorporated into early intervention assessment and progress monitoring practices. Similarly, various **general outcome measures** (GOMs) are being developed and validated to monitor progress related to early social interactions (e.g., Carta, Greenwood, Luze, Cline, & Kuntz, 2004), early literacy skills (e.g., Missall, McConnell, & Cadigan, 2006), early numeracy skills (e.g., Floyd, Hojnoski, & Key, 2006; VanDerHeyden et al., 2004), early motor skills (e.g., Greenwood, Luze, Cline, Kuntz, & Leitschuh, 2002), early language skills (e.g., Luze et al., 2001), and early problem-solving skills (e.g., Greenwood, Walker, Carta, & Higgins, 2006).

General outcome measures (GOMs) are assessment techniques commonly used to monitor the progress of an intervention for an individual child. GOMs such as the Individual Growth and Development Indicators (IGDIs) can be used to measure a child's continual progress toward outcome goals specified in the IFSP. Unlike criterion-referenced assessments, which have been used to evaluate the effectiveness of early intervention programs in the past, GOMs such as the IGDIs assess the same set of skills over time in order to identify growth toward identified outcomes. Results from IGDIs and other GOMs can be used to demonstrate an intervention's effectiveness to various stakeholders (Carta et al., in press).

Many of these GOMs are being developed in response to the current national attention given to a technique for providing prevention and intervention services to elementary-aged and older children. This technique is known as response to intervention, or RTI. The impetus for RTI focuses on a problem-solving approach to identification and evaluation of children who may benefit from various intervention services. RTI uses a tier-based implementation model in which the intensity and individuality of interventions is increased as an individual child's needs are recognized as being unmet. Moreover, repeated and continual progress monitoring of all students, but especially students whose needs have been identified as being unmet at any independent tier, is a crucial part of RTI. RTI grew out of a need to provide intervention and prevention services to children with learning difficulties prior to these children being labeled as learning disabled, which often did not occur until the second or third grade (Coleman, Buysse, & Neitzel, 2006; VanDerHeyden & Snyder, 2006).

A downward extension of the RTI model is currently being developed for use with very young children at risk for developing learning disabilities. This extension is known as the **recognition and response system.** It is based on the idea that "parents and teachers can learn to recognize critical early warning signs that a young child may not be learning in an expected manner and to respond in ways that positively affect a child's early school success" (Coleman et al., 2006, p. 3). Like RTI, the response and recognition system is a problem-solving process based on an intervention hierarchy that relies on screening, assessment, and progress monitoring, as well as research-based curriculum and instruction (Coleman et al., 2006).

Potential benefits of downward extensions of RTI, such as the response and recognition system, include the ability to improve child outcomes through problem-solving practices, the ability to provide larger numbers of children access to high-quality instruction, the enhancement of decision-making accuracy, and the improvement of child learning and growth. However, challenges to the implementation of downward extensions of RTI must be considered.

Currently, no consensus has been reached regarding what the desired outcomes of early education and intervention are. VanDerHeyden and Snyder contend that "Using early intervening models effectively in diverse early childhood settings will require policy makers, researchers, practitioners, and families to clarify desired outcomes and to specify indicators that will be used to evaluate whether benchmarks or instructional targets are being achieved" (2006, p. 529). Moreover, although various GOMs are being developed and validated for use as progress-monitoring tools, the development of sufficient progress monitoring tools is still in its infancy (VanDerHeyden & Snyder, 2006).

Because the field of early childhood education and care has not agreed upon desired outcomes, no consensus on which interventions are associated with desired outcomes has been reached. Without such consensus, the field of early education is missing a critical piece in the implementation of RTI systems. Similarly, the field of early education must agree upon standards against which to make judgments (VanDerHeyden & Snyder, 2006).

3. *Overall family outcomes:* Was the family satisfied with intervention? What are their attitudes regarding intervention? To what extent were the family's priorities addressed? With regard to overall family outcomes, Bruder and her colleagues (2005) postulate that early interventionists should assess whether families were provided the opportunity to make informed decisions concerning services and community opportunities. They also suggest assessment of whether a family's newly acquired or maintained quality of life will enhance the target child and his or her family's overall well-being. Next, there should be evaluation of whether families become self-sufficient as a result of early intervention services, whether families become knowledgeable about their child's special needs, and whether families received services that were individualized, coordinated, and effective (Bruder et al., 2005).

The Family's Role in Evaluation   Part C of IDEA recognized the importance of the family in providing early intervention services. Several studies (e.g., Able-Boone, Sandall, Loughry, & Frederick, 1990) confirmed that families want greater involvement in early intervention programs. Given the importance of the family in formulating objectives and implementing services, it is logical that families also should play a role in program evaluation. An obvious component of program evaluation that directly involves parents is consumer satisfaction. At a minimum, program evaluation should answer the question, "Are parents satisfied with the delivery of early intervention services?" Bailey (2001) asserts that program evaluation should consider three facets of family involvement: (1) Are legally mandated services provided? (2) Are the services provided utilizing practices that are recommended by professional organizations? (3) Are identified outcomes being achieved as a result of working with families?

Frequently, professionals use specially designed questionnaires and rating scales to assess family satisfaction. A number of questionnaires are available for this purpose (e.g., the *Family-Centered Program Rating Scale*) or FamPRS (Murphy, Lee, Turnbull, & Turbiville, 1995).

In general, parents who have greater involvement in the delivery of intervention services report greater satisfaction (Caro & Derevensky, 1991). In a study designed to isolate the source of parental satisfaction with early intervention programs, McWilliam et al. (1995) found that the individual case managers' behaviors were "often directly linked to families' positive impressions of early intervention services" (p. 53). Clearly, from the family's perspective, the individual early interventionist is a principal source of their satisfaction. This finding should come as no surprise, as the program manager typically is the primary channel through which the various intervention services flow. The program manager is the professional most visible to the family and represents the concerted efforts of everyone involved in the delivery of services. There is a need for further research to determine the specific personal and professional qualities of early interventionists that relate to parental satisfaction with services.

Planning the Evaluation. To answer evaluation questions adequately, the interventionist must plan ahead. Because special education law requires that IEPs and IFSPs address evaluation at the program planning stage, evaluation is a part of the intervention plan. By planning and implementing interventions with an eye toward evaluation, the early interventionist can make the process much less time-consuming and more systematic.

A first step in evaluation is to determine who will use the information provided by the evaluation. Different target audiences want different information, so different questions must be answered. For example, if the information is to be used internally (i.e., by service coordinators working in a particular local agency), some questions that may be asked include "Are the children served making suitable progress in meeting the objectives of the program plan?" and "Are families satisfied with the behaviors of the case manager?" However, if the information is to be used externally (e.g., by state education agencies), questions such as "What is the cost-effectiveness of service delivery?" and "What percentage of children have been diagnosed with developmental disorders?" might be asked. The expectations and needs of the target audience frame the content of questions to be answered by the evaluation.

The next step in planning an evaluation is to develop a design; that is, a systematic method for determining the format of the evaluation. This step in evaluation planning is crucial, yet it often is overlooked. Major problems in evaluating the effectiveness of early intervention programs include failure to employ a systematic methodology, inadequate evaluation tools, and lack of agreement about desired outcomes (Bagnato, 2007; VanDerHeyden & Snyder, 2006). A strong, systematic evaluation design not only provides insight into the overall quality of early intervention, but also helps determine which specific components of an intervention program are most effective. The design should follow logically from the questions to be answered. Some questions, such as those relating to parental satisfaction, are best answered by simple rating scales and questionnaires. Other questions, such as those concerning a child's progress, may best be answered through a series of repeated skills tests.

Still other questions are too complex to be answered with a single methodology. For example, a case worker may want to know whether parental involvement is related to the ongoing severity of a child's impairment. This question might best be answered with a combination of methods, including natural observations, structured and unstructured interviews, rating scales, and checklists. It may be necessary to further adapt the system of evaluation to the cultural characteristics of the family; for example, the professional may consider a combination of one-on-one interviews and short questionnaires in the family's native language. In all instances, the professional should seek input from outside sources, especially community members, local advocacy groups, and other human services agencies regarding their perceptions of the program's effectiveness and sensitivity.

Conducting the Evaluation.   Once the professional has isolated the target audience, formulated evaluative questions, designed a methodology, and selected the necessary instruments, it is time to conduct the evaluation. This step consists of collecting and analyzing data gathered from responses to the evaluation questions within the framework of the selected design. For the information collected during the evaluation to be useful, the professional must ensure that it is timely, reliable, and valid. Children develop rapidly; therefore, outdated information may simply not be relevant to the needs of the child. In addition, timely information cuts through bureaucratic red tape and facilitates decision making. To be considered reliable, information must be accurate and relatively free from error. For example, an early interventionist may wish to evaluate a child's play behaviors. One method of gaining the necessary information is for the professional to ask the mother to report on her child's play behaviors. Additionally, the early interventionist may decide to observe the child playing with other children and tabulate the number of times the child displays positive play behavior in a specified time frame. To be considered valid, information must be relevant to the evaluation question and lead logically to recommendations for practice. The more information that is obtained, the more likely it is that the evaluation will be reliable and valid.

Reporting Results of the Evaluation.   The final step in program evaluation is reporting the results to the target audience. The results should be reported in a clear, succinct, and understandable manner. The report also should offer suggestions and recommendations based on the results of the data analysis. An evaluation is worthless if it does not lead to improvements in the quality of intervention. Hanson and colleagues (2006) recommend providing decision makers with a brief executive summary as a means of calling attention to the significant findings of the evaluation. Naturally, the evaluation should be objective and not influenced by the biases of the interventionists who have a stake in the findings.

It is important to keep in mind that program evaluation is a process rather than a product. Ideally, evaluation should be conducted throughout the intervention program, not just at its conclusion. The purpose of such **formative evaluation,** occurring throughout program development and implementation, is to monitor the progress of the family and child and to provide feedback to the family and interventionists on a regular basis. Formative evaluation is particularly important in refining the delivery of services during the initial stages of program implementation (Anastasiow, 1981). **Summative evaluation,** on the other hand, refers to the measurement of outcomes at the end of the program. Summative evaluation provides an estimate of the overall quality and success of the service delivery. Both formative and summative evaluations are required to accurately assess the effectiveness of an intervention program.

Both formative and summative evaluations are required to accurately assess the effectiveness of an intervention program.

SUMMARY

In this chapter, the process of intervention as it pertains to infants and young children has been discussed. At any given point in history, education and the provision of social services are governed to some extent by the prevailing philosophies and trends of the times. Naturally, notions about what constitutes best practice are constantly changing, and predicting what tomorrow's priorities will be is a bit like fortune telling. Nonetheless, a review of the literature suggests that a number of trends in practice may influence the provision of services in the next several years.

Now that early intervention is no longer a new field, as it was immediately following the passage of P.L. 99–457, a number of programs have been developed that are devoted to the systematic training of early intervention professionals. Given the critical role of the individual interventionist in ensuring the success of intervention, the importance of maintaining high-quality professional training cannot be overstated. Reflecting the shift from child-centered to family-centered services, many of these programs are attempting to teach students the skills that are most valued by families.

If current trends continue, we can anticipate that inclusion will be an important force shaping the future of intervention with young children. As was indicated earlier in the chapter, inclusion refers to full incorporation of a child with special needs into normalized settings. If it is fully implemented (as it already has been in some states), not only will inclusion change the setting in which services are likely to be provided in the future, it also will change the very nature of children's needs and the ways in which they are met. For example, the skills necessary for a child to function appropriately in a regular classroom are very different from those that are necessary to function in a self-contained classroom with only a few other children who also have special needs. To meet these changing needs, intervention programs will need to be more flexible than ever before and interventionists will be called upon to embrace a spirit of cross-discipline cooperation.

As described earlier in the chapter, some professionals are not content with the current continuum of services and argue for the abolition of all special education for children. Although most early intervention experts agree that inclusion is the goal for all children, the removal of service delivery options infringes on other ideals of early intervention, particularly the legal mandate and commitment of professionals to provide services consistent with family goals and priorities. As the inclusion debate rages on, early interventionists will be called upon to maintain a reasoned approach to the complex—and all too often political—issue of determining the most appropriate setting for service provision.

The spirit and letter of IDEA contain a mandate for service provision that crosses the boundaries of traditional professional disciplines. Increasingly, professionals have been collaborating in early intervention and this trend seems likely to continue. In particular, the collaboration between medical professionals and other professionals is likely to increase. Improvements in medicine have led not only to increased survival and improved developmental outcomes for medically fragile children, but also to an increase in the number of technology-dependent young children. Given the complexities of such cases, improved collaboration between medical and nonmedical professionals can only contribute to more effective, less fragmented service delivery for children with special needs.

Further, as the number of ethnic and language minorities increases, so will the need for cultural sensitivity in the provision of early intervention services. Recruiting early interventionists from minority populations is likely to continue to be a pressing challenge for universities and agencies. In addition, early interventionists will be called upon to develop an awareness of their own cultures and values while learning to accept and appreciate the cultures and values of others from diverse backgrounds.

The competition for the ever-shrinking public dollar has forced local and state intervention agencies to prove their effectiveness in concrete and definitive ways. As a result, outcome-based evaluation is becoming more important as agencies struggle to ensure continued funding. Because of the nature of intervention with children with special needs, such evaluation efforts are unlikely to reflect the impact of intervention in valid ways. Therefore, early interventionists must approach evaluation proactively and begin to think creatively about efficient and accurate ways of demonstrating the effectiveness of their efforts. Given the current political climate, it seems likely that concerns about accountability will shape the way professionals provide services to children and families.

Despite the complications, that young children with special needs and their families continue to benefit from intervention remains the critical consideration of early intervention services. As described by the parent of a child with disabilities, the work is, in the end, worthwhile.

> Our arrival at Peter's diagnosis of autism has been circuitous and complex, but there is accounting here, for it speaks to the hopes, dreams, and schemes Public Law 99–457 is striving to accomplish for all children and their families. Our family has crawled through an incredulous maze in the last two-and-a-half years, through black holes and windows of light, and we still have a lot of traveling to do. The importance of intervention was a turning point for us. We felt rescued. (Bowe, 1995a, p. 369)

REVIEW QUESTIONS AND DISCUSSION POINTS

1. What are the theoretical and philosophical approaches that most commonly guide intervention with children? How would intervention planning differ depending on the approach taken?
2. What are the important components of an Individualized Education Plan (IEP) and an Individualized Family Service Plan (IFSP)?
3. What factors or considerations should educators take into account when developing interventions for children with special needs?
4. The role of the family in intervention is critical. Describe ways in which interventionists can involve families in meaningful ways.
5. Describe an evaluation plan for an intervention program. Who should be involved in the evaluation? How will the focus of the evaluation be determined?

RECOMMENDED RESOURCES

Professional Associations for Intervention

The Center for Improvement of Early Reading Achievement (*www.ciera.org*) is a consortium of educators at five universities committed to sharing the latest research in effective practices in literacy education for young children.

The Division of Early Childhood of the Council for Exceptional Children (DEC) is a not-for-profit organization for professionals who work with young children with special needs and their families. Their Web site (*www.dec-sped. org*) includes position and policy statements, recommended practices, legislative updates, a calendar of training opportunities, lists of resources, and applications for memberships.

The Head Start Bureau Web site (*www.acf.hhs.gov*) provides information for parents (e.g., how to enroll your child in Head Start), as well as professionals. Information on performance standards, publications, training opportunities, grant competitions, and related resources is provided online.

The National Association for the Education of Young Children (NAEYC) is a not-for-profit organization committed to promoting excellence in early childhood education. Their Web site (*www.naeyc.org*) contains information and updates on effective practices and public policies, guidelines for quality in early childhood education, an online store, and applications for membership.

The National Child Care Information Center (*www.nccic.org*) provides information and resources in hopes of ensuring that all children have access to high quality child care and education. Its Web site includes information for parents as well as tips for professionals working with young children. Links from the site allow the browser to find out more about other programs, grant opportunities, and publications.

The National Early Childhood Technical Assistance Center (NECTAC) is funded by the U.S. Department of Education to provide information, resources, and technical assistance to professionals working in early childhood education (*www.nectac.org*).

The Parent Advocacy Center on Educational Rights (PACER) is an organization committed to providing information to parents and professionals in order to ensure that individuals with disabilities have access to appropriate opportunities, care, and education. The early childhood link from its Web site (*www.pacer.org*) includes research updates, training opportunities, and an online newsletter, *Early Childhood Connection.*

Zero to Three's Web site (*www.zerotothree.org*) contains information and resources for parents and professionals about very young children, child care, and parenting, as well as briefs on breaking research and legislative updates.

REFERENCES

Able-Boone, H., Sandall, S. R., Loughry, A., & Fredrick, L. L. (1990). An informed, family-centered approach to Public Law 99–457: Parental views. *Topics in Early Childhood Special Education, 10*(1), 100–111.

Alberto, P. A., & Troutman, A. C. (2003). *Applied behavior analysis for teachers.* (6th ed.). Upper Saddle River, NJ: Pearson Education.

Anastasiow, N. J. (1981). *Socioemotional development.* San Francisco: Jossey-Bass.

Bagnato, S. (2005). The authentic alternative for assessment in early intervention: An emerging evidence-based practice. *Journal of Early Intervention, 28*(1), 17–22.

Bagnato, S. (2007). *Authentic assessment for early childhood intervention: Best practices.* New York: Guilford Press.

Bailey, D. B. (2001). Evaluating parent involvement and family support in early intervention and preschool programs. *Journal of Early Intervention, 24,* 1–14.

Bailey, D. B., Bruder, M. B., Hebbeler, K., Carta, J., Defosset, M., Greenwood, C., et al. (2006). Recommended outcomes for families of young children with disabilities. *Journal of Early Intervention, 28*(4), 227–251.

Bailey, D. B., Buysse, V., Edmondson, R., & Smith, T. M. (1992). Creating family-centered services in early intervention: Perceptions of professionals in four states. *Exceptional Children, 58*(4), 298–309.

Barnett, D., & Carey, K. T. (1992). *Designing interventions for preschool learning and behavior problems.* San Francisco: Jossey-Bass.

Bowe, F. G. (1995a). *Birth to five: Early childhood special education.* New York: Delmar.

Bredekamp, S. (1993). The relationship between early childhood education and early childhood special education: Healthy marriage or family feud. *Topics in Early Childhood Special Education, 13,* 258–273.

Bredekamp, S., & Copple, C. (1997). *Developmentally appropriate practice in early childhood programs.* Washington, DC National Association for the Education of Young Children.

Bricker, D. (1989). *Early intervention for at-risk and handicapped infants, toddlers, and preschool children* (2nd ed.). Palo Alto, CA: VORT Corp.

Bricker, D., & Cripe, J. J. (1998). *An activity-based approach to early intervention.* Baltimore: Brookes.

Bronfenbrenner, U. (1986). Ecology of the family as a context for human development: Research perspectives. *Developmental Psychologist, 22,* 723–742.

Brown, F., Evans, I. M., Weed, K. A., & Owen, V. (1987). Delineating functional competencies: A component approach. *Journal of the Association for Persons with Severe Handicaps, 12*(2), 117–124.

Brown, R. W., & Lenneberg, E. (1965). Studies in linguistic relativity. In H. Proshansky & B. Seidenberg (Eds.), *Basic studies in social psychology* (pp. 244–252). New York: Holt, Rinehart, and Winston.

Bruder, M. B., & Dunst, C. J. (2005). Personnel preparation in recommended early intervention practices: Degree of emphasis across disciplines. *Topics in Early Childhood Special Education, 25*(1), 25–33.

Burton, C. B., Haines, A. H., & Hanline, M. F. (1992). Early childhood intervention and education: The urgency of professional unification. *Topics in Early Childhood Special Education, 11,* 53–69.

Buysse, V., Bernier, K., & McWilliam, R. (2002). A statewide profile of early intervention services using the Part C data system. *Journal of Early Intervention, 25*(1), 15–26.

Caro, P., & Derevensky, J. L. (1991). Family-focused intervention models: Implementation and research findings. *Topics in Early Childhood Special Education, 11*(3), 66–80.

Carta, J. J., Greenwood, C. R., Luze, G. J., Cline, G., & Kuntz, S. (2004). Developing a general outcome measure of growth in social skills for infants and toddlers. *Journal of Early Intervention, 26*, 91–114.

Carta, J. J., Greenwood, C. R., Walker, D., Kaminski, R., Good, R., McConnell, S., et al. (in press). Individual growth and development indicators: Assessment that guides intervention for young children. In M. Ostrosky & E. Horn, (Eds.), *Assessment: Gathering meaningful information.* The *Young Exceptional Children Monograph* Series # 4. Longmount, CO: Sporis West.

Carta, J. J., Schwartz, I. S., Atwater, J. B., & McConnell, S. R. (1991). Developmentally appropriate practice: Appraising its usefulness for young children with disabilities. *Topics in Early Childhood Special Education, 11*(1), 1–20.

Coleman, M.R., Buysse, V., & Neitzel, J. (2006). Recognition and response: An early intervening system for young children at-risk for learning disabilities. Chapel Hill: University of North Carolina at Chapel Hill, FPG Child Development Institute.

Dempsey, I., & Dunst, C. J. (2004). Helpgiving styles and parent empowerment in families with a young child with a disability. *Journal of Intellectual and Developmental Disability, 29*(1), 40–51.

Dunst, C. J. (2002). Family-centered practices: Birth through high school. *The Journal of Special Education, 36*(3), 139–147.

Dunst, C. J. (1985). Rethinking early intervention. *Analysis and Intervention in Developmental Disabilities, 5*, 165–201.

Dunst, C. J., Bruder, M. B., Trivette, C. M., & Hamby, D. W. (2006). Everyday activity settings, natural learning environments, and early intervention practices. *Journal of Policy and Practice in Intellectual Disabilities, 3*(1), 3–10.

Dunst, C. J., Hamby, D., Trivette, C. M., Raab, M., & Bruder, M. B. (2000). Everyday family and community life and children's naturally occurring opportunities. *Journal of Early Intervention, 23*, 151–164.

Floyd, R. G., Hojnoski, R., & Key, J. (2006). Preliminary evidence of the technical adequacy of the preschool numeracy indicators. *School Psychology Review, 35*(4), 627–644.

Foster, M., Berger, M., & McLean, M. (1981). Rethinking a good idea: A reassessment of family involvement. *Topics in Early Childhood Special Education, 1*, 55–65.

Frisby, C. L. (1992). Issues and problems in the influence of culture on the psychoeducational needs of African-American children. *School Psychology Review, 21*(4), 532–551.

Green, J. W. (1982). *Cultural awareness in the human services.* Upper Saddle River, NJ: Prentice Hall.

Greenwood, C. R., Luze, G. J., Cline, G., Kuntz, S., & Leitschuh, C. (2002). Developing a general outcome measure of growth in movement for infants and toddlers. *Topics in Early Childhood Special Education, 22*, 143–157.

Greenwood, C. R., Walker, D., Carta, J. J., & Higgins, S. K. (2006). Developing a general outcome measure of growth in the cognitive abilities of children 1 to 4 years old: The early problem-solving indicator. *School Psychology Review 35*(4), 535–551.

Guralnick, M. J., & Albertini, G. (2006). Early intervention in an international perspective. *Journal of Policy and Practice in Intellectual Disabilities, 3*(1), 1–2.

Hanson, K., Morrow, C., & Bandstra, E. (2006). Early interventions with young children and their parents in the US: *Enhancing the well-being of children and families through effective interventions: International evidence for practice* (pp. 58–69). London, England: Jessica Kingsley Publishers.

Hanson, M. (1987). *Teaching the infant with Down syndrome: A guide for parents and professionals.* Austin, TX: PRO-ED.

Hanson, M. J., Lynch, E. W., & Wayman, K. (1990). Honoring the cultural diversity of families when gathering data. *Teaching of Exceptional Children in Special Education, 10*(1), 112–131.

Harry, B. (2002). Trends and issues in serving culturally diverse families of children with disabilities. *The Journal of Special Education, 36*(3), 138–147.

Hart, B., & Risley, T. R. (1975). Incidental teaching of language in the preschool. *Journal of Applied Behavior Analysis, 8*, 411–420.

Heward, W. L. (2005). *Exceptional children* (8th ed.). Upper Saddle River, NJ: Merrill/Prentice Hall.

Jacobs, G. M. (2001). Providing the scaffold: A model for early childhood/primary teacher preparation. *Early Childhood Education Journal, 29*(2), 125–130.

Jalongo, M. R., & Isenberg, J. P. (2008). *Exploring your role: An introduction to early childhood education* (3rd ed.). Upper Saddle River, NJ: Pearson, Merrill, Prentice Hall.

Johnson, B. H., Kaufman, R. K., & McGonigel, M. J. (1989). *Guidelines and recommended practices for the Individualized*

Family Service Plan. Bethesda, MD: Association for the Care of Children's Health.

LaParo, K. M., Sexton, D., & Snyder, P. (1998). Program quality characteristics in segregated and inclusive early childhood settings. *Early Childhood Research Quarterly, 13*, 151–167.

Luze, G. J., Linebarger, D. L., Greenwood, C. R., Carta, J. J., Walker, D., Leitschuh, C., et al. (2001). Developing a general outcome measure of growth in expressive communication of infants and toddlers. *School Psychology Review, 30*, 383–406.

Lynch, E. W., & Hanson, M. J. (1998). *Developing cross-cultural competence: A guide for working with young children and their families*. Baltimore: Brookes.

Lynch, E. W., & Hanson, M. J. (2004). *Understanding families: Approaches to diversity, disability, and risk*. Baltimore, MD: Brookes.

Margalit, M., Al-Yagon, M., & Kleitman, T. (2006). Family subtyping and early intervention. *Journal of Policy and Practice in Intellectual Disabilities, 3*(1), 33–41.

McWilliam, R. A., & Bailey, D. B. (1994). Predictors of service delivery models in center-based early intervention. *Exceptional Children, 61*(1), 56–71.

McWilliam, R. A., Tocci, L., & Harbin, G. L. (1998). Family-centered services: Service providers' discourse and behavior. *Topics in Early Childhood Special Education, 18*(4), 206–221.

Missall, K. N., McConnell, S. R., & Cardigan, K. (2006). Early literacy development: Skill growth and relations between classroom variables for preschool children. *Journal of Early Intervention, 29*(1), 1–21.

Murphy, D. L., Lee, I. M., Turnbull, A., & Turbiville, V. (1995). The Family-Centered Program Rating Scale: An instrument for program evaluation and change. *Journal of Early Intervention, 19*(6), 24–42.

Rathus, S. A. (2006). *Childhood: Voyages in development* (2nd ed.). Belmont, CA: Pearson, Thompson, Wadsworth.

Research and Policy Committee of the Committee for Economic Development. (1987). *Children in need: Investment strategies for the educationally disadvantaged*. New York: Author.

Rhodes, W. C., & Tracey, M. C. (1972). *A study of child variance: Intervention* (Vol. 2). Ann Arbor: University of Michigan Press.

Richmond, J., & Ayoub, C. (1993). Evolution of early intervention philosophy. In D. M. Bryant & M. A. Graham (Eds.), *Implementing early intervention: From research to effective practice*. New York: Guilford Press.

Rogers-Warren, A., & Warren, S. (1980). Mands for verbalization: Facilitating the generalization of newly trained language in children. *Behavior Modification, 4*, 220–245.

Sameroff, A., & Chandler, M. J. (1975). Reproductive risk and the continuum of caretaking casuality. In F. D. Horowitz, M. Hetherington, S. Scarr-Salapetek, & G. Seigal (Eds.), *Review of Child Development Research* (pp. 187–244). Chicago: University of Chicago Press.

Sandall, S., Hemmeter, M. L., Smith, B. J., & McLean, M. E. (2005). *DEC-recommended practices: A comprehensive guide*. Longmont, CO: Sopris West.

Sattler, J., & Hoge, R. D. (2006). *Assessment of children: Behavioral, social and clinical foundations* (5th ed.). San Diego, CA: Author.

Scarborough, A., Spiker, D., Mallik, S., Hebbeler, K., Bailey, D., & Simeonsson, R. (2004). A national look at children and families entering early intervention. *Exceptional Children, 70*(4), 469–483.

Smith, B. J., Miller, P. S., & Bredekamp, S. (1998). Sharing responsibility: DEC, NAEYC, and Vygotsky-based practices for quality inclusion. *Young Exceptional Children, 2*(1), 11–21.

Snyder, S., & Sheehan, R. (1993). *Family-centered early intervention with infants and toddlers: Innovative cross-disciplinary approaches*. Baltimore: Brookes.

Stainback, S., & Stainback, W. (1992). *Curriculum considerations in inclusive classrooms: Facilitating learning for all students*. Baltimore: Brookes.

Suran, B. G., & Rizzo, J. V. (1979). *Special children: An integrative approach*. Glenville, IL: Scott, Foresman.

Turnbull, A. P., Turnbull, H. R., Shank, M., & Leal, D. (2002). *Exceptional lives: Special education in today's schools*. Upper Saddle River, NJ: Prentice Hall.

Turnbull, S. K., & Turnbull, J. M. (1986). *Families, professionals, and exceptionality: A special partnership*. Upper Saddle River, NJ: Merrill/Prentice Hall.

U. S. Bureau of the Census. (1990). *Characteristics of the population: Vol. 1*. Washington, DC: United States Department of Commerce.

VanDerHeyden, A. M., Broussard, C., Fabre, M., Stanley, J., Legendte, J., & Creppel, R. (2004). Development and validation of curriculum-based measures of math performance for four-year-old children. *Journal of Early Intervention, 27*, 27–41.

VanDerHeyden, A. M., & Snyder, P. (2006). Integrating frameworks from early childhood intervention and school psychology to accelerate growth for all young children. *School Psychology Review, 35*(4), 519–534.

Wolery, M. & Wilburs, J. S. (1994). Introduction to the inclusion of young children with special needs in early childhood programs. In M. Wolery & J. S. Wilburs (Ed.). *Including children with special needs in early childhood programs* (pp. 1–22) Washington, DC: National Association for the Education of Young Children.

Wolery, M., Holcombe, A., & Werts, M. G. (1994). Effects of simultaneous prompting and instructive feedback. *Early Education and Development, 5,* 176.

Wolery, M., Werts, M. G., & Holcombe, A. (1993). Instructive feedback: A comparison of simultaneous and alternating presentation of non-target stimuli. *Journal of Behavioral Education, 3,* 187–204.

Wong, S. W., & Hughes, J. N. (2006). Ethnicity and language contributions to dimensions of parent involvment. *School Psychology Review, 35*(4), 645–662.

Woodruff, G., & Shelton, T. (2006). The transdisciplinary approach to early intervention. In G. M. Foley & J. Hochman (Eds.), *Mental health in early intervention: Achieving unity in principles and practice* (pp. 81–110). Baltimore: Brookes.

Partnerships with Families

Zolinda Stoneman, Mary E. Rugg,
and Katy Gregg

Chapter Outline

- Parent Emotions, Beliefs, and Parent-to-Parent Support
- Family-Centered Processes
- The Family as a System
- Factors That Influence the Family System
- Natural Environments as Sources of Everyday Learning Opportunities
- Skills for Effective Work in Partnership with Families
- Desired Family Outcomes

Tonya and Her Family

Tonya and her mother, Sheila, live in a mobile home in a rural area. Tonya, who is almost 3 years old, has two older sisters and a younger brother. Sheila works at a pancake restaurant from noon until eight in the evening, 5 days a week. While she is at work, her mother takes care of Tonya and her younger brother. The two older girls are in school during the day and are dropped off at their grandmother's house after school. Sheila picks up all of the children when she gets off work. On her days off, she is very busy doing laundry, grocery shopping, and taking care of the children. Tonya has large, bright eyes and a wonderful smile. She is quite delayed in her development. She does not yet walk. She makes sounds, but has no real words.

Tonya has received early intervention services since she was 14 months old. Parent to Parent connected Sheila with another single parent with a child with a substantial delay. When Sheila gets tired or discouraged, the two mothers talk on the phone and Sheila usually feels better. An early interventionist comes to Sheila's home on Saturday afternoons, one of Sheila's days off. She has helped Sheila think of ways that the limited time she has with Tonya can be the most fun for both of them, while, at the same time, teaching Tonya new skills. Sheila has learned to play sound games with Tonya when she bathes her and to help Tonya with her fine motor skills at mealtime. The interventionist helped Sheila find ways to incorporate all of her children into activities with Tonya so that the siblings would develop a close relationship with her. The interventionist also visits Tonya at her grandmother's home. She has arranged for Tonya to attend a local daycare center in the fall. The early interventionist is working with Sheila, the daycare provider, and with a physical therapist and speech-language therapist to create a developmentally stimulating inclusive preschool program for Tonya.

Families are the first and most important teachers of children. The family is responsible for the care of the child with a disability before interventionists, teachers, or therapists become involved with the child, and the family will remain the dominant force in the child's life long after these service providers have moved on to work with other children and families. Early interventionists are part of the child's life for a few years; families have a lifelong commitment. Bruder (2000) captured this thought when she wrote, "We must always remember that the children we serve belong to their families, and we are privileged to be in their lives for a short time" (p. 110).

When using a family-
centered approach,
providers recognize that
the family is the most
important decision maker
in the child's life and
respect the uniqueness of
each family and child.

For many years, educators and other professionals emphasized parent involvement in infant and preschool programs. Parents were encouraged to attend
educational and support-oriented meetings, to assist the teacher in the preschool
classroom, to implement intervention programs at home, and to provide information
about the child and family to professional staff. It was believed that involving parents
would serve the best interests of young children. These approaches to parent involvement retained professional control of services and programmatic decisions. In
recent years, there has been a dramatic change in the role of families in programs for
young children with disabilities. Parents, once seen as only "information providers,"
are now actively involved as decision makers (Blue-Banning, Summers, Frankland,
Nelson, & Beegle, 2004). An emphasis on parent involvement has helped pave the
way to a **family-centered approach,** in which families have the power to direct the
services that they—and their children—receive.

Changes in the role of families were the direct result of federal legislation.
When P.L. 99–457 was enacted into law in 1986, the role of families in the development and implementation of programs for young children with disabilities was
radically enhanced. Reauthorizations of this Act (e.g., P.L. 108–446; Individuals
with Disabilities Education Improvement Act [IDEA], 2004) have further codified
into law the central role of families in their children's early intervention programs.
The family is formally recognized as the most important constant in each child's life,
and the family environment as the richest context for social, emotional, cognitive,
and physical development. The role of the service delivery system is seen to be that
of supporting the family.

For children from birth through 2 years, served by Part C of IDEA, the individualized family service plan (IFSP) expands the intervention focus to include
families. A requirement of IDEA is that families are invited to be a member of the
team that develops the IFSP. Further, to facilitate this requirement, families are
asked for input regarding their priorities and concerns. Families have the options
of having their needs addressed in the IFSP, assisting in identifying the natural environments in which interventions will be delivered, reviewing the IFSP every 6
months, and declining or accepting early intervention services offered to the family and child. Families must be informed in writing before any change is made to the
child's services.

Part B of IDEA, which focuses on services to preschool children (aged 3
through 5) with disabilities, also stresses the important roles to be played by families. Parents of preschool children are given a significant role in the design and evaluation of services provided to their children, making them partners with the schools
in developing individualized education plans (IEPs). Parents are to be included as
members of teams making decisions about eligibility and placement of the child, as
well as members of the team developing the IEP. Parents must agree to and sign the
IEP. Due process and mediation procedures are in place if families disagree with the
IEP or with the child's placement. Both Part C and Part B of IDEA place strong emphasis on families and on family involvement in the early intervention process.

For a family-centered approach to become a reality, early intervention professionals must be sensitive to parent emotions and beliefs, embrace family-centered
values, understand family systems, appreciate factors that influence the family

system including family diversity, support learning in the natural environments experienced by families, work in partnership with families, and understand desired family outcomes. This chapter is organized around these themes.

:: PARENT EMOTIONS, BELIEFS, AND PARENT-TO-PARENT SUPPORT

The birth or diagnosis of a child with a disability is usually an unexpected life event. For many years, professionals focused only on the negative responses of families. Grief or mourning have often been addressed as a common response to learning that a child has a disability, due in part to cultural norms that maintain health and ablebodiness as necessary for happiness and acceptance (Partington, 2002). Grief has sometimes been viewed as the result of a family's attempt to cope with the loss of the "perfect" child they anticipated during pregnancy (O'Brien, 2007). Other parental responses that are viewed as negative include denial, blame, fear, guilt, grief, withdrawal, and rejection (Beaumont, 2006; Poehlmann, Clements, Abbeduto & Farsad, 2005). Scorgie and Sobsey (2000) caution that interventionists should avoid "catastrophizing" the effects of disability on the family. Although the initial re-action to the news is negative for many families, most families move on with their lives, accepting the child in her uniqueness. Scorgie and Sobsey found that for many families, the presence of a child with a disability is "transformational," accompanied by positive changes in the lives of individual family members and the family as a unit.

Family members vary in their initial response to diagnosis or birth of a child with a disability, and responses can change over time. There is no one correct reac-tion. Services and levels of involvement that are necessary at one stage of coping or decision making may be experienced as unnecessary, intrusive, or disrespectful at another stage. For example, some parents may be highly active and involved in planning and decision making immediately following the initial diagnosis of a dis-ability and later wish to alter their roles to allow them more time to focus on other aspects of their child's life. Other parents may withdraw after the initial diagnosis and want more time to make decisions or define their roles. These parents may gradually increase their levels of involvement with the service system over time.

Developmental milestones that provide a sense of accomplishment and satis-faction for family members, such as self-feeding, walking, talking, and toilet train-ing, may be delayed or never occur for children with disabilities, sometimes renewing parents' feelings of sadness or grief. Service providers must be careful to monitor such changes and adjust their roles accordingly. It is clear that not all fam-ilies are alike and that it is inappropriate to make assumptions about what families (or individual members of a family) are feeling or experiencing without talking with them and listening to their personal stories.

Parents often form their expectations for their children based on "facts" given to them by doctors, interventionists, and various other professionals. This is particu-larly true during infancy and early childhood. It is frequently the case, however, that unambiguous answers regarding the implications of the disability for the child's health or development are not available. These situations can be particularly difficult for families. In the past, many service providers have presented worst-case scenarios in order to prepare families for what might lay ahead. Although intended to save the family pain or disappointment later, this practice can limit child outcomes by creating self-fulfilling prophecies and can jeopardize the formation of healthy attachments in the family. Service providers must be straightforward regarding the limitations of available knowledge and provide parents and other family members the opportunity to talk about the challenges associated with living with a level of uncertainty. This should be a clear goal of any service provider.

Parents of children with disabilities face demands associated with parenting typically developing children, as well as additional challenges posed by parenting a child with a disability. The first choice of support for many parents of young children with disabilities is other parents in similar situations (Fox, Vaughn, Wyatte, & Dunlap, 2002). **Parent-to-parent programs** began in the early 1970s to meet this need and quickly expanded across the nation. The success of these programs is based on the personalized support offered by well-trained "veteran" parents who have children with similar disabilities and share similar life experiences (Beach Center on Disability, 2007; Santelli, Turnbull, Marquis, & Lerner, 2000). The emotional support and information received by the family reduces isolation and supports active decision making.

Parent-to-parent programs: "Veteran" parents provide support and encouragement for parents who are raising a child with a disability for the first time.

:: FAMILY-CENTERED PROCESSES

Implementing family-centered approaches to intervention requires a dramatic shift in the way many professionals think about families. To be successful, the interventionist must hold a set of attitudes, or values, that place the needs and desires of the family at the center of the intervention process. This value system is counter to the

Scott Cunningham/Merrill

Parents should be encouraged to take a leadership role on the intervention team.

child-centered approach historically endorsed by early intervention professionals, regardless of disciplinary background. Family-centered approaches require that professionals relinquish the "expert" role, creating instead a partnership with families in which both the professionals and the family members bring knowledge and expertise into the collaborative relationship.

Six primary values underlie family-centered early intervention.

1. Interventionists take time to get to know the family.
2. Family strengths are identified and emphasized.
3. Families are actively included in planning and decision making.
4. Services and supports are developed for the whole family, not just for the child.
5. Family priorities guide intervention goals and services.
6. The preference of the family concerning their level of participation is respected.

These values are discussed in the following sections.

Interventionists Take Time to Get to Know the Family

Before any formal assessments are made, before strengths can be identified, and before discussing potential services, the early intervention provider first needs to acquire a comprehensive understanding of the family and how it operates. For example, the early intervention provider in the opening vignette who is working with Tonya and her family may not have known about the grandmother's involvement and support without first listening to and talking with Sheila. Utilizing a family-centered approach requires that the provider first gain a thorough understanding of the child and the family. In this way, the interventionist can be more effective in finding supports for the family as well as in assisting the family to discover home learning opportunities for their child. It is essential for the interventionist to talk with the family in order to discover what the child's interests are and to discuss the child's motivations (Raab & Dunst, 2006). This makes it easier for the provider and family to integrate the child's favorite activities, toys, songs, games, and other preferences into learning opportunities.

Asking the family questions such as "How would you describe your child [and family]?" creates opportunities to see life through the family's eyes. Rugg (2004) suggests asking the family to discuss their hopes and dreams for their child in order to immediately get everybody involved in the child's life starting on a positive note. Responses to these questions and to follow up questions can provide insight into how the family currently interacts with the child. These responses also have the potential to inform the provider about how the family members care for and respond to the child prior to implementing suggestions that might change the family's current routines. When first interacting with a family, a conversation with the family members is a more comfortable and unbiased approach to discovering what the child already knows and what the family believes about their child's development than any assessment form or survey. In what ways is the family already using household items to interact with their child? What are some new connections that the family can be making? (Raab, 2003). For example, Sheila always thought that bath time with Tonya was such a chore. By talking with Sheila, the provider discovered that Tonya might be picking up on her mom's stress during bath time and becoming upset and resistant. Together they came up with ways to make bath time more fun for both mother and daughter.

Sandall & Ostrosky (2000) cite a service provider who has families ask themselves, "Is this routine working for my family? If not, what might make it easier or less stressful?" (p. 20). Questions such as these allow the interventionist to understand the family's perception of areas in which they need assistance. Bernheimer and Weisner (2007) suggest that one of the best ways to understand family adaptations and needs is to ask a parent to describe, in detail, the activities of a typical day, starting when the child wakes up in the morning and ending when the parents go to bed at night. They note that this is a more natural way of communicating with parents than directly asking about family needs, strengths, or administering family assessments. Creative solutions to challenging times during the day may include accompanying the parent and child to the grocery store and guiding the parent in ways to interact with the child in a positive fashion during this time of day. When Sheila's interventionist spent time with her and asked her to describe a typical day, the struggles that she was having with Tonya over bath time emerged as an area of frustration for Sheila and presented an opportunity for intervention.

Getting to know the family is important for discovering how different family members interact with the child. This may take place through speaking with family members individually, as a group, or by observing members interacting with the child (Center for Evidence-Based Research Practices, 2003). More generally, the intervention can build on how family members respond to their child/siblings and their level of parental sensitivity (Dunst & Kassow, 2004).

Family Strengths Are Identified and Emphasized

Family-centered early interventionists actively seek to identify and build on the assets and strengths of the families whom they serve. They focus their attention on learning about positive aspects of the family and reflecting back to the family the strengths of the family unit as well as the strengths and assets of the child with a disability. All families have strengths. All children, regardless of the severity of their disabilities, have strengths. Focusing on strengths does not mean that the interventionist denies or ignores the struggles and needs of the family. Rather, these challenges are addressed in the context of the strengths possessed by the family in order to meet and overcome the challenges.

Whereas the traditional intervention approach has often focused on the identification and remediation of deficits, the family-centered approach utilizes a positive focus in partnering with families. One tool that can assist the interventionist in identifying strengths is the Take a Look At Me™ Portfolio (Rugg, 2004). The portfolio provides a template on which family members can share thoughts, photos, and words to describe their child and family. The portfolio process encourages family members to observe their child in the home and community to determine and highlight their child's strengths, interests, hopes, and dreams. The completed portfolio can present a positive, holistic picture of the child and family that focuses on strengths.

Just as it is true that all families have strengths, it is also true that there are no perfect families. Consider, for a moment, your family of origin. Think about the feelings that would have been aroused in you and in your family if an interventionist had entered your home and talked with you about the things that were "wrong" about how your family was living: Too much fighting in front of the children? Meals consisting of too many unhealthy foods? Television playing too loudly for too many hours? Children staying up too late at night? Then, think about the effect of the same interventionist noting positive aspects of your family. Thinking back to Tonya, Sheila, and their family, what are some of the strengths that the interventionist might note? Grandparents are available to care for the children, as needed. Sheila clearly loves her children. The mother and the siblings are involved in Tonya's learning environment at home. Positive communications between the interventionist and the family, focusing on family strengths, set the tone for collaboration and partnership. Every person and every family wants to be valued and to be acknowledged as having a positive contribution to make.

For some families, strengths are easy to identify; for other families, strengths are less obvious. To see the strengths of some families, professionals must shift their concentration from the more obvious problems and risk factors and use a new "strengths-focused lens." With a family-centered focus, it is possible to discover strengths and assets in the most challenging family situations. Werner and Smith (1982, 1992), in their classic studies of resilient families and resilient children in Kauai, identified numerous strengths that helped families rear competent children in the face of adversity, including the following:

- One or more caring adults(s) were present in the child's life.
- Adults encouraged trust, independence, and initiative.
- There were clear and consistent rules and structure in the home.
- Parenting was characterized by warmth and high expectations.
- Harmony existed between parents and caregivers.
- Parents and caregivers possessed positive mental and emotional health.
- Families were stable over time.
- Kin and neighbors were available for emotional support.
- Family values were shared.
- There was a sense of family oneness.
- Strong, positive sibling relationships were intact.

These and other strengths, when identified and nurtured, form a foundation for successful interventions with families.

Families Are Actively Included in Planning and Decision Making

In family-centered programs, families hold the power to make key decisions about their children. Professionals believe that families are capable of making wise and responsible decisions about their children and about the family as a whole. Parents are encouraged to take a leadership role on the intervention team (Blue-Banning et al., 2004), rather than acting as passive participants. Family decisions are respected, even when they conflict with professional recommendations. Families are provided with the information and resources they need to make informed decisions. Further, and of major importance, information is provided in a manner that is culturally relevant for the family.

To make decisions, families need choices. Too often, the service options available to families are very limited (Hanson et al., 2000). Consider the example of a family of a 2-year-old child served in a Part C program. This family wants their child to be in an inclusive preschool program as the child ages and moves into the Part B early childhood special education system. However, the Part B program in their community administers only segregated programs. Under the old service model, the family would be told that an inclusive preschool was not an option. To continue to receive services after the child turned 3 years old, the family would have to accept a placement in one of the special education programs operated by the system. The interventionist working with Sheila, following a family-centered service delivery model, pursued the placement that she thought was in Tonya's best interests. From this perspective, she engaged in creative problem solving by working with Sheila and a local childcare center to develop an inclusive preschool placement for Tonya. In addition, when the interventionist makes a recommendation, she should make the rationale for that recommendation clear to the family.

Services and Supports Are Developed for the Whole Family

Supporting the whole family, including the mother, father, siblings, and extended family members, recognizes that family members are interdependent and that the development of the child is enhanced when the family is strong and when all members' needs are respected. It is unrealistic to expect that early interventionists will solve all of the family's problems or meet the needs of every family member. Early interventionists are not omnipotent. It is realistic, however, for early interventionists to serve as facilitators, connecting families to resources and assisting them in developing creative solutions to problems and needs. This includes helping families to use the resources of their natural circle of support (e.g., friends, relatives, clergy) to assist the family in achieving its goals. It also can include helping families expand these informal natural supports, linking them to others in the community who can provide support and assistance.

Family Priorities Guide Intervention Goals and Services

In family-centered early intervention programs, services reflect the choices and preferences of families and are tailored to their needs. Every child and every family is unique. The interventionist understands that two families with the same identified needs may prioritize these needs differently and may desire very different approaches to meet the needs (Shonkoff & Phillips, 2000). Each family's unique characteristics are revealed as families have the opportunity to be actively involved in all aspects of their child's program, including assessment, developing goals for the IFSP or IEP, selecting appropriate services and service providers, implementing the intervention, and evaluating intervention outcomes. The interventionist works with parents to generate intervention options and lets the family decide which options best fit their resources and desires (Dabkowski, 2004).

The Preferred Level of Family Participation Is Respected

Some families prefer to be actively involved in all aspects of their child's program; others want professionals to plan and implement the intervention with little family involvement. In family-centered intervention programs, all families are given the option of controlling their child's program. However, not all families want this level of responsibility. The extent to which families choose to engage in intervention activities varies greatly; the level also may change over time. For example, some parents may decline a particular service in order to have time for the family to participate in much-needed recreation or leisure or to engage in other nondisability-related activities. The importance of such activities for the resilience and well-being of all family members is recognized and their choices are validated.

Family members may choose to have very limited participation in their child's program. This does not necessarily imply that they are "bad" or "uninterested." Interventionists are respectful of family routines and commitments, scheduling evening meetings, weekend home visits, or whatever is needed to accommodate the family's schedule (Blue-Banning et al., 2004; Sebald & Luckner, 2007). Families are never pressured into any choice of services or denied those services at a later date if their needs or choices change.

:: THE FAMILY AS A SYSTEM

In addition to adopting a family-centered values base, it is important that early interventionists appreciate the systemic nature of the family. A family is more than a collection of individual members. **Family systems theory** (Broderick & Smith, 1979; von Bertalanffy, 1968) recognizes that there are complex interconnections among family members. In the family system, many roles and rules guide individual and family functioning. Within the larger system of the family are subsystems made up of smaller groups of family members. For instance, there may be a husband and wife subsystem, a parent and child subsystem, a grandparent and parent subsystem, and a sibling subsystem all within the same family.

Each family subsystem influences other subsystems and the family as a whole. Thus, change or intervention in one part of the family can positively or negatively affect the entire family (Minuchin, 1974). "Each family member influences the family as a whole. To separate one from another is like trying to put together a puzzle without all the pieces" (Beach Center on Families and Disability, 1997). A change in the relationship between the parent and one child, for example, might also affect the parents' marriage and the sibling relationship. Similarly, when events impact one

Family systems theory: Multiple subsystems make up the family, including parents, children, siblings, and extended family.

family member, all family members are affected in some way. If, for example, Tonya's mother were to lose her job, every member of the family would be affected.

This conceptualization of the family as a system is important when intervention programs for young children are being planned. Interventions designed to help children learn, for example, can have unintentional negative effects if those interventions create stress or conflict in the family. Expecting parents to perform painful physical exercises with their child or to implement certain demanding behavior modification strategies or intensive educational strategies may have short-term benefits for the child. In the long term, however, the developmental progress of the child may be compromised by the stress and conflict created in the child's family by these demands.

Service providers who wish to deliver the most appropriate and helpful services to families of children with disabilities must spend time talking with all available family members in an informal, open, and respectful manner before suggesting interventions. Fialka (2001) suggests asking the family a series of questions when discussing possible in-home interventions: "How will this disrupt or change your life?" "How will this complicate your daily living?" "What do I need to understand from your side as the parent?" (p. 26). In general, families will be more open to suggestions, interventions, and changes that closely fit their already established values and behaviors.

Parental Roles

Young children can place heavy time demands and role restrictions on families, including feeding, bathing, and dressing; the time demands of parenting can be intensified when a child has a disability. These added role responsibilities fall disproportionately on mothers (Curran, Sharples, White, & Knapp, 2001; Hauser-Cram, Warfield, Shonkoff, & Krauss, 2001; Porterfield, 2002). It is important to note, however, that in some couples, the father is the primary caregiver of the child. Single fathers are the head of household in other families. Parents of children with disabilities often are expected to be educators, speech therapists, physical therapists, medical technicians, advocates, and service planners, and to fill numerous other roles not usually assumed by parents of typically developing children. Parents are asked by interventionists to perform these roles, sometimes to the exclusion of the primary and most important role of all parents: that of nurturer.

One of the most important roles of early interventionists is to support positive, developmentally enhancing relationships between parents and their young children with disabilities. Trivette (2003) analyzed multiple early intervention outcome studies and found that enhanced parental responsiveness can positively influence early childhood development in cognitive and social-emotional domains. Responsive parent–child interactions can be disrupted by many factors, including parent stress or fatigue, hard-to-interpret child cues, lack of responsiveness from the child with a disability, absence of positive parenting models, and lack of parenting information or skill. Parent responsiveness includes behaviors such as turn-taking, expressions of warmth, responding to the child's vocalizations, using the child's interests to guide the interaction, sensitivity to the child's cues, and minimal use of directives or

Courtesy of Lisa Harris

Siblings can be a positive factor in young children with special needs.

commands. Intervention based on enhancing these parenting behaviors is often termed **relationship-focused early intervention** (Mahoney & Perales, 2005).

Early interventionists often use the term *parents* when, in practice, they usually mean *mothers* (Porterfield, 2002; Turbiville & Marquis, 2001). It is not uncommon for interventionists to never meet the child's father, even if he is living in the home and is actively involved in the care of his child. Turbiville and Marquis (2001) suggest that early interventionists often are not well prepared to work with mothers and are even less prepared to work with fathers. It is vital that fathers be supported in their efforts to participate in their child's intervention, consistent with their preferred roles or level of involvement. This may mean scheduling meetings when fathers can attend or communicating directly with fathers over the phone rather than immediately asking to speak with the mother. It also may mean planning activities that can be shared by both parents.

> Relationship-focused early intervention involves providing parents with techniques to enhance their responsiveness to child-directed behaviors.

Marital Roles

In two-parent families, parents are partners with each other as well as with their children. The relationship between parents is an important predictor of overall family functioning. A positive marital relationship and positive coping strategies have been found to be associated with less familial stress in families with children with disabilities (Gavidia-Payne & Stoneman, 2006). The importance of the marital relationship must be recognized. Service providers should support the maintenance of healthy marital partnerships through provision of services such as respite care, which allows the couple to spend time away from parenting duties. Some marriages experience additional stressors related to parenting a child with a disability. It is important to recognize, however, that many marriages are not adversely affected by disability and many even become stronger (O'Brien, 2007). For single parents, it is important to recognize the parent's need for time away from child-related responsibilities and to support the parent in maintaining a healthy network of social relationships. Supporting positive relationships between family co-caregivers is important regardless of the composition or lifestyle of the family.

Sibling Roles

Brothers and sisters are an important part of the lives of children with disabilities, but they also need to be celebrated for their uniqueness and individual successes outside of disability-related activities.

Brothers and sisters serve as teachers, caretakers, friends, and playmates to each other. The relationships between the siblings in families of children with disabilities are similar to all sibling relationships. Few differences have been found in the levels of play, social activities, or conflicts (Stoneman, 2005). It is important for families and early interventionists to recognize the needs of siblings, and to avoid an exclusive focus on the child with the disability or disability-related issues and activities. Children without disabilities need the freedom and the support from their families to pursue their own interests and activities. Siblings benefit when parents are supportive and open in talking with them about their brother or sister with a disability. Interventionists should consider the impact of goals and strategies on siblings while planning services and recognize the importance of family involvement in nondisability-related activities, including leisure time.

Brothers and sisters of children with disabilities have developmental needs of their own that can be addressed by early intervention. During home visits, it is helpful for the interventionist to include siblings in ongoing activities, listening to the siblings' communications and providing play materials for siblings as well as for the child with a disability. By actively including siblings in the visit, interventionists can help them understand that they are an important part of the family, worthy of the interventionist's time and attention. *Sibshops,* which are sibling support groups offered across the country, can help children share their experiences and realize that there are many other children in similar family situations (Meyer & Vadasy, 1994).

Although there is still much to learn about the brothers and sisters of children with disabilities, we do know that, given appropriate support and opportunities, sibling relationships in these families are characterized by many of the same strengths and challenges found in all other families. Brothers and sisters of children with disabilities can benefit from the expanded opportunities for role enactment and personal growth when the family system responds positively to the child with the disability. Early interventionists can help make that happen.

The Role of the Child with a Disability

Parents, siblings, grandparents, and other family members develop relationships with the child with a disability based on their understanding of who the child is and what her unique qualities are. The formation of a holistic view of a child, along with clear and accurate information about the disability, reduce the possibility that the child could be labeled as the "vulnerable," "needy," or "special" one in the family, and have areas of strength and potential go unrecognized. Interventionists can promote this holistic perspective by frequently engaging in conversations with family members regarding characteristics of the child that are not directly related to the disability including strengths, interests, and personality traits. Interventionists who cannot see beyond the child's disability cannot support a family in taking a more holistic view. Because of the daily opportunity that families have to observe their child in multiple contexts, it is often the members of the family who naturally develop a comprehensive, holistic view of the child. Ironically, it can be the family's task to help the interventionist see beyond the disability and appreciate the complexity of the "whole child." Finally, as with all children, children with disabilities frequently shape their own roles in their families by their interests, personalities, and talents. The unique characteristics of each child must be recognized and celebrated.

The Role of the Extended Family

Shelia is fortunate to have her own mother, Tonya's grandmother, as an informal support to help with the children. Their early intervention provider should remain vigilant in allowing for time for Sheila and Tonya's grandmother to spend time together, away from the children, in order to enhance their already supportive relationship. Increased family mobility and an emphasis on independence rather than interdependence have functioned to limit extended family networks as sources of support (Taylor, 2000). Many families, however, do continue to strongly rely on extended family members to provide emotional and practical help with child rearing.

In some families, including those with young single parents or parents with multiple life stresses, grandparents may be the primary caregivers for the child with a disability. With this in mind, it is important that interventionists ask specific questions regarding the involvement of extended family members and their attitudes and behaviors toward the child. Grandparents, aunts, uncles, and other relatives often have emotional and informational needs related to the child's disability that can be met through involvement in early intervention. Additionally, they frequently have unique perspectives on the child and can be sources of additional information for the interventionist, as well as sources of family support. All people identified as members of the family should be offered the opportunity to participate in support groups, educational activities, or IFSPs and IEPs, *when such involvement is desired by the parents.* Interventionists understand that families from different cultures may have differing views concerning the roles of family members and the manner in which family members interact with service providers. It is essential that these cultural and familial norms are respected.

Courtesy of Stephen Hooper

Extended family involvement can be critical to the on-going development of children.

:: FACTORS THAT INFLUENCE THE FAMILY SYSTEM

Early interventionists who understand and respect cultural influences on a family are more likely to provide culturally sensitive and effective services.

Respect for family diversity is critical to the provision of sensitive and effective intervention services. Early interventionists are called upon to serve families representing a wide variety of situations, backgrounds, and philosophies. The following sections address changing family demographics, serving families from different cultures, and the interconnections of families, disability, poverty, and early intervention.

Changing Family Demographics

Historically, the provision of human services has been based on the traditional definition of a family as a married couple with children living in the same household. Many different types and structures of families are present in today's society. The 2000 U.S. census revealed that 10 million children under age 18 live in single-mother households; 2 million children live with single fathers (U. S. Census Bureau, 2001). Many other children live in blended families with stepparents, in foster or adoptive families, with grandparents or other relatives, with gay and lesbian couples, in families built around nonmarital relationships and parenting partnerships, and in multigenerational households. Service providers must be prepared to recognize and honor each family's unique definition of membership. Such recognition will entail taking time to get to know each family, withholding judgments that criticize any nontraditional family form, and fashioning services that allow for the participation of all family members. As Smith, Boutte, Zigler, and Finn-Stevenson (2004) point out, "the dynamic nature of families in the United States does not negate the influence of family, but instead draws more attention to the need to understand and help strengthen families for their critical roles in children's lives" (p. 215).

Serving Families from Different Cultures

America is becoming increasingly diverse. "Five and half million children in America speak nearly 400 languages other than English . . . these children are a bridge between two cultures" (Ready at Five Partnership, 2004, p. 9). In the 2000 census, approximately 75% of the population—211,460,626 people—described themselves as White. African Americans comprised 12.3% of the population (34,658,190 people). More than 35.3 million people, 13% of the population, described themselves as Hispanic or Latino/Latina. Slightly over 3.5% of the population are of Asian origin (10,242,998 people); approximately 1% are American Indian (2,475,956 people). Almost 1.5%, or 6.8 million people, responded that they were of two or more races. If current population trends continue, no racial or ethnic group will be a majority in the U. S. population by mid-century. The increase in the proportion of the population that is non-White is especially dramatic for the age group of most interest to early interventionists, namely, infants and young children (U. S. Census Bureau, 2001).

> Cultural competence: Being open and respectful to expected and unexpected differences in families even if they are outside your level of familiarity.

It is critical that early interventionists have the competence to support families from diverse cultural backgrounds, including families who are recent immigrants and speak a language other than English. It is not necessary for an interventionist to know everything about a particular culture in order to provide sensitive and appropriate

---

BOX 10.1   CULTURAL COMPETENCE IN EARLY INTERVENTION

Cultural competence is a set of personal beliefs and attitudes that shape behavior. Service providers who are open and eager to learn, respectful of differences, and willing to conduct thoughtful self-examinations and make personal change are most capable of developing cultural competence (Hepburn, 2004). These traits allow early interventionists to identify and use cultural resources, strengthen their relationships with families, and provide the most effective services. A focus on the development of these personal characteristics, rather than on the acquisition of detailed knowledge of a culture, will also discourage service providers from stereotyping families based on their membership in a cultural group. Each family is unique and any one family may be as different from a family in their own cultural group as they are from a family from another cultural group (Zionts, Zionts, Harrison, & Bellinger, 2003).

services (Hepburn, 2004; Ready at Five Partnership, 2004). Several strategies enable early interventionists to work sensitively and effectively with families from diverse cultural backgrounds, including the following:

- Learn to view cultural diversity as an asset—something to celebrate—rather than as a problem to be overcome.
- Focus on the uniqueness and individuality of each family and of each child.
- Be aware of your own cultural beliefs and customs, including the beliefs that you hold about what constitutes a "strong" or "ideal" family.
- Encourage families to share their stories, their hopes, and their histories. Try to understand what they want for their children and the cultural meanings they have concerning disability.
- Be sensitive to the ways that social interactions may differ across cultures. This may include personal space (how close to stand to someone), use of eye contact, gender roles, comfort in talking about oneself, comfort with silence, and use of touch.
- Learn to be comfortable around people who look or think differently than you do. Learn to make others feel comfortable. Show acceptance.
- Fight against the tendency to stereotype families, even if the stereotypes are positive.
- Be sensitive to the strong impact that current, as well as historic, discrimination has on families.
- Learn about what it means to emigrate to the United States. Think about the challenges of living in a country where you do not speak the dominant language. Learn to work with a language interpreter.
- Learn who makes the decisions in the family and how decisions are made (i.e., what factors are important in making decisions).

Families, Disability, Poverty, and Early Intervention

Although the United States is an affluent country, many families live in poverty. Young children are more likely to be poor than any other age group. Contrary to many stereotypes, the majority of poor young children live in working households; only 11% of poor children under age 3 live in families that rely primarily on public assistance (Song & Lu, 2002). Approximately 18% of all children live in poverty in the United States. Young children living with single mothers are five times more likely to be poor than those living with married parents; 45% of young children living in mother-headed families are poor, whereas only 9% of young children living with married parents experience poverty (Song & Lu, 2002).

Poor children are more likely than affluent children to have disabilities. This is true for many reasons, including maternal and child malnutrition, inadequate prenatal care for the mother, exposure to environmental toxins, poor access to health care, maternal drug and alcohol abuse, trauma related to unsafe environments, compromised parenting, and lack of developmental opportunities. Poverty, by itself, does not cause disabilities in children, but the consequences of poverty place young, poor children at heightened risk for disabilities (Harry & Klingner, 2006).

For many early interventionists, the majority of families they serve are living in poverty. Yet, most interventionists come from middle-class backgrounds and have limited understanding of what it means to live in persistent poverty.

Homelessness is a poverty-related issue of importance to early interventionists. It is estimated that each week, more than 200,000 U. S. children experience homelessness; 42% of these children are under 5 years of age (Burt et al., 1999). Young children whose families are poor and often homeless are at high risk of developmental delays and emotional and behavioral disabilities. Developing early intervention strategies for families who are homeless (Kelly, Buehlman, & Caldwell, 2000) can support these families during trying times and can prevent or reduce developmental difficulties in their children.

Homelessness and/or living in poverty increases a child's chance for developmental delays and other disabilities.

Families of minority young children have significantly higher rates of poverty than do nonminority families (Harry & Klingner, 2006), and those with special health care needs have additional stressors affecting their family's quality of life (Deboba, McPherson, Kenney, Strickland, & Newacheck, 2006). The percent of children living in poverty increases tremendously for African American (36%) and Hispanic (29%) children (Annie E. Casey Foundation, 2006). In two-parent families, Hispanic young children are three times more likely (24%) to experience poverty than African American children (8%), and almost five times more likely to be poor as white children (5%). In single-parent families, over half of all African American children aged 3 and under, and nearly half of young Hispanic children, are poor (Song & Lu, 2002). These high poverty rates lead to increased rates of disability among minority children (Harry & Klingner, 2006). Harry and Klingner contend that the "disability label is seen as undesirable, particularly by people who are already stigmatized on grounds of ethnicity" (p. 13).

It is important for early interventionists to understand the complex relationships among disability prevalence, poverty, and minority status and to be able to differentiate the effects of poverty from those of cultural or ethnic differences among families. Emerson, Hasson, Llewellyn, Blacher, & Graham (2006) found that differences in well-being between mothers of children with and without disabilities often are due to income differences and poverty-related stresses rather than to the effects of having a child with a disability. Without an understanding of the overwhelming effects of poverty on children and families, it is impossible to provide early intervention services that are effective and that make sense for the family.

:: NATURAL ENVIRONMENTS AS SOURCES OF EVERYDAY LEARNING OPPORTUNITIES

The role of families in the delivery of early intervention was changed dramatically by Part C of the 1997 reauthorization of IDEA, which stated that

> To the maximum extent appropriate, early intervention services must be provided in natural environments, including the home and community settings in which children without disabilities participate . . . . Services can only be provided in a setting other than a natural environment when early intervention cannot be achieved satisfactorily in a natural environment. [Sec. 303.12(b)(1)(2)]

Natural environments are settings in which children with and without disabilities spend their time in the home and community, including daily activities and routines.

The focus on natural environments continues under the 2004 reauthorization of IDEA. In most states, programs and services for infants and toddlers have shifted from a clinic-based model to a model in which services are delivered in **natural environments,** those settings where children without disabilities spend their time (e.g., the home, community programs, childcare, and other settings in which the child and family live, learn, and play). Families no longer experience the stresses associated with taking their child to different therapy settings. Rather, the intervention comes to the child and family. Because most young children spend large amounts of time with their families, the family becomes a primary setting for early intervention. Team members, along with the family, collaborate to develop IFSP outcomes that can be integrated throughout the day in naturally occurring activities using the child's interests, favorite toys, and other interesting materials. Care providers implement intervention within the context of changing diapers, reading books, folding laundry, or riding in the car. Service providers serve as "coaches" to family members, helping them gain confidence and competence to meet the needs of their child with a disability.

Addressing early intervention outcomes in the natural environment requires more than a change in location. It requires providers to consider the routines, materials, activities, and people common to the child and family in order to determine the best opportunities for teaching and learning. Family routines are the activities of daily living (e.g., eating, grocery shopping, bathing, etc.) that relate to family interests and priorities. For infants and young children, naturally occurring events include child-initiated actions and play (e.g., climbing into cupboards to play with the pots and pans, activating the mobile on the crib), daily routines (e.g., diapering, traveling to the childcare center, washing up), and planned activities (e.g., shopping) (Sandall & Ostrosky, 2000). Children learn throughout the day. Parents can be very creative in adapting everyday activities to create learning environments for their children; an important role of interventionists is to help parents adapt their everyday activities to maximize learning (Keilty & Galvin, 2006).

A role of early interventionists is to help care providers and parents identify teachable moments and learning activities within daily routines and everyday experiences.

Playtime provides opportunities for the child to develop and practice skills with her family members in a positive, natural, mutually satisfying context (McWilliam, 2000). Children learn about water while playing in the bathtub, washing hands in the sink, getting a drink, splashing in a puddle, or swimming in a pool. In addition to understanding what water is, children are learning self-help skills like drinking from a cup, hand and face washing, or motor skills like walking and jumping. Early interventionists listen to families and support them in identifying priorities and concerns, family and child preferences, comfortable routines, and when and how to embed training within routines. Families share information about the day-to-day settings and activities that are of interest to the child and family and are potential sources of learning.

As the child experiences different places, she experiences multiple kinds of natural learning environments. It is also true that any one learning environment can be the source of multiple kinds of learning opportunities. For example, a kitchen table is a place that affords a child opportunities to listen to others talk, to ask for a drink, to learn to use a spoon, to play with toys, or to draw with crayons (Dunst, Bruder, Trivette, & Hamby, 2006). Many of these opportunities occur as part of daily living, family routines, family rituals, and family and community celebrations and traditions

(Chai, Zhang, & Bisberg, 2006). What is especially appealing about using natural environments for promoting and enhancing learning is that these sources of children's learning opportunities are literally everywhere in a child's family and community (Dunst et al., 2006).

Although the natural environments provisions of IDEA are focused on children birth through age 2, there is no magical change in the way that families function when the child turns 3 that makes these interventions any less appropriate or effective. Working collaboratively with families to embed intervention activities in the ongoing daily activities of the child is important throughout the preschool years. These strategies are as relevant to interventionists working with children with disabilities aged 3 through 5 as they are to interventionists working under Part C.

∷ SKILLS FOR EFFECTIVE WORK IN PARTNERSHIP WITH FAMILIES

The Division for Early Childhood of the Council for Exceptional Children identified four family-based practices that form the foundation for quality services to young children with disabilities and their families (Trivette & Dunst, 2005). The first of these, *families and professionals share responsibility and work collaboratively*, focuses on partnership. This partnership rests on the strong positive regard and trust that develops between the interventionist and parents, which Trute and Hiebert-Murphy (2007) have termed the "working alliance." The second recommendation, *practices strengthen family functioning*, highlights positive practices such as respecting family choice and decision making, building supports and resources, and working to avoid interventions that disrupt family life. The third recommendation, *practices are individualized and flexible*, focuses on practices that are attuned to the priorities of different family members and that build on family values and cultural mores. The final recommendation, *practices are strengths- and assets-based*, stresses a positive approach that focuses on child and family strengths rather than deficits and that builds on the competence of families and children.

To implement these recommended practices, interventionists need skills that build on the family-centered values discussed earlier. These skills include demonstrating respect, being realistic, using good listening and communication skills, helping the family to build natural support networks, being sensitive, forming partnerships and collaborations, and being flexible.

Demonstrating Respect

Respect for the family is the hallmark of all positive and effective intervention efforts. It is created and sustained by a fundamental belief in the importance of families and trust in the ability of families to make the most appropriate choices for their children. Early interventionists demonstrate respect when they ask families what they see as priority areas for intervention before offering an opinion. They offer their own opinions in a way that allows parents to comfortably disagree

BOX 10.2   DEC-RECOMMENDED PRACTICES: FAMILY-BASED PRACTICES

Families and professionals share responsibility and work collaboratively.

F1. Family members and professionals jointly develop appropriate family-identified outcomes.

F2. Family members and professionals work together and share information routinely and collaboratively to achieve family-identified outcomes.

F3. Professionals fully and appropriately provide relevant information so parents can make informed choices and decisions.

F4. Professionals use helping styles that promote shared family/professional responsibility in achieving family-identified outcomes.

F5. Family/professionals' relationship building is accomplished in ways that are responsive to cultural, language, and other family characteristics.

Practices strengthen family functioning.

F6. Practices, supports, and resources provide families with participatory experiences and opportunities promoting choice and decision making.

F7. Practices, supports, and resources support family participation in obtaining desired resources and supports to strengthen parenting competence and confidence.

F8. Intrafamily, informal, community, and formal supports and resources (e.g., respite care) are used to achieve desired outcomes.

F9. Supports and resources provide families with information, competency-enhancing experiences, and participatory opportunities to strengthen family functioning and promote parenting knowledge and skills.

F10. Supports and resources are mobilized in ways that are supportive and do not disrupt family and community life.

Practices are individualized and flexible.

F11. Resources and supports are provided in ways that are flexible, individualized, and tailored to the child's and family's preferences and styles, and promote well-being.

F12. Resources and supports match each family member's identified priorities and preferences (e.g., mother's and father's priorities and preferences may be different).

F13. Practices, supports, and resources are responsive to the cultural, ethnic, racial, language, and socioeconomic characteristics and preferences of families and their communities.

F14. Practices, supports, and resources incorporate family beliefs and values into decisions, intervention plans, and resources and support mobilization.

Practices are strengths- and assets-based.

F15. Family and child strengths and assets are used as a basis for engaging families in participatory experiences supporting parenting competence and confidence.

F16. Practices, supports, and resources build on existing parenting competence and confidence.

F17. Practices, supports, and resources promote the family's and professional's acquisition of new knowledge and skills to strengthen competence and confidence.

Source: From "DEC-Recommended Practices: Family-Based Practices," by C. M. Trivette and C. J. Dunst, in *DEC-Recommended Practices* (pp. 113–118), in S. Sandall, M. L. Hemmeter, B. J. Smith, & M. E. McLean, 2005, Longmont, CO: The Division for Early Childhood of the Council for Exceptional Children. Used with permission.

(Blue-Banning et al., 2004). Service providers who respect families honor their decisions, lifestyles, values, beliefs, and efforts to care for their children, even when this entails supporting choices the service provider would not have made. Interventionists must not only *feel* respect toward families; they also must actively *demonstrate* that respect in their interactions with family members and in the way they talk about the family to others.

> Treating a family with respect, dignity, and without judgment will increase the likelihood of providing individualized, family-centered services.

Being Realistic

It is easy for interventionists to forget that parents have roles and responsibilities in addition to parenting a child with a disability. The daily demands of rearing children and managing careers, finances, and households, as well as meeting other family responsibilities, can sometimes be overwhelming. Even more is demanded of parents of children with disabilities than is demanded of parents of typically developing children, and it is demanded for a longer period. Parents of children with disabilities often are expected to be "super parents" who attend meetings, work in their children's classrooms, advocate for their children's rights, implement home-based therapy programs, collect daily data, attend workshops, support other parents, plan and implement IFSPs and IEPs, and transport their child to see doctors, therapists, and other service providers.

Most families welcome the opportunity to actively participate in planning and implementing intervention activities. For some families, however, these extra parenting tasks become overwhelming. When families are overburdened with intervention plans they cannot possibly implement or when such plans have negative impacts on other areas of family functioning, family members often feel guilty and discouraged and may avoid contact with the service provider they feel they have failed. Families that decline or fail to complete services may be labeled inappropriately by interventionists as "resistant" or thought to care less for their child. It is important to consider the many aspects of a family's life when suggesting services or levels of involvement. Being realistic means working together with the family to design intervention strategies that make sense and can be easily implemented in the everyday life of the family.

Using Good Listening and Communication Skills

Listening skills are critical for successful work with families. To be effective, service providers must want to hear what family members have to say and be truly interested in understanding each family's unique needs and concerns. While family members are talking, the provider should concentrate fully on what they are saying. This means paying careful attention to what is being communicated and being sensitive to both verbal and nonverbal cues. It is often helpful for the provider to repeat what she hears family members saying so that they have the opportunity to correct or clarify the provider's interpretation. Whenever possible, service providers should make notes after, rather than during, conversations and review any notes with the family. Ample time should be allowed for talking with family members. Silences in conversation should not be filled because important information is often revealed after a period of silence. The provider should ask herself, "Do I really listen to families? Do I accept and respect what family members tell me or am I actively trying to influence their beliefs or ideas?"

Service providers should be keenly sensitive to how their negative attitudes or disagreements with a family may be communicated, either directly or in more subtle ways. Such thoughts can undermine family confidence, causing members to feel inadequate or defensive and seriously limiting the extent to which services will be used effectively. Interventionists who always keep the overall goal of family empowerment in mind and who derive personal rewards from seeing families become more competent and self-sustaining are most likely to provide the most appropriate and effective services (Dunst & Trivette, 1994).

The provision of services to families of children with disabilities often necessitates the involvement of numerous service providers, many of whom have access to confidential and intimate information about the families. Boundary conflicts can arise when service providers fail to recognize the roles and rights of all family members or when professionals intrude too far into the lives of families. For example, parents of children with disabilities are sometimes asked very personal questions about their marriages, finances, and family relationships. These areas of discussion can be viewed by the family as intrusive and unhelpful unless approached with sensitivity and a clear statement of purpose. Asking questions about family coping and marital adjustment is often unnecessary and can send a message that the interventionist believes that because the child has a disability, the parents must have problems as well (Blue-Banning et al, 2004). On the other hand, some families want to share this personal information with the interventionist. Sensitive communication and good listening skills allow the interventionist to understand the family's feelings and to be responsive to their desired level of disclosure.

Helping the Family Build Natural Support Networks

> The ecological model involves looking at a child's development within the layers of the contexts and relationships that form her environment.

> Natural support systems are the unpaid resources in a family's life, such as friends and relatives, who can provide assistance in helping the family achieve their goals.

Families and their children live within neighborhoods and communities. They have many social connections, including religious organizations, school and work, clubs and civic organizations, and recreational settings. Bronfenbrenner (1979) developed an ecological model of human development that has had a major impact on public policy and on services for children with disabilities and their families. The **ecological model** stresses the important developmental influences exerted by the settings in which children and families live and by the larger contexts in which those settings are embedded. It is possible for families, with the support of early interventionists, to utilize people and organizations in the family's ecology to provide important support. In the disability field, drawing upon people already present in the family's environment to help the family achieve their goals is referred to as **natural support**. Members of a natural support network are not paid. They provide assistance from a sense of community and from a caring relationship they have developed with the family (Santos & Zhang, 2001).

It is important that early interventionists encourage the family's use of natural support networks such as friends, neighbors, community or church resources, and extended family relationships when they are available. Although utilization of natural supports can decrease reliance on paid service provision, this is not a primary purpose for nurturing these supports. Involvement with these sources of support can enhance a sense of connection and community and normalize the need for support as something common to all families. Some families develop natural support networks with little assistance from the interventionist. For other families, the skill of the interventionist will be called upon to invite community members into the life of the family.

Being Sensitive

Being sensitive to families includes carefully listening and then responding in a way that is consistent with the messages that families are sending. Interventionists must communicate a sincere sense of caring, warmth, and encouragement. Support is much easier to accept when the person offering the support is perceived to have a positive attitude and to be genuinely interested in helping (Dunst & Trivette, 1994). The interventionist must listen to herself talk to the family, making sure that her words communicate a strengths-based approach that is positive toward the family and toward the child and focuses on assets rather than on deficits or problems.

Fox et al. (2002) interviewed parents of young children with disabilities receiving services related to problem behaviors. They found that the professionals described as being the most helpful to the families were those who provided support and encouragement. Encouragement can be communicated by helping the family identify and successfully solve small problems or achieve short-term goals before moving on to tackle more difficult or long-range issues. Such successes bolster the self-esteem and confidence of family members and increase their investment in the intervention process (Dunst & Trivette, 1994).

It is important that providers envision what life is like for families (Bruder, 2000) without implying that they know what the family is experiencing. Consider a scenario such as this for a parent: You missed an IEP or IFSP meeting because your car wouldn't start. Earlier in the day, your babysitter canceled and you have no option but to take your three young children to the meeting. But now you have no transportation. You are tired, one of your children is crying, and you really don't understand what this meeting is about and feel rather intimidated by the group of professionals who will probably attend. Wouldn't you be tempted to just stay home? Thinking about life from the point of view of the family often helps interventionists to identify support needs and to put a positive frame on the behavior of the family. Sensitivity is based on understanding and understanding is based on a vision of the world as experienced by the family.

It often is a powerful experience for interventionists to spend a day (and a night) caring for the child with a disability and her siblings or to accompany the family throughout a typical day that might include a trip to the doctor or to the Social Security office. After this type of personal experience, the provider's point of view may never be the same. Looking at family life from the outside presents a very different view than that obtained when walking beside the family, experiencing what their life is really like.

Reaching Out—Forming Partnerships and Collaborations

Early intervention is not a one-person or single-agency endeavor. In addition to forming partnerships with families, interventionists must develop collaborations with other community agencies and resources. Teams whose members are employed by different agencies or departments often deliver early intervention services. Team members must be able to work together with mutual respect to implement family-centered early intervention.

Developing community partnerships is especially critical for families with complex living situations. Some families served by early interventionists are characterized by disorganization, multiple stressors, and severely limited resources (Oelofsen & Richardson, 2006). These families may reside in substandard housing in neighborhoods where the crime rate is high and hope for the future is low. An interventionist may suspect, or may know, that a family is engaging in child abuse or neglect; such knowledge confers legal requirements for appropriate reporting. Subsequent renegotiation of relationships with family members also will be necessary. Other families may be impacted by substance abuse, high levels of family conflict, homelessness, serious mental health problems in a parent, entanglement with the legal system, or extreme poverty. Thompson (1992) suggested that, "Tackling problems associated with poverty is not a challenge for the faint of heart" (p. 9). Complex family issues, such as those described above, are not challenges to be handled alone. Interventionists must be familiar with the resources available in their communities and have the skills necessary to interact with other professionals and agency personnel to obtain the supports and services that are needed for the children and families that they serve.

Being Flexible—Doing Whatever It Takes

The *Statement in Support of Families and Their Children*, published by the Center on Human Policy (1987), introduced the principle of "whatever it takes," stating that family services should be "flexible, individualized, and designed to meet the diverse needs of families." Interventionists working with families must be creative and adaptable. Implementing family-centered early intervention requires a willingness to create positive visions for the future with families and to listen to and share their dreams.

∷ DESIRED FAMILY OUTCOMES

To this point in the chapter, we have considered issues related to the family in the early intervention process. Several important questions remain to be addressed: What are we trying to achieve through these efforts? What difference are we trying to make in the lives of families? To design intervention goals for individual families, we need to ask family members what they want and use their responses to guide the selection of intervention goals and outcomes. Because interventionists are employed by publicly financed state and national programs, however, clear family outcomes need to be developed to guide early intervention systems and to determine if early intervention programs are having the desired positive effects on families. To be accountable for the use of public funds, early intervention systems must identify and define their desired outcomes for families.

Summers et al. (2005) define **family outcomes** as positive or negative impacts experienced by families that result from the provision of services and supports. A major effort toward defining early intervention outcomes has been undertaken by the Early Childhood Outcomes (ECO) Center (Bailey et al., 2006). The ECO Center identified five desired family outcomes for early intervention services: (1) understand their child's strengths, abilities, and needs; (2) know their rights and advocate effectively for their child; (3) help their child develop and learn; (4) have support systems; and (5) gain access to desired community services and activities. These outcomes were proposed as a framework to be used to evaluate the success of early intervention programs. Summers and colleagues (2006) argue that these short-term, intermediate family intervention outcomes lead to a longer-term, ultimate outcome: improved family quality of life. The following sections briefly explore each of these desired family outcomes.

Family outcomes are the effects that services and supports have on the family.

Families Understand Their Child's Strengths, Abilities, and Needs

Parents know their child better than interventionists and others who enter the child's life for a limited time. This in-depth parent knowledge forms the foundation for successful intervention efforts. Even though families have great understanding of their child's personality and activities, they are not always familiar with developmental issues related to their child's specific disability. In addition, parents may not be aware of the ages at which typical developmental milestones are achieved or know how to help a child who is delayed in reaching those milestones. Interventionists can help parents gain this information, linking them with informational resources and sharing their professional experience. Zaidman-Zait and Jamieson (2007) suggest that parents of young children with disabilities increasingly are turning to Web-based resources to obtain information and support from other parents via chat rooms, bulletin boards, and listserves. The early interventionist can help families access these resources. Informed parents are better able to effectively parent their children.

With the increase in Internet use, it is important for service providers to assist families in evaluating acquired information without disregarding new and innovative ideas.

Families Know Their Rights and Advocate Effectively for Their Child

The opening section of this chapter described some of the rights enjoyed by families under federal regulations and laws. Parents are not always aware of their rights. Additionally, parents who know their rights may not know how to exercise those rights to advocate for their child. Interventionists can link parents to information, help them become comfortable with the service system, link the family with peer mentors, and help parents prepare to help develop the IFSP/IEP. Parents who are aware of their rights and know how to advocate for their child are better prepared to work in partnership with professionals to design and access the services and supports needed by the child and family.

Families Help Their Child Develop and Learn   Families are the primary teachers of young children. Interventionists can help parents think about ways to incorporate learning objectives into the everyday activities of the child and family. For certain children, such as those with challenging behaviors, muscle contractions, or feeding problems, parents may request assistance from interventionists in order to know how to appropriately address these issues. Children learn best when their parents make use of everyday activities and settings to stimulate learning in developmentally appropriate ways.

Families Have Support Systems   Support for families can take many forms. Interventionists may link parents with peer networks such as Parent to Parent so that families can have ongoing support from parents who are experiencing similar disability-related issues. Accessing services, such as skilled babysitters, financial supports, or parenting groups, can alleviate stress and feelings of isolation. Parents who feel supported have more energy and emotional strength to devote to the important tasks of parenting. All members of the family, including siblings and extended family members, benefit when families have adequate support.

Families Gain Access to Desired Community Services and Activities
There are numerous generic community resources available to families of typically developing children. These community resources include professional services such as pediatricians and dentists. Community resources also include childcare, recreational opportunities, religious services, and places of business such as grocery stores. For some families of young children with disabilities, there are barriers to accessing these common community services. Interventionists can help families address these barriers and help community service providers feel confident in their ability to serve the child and family. As community settings become fully inclusive of children with disabilities and their families, families can live more ordinary lives and community members can get to know these children and their families, enriching all involved.

Families Have Improved Quality of Life   Summers et al. (2005) conceptualize family quality of life as consisting of five domains: (1) family interactions, (2) parenting, (3) emotional well-being, (4) physical–material well-being, and (5) disability-related support. When family quality of life is high, enjoyment, open communication, constructive problem solving, and mutual love and caring characterize *family* interactions. *Parenting* addresses the individual needs and strengths of each child and helps children learn to be independent, get along with others, and make good decisions. The *emotional well-being* that accompanies positive family quality of life is characterized by friends and others who help to relieve stress, time to pursue individual interests, and help from others outside the family. Families have physical–material well-being when they are financially secure, safe, receive medical and dental care, and have access to transportation. *Disability-related support,* such as effective early intervention and a positive relationship with interventionists, is the final component of positive family quality of life.

SUMMARY

This chapter has provided an overview of key issues for the early interventionist to consider when working with young children with disabilities. In one sense, it is natural for service providers to care deeply about the families and children they serve and to have their own values and beliefs about what is best for them. As mentioned in several sections of this chapter, however, there will be times when family choices, goals, practices, or values will be different from those of the professional. This is not undesirable and, in fact, should be expected when a family is actively involved in early intervention services. How the early interventionist responds to these situations will contribute significantly to the strength of the family-centered services.

Across the nation, states are struggling to turn the promise of family-centered intervention into reality for families and young children. We have made much progress, but there is still much work to be done. Progress toward this goal will be enhanced when a new generation of early intervention professionals is trained to be sensitive to parent emotions and beliefs, embrace family-centered values, appreciate family diversity, understand family systems, support learning in natural, everyday environments, work in partnership with families, and achieve success in achieving desired family outcomes.

REVIEW QUESTIONS AND DISCUSSION POINTS

1. Why is it so important for families to be in decision-making roles concerning the early intervention services received by their children with disabilities?
2. How would you go about helping parents become more responsive to their child with special needs using relationship-based early intervention? How would you implement this intervention while still maintaining a family-centered, partnership perspective?
3. How does your own cultural background influence how you interact with families? Think of an experience where cultural differences may cause you to judge a family negatively because a culturally based

practice was new to you. What would you do if this happened? How could you better understand the family's point of view?
4. Think of challenges families may have during everyday routines when they have a child with special needs. How can natural learning opportunities be incorporated into these routines to assist both parent and child?
5. Think of other skills, not mentioned in this chapter, that are important for early interventionists who are implementing family-centered early intervention. What are those skills?

RECOMMENDED RESOURCES

Books

Dunst, C. J., Trivette, C. M., & Deal, A. G. (Eds.). (1994). *Supporting and strengthening families: Volume 1: Methods, Strategies, and Practices.* Cambridge, MA: Brookline Books, Inc.

Horn, E., Ostrosky, M. M., & Jones, H. (2004). *Young exceptional children: Family-based practices: Monograph Series No. 5.* Denver, CO: Division of Early Childhood of the Council for Exceptional Children.

Sandall, S., & Ostrosky, M. (Eds.). (2000). *Young exceptional children: Natural environments and inclusion: Monograph Series No. 2.* Denver, CO: Division of Early Childhood of the Council for Exceptional Children.

Shonkoff, J. P., & Phillips, D. A. (Eds.). (2004). *From neurons to neighborhoods: The science of early childhood development.* Washington, DC: National Academy Press.

Websites

Division of Early Childhood of the Council for Exceptional Children
www.dec-sped.org

Take a Look at Me!: A strengths-based portfolio
www.takealookatmeportfolio.com

Family Involvement Network of Educators (FINE)
www.gse.harvard.edu/hfrp/projects/fine.html

The Beach Center on Disability
www.beachcenter.org

The Center on Disability and Community Inclusion at the University of Vermont
http://www.uvm.edu/~cdci/?Page=programs/familysupport/index.htm

The Fathers Network
www.fathersnetwork.org

Parents Helping Parents
www.php.com

The Sibling Support Project
www.siblingsupport.org

REFERENCES

Annie E. Casey Foundation. (2006). *Kids count data book: States profiles of child well-being.* Baltimore: Annie E. Casey Foundation.

Bailey, D. B., Bruder, M. B., Hebbeler, K., Carta, J., Defosset, M., Greenwood, C., et al. (2006). Recommended outcomes for families of young children with disabilities. *Journal of Early Intervention, 28,* 227–251.

Beach Center on Families and Disability. (1997). Family-centered service delivery. *Families and Disability Newsletter, 8*(2), 1–3.

Beach Center on Disability. (2007). Characteristics of Parent to Parent programs. Retrieved May 11, 2007, from *http://www.beachcenter.org/families/parent_to_parent/default.aspx*

Beaumont, D. (2006). Exploring parental reactions to the diagnosis of cleft lip and palate. *Paediatric Nursing, 18,* 14–18.

Bernheimer, L. P., & Weisner, T. S. (2007). "Let me just tell you what I do all day. . . " The family story at the center of intervention research and practice. *Infants & Young Children, 3,* 192–201.

Blue-Banning, M., Summers, J. A., Frankland, H. C., Nelson, L. L., & Beegle, G. (2004). Dimensions of family and professional partnerships: Constructive guidelines for collaboration. *Exceptional Children, 70,* 167–184.

Broderick, C., & Smith, J. (1979). The general systems approach to the family. In W. R. Burr, R. Hill, F. I. Nye, & I. L. Reiss (Eds.), *Contemporary theories about the family* (Vol. 2, pp. 112–129). New York: Free Press.

Bronfenbrenner, U. (1979). *The ecology of human development: Experiments by nature and design.* Cambridge, MA: Harvard University Press.

Bruder, M. B. (2000). Family-centered early intervention: Clarifying our values for the new millennium. *Topics in Early Childhood Special Education, 20,* 105–115.

Burt, M. R., Aron, L. Y., Douglas, T., Valente, J., Lee, E., & Iwen, B. (1999). *Homelessness: Programs and the people they serve.* Washington, DC: Interagency Council on the Homeless.

Center for Evidence-Based Research Practices. (2003). *Success breeds happiness.* Asheville, NC: Orelena Puckett Institute.

Center on Human Policy. (1987). *Statement in support of families and their children.* Syracuse, New York: Author.

Chai, A.Y., Zhang, C., & Bisberg, M. (2006). Rethinking natural environment practice: Implications from examining various interpretations and approaches. *Early Childhood Education Journal, 34*(3), 203–208.

Curran, A. L., Sharples, P. M., White, C., & Knapp, M. (2001). Time costs of caring for children with severe disabilities compared with caring for children without disabilities. *Developmental Medicine & Child Neurology, 43,* 529–533.

Dabkowski, D. M. (2004). Encouraging active parent participation in IEP team meetings. *Teaching Exceptional Children, 36*(3), 34–39.

Deboba, D., McPherson, M. G., Kenney, M. K., Strickland, B., & Newacheck, P. W. (2006). Achieving family and provider partnerships for children with special health care needs. *Pediatrics, 118,* 1607–1615.

Dunst, C. J., & Kassow, D. Z. (2004). Characteristics of interventions promoting parental sensitivity to child behavior. *Bridges: Practice-Based Research Synthesis, 3*(3), 1–17.

Dunst, C. J., & Trivette, C. M. (1994). What is effective helping? In C. J. Dunst, C. M. Trivette, & A. G. Deal (Eds.), *Supporting and strengthening families, Vol. 1: Methods, strategies and practices* (pp. 162–170). Cambridge, MA: Brookline Books.

Dunst, C. J., Bruder, M. B., Trivette, C. M., & Hamby, D. (2006). Everyday activity settings, natural learning environments, and early intervention practices. *Journal of Policy and Practice in Developmental Disabilities, 3,* 3–10.

Emerson, E., Hasson, C., Llewellyn, G., Blacher, J., & Graham, H. (2006). Socio-economic position, household composition, health status and indicators of the well-being of mothers of children with and without intellectual disabilities. *Journal of Intellectual Disability Research, 50,* 862–873.

Fialka, J. (2001). The dance of partnership: Why do my feet hurt? *Young Exceptional Children, 4,* 21–27.

Fox, L., Vaughn, B. J., Wyatte, M. L., & Dunlap, G. (2002). "We can't expect other people to understand": Family perspectives on problem behavior. *Exceptional Children, 68,* 437–450.

Gavidia-Payne, S., & Stoneman, Z. (2006). Marital adjustment in families of young children with disabilities: Associations with daily hassles and problem-focused coping. *American Journal on Mental Retardation, 111,* 1–14.

Hanson, M. J., Beckman, P. J., Horn, E., Marquart, J., Sandall, S. R., Greig, D., et al. (2000). Entering preschool: Family and professional experiences in this transition process. *Journal of Early Intervention, 23,* 279–293.

Harry, B., & Klingner, J. (2006). *Why are so many minority students in special education? Understanding race and disability in schools.* New York: Teachers College Press.

Hauser-Cram, P., Warfield, M. E., Shonkoff, J. P., & Krauss, M. W. (2001). Children with disabilities: A longitudinal study of child development and parent well-being. *Monographs of the Society for Research in Child Development, 66* (3, Serial No. 266).

Hepburn, K. S. (2004). *Building culturally linguistically competent services to support young children, their families, and school readiness.* Baltimore: The Annie E. Casey Foundation.

Individuals with Disabilities Education Act, Amendments of 1997. IDEA final regulations—34 CFR Part 303, Early Intervention Program for Infants and Toddlers with Disabilities.

Individuals with Disabilities Education Improvement Act, Amendments of 2004, Pub. L. No. 108–446, U.S.C. 20, §1400 et seq.

Keilty, B., & Galvin, K. M. (2006). Physical and social adaptations of families to promote learning in everyday experiences. *Topics in Early Childhood Special Education, 26,* 219–233.

Kelly, J. F., Buehlman, K., & Caldwell, K. (2000). Training personnel to promote quality parent-child interaction in families who are homeless. *Topics in Early Childhood Special Education, 20,* 174–185.

Mahoney, G., & Perales, F. (2005). Relationship-focused early intervention with children with pervasive developmental disorders and other disabilities: A comparative study. *Journal of Developmental and Behavioral Pediatrics, 26,* 77–85.

McWilliam, R. A. (2000). It's only natural . . . to have early intervention in the environments where it's needed. In S. Sandall & M. Ostrosky (Eds.), *Young exceptional children: Natural environments and inclusion* (Monograph Series No. 2 ed., pp. 17–26). Denver, CO: Division of Early Childhood of the Council for Exceptional Children.

Meyer, D. J., & Vadasy, P. F. (1994). *Sibshops: Workshops for siblings of children with special needs.* Baltimore: Brookes.

Minuchin, S. (1974). *Families and family therapy.* Cambridge, MA: Harvard University Press.

O'Brien, M. (2007). Ambiguous loss in families of children with autism spectrum disorders. *Family Relations, 56,* 135–146.

Oelofsen, N., & Richardson, P. (2006). Sense of coherence and parenting stress in mothers and fathers of preschool children with developmental disability. *Journal of Intellectual & Developmental Disability, 31,* 1–12.

Partington, K. J. (2002). Maternal responses to the diagnosis of learning disabilities in children: A qualitative study using a focus group approach. *Journal of Learning Disabilities, 6,* 163–173.

Poehlmann, J., Clements, M., Abbeduto, L., & Farsad, V. (2005). Family experiences associated with a child's diagnosis of fragile X or Down syndrome: Evidence for disruption and resilience. *Mental Retardation, 43,* 255–267.

Porterfield, S. L. (2002). Work choices of mothers in families with children with disabilities. *Journal of Marriage and Family, 64*(4), 972.

Raab, M. (2003). Relationships between types of toys and young children's social behavior. *Bridges: Practice-Based Research Synthesis, 1*(8), 1–13.

Raab, M., & Dunst, C. J. (2006). Influence of child interests on variations in child behavior and functioning. *Bridges: Practice-Based Research Synthesis, 4*(4), 1–22.

Ready at Five Partnership. (2004). *What works? Promising practices for improving the school readiness of English language learners.* Baltimore: The Annie E. Casey Foundation.

Rugg, M. (2004). Creative early intervention: Building on the hopes and dreams of families. *Update: Making a*

Difference in the Lives of People. Athens, GA: Institute on Human Development and Disabilities.

Sandall, S., & Ostrosky, M. (Eds.). (2000). *Young exceptional children: Natural environments and inclusion: Monograph Series 2*. Longmont, CO: Sopris West.

Santelli, B., Turnbull, A., Marquis, J., & Lerner, E. (2000). Statewide Parent-to-Parent programs: Partners in early intervention. *Infants & Young Children, 13*(1), 74–88.

Santos, R. M., & Zhang, C. (2001). *An individualized perspective of family service supports: A review of the literature: Technical Report 10*. Champaign, IL: Culturally & Linguistically Appropriate Services Early Childhood Research Institute.

Scorgie, K., & Sobsey, D. (2000). Transformational outcomes associated with parenting children who have disabilities. *Mental Retardation, 38,* 195–206.

Sebald, A., & Luckner, J. (2007). Successful partnerships with families of children who are deaf. *Teaching Exceptional Children, 39*(3), 54–60.

Shonkoff, J. P., & Phillips, D. A. (Eds.). (2000). *From neurons to neighborhoods: The science of early childhood development*. Washington, DC: National Academy Press.

Smith, E. P., Boutte, G. S., Zigler, E., & Finn-Stevenson, M. (2004). Opportunities for schools to promote resilience in children and youth. In K. I. Maton, C. J. Schellenbach, B. J. Leadbeater, & A. L. Solarz (Eds.), *Investing in children, youth, families, and communities: Strengths-based research and policy*. Washington, DC: American Psychological Association.

Song, Y., & Lu, H. (2002). *Early childhood poverty: A statistical profile*. New York: Columbia University, National Center for Childhood Poverty.

Summers, J. A., Poston, D. J., Turnbull, A. P., Marquis, J., Hoffman, L., Mannan, H., & Wang, M. (2006). Conceptualizing and measuring family quality of life. *Journal of Intellectual Disability Research, 49,* 777–783.

Taylor, G. (2000). *Parental involvement: A practical guide for collaboration and teamwork for students with disabilities*. Springfield, IL: Charles C. Thomas Publisher, Ltd.

Thompson, T. (1992). For the sake of our children: Poverty and disabilities. In T. Thompson & S. C. Hupp (Eds.), *Saving children at risk: Poverty and disabilities*. Newbury Park, CA: Sage.

Trivette, C. M. (2003). Influence of caregiver responsiveness on the development of young children with or at risk for developmental disabilities. *Bridges: Practice-Based Research Synthesis, 1*(6), 1–13.

Trivette, C. M., & Dunst, C. J. (2005). DEC-recommended practices: Family-based practices. In S. Sandall, M. L. Hemmeter, B. J. Smith, & M. E. McLean, *DEC-recommended practices: A comprehensive guide for practical application* (2nd ed.). (pp. 113–118). Longmont, CO: Sopris West.

Trute, B., & Hiebert-Murphy, D. (2007). The implications of "working alliance" for the measurement and evaluation of family-centered practice in childhood disability services. *Infants and Young Children, 20,* 109–119.

Turbiville, V. P., & Marquis, J. G. (2001). Father participation in early education programs. *Topics in Early Childhood Special Education, 21,* 223–231.

U.S. Census Bureau. (2001). *America's families and living arrangements*. Washington, DC: U.S. Department of Commerce.

von Bertalanffy, L. V. (1968). *General systems theory*. New York: George Brazilles.

Werner, E. E., & Smith, R. S. (1982). *Vulnerable but invincible— a longitudinal study of resilient children and youth*. New York: McGraw-Hill.

Zaidman-Zait, A., & Jamieson, J. R. (2007). Providing Web-based support for families of infants and young children with established disabilities. *Infants & Young Children, 20,* 11–26.

Zionts, L. T., Zionts, P., Harrison, S., & Bellinger, O. (2003). Urban African American families' perceptions of cultural sensitivity within the special education system. *Focus on Autism and Other Developmental Disabilities, 18,* 41–50.

Name Index

Subject Index